**LABOR AND EMPLOYMENT
RELATIONS ASSOCIATION SERIES**

Union Organizing and Collective Bargaining at a Critical Moment: Opportunities for Renewal or Continued Decline?

Edited by

Howard R. Stanger
Paul F. Clark
John T. Delaney

Union Organizing and Collective Bargaining at a Critical Moment: Opportunities for Renewal or Continued Decline? Copyright © 2024 by the Labor and Employment Relations Association. Printed in the United States of America. All rights reserved. No part of the book may be used without written permission, except in the case of brief quotations embodied in critical articles and reviews.

First Edition
ISBN 78-0-913447-29-1
Price: $39.95

LABOR AND EMPLOYMENT RELATIONS ASSOCIATION SERIES
  LERA *Proceedings of the Annual Meeting* (published online annually, in the fall)
  LERA *Annual Research Volume* (published annually, in the summer/fall)
  LERA Online Membership Directory (updated daily, member/subscriber access only)
  LERA *Labor and Employment Law News* (published online each quarter)
  LERA *Perspectives on Work* (published annually, in the fall)

Information regarding membership, subscriptions, meetings, publications, and general affairs of LERA can be found at the Association website at www.leraweb.org. Members can make changes to their member records, including contact information, affiliations, and preferences, by accessing the online directory at the website or by contacting the LERA national office.

LABOR AND EMPLOYMENT RELATIONS ASSOCIATION
University of Illinois Urbana-Champaign
School of Labor and Employment Relations
121 Labor and Employment Relations Building
504 East Armory Ave., MC-504
Champaign, IL 61820
Telephone: 217/333-0072   Fax: 217/265-5130
Website: www.leraweb.org
E-mail: LERAoffice@illinois.edu

Acknowledgments

I would like to thank the following people and organizations for making this research volume possible. Paul Clark and John Delaney were wonderful and skilled co-editors who helped launch this research volume and provided keen insight and expert guidance along the way. It was a pleasure to work with them on this volume.

The authors and commentators in this volume provided their expert analysis on organizing and collective bargaining in a variety of industries that will inform scholars, professionals, and students for many years.

The LERA editorial team, headed by Ryan Lemare, supported our proposal to continue IRRA/LERA's long tradition of research volumes that focus on collective bargaining, which are published every dozen years or so.

Peggy Currid expertly improved our grammar and use of acronyms and herded us cats in the right direction to stay on schedule.

Alex Colvin and Ariel Avgar of the ILR School at Cornell and Jon Schleuss and the staff at The NewsGuild were most generous in providing me with access to critical information for my chapter on newspapers.

Finally, John, Paul, and I owe an intellectual debt to the many authors and editors who have shared their knowledge and insight of a variety of industries in previous research volumes on collective bargaining. We are honored that we can keep this tradition alive in LERA.

—Howard Stanger

Contents

Introduction
Union Organizing and Collective Bargaining at a Critical Moment: Opportunities for Renewal or Continued Decline?...................1
Howard R. Stanger, Paul F. Clark, and John T. Delaney

Chapter 1
Collective Bargaining in Autos: Electrification, a Reformed UAW, and New Union Leadership in a Turbulent Industry..........................13
Marick F. Masters, Frank Goeddeke, Jr., and Ray Gibney

Chapter 2
Collective Bargaining in the US Construction Industry......................49
Dale Belman and Mark Erlich

Chapter 3
Regenerating The NewsGuild: Organizing and Bargaining in the Newspaper Industry Since 2015...75
Howard R. Stanger

Chapter 4
Achieving Harmony: The Role of Collective Bargaining in the Symphonic Music Industry..125
Timothy Chandler and Rafael Gely

Chapter 5
Trucking Collective Bargaining: The Problem of Conflicting Labor Market Governance...151
Michael H. Belzer

Chapter 6
Labor Relations in the Healthcare Industry: A Portrait of Contradictions..185
Ariel Avgar, Adrienne E. Eaton, Rebecca K. Givan, and Adam Seth Litwin

Chapter 7
Teachers and Unions: Collective Bargaining in the Schools and the Politics of Public Education..211
Clifford B. Donn and Brenda J. Kirby

Chapter 8
Police Collective Bargaining: An Integral Part of US
Law Enforcement 229
Paul F. Clark

Chapter 9
Collective Bargaining in the Grocery Industry and the Growth
of the Nonunion Sector 255
Michael Schuster

Chapter 10
Emerging Labor Relations in High-Tech Industries 275
David Lewin and Tingting Zhang

Chapter 11
Labor Relations and Collective Bargaining in the Museum
Industry 299
Daniel J. Julius, Jai Abrams, and James N. Baron

Chapter 12
The Status of Unionization Among Undergraduate Students 317
Daniel J. Julius, Nicholas DiGiovanni, and Jai Abrams

Commentaries 333

About the Contributors 377

LERA Executive Board Members 2024–25 386

Introduction

Union Organizing and Collective Bargaining at a Critical Moment: Opportunities for Renewal or Continued Decline?

Howard R. Stanger
Canisius University

Paul F. Clark
Pennsylvania State University

John T. Delaney
Saint Vincent College

Which is the reality? Ours is a time when 70 years have passed since union density reached a peak of 34.8% in 1954 (US Bureau of Labor Statistics 2024). It is also a time when workers have organized their workplaces in the face of substantial employer animus, and a wave of strikes has produced notable gains for unionized and nonunionized employees. The interests of workers and employers diverge in many new ways today, including whether to work remotely and whether artificial intelligence–infused technology will reinforce old stereotypes and biases in making work decisions. We live in an age where the courts have methodically reduced the role and rights of unions and their workers while expanding the personhood of corporations. We live in an era in which it is difficult for young workers to afford a home, and social media seems to divide people.

This is also a period when the number of union representation elections has increased 83% over the past three years and when unions have won over 70% of elections for eight years in a row (peaking in 2023 at 79%). Notably, workers in industries that traditionally have been viewed as unorganizable, such as food services, retail stores, and high tech, have rapidly voted for union representation. This period has also seen growth in union bargaining power, which has fueled more strike activity and substantial improvements in collective agreements.

This research volume chronicles the current dual reality for workers and unions. Its composition reflects the emerging labor and employment relations landscape. Chapters cover collective bargaining in the industries of lore, such as automobile manufacturing, newspapers, and trucking; in industries that have grown an intense labor presence over time, such as police and some healthcare occupations; and in those being sought by unions as areas of the future, such as high technology and among students in higher education. The chapters document current successes and glimmers of hope for the future of the labor movement.

Yet for all the successes, there remain many disappointments for workers and unions. Givebacks during negotiations in hard times—such as the Great Recession (2007–2009) or the recent coronavirus pandemic—have yet to be recovered. Job loss has resulted from the extensive deployment of new technology. And worker attitudes, shaped by extensive employer animus, have led to extremes of worker acceptance or willingness to fight to the end. Many of society's challenges in the United States are reflected in the workings of the labor movement.

BACKGROUND

The past half-century has been a mostly sad story for organized labor in the United States. Union density, the percentage of the workforce belonging to unions, declined from 34.8% in 1954 to 10% in 2023 (US Bureau of Labor Statistics 2024). Union density in the private sector workforce was reported to be 6%, which is lower than in 1890 (Gordon 2019; US Bureau of Labor Statistics 2024). Total union membership stood at 14.4 million, down from 21 million in 1979 and 17.7 million in 1983 (Mayer 2004; US Bureau of Labor Statistics 2024).

For several decades, the decline of private sector unionism has been offset by the strength and stability of public sector unionization. Public sector union membership grew rapidly in the 1960s and 1970s, when state legislatures passed collective bargaining laws for public employees. From slightly over 3 million in 1973, public sector union ranks almost doubled to 5.8 million by 1980 and to 6.5 million a decade later. By 2010, it had reached 8.4 million. Yet in 2023, public sector union membership had fallen to 7 million (Hirsch, Macpherson, and Even 2024; US Bureau of Labor Statistics 2024) as a result of the Great Recession, state bargaining law changes that made unionization more difficult, and the US Supreme Court's 2018 ruling in *Janus* that effectively made the public sector an open shop (Supreme Court of the United States 2018). Still, compared with the private sector, public sector density rates have been robust, hovering at around 35% for the past four decades. In 2023, it was about 33% (US Bureau of Labor Statistics 2024).

There is general agreement that several factors, some operating independently and others negatively reinforcing each other, have contributed to union decline over the past 70 years. Among the more notable ones are structural shifts in the economy, employer opposition, weak labor laws, federal and state legislation that has substituted for union protection, the growth of the field of human resources management, and the limited success unions have had in responding to institutional threats with new and successful organizing and political strategies.

Although overall union density has fallen to 10%, considerable variation in density exists across industries. Unions still have a significant presence in some major US industries, where the percentage of union membership is significantly higher than the national average. For example, over 150,000 employees (about 17% of the auto industry workforce) are union members (Carey 2019; Reuters 2021; Snitkoff 2021). About 230,000 registered nurses (RNs), or 20.4% of the RN workforce, are represented by unions. And 7 million workers employed in local, state, and federal government belong to a union (34% of government employees) and work under a union contract. Within the public sector, union density for police officers is 57.5%, which is the highest percentage of union membership of any occupation in the United States (DiSalvo 2020). Clearly, the unionized segment of the US workforce and the process of collective bargaining that occurs in unionized workplaces are important and relevant in many workplaces. Chapters in this volume describe the nature and unique features of labor relations in the auto industry, in healthcare industries, and in law enforcement.

Even in sectors with lower union density, such as newspapers and retail food, which are addressed in chapters of this volume, contemporary developments have fostered a revival of interest in unions. In part, this may be due to changing attitudes. For example, the data show an increasingly favorable view of unions among the public at large. The percentage of people in the United States who approve of unions, as measured annually by Gallup since 1937, has stood above 50% each year, except 2009. Approval has increased in recent years. It reached 71% in 2022—its highest level since 1965. The 2023 poll revealed that support for unions exceeded its long-term average for the fifth consecutive year. The 2021 poll also found that 77% of young workers (18 to 34 years old) approved of unions. And consistent with academic research, the poll also revealed high support of unions by union members (86%) (Brenan 2021; Pendell 2024).

Other evidence of changing public opinion about unions is found in a 2021 Pew Research Center poll that reported a "majority of US residents continue to say the long-term decrease in the percentage of workers represented by unions is bad for working people in the United States, and for the country as a whole" (Gramlich 2021). The Pew Survey also revealed that 68% of Black adults and 64% of Hispanic adults believe that unions have a positive effect on society (Gramlich 2021).

The interest of younger workers in unions and collective bargaining is also important. Drawing from US Bureau of Labor Statistics data on unions from 2017, Economic Policy Institute economist John Schmitt (2018) reports that younger workers are transforming the US labor movement. Three-fourths of the gains (198,000) in union members between 2016 and 2017 were among workers under the age of 35. In a 2020 *New Yorker* article titled "The Faces of a New Union Movement," labor journalist Steven Greenhouse (2020) documents how labor market and economic insecurities have led younger workers to organize unions in sectors with little previous union activity, such as art galleries, museums, high-tech firms, digital media, political campaigns, cannabis shops, and elsewhere.

Writing in *The Guardian* in 2022, Greenhouse turned his attention to path-breaking union organizing victories at several locations: Starbucks stores in Buffalo, New York; a cavernous Amazon warehouse on Staten Island; an REI retail store in Manhattan; and a tech group at *The New York Times*. The key activists and employees at these workplaces were mainly young workers.

Recent years have also seen an increase in worker militancy (Combs 2024). An explosion of strikes occurred nationally in 2018 and 2019, including the "Red for Ed" strikes involving thousands of teachers across the country who walked out over school funding and pay (Johnston 2022). The number of workers involved in strikes jumped from 25,000 in 2017 to 485,000 in 2018. In 2019, the number of striking workers dropped slightly to 426,000. Over the years 2020 through 2022, the numbers declined, but significant stoppages continued to occur. Strike activity was so high in October 2021 that the month was dubbed "Striketober" by the media as workers at John Deere and Kellogg went out on long strikes, and employees of the largest health system in the nation, Kaiser Permanente, threatened a massive strike (Greenhouse 2021). Subsequently, strategic strikes in 2023 by the United Auto Workers (UAW) and a major strike threat by the Teamsters union at UPS led to substantial union bargaining gains.

The limitations of the US Bureau of Labor Statistics work stoppage data—which record only large stoppages—have led other groups to fill in the data void by tracking labor disputes more extensively. For example, *Pay Day Report*, founded by labor journalist Mike Elk (2022), identified 1,900 strikes since it began tracking in March 2020. In 2023, Cornell University's *Labor Action Tracker* documented 470 work stoppages involving 539,000 workers and about 25 million strike days. The number of work stoppages increased by about 9% between 2022 and 2023, mainly because of a few large, high-profile disputes, such as the SAG-AFTRA strike, the Coalition of Kaiser Permanente Unions strike, the Los Angeles Unified School District strike, and the UAW "stand-up" strike. These four largest strikes accounted for approximately 350,100 of the 539,000 workers, or about 65% of all workers involved in work stoppages (Cornell University 2022, 2023). Combined, these three sources have reported an increase in labor disputes and activism before and during the pandemic as the labor market tightened, giving workers more power than they had experienced in decades (Schreiber 2021).

Labor activism can also be seen in workers' attempts to form unions. The number, size, and outcome of organizing drives have long been looked at as indicators of the state of the US labor movement. Over the past several years, the number of unionization efforts has grown. Some of these efforts (like the ones at Amazon) have involved relatively large groups of workers, but most have involved relatively small workplaces.

A 2024 Bloomberg Law report noted that the National Labor Relations Board (NLRB) held 1,020 representation elections in 2021 and that unions won 75.3% of the ballots. The number of elections jumped to 1,572 in 2022, with unions winning 76.7%; elections rose further in 2023 to 1,866 elections, with unions successful in 78.9% of the cases. The year 2023 was the eighth straight in which unions won over 70% of representation elections. Before 2016, by contrast, the union win rate had not exceeded 70% since 1950 (Bloomberg Law 2024: 1).

Evidence of unions winning such a high percentage of organizing drives has led some observers to conjecture that labor was experiencing a revitalization or even a rebirth. But equally of interest is that these organizing campaigns have been taking place in nontraditional industries with little to no history of unions, such as digital media (2015–), Starbucks (2021–), REI (2022–), Amazon (2022–), Apple (2022–), Activision (2022–), and elsewhere (National Labor Relations Board 2022). This volume includes chapters covering several of these industries to provide a perspective on this ongoing development.

Employers' responses to these organizing drives have varied, from outright opposition to neutrality. Writing about the organizing campaigns at prominent high-tech firms, *The Washington Post* observed, "Faced with the threat of unionized workforces, tech companies—some of the most valuable and fastest-growing in the world—are increasingly turning to classic union-busting tactics to preserve control over their workforces" (Tiku, Albergotti, Jaffe, and Lerman 2022).

Aggressive opposition has also been the response of retail coffee giant Starbucks, which reacted to the efforts of employees to organize at a handful of stores in Buffalo in 2021 with a hostile anti-union campaign. Despite the company's efforts, one of the Buffalo stores became the first Starbucks in recent years to unionize when its baristas voted 19 to 8 in favor of union representation. Since then, about 400 company-owned stores have organized. Since July 2022, however, the rate of organizing has noticeably declined. In February 2024, in a sharp reversal of the labor strategy, Starbucks agreed to negotiate a framework for a possible master contract with Workers United, the union that represents Starbucks baristas (Bruenig 2022; Eidelson 2023; More Perfect Union 2022).

Not all high-tech companies have responded harshly to union organizing. In June 2022, Microsoft, a high-tech company with no history of formal labor unions, announced that it would remain neutral in the face of efforts by its employees to organize. This unusual response is possibly related to the failure of Starbucks' hostile and aggressive response to its organizing drive and the backlash that the approach has received. Microsoft's conciliatory position was also probably related to its controversial effort to acquire the video game maker Activision Blizzard, where a small group of 22 quality-assurance testers voted 19 to 3 in favor of a union, despite Activision management's strong opposition. In return for neutrality, the Communications Workers of America, the union that organized the Activision workers, agreed to drop its anti-trust–based opposition to Activision's merger with Microsoft (Scheiber and Weise 2022).

This fast-changing and dynamic environment is an appropriate time to examine union organizing and bargaining across US industries. Compared with the 1950s and 1960s, when union membership and influence were at their peak, the US labor movement today is less powerful but also shows strong signs of life in certain sectors of the economy. Young workers in a number of workplaces are employing nontraditional approaches to collective action, which suggests the possibility of a change in fortune for unions after decades of stagnation and decline. After the disruption and trauma of the pandemic years, there is evidence that the way many workers view their lives at work is changing. In particular, there seems to be a greater desire for equity facilitated through workplace voice and engagement. Shaped by a changing labor market and a pandemic, it is unclear whether these changes will endure. But it is clear that the US labor movement now has more momentum than it has had in decades.

The chapters of this volume document the state of labor organizing and collective bargaining in selected US industries. The chapters provide insight into whether this current interesting point in time is an inflection point, and the authors and commentators identify lessons and themes that emerge from the analyses. The industries covered in the volume reflect a mix across the economy. They were selected in part because of evolving labor activism. The industries are auto manufacturing, construction, healthcare, high technology, students in higher education, K–12 education, museums, newspapers, police, retail food, symphonies, and trucking. The chapters have been produced by labor and employment relations scholars to chronicle this interesting time. We have also enlisted expert commentators to discuss developments in many of these industries and to provide context on what the situation may precipitate. The volume updates similar assessments conducted in 1994, 2002, and 2013 and published as IRRA/LERA research volumes. We structured the chapters to focus on a common set of issues (parties, bargaining structure, critical issues, challenges to the bargaining relationship, and unrest) that will both elucidate the situation in that industry and facilitate comparison across and between industries.

INSIGHTS FROM THE CHAPTERS

Although displaying an interesting picture of the differences across industries, the chapters in this research volume suggest seven common insights. First, despite many glimmers of hope for the labor movement, the specific sectoral and general challenges unions have faced in recent decades may still outweigh opportunities. For example, unions organized nearly 100,000 workers in the 2023 NLRB elections, labor's largest gains in a quarter century (Combs 2024). And large organizing gains have occurred in the case of workers younger than 25 years old, such as baristas, students, and interns (Purifoy 2023). Yet, in that same year, the overall union density fell.

And while the successful organizing campaign at Starbucks generated significant attention and enthusiasm, in the three years since the first store organized in 2021, Starbucks employees have yet to win a union contract—though as noted earlier, Starbucks and the Workers United union have agreed to begin discussions on a "foundational framework" for bargaining that could lead to a national contract (Cunningham and Wiessner 2024).

The aggressive anti-union approach that most employers continue to take in dealing with unions may partly explain the increase in strike activity in recent years (Eidelson 2023). The reality is that, given weaknesses in US labor law enforcement, the traditional game plan employers have followed to oppose unions has continued to be generally effective. In combination with conservative court rulings and the growth of Sun Belt states relative to other parts of the United States, organized labor has remained at a disadvantage, with union density continuing to shrink despite current popularity

(Johnston 2022). Clearly, unions need changes in the legal and regulatory environment to overcome these challenges. This need may partly explain why the Teamsters union made a donation to the Republican Party in 2024 (Gurley 2024).

In the construction industry, employer opposition has grown to include seeking changes in government policy on prevailing wages and amended tax policies regarding independent contractors, which directly benefit the nonunion sector. The transient nature of the construction workforce in many trades has also created a situation in which some employers rely on undocumented or immigrant workers who are paid low wages. Although some locations still display effective traditional construction labor relations, intense competition across employers for business increasingly endangers the viability of the unionized sector of the industry.

Second, many of the chapters in this volume underscore the power of union leadership to engage members and generate union gains. In the past, union leaders were national figures, mentioned in the press for good reasons (Walter Reuther) and bad reasons (Jimmy Hoffa)—and always aligned with the struggles of the times, from workplace equity to civil rights. Today, the average person would be hard pressed to name a major union leader. Yet the emergence of new leaders has galvanized union efforts in some industries. For example, there was a clear change in direction at the UAW under its new president, Shawn Fain, which increased militancy coupled with strategic strike engagement. This resulted in substantial gains in the 2023 negotiations with the Big 3 auto companies and beyond. Next up for the UAW is an effort to leverage those gains into membership growth, with a bull's-eye painted on foreign transplants in the South, and Tesla and its larger-than-life CEO, Elon Musk.

Similarly, the leadership of Sean O'Brien, elected president of the Teamsters in 2021, appeared to make a decisive difference in the union's high-profile bargaining with UPS in 2023. The aggressive approach he took in those negotiations led to one of the strongest contracts that any union has won in recent decades.

It also seems apparent that the days of corporatist union leaders are ending, as workers seek better outcomes, and the legal framework increasingly gives workers the option to choose not to support their union. Such a situation likely portends more aggressive tactics by leaders who are judged by whether they win or lose. It also requires efforts to shape political outcomes in ways that provide more pro-union regulatory and legislative outcomes.

Third, the chapters suggest that the past several years have seen a rekindling of enthusiasm for unions. The economic uncertainty and inequality facing workers, an increased focus on social justice, the anti-union policies of the Trump administration, and the pro-union actions of the Biden administration's policies appear to have galvanized the labor movement. This is evident in most of the sectors covered in this volume, though the impact is stronger in some than others. Labor strife in K–12 education expanded, particularly in states that had been unsupportive of unions. Efforts to leverage social justice also seemed to increase labor activism. The efforts also caused challenges to police unions, which struggled to deal with the legacy of George Floyd's death while addressing increasing crime rates.

The injection of issues outside of the workplace into labor–management relations creates challenges and opportunities for unions. For example, social issues appear to have enhanced engagement with unions by younger workers and those who have college degrees. Given the nature of these employees, social justice issues have become more important for organizing. It is less clear how important these issues will be in negotiating agreements.

Fourth, unions have gained strength recently in organizations and industries that have historically shown less proclivity to embrace full-scale anti-union approaches. Museums, symphonies, higher education, K–12 education, and healthcare are battleground industries for organized labor. To some extent, these industries have become attractive to unions because they tend to employ educated workers who support progressive causes and disapprove of the way their organizations handled aspects of the pandemic. Sometimes, opportunistic partnerships have occurred here too, which seems to explain Microsoft's neutrality pledge on union organizing in return for the union's pledge not to oppose the acquisition of Activision Blizzard.

Fifth, the pandemic affected unions in contradictory ways. For example, it ignited additional public support for workers deemed "essential" in retail food and other industries, which led to compensation gains at the same time that it changed the nature of many industries. The retail sector's transformation to e-commerce shuttered many stores, including some name brands. Nonunion giants Walmart and Amazon gained substantially from this shift, while workers in traditional stores lost opportunities. Some union workers benefited from the e-commerce boom as drivers and pilots for UPS and FedEx struggled to deliver the volume of goods ordered online. Union organizing spiked in healthcare as workers, including physicians, sought ways to counter the danger they faced from the coronavirus and the societal attitudes that created regular work challenges. As symphonies and museums reduced their staff and cut hours, worker efforts to secure community support expanded dramatically and, in some cases, led to bargaining gains as the pandemic eased.

Clearly, the pandemic accelerated technology-based changes that have the potential to alter opportunities for workers in the future. For example, many toll roads have switched to wireless tolling. The increase in online education's availability created opportunities for K–12 education to substitute remote learning for snow days.

Sixth, technological advances continue to affect workers' experience on the job and their interest in unions. For example, there is considerable concern about the use of artificial intelligence (AI) platforms by employers to select workers or monitor productivity and performance. Biases in the data used to train AI interfaces, such as anti-union animus, could be leveraged by employers to avoid workers interested in unions or voice. At the same time, this could generate worker demands to be free from such monitoring, which could create more militancy and strikes. And if the use of driverless trucks becomes common in the future, a substantial number of jobs would be threatened. As the recent Hollywood writers' strike revealed, collective bargaining will be one way that workers attempt to regulate the use of AI in the workplace. They will also aggressively lobby the government for public policies that protect their members. Whether unions will be effective in these approaches is difficult to predict.

Seventh, the chapters illustrate how, for decades, the legal framework governing unionization and bargaining has been significantly and consistently tilted in favor of employers. Judicial interpretations in the private sector and recent conservative legislative changes in public employee labor law in several states have contributed to this uneven situation. The changes often suggest a theoretical victory of individual rights over collective ones, even when individuals are worse off as a result. To some extent, many of the individual rights supported by labor over time—civil rights, LGBTQ rights, fair housing, etc.—have contributed to the decline of collective rights, which arm the core of our labor relations legal system. Powerful interests of the right have used the goals of individuals to subvert the power of organized labor.

Unions have seen some progress in reversing the long-term trends under the Biden administration. President Biden has often proclaimed his intention to be the "most pro-union president" in the nation's history. And while Republicans have prevented the passage of his signature labor law reform bill, the Promoting the Right to Organize Act, the appointments he has made to the NLRB, notably general counsel Jennifer Abruzzo, have led to several important pro-union changes in the administration of labor law (Gurley 2022; Meyerson 2023).

Overall, it remains unclear whether the recent interest in unions is sustainable in the face of employer opposition, conservative judicial decisions, and an uncertain regulatory and legal environment. Even when workers made substantial gains, such as at UPS, workforce reductions followed to address increased costs. The chapter authors and commentators have provided excellent insights into the gains made in specific sectors and the nuance of ongoing activity. Yet the many highlights described do not prove a paradigm shift in union–management relations. Contributing to this lack of clarity are findings that unions have not addressed key issues in certain sectors, including the development of a more diverse K–12 education workforce, overcoming a "bro" culture in high technology that has been disrespectful to women and other underrepresented groups, and substantial variation in outcomes across bargaining locations. Whether unions can address these and the many other challenges they face has yet to be seen.

UNION ORGANIZING AND COLLECTIVE BARGAINING IN 2024 AND BEYOND

For decades, the labor and employment relations field has speculated about the possible resurgence of the US labor movement. Evidence in this volume suggests that, despite some union gains in recent years, there appears to be little reason to predict that we will see the return of widespread unionization, at least in the short term. Yet increasing union strength in the face of employer opposition in some industries and sectors noted in this volume is evidence that unions will continue to have an important role to play in US society.

The future relevance of unions is also underscored by the increasing support unions have received from the public (Johnston 2022). Clearly, people seek some (or many) of the outcomes unions provide—better compensation, fairness and protection from arbitrary treatment, and a voice at work—while also valuing their individual rights. These dual preferences create conditions for anti-union employers to exploit and have facilitated a great reduction in union density. Many employers remain committed to fighting unions aggressively because the strategy has proven very effective over the past half century. Any significant and sustained resurgence of the labor movement will require employers to drop their active opposition to unions, unions to find new strategies that can overcome that opposition, or the federal government to reform labor law with greater enforcement and stiffer penalties. Employers' opposition to unions seems unlikely to subside in the short run, so we are likely to witness more examples of unions implementing "outside of the box" strategies that may or may not be effective, especially without a supportive legal framework.

It is not time for supporters of organized labor to be dismayed, however, as changing conditions sometimes create surprising results—as the 1930s demonstrated. For this reason, the lessons of the last chapter in the volume are of special interest. The growing unionization among college students has the potential to seed unionism in many areas in coming years. That the interest includes students working in traditional university jobs, as well as athletes, suggests a broader circumstance than in earlier years. Combined with localized union successes across industries and occupations in locations such as Las Vegas, there is the potential for a new brand of labor activism to emerge and grow. While we expect this brand to be unlocked and spread by technology, it is rooted in the concerns of young people about equality and equity. Efforts by conservatives to eliminate diversity, equity, and inclusion offices and programs may cause more students to turn to unions and build a future labor coalition.

Absent dramatic changes in the approaches of employers and unions, we expect to see a continuation of the long-run trend in which unions in some sectors have strong outcomes and gains, while unions in other sectors stagnate or decline. We also expect an ebb and flow of organizing driven by changing conditions. For example, the increasing involvement of private equity in healthcare and newspapers has the potential to alter employee and public attitudes in ways that are supportive of labor. We also expect demographic changes, concerns about climate change, and social concerns to inject themselves into the labor and employment relations debate in fits and starts in the coming years. If this is indeed the case, unions will remain relevant but more so in specific sectors and industries than in others. This underscores the importance of examining the circumstances of specific industries and sectors in assessing the health and effectiveness of union organizing and collective bargaining in the US context.

REFERENCES

Bloomberg Law. 2024. "NLRB Election Statistics: Year-End 2023." Labor Data Series.
Brenan, M. 2021. "Approval of Labor Unions at Highest Point Since 1965." Gallup. September 2. https://tinyurl.com/45ypbxaw
Bruenig, M. 2022. "Starbucks Union Drive Slowed Down in July." People's Policy Project. August 4. https://tinyurl.com/4jscn7b7
Carey, N. 2019. "Fiat Chrysler's UAW Members Ratify New Four-Year Contract." Reuters. December 11. https://tinyurl.com/ycxkhzu8
Combs, R. 2024. "Analysis: Workers Spent 2023 Unionizing—and Striking—in Droves. Bloomberg Law Analysis. February 13.
Cornell University. 2022. "Labor Action Tracker." Cornell ILR School. https://striketracker.ilr.cornell.edu
Cornell University. 2023. "Labor Action Tracker." https://tinyurl.com/4x3xhazf
Cunningham, W., and D. Wiessner. 2024. "Starbucks Union Seeks National Template for U.S. Bargaining." Reuters. March 1. https://tinyurl.com/2hahfmub
DiSalvo, D. 2020. "The Trouble with Police Unions." National Affairs. Fall. https://tinyurl.com/yzj29jrz
Eidelson, J. 2023. "Summer of Strikes: American Firms Face 650,000 Worker Walkouts." Bloomberg Law. Daily Labor Report. July 20. https://tinyurl.com/3xfe3ryp
Elk, M. 2022. "Payday Tracks 1,900th Strike—8,000 Nurses Strike in CA—Inspired by Starbucks Workers, Verizon Retail Workers Win Rare Union Election." Payday. April 18. https://tinyurl.com/5h7nckd9
Gordon, C. 2019. "The State of the Unions." Dissent. February 13. https://tinyurl.com/4e8bn6dy
Gramlich, John. 2021. "Majorities of Americans Say Unions Have a Positive Effect on U.S. and That Decline in Union Membership Is Bad." Pew Research Center. September 3. https://tinyurl.com/zfr83j4t
Greenhouse, Stephen. 2020. "The Faces of a New Union Movement." *New Yorker*. February 28. https://tinyurl.com/mwyywkrh
———. 2021. "'Striketober' Is Showing Workers' Rising Power—But Will It Lead to Lasting Change?" *Guardian*. October 23. https://tinyurl.com/5h6ce7ss
———. 2022. "US Unions See Unusually Promising Moment amid Wave of Victories." *Guardian*. March 16. https://tinyurl.com/39s2d6ac
Gurley, L.K. 2022. "The Lawyer Who Could Deliver on Biden's Wish to Be the Most Pro-Union President." *Washington Post*. October 17. https://tinyurl.com/ndn3wk3m
———. 2024. "Teamsters Give GOP First Major Donation in Years with $45,000 to GOP." *Washington Post*. February 21. https://tinyurl.com/4vru47k9
Hirsch, B., D. Macpherson, and W. Even. 2024. "Union Membership, Coverage, and Earnings from the CPS." https://www.unionstats.com
Johnston, T. 2022. "The U.S. Labor Movement Is Popular, Prominent and Also Shrinking." *New York Times*. January 25. https://tinyurl.com/2tcnbp69
Mayer, G. 2004. "Union Membership Trends in the United States." Congressional Research Service. https://tinyurl.com/3ynn7bp7
Meyerson, H. 2023. "Biden's NLRB Brings Workers' Rights Back from the Dead." *American Prospect*. August 28. https://tinyurl.com/56zdy859

More Perfect Union. 2022. "Map: Where Are Starbucks Workers Unionizing." February 3. https://tinyurl.com/33dtcyrb

National Labor Relations Board. 2022. "Correction: First Three Quarters' Union Election Petitions Up 58%, Exceeding All FY21 Petitions Filed." NLRB Office of Public Affairs. July 15. https://tinyurl.com/mwmp7szz

Pendell, R. 2024. "Are Unions Experiencing a Renaissance? Not Quite." Gallup. January 23. https://tinyurl.com/bkkudc6a

Purifoy, P. 2023. "Unionization Nears Record Levels as Students, Interns Organize." Bloomberg Law. Daily Labor Report. August 24. https://tinyurl.com/2ae2py7r

Reuters. 2021. "GM Says UAW 'Well Positioned' to Represent Workers at Battery JV." Reuters. May 25. https://tinyurl.com/yvj9w59k

Schmitt, J. 2018. "Biggest Gains in Union Membership in 2017 Were for Younger Workers." Economic Policy Institute. January 25. https://tinyurl.com/2he8z2tv

Scheiber, N. 2021. "How the Pandemic Has Added to Labor Unrest." *New York Times*. November 1. https://tinyurl.com/2tezee8f

Scheiber, N., and K. Weise. 2022. "Microsoft Pledges Neutrality in Union Campaigns at Activision." *New York Times*. June 13. https://tinyurl.com/4d5vcj2f

Snitkoff, E. 2021. "Ford Has the Most UAW Represented Workers of Any Automaker." Ford Authority. March 21. https://tinyurl.com/bdh33bnm

Supreme Court of the United States. 2018. *Janus v. American Federation of State, County, and Municipal Employees Council 31, et al.* https://tinyurl.com/2673txab

Tiku, N., R. Albergotti, G. Jaffe, and R. Lerman. 2022. "From Amazon to Apple, Tech Giants Turn to Old-School Union-Busting." *Washington Post*. April 24. https://tinyurl.com/2ex93kuw

US Bureau of Labor Statistics, 2024. "Report on Union Membership." https://tinyurl.com/bdfzvsw9

Chapter 1

Collective Bargaining in Autos: Electrification, a Reformed UAW, and New Union Leadership in a Turbulent Industry

Marick F. Masters
Frank Goeddeke, Jr.
Wayne State University

Ray Gibney
Pennsylvania State University, Harrisburg

Abstract

The United Auto Workers experienced historic changes and events during the past ten years. It suffered a major scandal involving misconduct among several high-ranking officials that forced a partial government takeover of operations in 2021 and the introduction of significant constitutional and administrative reforms. A federal monitor supervised the first direct election of international officers in 2022 and 2023, which resulted in the election of dissident candidates to the presidency and six other top-level positions. Under new leadership, the union launched an aggressively novel "stand up" strike strategy in bargaining the contracts with the Big 3. Its strategy proved effective in negotiating record contracts from companies making record profits. The United Auto Workers exploited the companies' profitability in the midst of the economic challenges in financing the transition to electric vehicles. After the ratification of the contracts in late November 2023, the union launched a massive organizing campaign to represent more than 160,000 workers at 13 nonunion companies with manufacturing operations in the United States.

INTRODUCTION

Collective bargaining in the auto industry has a history of confrontation and turbulence, responding to powerful economic, political, social, and technological forces (Barnard 2004; Stieber 1962). Since the 1950s, attention has centered on the relationships between the unionized Big 3 (Ford, General Motors, and Chrysler, the latter now operating as Stellantis) and the United Auto Workers (UAW). More than a dozen major foreign- and domestic-based manufacturers have nonunion plants in the United States, whose total hourly employment exceeds the combined unionized workforces of the Big 3 (a term we use rather than the Detroit 3 because Stellantis is headquartered in the Netherlands). This iconic union has fluctuated in power and stature based on structural, cyclical, and other critical developments. In recent years, the disruptive changes in technology (i.e., electrification pursued to address climate change) and the COVID-19 pandemic have combined with intensifying competition to challenge the companies and UAW across the US auto industry. On top of this, the UAW has grappled with a major scandal implicating high-level officials in financial malfeasance for personal gain and political ambition, forcing partial government oversight with mandated reforms aimed at further democratizing the union and establishing rigorous ethical and financial protocols (Goeddeke and Masters 2021).

This chapter provides an overview of the state of collective bargaining in the US auto industry. We include some historical perspectives but concentrate on more recent developments. Thus, we update the work of Katz, MacDuffie, and Pil (2013) in "Crisis and Recovery in the U.S. Auto Industry: Tumultuous Times for a Collective Bargaining Pacesetter," which was published in LERA's 2013 research volume, *Collective Bargaining Under Duress* (Stanger, Clark, and Frost 2013). Katz, MacDuffie, and Pil conclude their analysis by observing that "although the influence of the Big Three and the UAW may decline, the auto sector remains a sizable employer and a source of revealing information concerning the evolution of production practices and industrial relations" (2013: 75).

The Big 3 have recovered from the Great Recession and concomitant bankruptcy (General Motors and the former Fiat Chrysler) or wholesale leveraging (Ford), but they face an even more challenging future in an industry where the dominant union, the UAW, has had to undergo massive internal reforms in response to what federal prosecutors referred to as a "culture of corruption" (UAW Monitor Initial Status Report 2021). We examine the overall state of the industry with its major challenges; the background of bargaining history, strategy, structure, and strikes; the principal industry parties; recent rounds of contract negotiations between the Big 3 and the UAW; current trends in union organizing; and the future of collective bargaining. Our focus is on how recent changes in the industry and parties have impacted collective bargaining, particularly in the most recent rounds since 2015. The challenges facing the parties set the stage for the future, influencing the economic viability of the companies and the prospects of the UAW in organizing nonunion auto producers with manufacturing facilities in the United States, such as Toyota, Honda, BMW, Hyundai, and Tesla.

INDUSTRY OVERVIEW

The nature and scope of the auto industry exerts powerful influences on labor–management relations among companies operating in the United States. The practical ubiquity of its products raises sensitivities to labor conditions that affect cost and availability. Employment associated with the distribution and supply chains magnifies the potential effects of worker stoppages and expensive collective bargaining contracts that may adversely affect job security. Market concentration affects the ability of firms to pass on higher employee compensation to consumers, accounting in part for their resistance to rising labor costs. The high cost of entry and sustained competitiveness require companies to ensure labor costs do not crowd out capital to their relative disadvantage, which has implications for their incentive to operate nonunion. Global pressure to transition to EVs affects the competitiveness of legacy companies such as the Big 3 and their vulnerability to labor disruptions. We focus on recent trends in industry employment, market conditions, the transition to EVs, wage levels, and aggregated unionization rates.

Structural shifts in the industry have changed collective bargaining. After several rounds of essentially concessionary bargaining from 2007 through 2019, the UAW exploited the Big 3's recent string of profitability to make "audacious" demands in 2023. It changed its bargaining strategy, used a novel approach to strikes, and engaged in publicized bargaining to impel the companies to make continual concessions to meet the members' demands. Immediately on the heels of "record contracts" ratified by the rank and file, the UAW launched a public campaign to organize the growing nonunion segment of the industry, targeting 13 specific companies and quickly following up by filing unfair labor practice charges against Honda, Hyundai, and Volkswagen for violating workers' organizing rights under the National Labor Relations Act (NLRA).

The relative bargaining power of the parties (principally the UAW and the Big 3) depends on several varyingly interconnected factors. One is the profitability of the companies, which correlates with sales. A second involves the market concentration of the industry, while a third concerns the level of unionization across manufacturers, primarily the original equipment manufacturers (OEMs) but also the parts suppliers. Fourth is the role of environmental public policy in pushing the companies to produce EVs. A fifth influencing factor is the application and interpretation of labor law to encourage union representation.

Industry Economic and Employment Import

At the macro level, the auto industry has a significant economic impact domestically and globally, far beyond the direct operation and employment of the OEMs. The industry includes hourly and salaried employees who work for the OEMs and the multitude of parts suppliers, including the growing number of electric vehicle (EV) battery producers. In addition, the auto sector encompasses the dealerships that sell at the wholesale and retail levels and companies that repair and service vehicles. Distribution and supply chains are increasingly global in nature, with domestic-based firms having extensive international operations. On top of this, numerous foreign-based OEMs operate in the United States. These producers rely heavily on foreign-based suppliers for parts and raw materials, a trend accelerated by electrification.

The auto industry, including the OEMs and the parts suppliers, exerts a multiplicative economic impact, directly employing hourly and salaried workers and generating additional jobs through spillover effects. Eighteen OEMs (13 of which are foreign based) produce in the United States, with facilities in 19 states (*Automotive News* 2023). According to the Alliance for Automotive Innovation 2022 industry report (Alliance for Automotive Innovation 2023), the US auto industry contributed 4.9% to the total GDP of the United States. It generated 9.6 million jobs directly and indirectly that paid $650 billion in payroll compensation in 2022. Because of its important economic role, auto manufacturing draws the attention of policy makers and others with an interest in its footprint on jobs, wages, communities, and the environment.

We break down direct auto industry employment into manufacturing and nonmanufacturing segments (Table 1). As of September 2023, the industry employed more than 5.6 million workers, nearly 1.1 million of whom are in manufacturing (OEMs and parts suppliers). More than 370,000 work in wholesale and retail trade, with slightly more than 2 million in dealerships. Just over 1 million are in auto repair and maintenance.

In the manufacturing segment, the total number of production-related employees increased by nearly 30% between September 2013 and September 2023 (Figure 1), rising to nearly 1.1 million. The number of workers in the motor vehicle (assembly) segment rose by 73.5% over the same period. Employment rose 21.4% to 164,500 in the body and trailer parts segment. At the end of the period, nearly 584,000 worked in the other parts components of the industry, compared with almost 545,000 at the start. But employment in this segment peaked at more than 601,000 in 2018.

Table 1
Employment in Auto Industry, September 2023
(in thousands)

Manufacturing	
Motor vehicles and parts manufacturing	1,083.7
Motor vehicles manufacturing	335.6
Motor vehicle bodies and trailers	164.5
Motor vehicle parts manufacturing	583.6
Wholesale trade	
Motor vehicle and parts wholesalers	370.3
Retail trade	
Motor vehicle and parts dealers	2,058.6
Other services	
Automotive repair and maintenance	1,030.5
Total	**5,626.8**

US Bureau of Labor Statistics, "Automotive Industry: Employment, Earnings, and Hours."

Figure 1
Employment (in thousands) in Auto Manufacturing,
September 2013 through September 2023

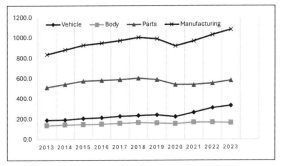

US Bureau of Labor Statistics, "Automotive Industry: Employment, Earnings, and Hours."[1]

These data do not reflect that step decline that occurred in motor vehicle employment during the Great Recession/bankruptcy years (2007 through 2010), when employment in the assembly part of the industry dropped. Nor do they reflect long-term trends in the erosion of the Big 3's employment. For example, General Motors' employment, which included hourly workers with its parts subsidiary (Delphi) at the time, shrank from 457,000 in 1985 to 182,000 in 2002 (McAlinden 2004). This erosion occurred due to cyclical effects, rising international competition, and improvements in labor productivity resulting from production-process efficiencies and technology. A report from the St. Louis Federal Reserve stated that "economic research concludes that increased productivity—for example, producing the same output with fewer workers—explains most of the decline in overall manufacturing employment. Indeed, we find that labor productivity has increased in motor vehicle assembly production as well" (Federal Reserve Bank of St. Louis 2019). Nor do aggregate trends in data reflect that shift in employment between OEMs, which manifested significant growth in the nonunion companies. Though the UAW and auto executives have suggested that electrification will result in job losses in the industry, evidence on this proposition is not clear cut (Economic Policy Institute 2021). Changes in market conditions and pressures to eliminate redundancies among production—and salaried—workers have a lot to do with fluctuations in the companies' employment levels. Technology, however, and related improvements in production processes to generate higher levels of labor productivity, continually mean fewer workers for given levels of output.

Further complicating the structure of the auto manufacturing industry is the emergence of numerous joint ventures between the Big 3 and the nonunion OEMs with foreign-based battery producers. All of these joint ventures except Ultium Cells (a joint venture between General Motors and LG Energy in Warren, Ohio) are nonunion. The UAW has pledged to organize the joint ventures, particularly those involving the Big 3, and fold their workers under the national agreements with Ford, General Motors, and

Stellantis. More broadly, non-Big 3 companies are investing heavily in building both battery and EV manufacturing sites. As an illustration of the scope of this investment, EV and battery manufacturers such as Rivian, Hyundai, and Kia have announced $24.6 billion in capital investments in the state of Georgia alone, involving projects that could create an estimated 29,700 new jobs (State of Georgia 2023).

Market Conditions and Concentration

The Big 3 operate in an increasingly global market in which their position has shrunk in relative terms by vast amounts. China has become the world's largest market for motor vehicles and has taken the lead in the production of EVs and batteries. As shown in Figure 2, China's motor vehicle sales market was nearly twice as large as that of the United States in 2022. Sales of EVs (battery and plug-in hybrids) were more than five times as large in China as in North America in 2022 and more than twice the total sales in Europe. Some analysts project that nine of the top ten automakers in the world will be based in China in the not too distant future (Mollman 2023).

US Motor Vehicle Sales, Big 3 Market Share, and Market Concentration

Several aspects of the US market for motor vehicles since the early 2000s merit note. First, US sales fluctuate widely based on cyclical and structural conditions. Second, China has surpassed the United States as the world's market and has a vast lead in EVs. Third, the Big 3's market share in the United States has continued shrinking, as nonunion, foreign-based, and domestic EV producers have grown. Market concentration within the industry has declined. These realities demonstrate the global scope of the competition facing the Big 3 and the concomitant decline in their ability to simply pass on rising labor costs to consumers through higher prices. These

Figure 2
Motor Vehicle Sales by Country, 2022

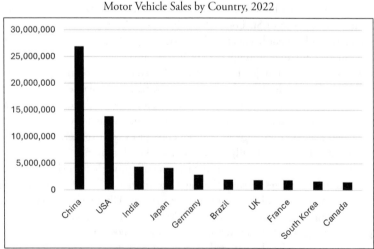

Factory Warranty List (no date).

companies compare their labor costs to nonunion foreign transplants, domestic EV producers, and emerging foreign competitors that are poised to sell in the US market. Total light vehicle sales in the United States took a nose dive during the Great Recession, when the volume was just barely above 10.4 million in 2009, before rising to nearly 17.5 million in 2016 (Figure 3). Sales had dropped to 17.0 million in 2019, before falling to 14.4 million in 2020, the year the pandemic had its most severe economic effects. Sales recovered somewhat in 2021, but in 2022 they stood at 13.7 million (*Automotive News* 2023).

In the past decade, the combined US market share of the Big 3 in light vehicle sales continued its decades-long decline, falling from 44.3% in 2013 to 40.8% in 2022 (*Automotive News* Data Center, no date). To put this drop in historical perspective, these three companies combined accounted for 90% of the US market in 1966 (WardsAuto 2019). The share among five of the largest foreign-owned companies in the United States—Toyota, Hyundai, Honda, Nissan, and Volkswagen—stood at 42.3% in 2022. Two nonunion electrical vehicle companies—Tesla and Rivian—in the United States constituted 3.6% of those sales in 2022, from negligible levels in 2016 (*Automotive News* Data Center 2023).

Over the past two decades, market concentration in the US industry has shrunk, declining 18 percentage points from 75.5% among the top four producers in 2002 to 57.5% in 2017 (Atkinson and Lage de Sousa 2021). Along with other factors, such as the steep decline in union density in the industry, this development has had profound effects on collective bargaining and labor relations because it affects the pricing power of manufacturers to pass along rising labor costs to consumers.

Figure 3
US Sales of Light Vehicles, 2004 to 2022 (in millions)

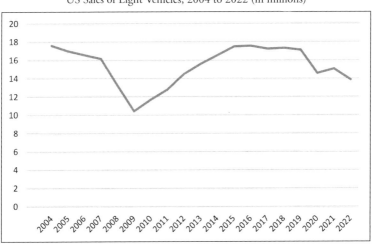

Automotive News Data Center, "2024 *Automotive News* Dealer Census" (2023).

Wages and Unionization

Regarding wage levels for motor vehicle workers, the average hourly wage climbed from $27.64 in January 2013 to $32.51 in November 2023; however, if adjusted for inflation, the average wages would have risen to $36.85. For workers in parts and manufacturing together, average wages grew from $20.93 in 2013 to $28.64 in November 2023, which is just slightly above $27.91 when adjusted for inflation (US Bureau of Labor Statistics, "CPI Inflation Calculator").

Figure 4 provides data on union membership as percentage of various segments of the workforce (i.e., union density rates) for selected years between 1983 through 2022. It shows density rates in each of these years for the total workforce, the private sector, the manufacturing sector, and then in auto manufacturing to provide a comparative perspective on trends. Union density has declined significantly across the board. Total union density fell from 20.1% in 1983 to 10.1% 40 years later. Private sector density dropped from 16.5% to 6%, and density in manufacturing declined from 27.8% to 7.8%, while density in auto manufacturing plummeted from 58.5% to 15.8% (Hirsch, Macpherson, and Even 2024).

Several major structural factors contributed to the decline in unionization in the United States (Goeddeke and Masters 2021; Greenhouse 2019; Rosenfeld 2014). First, international competition reduced the Big 3's market dominance and contributed to the shrinkage in unionized employment levels (Congressional Research Service 2010). Second, improvements in production and the introduction of automation and other technologies enabled the companies to raise productivity at given levels of labor input (Federal Reserve Bank of St. Louis 2019). Third, the UAW has failed to organize the

Figure 4
Union Membership Density Rates by Industry, 1983–2022

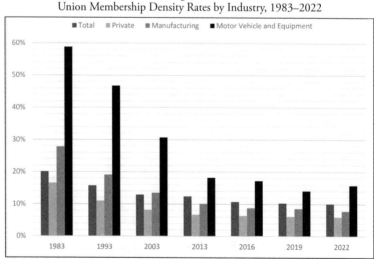

Hirsch, Macpherson, and Even (2024).

nonunion companies in the industry that have substantially increased employment at the same time the Big 3 have downsized (Press 2023).

Transition to Electrification

Because the auto industry is a major user of fossil fuels and producer of products that use such fuels, it receives considerable attention for its so-called carbon footprint. The electrification of motor vehicle fleets thus becomes an integral means of reducing carbon dioxide emissions, and numerous automakers worldwide have announced ambitious plans in that direction (Motavalli 2021).

Electric vehicles constitute a growing share of US and global vehicle sales, with many countries setting bold goals to electrify a sizable segment of industry sales by 2030. The Biden administration has endorsed making 50% of all vehicles sold domestically be electric by 2030 (US White House 2021). Major US auto producers have retooled old or built new plants to produce EVs, with 34,761 employees working in battery-producing sites (IBISWorld 2023). Legacy OEMs (Ford, General Motors, and Stellantis/Chrysler) have a total of nine plants capable of producing electrical vehicles; foreign-owned transplants have eight such sites; Tesla and other EV startups in the United States have five production plants *(Automotive News* Data Center, no date). Indeed, each of the Big 3 is committed to accelerating the transition, investing in facilities to produce relevant products, and making necessary changes in personnel to align with this transformation. General Motors, for example, announced in 2022 that it planned to produce one million EVs in North America by 2025 (PR Newswire 2022). The potential displacement of workers employed in the internal combustion engine (ICE) sector of the industry, the rise in nonunion employment in producing EVs, and significantly lower wages of EV battery workers (United Auto Workers, "Taking the High Road"²) have major implications for collective bargaining.

Figure 5 shows the rise in EVs as a percentage of total light vehicle sales in the United States [battery EVs and plug-in hybrids (PHEVs)] between 2011 and 2022. They rose from a mere 206,000 in 2013 to more than 10.52 million in 2022. This represents an increase from 0.2% of the total market sales to 13% (World Economic Forum 2023). China accounted for 59% of sales and 64% of the production of EVs around the globe in 2022. In the United States, the sales of EVs (battery EVs, PHEVs, and hybrids) grew to 12.2% by the first half of 2022, up from 11.9% in 2021 (Bush 2022).

According to the UAW, the production of EV powertrains will require 80% fewer parts and 30% fewer hours of labor than ICE vehicles (United Auto Workers, "Taking the High Road"). The transition to EVs may thus not only require fewer workers but also result in the displacement of those employed in ICE assembly and parts. The net effects of the transition to EVs, however, depends on ultimate demand for the product, suggesting the possibility of potential job increases (Economic Policy Institute 2021). Regardless, the UAW has deep concerns about potentially displaced workers and the sheer amount of capital investments required to transition to EVs. This leads to major concerns in collective bargaining to protect autoworkers. To protect jobs

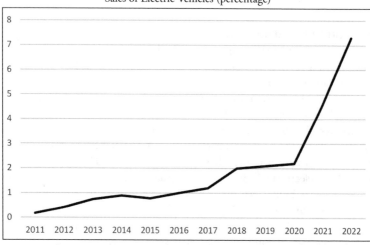

Figure 5
Sales of Electric Vehicles (percentage)

US Bureau of Labor Statistics, "Charging into the Future."

from displacement, the UAW has an interest in ensuring that the Big 3 make the investments to retool existing ICE facilities for EV production—encouraging the companies to build their own battery-production facilities that would be union represented, as opposed to entering into nonunion joint ventures for that purpose, and guaranteeing that workers employed in EV assembly and battery production are paid the same rate as those in UAW-represented ICE facilities.

THE PARTIES
Unions

The dominant union within the US auto industry is the UAW. Since the 1930s, when the nascent union solidified itself as a national organization representing autoworkers across the industry, the UAW has occupied a central position. But a few other unions also represent workers in auto manufacturing—or have attempted to do so. They include the International Association of Machinists, which represents workers such as auto mechanics, and the International Brotherhood of Electrical Workers. In addition, numerous other unions, such as the United Steelworkers, which merged in the 1990s with the former United Rubber Workers, represent workers among suppliers in the industry. Finally, the Workers United union, affiliated with the Service Employees International Union, has recently made efforts to unionize workers at Tesla.

United Auto Workers

Figure 6 reports data on UAW membership from 1936 through 2021. Membership peaked in the late 1970s but dropped significantly thereafter with the job losses forced

Figure 6
UAW Membership, 1936–2021

United Auto Workers, "Secretary–Treasurer's Report."[3]

by the confluence of stagflation, rising energy prices, and accelerating foreign competition in the US motor vehicle market. Membership rose slightly as the economy rebounded between 1983 and 1985, but it fell continuously to its low point of 355,191 in 2010. Membership rose from this low point to 430,871 in 2017 before falling back to 372,254 in 2021 and inching up to 383,003 in 2022, as reported in the UAW's latest LM-2 financial disclosure report filed with the US Department of Labor.

The number of members in a union, especially in conjunction with its density within its industry, is an important indicator of the union's capacity to threaten the production or delivery of services of a company through a strike or other job action. A large union with significant density has the potential to do extensive damage to an employer through strikes and to mobilize community support for its bargaining stances.

Another aspect of membership relevant to a union's power is its composition. Unions with occupationally and industrially diverse memberships may find themselves spread thinner in trying to service members in units with divergent needs and expectations. UAW membership has grown more industrially and occupationally heterogeneous as it has broadened its organizing paths, partly in response not only to new opportunities but also to declining employment in the Big 3 over several decades.

Figure 7 shows the percentage of the UAW membership circa 2021 by sector. It reveals that 35% comes from auto manufacturing, while 21% emanates from technical, office, and professional workers, many of whom are in the public sector. Thirty-one percent of UAW members work for independent parts suppliers or in other manufacturing sectors, with 10% in aerospace and agricultural and construction equipment combined.

Figure 7
UAW Membership by Sector

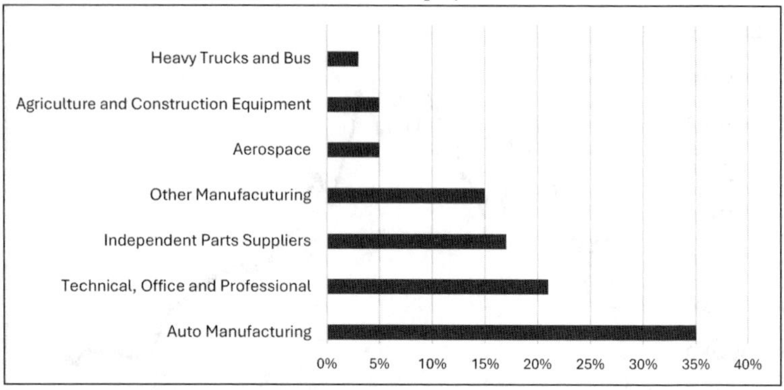

Sector	Percentage
Heavy Trucks and Bus	~2%
Agriculture and Construction Equipment	~4%
Aerospace	~5%
Other Manufacuturing	~15%
Independent Parts Suppliers	~17%
Technical, Office and Professional	~21%
Auto Manufacturing	~36%

United Auto Workers, "UAW Basics."

UAW Scandal, Government Monitoring, and Direct Elections

The current state of labor–management relations in the industry cannot be fully appreciated without reference to the scandal that engulfed the union for more than a decade. News of the scandal broke in the media in July 2017 (for detailed information on the nature, scope, prosecution, and government remedy of the scandal, though the underlying criminal activity began several years earlier, see Goeddeke and Masters 2021). The criminal wrongdoing involved the misuse of union-connected finances, especially those associated with the joint training centers administered by the UAW and the Big 3 by the union and each company. Eventually, federal prosecutors secured the indictment, conviction, and imprisonment of a dozen UAW officials, including two former international presidents, Dennis Williams and Gary Jones, and a handful of high-ranking corporate officials with the former Fiat Chrysler Automobiles.

As a result of criminal investigations that began nearly a decade ago, the UAW was brought under partial government control to implement major reforms, which led to its first-ever direct member elections of its governing international executive board (IEB) in 2022–2023. These elections ended 70 years of one-party rule by the administration caucus of the UAW, putting into office top leaders who led the equally historic bargaining in 2023. Under these new election procedures, dissidents affiliated with the Unite All Workers for Democracy (UAWD), which formed in 2018 to advocate constitutional revision in the UAW with a focus on direct elections of the IEB and an end to excessive collaboration with management, captured seven of the 14 IEB positions, including the presidency, two international vice presidents, secretary-treasurer, and three regional directors. Shawn Fain, an international representative of the UAW support by the UAWD, was declared winner in the run-off presidential election by a court-appointed federal monitor on March 25, 2023—just in time to preside over the union's special bargaining convention convened to set priorities for the 2023 round of bargaining with the Big 3, which kicked off in mid-July, two months before the contract expiration date of midnight September 15, 2023.

Employers

The automotive industry is divided into several categories based on the companies' positions in the supply chain. At the apex lie the manufacturers that assemble parts into final products destined for sale. To varying degrees, these companies may also produce vehicular parts. In the United States, the dominant players in this category include the unionized Big 3. Multitudes of suppliers fit into tiers defined in terms of their proximity to the OEMs (i.e., those that assemble parts into cars or trucks for sale). In the United States, the OEMs include domestic-owned and foreign-owned producers that manufacture and sell vehicles. Suppliers of numerous parts and raw materials provide the parts to assemble vehicles for market distribution. Logistics and transportation companies play an important role in distributing the goods required at various stages of supply chain and production processes.

Manufacturers: Big 3 and Nonunion

The principal OEMs that sell vehicles in the United States fall into three segments: (1) the unionized Big 3 (Ford, General Motors, and Chrysler/Stellantis); (2) the nonunion, domestic-owned EV manufacturers (e.g., Tesla and Rivian); and (3) the foreign-owned companies that both prodtabluce and sell vehicles in the US market. We also identify the top-ranked suppliers in the United States, comparing the rankings in 2011 to 2022, as reported by *Automotive News*. In addition, our analysis covers the various joint ventures between the Big 3 and other companies engaged in various phases of the manufacturing of EVs.

In the past several decades, the Big 3 have experienced a continual decline in their share of domestic light vehicle sales. As a result, they suffered financial losses and changed the geography of their manufacturing base, resulting in sizable reductions in their plants in the United States. Their employment, both hourly and salaried, also dropped, contributing to the loss of hundreds of thousands of union jobs.

Figure 8 shows the dramatic drop in the Big 3's market share from the early 1960s to 2016. The drop has been staggering. In combination, their market share dropped from 90% in 1966 to closer to 80% in the 1970s, falling to just above 70% in the 1980s, where it held until the early 2000s. By 2007, the Big 3's share had fallen below 50%, and in 2022, it stood at barely above 40% (*Automotive News*).

As their share of the market declined and companies introduced various improved manufacturing processes and increased automation, the Big 3 also significantly reduced the number of car and truck assembly plants in the United States to correct for overcapacity. The three companies had 46 such plants in the United States in 2007 but only 27 in 2023 (Table 2).

As noted, the shift to EVs resulted in new competitors entering the domestic market and spawned a wave of new joint ventures to produce EV components and assemble such vehicles. Rivian and Tesla employ 14,122 and 127,855, respectively, worldwide. The joint ventures between the Big 3 and foreign-based manufacturers opened more than a dozen such plants in the United States, and numerous others are in various stages of development. More broadly, the Big 3 and other companies

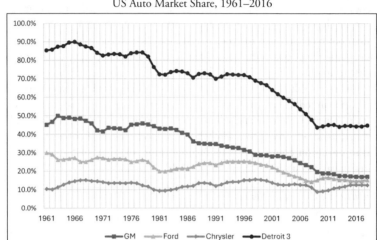

Figure 8
US Auto Market Share, 1961–2016

WardsAuto (2019).

Table 2
Number of Big 3 Car and Truck Assembly Plants in North America

	2007			2023		
	United States	Canada	Mexico	United States	Canada	Mexico
Ford	13	2	3	12	2	2
General Motors	21	3	4	13	2	3
Chrysler	12	3	2	5	2	3
Total	**46**	**8**	**9**	**27**	**6**	**8**

Automotive News Data Center (2023).

recently made announcements pertaining to manufacturing sites for the production and assembly of EV components, including batteries. Table 3 provides a partial list of recent announcements to show the magnitude and scope of such initiatives. These investments have implications for the allocation of financial, human, and physical resources, impacting employment and wages. Increasingly, the emerging EV companies compete with the Big 3 for market share and factors of production. Thus, the Big 3 will gauge their potential competitiveness by comparing their financial performance and labor costs to the nonunion domestic EV companies as well as the foreign-based transplants in the United States.

Table 3
New Battery Plants in United States Announced by October 25, 2021

Manufacturer	Location	Expected opening
Ford	TN	2025
Ford and SK	KY	2025
Ford and SK	KY	2026
General Motors and LG Chemical	OH	2022
General Motors and LG Energy	TN	2023
General Motors and LG Energy	TBD	TBD
General Motors and LG Energy	TBD	TBD
SK Innovation	GA	2022
SK Innovation	GA	2023
Stellantis and LG Energy	TBD	2024
Stellantis and Samsung SDI	TBD	2025
Toyota	NC	2025
Volkswagen	TN	TBD

Source: US Department of Energy 2021.

Suppliers

Approximately 30,000 components go into the building of a vehicle (Figure 9). US-based manufacturers import those components from 186 countries. The supply chain consists of three basic tiers. Tier 1 supplies basic parts to the assembly of vehicles, with its suppliers dealing directly with the OEMs. Tier 2 includes companies that provide parts to Tier 1 suppliers and includes producers that may serve a variety of industries. Tier 3 provides raw materials for the production of vehicles and other products with similar requirements. Globalization, electrification, macroeconomic conditions, demography, and geopolitical developments influence the composition and structure of the market of producers in these supply tiers. According to a recent study by Deloitte (Coffman, Iyer, and Robinson 2023), the auto supplier industry is facing structural challenges relating to the rising cost of capital, aligning production strategies to meet changing product demands, and streamlining costs to increase profit margins.

Three developments highlight the changing composition of the supply chain. First, the number of US-based companies in the top 20 global suppliers in auto has fallen, along with their respective share of the sales revenues of these companies. In 2011, five US-based companies (Cummins, TRW, Lear, Johnson Controls, and Delphi) (*Automotive News* Research and Data Center "Tables and Lists," no date) fell into the top 20, comprising nearly 20% of this group's sales revenue. By 2021, only three US-based companies (Lear, Tennoco, and Borg Warner) made this ranking.

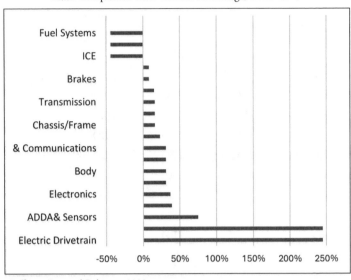

Figure 9
Auto Component Sales Growth Percentage, 2022–2027

Coffman, Iyer, and Robinson 2023.

Second, the shift to electrification increases the dependence of the OEMs on suppliers of batteries (Vendetti 2022). The five largest manufacturers of battery cells (CATL, LG Energy Solutions, Panasonic, BYD, and Samsung) comprise 81% of the market share for this product; China is responsible for 66% of the global production of vehicles.

Third, the components used to produce batteries and the natural resources extracted and processed for their production are also concentrated in suppliers based in a handful of countries outside the United States (Dungs 2023). China makes 77% of the cathodes and 92% of the anodes used in battery cell production, and it refines 66% of lithium and 73% of cobalt, which are vital natural resources in this process (King 2023).

Government

Government at federal, state, and local levels in the United States has a major influence on the auto industry, the UAW, and labor–management relations. Because of the economic impact of the industry, all levels of government have an interest in securing employment in the industry. Concerns about climate change and the role of fossil fuels as a contributing factor led to policies and programs to encourage the rapid transition to EVs. To promote industrial commerce and secure workers' ability to organize collectively into unions, lawmakers also enact various labor statutes to define the relative rights and powers of unions and employers in the process of achieving bargaining recognition, negotiating contracts, and resolving disputes. Appointments to independent agencies, such as the National Labor Relations Board (NLRB), which oversee these laws, have an important effect on rulings and legal interpretations.

The federal government has played a major role in providing financial assistance to the Big 3 to save them from liquidation and attendant additional plant closures and job losses. Deep concerns about the adverse effects of financial distress in the auto industry led the federal government in December 2008 to provide what amounted to almost $80 billion in assistance to General Motors and Chrysler through the Targeted Asset Relief Program (Cannis and Webel 2013). Federal aid could not avert General Motors' and Chrysler's bankruptcies, which forced the companies to restructure and shed assets, including plants and dealerships.

As a major user of fossil fuels in producing products that contribute substantially to environmental concerns, the auto industry receives considerable attention from policy makers and regulators addressing environmental protection. The electrification of motor vehicle fleets thus becomes an integral means of reducing carbon dioxide emissions (Motavalli 2021). Policy makers target it for prescriptive measures to reduce the producers' adverse environmental effects, encouraging acceleration in the transition from ICEs, which rely on fossil fuels, to electric EVs. In the United States, for example, numerous federal policies encourage the production and purchase of EVs, which have required changes in manufacturing facilities and personnel. The Biden administration endorses making 50% of all vehicles sold domestically be electric by 2030 (US White House 2021).

On May 2, 2023, UAW president Shawn Fain sent a memo to all UAW employees, "Talking Points on President Biden and EVs" (Lawrence 2023) He discussed his recent visit to Washington, D.C., to speak to the importance of having a "just transition." Fain enumerated recent plant closures by Stellantis, Ford, and General Motors and the lower wages paid to employees at the joint ventures to produce batteries, including General Motors' Ultium joint venture with LG Chemical, which (before recent contract agreements with the UAW) started its hourly workers at $16.50 an hour with a seven-year progression to $20. In the memo, Fain observed that President Biden had announced his bid for re-election on April 25, 2023, but noted, "We want to see national leadership have our back on this before we make any commitments" (Hall and Beggin 2023).

Another set of policy considerations pertains to labor laws that affect worker organizing. Here the major applicable statute is the NLRA, as amended, which establishes policies about the organizing of workers in industries such as auto manufacturing (OEMs and suppliers). A key issue now facing the UAW is organizing nonunion parts of the auto sector in the United States, including workers employed by newly formed joint ventures with the Big 3 to produce batteries and assemble EVs. For example, Ford has invested in the joint ventures with SK Innovation of South Korea to establish three battery sites and an assembly plant in its Blue Oval City and Blue Oval SK locations in Tennessee and Kentucky, respectively. General Motors has invested in four battery manufacturing joint venture sites with LG Chemical of South Korea. Stellantis has battery-producing joint ventures with Samsung SDI. Under existing labor law, the UAW typically needs to organize each of these ventures on a case-by-case basis through a certification-election process that can prove challenging in many dimensions. It would prefer to have a system in which bargaining recognition could be achieved if a majority of the employees of a prospective bargaining-unit sign cards authorizing the UAW to represent them. But employers are under no legal obligation to grant such recognition and may insist on holding a form election under the supervision of the NLRB.

To encourage union organizing, including the recognition of workers through the demonstration of majority status via authorization cards, the current NLRB under President Biden's recent appointments took steps through its decision and the NLRB's General Counsel's guidance in the case of *Cemex Construction Materials Pacific, LLC* (372 NLRB No. 130, August 25, 2023). The guidance issued on November 2, 2023, echoed the two goals of public policy regarding union organizing under the NLRA: "Effectuating ascertainable employee free choice and deterring employer misbehavior" (National Labor Relations Board, "Guidance"[2]). The upshot of the new standard adopted by the board to promote the recognition of labor unions is to shift the burden to the employer to request an election if it doubts a claim of majority status by a union based on authorization cards. If it does not do so, then the board may grant recognition and order bargaining if the claim of majority status has merit. Furthermore, if a company interferes with workers' right to form a union and thus prevents a fair certification election, then the board may grant recognition. If an election is held, the board will scrutinize the company's conduct if allegations of unfair labor practices arise. In another development, the NLRB also restored expedited election procedures for union recognition that require the parties to proceed with an election before unfair labor practice charges are resolved. Delaying the election until such resolution may damage the union's chances of winning, as support among workers tends to erode over time (Lawrence and LaReau 2024; Weissner 2023).

BARGAINING STRUCTURE, STRATEGY, AND STRIKES

Bargaining in auto manufacturing reflects the relative position and power of the parties in the industry. During UAW's formative years, when it struggled through the "sit down" strikes to gain recognition and Walter Reuther tamed internal factionalism to consolidate his political base, the parties established the contours of a bargaining structure that still prevails (Barnard 2004; Stieber 1962). The UAW also initiated its fundamental strategy of "targeting" companies for bargaining to lay the basis for a pattern agreement in the industry. The union exploited its power to negotiate precedent-setting contracts that raised wages and innovated benefits that built the middle class.

Structure and Strategy

The structure of contemporary bargaining in the US auto industry represents a version of pattern bargaining, in which the UAW attempted to standardize major contractual provisions across the Big 3. The parties bifurcated negotiations between the national and local levels. The UAW is internally organized around the major OEMs, with each of its three international vice presidents assigned by the UAW president to cover one of the three companies. The UAW has typically "targeted" one of the Big 3 for launching negotiations, with the contracts having a common expiration date. It strives to target the company that could yield the best contract, which it can then use to "whipsaw" the other two.

The national contracts cover major economic issues, including wages and benefits, and address matters that directly or indirectly affect capital investments to secure jobs among the rank and file. Local negotiations supplement national bargaining. Local plant bargaining focuses on work rules, production specifications and schedules, and other terms and conditions relevant to plant-level conditions (Katz, MacDuffie, and Pil 2013). The UAW sets strategies for national negotiations across major industries and employers through "bargaining conventions" that are held before the start of the negotiations with the Big 3 and other major employers. Delegates to this special convention are members of the union's previous constitutional convention, who are elected at the local level by secret ballot of the membership.

The UAW national contract negotiations with the Big 3 have historically established a pattern to affect key suppliers of auto parts and adjacent manufacturing industries, such as aerospace and agricultural equipment (Budd 1992). Because unionization in auto and other manufacturing industries has fallen dramatically in recent decades, the pattern effects of the UAW have waned, even within the top domestic auto manufacturers. Each of the companies has faced increasing pressures to adapt contractual provisions to specific organizational circumstances.

Strikes

As the dominant domestic automakers gained market share and the UAW increased its density in the assembly and parts supplier segments, bargaining took on a ritualistic quality in which frequent strikes at the national and local plant levels occurred. As shown in Table 4, the UAW struck at least one of the Big 3 in each round of national bargaining between 1955 and 1976. Afterward, in the face of stiffening international competition, strikes became much less frequent at both the national and local levels, reflecting the more general decline in organized labor's position in the United States. Union density and strike frequency plummeted in the 1980s as companies became much more resistant to labor's demands and willing to replace strikers to weaken their bargaining resolve (Greenhouse 2019; Noble 1985; Rosenfeld 2014).

As the Big 3 lost market share and faced periods of declining sales and profitability, they had to close plants and lay off workers. The companies faced not only cyclical fluctuations in consumer demand but structural forces that overwhelmed them by the early 2000s. Domestic vehicle sales had begun to decline before the US economy dipped into the Great Recession in late 2007, and by then, the companies had experienced significant losses. In fact, between 2001 and 2007, the companies laid off nearly 160,000, or close to 39% of their hourly workers (Figure 10). As the economy dove deep into recession, the Big 3 faced existential financial threats (Canis et al. 2009). Chrysler and General Motors were forced to declare bankruptcy in 2009 after receiving federal assistance (Canis and Webel 2013). In late 2006, Ford secured $23.6 billion in loans, having suffered huge losses in that year of $12.7 billion, which gave it the capital to escape bankruptcy (Vlasic 2009). Between 2007 and 2010, the Big 3 and the UAW had to negotiate contracts imposing major economic concessions on workers. As a condition for receiving federal aid and emerging from bankruptcy, Chrysler and General Motors had to engage in major restructuring, close plants, reduce employment, and shed dealerships (Canis and Webel 2013). To remain competitive, Ford had to impose comparable cutbacks (Cutcher-Gershenfeld, Brooks, and Mulloy 2015b).

Table 4
UAW Strikes Against the Big 3, 1950–2019

Year	Company	Number of days	Number of strikers	Level
1950	Chrysler	102	95,000	Local
1955	Ford	1	78,000	Company
	General Motors	12	160,000	Company
	Chrysler	1	14,000	Local
1958	Ford	13	75,000	Company
	General Motors	26	270,000	Company
	Chrysler	6	56,000	Company
1961	General Motors	20	239,000	Company
	Ford	19	116,000	Company
1964	General Motors	8	15,000	Local
	Chrysler	2	12,000	Local
	General Motors	45	275,000	Company
	Ford	19	25,000	Local
1967	Ford	65	159,000	Company
	General Motors	13	44,000	Local
	Chrysler	10	17,000	Local
	General Motors	1	15,000	Local
1970	General Motors	134	355,000	Company
1973	Chrysler	9	111,400	Company
	Ford	68	166,300	Company
	General Motors	1	66,700	Company
1976	Ford	28	166,300	Company
1998	General Motors	54	152,200	Local
2007	General Motors	2	74,000	Company
2019	General Motors	42	46,000	Company

Annual reports on strikes prepared by US Bureau of Labor Statistics, 1950 through 1980 and various other US BLS reports since, including information at https://www.bls.gov/wsp.

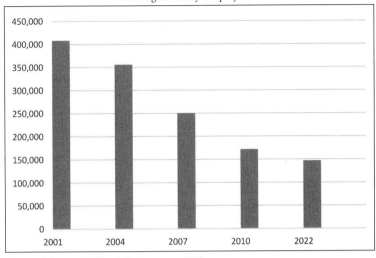

Figure 10
Total Big 3 Hourly Employment

Companies' annual 10K and 20-F reports to SEC.

The Great Recession, Bankruptcy, and Recovery: 2007 and 2009 Negotiations

The United States suffered a steep recession between December 2007 and June 2009 in which the nation's GDP shrank by 4.3%; unemployment peaked at 10% in October 2009 (Goeddeke and Masters 2021). This cyclical factor exacerbated the structural problems encountered by the Big 3.

As the 2007 negotiations approached, the companies faced labor-cost structures that were uncompetitive relative to their foreign-based competitors, several of which had established manufacturing sites that operated nonunion in the United States over recent decades. The Big 3 had average hourly compensation levels that vastly exceeded those of employees of nonunion transplants. In the 2007 contracts (as amended in 2009), the Big 3 and the UAW took several notable measures to reduce labor costs. They introduced a two-tier compensation system to provide lower wage and benefit levels for new hires and more flexibility to hire part-time and temporary workers. The parties negotiated the replacement of traditional benefit defined pension plans with defined contribution plans for new hires. In addition, they agreed to shift the liabilities of retiree healthcare obligations from the companies' balance sheets to separate entities known technically as voluntary employee beneficiary associations, to be financed by the contributions from the companies.

The Big 3's market share shrunk even further during the depths of the Great Recession, which caused the volume of sales to plummet. Despite efforts to avoid doing so, Chrysler declared Chapter 11 bankruptcy on April 30, 2009, and General Motors followed suit on June 1, 2009. Through a massive infusion of federal financial assistance, the companies survived bankruptcy but had to massively reduce their footprint in terms of plant capacity, hourly and salaried workers, and dealerships. Through the bankruptcy process, the old Chrysler and the old General Motors emerged as the New Chrysler Group LLC and the New General Motors Company with significantly fewer employees, plants, and dealerships, and with lower production.

In 2009, the UAW and the Big 3 reopened their contracts to agree to new cost-saving terms. They suspended cost-of-living allowances and performance bonuses, froze wages for new employees, and pledged not to strike (at least in the case of General Motors and Chrysler). Ford, which did not undergo bankruptcy, was not able to secure a no-strike pledge; its workers rejected a tentative contract with such a stipulation in the 2009 negotiations. In addition, the Big 3 and the UAW agreed to eliminate the so-called jobs bank that essentially guaranteed workers who were laid off from their regular jobs the pay and benefits equivalent to what they were earning while at work.

Contract Negotiations 2011–2019

By 2009, the three companies had regained profitability by increasing their sales significantly from the depths of the Great Recession while having cut their labor costs extensively. In 2011, the companies and the UAW renegotiated their respective four-year contracts (Goeddeke and Masters 2021). While they had avoided collapse, they still faced relentless international competition, as their collective market share in the United States had fallen below 50%. In addition, compared with the transplants, the Big 3 still had sizable labor-cost disadvantages (Table 5). After weeks of intense negotiations across the three companies, the parties agreed to pattern contracts that maintained the two-tier wage structure but increased the base by a slight amount at the second tier. Base wages at Tier 1, or among legacy (pre-2007) workers, were frozen for the life of the contracts (four years). Profit-sharing formulas were changed to be based on earnings before interest and taxes.

Overall, the Big 3 generated more than $65 billion in net income in 2011 through 2014. Their total sales grew pronouncedly since the nadir in 2009, which enabled them to add more hourly workers. One of the biggest sore points that festered in these years was disgruntlement over the two-tier wage structure. It created considerable friction among rank-and-file members and eroded confidence in the union's capacity to champion solidarity. In addition to having a lower base wage, the second-tier workers lacked a defined benefit pension plan, instead having the defined contribution variety. As the 2015 negotiations drew near, there were demands for collapsing the wage differential and providing a general wage increase.

The 2015 Negotiations

By 2015, Fiat Chrysler had closed the gap with the transplants, having lowered its costs from $52 per hour to just $47, representing a $5 drop compared with the transplants' $3 reduction (Table 4; Goeddeke and Masters 2021). Ford's total labor costs dropped one dollar, while General Motors' rose two. Thus, General Motors and

Table 5
Hourly Labor Costs for Auto Manufacturers

Manufacturer	2007	2011	2015	2019
Fiat Chrysler		$52	$47	$50
Ford	$71	$58	$57	$61
General Motors	$78	$56	$55	$63
Transplants, average	$49	$50	$47	$50

Automotive News, no date; Cannis et al. 2009; Ford Motor Company 2019; Goeddeke and Masters 2021.

Ford each had at least a 21% disadvantage in labor costs compared with those of Fiat Chrysler and the transplants.

The UAW surprised most auto industry analysts in 2015 by selecting Fiat Chrysler as its target. On September 15, 2015, the day the contract was set to expire, the parties reached a tentative agreement. The Fiat Chrysler workers, however, rejected the proposed contract by 65%. A principal objection centered on the two-tier wage structure. Opponents of the tentative agreement objected that the Tier 2 workforce would not be shrunk to the 25% cap presumed to take effect at that time and that the wage gap would not be fully closed but would fall short of the $28 per hour goal at the designated rate of slightly above $25 per hour.

The Fiat Chrysler–UAW contract that was finally approved by the rank and file in October included an eight-year pathway to close the gap between the two tiers. It retained two 3% general wage increases and two 4% lump sum payments, as initially negotiated. The parties also kept the improvement in the profit-sharing arrangement, which provided for the payouts to be based on 100% of North American profits, as opposed to 85% in the 2011 accord.

The ratification of the second Fiat Chrysler tentative agreement paved the way for negotiations to proceed with the other two Big 3. Negotiations moved to General Motors immediately afterward and then to Ford. These companies followed the pattern, providing for the collapsing of the two-tier wages within eight years, including lump sum and general wage increases of 4% and 3%, respectively, and maintaining healthcare benefits without additional cost-shifting. General Motors followed Fiat Chrysler and eliminated the cap on profit-sharing payouts, though Ford did not. General Motors and Ford also provided healthcare for Tier 2 workers, and Ford followed Fiat Chrysler's lead in raising its contributions to the Tier 2 workers' 401(k) plans.

The 2019 Negotiations

When the 2019 contract negotiations kicked off in July, the tone differed sharply from the amicability shown in 2015 (Goeddeke and Masters 2021). Despite profitability, Ford and General Motors had announced significant downsizing in 2018. General Motors had announced a plan to shutter five plants, four in the United States and one in Canada. Auto sales had declined, and the industry was buffeted by disruptive technological changes connected with increasing pressures to transition to EVs.

The UAW announced on September 13, 2019, that it was "targeting" General Motors, which had provoked the most animosity among rank-and-file members because of its earlier announced plant closures. The UAW had primed the rank and file to prepare for a strike, having raised its dues in 2014 to shore up its then-dwindling strike fund. The companies, also in anticipation of a strike, built inventory to give them a cushion in case of a disruption in production from a strike. Lasting 40 days, 48,000 UAW members struck at 34 General Motors plants, costing the company $3 billion.

To get a deal, General Motors made significant cash payouts, which were followed at Ford and Fiat Chrysler. The parties expedited the path to closing the tiered wage gaps, established a path for temporary workers to earn permanent status, offered a healthcare plan to temporary workers, preserved healthcare benefits, procured sizable product investments ($7.7 billion in the case of General Motors), granted general wage increases and lump sum payments, continued profit sharing, and paid hefty ratification bonuses.

BARGAINING 2023

The more ideologically militant leadership at the UAW exploited key economic, political, and technological realities in implementing a novel bargaining strategy. First, the union argued that because the companies had achieved record profits over the past decade, the workers deserved record contracts to recompense them for the sacrifices made during the recession/bankruptcy years. The UAW exclaimed that the companies had generated $250 billion in profits in their North American operations over the past decade. In their North American markets in 2022, the respective companies generated net income (earnings before interest and taxes, in the case of Ford and General Motors) of nearly $13 billion (General Motors), $9.2 billion (Ford), and $14.93 billion (Stellantis), which enabled the companies to make average profit-sharing payments to hourly workers of $9,176, $12,750, and $14,760, respectively, for 2022 (Noble 2023).

Second, the UAW recognized that the enormous capital demands to finance the accelerating transition to EVs made the companies more vulnerable to the adverse effects of strikes than they would have been in less-disruptive periods of technological/product change. It urged policy makers to give labor a place at the decision-making table to create a "fair and just transition" rather than a "race to the bottom" (Eisenstein 2023).

Third, the UAW tapped an increasingly favorable public opinion toward unions to advocate wage increases commensurate with raises in executive compensation in the Big 3; the Big 3's CEOs had reaped increases averaging 40% in the years between 2019 and 2022. The union justified its operational and symbolic militancy on the grounds that workers deserved not to have to live paycheck to paycheck while the companies were sufficiently flush to heap large rewards on their CEOs while autoworkers' wages had declined 20% in real purchasing power since the 2019 contracts.

The strategy developed by the UAW, encapsulated by the "stand up" strike reminiscent of its "sit down" precursor, replaced the traditional approach of targeting one company at the start of negotiations with concurrent bargaining across the Big 3 to set the "pattern." In a clear break with the past, UAW president Shawn Fain announced on July 10, 2023, that the UAW was dispensing with the ceremonial handshake openings between the union's and the three companies' bargaining teams in what had become a photo-op ritual. Instead, the UAW International's leadership would hold member-handshake meetings at a plant of each of the companies to kick off bargaining. In announcing this change, Fain said, "The members come first. … I'll shake hands with the CEOs when they come to the table with a deal that reflects the needs of the workers who make this industry run. When the 150,000 autoworkers at Ford, General Motors, and Stellantis receive the respect they are due for their sacrifice in generating the historic profits of the past decade, then we can proceed with a handshake" (Strong 2023).

UAW's new bargaining strategy involved publicizing member demands to arouse membership support and galvanize favorable public opinion. The initial demands included the following: increase in wages (reportedly 46% over the life of the contract), restoration of the cost-of-living allowance, restoration of defined benefit plans and retiree healthcare, more paid time off (eventually construed as meaning a 32-hour work week with pay at 40 hours), increase in payments to retirees on pensions, enhancement of profit-sharing-formula payments, limits on the use of temporary employees, job security for laid-off workers, and the right to strike over plant closures (United Auto Workers "News, Resources, and Actions"). Industry analysts reported that these proposals, if fully adopted, would raise the hourly cost of autoworkers at the Big 3 from roughly $65 to $150 (Martinez 2023), compared with $55 at the foreign transplants and $45 to $50 at Tesla (Lawrence and LaReau 2023).

Although the union publicized its demands on August 1, the companies waited for several weeks before putting their counteroffers on the table. During the period between August 31 and September 8, the three companies made their counters public. Member demands vastly exceeded the companies' offers, though some differences emerged across the Big 3. The UAW quickly rejected the offers as insulting. Shawn Fain had chastised the Big 3 for stalling negotiations by waiting so long to make their initial proposals, thus making it increasingly unlikely that tentative agreements could be reached before the contracts expired. Fain emphasized that the contract expiration date of midnight on September 15, 2023, was a deadline not a reference point. The UAW held open the extent to which it might strike one or more of the companies at any of their specific facilities, depending on the progress of negotiations.

When the contracts expired on September 15, 2023, without tentative agreements, the UAW launched its first wave of strikes. Over the next six weeks, it conducted five waves of strikes, gradually escalating the pressure on the companies over time to force more concessions. Symbolically, Shawn Fain illustrated the rising tension in a Facebook LiveStream appearance on October 6, 2023, in which he wore a T-shirt that read "Eat the Rich." If the union felt a company had been particularly forthcoming in negotiations (as it did when Stellantis made concessions granting the union the right to strike over plant closures), then it would exempt it from a strike action taken during that specific time.

Over the course of the strikes, which ended on October 30 with the tentative agreement at General Motors, the union called on 48,313 workers to strike at nine plants and 38 parts distribution centers. The waves varied in length, from more than 40 days to just two days, depending on the company and location. Together, the strikes impacted between nearly 31% and 36% of the companies' production based on the first eight months of 2023, according to data from the *Automotive News* Data Center.

The companies reported that the strikes cost them billions in revenue losses in the third quarter of 2023 (Knutson 2023). General Motors reported losing $1.1 billion, Ford lost $1.7 billion, and Stellantis $3.2 billion. However, each of the companies is still expected to make significant profits in 2024, though somewhat below previously projected levels. The negotiated contracts were estimated to raise labor costs by billions: General Motors reported that its contract with the UAW would raise its labor costs by $9.3 billion through 2028, when the new agreement expires (Walz 2023).

The Anderson Economic Group (2023) estimated that the strikes cost the US economy over $10.4 billion, with the Big 3 losing over $4.34 billion. Based on strike benefit payments of $500 per striker per week, we estimate that the UAW spent more than $82 million.

Eventually, the strikes produced the effect the UAW wanted, compelling the companies to make sufficient concessions to reach tentative agreements with Ford (October 25), Stellantis (October 28), and General Motors (October 30). The UAW won a 25% increase in general wages (not compounded) for the roughly four-and-half-year contracts (United Auto Workers, "News, Resources, and Actions"). It secured the restoration of the cost-of-living allowance, reductions in the time to reach the top wage rate to three years from eight, and the transition of temporary workers to full-time status with pay increases for such workers until their transition. The companies further agreed to eliminate wage tiers, grant the right to strike over plant closures, increase contributions to 401(k) plans, increase payments to legacy retirees in defined benefit pension plans, and provide for a path to recognition of joint venture battery plants in selected sites at General Motors and Stellantis. Each of the companies made commitments to invest billions of dollars in North American plants over the life of the contracts, with Stellantis agreeing to reopen its Belvidere, Illinois, plant (Isadore 2023a).

The union quickly started the ratification process as tentative agreements were reached at each company (United Auto Workers, "UAW Members Ratify"). Members, including temporary workers in good standing, had the right to vote by secret ballot at the meetings convened across local unions to consider contractual provisions. Voting took place over several weeks, with the final votes publicized on November 20, 2023. Rank-and-file members approved the contracts in each of the three companies by a solid majority. At Ford and Stellantis, roughly 70% of the members supported the contracts, while almost 55% did so at General Motors.

UNION ORGANIZING IN NONUNION AUTO INDUSTRY

The decline in UAW membership over several decades and the decrease in its density in the auto manufacturing and parts equipment industry revealed the inability of the union to offset these adverse trends by organizing new members. The UAW had failed in previous attempts to penetrate the foreign transplants and domestic EV producers. It has had a modicum of success of organizing in other industries, such as the public sector, healthcare, and gaming, but nowhere near the level to compensate for overall shrinkage. More than half of the autoworkers employed by OEMs in the United States remain union-free. Reduced density shrunk the union's bargaining power compared with what it was when the Big 3 had a lopsided market position. Acutely aware of its vulnerable status, the UAW wasted no time announcing its intention to organize these companies.

On November 29, 2023, the UAW launched a major public campaign to organize 13 targeted nonunion auto producers with facilities in the United States. These included seven Asian-based companies (Honda, Hyundai, Nissan, Subaru, Toyota, Hyundai-Kia), four European-based companies (BMW, Mercedes-Benz, Volkswagen, Volvo); and three US-based companies (Lucid, Rivian, and Tesla). Collectively, these companies operate 37 manufacturing facilities in 16 states. They employ an estimated 168,227 workers (see appendix for a breakdown of available employment data and sources).

In announcing this campaign, the UAW issued a press release and a video explaining the rationale for union representation. The announcement stated, "In an unprecedented move, autoworkers at more than a dozen nonunion automakers have announced simultaneous campaigns across the country to join the UAW. Thousands of non-union autoworkers are signing cards at the new UAW website, UAW.org/join, and are publicly organizing to join the UAW. The organizing drive will cover nearly 150,000 autoworkers across at least thirteen automakers." The case for union representation at those firms rests on the same basis used to bargain record contracts with the Big 3: the companies had amassed huge profits on the backs of workers whom they failed to appropriately compensate. Only through collective bargaining backed with the right to strike will workers be able to ensure a fair distribution of corporate abundance.

The campaign centers on generating "authorization cards" as a means of demonstrating sufficient interest in holding an NLRB certification election or claiming majority status. The UAW noted that it would mobilize card-checking efforts at each of these companies and approach management with a request for recognition when they secured 70% of the proposed bargaining-unit employee signatures; when 30% of the workers signed such cards, the UAW would go public, as it has done at Volkswagen in Chattanooga, Tennessee; when the 50% mark was reached, the union would hold a rally at the site (United Auto Workers, "Non-Union Autoworkers").

The union's track record of organizing in recent decades has been weak across the board. While it has picked up some members in nonauto sectors, such as public education, healthcare, and gaming, it failed to penetrate the nonunion auto OEM and parts segments. Since 2013, for example, the UAW has been involved in 77

NLRB-supervised elections with employees of 100 or more in the proposed bargaining units, only three of which involved foreign-based OEMs, losing two at Volkswagen and Nissan, while winning one at a smaller unit at Volkswagen (National Labor Relations Board, "Recent Election Results").

Among parts suppliers (which the UAW refers to as independent parts suppliers), the UAW won 17 of 45 elections over the past decade, but those election-unit victories involved only 5,040 employees. It also won three elections among academics and ten among employees in the gaming industry. Altogether, the 34 units where it won elections have only 14,101 employees.

The UAW has launched organizing drives among other foreign transplants, such as Toyota, Mercedes-Benz, Honda, Hyundai, and Kia, but has not had success at this point. It did win an election in December 2022 by a lopsided 710–16 vote to represent employees at the battery manufacturing plant operated by Ultium, a joint venture between General Motors and LG Chemical of South Korea, at a former UAW-represented location in Lordstown, Ohio.

According to union certification-election data reported by the NLRB, the UAW won only 15 certification elections in the past year (December 2022 through December 2023). This represents a total of only 1,111 employees as possible new members. Between 2013 and 2023, it secured only four elections of nonunion auto OEM-connected facilities, of which it lost two: Nissan (Canton, Mississippi, in 2017) and Volkswagen (Chattanooga, Tennessee, in 2019) (National Labor Relations Board, "Recent Election Results").

As noted earlier, under the administration of President Biden, the NLRB has taken important steps through its *Cemex* decision and NLRB General Counsel's guidance to facilitate union organizing by changing the standard by which a union can be recognized. In filing unfair labor practice charges against Honda, Hyundai, and Volkswagen so soon after launching this multi-employer organizing campaign, the UAW showed its intent to exploit a potential advantage in this new legal interpretation to secure recognition if could show that the companies violated the workers' right to form a union through a show of majority status (Garsten 2023). In addition, the NLRB held that if an employer's unfair labor practices render a future certification election unlikely to reflect workers' genuine preferences, it may order recognition and bargaining.

In relatively quick order, the UAW achieved a major success in this newly launched campaign to organize nonunion auto producers in the United States. It won an NLRB certification election at the Volkswagen plant in Chattanooga, garnering 73% of the vote, as announced on April 19, 2024. In addition (as of this writing), the NLRB has granted its petition to hold a certification election at the Mercedes-Benz plant between May 13 and 17, 2024 (United Auto Workers, "Volkswagen Workers").

THE FUTURE OF COLLECTIVE BARGAINING IN THE AUTO INDUSTRY

The future of collective bargaining in the auto industry depends on the relative position and power of the principals: the UAW and the Big 3. Their position and power, in turn, depend on how they meet three existential challenges. The first challenge is the success the companies have in competing in the transition to EVs. Will Tesla and other emerging domestic EV producers gain more market share? Will the Big 3 lose more ground to the major foreign-based producers in Europe and Asia? If the center of gravity moves increasingly away from the Big 3, then they might suffer reduced profitability that forces downsizing and other forms of restructuring. The second challenge is the omnipresent state of the interdependent US and global economies. A recession could harm the companies and the union alike, slowing their capacity to adapt to EV transition and reducing nonunion workers' willingness to take risks to support unionization. The third challenge is whether the UAW can penetrate the nonunion automakers.

The UAW came off bargaining in 2023 with its "stand up" strikes, exuding more optimism than it had shown in decades. Reformed and revitalized under new leadership, the union declared organizing the nonunion automakers as its next mission. It publicly identified 13 targets that collectively employ more hourly workers than the Big 3 (see appendix). To demonstrate its resolve, the UAW promptly filed unfair labor practice charges against Honda, Hyundai, and Volkswagen. Six of the 13 companies sought to preempt the union by announcing major wage increases.

The rising optimism of labor protagonists stems from a confluence of factors. They include favorable public opinion toward unions (Saad 2023), rising activism in organizing and striking (Shierholz, Poydock, and McNicholas 2023), a pro-union president and NLRB (Meyerson 2023), and a string of negotiated agreements raising wages and making other improvements in working conditions in industries ranging from entertainment and package delivery to healthcare, hospitality, and auto manufacturing (Isidore 2023b). Do these developments point to labor's revitalization or represent just a temporary uptick in an otherwise continuing downward slide?

To offer perspective, while the level of public approval was at 67% in 2023 (according to Gallup) is impressive, it fell from 71% and fluctuates widely (48% in 2010 compared with 75% in 1965). Moreover, general approval does not easily translate into support in actual organizing campaigns, especially where workers face employer opposition and must evaluate the merits of having a specific union as a bargaining representative. Another caveat in interpreting the favorableness of the current environment lies in its historic comparison. Though the level of major strikes (involving 1,000 or more workers) in 2023 exceeded the number in 2022 (31 compared with 22) and the number of actual workers is significantly higher (nearly 460,000 compared with data from the US Bureau of Labor Statistics, "Work Stoppages"), they pale compared with historic highs. For example, in 1970, there were 383 major strikes involving nearly 2.5 million workers. As recently as 2018, there were more workers involved in such strikes (over 481,000) than in 2023.

Similarly, though there has been an uptick in union certification elections in recent years, they amount to just a sliver of the overall workforce. Fewer than 93,000 workers were eligible to vote in certification elections conducted by the NLRB in fiscal year 2023, and that amounts to less than one-tenth of 1% of the total number of employed people in the United States (National Labor Relations Board, "Election Results").

The hard reality is that organized labor in the United States has continued to decline for decades as a percentage of the workforce. Just 6% of the private sector workforce belongs to a union. In durable goods manufacturing, only 8% are unionized (US Bureau of Labor Statistics, "Union Members—2023"). And the "record contracts" come after years of bargaining concessions and job losses in many industries. In the case of the UAW, the 25% increases in wages came after several contracts in which wages were frozen, cost-of-living allowances eliminated, and two-tier pay systems introduced. And, as the UAW noted in making its members' demand to have the contractual right to strike over plant closures during the 2023 negotiations, the Big 3 had closed 65 plants in the United States over the past 20 years (United Auto Workers, "News, Resources, and Actions"). But the ink had hardly dried on the recently ratified Big 3 contracts when General Motors and Stellantis announced layoffs affecting more than 4,800 workers, while Ford reduced the number of new jobs by 800 from a projected 2,500 at its new EV battery plant planned for Marshall, Michigan, which has been paused (Boucher 2023).

If the past is prologue, the future portends a diminishing role for the Big 3 and the UAW. If anything, the level of competition in the auto industry has escalated significantly with the advent of EVs and the growth in nonunion domestic and foreign-based EV producers. The UAW, while having shown signs of revitalization under newly elected leadership as a result of court-mandated constitutional reforms, still has the stigma of the recent scandal to overcome. The nonunion producers in the United States targeted by the UAW have only begun to mount their efforts to counter the organizing campaign. They can be expected to challenge the union through vocal campaigns, aided in the process by a plethora of rabidly anti-union lawmakers and advocacy groups (McNicholas, Poydock, Sanders, and Zipperer 2023).

APPENDIX: MANUFACTURING EMPLOYMENT BY SITE OF NONUNION AUTOMAKERS IN THE UNITED STATES

Company	Location	Employment
Tesla	Fremont, CA	22,000
	Austin, TX	20,000
	Reno, NV	10,521
	Buffalo, NY	1,948
Lucid	Casa Grande, AR	7,200
Rivian	Normal, IL	8,000
Hino-Toyota	Marion, AR	1,096
	Mineral Wells, WV	377
Honda	Marysville, OH	3,600
	Marysville, OH	100
	East Liberty, OH	2,900
	Anna, OH	2,600
	Russells Point, OH	1,000
	Lincoln, AL	4,500
	Tallapoosa, GA	400
	Greensburg, IN	2,500
Mazda-Toyota	Huntsville, AL	4,108
Nissan	Smyrna, TN	7,400
	Decherd, TN	2,100
	Decherd, TN	270
	Canton, MS	4,900
Subaru	Lafayette, IN	6,217
Toyota	Long Beach, CA	278
	Georgetown, KY	9,424
	Troy, MO	409
	Jackson, TN	935
	Buffalo, WV	2,073
	Princeton, IN	7,764
	San Antonio, TX	3,747
	Blue Springs, MS	2,260
Hyundai-Kia	Montgomery, AL	3,600
	West Point, GA	2,700
BMW	Spartanburg, SC	11,000
Mercedes-Benz	Tuscaloosa, AL	3,700
Volkswagen	Chattanooga, TN	3,800
Volvo	Ridgeville, SC	2,800
Total		168,227

ENDNOTES

1. For ease of referencing, sources from the US Bureau of Labor Statistics are listed in a separate section of the references at the end of this chapter.
2. Sources from the National Labor Relations Board are listed in a separate section of the references at the end of this chapter.
3. Sources from the United Auto Workers are listed in a separate section of the references at the end of this chapter.

REFERENCES

Alliance for Automotive Innovation. 2023. "Driving Force Annual Report." November 29. https://tinyurl.com/5n87s3t7

Anderson Economic Group. 2023. "Week Six: Economic Losses from UAW Strike Top $10.4 Billion." November 1. https://tinyurl.com/rpcdpnsm

Atkinson, R.D., and F. Lage de Sousa. 2021. "No, Monopoly Has Not Grown." Innovation Technology & Innovation Foundation. June 7. https://tinyurl.com/ymwkuptw

Automotive News. No date. "The UAW-Detroit 3 2019 Negotiations." https://tinyurl.com/44hsym2m

Automotive News Data Center. 2023. "2024 *Automotive News* Dealer Census." https://www.autonews.com/data-center

———. 2023. "North America Car and Truck Assembly Plants, as of 10-15-23." October 15. https://tinyurl.com/2k9dn9jt

Automotive News Research and Data Center. No date. "Tables and Lists." https://www.autonews.com/data-lists

Barnard, J. 2004. *American Vanguard: The United Auto Workers During the Reuther Years, 1935–1970.* Detroit, MI: Wayne State University Press.

Boucher, D. 2023. "Ford to Drastically Scale Back Jobs, Investment Plans for Marshall EV Battery Plant." *Detroit Free Press.* November 21. https://tinyurl.com/ye39wphp

Budd, J. 1992. "The Determinants and Extent of UAW Pattern Bargaining." *Industrial and Labor Relations Review* 45, no. 3: 523–539.

Bush, J. 2022. "Automakers Invest Billions in North American EV and Battery Manufacturing Facilities." Center for Automotive Research. July 21. https://tinyurl.com/yc5k2bsu

Canis, B., J.M. Bickley, H. Chaikind, C.A. Pettit, P. Purcell, C. Rapaport, C., and G. Shorter. 2009. "U.S. Motor Vehicle Industry: Federal Assistance and Restructuring." R40003. Congressional Research Service. May 29. https://tinyurl.com/3yjp6aur

Canis, B., and B. Webel. 2013. "The Role of TARP Assistance in the Restructuring of General Motors." Congressional Research Service. May 9. https://tinyurl.com/ypbwfv9f

Coffman, J., R. Iyer, and R. Robinson. 2023. "2023 Deloitte Automotive Supplier Study: Transforming Business Models Amidst Rising Operational Challenges." Deloitte. https://tinyurl.com/26mhj6je

Congressional Research Service. 2010. "The U.S. Motor Vehicle Industry: Confronting a New Dynamic in the Global Economy." March 26. https://tinyurl.com/23nvejjk

Cutcher-Gershenfeld, J., D. Brooks, and M. Mulloy. 2015a. "Inside the Ford-UAW Transformation: Pivotal Events in Valuing Work and Delivering Results." EBIN. https://tinyurl.com/5495yfat

———. 2015b. "The Decline and Resurgence of the U.S. Auto Industry." Economic Policy Institute. Briefing Paper #399. May. https://tinyurl.com/3s3pc4kp

Dungs, J.J. 2023. "China Has Perfectly Tangled the Battery Value Chain with EVs." *Forbes.* August 17. https://tinyurl.com/5xbt9kff

Economic Policy Institute. 2021. "The Shift to All-Electric Vehicles Could Create over 150,000 Jobs by 2030—If Policymakers Make Smart Investments to Secure U.S. Leadership in the Auto Sector." September 22. https://tinyurl.com/52bhtu6b

Eisenstein, P. 2023. "New UAW President Threatens to Withhold Biden Endorsement over EV Transition." Detroit Bureau. May 4. https://tinyurl.com/mtbvwbxb

Factory Warranty List. No date. "Car Sales by Country, 2023 Full Year." https://tinyurl.com/37f5yatm

Federal Reserve Bank of St. Louis. 2019. "The U.S. Labor Market Since NAFTA." April 15. https://tinyurl.com/bddna96u

Ford Motor Company. 2019. "2019 UAW-Ford: National Negotiations Media Fact Guide." https://tinyurl.com/4wfrdhk5

Garsten, E. 2023. "UAW Files Union-Busting Complaints Against Honda, Hyundai and Volkswagen." *Forbes*. December 11. https://tinyurl.com/6638cjpb

Goeddeke, F., and M.F. Masters. 2021. "The United Auto Workers: From Walter Reuther to Rory Gamble." *Perspectives on Work* 24: 40–44.

Greenhouse, S. 2019. *Beaten Down, Worked Up: The Past, Present, and Future of American Labor*. New York, NY: Alfred A. Knopf.

Hall, K., and R. Beggin. 2023. "UAW Demands Biden Support 'Top Wages' for EV Workers Before Endorsing." *Detroit News*. May 3.

Hirsch, B.T., D.A. Macpherson and W. Even. 2024. "Union Membership and Coverage Database from the Current Population Survey." https://www.unionstats.com

IBISWorld. 2023. "Battery Manufacturing in the US—Employment Statistics 2004–2029." April 24. https://tinyurl.com/3vzhe9dd

Isidore, C. 2023a. "Here's Why Saving This Illinois Auto Plant Is a 'Gigantic Deal.'" CNN Business. November 10. https://tinyurl.com/yc6mfmsw

———. 2023b. "Unions Are the Strongest in Decades. Nearly a Million Americans Got Double-Digit Raises as a Result." CNN Business. November 21. https://tinyurl.com/5n8433uw

Katz, H.C., J.P. MacDuffie, and F.L. Pil. 2013. "Crisis and Recovery in the U.S. Auto Industry: Tumultuous Times for a Collective Bargaining Pacesetter." In *Collective Bargaining Under Distress: Case Studies of North American Industries*, edited by H.R. Stanger, P.F. Clark, and A.C. Frost, 45–80. Champaign, IL: Labor and Employment Relations Association.

King, R.E. 2023. "China: The Linchpin of the World's Electric Vehicle Production." Jalopnik. May 17. https://tinyurl.com/4sbmf63j

Knutson, J. 2023. "Cost of UAW Strike: GM, Ford and Stellantis Report Billions in Losses." Axios. November 30. https://tinyurl.com/ypubj87x

Lawrence, E.D. 2023. "UAW Isn't Ready to Endorse Biden for Another Term Yet, UAW president Says. Here's Why." *Detroit Free Press*. May 5. https://tinyurl.com/2ry9kx5a

Lawrence, E.D., and J. LaReau. 2023. "As UAW, Detroit 3 Fight over Wages, Here's a Look at Autoworker Pay, CEO Compensation." *Detroit Free Press*. September 21. https://tinyurl.com/2s45p8rn

———. 2024. "UAW's Push to Organize Workers at Nonunion Carmakers Is a Race Against Time." Yahoo. January 10. https://tinyurl.com/mtd2548f

Martinez, M. 2020. "Detroit 3 Labor Costs to 'Rise Steadily' over Next 4 Years Under New UAW Contract." *Automotive News*. January 15. https://tinyurl.com/4czf8dbn

———. 2023. "UAW Demands Would Mean 'Unsustainable' Labor Costs for Detroit 3, Sources Say." *Automotive News*. August 9. https://tinyurl.com/3btffcch

McAlinden, S. 2004. "The Meaning of the 2003 UAW–Automotive Pattern Agreement." Center for Automotive Research. June. https://tinyurl.com/3ktz2459

McNicholas, C., M. Poydock, S. Sanders, and B. Zipperer. 2023. "Employers Spend More Than $400 Million per Year on 'Union-Avoidance' Consultants to Bolster Their Union-Busting Efforts." Economic Policy Institute. March 29. https://tinyurl.com/4a54vwcc

Meyerson, H. 2023. "Biden's NLRB Brings Workers' Rights Back from the Dead." *American Prospect.* August 28. https://tinyurl.com/4wxvwt5t

Mollman, S. 2023. "Elon Musk Suggests Tesla and 9 Chinese Companies Will Be Top 10 Carmakers." *Fortune.* November 30. https://fortune.com/2023/11/30/elon-musk-china-ev-future-tesla-byd-top-global-carmakers/?n=%40

Motavalli, J. 2021. "Every Automaker's EV Plans Through 2035 and Beyond." *Forbes.* October 4. https://tinyurl.com/ybju4558

Noble, B. 2023. "Stellantis Workers Could Receive $14,760 in Profit Sharing." *Detroit News.* February 22. https://tinyurl.com/yuf4uayj

Noble, K.B. 1985. "Big Strikes Found on Decline in U.S." *New York Times.* February 22. https://tinyurl.com/msauv95c

Press, A.N. 2023. "The UAW's Next Fight. Organizing Nonunion Companies Like Tesla." *Jacobin.* November 14. https://tinyurl.com/2kaccnf3

PR Newswire. 2022. "GM Raises 2022 Guidance and Expects North American EV Portfolio to Be Profitable in 2025 as Annual Capacity Tops 1 Million." November 17. https://tinyurl.com/mvn2w5m5

Rosenfeld, J. 2014. *What Unions No Longer Do.* Cambridge, MA: Harvard University Press.

Saad, L. 2023. "More in the U.S. See Unions Strengthening and Want It That Way." Gallup. August 30. https://tinyurl.com/mrcm7fbv

Shierholz, H., M. Poydock, and C. McNicholas. 2023. "Unionization Increased by 200,000 in 2020." Report. Economic Policy Institute. January 19. https://tinyurl.com/43apyxv4

Stanger, H.R., P.F. Clark, and A.C. Frost, eds. 2013. *Collective Bargaining Under Duress: Case Studies of Major North American Industries.* Champaign, IL: Labor and Employment Relations Association.

State of Georgia, Department of Community and Economic Development. 2023. "Electric Transportation Ecosystem." https://tinyurl.com/yc56952u

Stieber, J. 1962. *Governing the UAW.* New York, NY: John Wiley and Sons.

Strong, M. 2023. "UAW Skipping Ceremonial Handshake to Start Contract Talks." Detroit Bureau. July 10. https://tinyurl.com/49n7tcu4

US Department of Energy 2021. "FOTW #1217, December 20, 2021: Thirteen New Electric Vehicle Battery Plants Are Planned in the U.S. Within the Next Five Years." https://tinyurl.com/35nuu6y3

US White House. 2021. "Executive Order on Strengthening American Leadership in Clean Cars and Trucks." Executive Order 14027. August 5. https://tinyurl.com/46wwyy68

Vendetti, B. 2022. "The Top 10 EV Battery Manufacturers in 2022." Visual Capitalist. October 5. https://tinyurl.com/27yt86fb

Vlasic, B. 2009. "Choosing Its Own Path, Ford Stayed Independent." *New York Times.* April 8. https://tinyurl.com/yzr76dy5

Walz, E. 2023. "GM Says UAW Labor Agreement Will Cost $9.3B Through 2028." Automotive Dive. November 29. https://tinyurl.com/3h99eb5x

WardsAuto. 2019. "Animated Chart of the Day: Market Shares of US Auto Sales, 1961 to 2018." June 28. https://tinyurl.com/yx8mzwdm

Weissner, D. 2023. "NLRB Restores Obama-Era Rule Speeding Up Union Election Process." Reuters. August 24. https://tinyurl.com/bdzch83p

World Economic Forum. 2023. "Electric Vehicle Sales Leapt 55% in 2022—Here's Where That Growth Was Strongest." May 11. https://tinyurl.com/3aumydb8

National Labor Relations Board Sources Cited/Consulted

"Election Results." https://tinyurl.com/53aabxa6

"Guidance in Response to Inquiries about the Board's Decision in Cemex Construction Materials Pacific, LLC." https://tinyurl.com/36sr8wx3

"Recent Election Results." https://tinyurl.com/m28mzyjs

United Auto Workers and Additional Sources Cited/Consulted

"2019 Contracts with Hourly Employees for FCA, Ford, and GM."

"Constitution of the International Union." https://uaw.org/uaw-constitution-2

Making EVs Work for American Workers." March 2021 Update to UAW EV White Paper. https://tinyurl.com/3wtnjyv5

"New UAW Video Highlights Big 3's Massive Profits, Makes Clear They Can Easily Afford Union's Contract Demands." https://tinyurl.com/4yy2xz4f

"News, Resources, and Actions for 2023 Big Three Bargaining." https://uaw.org/uaw-auto-bargaining

"Non-Union Autoworkers Are Being Left Behind. Are You Ready to Stand Up and Win Your Fair Share?" https://uaw.org/join

"Secretary–Treasurer's Report to the 38th UAW Constitutional Convention." https://uaw.org/convention

"Taking the High Road: Strategies for a Fair EV Future." https://tinyurl.com/f4mdn57w

"UAW Basics." Publication #515. May 21, 2021.

"UAW Members Ratify Historic Contracts at Ford, GM, and Stellantis." https://tinyurl.com/4rdnp2jm

"UAW Statement on Court Filing of Former UAW Member Gary Jones." Press Release. March 5.

"Volkswagen Workers Are Making History. Mercedes Workers Got Next." https://tinyurl.com/fd3k8dzj

Reports, *United States District Court, Eastern District of Michigan, Southern Division, USA v. UAW,* Case No. 20-13293

"UAW Anti-Fraud Complaint." December 14, 2021.
"UAW Appointment of Monitor." May 12, 2021.
"UAW Consent Decree." January 29, 2021.
"UAW Monitor Referendum Report." 3. January 7, 2022.
"UAW Monitor Initial Status Report." November 11, 2021.
"UAW Monitor Second Status Report, Election Rules." May 11, 2022.
"UAW Monitor Third Status Report." July 19, 2022.
"UAW Monitor Fourth Status Report." December 5, 2022.
"UAW Monitor Fifth Status Report." March 17, 2023.
"UAW Monitor Sixth Status Report. March 25, 2023, amended May 2, 2023.
"UAW Monitor Seventh Status Report." June 16, 2023.

US Bureau of Labor Statistics and Additional Sources Cited/Consulted

"Automotive Industry: Employment, Earnings, and Hours." https://www.bls.gov/iag/tgs/iagauto.html

"Charging into the Future: The Transition to Electric Vehicles—Beyond the Numbers." https://tinyurl.com/ycxpw2we

"CPI Inflation Calculator." https://www.bls.gov/data/inflation_calculator.htm

"Union Members—2023." https://tinyurl.com/ye2a3zbf

"Work Stoppages." https://www.bls.gov/wsp

CHAPTER 2

Collective Bargaining in the US Construction Industry

Dale Belman
Michigan State University

Mark Erlich
Harvard Center for Labor and a Just Economy, Carpenters Union

Abstract

The union construction industry has had a reputation as a predominantly White male workforce that resisted diversity as well as technological innovation. Although this characterization may once have been accurate, the unionized side of construction has undergone social and technological transformation since the 1980s. Under fierce pressure from the open shop and its corporate supporters, the leaders and members have accepted that to maintain their wages, benefits, and status, they must embrace changes in technology and techniques needed to support the union productivity advantage. While once viewed as among the most strike-prone industries, labor–management programs have been incorporated throughout the industry and into daily work routines. The apprenticeship system has been modernized and is among the largest and best technical training systems in North America. The introduction of Black and Latino workers, particularly in the basic trades, has altered the composition of the workforce. The introduction of Black and Latino workers, particularly in the basic trades, has altered the composition of the workforce. Recent efforts to bring women into the crafts have included accelerated pre-apprenticeship training, effective support groups, and a heightened understanding of women's issues, such as pilot daycare programs. Although the union sector remains under many pressures, it has held its own for 30 years and has demonstrated a much greater willingness to adopt new policies and programs.

INTRODUCTION

Construction represents 4% to 5% of the gross domestic product (GDP) and is one of the core industries in the US economy. From building homes to highways to schools to skyscrapers, the construction industry touches lives in nearly universal ways. Construction is a risk-filled, volatile, and potentially lucrative business, but companies in the industry would not be able to generate a single dollar of profit were it not for the millions of skilled and unskilled construction workers who show up every day on the nation's construction sites. The best paid of these workers belong to America's building trades unions. Their pay, benefits, and working conditions are determined by periodic negotiations between these unions and building contractors. This chapter discusses in detail the collective bargaining mechanisms in the US construction industry. The chapter also identifies the unions and employers that engage in this process; the historical, economic, and legal context; and the issues and outcomes that flow from the process.

Whenever unions and employers meet to engage in collective bargaining, they typically sit on opposite sides of the table. In addition to the participants, there are often other voices in attendance—even if they are not physically at the table. These are the proverbial elephants in the room. When factory owners and manufacturing union leaders face off in bargaining, the threats of globalization, outsourcing, offshoring, automation, and mechanization hover over the table in the air like Banquo's ghost at Macbeth's banquet. When Teamsters officials meet with UPS executives, the competitive reality of nonunion FedEx and Amazon delivery services is in the back of everyone's minds. Management spokespeople often elevate the menace of market competition from outside forces—whether legitimate or not—as a means of dampening union demands.

In collective bargaining in the contemporary construction industry, there is a genuine elephant in the room. That elephant is the presence of a firmly established nonunion sector characterized by lower wages and poorer working conditions. This was not always the case. From roughly 1900 through 1975, building trades unions enjoyed a near monopoly on construction work in the United States. In most parts of the country, the union market share exceeded 80% (Erlich and Grabelsky 2005). The challenge of the nonunion competition was, at worst, a minor annoyance. In the past 50 years, the context has changed. Union density has tumbled, and the industry has become bifurcated. There continue to be strong union outposts in major metropolitan areas in the Northeast, Midwest, and West Coast, but outside of those cities and certainly below the Mason–Dixon line, nonunion contractors and their workforce build the majority of the nation's buildings and infrastructure (Erlich 2023).

When contractors raise the issue of nonunion competition in contract negotiations, union leaders inevitably consider the concern about excessive raises potentially pricing union contractors out of the market. With the exception of those operating in a handful of strong union cities or on highly specialized projects, owners have a choice. They can select a unionized general contractor/construction manager with a set of unionized subcontractors, they can choose a contractor that will employ nonunion workers, or they can opt for a hybrid (i.e., a mix of union and nonunion subcontractors). The owners' menu of choices casts a shadow on the bargaining table. Union negotiators will argue that their members are more skilled, more productive, more readily available and likelier to meet scheduling requirements. While those assertions are generally well founded, the difference in union and nonunion compensation frequently produces lower nonunion bids and serves as the ultimate source of owner motivation, particularly for owners that are less concerned with quality than with the bottom line (Erlich 2023).

Rather than bargain a single master agreement covering all construction work, each of the 15 building trades unions negotiates its own contract, generally on a regional geographic basis. The wage and benefit trends tend to be similar among trades in a given area but vary widely from region to region, depending on the level of union market share. There may be unusually large and influential employers in a locality but, for the most part, each union bargains with a multi-employer association seeking a master agreement for a particular trade in a particular area. While some of the basic crafts—carpenters, laborers, and operating engineers—may sit across the table from general contractors, the majority of the crafts (including those same basic crafts) bargain with specialty subcontractors. The owners ultimately pay the bills for construction services, and the general contractors/construction managers oversee the project and retain the subcontractors, but the subcontractors employ the bulk of the craft workforce and are most concerned with managing labor relations.

Subcontractors bring mixed experiences to the table. Many of them began their careers in their crafts as union members before becoming subcontractors. Because of their background, they identify with their workforce to a greater degree than most employers do. In settings where general contractors and subcontractors sit together to bargain with a union, their conflicting agendas may be as severe as joint opposition to union demands. The alignment of interests on the employer side is not always clear. As clients, subcontractors have to balance the need to sustain decent relations with the general contractors with the realization that margins may actually rise as worker compensation increases if profits are figured as a percentage of total bids. As employers, subcontractors focus on the contractual language determining daily conditions on the jobsite, whereas general contractors concentrate more on limiting raises so that owners do not complain about spiraling costs.

Over time, trade-specific contract terms and conditions have become increasingly universal, as agreements cover larger swaths of territory based on an informal practice of pattern bargaining. Still, the agreements will be in effect only for union jobs. Over the term of an agreement, some projects in an area will be built in accordance with the contract, and others will be built on a nonunion basis outside that bargaining structure—depending on owner/contractor preference. Unlike a factory agreement in which the terms and conditions apply to all the covered work for the duration, it is possible in a weak market share area to have an agreement that is not enforced. Most of the work may be nonunion, and some of the union work might even have concessions deviating from the basic contract. Thus, every project built in a given area during the term of an agreement may or may not be covered—an essential difference from collective bargaining environments in other industries.

THE PARTIES: CONSTRUCTION UNIONS

The construction sector created $954 billion in value added in 2021, accounting for 4.1% of the US GDP (US Bureau of Economic Analysis 2021). Of the 7.8 million workers employed in construction, 5.7 million were employed as production workers in December 2022 (Flood et al. 2022).[1] There were, in addition, 2.5 million self-employed workers (Flood et al. 2022). The NAICS system divides construction into the construction of buildings (NAICS 236), heavy and civil engineering (NAICS 237), and specialty trades contractors (NAICS 238). Table 1 provides the employment, earnings, and national union density (the percentage of the workforce belonging to a union) of the broad standard operational code construction occupations.

The 15 international building trades unions have a membership of 4.1 million. With the exception of the Teamsters, who have members in a wide range of industries and occupations, the members of building trades unions primarily work in construction. However, most have at least some members who are not construction workers—for example, the International Union of Operating Engineers (IUOE) represents registered nurses, and the International Association of Sheet Metal, Air, Rail and Transportation Workers (SMART) represents bus drivers and railroad employees. Each of the unions has members in Canada, as well as in the United States. Table 2 lists the building trades by membership size. All but the United Brotherhood of Carpenters (UBC) are members of the North American Building Trades Unions (NABTU) of the AFL-CIO.

Hirsch, Macpherson, and Even (2023) reported that US national union membership declined from 18.1 million members in 1973 to 14.3 million members in 2022, causing union density to drop from 24% in 1973 to 10.1% in 2022. They also report that union membership in the construction industry fell from 1.8 million in 1973 to 1.1 million in 2022. As a consequence, union density in construction declined from 38.1% in 1973 to 12.6% in 2023.

Although overall union density is an important metric of the role construction unions play in the industry, unions play a much larger role in some construction subsectors and a much smaller role in others. For example, most residential construction is done by nonunion workers; construction unions only play a small role in this subsector and have little to no influence on wages or working conditions in the residential sector. However, a significant percentage of more specialized construction, including semiconductor facilities, large bridges and tunnels, large urban buildings, pipelines, and power plants continue to be dominated by unionized contractors (Ormiston, Belman, Brockman, and Hinkel 2019).

THE PARTIES: CONSTRUCTION EMPLOYERS

The employer side of the industry consists of very large numbers of small contractors whose work is coordinated by general contractors or by construction managers. Of the 740,000 firms in the NAICS construction industry (NAICS 23), 91% have fewer than 20 employees, and only 0.2% have 500 or more employees. The distribution of employment is weighted toward larger firms: 34% have 20 or fewer employees, 30% have 21 to 99 employees, 18% have 100 to 499 employees, and 19% have 500 or more employees (may not add to 100% due to rounding). Sixty-four percent of industry employment is provided by specialty trades and 20% by residential construction; the balance is in nonresidential buildings (NAICS 2362) and heavy and civil engineering (NAICS 2367) (US Bureau of the Census 2020).

Table 1
Employment, Hourly Wages, and Union Density in Construction, 2021

Occupation	2021 employment	Hourly wage	Union density (%)
First-line supervisors	665,870	28.45	15.7
Boilermakers	12,920	29.18	48.7
Brick masons, block masons, and stone masons	64,950	24.71	18.5
Carpenters	668,060	23.59	15.5
Floor and tile installers and finishers	83,600	22.19	7.9
Cement masons, concrete finishers, and terrazzo workers	189,240	24.66	15.2
Construction laborers	968,760	21.42	12.1
Construction equipment operators	404,820	25.79	23.7
Drywall and ceiling tile installers	111,650	21.17	11.7
Electricians	650,580	28.06	32.4
Glaziers	52,700	25.63	15.6
Insulation workers	58,370	23.93	11.3
Painters and paper hangers	216,560	20.75	6.8
Pipe layers	33,330	25.90	17.5
Plumbers, pipefitters, and steamfitters	417,620	27.37	29.3
Plasterers and stucco masons	26,980	25.04	15.2
Roofers	129,890	19.60	9.5
Sheet metal workers	122,630	24.69	26.6
Structural iron and steel workers	68,620	25.76	49.4
Solar photovoltaic installers	16,420	20.96	7.7
Helpers, construction trades	206,900	19.73	10.1
Construction and building inspectors	117,830	29.19	29.3
Elevator and escalator installers and repairers	22,510	39.79	72.3
Hazardous materials removal workers	44,240	21.56	15.0

Flood et al. (2022).

Although there are very large national and international construction firms whose names appear prominently on signs around large construction sites, few of these firms hire craft workers directly. Instead, they partner with local, regional, and national firms that employ and direct the craft labor force. A review of the Bechtel postings on Indeed.com on March 9, 2024, found eight craft postings among hundreds of Bechtel job openings. Almost all craft employment is provided by the smaller operative firms that undertake craft work on a project. These firms are specialized

Table 2
US Unions with Significant Building Trades Membership

Union	Membership in building trades
International Brotherhood of Teamsters (Teamsters)	1015775
International Brotherhood of Electrical Workers (IBEW)	688937
Laborers International Union of North America (LIUNA)	603,921
United Brotherhood of Carpenters (UBC)	430605
International Union of Operating Engineers (IUOE)	396446
United Association of Plumbers, Pipefitters and Steamfitters (UA)	359037
International Association of Sheet Metal, Air, Rail and Transportation Workers (SMART)	193681
International Association of Bridge, Structural, Ornamental and Reinforcing Iron Workers Union, AFL-CIO (IW)	124937
International Union of Painters and Allied Trades (IUPAT)	106779
International Union of Bricklayers and Allied Craftworkers (BAC)	70769
Operative Plasterers' and Cement Masons' International Association (OPCMIA)	44160
International Union of Elevator Constructors (IUEC)	30738
International Association of Heat and Frost Insulators and Allied Workers (HFIAW)	22557
United Union of Roofers, Waterproofers, and Allied Workers (UURWAW)	22231
Total	**4110573**

Office of Labor–Management Standards LM-3 and LM-4 (2023).

by craft, with distinct firms undertaking tasks such as inside electrical work, drywall installation, plumbing, iron erection, and concrete work. Coordination between the firms is provided by the general contractor or construction manager. It is often a flash point on the project, with differences between subcontractors on their scope of work leading to inefficiencies and litigation (Indeed.com 2024).

Because the operative firms are small, they formed employer associations to represent their member firms in bargaining with local unions. The structure of the employer association parallels that of the building trades unions, with local chapters, state associations, and national associations that coordinate activities such as lobbying, tracking legislation, updating licensing standards, and providing shared services to local chapters. Among the most prominent employer organizations are the Associated General Contractors (AGC), the National Electrical Contractors Association (NECA), and the Mechanical Contractors Association of America (MCAA). Bargaining takes place at the local level, with regular communication between local bargainers and regional and national organizations. In some instances, national employers' organizations and their counterpart unions directly regulate frictions in bargaining through national organizations, such as the NECA/IBEW Council on Industrial Relations. The main employer association for nonunion contractors is the Associated Builders of America (ABC) and the Independent Electrical Association (IEA). The AGC differs from many other employer associations in that it has both union and nonunion members. A majority of its current members are nonunion.

NEGOTIATING COMPENSATION IN CONSTRUCTION

Construction contracts are bargained separately for each by trade (e.g., plumbing, electrical, carpentry) between local or regional employer trade associations and their counterpart union locals every two to five years.[2]

Bargaining in construction differs from that in many other industries. The compensation package is negotiated as a total labor cost per hour, inclusive of hourly wages, pension and healthcare benefits, apprenticeship training, and industry competitiveness funds. Once the total cost is agreed on, the union, with the advice of consultants, determines the allocation of total compensation between wages, benefits, apprenticeship, and other claims. The Construction Labor Research Council (CLRC) reports that total compensation package costs across all crafts and regions rose at an annual rate of 2.9% in 2019 and 3.1% in 2022 (Table 3). The council predicts total costs will increase 3.7% in 2024.[3]

While construction bargaining is local by trade, there are strong patterns across crafts and regions. The CLRC found that, over the past decade, the largest dollar increases were negotiated by plumbers, operating engineers, and glaziers, and the lowest by roofers, laborers, and plasterers. There are, however, strong patterns between the crafts. With a few exceptions, craft settlements were within one-half of a percentage point of the national

Table 3
Annual Negotiated Increases in Total Package Compensation

Year	Percentage increase	Dollar amount
2013	2.3	$1.00
2014	2.5	$1.10
2015	2.5	$1.20
2016	2.6	$1.25
2017	2.6	$1.63
2018	2.8	$1.73
2019	2.9	$1.68
2020	2.9	$1.63
2021	2.9	$1.84
2022 (through June)	3.1	$2.17

Construction Labor Research Council (2022).

average, and 15 out of 17 settlements were within $0.30 of the national average. In 2022, the largest dollar settlements, $2.28 and $2.30, were negotiated in the Pacific Southwest (Arizona, California, Hawaii, and Nevada) and the Pacific Northwest (Alaska, Idaho, Oregon, and Washington); the lowest were $0.88 in the South Central states (Arkansas, Louisiana, New Mexico, Oklahoma, and Texas) and $1.32 in the Southeast (Alabama, Florida, Georgia, Kentucky, Mississippi, North Carolina, South Carolina, Tennessee, and Virginia) (Construction Labor Research Council 2022).

STRUCTURE OF NEGOTIATIONS (THE PARTIES)

Construction employers are represented in bargaining by local or regional employer associations. In the electrical trade, for example, bargaining is carried out by a local chapter of NECA. In other crafts, employer associations are subdivided by specific types of work. For example, operating engineer employer associations are often divided between heavy/highway and general construction. These divisions run along important divisions in the construction market or in the type of work.

On the union side, all workers are represented by a group of locals with geographic jurisdiction. Where there are multiple employer associations, the contracts are specific to that association, with terms, conditions, and compensation adapted to the conditions of work. Compensation follows strong patterns across contracts. Even when there is a single union and employer association, contracts may be adapted to specific markets. Electrical contracts may distinguish between commercial contracts and residential contracts, with differences between work rules and compensation. Because workers in the crafts move back and forth between employers, the existence of different pay rates for different types of work may cause conflict within locals. For that reason, some carpenter locals have spun off residential work into separate locals with separate contracts (Erlich 2023).

With some notable exceptions, most crafts have consolidated bargaining into regions of multiple locals. This reflects the need for the union to cover the labor market from which craft workers are drawn and establish shared terms and conditions within the market. The carpenters have moved toward ever larger regions; the New England Region was recently enlarged to include New York State, with the exception of New York City locals. The movement toward regions allows for more effective bargaining and servicing of locals at a time when local structures became an impediment to the smooth movement of labor within a labor market. This consolidation reduces the role of the union locally and can result in less local autonomy and less direct input by the membership (Strauss 1991).

What has collective bargaining accomplished for construction union members? Two metrics are used to address this question: a comparison of average hourly earnings in construction with manufacturing, another industry with a significant union presence, and a comparison of average hourly earnings of construction workers with all workers throughout US industry (Table 4). Both comparisons are limited to earnings and do not incorporate the costs of benefits. In 1963, the average construction

Table 4
Average Hourly Compensation of Construction, Manufacturing, and All Employees

	Average hourly earnings			Ratios	
Year	Construction	Manufacturing	All	Construction/ manufacturing	Construction/ all
1962	$2.89	$2.27		1.27	
1967	$3.63	$2.71	$2.86	1.34	1.27
1972	$5.54	$3.70	$3.90	1.50	1.42
1977	$7.55	$5.55	$5.44	1.36	1.39
1982	$11.04	$8.36	$7.87	1.32	1.40
1987	$12.15	$9.77	$9.14	1.24	1.33
1992	$13.80	$11.40	$10.77	1.21	1.28
1997	$15.65	$13.14	$12.50	1.19	1.25
2002	$18.51	$15.29	$14.96	1.21	1.24
2007	$20.94	$17.26	$17.41	1.21	1.20
2012	$23.96	$19.08	$19.72	1.26	1.21
2017	$26.72	$20.90	$22.04	1.28	1.21
2022	$31.81	$24.85	$26.96	1.28	1.20

US Bureau of Labor Statistics, "Average Hourly Earnings" (no date).

worker earned 124% of the earnings of a manufacturing worker. This peaked in 1972, with construction workers earning 150% of manufacturing earnings, and then declined to 120% in the mid-1990s. It recovered to 128% in the late 2010s and early 2020s. Construction worker earnings followed a similar path relative to the earnings of all worker pay, peaking at 143% in 1975, declining to a 120% range from 1992 to 2019, and remaining slightly below that currently. The trends of construction wages relative to both manufacturing workers and all workers reflect the strength of the building crafts following World War II, their decline following the 1981–1983 recession, and the stabilization of their position from the 1990s forward.[4]

STRIKE ACTIVITY IN CONSTRUCTION

There have been very few strikes or lockouts in the construction industry over the past 30 years. Since 2012, only four work stoppages involving 1,000 or more employees have occurred. The current low level of work stoppage activity contrasts with the industry's historic reputation for being strike prone. The decline in strikes in the construction industry parallels the decline in strikes throughout the US economy; similar factors explain both. These include a weak economy with sufficient unemployment to make strikes increasingly risky from the union and union members' points of view. The drop in strikes in construction is also linked to factors that set back the industry as a whole beginning in the 1980s, particularly the high interest rates the Federal Reserve used to wring inflation out of the economy between 1979 and 1983. This hit construction particularly hard, given its dependence on borrowing money for building projects. Unemployment in construction spiked into the 18% to 20% range in 1982–1983 (US Bureau of Labor Statistics 1988) and remained above 13% until 1987 (US Bureau of Labor Statistics 2023).[5]

The period of high unemployment coincided with nonunion contractors increasingly moving from residential and light commercial into the union-dominated commercial and industrial construction sectors and helped the nonunion sector establish itself as a fierce competitor in these sectors. Union members often "stuck their card in their shoe" (left the union sector) and worked nonunion jobs when they were available, further increasing the capacity of the nonunion sector by providing a ready supply of trained and experienced labor (Allen 1988).

With the increasing threat from nonunion construction in core union segments, strikes became too costly to undertake, except in exceptional circumstances. Union leaders shifted to promoting their members as a dependable source of skilled labor. This manifested itself in the development of "codes of excellence" for craft workers on the worksite. These codes stressed the dependability and quality of highly trained union workers and included assurances that projects would be built without strikes or other disruptions. These were an important selling point for union labor, as was the use of project labor agreements (PLAs) with no-strike clauses and of labor–management committees that worked to avoid jurisdictional issues between crafts and served the purpose of making union construction a benchmark for successful projects. One result of this has been the continued growth of the system of labor–management committees in the industry.

HOW THE INDUSTRY CHANGED: INTERVENTION OF THE OWNERS

In the wake of the strike activity of the late 1960s, a group of executives from most of the nation's largest corporations—clients or "users" of the construction industry—formed the Construction Users Anti-Inflation Roundtable in 1969, renamed the Business Roundtable in 1972. Prior to becoming one of the country's principal corporate voices on national policy discussions, the organization's founding goal was to reduce inflationary building costs and rein in what was perceived as excessive union power in the building crafts—that is, the power to elevate wages and to control the day-to-day culture of the jobsite (Linder 2000). These owners wanted to realign the interests and power relations among owners, contractors, and unions. They rebelled at what they viewed as an excessively cozy relationship between contractors and unions. The long-standing and relatively stable system of labor relations that predated the Business Roundtable may have been effective in terms of developing and retaining a skilled workforce, but owners chafed at the power ceded to the unions. Unlike their manufacturing counterparts, construction users were not focused on introducing advances in mechanization. Instead, they adopted a laserlike focus on creating an environment in which construction employers pledged obeisance to the client who was paying the bills rather than to the labor organizations that represented the employees (Business Roundtable 1983).

The Roundtable issued a series of reports titled "More Construction for the Money," in which they bemoaned the "inordinate fragmentation" of the industry. In the absence of cost-effective management systems, the reports concluded that "the big losers are owners" (Business Roundtable 1983). In 1968, Winton Blount, head of one of the nation's largest general contracting firms, described construction labor relations as "chaotic at best" and went on to suggest that "despotic or unbelievable may be better terms" (Bloomberg Industry Group/BNA 1968). Blount and other Roundtable members wanted to place supervision firmly in management's hands, both in the executive office and on the jobsite.

One method of doing so was to restructure industry responsibilities and move from the traditional self-performing general contractor system to construction management, in which the prime contractor worked for a fee and transferred estimating risks and managing the workforce onto subcontractors. The shift was consistent with a deregulatory environment and the fissuring business strategy that transferred the coordination of employment relations and product standards to a multitude of franchisees, labor brokers, and other third-party managers—all in the name of freedom from direct responsibilities for a workforce, along with the resultant cost savings. The transition was, in many ways, complete by the end of the century. A 2000 textbook on project management suggested that the era in which general contractors "performed significant amounts of work with their own forces is largely over" (Levy 2000). The construction manager was now an extension of the owners' vision and wallet.

In conjunction with this approach, the Roundtable developed a political agenda to limit union power. They supported the expansion of the ABC as a counterweight to the existing employer associations dominated by contractors with collective bargaining agreements. The ABC would serve as an anti-union political voice in the halls of Congress and state legislatures around the country (Linder 2000).

While failing to repeal or weaken the Davis–Bacon Act, a 1931 law that mandated hourly wage rates (usually the union scale in a given locality) on federally financed construction projects, the ABC and its business allies successfully supported efforts to repeal state prevailing wage or "mini Davis–Bacon" laws. These laws insured that the wage rates on union sites served as the standard for the entire industry in a given state. Legislative or referendum-based campaigns to repeal such laws gained momentum in the 1970s and 1980s. Nine states rolled back state prevailing wage laws between 1979 and 1989. Six more have taken similar action since then. Today, 24 states do not have a prevailing wage law.

Just as significantly, lobbyists were able to convince Congress to enact Section 530 of the Revenue Act of 1978. Congressional supporters argued that the Internal Revenue Service (IRS) had inappropriately increased vigilance in the enforcement of employment tax laws over the previous decade. Companies that treated workers as independent contractors complained that the IRS was imposing costly reclassification penalties that created past and future liabilities. Section 530, and additional amendments in 1982, granted a "safe harbor" to employers that had a "reasonable basis" for treating workers as nonemployees. Congress explicitly defined reasonableness as the standard in situations in which the use of independent contractors was a "longstanding recognized practice of a significant segment" of an industry. From the perspective of a formerly compliant construction contractor, Section 530 gave a green light to reclassifying its workforce as independent contractors (Erlich 2023).

MISCLASSIFICATION AS A BUSINESS MODEL

Using independent contractors on building projects limited risk and shifted the employment burden through the expansion of multi-tier subcontracting. While misclassification has emerged as a business model in many industries, including the gig sector, construction already depended on a long-standing system of subcontracting that thus allowed a simpler extension of an existing set of contractual relations. Stan Marek, CEO of Houston-based Marek Co., one of the largest interior systems contractors in the South, termed Section 530 "by far the most abused change in the history of the IRS" (Steffy and Marek 2020). He attributed the destruction of the union sector of the building industry in Texas in the 1980s to the growth of independent contracting enabled by the amended tax code.

The newly emboldened nonunion contractors opted to lower labor costs by compensating tradesmen as independent contractors, even though their daily tasks and methods of work remained unchanged. Responsible nonunion employers like Marek complained that it was becoming "impossible for companies like ours that play by the rules to compete" when, by his estimation, half of his competitors' workers were hired as independent contractors (*Engineering News-Record* 2013).

The motivation driving the elimination of employee status was simple. The various state and federal tax and insurance obligations associated with hiring employees constituted a significant portion of total compensation costs. The ability to eliminate as much as or more than 30% of labor costs by simply reclassifying a company's workforce as independent contractors was a clever and effective method to gain a competitive edge over other contractors who continued to bear the burden of required mandates. Like employers in other industries, construction contractors abandoned the obligations to pay their share of income, unemployment, and Social Security and Medicare taxes (as well as earned sick time in some states) by redefining employees as independent contractors.

Construction firms have an incentive to misclassify beyond the usual labor savings of state and federal tax obligations. They also shed the burden of workers compensation insurance policies that, owing to the risks inherent in the dangerous construction industry, carry above-average premiums. For nonunion contractors that already pay lower wages than their union counterparts and provide few, if any, benefits, the temptation to realize 30% to 35% in labor cost savings and further extend the compensation gap and competitive edge is virtually irresistible. Independent contractors are no longer confined to building backyard decks or even single-family homes in suburban developments; misclassified workers have become a regular presence on multimillion-dollar projects working for sizable construction employers.

A cottage industry of lawyers and accountants advised contractors to alter their employment practices, moving the workforce from employees to independent contractors. The American Bar Association's Construction Lawyers Guide even developed a five-page boilerplate independent contractor agreement for construction contractors (Seeman, Hennessey, and Cooper 2001). Though the character of the work remained unchanged in terms of the underlying criteria of direction and control, many courts accepted the existence of this type of document as solely determinant.

As an example, a Pennsylvania carpenter named Mulzet was hired in 1998 by drywall contractor R.L. Reppert. According to subsequent court documents, the company supplied all the necessary power tools, while Mulzet brought his hand tools—standard practice in the industry. The federal judge in the case acknowledged that Mulzet performed the same work as company employees, was paid hourly as were company employees, and that his work was assigned and evaluated by the same supervisors. But Reppert had required Mulzet to sign an independent contractor agreement as a condition of employment, and, as a result, the judge ruled that the document alone "tips the scales decidedly in favor of the conclusion that Mulzet was an independent contractor" (Bloomberg Industry Group/BNA 2002).

The use of misclassification was further accelerated as a result of the passage of the 1986 comprehensive Immigration Reform and Control Act (IRCA), a bill intended to stem the flow of migrants crossing the Mexican border into the United States. Many business associations opposed the IRCA because it contained penalties against employers who knowingly hired undocumented workers. The provision was intended to pressure employers to abandon the practice of exploiting the lack of citizenship status as a means of reducing labor costs. The attempt was largely unsuccessful because the legal standard of "knowingly" was difficult to prove, but businesses found an additional unintended consequence of the legislation. Because employer sanctions were triggered only if the new hire was an employee, one obvious conclusion was to hire new workers as independent contractors rather than employees.

IMMIGRATION AND THE CHANGING WORKFORCE

In a 1987 AGC question-and-answer sheet on the new legislation, one of the questions posed was, "What if I decide just to give up and have no one in my business other than independent contractors and leased employees?" (Hyman 2018). The answer was self-evident. In the wake of IRCA, immigration and misclassification became inextricably linked.

As early as 1984, a Rice University economist claimed that one-third of all commercial construction jobs in the Houston area were filled by undocumented workers from Mexico, Central America, and South America. His study suggested that those workers were being treated as independent contractors so that employers could avoid paying taxes (*U.S. News and World Report* 1984). According to many Pew Research Center studies on immigration, the proportion of Hispanic male workers in construction increased four times as fast as the increase of White male workers between 1990 and 2000 (Kochhar 2005). By the end of 2006, nearly a third of recently arrived foreign-born Hispanic workers were working in construction, predominantly in the South and, to a slightly lesser extent, in the West (Pew Research Center 2007).

The Center for Migration Studies and the Migration Policy Institute estimated that there were 1.7 million undocumented workers in Texas alone in 2014, 24% of whom worked in construction (Warren 2016). Undocumented immigrants made up 15% of the national construction workforce, outnumbering immigrant workers with valid working papers (Passell and Cohn 2016). Construction continues to employ more undocumented workers than any major industry.

The Austin-based Workers Defense Project has conducted two studies on construction workers' conditions—one in Texas and one across the South. Their findings demonstrated that half of the workforce in Texas was foreign born and that, in six Southern states, nearly one-third were undocumented. In certain nonlicensed crafts with a tradition of piecework—drywall, ceilings, wood framing, roofing, bricklaying, painting, and taping—the numbers were even higher. The lack of acceptable immigration documentation exposed these workers to unsafe conditions, poverty-level payments, and wage theft. Over 40% of the surveyed group in Texas reported that they routinely experienced nonpayment of overtime and, in many cases, nonpayment of any wages (Workers Defense Project 2013, 2017).

The tectonic shift in construction workforce demographics depended on a steady labor supply chain. The people who recruited workers and their families to cross the border illegally were referred to as "coyotes," a colloquial term dating back to the 19th century. The coyote system of smuggling groups of people for a fee was well suited for the multi-tier subcontracting system of construction. Coyotes graduated to become labor brokers, using smartphones with hundreds of contacts to function as informal hiring halls and supplying subcontractors with workers wherever and whenever they were needed. The relationship between subcontractors and labor brokers also provided a shield against legal liability unless overtaxed regulators and auditors took on the Herculean task of applying joint employer or criminal conspiracy standards connecting the two entities (Erlich 2023).

The growth of the immigrant workforce had begun to undermine the rationale for a "paper-intensive" legal approach to misclassification. If there was already a question of uncertain citizenship status, many employers and labor brokers began to wonder why they should bother with lengthy legal documents and 1099 forms. Entering the world of the underground economy through a system of straight cash or paychecks without deductions was a simpler and more cost-effective method of compensation. The transition from independent contracting with a legal paper trail to off-the-books unrecorded cash compensation further complicated regulatory options. Active enforcement agencies had been able to track the advance of independent contracting by monitoring the issuance of 1099 forms. But the descent into the underground economy and under-the-table payments posed new and nearly insurmountable obstacles. The challenge of measuring, let alone regulating, employer behavior when the entire system of compensation was unrecorded stymied investigators accustomed to building cases through documentation (Erlich 2023).

The growing use of undocumented workers, coupled with the practice of payroll fraud and wage theft, spread from the South to the Midwest and Northeast in the early 2000s. By 2010, for example, a New York Building Congress analysis claimed that 45% of the city's crafts workers were not US citizens, and a Fiscal Policy Institute study suggested that the level of payroll fraud was particularly acute in the city's affordable housing industry, where fully two thirds of the workforce were either independent contractors or paid off the books (Fiscal Policy Institute 2007; Real Deal 2011).

The most recent and comprehensive national study estimated conservatively that, in 2017, between 12.4% and 20.5% of the construction industry workforce (1.3 to 2.2 million workers) were either improperly classified as independent contractors or employed informally off the books. Depending on worker income assumptions, the study concluded that fraudulent employers may have realized between $6.2 and $17.3 billion in labor cost savings, figures that are the basis of estimates of tax revenues lost annually to state and federal coffers, as well as premiums unpaid to workers compensation insurers (Ormiston, Belman, and Erlich 2020).

The spread of misclassification and cash payments predated the influx of undocumented workers into construction, but the two have evolved to be mutually reinforcing. The availability of large numbers of workers lacking legal standing has driven down wages and working standards in construction—not only for those who are undocumented but for citizens and documented workers as well. Contractors threaten those who complain about substandard working conditions and payroll theft by being replaced with more docile workers willing to endure substandard conditions. A reputation for "standing up" also affects current employees' ability to be hired for the next project.

REINFORCING THE INSTITUTIONS OF COLLECTIVE BARGAINING IN CONSTRUCTION

The unionized construction industry, its unions, and its employers face ongoing challenges in the labor and product markets. These challenges are accompanied by unfavorable changes in the legal structures within which they operate. In contrast to much of the labor movement and its employing firms, the unionized construction industry has been successful in maintaining union membership since the 1980s, in continuing to provide good union jobs that allow workers to support their families, and in providing a foundation for economic success for its contractors. The success of labor and management arises from three distinct sources: maintaining the unionized sectors' productivity advantage; bringing in under-represented groups, particularly African Americans, Latinos, and women; and altering the government policies and the owner perceptions that have limited its ability to compete successfully.

IMPROVING CRAFT WORKER PRODUCTIVITY

In his article "Declining Unionization in Construction: Facts and Reasons," Allen (1988) noted that unionized construction workers enjoyed an 83% to 109% compensation premium, as well as a 24% to 32% productivity advantage over nonunion construction workers. This is critical to unionized sector employers, for whom maintaining productivity has become the key to maintaining good jobs. Convincing owner/principals of the cost effectiveness of unionized construction has required a rethinking of the strengths and weaknesses of the unionized sector.

The unionized sector needs, on an ongoing basis, to demonstrate that union projects cost no more than those of nonunionized competitors, that the completed projects are of higher quality, and that projects will not be impeded by labor shortages or jurisdictional disputes that hamper progress, raise costs, and raise owners' concerns. Achieving those goals requires more deliberate and increased investment in the hard and soft skills of apprentices and journey workers, greater insistence on professionalism by craft workers on the job, taking advantage of the skills and knowledge of the labor force to allow the craft workforce to explicitly support the management of projects, and developing institutions to better coordinate projects across crafts.

The labor movement has worked to modernize its apprentice and journey worker training programs and facilities. This has encompassed bringing new instructional and construction technologies into the curriculum, incorporating contemporary adult learning strategies in the classroom and on the job, and taking advantage of distance learning and contemporary IT to make training richer and more flexible. The UBC, for example, has built one of the largest training facilities in the world. The International Training Center (ITC) in Las Vegas is a 1.2 million-square-foot campus that offers skill and leadership training for 15,000 members a year. The ITC is a state-of-the-art publisher of craft training manuals for internal union, as well as vocational, school use (Belman 2022).

The building trades, including the UBC, invest $2 billion annually in training programs in 1,900 training centers in the United States and Canada. Many of these centers incorporate remote teaching to allow students to obtain knowledge and practice with advanced skills that are not available locally. Completion of a registered apprenticeship takes three to five years and involves 32 hours of on-the-job training and eight hours of classroom instruction per week (Belman 2022).

To successfully train young workers in a craft, apprenticeship instructors need to remain abreast of developments, master them, and effectively teach the skills necessary to successfully develop workers. The curriculum for apprenticeship instructors in the International Pipe Trades Joint Training Committee (IPTJTC) requires 200 hours of classes, takes five years to complete, and involves both in-person training at the national training center and online training in adult and technical education. Great emphasis is placed on instructor effectiveness in conveying technical skills and in using contemporary teaching techniques, including a full range of in-person and distance-learning methods (Belman 2022).

Construction apprenticeship training increasingly includes classes in leadership and management roles. The IPTJTC includes teaching craft workers to undertake a "look ahead" approach to ensure they have the plans, blueprints, tools, and supplies needed to remain engaged for the following three days. This both reduces costly waiting times and the burden on supervisors and forepersons to address these matters, in addition to their other duties. The Laborers Union includes foreperson training in its apprenticeship program (Belman 2022).

NABTU and their contractor partners developed the Multi-Craft Core Curriculum (MC3) to be used in public career and technical education (CTE) schools to expand the numbers and diversity of the pipeline from secondary schools to construction registered apprenticeships. NABTU's MC3 program is an apprenticeship-readiness program that provides a mixture of hard and soft skills to prepare participants for successful entry into registered apprenticeships, acquaints them with the crafts that have registered apprenticeship programs, and provides exposure to help participants decide whether construction is a good fit for their long-term career goals (Belman 2022).

The MC3 program includes an introduction to the construction industry, tools, and materials, construction health and safety, blueprint reading, basic math for construction, heritage of the US workers, diversity in the construction industry, green construction, and financial literacy. The program requires a minimum of 120 classroom hours. This curriculum is currently available in several settings, including high schools, community colleges, adult re-entry programs, and programs for those involved in the justice system.

The MC3 can be taught face-to-face, but it is also available to all approved apprenticeship readiness programs in a web-based learning management system. All student and instructor materials for the updated MC3 program are available in one integrated learning management system, modeled on the Blackboard platform used at many colleges and universities.[6] Much of the effort to use the MC3 program to recruit underrepresented groups has been consolidated in TradesFutures, a program that helps women, veterans, and people of color establish and maintain careers in the construction industry.

These efforts to have borne fruit. In their 2022 report, "Quantifying the Value of Union Labor in Construction Projects, Independent Project Analysis," McFadden, Santosh, and Shetty) found that, in the pipe trades, union labor is 14% more productive than nonunion labor and reduces total project costs by 4%. Mixed union/nonunion labor was 8% less productive than union labor. Although additional research is needed in other trades, this supports the union contention that high-skilled union workers are both more productive and less expensive than their nonunion counterparts.

THE PENSION CRISIS WITHIN UNIONIZED CONSTRUCTION

Unionized construction workers participate in multi-employer pension plans that manage the pension contributions made by their employers. These plans are jointly overseen by employers and union representatives. Prior to the American Rescue Act of 2021, 200 multi-employer plans covering 2 to 3 million union members and their families were on pace to become insolvent by 2026 (White House 2022). Overall, 1,229 active multi-employer plans had $1.145 billion in liabilities and $494 in assets. Although 57.7% of multi-employer plans were not considered underfunded by the US Department of Labor, 132 (9.6%) were considered endangered or seriously endangered, 190 (20.8%) were critical, and 113 (11.8%) were classified as critical and declining.[7] Insolvent plans are unable to continue paying benefits—with severe consequences for current retirees, current paying members, and unionized employers participating in the plans. Plans that became insolvent have their payments taken over by the Pension Benefit Guaranty Corporation; the statutory maximum payout per worker is $12,870 annually. Eighty percent of participants in multi-employer plans will receive less than the PGBC maximum (Congressional Research Service 2020).

The issue with the funding of pension plans dates to the Pension Reform Act of 1986. This reform placed a 40% tax on the overfunding of plans. Single-employer plans could address this by stopping payments into the plan until the plan was correctly funded. Multi-employer plans were not able to do this because of their contractual obligation to pay into the plan. Instead, overfunding was addressed by increasing retiree benefits. For the plans in critical status, the requirement for increased contributions forced unions to allocate the bulk of contractual increases to pension funds, even as health insurance costs were also escalating. Active members would face reductions in their pensions. In addition, recruiting new unionized employees became very challenging because signing a collective agreement would immediately saddle a firm with millions of dollars of withdrawal liabilities. If plans liquidated, firms could face crippling immediate payments (Federal Register 2022).

In 2021, the American Rescue Act provided special financial assistance amounting to $44.3 billion to plans in the endangered and critical category. Under reasonable assumptions about the returns of new and legacy assets, plans that receive these payments will be solvent and continue paying benefits to 2051. This has been somewhat complicated by the decline in the value of bonds in the face of rising interest rates, but matters are far better than before the American Rescue Act (Pension Benefit Guaranty Corporation, no date).

OPENING CRAFTS TO UNDER-REPRESENTED POPULATIONS

The early craft guilds maintained their monopoly on their trade by limiting access to knowledge and skills. Entering the trade often required prior family involvement; exclusion became intermixed with discrimination by race, ethnicity, and gender. *De jure* or *de facto* exclusions were common among the building trades.

The current need for skilled crafts workers in the construction industry is estimated at more than 646,000 annual occupational openings from 2023 through 2032 (US Bureau of Labor Statistics, "Employment by Detailed Occupation," no date). It will provide an opportunity for registered apprenticeship programs to bring in a new generation of more diverse workers into the industry and rebuild the market share of employers who provide family-supporting employment. The trades are moving toward greater inclusion by bringing in previously excluded racial and ethnic groups, as well as encouraging women to enter the trades (Bilginsoy, Bullock, Wells, and Zullo 2022).

New York City provides an example of how the demographics of the union workforce in construction are changing. In the construction boom of the 1960s, discriminatory hiring resulted in a construction labor force that was 92% White; some skilled trades had virtually no African American members (Mishel 2017).

Gary LaBarbera, president of the Building and Construction Trades Council of Greater New York, frankly acknowledged this problem, while citing steps the trades in that city have taken to open up the industry to workers of color:

> We recognized years ago that New York's construction industry, like many others, had long suffered from a diversity problem. … Through initiatives like the Edward J. Malloy Initiative for Construction Skills, we have welcomed thousands of skilled African American and Latino workers into our ranks, and we are proud to say that today, 65 percent of local apprentices are minorities. (*Real Estate Weekly* 2015)

In 2017, the Economic Policy Institute reported that 21.2% of union construction workers in New York City were African American, compared with only 15.8% of the nonunion construction workforce. African American participation in apprenticeship programs virtually doubled from 18.3% to 35.1% from 1994 through 2014. The economic benefits of this trend are significant, with Black union construction workers earning 36% more than their nonunion counterparts (Mishel 2017).

The picture is different for Hispanic workers, who composed 30.5% of the union workforce in New York in 2006 through 2015. Hispanic participation in union-registered apprenticeship rose from 16% in 1994 to 22% in 2015. Union Hispanic construction workers had a 53% wage advantage over nonunion Hispanics: $24.18 versus $15.84. Hispanic workers represent a higher percentage of the nonunion labor force, accounting for 50% of employment. Hispanic workers who are union members are older, better educated, and have been in the United States longer than their nonunion counterparts. Although these results pertain only to New York City, similar changes are taking place in other urban areas (Mishel 2017).

Unions have taken steps to be more welcoming to Hispanic workers. This includes hiring bilingual local staff, translating apprenticeship materials into Spanish, teaching in Spanish, and reaching out to undocumented workers in conjunction with worker centers. Many unions accept undocumented workers with whatever Social Security numbers they provide and refer them to contractors who are not cautious about verifying their legal immigration status. The UBC uses programs such as Fast Justice to recover stolen wages. In addition, unions have undertaken a host of initiatives to work with state and federal regulatory agencies to assist workers subject to wage theft as a means of sending a message that unions represent all construction workers and to achieve a more level playing field with regard to bidding (Belman 2022).

Women's participation has been particularly challenging for the unionized industry. The long-established culture of construction has been hostile to women's participation, and many of the barriers created to keep women from working in the industry remain. A number of programs have been established to encourage women interested in careers in construction and to support those currently working in apprentice and journey worker positions. For the past decade, NABTU has sponsored an annual conference, Tradeswomen Build Nations (TWBN), to bring together women who are actively involved in NABTU member unions. More than 3,000 women participated in the 2022 conference in Chicago. In addition to the annual conference, TWBN provides mentoring, support, and connection through lean-in circles and support to women's committees in local unions (Lean In, no date).

Among the impediments for women working in construction is finding accessible daycare that fits their working hours. Several metropolitan trades councils now provide daycare to assist women members. Important daycare pilots, a site facility in Milwaukee, and a voucher program in New York City were announced at the Opportunity Pipeline Forum on January 18, 2023. The cost of the two pilots is $1 million (TradesFutures, no date). Also, the challenges of physical work associated with the iron-working trade create unique health challenges that can jeopardize a pregnancy. Responding to the needs of craft workers and their families, the Iron Workers Union and the Ironworker Management Progressive Action Cooperative Trust established the first national paid maternity leave benefit in 2017. The paid maternity benefit includes a maximum of six months of pre-delivery leave and six to eight weeks of post-delivery leave. This is the most generously paid maternity leave benefit in the building trades (North American Building Trades Unions 2022).

The challenge for the unionized industry is clear. Women, Asian, Native American, and African American workers are under-represented in the construction trades and have been for decades. The construction sector remains one of the few industries where an individual without a college degree can earn a family-supporting wage and build a career. Under-representation equates to lost opportunities for nontraditional workers to secure jobs with the middle-class earnings and benefits that have long represented the economic backbone of communities across the United States. The inequality of opportunities—and even inequality within the industry—also contributes to the nation's overall sizable and persistent gender and racial pay gaps. Much of the effort to promote diversity in the unionized trades, in particular their recruitment of under-represented groups, has been consolidated in TradesFutures (TradesFutures, no date).

USING LABOR-MANAGEMENT COOPERATION TO CREATE COMPETITIVE ADVANTAGE

Construction projects require a complex choreography between craft workers, supervisors from as many as 14 trades, and engineers, architects, suppliers, and owners. Problems on projects often arise from errors in coordination and cause excessive downtime, rework, and increased costs. A well-coordinated project helps parties achieve on-time results at or below contractually established costs. The unionized sector has argued that the superior training of the union workforce can achieve this desirable result.

Because of the degree of coordination, construction projects are vulnerable to stoppages, but traditional means of averting this problem have not been widely used in the sector. Lange and Mills noted:

> Historically, construction has made little use of binding arbitration by neutrals as a means of settling grievances. Instead of the usually lengthy process of grievance handling and arbitration, there is the "instant justice of construction." When the job steward and the employer's superintendent fail to settle grievances, the business agent of the local union intervenes. If he is also unsuccessful, a strike is likely to be called on the spot. (1979: 88)

While highly effective in achieving short-term goals, strikes have long-term consequences. They injure the reputation of unionized construction and discourage owners from using unionized sector contractors. This issue has long been acknowledged and has resulted in advances in labor relations in the unionized sector.[8]

The unionized construction sector has developed and reinforced institutions that facilitate cooperation between employers and their craft workers as well as across trades. These institutions provide a strong foundation for successful projects. Some aspects of labor–management cooperation accrue naturally. Most contractors are small and use their craft workers in managerial positions, such as foremen, supervisors, and estimators. Small firm size, experience with some dimensions of management, and training in small business operations through apprenticeship programs make craft workers aware of their employer's situation and also facilitate craft workers moving into owning their own firm. The link between an employer and its workforce is stronger than in most industries (Belman and Ormiston 2021).

Labor–management cooperation has been reinforced by local healthcare plans, pension plans, and apprenticeship programs that are organized as Taft–Hartley trusts[9] and are overseen by labor–management committees. Trustees make decisions about the generosity of the benefits and the amount of compensation required, which comes out of the negotiated settlement. Cooperation is carried further into joint labor–management committees organized by local building trades councils and employers to address cross-trade issues on specific projects and promote the industry. Jurisdictional issues between trades on specific projects that once would have resulted in a strike are now worked out in pre-project conferences. Project joint labor–management committees are also used to resolve unanticipated matters that arise in the course of the project. Committees place particular emphasis on resolving issues without the owner knowing about the dispute.

While the dangers of jurisdictional strikes or general contract strikes have discouraged owners from using unionized contractors in the past, the decline in strike activity in construction and the use of PLAs have helped ensure owners that using unionized contractors will be advantageous. PLAs signed by an owner and the local building trades council uniformly incorporate clauses that forbid any strikes or lockouts in the course of the project. PLAs also include clauses that commit unions to providing labor within 48 to 72 hours. In a period in which labor shortages regularly delay or cause the cancellation of nonunion projects, there is a strong record of PLA projects being sufficiently staffed, uninterrupted by labor issues, and benefiting from the superior coordination arising from craft workers, their unions, and management identifying with the success of the project (Ormiston and Duncan 2022).

Diverging from the "instant justice" common to construction, the electrical, plumbing and pipefitting, and sheet metal specialty trades have long-standing councils operating to address issues over grievance and contract matters that might result in a strike. In the electrical industry, the Council on Industrial Relations (CIR) resolves grievances—and often contract issues—between IBEW locals and NECA contractors. Dating to 1920, the CIR currently hears about 100 grievance and negotiation cases annually. The parties to a dispute typically submit a joint application to the CIR, which provides a detailed wage history and the CLRC's estimate of the local market share of the parties. Parties are urged to continue local negotiations and may receive help from local or regional offices (Bodah and Grob 2020).

If an issue cannot be settled at lower levels, the CIR will form a 12-member panel, equally divided between management and union representatives, to hear a case at its quarterly meeting. The parties to the dispute each have an opportunity to succinctly make their case before their panel, and panel members can ask questions of the presenters. Questions are intended to uncover the sources of the conflict and resolve cases quickly and may include questions about organizing activities, nonunion rates, benefit funds, and apprentice/journey worker ratios. The CIR panel retires to executive session and typically reaches a unanimous decision within a day. Although the decision is provided to the parties, the logic of the decision is not discussed (Bodah 2002).

There are many reasons for the decline in strikes in construction. The efforts of the unionized industry to protect their market by reassuring owners that their projects will be built on time at cost have played an important role in reducing the level of disputes in a historically disputatious and litigious industry but have also contributed to an ability of the sector to expand their list of return clients to major manufacturing companies and utilities.

CONCLUSION

Through the first three-quarters of the 20th century, industrial relations experts touted construction's collective bargaining system as a paragon of effective labor–management collaboration. In 1961, Harvard economist and future Secretary of Labor John T. Dunlop promoted the "inner unity and logic" to the interactions among building trades unions, contractor associations, and public agencies. "No single major feature of collective bargaining in this industry," Dunlop wrote, "can be understood apart from the … system as a whole … [based on] a common body of ideas and values" (1961). The component pieces of the system—multi-employer bargaining, skill training, job dispatching, benefits administration, and dispute resolution—were hailed as a model of successful industrial relations to be emulated in other industries. As late as 1979, scholars Julian Lange and D. Quinn Mills published an optimistic anthology emphasizing the success of the building trades system, titled *The Construction Industry: Balance Wheel of the Economy* (Lange and Mills 1979).

But not long after the book's publication, it became clear that the wheels were falling off the long-standing system of labor relations in construction. Owners had coalesced around what they perceived as excessive union power, misclassification was emerging as a rival business model to conventional employment relations, a new low-waged immigrant population was entering the workforce, and nonunion contractors were replacing union firms in many parts of the country.

Today, the landscape is bifurcated. In many metropolitan areas, the arrangements that Dunlop and others described still exist, functioning relatively smoothly and successfully. Trades workers can make a decent living with good benefits and work under safe conditions. This chapter described the mechanics of that procedure. But in geographical areas dominated by nonunion employers, there is no comprehensive system. Training is limited, wages have been reduced, safety is often compromised, and workers have no organized voice. The only way to describe the contemporary process of collective bargaining in construction is to recognize its continuing vitality in some jurisdictions and its collapse in others. The wheel is wobbling and needs rebalancing.

ENDNOTES

1. Production workers operate machines and other equipment to assemble goods or distribute energy; production workers include, but are not limited to, craft workers (US Bureau of Labor Statistics, https://tinyurl.com/yxef4tzf).

2. For example, when Michigan passed a right-to-work law in 2013, a number of construction contracts were extended to avoid being subject to the requirements of the new law. Extensions of up to ten years, the maximum allowed, were common.

3. The CLRC collects data on contract settlements for unionized employers and summarizes its data in quarterly reports. It is supported by national associations of construction employers, including the National Electrical Contractors Association, the Sheet Metal and Air Conditioning Contractors' National Association, the Associated General Contractors of America, the Association of Union Constructors, and others. The publications include the quarterly *CLRC Settlement Reports* and *CLRC Labor Costs in Construction*.

4. The higher earnings of construction workers reflected both their craft skills and their higher incidence of unemployment as they moved between projects and during the winter season.

5. Changes in BLS reporting criteria for strikes beginning in 1984 have made comparison of strike activity over time challenging. The reputation of being strike prone in the 1960s and 1970s is well documented in BLS data. Between 1962 and 1973, there were 54 work stoppages involving 10,000 or more workers in the construction industry, 12 of which occurred in 1972 alone. Between 1984 and 1988, there were never more than seven "major" work stoppages (involving 1,000 or

more workers) in a year, and these collectively never involved more than 20,000 employees. Since 2012, only four work stoppages have involved 1,000 or more employees (US Bureau of Labor Statistics 1975, 2023).

6. Fifty CTE high schools and community colleges across the United States have adopted MC3 as part of their curriculum. NABTU has received formal approval for the MC3 by state education departments in California, Louisiana, Maryland, Michigan, and Ohio. State approval is pending in Floria, New York, and Texas. How the MC3 fits into a school's CTE curriculum and academic calendar is up to the school district and the local Building Trades Council, which has local jurisdiction over the MC3 (discussion with T. Kriger, director of research and education, NABTU).

7. Endangered plan benefits were no more than 80% funded or were expected to have a serious deficiency in six years or fewer. The critical plan value of benefits was less than 65% funded or were expected to be insolvent in five years or fewer. Critical and declining plans were those expected to be insolvent within the next year (Congressional Research Service 2020).

8. There is a very long history of litigious behavior between owners and general contractors, between general contractors and subcontractors, and among subcontractors. Construction is not one big, happy family on the employer side (LePatner 2007).

9. A Taft–Hartley trust is a multi-employer benefit trust fund created solely for the benefit of collectively bargained employees working for many employers. The fund is maintained pursuant to a trust agreement and one or more collective bargaining agreements. Employers negotiate the fund into the applicable collective bargaining agreement and agree to contribute to the fund at certain specified rates for the benefit plans that are negotiated (medical, dental, vision, apprenticeship, and industry promotion). It is administered jointly between an employer association and a union.

REFERENCES

Allen, S. 1988. "Declining Unionization in Construction: Facts and Reasons." *ILR Review* 41, no. 3: 343–359.

Belman, D. 2022. "Registered Apprenticeship: Built to Last?" Report. East Lansing, MI: Institute for Construction Employment Research. http://tinyurl.com/bpasfv7m

Belman, D., and R. Ormiston. 2021. "Creating a Sustainable Industry and Work Force in the U.S. Construction Industry." In *Work and Labor Relations in the Construction Industry: An International Perspective*, edited by D. Belman, J. Drucker, and G. White: New York, NY: Routledge.

Bilginsoy, C., D. Bullock, A. Wells, and R. Zullo. 2022. "Diversity, Equity, and Inclusion Initiatives in the Construction Trades." Report. East Lansing, MI: Institute for Construction Employment Research. http://tinyurl.com/3sk2yj2r

Bloomberg Industry Group/BNA. 1968. "Construction Labor Report." Newsletter, Bureau of National Affairs. November 20.

———. 2002. "Construction Labor Report." Newsletter. Bureau of National Affairs. January 2.

Bodah, M., and H. Grob. 2020. "An Alternative to Industrial Dictatorship: 100 Years of the Council for Industrial Relations." *Perspectives on Work* 24: 54.

Business Roundtable. 1983. "More Construction for the Money: Summary Report of the Construction Industry Cost-Effectiveness Project." January.

Congressional Research Service. 2020. "Data on Multiemployer Defined Benefit (DB) Pension Plans." May 22. https://tinyurl.com/4ty7u8j7

Construction Labor Research Council. 2022. "Total Package Increases for Union Craft Workers in Construction. June. (See also "Settlement Reports and CLRC Union Labor Costs in Construction," various dates.)

Dunlop, J. T. 1961. "The Industrial Relations System in Construction." In *Structure of Collective Bargaining: Problems and Perspectives*, edited by A.R. Weber. New York, NY: Free Press of Glencoe.

Erlich, M. 2023. *The Way We Build: Restoring Dignity to Construction Work*. Urbana, IL: University of Illinois Press.

Erlich, M., and J, Grabelsky. 2005. "Standing at a Crossroads: The Building Trades in the Twenty-First Century." *Labor History*. November.

Engineering News-Record. 2013. June 3.

Federal Register. 2022. Vol. 87, no. 130. July 8. "Pension Benefit Guaranty Corporation." https://tinyurl.com/bddwsvk6

Fiscal Policy Institute. 2007. "The Underground Economy in the New York City Affordable Housing Industry." April 17. https://tinyurl.com/5f9z5wtu

Flood, S., M. King, R. Rodgers, S. Ruggles, J.R. Warren, and M. Westberry. 2022. "May 2021 National, State, Metropolitan, and Nonmetropolitan Area Occupational Employment and Wage Estimates." Integrated Public Use Microdata Series, Current Population Survey: Version 10.0 [dataset]. Minneapolis, MN: IPUMS. https://tinyurl.com/yc39ck55

Hirsch, B.T., D.A. Macpherson, and W.E. Even. 2023. "Union Membership, Coverage, Density, and Employment by Industry, 1983–2022." http://www.unionstats.com

Hyman, L. 2018. *Temp: How American Work, American Business, and the American Dream Became Temporary*. New York, NY: Viking.

Indeed.com. 2024. "Bechtel: Work Wellbeing." March 9. https://www.indeed.com/cmp/Bechtel

Kochhar, R. 2005. "The Occupational Status and Mobility of Hispanics." Pew Research Center. December 15.

Lange, J., and D.Q. Mills. 1979. *The Construction Industry: Balance Wheel of the Economy*. Lexington, MA: Lexington Books.

Lean In. No date. "Lean In Circles for Union Tradeswomen." https://tinyurl.com/2s3jf62a

LePatner, B.B. 2007. *Broken Buildings, Buster Budgets: How to Fix America's Trillion-Dollar Construction Industry*. Chicago, IL: University of Chicago Press.

Levy, S. M. 2000. *Project Management in Construction*, 5th edi. New York, NY: McGraw-Hill.

Linder, M. 2000. *Wars of Attrition: Vietnam, the Business Roundtable, and the Decline of Construction Unions*. Iowa City, IA: Fanpihua Press.

McFadden, S. Santosh, and R. Shetty. 2022. "Quantifying the Value of Union Labor in Construction Projects." December. Ashburn, VA: Independent Project Analysis.

Migration Policy Institute. No date. "Profile of the Unauthorized Population: Texas."

Mishel, L. 2017. *Diversity in the New York Union and Non-Union Construction Sector*. Washington, DC: Economic Policy Institute.

North American Building Trades Unions. 2022. "Iron Workers and Contractors Announce Paid Maternity Leave Benefit." https://tinyurl.com/5h7vukdn

Office of Labor–Management Standards, US Department of Labor. 2023. "LM-3 and LM-4 Reports, 2022–2023." https://tinyurl.com/tu3cwp9n

Ormiston, R., D. Belman, J. Brockman, and M. Hinkel. 2019. "Rebuilding Residential Construction." In *Creating Good Jobs: An Industry-Based Strategy*, edited by P. Osterman. Cambridge, MA: MIT Press.

Ormiston, R., D. Belman, and M. Erlich, 2020. "An Empirical Methodology to Estimate the Incidence and Costs of Payroll Fraud in the Construction Industry." Report. East Lansing, MI: Institute for Construction Employment Research. https://tinyurl.com/56re325j

Ormiston, R., and K. Duncan. 2022. "Project Labor Agreements: A Research Review." Report. East Lansing, MI: Institute for Construction Employment Research.

Passell, J., and D. Cohn. 2016. "Occupations of Unauthorized Immigrant Workforce." Report. Pew Research Center. November 3.

Pension Benefit Guaranty Corporation. No date. "American Rescue Plan Act of 2021." https://tinyurl.com/33dzemk4

Pew Research Center. 2007. "Construction Jobs Expand for Latinos Despite the Slump in Housing Market." Report. March 7.

Real Deal, The. 2011. "Non-US Citizens Make Up 39 Percent of NYC's Construction Workforce." December 21.

Real Estate Weekly. 2015. "Apprenticeship Offers a Path to the Middle Class." November 15. https://tinyurl.com/5bfh9vz2

Seeman, C., E. Hennessey, and R. Cooper, eds. 2001. *The Construction Lawyer's Guide to Labor and Employment Law*. Chicago, IL: American Bar Association.

Steffy, L., and S. Marek. 2020. *Deconstructed: An Insider's View of Illegal Immigration and the Building Trades*. College Station, TX: Texas A&M Press/Stoney Creek.

TradesFutures. No date. https://tradesfutures.org

US Bureau of the Census, US Department of Commerce. 2020. "The Number of Firms and Establishments, Employment, and Annual Payroll by State, Industry, and Enterprise Employment Size." https://tinyurl.com/369uhhf2

US Bureau of Economic Analysis, US Department of Commerce. 2021. "Value Added as a Percent of US GDP." https://tinyurl.com/25vfp9nn

US Bureau of Labor Statistics, US Department of Labor. 1975. "Work Stoppages in Contract Construction 1962–1973." *Bulletin 1847*. https://tinyurl.com/5n6ssyrd

———. 1988. "Table 32, Unemployment Rates by Industry and Class of Worker." *Handbook of Labor Statistics*, p. 145.

———. 2023. "Annual Work Stoppages Involving 1,000 or More Workers, 1947–Present." September. https://tinyurl.com/v28bk9dh

———. No date. "Average Hourly Earnings of Production and Nonsupervisory Employees, Construction and Manufacturing, NAICS Code 23 and All Private Workers." https://tinyurl.com/y64kncky

———. No date. "Employment by Detailed Occupation: Table 1.2 Employment by Detailed Occupation, 2022 and Projected 2032." https://tinyurl.com/bde7why5

U.S. News and World Report. 1984. "Crackdown on Illegal Aliens—The Impact." July 2.

Warren, R. 2016. "US Undocumented Population Drops Below 11 Million in 2014, with Continued Declines in the Mexican Undocumented Population." *Journal on Migration and Human Security* 4, no. 1: 1–15.

White House. 2022. "FACT SHEET: President Biden Announces Historic American Rescue Plan Pension Relief for Millions of Union Workers and Retirees." July 5. https://tinyurl.com/mr4886md

Workers Defense Project. 2013. "Build a Better Texas: Construction Working Conditions in the Lone Star State. A Report from the Workers Defense Project in Collaboration with the Division of Diversity and Community Engagement at the University of Texas at Austin."

———. 2017. "Build a Better South: Construction Working Conditions in the Southern U.S." Workers Defense Project and the Partnership for Working Families.

Chapter 3

Regenerating The NewsGuild: Organizing and Bargaining in the Newspaper Industry Since 2015

Howard R. Stanger
Canisius University

> *Once upon a time, newspapers were the first, best source of news for the public.... That's not the case anymore. Newspapers have seen an alarming shrinkage of their revenue, their resources, their staff, and their readership. And while smaller, local papers are hit especially hard by this, it is by no means limited to certain areas. This is a nationwide problem.*
>
> —Demkovich 2022

> *After suffering a historic meltdown a decade ago in the financial crisis, American newspapers began racing into digital businesses, hoping that strategy would save them from the accelerating decline of print. The results are in: A stark divide has emerged between a handful of national players that have managed to stabilize their businesses and local outlets for which time is running out.... Local papers have suffered sharper declines in circulation than national outlets and greater incursions into their online advertising businesses from tech giants such as ... Google and Facebook.... The result has been a parade of newspaper closures and large-scale layoffs.*
>
> —Hagey, Alpert, and Serkez 2019

Abstract

This chapter delves into labor relations in the newspaper industry post 2015, marked by significant changes leading to a resurgence in organizing by The NewsGuild. It builds on two previous studies within this research volume: one covering 1975 through 2001 and the other focusing on 2001 through 2013. These periods saw union decline, contract concessions, and shifts in ownership from family-owned to investment company–owned chains. The rise of the Internet drastically reduced print advertising revenue, with a peak of $49.3 billion in 2006 plummeting to $9.6 billion in 2021. This decline accelerated after the Great Recession, impacting circulation and digital ad revenue. Bankruptcies during the recession led to ownership consolidation, exacerbated by COVID-19's effects on print-to-digital transition and job cuts. Between 2005 and 2023, industry employment dropped significantly, especially in newsrooms and production roles. Journalists, particularly at metro and regional dailies, faced job cuts and inequities, prompting increased unionization efforts post 2015. The NewsGuild made substantial organizing strides from 2015 onward, adding thousands of new members annually across digital and print media outlets. Despite challenges in securing first contracts, the Guild negotiated new agreements at various newspapers, including major national ones. The Guild's organizing successes spanned diverse regions and employer types, with tactics ranging from walkouts to social media campaigns. As the industry seeks a sustainable business model for quality journalism and stable employment, navigating complex labor relations remains crucial.

INTRODUCTION

The newspaper industry's economic problems noted in the epigram stem from the rapid decline in print classified advertising revenue over the past two decades. These problems led billionaire investor and newspaper company owner Warren Buffet to declare in 2019 that newspapers were "toast" (Chiglinsky and Smith 2019). According to the Pew Research Center, which tracks media, US newspaper advertising revenue peaked at $49.3 billion in 2006 but fell by 80% to $9.6 billion in 2021. Ad revenue for publicly traded newspaper companies declined 40% from 2019 compared with 25% for the industry as a whole (Matsa and Worden 2022; Pew Research Center 2023).

Despite the industry's economic struggles, its decent cash flow has attracted investment firms—mainly private equity and hedge funds—that have purchased individual newspapers and entire chains, a recent and major departure when large, publicly traded media companies dominated the industry (Abernathy 2020a; Abernathy and Franklin 2022).

The rapid evaporation of the industry's revenue has adversely impacted employment, but it has also stimulated union growth and sometimes tense labor–management relationships. This chapter will document the significant growth in union organizing and the current state of collective bargaining in the US daily newspaper industry, which includes both print and digital operations. Central to the story is The NewsGuild (Guild, or TNG), the main union representing newsroom and business-side employees in the industry. The Guild has experienced membership growth in recent years from new organizing in unlikely places, while the unions representing the older production and distribution trades in the industry have undergone drastic job losses, as newspaper companies have shifted resources from print to digital operations.

Still, since 2005, 60% (or 43,140) of newspaper journalists have left the industry because of retirements, layoffs, or other forms of severance. Most of these journalists were employed by large metro and regional daily newspapers (Abernathy 2023: 5, 19). Both nonunion and union newsrooms have experienced job losses owing to layoffs, buyouts, outsourcing, and closures. Over the past four decades, newspaper industry collective bargaining has been mainly concessionary, and there has been little union organizing (see Stanger 2002, 2013). This situation changed after 2015, when the cumulative impact of two recessions, corporate restructurings, years of job cuts, pay freezes, reductions in benefits, and growing job insecurity drove workers to organize unions in newspapers all across the country.

THE NEWSGUILD–COMMUNICATIONS WORKERS OF AMERICA

The NewsGuild–CWA was founded by New York City–based journalist Heywood Broun and his colleagues as the American Newspaper Guild (ANG) in 1933. The Guild is currently one of seven industry sectors of the Communications Workers of America (CWA). Originally a union of telephone workers, CWA currently represents workers in all areas of communications, including media, as well as in healthcare and public service, customer service, and other fields. In 2022, CWA reported 652,581 total members/fee payers (US Department of Labor, LM-2, Schedule 13, 2022).

The ANG became the Newspaper Guild in 1970 to reflect the inclusion of Canadian membership. The Newspaper Guild reached its membership peak of about 34,000 in the 1980s, and in 1997, it was absorbed by the CWA. That same year, Linda K. Foley was elected the Guild's first female president.

In January 2015, delegates representing Guild membership in the United States, Canada, and Puerto Rico voted to change the union's name to The NewsGuild–CWA to reflect the growing diversity of the Guild's membership, which includes workers in nonprofit organizations, social justice organizations, broadcast news, news agencies, public sector organizations, and, most recently, digital-only news. Owing to employment cuts that followed declines in advertising and circulation revenue, the Guild lost 28% of its membership between 2000 and 2010 (Richardson 2015c; Stanger 2103: 220). Since 2015, however, its ranks have grown by around 7,000 to over 26,000 members in 275 media, 57 nonprofit, 55 labor, and 45 other organizations (The NewsGuild, "History," "Members").

Historically, the Guild has represented newsroom workers in larger and more urban national and local newspapers. It generally did not represent journalists in smaller cities, rural areas, or the South until after 2015 (Leab 1970; Mari 2021; Stanger 2002, 2013). The NewsGuild is currently composed of 46 US and 17 Canadian locals, based largely on geography. Some locals represent workers of a single publication, while others include multiple workplaces, with each one considered a "unit" within the local (The NewsGuild, "Locals").

At the five largest chains—Gannett, Digital First Media, Tribune Publishing, Lee Enterprises, and McClatchy—the Guild currently represents over 2,500 workers in 97 bargaining units. Of this group, the Guild represents the most workers at Gannett (42 units and 1,065 employees) and the fewest workers at McClatchy (225 in 13 units) (The NewsGuild, personal correspondence, 2023).

In 2019, Jon Schleuss, a 32-year-old digital data reporter at the *Los Angeles Times*, defeated 12-year incumbent president Bernie Lunzer in the first contested (and a re-run) Guild election in over a decade. The year before, Schleuss and his colleagues won a historic organizing campaign at the *Times*, which had been nonunion for 130 years (The

NewsGuild, 12/10/19).[1] Schleuss sought to reverse the Guild's membership decline and stagnant wages, respond to ongoing political attacks on the news media and journalists, and promote greater democracy and transparency within the union. He also stated that "Guild headquarters needs to finally get in step with the digital revolution reshaping our industry ... and dramatically expand the use of the Guild website, social media, and other forms of digital communications" (Lenz 2019; Schleuss, "Candidate Statement," 2019).

UNION DENSITY IN THE NEWSPAPER INDUSTRY

Using three-year averages from 2011 through 2022, union density data for the newspaper industry reveal a U-shaped pattern. The three-year average for union density between 2011 and 2013 was 7.5%; between 2014 and 2016, it was 7.1%; between 2017 and 2019, density averaged 6.4%; but from 2020 through 2022, the three-year moving average rose to 10.1%, an increase that likely reflects the Guild's successful organizing initiatives (www.UnionStats.com).

A 2022 Pew survey of about 12,000 working US-based journalists offers a broader view of unionization across different media segments of the industry. Pew found that 16% of journalists employed at least part time—excluding freelancers—at news organizations were union members. But another 41% indicated they would join a union if one were available to them, for a potential union density rate of 57%. In addition, 26% of journalists reported working for a news organization that has a union (Liedke 2022).

Younger (ages 18–29) journalists were more desirous of joining a union than their older (ages 65 and older) peers. For example, 77% of younger journalists were either already in a union (20%) or would join one if one were available to them (57%), nearly twice the share of older workers. The results also showed that women, Black, Hispanic, and Asian journalists are likelier than White journalists to say they were either in a union or would join one if available to them. Journalists who worked in larger media outlets were far likelier to be in a union than those in smaller media organizations, which is consistent with historical patterns (Liedke 2022).

Newspaper Industry Dynamics
Industry Ecosystem

There are four national newspapers—the *New York Times*, *Wall Street Journal*, *Washington Post*, and *USA Today*. Of these, the *Times*, the *Post*, and the *Journal* are organized; *USA Today*'s newsroom is nonunion. There are also approximately 150 metro and regional dailies, 1,063 small and mid-sized dailies, and 4,792 weeklies and nondailies across the United States. One of the more significant outcomes of the industry's ongoing economic difficulties has been the high number of local newspaper closings. Since 2005, almost 2,900 newspapers have ceased publication, including over 130 properties that have either closed or merged between 2022 and 2023. All but about a hundred are weeklies. The rate of closings has accelerated because a handful of big chains and regional companies have shuttered multiple papers in a single episode. Moreover, between 2019 and May 2022, which included the COVID-19 pandemic, an additional 360 papers ceased publication. Over 200 counties in the United States have no newspaper, and more than 1,600 have only one (typically a weekly). Newspaper closures create "news deserts," or situations where residents have very limited access to credible news. Roughly 70 million people live in a news desert or what will soon become one. Many newspapers that have survived have been stripped of resources and produce "ghost newspapers" that are shells of their former selves (Abernathy 2020a, 2023: 3–5, 17; Abernathy and Franklin 2022: 5, 12, 18).

Newspaper Industry Economics

Historically, the lifeblood of the newspaper industry has been revenue derived from two main sources—advertising and circulation. Advertising revenue has traditionally composed roughly two-thirds of the total, but this has changed in recent years. In 2020, for the first time, newspapers earned more money from circulation than from advertising. Moreover, Axios predicts that US digital newspaper advertising revenue will surpass print ad revenue by 2026 (Barthel 2021; Fischer 2022).

Aggregate revenue for newspaper publishers was slightly over $20 billion ($9.6 billion from advertising and $11.1 billion from circulation) in 2020, the lowest amount since it peaked in 2005 at about $60 billion ($49.4 billion from advertising and $10.7 billion from circulation), a decline of 67%. The reduction in advertising revenue, however, was even greater, at 81% (Demkovitch 2022) (Figure 1). The largest drop in revenue occurred during the Great Recession between 2007 and 2009. Revenue problems continued after the recession, however. According to Statista, between 2013 and 2020, US newspaper advertising revenue fell from $16.13 billion to $10.22 billion, a drop of about 58% (Statista 2023).

Figure 1
Total Revenue of US Newspapers

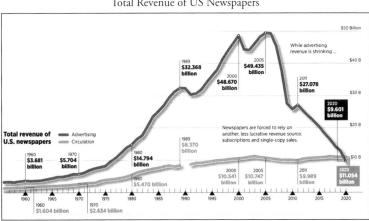

The Spokesman-Review 2022.

As advertising revenue has declined over the past two decades, the share of digital advertising revenue has increased from 17% in 2011 to 39% in 2020, but this increase has not compensated for the dramatic decline of print advertising revenue because Google, Meta's Facebook, and Amazon have taken about 65% of total digital revenue, while Microsoft's $10 billion in revenue in 2021 has placed it fourth on the list (eMarketer 2021; Mandese 2022). As recently as 2017, digital advertising accounted for one third of overall US ad spending, about the same as newspaper, radio, magazine, and local television ad revenue combined. By 2020, however, the four media sectors' combined share of the market fell to 21%. In 2017, Google and Facebook alone accounted for 86% of all digital ad growth in the industry. While these companies have siphoned off ad dollars from all publishers, local newspapers have borne the brunt of the decline. For example, the two tech giants have combined for 77% of digital ad dollars in local markets, compared with 58% at the national level (Hagey, Alpert, and Serkez 2019; Vranica 2020).

While the newspaper industry's advertising-centric business model has generally collapsed, there have been some improvements in circulation—but not enough to reverse overall revenue decline. For example, daily print newspaper circulation peaked at roughly 60 million in 1990, leveled off to 55 million in 2004, and then trended downward to 24 million in 2020, a decline of 62% since 2004. Between 2000 and 2020, the paid circulation of Sunday newspapers dropped 57%, from 59.4 to 25.8 million. Overall circulation revenue peaked at $11.23 billion in 2003 and has mostly held steady since then. In 2020, it registered $11.09 billion, the first time circulation revenue surpassed advertising revenue (Statista 2023).

Even with the fading effects of the pandemic, print circulation for the top 25 largest newspapers fell 14% between March 2022 and March 2023.[2] The combined average daily circulation for the top 25 was 2.6 million, down from three million during the same period. No newspaper in this group increased its year-to-year circulation. Between the first quarter of 2019 through March 2023, overall print circulation dropped 32%. Data on digital circulation showed a more positive trend, but print remains the most important revenue stream for both circulation and advertising (Majid 2023).

As Abernathy reports, "Many metro newspapers that once had hundreds of thousands of print subscribers have been able to entice only a few thousand subscribers to pay for their online editions, at only 23% of the price charged print subscribers" (2020a: 24). This is problematic because, since 2010, the number of people reading news online has surpassed those reading local newspapers. And the portion of people who consume news from digital devices continues to outpace those who receive their news from television, radio, and print publications (Abernathy 2020a).

Overall, daily newspaper publishers are replacing high-margin print advertising revenue with low-margin subscription and digital revenue, further reducing profits. By contrast, national newspapers such as the *New York Times*, *Wall Street Journal*, and *Washington Post* have had more success converting print readers to digital subscribers and have used the added revenue to invest in news-gathering and other businesses (Abernathy 2020b; Abernathy and Franklin 2022; Statista 2023).

Employment Decline

The steep decline in industry revenue has led to a concomitant loss in employment. Newspaper employment, for example, has fallen dramatically since the early 2000s. Between 2005 and 2023, overall employment dropped by over 70%, while the number of newsroom jobs fell by 57%, from 75,000 to 31,860. The loss of production-related jobs was even steeper—85% from 98,540 to 14,750 over the same time (Abernathy 2023) (Figure 2). The most precipitous drop in employment occurred during the depths of the Great Recession, around 2008 and 2009 (Mutter 2012).

In a comparative analysis of five media segments—newspapers, television, digital only, radio, and cable television—between 2008 and 2018, Pew found that only digital-only news experienced employment growth—from 7,400 to 13,500 employees, or an increase of 82%. By contrast, during this ten-year span, newspaper newsroom employment fell 47%, from 71,000 to 38,000, compared with a 25% decline for overall newsroom employment across the five media segments. Overall, across media sectors, newsroom employment in the United States dropped 26% between 2008 and 2020 (Grieco 2018a, 2019a, 2019b; 2020; Statista 2022; Walker 2021).

The year 2019 witnessed more employment losses in the media. On a single day in January, over 1,000 jobs disappeared. By early July, about 3,000 news workers had either been laid off or offered buyouts, the highest number since the Great Recession a decade earlier (Smith 2019). By the end of 2019, *Business Insider* reported that 7,800 workers had lost their jobs across the entire news media landscape (Goggin 2019).

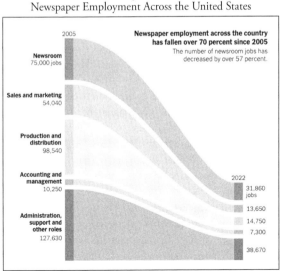

Figure 2
Newspaper Employment Across the United States

Local News Initiative, Northwestern University (by Taylor Maggiacomo).

The Financialization of Newspapers: The Rise of Private Investment Firms and Their Impact on Labor

Over the past half century, the newspaper industry has experienced noticeable shifts in ownership structure from family-based publishers to publicly traded ones and, since the Great Recession, to investment firms that have acquired hundreds of newspapers through mergers and acquisitions, direct purchases, and sales out of bankruptcy. Large regional chains also play a significant role in the industry, although they typically own smaller dailies and weeklies and are virtually nonunion (Abernathy and Franklin 2022). Greater industry concentration has accompanied ownership changes (see Stanger 2002, 2013 for more on ownership patterns before 2015).

Investment firms, like their previous owners, seek to earn profits, but their business models are generally different. For example, hedge funds and private equity firms often finance acquisitions with significant amounts of debt and manage their properties with aggressive cost cutting and lofty revenue goals. To achieve these financial targets, they rapidly cut jobs, pay, and pension plans; make use of bankruptcy courts to restructure balance sheets; consolidate sales and other business functions; sell off real estate, including newsrooms; outsource labor; and centralize editorial functions in regional hubs away from the communities that their newspapers serve. Moreover, they tend to be complex business entities that lack transparency, accountability, and civic mission. The bottom line: "Profits derived from cost cutting (are) not reinvested; instead, they [are] used to pay loans, management fees and shareholder dividends" (Abernathy 2020a: 3, 37; Kuttner and Zenger 2017).

The growing consolidation of the newspaper industry by investment firms and its impact on labor can be seen in a few recent large mergers and acquisitions and other newspaper transactions.

The New Gannett

Gannett, the largest newspaper chain, was purchased by GateHouse Media's private equity company's parent firms, New Media Investment Group and Fortress Investment Group, in 2019, for $1.1 billion and the assumption of $1.8 billion in debt financed by another private equity firm, Apollo Management. The new company kept the Gannett name. In 2022, the new Gannett owned 236 dailies (and 487 weeklies). Among its more notable newspapers are the *Arizona Republic, Columbus Dispatch, Detroit Free Press, Des Moines Register, Indianapolis Star, Milwaukee Journal Sentinel, USA Today*, and Gannett's original flagship property, the *Rochester Democrat & Chronicle*.

Since the GateHouse merger, Gannett has reduced the number of markets in which it operates, creating more local news deserts. For example, it owned 261 daily and 302 weekly newspapers in 2019. By the end of 2022, however, it cut 171 properties, a decline of about 30%. Gannett derives 90% of its newspaper revenues from its top 100 daily markets and, according to CEO Mike Reed, is likely to continue to shed properties in smaller markets.

At the end of 2018, the last full year before the merger, the two companies had 27,600 employees combined. Since the merger, Gannett has slashed over 10,000 jobs; by the end of 2022, it employed only 11,200 employees in the United States. Employment cuts were substantially deeper than the rate of its newspaper revenue decline because of its heavy merger-related debt load, the reduction in local markets, and its reorientation toward a digital news company.

Union density rates at Gannett, however, increased from 12% in 2018 (pre-merger) to 17% at the end of 2022, as workers organized new units in response to the merger, cost cutting, and job instability (Benton 2023; Fischer 2023b; Fischer and Flynn 2023; Wikipedia, "Gannett").

Alden Global Capital

The second largest newspaper chain, and one that also employs many union members, is the New York City–based hedge fund Alden Global Capital (Alden) and its newspaper chain unit Media News Group (MNG), formerly known as Digital First Media (DFM). Media News Group publishes 66 daily newspapers and more than 300 weeklies, including the *Boston Herald*, *Denver Post*, *Hartford Courant*, *New York Daily News*, *Orange County Register*, *San Jose Mercury News*, and *St. Paul Pioneer Press* (Media News Group, no date).

In 2021, Alden purchased Tribune Publishing for $630 million in a hostile takeover after failing to buy Gannett in 2019. NewsGuild president Jon Schleuss expressed concern about the hedge fund's business practices, saying, "Alden has a history of running newspapers into the ground. … This isn't good for workers, for the company, shareholders, or the communities" (Alpert and Lombardo 2021; Channick 2021a, 2021b).

From the time that Alden acquired a 32% stake in Tribune in late 2019 through April 2021, employment at Tribune dropped 30.4% (Edmonds 2021). At that time, the Guild represented 600 employees at eight of Tribune's nine major metros and 450 employees at MNG newspapers. Layoffs continued even as journalists organized unions at multiple Tribune papers. Between May 2018 and June 2021, for example, 287 union jobs were cut in 16 new bargaining units of various sizes (Edmonds 2021; Peck 2022; Reynolds 2021a, 2021b).

Large private investment firms generally do not have good reputations for their commitment to journalism and business practices, but they differ in degree. Veteran media analyst Ken Doctor argues that Alden "has been manifestly worse. … While GateHouse has cut, it is mindful of trying to improve the editorial product. There's more strategy there. But Digital First [MNG] papers tend to spiral down more quickly than others" (quoted in Zenger 2018).

Alden's newspaper strategy of buying distressed and bankrupt newspapers, slashing jobs, and selling newspaper real estate has led some to refer to it as "mercenary," a "vulture," and "the grim reaper of American newspapers" (Benton 2021; O'Connell and Brown 2019; The NewsGuild, "Hedgepapers," 2020). Alden-owned newspapers have disinvested in newsrooms at twice the rate of their competitors. For example, between 2012 and December 2018, DFM cut its Guild-represented workforce at the 12 newspapers by about 70%, from 1,552 to 478. And in the short window between 2015 and 2017, it reduced employment by 36% (Coppins 2021; Reynolds 2019).

DFM, however, was highly profitable, according to Ken Doctor. In fiscal year 2017, it reported a 17% operating margin—well above its peers—and profits of $159 million. In the same year, GateHouse's $1.3 billion in revenue exceeded DFM's $939 million, but it earned only $34.6 million in operating income. DFM's margin ranked highest among the four major chains at the time—New York Times Co., Gannett, Tronc (Tribune's short-lived name), and McClatchy—with each posting operating margins under 10%. DFM also had positive margins in all the geographic regions in which it operated (Doctor 2018; Reynolds 2018b).

High profits and repeated cuts have left DFM's diminished newsrooms hamstrung in their ability to provide effective news coverage and have led to numerous union-organized public protests, the most notable of which occurred at the *Denver Post* in April 2018. Alden acquired the *Denver Post* in 2011 and has cut newsroom employment multiple times since then. In 2016, for example, it eliminated 26 positions, which reduced the headcount to below 100, or about one third of the total from a decade earlier. About two years later, it cut another 30 newsroom jobs (25 union workers), or a third of the staff. The layoffs left the newsroom with only 69 employees to cover Denver's population of 2.9 million. At its peak, by contrast, the paper employed 300 journalists (Dean 2018; Sanchez 2016).

The Denver Newspaper Guild claimed that the layoffs were driven by Alden's "greed and its desperate attempt to recoup more than $130 million in investment losses from [its] Fred's Pharmacy [purchase] fiasco. … Such gambles in unrelated business ventures—Fred's Pharmacy, Payless Shoes, and Greek sovereign bonds—are draining DFM newspapers of the resources they need to survive" (quoted in Reynolds 2018a; Sullivan 2018).

The multiple rounds of cuts at the 125-year-old **Denver Post** sparked a newsroom rebellion in 2018 that included mass protests outside the *Post*'s building, a trip to Alden's New York City offices, and a long editorial that was approved by Chuck Plunkett, the *Post*'s editorial page editor, who resigned a month later (*Denver Post* Editorial Board 2018; Healy 2018; Rosman and Peiser 2018; Wenzel 2018).[3]

Lee Enterprises

The third-largest newspaper chain is Lee Enterprises, which purchased Warren Buffet's newspaper company, BH Media, in January 2020, for $140 million. Prior to the sale, BH Media hired Lee to manage its newspaper operations. After the purchase, Lee owned 77 dailies and roughly 150 total newspapers, including the *Arizona Daily Star*, *Buffalo News*, *Omaha World-Herald*, *Richmond Times-Dispatch*, *St. Louis Post-Dispatch*, and *Tulsa World* (Reynolds 2020). In 2022, Lee successfully rebuffed Alden's hostile bid, but Alden and other investment firms still own shares in Lee and continue to pressure it to cut costs and move toward a profitable digital-first strategy (Abernathy 2020b; Edmonds 2022; Funk 2022).

In May 2022, for example, in the wake of poor financial performance and a lower-than-expected reported number of digital subscribers, Lee announced 400 layoffs—or 10% of its total employment base of about 4,793 full-time equivalent employees, which included about 800 Guild members at 12 union newspapers. It also offloaded pension liabilities (Fischer and Flynn 2022; Fu 2022d).

Lee's disinvestment in the *Buffalo News*, once the "crown jewel of Warren Buffett's news empire," shows the effects of both financialization and the economic challenges facing the newspaper industry. Buffett purchased the *News* in 1977 and kept it separate from other acquired newspapers until Buffet folded it and 31 other papers into Lee Enterprises. The *News* then became just one of 77 newspapers under the company's centralized control and was soon subject to employment cuts and outsourcing. When Lee took over in January 2020, the Buffalo Newspaper Guild represented 158 employees, including 82 in the newsroom. But by early 2023, the union represented only 90 employees, including 57 in the newsroom—a decline of 43%. In 2011, the *News* employed 145 journalists. The drop in employment mirrored daily print circulation declines, which stood at about 35,000 in October 2023 from 56,000 a year earlier, and from a peak of 310,000 in the mid-1990s.

In January 2023, Lee announced additional newsroom cuts and the outsourcing of the printing of the *Buffalo News* to Advance Publications' Cleveland facility, which cut roughly 160 union production and distribution jobs in Buffalo. In addition, Lee sold the *News*'s marketing business, put its downtown office building up for sale, and moved staff to a nearby office building. Lee also slashed employment across its portfolio of newspapers. Between 2021 and 2022, it reduced its workforce by 15%, from 5,130 to 4,365. At its largest newspaper, the *St. Louis Post-Dispatch*, the United Media Guild now represents only 77 employees, down from a high of 450 in 2005, when Lee purchased the paper from the Pulitzer family (Fu 2023a; Heaney 2023).

In June 2023, the Unions of Lee Enterprises, an organization of employees from all 12 unionized newsrooms, launched a public campaign against Lee for cutting print circulation at most of its papers to thrice weekly, with all printed papers to be delivered by the US Mail. The unions also objected to Lee's outsourcing to out-of-state and foreign hubs, cutbacks to customer service, and, especially, for its ongoing disinvestment in newsrooms. "None of these drastic cuts will serve the company, its investors, its readers, or its employees in the long term," argued the union group (Unions of Lee Enterprises 2023).

McClatchy

The last major unionized chain is McClatchy, which ranks 18th overall with 30 dailies but is a major employer of union labor in 17 of its newsrooms. Among McClatchy's larger newspapers are the *Charlotte Observer*, *Fort Worth Star-Telegram*, *Kansas City Star*, *Miami Herald*, and *Sacramento Bee*. In 2020, the investment firm Chatham Asset Management purchased McClatchy out of bankruptcy for $312 million after initially investing in it in 2009. At the time McClatchy exited bankruptcy, it employed 24,000 people, carried $700 million in debt and high pension obligations, and had only six newsrooms represented by The NewsGuild. Financial troubles for McClatchy originated in 2006, when it paid $4.5 billion (plus $2 billion in debt) for the Knight Ridder chain. But drastically changed industry conditions soon after saddled the company with heavy debt and diminished revenue. In response, McClatchy offered voluntary buyouts to 450 employees in 2019. Following Chatham's acquisition, workers organized unions at about a dozen of McClatchy's newspapers (Abernathy 2020b: 31–32; Abernathy and Franklin 2022: 22–24; Robertson and Tracy 2020; Smith 2019; Tracy 2020a, 2020b).

GROWING INDUSTRY CONCENTRATION IN A FINANCIALIZED INDUSTRY

More than half of all dailies and a quarter of all newspapers are owned by the ten largest chains. Four of those chains—Gannett, MediaNews Group, Lee Enterprises, and CNHI—are either owned by or indebted to private investment firms. The other six are large private regional chains that each own between 46 and 148 papers (Abernathy 2023: 21–23).

Mergers and acquisitions carried out by three of the top five largest chains and McClatchy have led to further consolidation of the industry. For example, Gannett, Alden, and Lee currently own over 700 papers, about a third of all dailies in the country, with many in the largest markets. Postmergers, these firms have been active in making additional transactions, including shedding unprofitable properties. For example, between 2022 and 2023, Gannett, Alden, and Lee have divested themselves of over 100 newspapers. Still, only ten of the largest dailies in the United States remain independently owned. Some of these newspapers were purchased by billionaires, such as the *Washington Post* (Jeff Bezos); *Boston Globe* and *Worcester Telegram & Gazette* (John Henry); *Minneapolis Star-Tribune* (Glen Taylor); and *Los Angeles Times* (Patrick Soon-Shiong) (Abernathy 2023: 21–22; Abernathy and Franklin 2022: 7, 24; Dirks, Van Essen & April, press releases, various years; Jacob 2021; Kennedy 2018).

What Else Hath Investment Firms Wrought?

Ewens, Gupta, and Howell (2022) found that the share of newspapers owned by private equity firms increased from about 5% in 2002 to around 23% in 2019. A major finding of their study was that reporting on local governance issues declined in favor of more centrally produced and syndicated national news stories, owing to cost savings. Overall, the number of articles published fell by 16.7%. The researchers also found that the number of local reporters declined by 7.3% and editors by 8.9%. Private equity ownership was also associated with print circulation declines but large increases in digital circulation and higher survival rates for local papers. Following private equity buyouts, however, the authors found less citizen participation in local democracy and a lower awareness of local politicians. The researchers summarize their findings this way:

Overall, the operational changes we see appear to have ambiguous social welfare consequences. The bright side is that private equity ownership leads to higher newspaper survival rates and more digital content, consistent with investing to help turn around and modernize a struggling industry. A downside is that civic engagement appears to decline because readers of newspapers and the outlets that rely on their reporting have less information about local government. (Ewens, Gupta, and Howell 2022: 6)

COVID-19 ACCELERATED NEWSPAPER INDUSTRY CHALLENGES

The COVID-19 pandemic that began in March 2020 worsened industry and employment conditions. Among the few remaining publicly traded newspaper companies that Pew tracks—major chains that own over 300 dailies—year-over-year advertising revenue fell by a median of 42%. In addition, the ten largest newspapers saw print circulation fall by an average of 20% during the pandemic. Even digital ad revenue declined by a median of 32%. In contrast, the three major cable news networks' ad revenue held steady (Barthel, Matsa, and Worden 2020; Schultz 2021).

The pandemic also accelerated the move from print to digital delivery, such that 42 of the largest 100 newspapers now deliver print editions six or fewer times per week, while 11 print editions only one or two times weekly and deliver e-editions the rest of the time. But the trade-off is uneven. Media researcher Iris Chyi examined the impact of the pandemic on print and digital circulation for 20 metro dailies. She found that digital subscriptions grew 64% between 2019 and the third quarter of 2020, but the rapid decline in print circulation (–21%) and the wide gulf between the more expensive print subscriptions and cheaper digital ones contributed to an overall decline in subscription revenue. The price gap means that it takes almost six new digital subscribers to compensate for the loss of one print subscriber (Chyi 2021: 1–6).

Similar to her earlier study, Chyi found that consumers still prefer print to digital news: "This pandemic has made it clear that when digital transformation finally happens, the net result is unfortunately 'exchanging analog dollars for digital dimes,'" such that the industry must continue to find a viable business model (quoted in Abernathy and Franklin 2022: 7).

Between the onset of the pandemic and August 2021, at least 6,154 news workers, both editorial and noneditorial, were laid off, about 100 news outlets closed (with 14 subsequently reopening to some extent), and another 42 were absorbed in mergers and acquisitions. The NewsGuild reported that 33,000 news employees had been impacted by layoffs, furloughs, or pay cuts when the pandemic hit. The federal Paycheck Protection Program (PPP), which provided loans to small businesses to cover payroll expenses, assisted 2,800 newspaper companies that employed 40,000 workers between March and August 2020. PPP loans enabled many newspapers to stay open. But newspapers representing over 80% of US circulation were ineligible for PPP loans because many were owned by large chains excluded from the loan program (Hagey, Trachtenberg, and Wise 2020; Miller 2021; The NewsGuild 5/4/20).

PPP loans and economic recovery minimized job losses, however. According to Pew, only 11% of larger newspapers experienced layoffs in 2021, compared with 33% in 2020 and 24% in 2019. Unlike in previous years, major newspapers did not undertake multiple rounds of layoffs in 2021 (Shearer and Tomasik 2022).

The employment situation in the larger media industry has not recovered since the receding of the pandemic. In mid-June 2023, the outplacement firm Challenger, Gray & Christmas reported that there were 17,436 media job cuts, the highest year-to-date level of loss on record. Print, broadcast, and digital outlets collectively announced 1,972 job cuts by mid-June 2023, surpassing the 1,808 jobs lost for all of 2022 (Fischer 2023b).

The economic and other challenges that have roiled the newspaper industry and created precarious employment conditions over the past two decades have led to an upsurge in union organizing, mainly by newsroom workers.

Union Organizing and Rebirth of The NewsGuild

In late 2015, the CWA granted The NewsGuild $500,000 to organize digital media newsrooms. At the time, the Guild represented about 2,000 digital journalists, including those at major newspapers, although the vast majority of its members worked at traditional print newspapers (Richardson 2015b; Sterne 2015).

Until that time, the Guild had done little organizing in newspapers because it focused on protecting the integrity of existing contracts and limiting job cuts. Between 2015 and 2017, however, it made gains in organizing in both digital and print news, averaging about 342 new members a year. It made even more significant advances thereafter, averaging over 1,500 new members a year between 2018 and 2021, when it broke its annual organizing record, with 1,542 new journalists at 26 media outlets. Moreover, over 8,500 of the Guild's 26,000 members had joined the union after 2015, although not all of these new members worked in the news industry (Figure 3) (Fu 2021e; The NewsGuild 2021; The NewsGuild 5/13/22).

A number of factors have spurred newspaper journalists to unionize. Among them are the industry's financial challenges and the takeover of newspaper chains by investment companies, low pay and years without raises, and employment and compensation cuts. The social isolation of the pandemic and the desire to preserve journalism's vital role in American democracy in the face of disinvestment in news-gathering were additional motivations. Organizing victories begat more organizing, as NewsGuild president Jon Schleuss noted: "People see other campaigns winning unionization votes and good contracts. ... That has helped this spread like a wildfire, with people asking, 'Would a union be possible here?'" (Greenhouse 2019, 2022; Knolle 2018; The NewsGuild 1/28/19). This question was most appropriate for journalists at some large newspapers with long histories of anti-unionism.

The Fall of Anti-Union Citadels in Los Angeles and Chicago

In October 2017, journalists at the *Los Angeles Times* announced their intention to unionize. They had a majority of authorization cards signed and expected additional

Figure 3
Workers Unionizing with The NewsGuild–CWA

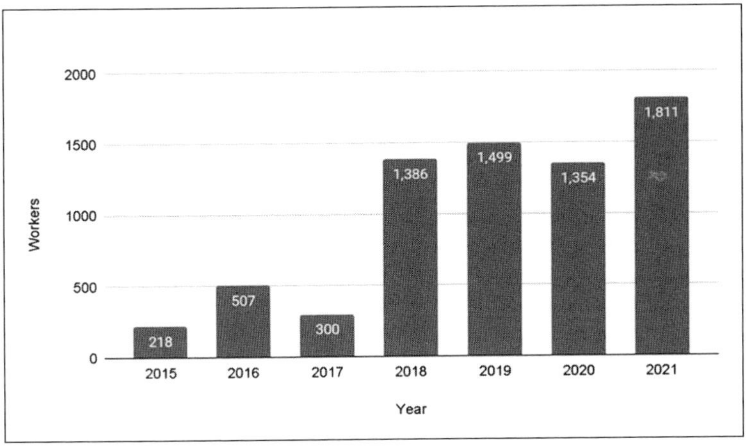

Year	Workers
2015	218
2016	507
2017	300
2018	1,386
2019	1,499
2020	1,354
2021	1,811

The NewsGuild.

employees to sign cards. *Times* journalists declared a number of key bargaining objectives, such as annual pay increases and guaranteed minimum salaries, equal pay for all employees, improved vacation time, competitive parental leave, fair notice of layoffs, guaranteed severance packages, and recall rights. The latter three demands were critical in the context of unstable industry conditions (L.A. Times Guild, "Letter to the Newsroom," 2017).

The Los Angeles Times's owner, media company Tronc, was headquartered in Chicago and had recently changed its name from Tribune Publishing to reflect its new focus as a digital-first company.[4] Management had angered newsroom employees with multiple rounds of cost cutting and layoffs, an abrupt decision to eliminate accrued vacation days, termination of newsroom leaders and installation of new executives who clashed with employees, and alleged mismanagement that had begun after Tribune purchased the paper in 2000 from longtime owners, the Chandler family. The Times also struggled during the stormy five-year reign of real estate magnate Sam Zell, whose highly leveraged buyout of Tribune in 2007 saddled the company with heavy debt and hurt the paper's journalistic reputation. The multiple rounds of layoffs over the years cut newsroom employment from a peak of 1,200 to 500 in 2017 and further handicapped the Los Angeles Times (Ember 2017; Mohajer 2017).

Tronc deployed an interim executive director from Chicago to Los Angeles to counter the union drive, sent a series of e-mails, posted webpages and videos to workers, and held captive-audience meetings opposing the union. The Los Angeles Guild, in turn, mounted a counter-offensive in which journalists used their investigative skills to expose mismanagement and personal misconduct as well as executive excesses at the *Times* and at Tronc. Journalists also employed a coordinated and effective online strategy to share their pro-union views, trumpet executives' misdeeds, and connect workers with their local communities. Kristina Bui, a *Times* copy editor and local Guild leader, remarked, "Social media allowed us to reach our co-workers, our subscribers and our bosses" (The NewsGuild, 1/28/19). Social media as an organizing tool was initially used extensively and effectively by editorial workers at digital-only media outlets and then adopted by editorial employees at newspapers (Jaffe 2019).

The *Los Angeles Times* certification vote, held in early January 2018, was 248 to 44, or 5 to 1, in favor of the union. For the first time since the *Times*'s initial edition was printed in 1881 (136 years before), newsroom employees at the *Los Angeles Times* had union representation. *Times* reporter Bettina Boxall told HuffPost, "The overwhelming majority voted to finally give this newsroom a voice. ... Having a union won't stop layoffs, but we have a collective voice and the days of the newsroom passively standing by while corporate management did whatever they wanted are over" (quoted in Jamieson, Brenoff, Ferner, and Strachan 2018). The West Coast "citadel of the open shop" had finally been breached.

About a year later, after the union's victory at the *Los Angeles Times*, The NewsGuild turned its attention to organizing another Tronc property—the 170-year-old *Chicago Tribune*, once called the "World's Greatest Newspaper"—and another anti-union fortress. The decision to organize the *Tribune*'s newsroom came in the wake of the company's sale of the *Los Angeles Times* to medical entrepreneur Patrick Soon-Shiong for $500 million, the resignation of Tronc's chairman for alleged sexual harassment, financial problems, and a series of job cuts (Eidelson 2018). In a letter to newsroom staff, the 46-member organizing committee that included four Pulitzer Prize winners cited a number of grievances: irregular raises and pay inequities, rising healthcare costs, inadequate parental leave, lack of professional development, high turnover, lack of diversity, job insecurity, and "a series of corporate owners [who have] jeopardized our ability to do great work" (Eidelson 2018; Feder 2018).

Organizing efforts at the *Chicago Tribune* and a few sister publications, which combined to form a 300-person bargaining unit, were coordinated by the Chicago News Guild, the union that represents editorial employees at the *Chicago Sun-Times* and the *Chicago Reader*. The *Tribune* drive also followed a few successful union victories at other Chicago media outlets. With the sale of the *Los Angeles Times*, the *Baltimore Sun* (unionized since 1934) was the only major unionized newsroom owned by Tronc (Bologna 2018; Charles and Wilusz 2018; Folkenflick 2018a).

Chicago Tribune workers faced a politically conservative corporate owner with a long history of anti-unionism. Former *Chicago Tribune* managing editor James Warren encapsulated the newspaper's ideological leanings under Robert R. McCormick, who controlled the paper between 1910 until his death in 1955:

> McCormick, a notorious ideological foe of President Franklin Roosevelt, hated unions. And while unions did represent production employees at his flagship *Chicago Tribune*, they never got footing among journalists since the company melded a distinct and soothing paternalism with the pragmatism of

always matching or exceeding whatever unions bargained for reporters and editors and its rival papers." (quoted in Folkenflick 2018a; Wikipedia, "Robert R. McCormick")

During the 1980s, Tribune Publishing's anti-union animus was evident during strikes by production workers at the *Chicago Tribune* and the *New York Daily News*. Following the strike in New York, Tribune sold the *Daily News*. Nevertheless, hostility toward unions continued after these disputes, however (Folkenflick 2018a).

By April 2018, the Chicago Guild had signed up 85% of the newsroom employees. Management, however, refused voluntary recognition, setting up a National Labor Relations Board (NLRB) election. Within two weeks, though, Tronc reversed course and agreed to recognize the union for the first time since the paper's founding in 1847. The victory at the *Chicago Tribune* inspired journalists at other major Tronc properties in Hartford, Orlando, and South Florida, and smaller ones in the Mid-Atlantic region, to start organizing drives of their own that also resulted in successful elections (Bologna 2018; Bologna and Diaz 2018; Folkenflick 2018b).

In the fall of 2018, after initially refusing to voluntarily recognize the Tidewater Media Guild at two smaller Virginia newspapers—the *Virginian-Pilot* in Norfolk and the *Daily Press* in Newport, where 83% of eligible employees backed the union—Tribune Publishing, which switched back from the name Tronc in June 2018, reversed course again and recognized the unions (Schneider 2018; Statt 2018).

In December 2018, Tribune also voluntarily recognized editorial employees at the *Capital Gazette* and the *Carroll County Times*, both part of its Sun Media Group. Editorial employees at the *Hartford Courant* and a sister publication also won recognition in February 2019. And newsroom employees at the *Orlando Sentinel* won an NLRB election in May 2020 by a 36–8 vote. Six months later, Alden purchased Tribune Publishing (The NewsGuild 2021).

Newsroom Organizing at Other Major Chains

In addition to organizing a number of Tribune properties, the Guild also embarked on numerous other drives at small publishers and major newspaper chains, especially where mergers and acquisitions were involved. For example, between 2017 and 2022, roughly 40% of new units formed at newspapers that had changed ownership in the year before or soon after, according to a University North Carolina study (Mahone 2022: 2). Guild units won voluntary recognition at over 40 newspapers and won more than 60 NLRB elections.[5]

The organizing wave of newsrooms at papers owned by the big chains continued in the years ahead, with unions forming at dozens of newspapers owned by McClatchy, Alden, GateHouse, and Gannett between 2018 and 2022. As significant was that many of these organizing drives occurred in right-to-work states, including a number in the South.

For example, five Guild units at McClatchy were voluntarily recognized in 2020 and 2021, and four won NLRB elections between 2019 and 2022. The *Miami Herald* was the largest unit, with 99 employees; the *Kansas City Star* was the second largest, with 39 employees.

At Alden's Southern California News Group (SCNG), the Guild won a large, consolidated unit of 143 employees at 11 newspapers in 2021 by a vote of 64 to 19. Organizing at the SCNG came in response to layoffs, high turnover and staffing shortages, stagnant wages and diminished benefits, and Alden's acquisition of Tribune Publishing (Fu 2021b).

There were only a few organizing drives at Gannett until it was acquired by GateHouse in 2019. Most of the newspapers were small, but the Guild won the largest unanimous vote in its history at the *Palm Beach Post* and *Palm Beach Daily News*, 55 to 0. The Guild's largest new unit at Gannett was the *Arizona Republic*, with over 100 employees, in 2019 (Bloomberg Law, "Labor Plus," various dates; Krupat 2021: 55).

The NewsGuild won all six NLRB elections at Lee Enterprises between 2018 and 2022, including the *Omaha World-Herald*, Warren Buffett's former hometown newspaper and the largest Lee unit organized, with over 90 employees. In addition, in the fall of 2020, the Guild won an election at the *Dallas Morning News*, owned by the DallasNews Corporation. This was the first and largest (128 employees) of the newsrooms organized in Texas (Bloomberg Law, "Daily Labor Report," "Labor Plus," various dates; The NewsGuild 2021; The NewsGuild, 10/16/20).

Table 1 shows the ten largest newsrooms organized by the Guild since 2018, which collectively yielded over 1,500 newly represented employees.

Organizing Summary and Implications

The NewsGuild's organizing successes in the newspaper industry is notable for a few reasons. First, according to a University of North Carolina report,

> This unionization momentum has happened against the backdrop in the decline of local news, increasing consolidation of local news media, and the acquisition of local newspapers by investment firms [since 2019)]. ... [T]hree mergers and acquisitions have placed approximately 850 local newspapers in the hands of investment companies that mainly focus on maximizing profits at the expense of supporting journalism's civic mission. (Mahone 2022: 1)

Second, the Guild has added new members at newspapers of all sizes, including those owned by small publishers and the largest chains. Third, many newly organized units have been formed in parts of the United States with little history of unionization and in states with right-to-work laws. One study found that media unions have had more success organizing in right-to-work states (100%) than they have in union-friendly states (85%) between 2017 and 2022 (Mahone 2022: 9).

Table 1
The Ten Largest Newsrooms Organized by The NewsGuild Between 2018 and 2021

Newspaper/group	Year	Size of collective bargaining unit	Ownership at time of certification
Los Angeles Times	2018	389	Tronc
Chicago Tribune	2018	280	Tronc
Southern California News Group	2021	143	DFM/Alden
Dallas Morning News	2020	128	DallasNews Corporation
Arizona Republic	2019	101	Gannett
Daily Press (Newport News, Virginia; Virginian-Pilot and two others)	2018	100	Tribune Publishing
Miami Herald and El Nuevo Herald	2019	99	McClatchy
Omaha World-Herald	2018	91	BHM
North Jersey Media Group (Bergen Record and others)	2021	83	Gannett
Daily Hampshire Gazette and Valley Advocate	2018	80	Newspapers of New England

Fourth, membership gains occurred during a severe pandemic and a related short but sharp recession. Finally, aside from very recent union membership gains overall nationally, both union membership and union density have been trending down for over four decades (UnionStats).

The Guild has been able to overcome resource limitations and geographical disadvantages by using both traditional and nontraditional organizing techniques, especially the use of digital technologies. Asked by an interviewer about helpful organizing techniques, President Jon Schleuss remarked,

> Social and digital media have provided great opportunities, especially during the pandemic. We've successfully organized places pretty much start-to-finish online. ... Organizing is about the one-to-one connection. Or, if we can't do it in person, we have to do it another way. That involves a lot of Zoom meetings, encrypted chat, where workers are sharing information with each other; and one-on-one phone calls to check in (quoted in Krupat 2021: 55).

COLLECTIVE BARGAINING STRUCTURES: TRADITIONAL AND EXPERIMENTAL

Historically, bargaining structures in the newspaper industry have been decentralized, with separate contracts for newsroom workers and multiple production and distribution units. In some cases, there could be a dozen contracts at a single newspaper. In recent years, however, there have been some notable examples of more centralized bargaining units, but these remain the exception to the historical norm of decentralized bargaining.

For example, in August 2016, NewsGuild members ratified a three-year national agreement with Alden's DFM, which included the first pay raise in nearly a decade. The contract that expired on July 31, 2019, covered 870 workers at 12 newspapers. According to Guild leaders, "this nationally coordinated bargaining framework represents a fundamental advance for members at all locations" (Lunger 2017). This unprecedented agreement followed protests and petitions against Alden and DFM executives under the banner of #NewsMatters, a NewsGuild project financed by the CWA and designed to combat newsroom staff reductions and rampant cost cutting (Digital First Media Workers 2016; Richardson 2016). Despite the Guild's coordinated campaign to counter Alden's business and labor practices, the agreement has not yet been renewed.

A similar "global settlement" between GateHouse and The NewsGuild was ratified in February 2018. This single, centralized labor agreement covered 16 newspapers, seven local Guild units, and 730 employees. NewsGuild's then-president Bernie Lunzer touted the agreement: "By negotiating a single agreement for 16 newspapers, we have significantly enhanced workers' power now and for the future. ... Rather than negotiating separately in small groups, our members are facing a common adversary together. This agreement provides a great platform for future negotiations" (Lunzer 2017).

The pact provided for a second round of bargaining to address other issues with a novel arrangement: the locals were divided into three separate categories—long-term GateHouse units, recently acquired units, and newly organized units. The NewsGuild agreed to refrain from any coordinated national campaign against GateHouse until on or after June 30, 2018 (Lunzer). This agreement has not yet been renewed.

The most recent centralized bargaining unit was formed in June 2021, when a new union, the SCNG Guild, was created to represent 140 journalists employed by the Southern California News Group, which includes 11 Alden-owned newspapers. This unit has yet to win a first contract (Fu 2021e; The NewsGuild, 2/24/21).

BARGAINING FIRST CONTRACTS: FAILURES AND SUCCESSES

As of July 2023, there were seven first contacts signed at McClatchy, six at Lee Enterprises, two at GateHouse/Gannett, and none at Alden. The former Tronc/Tribune Publishing *Los Angeles Times* is the largest newsroom to have won a first contract.

As of November 2023, 34 new Guild units had yet to conclude their first contracts. Fifteen units, or 44% of the total, are in GateHouse's Gannett newsrooms—the most of any chain. Alden's Tribune Publishing was second, with eight (23%) of the total. Lee Enterprises (two) and McClatchy (one) together were responsible for under 9% of the total number of new units currently without first contracts.[6]

Getting first contracts is neither easy nor quick. A Poynter study of media organizing drives between January 2012 and June 2021 found that it took the 47 successful bargaining units on average almost 19 months to secure first contracts. Thirteen units won contracts within a year, while another 13 took two years. The fastest time to a first contract—four months—occurred at the Lee Enterprises–owned *Billings Gazette* in Montana in 2020 (Fu 2021b). The majority of new Guild contracts have been ratified within two years of organizing, in line with a recent Bloomberg Law analysis of 391 first contracts since 2005 (Combs 2022).[7]

The largest and most significant first contract was signed by the *Los Angeles Times* in 2019. The L.A. Times Guild trumpeted the landmark settlement in a message to its members: "After 15 months at the bargaining table, the union representing nearly 500 journalists at the *Los Angeles Times* tentatively agreed to the first newsroom contract since the newspaper began publishing in 1881" (L.A. Times Guild 2019). A *Los Angeles Times* article called the three-year contract "a milestone for a newspaper that for generations was known as a bastion of anti-unionism" (James 2019).

The first contract contained important gains for workers. For example, they received average raises over $11,000, with about 200 people getting raises of at least $10,000; a 5% ratification bonus, followed by across-the-board raises of 2.5% in each of the next two years; pay minimums for all newsroom positions and step raises by industry experience, a traditional Guild pay policy; job protections such as just-cause discipline, seniority-based layoffs, limits on outsourcing and subcontracting, and guaranteed severance packages; protections against harassment and retaliation; and the right of journalists to pursue personal book projects and retain intellectual property rights to them (L.A. Times Guild 2019: 1). Union members overwhelmingly ratified the contract, 388 to 3 (McAlevey and Lawlor 2021: 81).

The parties began negotiating a second contract in September 2022 but had not yet reached a settlement when, in early June 2023, *Times* executives announced 74 layoffs as part of a restructuring prompted by "the economic climate and the unique challenges." The message coincided with the fifth anniversary of Patrick Soon-Shiong's purchase of the paper and a few weeks after the *Times* celebrated earning two Pulitzer Prizes, but it also occurred in the middle of a large wave of media layoffs (Fu 2023b; James 2023; L.A. Times Guild 2023).

Across the bargaining landscape for first contracts, Guild units won improvements in wages, job security protections, severance pay, healthcare, paid leave, grievance arbitration, and just-cause discipline. The new collective bargaining agreements also provide for minimum salaries, salary increases, pay equity adjustments, and a weekly pay differential for language certification. The *Los Angeles Times* contract included abortion and gender-affirming care and paid time off for new holidays and, for the first time, employees are now eligible for paid parental leave.

Another large first contract was ratified in mid-June 2023, when journalists at the *Dallas Morning News* voted 122 to 0 (99% turnout) on the three-year contract after 900 days of bargaining and a long mediation session. The collective bargaining agreement covers over 130 employees at both the *Dallas Morning News* and *Al Dia* who, in October 2021, voted by over a 75% margin to become the first major newspaper in Texas to unionize in the modern era (The NewsGuild, 6/15/23).

There were also notable first contracts in mid-sized bargaining units, including McClatchy's *Kansas City Star*, located in Missouri, a state that passed a right-to-work law in 2017. About 40 journalists announced an organizing drive at the *Star* in May 2021 and were voluntarily recognized by management 23 days later. But it wasn't until early January 2023, after six months of bargaining, that members of the Kansas City News Guild, a unit of the United Media Guild, located in St. Louis, unanimously ratified their first labor contract, 51 to 0. The three-year deal provides across-the-board raises and a ratification bonus, pay raises and new benefits for part-time employees, and important workplace protections (Kansas City News Guild 2023; The NewsGuild, 5/10/21, 6/2/21).

The Guild also had success in Nebraska, another right-to-work state. In 2018, about 90 newsroom employees at Warren Buffet's *Omaha World-Herald* organized and, two years later, in May 2020, unanimously ratified their first contract. The union won small pay raises, a new pay scale with higher starting minimums and step increments, extended severance pay for more senior employees, job security protections, just-cause discipline, a grievance arbitration procedure, and a temporary freeze on employee-paid healthcare costs (The NewsGuild, 5/12/20).

The Guild also signed first contracts in non-right-to-work states. For example, after forming a union in 2018, about 80 Pioneer Valley NewsGuild members working at the *Daily Hampshire Gazette* and *Valley Advocate* in Massachusetts unanimously ratified a two-year deal in 2021, after engaging in a work-to-rule campaign and picketing in front of the newspaper's offices. The contract provided pay raises of 3% and 2% in 2022 and 2023, respectively, top minimum weekly pay, a paid holiday for Martin Luther King Day, and additional vacation time for longer-tenured employees. It also contained employment protections, such as just-cause dismissal, protections against outsourcing, and severance guarantees that included three months of fully paid health insurance. The collective bargaining agreement was the first in the *Gazette*'s 235 history (The NewsGuild, 12/29/21; The NewsGuild 2023c).

The Guild also negotiated first contracts at smaller newspapers in right-to-work states, such as Idaho, Montana, South Carolina, and Virginia. In September 2020, following organizing victories at McClatchy's *Miami Herald*, *Bradenton Herald*, and *Idaho Statesman*, news workers at two small McClatchy papers in South Carolina—the *Island Packet* (Hilton Head) and *Beaufort Gazette*—won voluntary recognition. The local union, the Packet/Gazette Guild, became a unit in the large Washington–Baltimore Guild local.

Eighteen months later, in March 2022, journalists in Hilton Head and Beaufort ratified their first collective bargaining agreement, covering about 30 workers. The three-year agreement established an annual salary minimum of $45,000, which raised pay for most unit members, and guaranteed raises of 2% over the next two contract anniversaries. Not much else was reported, but union members exclaimed, "We're so proud to have McClatchy's first union contract in the Southeast" (The NewsGuild, 9/11/20, 3/18/22, 4/4/22, 4/12/22).

Taken together, these and other new contracts generally accomplish The NewsGuild's objectives: "Forming a union gives workers the opportunity to negotiate contracts with raises, parental leave, greater diversity, more job security, 'just cause' protection, and severance pay. It gives workers a voice at work" (The NewsGuild, "Organize With Us").

As these new bargaining relations mature, they can become more sophisticated and add better terms and conditions. But this is not guaranteed in an industry struggling to find a viable business model. Even for union journalists employed at the more stable large national newspapers—the *New York Times*, *Wall Street Journal*, and *Washington Post*—concessions continued in certain areas and contractual improvements in others, but they were not easy to achieve.

RECENT CONTRACT SETTLEMENTS AT THREE NATIONAL NEWSPAPERS

Dow Jones/*Wall Street Journal* and the Independent Association of Publishers' Employees

The local union representing newsroom employees at Dow Jones & Company's *Wall Street Journal* is the Independent Association of Publishers' Employees (IAPE), a once-independent union that became part of The Newspaper Guild in 1996. The IAPE has about 1,300 members in multiple locations in the United States and Canada and has been representing Dow Jones employees for over 80 years (Independent Association of Publishers' Employees, no date).

The IAPE and Dow Jones signed a three-year contract renewal retroactive to July 1, 2019. The agreement provided minimum salary increases of about 6.5% over three years, a ratification bonus of $700 for each full-time IAPE-represented employee (prorated for part-time employees), and a small, lump-sum bonus tied to Dow Jones's performance and the funding level of management's bonus pool. Other pay adjustments included increases in the salary scales for reporting and information technology jobs, higher minimum scales for other select job titles, and a general increase in minimum salary scales in each year of the contract.

The collective bargaining agreement extended the 2019 health insurance plan through 2020 with a freeze of health insurance premiums, deductibles, and co-payments. Premium increases and plan design changes were capped in 2021 and 2022. The union also limited the company's right to employ temporary employees for more than one year and obtained enhanced job security rights in certain situations and greater notice requirements for work-schedule changes (Dow Jones 2019).

In August 2022, the parties signed a one-year deal that called for a 4% wage increase (a minimum increase of $40/week), a 1% lump-sum payment, and an additional 0.5% wage increase, effective January 1, 2023. The pact also extended the company's 2022 health insurance plan through 2023; froze current health insurance premium rates, deductibles, co-payments, and other plan terms; and increased the reimbursement for physical fitness expenses for all IAPE-represented employees.

The parties also resolved a couple of pandemic-related issues, such as the return-to-office policy, with the company agreeing to provide the union 45 days' advance notice of any intention to increase in-office working days and 30 days' notice of changes to the existing COVID vaccination policy. The contract also included gender-neutral language and added Juneteenth and Truth and Reconciliation Day holidays for employees in the United States and Canada, respectively (Dow Jones 2022; Roush 2022). Contract negotiations that began in June 2023 have not yet resulted in a renewed contract.

Washington Post and the Washington Post Newspaper Guild

The Washington Post Newspaper Guild has represented newsroom employees since 1934 and currently represents over 1,000 workers. The *Post* unit is one of 27 in the Washington–Baltimore News Guild. It signed its first collective bargaining agreement with the *Washington Post* in 1938 (Washington Post Guild, "About the Guild").

In August 2013, the Graham family, owners of the *Washington Post* since 1933, sold the *Post* to Jeff Bezos, the billionaire founder of the e-commerce company Amazon. In November of that year, after strained negotiations, the union and management agreed to a one-year contract. At that time, the bargaining unit included 820 employees, down from 920 from 2011 and from 1,400 from about a decade earlier. The *Post* had reported negative profits for the previous seven years, so job security was a salient issue for the union. The Guild retained job security provisions "that define severance benefits, return-to-work or buyout guarantees and maintain seniority considerations during layoffs." Management, however, secured the right to exempt 25% of the workforce from seniority considerations for layoffs (Hobbs 2013).

The subsequent contract ran for two years and was signed after eight months of intense negotiations. Announced in June 2015, the collective bargaining agreement included a ratification bonus and a 4.5% pay raise over the life of the agreement, which the Guild trumpeted as "the largest such general pay increase in at least a decade." Management won a freeze of pension benefits and the implementation of a cash-balance retirement plan, but the union prevailed with the continuation of healthcare benefits for part-time workers, the addition of gender identity to the contract's nondiscrimination clause, and the deletion of language that prohibited remote workers from assisting with child or eldercare (Richardson 2015a).

After 14 months of negotiations, the parties reached a two-year renewal in June 2018 that union leadership believed to be adequate, given management's stiff resistance at the bargaining table. The union won improved paid parental leave for spouses and defeated management's attempt to impose a new discretionary pay system that could have excluded some employees from getting raises. The union was unable to fend off adverse terms in the areas of overtime, retirement benefits, job security, and severance. Despite local union leadership's displeasure with the contract, it recommended that the membership ratify it (Kanu and Diaz 2018; Washington–Baltimore News Guild, "Bulletin," 2018).

The 2018–2020 contract was followed by two short extensions—one for ten months that expired April 30, 2021, and a second one-year extension that expired on June 30, 2022. These continuations provided pay increases and evening/night-shift differentials. The most recent extension granted workers 15 sick leave days per year, enhanced vacation days, 20 weeks of paid parental leave, and 15 to 45 weeks of severance pay, depending on seniority (Bloomberg Law, "Labor Plus, Settlement Summaries," 2022).

The contract had not yet been extended or renewed, but management announced job cuts at the end of December 2022. In late January 2023, facing stalled subscriber growth, falling ad revenue, and the departure of key personnel, management announced additional cuts as part of its ongoing strategic shift to online readership that the union strongly opposed. In October 2023, the *Post* offered buyouts in order to cut an additional 240 jobs in the face of rapid expansion; lower-than-expected subscriptions, advertising revenue, and overall traffic; and an expected financial loss of $100 million for the year (Izadi and Ellison 2022, 2023; Mullin and Robertson 2023; Sommer and Izadi 2023).

By early December 2023, the voluntary buyouts had not reached the planned 240, so management announced the prospects for layoffs. The union responded with a one-day strike on December 7 to protest the expected layoffs and stalled contract negotiations that had been dragging on for 18 months. The walkout by 700 employees was the first at the *Post* since press operators struck the paper for 20 weeks in 1975. That strike had episodes of violence and led to the union's permanent ouster (Fu 2023d; Robertson 2023b).

Washington Post Guild chief steward and science reporter Sarah Kaplan announced at a press conference: "We deserve a contract with good pay that keeps up with inflation and is competitive with other workplaces. We deserve a contract that has job security protections and that respects seniority." Other outstanding issues include mental health benefits and remote work policies (Fu 2023d).

After 18 months of sometimes tense negotiations that included a one-day walkout and "digital" strike, the parties renewed the labor agreement, which included pay raises (Mullin 2023).

The *New York Times* and the NewsGuild of New York

The NewsGuild of New York (NGNY) was co-founded by the famous columnist Heywood Broun in 1934. Broun was also one of the key founders of the ANG in 1933. The New York union signed its first labor agreement with the *New York Times* in 1941. The local currently represents close to 3,000 media workers, including digital-only journalists, in the New York City area (Leab 1970; NewsGuild of New York; Wikipedia, "New York Times Guild").

In December 2017, the NGNY signed a four-year deal that provided a 2.5% signing bonus and 2% raises in 2018, 2019, and 2020. For the first time, employees secured guaranteed medical coverage for up to one year for any laid-off member. In addition, the company agreed to provide both short- and long-term disability benefits for medical leaves. Vacation benefits were enhanced, and *Times* employees who remained for 15 or more years would be eligible for five weeks of paid vacation. Bargaining unit members also won an additional paid holiday and personal day. The union added workers in the video and audio departments to the bargaining unit of 1,100. NGNY president Grant Glickson commented on the 2017 renewal: "The negotiating committee worked incredibly hard. … It was a tough fight. But I commend our committee and our membership for hanging in there and securing a contract during a time when union protections for media professionals across the nation are crucial for those working in this industry" (NewsGuild of New York 2017).

The contract negotiations that followed in 2021 were contentious and complicated by representation-related issues at two of the company's new digital units—Wirecutter, a product-review website, where workers formed a union in 2019 but had not yet signed a first contract, and a large group of software engineers, data analysts, and product managers who were part of a new 650-member unit organized in April 2021 and whose NLRB election result was still pending. By this time, the *Times* unit had grown to about 1,300 employees. In November 2021, about 100 people, including Wirecutter and tech workers, joined *Times* employees outside the paper's headquarters to protest anti-union tactics at the three units (Fu 2021d; Robertson 2021).

Contract negotiations faced another challenge when union members defied *Times*'s management's post-pandemic return-to-office plans in September 2022. The local union stated that it had obtained 1,280 signatures from union members from the *Times*, Wirecutter, and the tech unit pledging to stay home. The three units had a total of about 2,000 members. Their petition was part of a coordinated attempt by *Times* union members to achieve a contract renewal that included the filing of an unfair labor practice for management's alleged failure to negotiate a return-to-office policy (Bruell 2022a; Iafolla 2022).

Tensions between labor and management escalated at the end of 2022, when *Times* staffers engaged in a one-day strike in response to 20 months of stalled negotiations—the first walkout at the *New York Times* in over 40 years. By late March 2023, their frustration with management, and divisions within the union extended negotiations past the two-year mark. Workers took to the messaging app Slack to vent about the stalled negotiations. For the first time, *Times* publisher A.G. Sulzberger intervened, expressing his concerns in a note to the union about the lengthy negotiations and alleged that the union was refusing to negotiate in small groups "to lock eyes, shake hands and hash out a deal." He—along with some union members—advocated for the use of a mediator, which had helped during the stalled negotiations in 2012 (Bruell 2022a, 2023a; Jones 2022).

In April 2023, *New York Times* and *Washington Post* employees engaged in coordinated but separate collective actions to get their respective managements to agree to raise minimum pay and sign new contracts (The NewsGuild, 4/28/23). By the end of May, exhausted from years of negotiations and job actions, the NGNY and *New York Times* management agreed to a five-year contract (2021–2026) that the union called "groundbreaking," in part because of the $100 million newsroom investment (NewsGuild of New York 2023a).

The contract, which contained no union concessions, provides for a higher minimum salary of $65,000; immediate raises of at least 10.6% for all members, with 12.5% increases for the lowest earners; and annual pay increases based on an employee's actual pay rather than contract minima. Union members also received a one-time retroactive bonus of 7% of their base pay. Improved employee benefits include $50,000 in fertility coverage and paid sabbaticals of four weeks for every ten years worked at the *Times*. The agreement is the first in the unit's history to include language on hybrid work that permits management to require employees to be present in the office three days per week. It also bans the use of nondisclosure agreements in cases of workplace abuse or harassment. Additionally, the contract expands the newsroom into local markets across the country, with the new union jobs paid at "fair" minimum salaries (Izadi and Scribner 2023; NewsGuild of New York 2023a; Robertson 2023a).

JOURNALISTS' PAY AND GUILD MINIMUM SALARIES

The median annual wage for news analysts, reporters, and journalists was $48,370 (roughly $930 per week) in May 2021, according to the US Bureau of Labor Statistics' *Occupational Handbook* (2023). Newsroom workers are over twice as likely to hold a college degree and earn higher median annual earnings across education levels than the average US worker—$48,050 versus $39,296. But college-educated newsroom employees earn less than all other college-educated workers—$50,696 versus $59,448, according to Pew (Grieco 2018b).

NewsGuild's top minimum salaries from more than 100 of its collective bargaining agreements in the United States and Canada show a wide range of pay, driven mainly by the size and resources of the newspaper, history, and other factors. As of January 1, 2023, the five highest minimum weekly salaries (rounded up) at daily newspapers are at the *Los Angeles Times* ($2,236), *New York Times* ($2,042), *Wall Street Journal* ($1,602), *Minneapolis Star-Tribune* ($1,498), and *Boston Globe* ($1,469).

By contrast, the five lowest weekly salaries (rounded up) are significantly lower than the median weekly pay for journalists of $930 reported by the US Bureau of Labor Statistics: *Pottstown Mercury* ($613), *Wilkes-Barre Citizens' Voice* ($647), *Hazelton Standard-Speaker* ($666), *Daily Hampshire Gazette* ($694), and *Monterey Herald* ($717). Overall, the average top minimum weekly pay across all 112 collective bargaining agreements in the United States and Canada is $1,208, or about $62,800 annually (The NewsGuild 2023c).

NEWSROOM DIVERSITY AND PAY INEQUITIES: BARGAINING FOR A FAIRER WORKPLACE

In 1978, the American Society of News Editors (ASNE) conducted its first survey on staffing and minority representation in newsrooms. At that time, 43,000 people worked in newsrooms, with 1,700 (3.95%) of them minorities. ASNE's 40th survey, in 2018, was its last because of very low response rates. The sample does not permit generalization, but people of color represented 22.6% of newsrooms, compared with 16.5% in 2017. Among daily newspapers, 22.2% of employees identified as racial minorities versus 16.3% in 2017. In addition, the final survey found that women composed 41.2% of the daily newspaper workforce in 2018, up from 38.9% in 2017 (News Leaders Association 2018).

The most recent diversity survey, in 2019, was conducted by the News Leaders Association (NLA), ASNE's successor. Among daily newspapers, about 21.0% of salaried employees were racial minorities (compared with 21.6% in 2018). Overall, representation among women in newsrooms held steady at 41.8%, similar to the 2018 survey (News Leaders Association 2019).

While there have been some improvements in diversifying newsrooms and reducing pay inequities, The NewsGuild and its locals acknowledge that more progress needs to be made at the bargaining table.

Closing Gender- and Race-Based Pay Gaps in Newsrooms

In early August 2017, NewsGuild representatives convened in Pittsburgh to address pay disparities in newspapers across the country. Some publishers, without admitting structural pay inequities, had made individual salary adjustments, but according to the Guild, gender- and race-based pay inequities remained widespread. The NewsGuild's then-president Bernie Lunzer stated that "pay equity is a fundamental human rights issue" (The NewsGuild, 8/17/17). Current Guild president Jon Schleuss reaffirmed the union's priority of pay equity, noting that it has become "a huge issue" with the thousands of Guild-represented media workers in about 180 news outlets. He said, "We see it in a lot of organizing conversations that we have with people who are joining our union" (Chick 2020).

The IAPE unit at the *Wall Street Journal* made this concern salient in 2016, when its pay study showed that, on average, women earned 86.8% of men's earnings, up from 76% in 1991, but still not close enough to parity. Dow Jones, the *Journal*'s parent, granted equity adjustments to 31 of 1,300 union employees, but large disparities remained. The IAPE commissioned a compensation study that revealed an "alarming" gender pay gap, notably for women in their 30s. A follow-up study in 2019 found a similar disparity: median salaries for all full-time, unionized male employees were about 15% higher than those of unionized female employees. In March 2023, the IAPE released a fourth pay study that discovered that the overall gender pay gap had increased over the past four years (Independent Association of Publishers; Employees 2023; The NewsGuild, 8/17/17).

Guild units at the *Minneapolis Star-Tribune, New York Times, Philadelphia Daily News, Philadelphia Inquirer, San Francisco Chronicle,* and *Washington Post,* as well as Philly.com, uncovered similar gender- and race-based pay inequities in their respective studies (The NewsGuild, 8/17/17; Waggoner 2019).

Since 2017, The NewsGuild and a number of its locals have employed a variety of tactics to reduce pay inequities and increase workplace diversity, including pay studies, member mobilization, legal actions, and collective bargaining. For example, in late 2020, a year after attaining their first contract, journalists at the *Los Angeles Times* won a $3 million class-action settlement to remedy-pay discrimination claims (The NewsGuild, "Pay Equity"). The NewsGuild of Greater Philadelphia bargained to reduce pay inequities. In 2021, the *Philadelphia Inquirer* announced that it would allocate $300,000 to 70 employees whose pay was considered inequitable, although the company did not admit to racial or gender pay discrimination. Despite the re-establishment of a diversity committee and some pay adjustments in 2020, pay gaps remained, which led the Philadelphia union to file grievances against the *Inquirer* (The NewsGuild, "Pay Equity"; The NewsGuild, 3/21/22).

At the *Washington Post,* a follow-up pay study in 2022 concluded that women and people of color were still paid considerably less (13% to 16%) than their White male counterparts. Despite the *Post*'s success in hiring more people of color, it has failed to retain a number of them (The NewsGuild, "Pay Equity;" The NewsGuild, 4/13/22). A Nieman Reports article backed the Washington Guild's findings on retention:

> The refusal of many media companies to address the pay problem head-on has contributed to the current crisis in newsrooms: Inequity is one of the reasons many organizations have trouble retaining journalists of color, contributing to the lack of diversity in the top ranks, where decisions are made and coverage is shaped. (Chick 2020).

Equity and diversity issues are not limited to individual newspapers. In August 2020, for example, Gannett launched a company-wide initiative to make its workforce as diverse as the nation as a whole (Bomey 2020; Tameez 2020). The NewsGuild conducted an independent study of 14 unionized Gannett newsrooms that employed 450 people in 41 newsrooms, while the NewsGuild of New York carried out a similar investigation that involved six unions and over 200 journalists at nearly a dozen union newspapers in the Atlantic region. The larger study found that the median salaries (in fall 2020) of women and people of color were at least $5,000 less than those of their White and male colleagues. The New York local also undertook a smaller study of Gannett's six Atlantic region newsrooms and found similar pay and staffing disparities. Gannett strongly disputed the union's methodology and findings of both studies, however (Fu 2021a, 2022e).

A group of unions at Tribune papers called the Tribune Publishing Guild released a study of 12 newsrooms that employed 380 people in early March 2022. The data were collected in 2021, a few months before Alden acquired Tribune Publishing in 2021, and used to identify bargaining goals. In general, the findings revealed gender and racial pay gaps between $4,000 and $8,355. The Tribune Guilds called on Tribune and Alden to work with The NewsGuild to increase diversity and inclusion across the chain (Fu 2022c; The NewsGuild, "Pay Equity Study," 2022).

Overall, despite the surveys' methodological shortcomings, the results generally show that management and labor have more work to do to reduce existing pay inequities and further diversify newsrooms.

INCREASING LABOR MILITANCY

There have been only a few major strikes in the newspaper industry since notable ones in Detroit in 1995 and Seattle in 2000. Over the past few years, however, there have been over 20 strikes and strike threats conducted by all types of media unions, according to a Poynter analysis. Unionized journalists, after a few decades of labor quiescence and concession bargaining, have increased their solidarity and militancy, especially given protracted negotiations for first contracts. According to NewsGuild president Jon Schleuss, "These media companies have been refusing to bargain in good faith, and so they drag out the process as much as possible. All these journalists and other media workers are extremely frustrated by the time it takes to get a contract" (quoted in The NewsGuild, 12/29/21; Fu 2022f; Peck 2022).

In response to stalled contract negotiations, journalists have resorted to a variety of tactics, including short lunchtime and one-day walkouts, lobbying, e-mail campaigns, social media and messaging apps and, as a last resort, conducting traditional open-ended strikes. Because strikes are inherently risky, especially in a weakened industry, newspaper unions have tried to offset risk by encouraging reader and advertising boycotts, starting their own news outlets, employing short walkouts that prevent management from replacing workers, and by engaging in public protests and other performative actions (Eidelson 2022; Fu 2022f; Peck 2022; The NewsGuild, 4/4/22).

The following cases illustrate some of the different manifestations of the growing labor conflict in the newspaper industry in recent years.

Fort Worth Star-Telegram Strike

In 2020, McClatchy, owner of the *Fort Worth Star-Telegram*, voluntarily recognized the Fort Worth NewsGuild. After two years of bargaining, the 21-member bargaining unit (1,400 at its peak) filed unfair labor practices and voted to strike by a 91% margin. The strike was the first in a Texas newsroom, the first against McClatchy since Chatham Asset Management acquired it in 2020, and the third overall in the prior four months, which included roughly 100 journalists and other workers at the *Pittsburgh Post-Gazette* and about 300 journalists at Reuters who walked out for a day in August 2020 (Erickson 2022; Fu 2022b).

Pay was the main outstanding issue. The union demanded a minimum annual salary of $57,000, an amount it claimed a journalist needed to earn to afford a one-bedroom apartment in the area. Management offered a base wage of $45,000. Other contested issues included severance pay and sick-leave policies. Once the strike began, McClatchy cut off workers' health insurance and advertised for temporary journalists, while the union raised funds in a GoFundMe campaign.

After 24 days, the parties reached a settlement. McClatchy conceded a minimum salary of $52,000 for current employees and $50,000 for future hires, along with improvements in layoff procedures and bereavement leave. Kaley Johnson, a local Guild vice president, referred to the three-year deal as a starting point: "They definitely still did not move enough to create equitable conditions, but it's enough for a first contract." The pact was also significant because it was the first newsroom labor contract in Texas since the *San Antonio Light* shut down in 1993 (Bova 2023).

Pittsburgh Post-Gazette

In August 2020, journalists at the *Pittsburgh Post-Gazette*, the largest newspaper in western Pennsylvania, voted 88 to 31 to strike after Block Communications, Inc. (BCI), owners of the *Post-Gazette* since 1927, unilaterally imposed new working conditions on employees represented by the Newspaper Guild of Pittsburgh. Specifically, the Block family–owned newspaper cut wages and vacation time, outsourced work to non-Guild personnel, and forced workers into a more expensive health insurance plan with less coverage. For two years, the company had refused to pay workers' health insurance premiums, arguing that the *Post-Gazette* had lost almost $264 million since 2007. The union countered that BCI was a highly profitable media company that also owns the *Toledo Blade*, Internet, telephone, and cable TV properties. Unionized mailers, typographers, advertising workers, and distribution employees also voted to strike, but their parent unions—CWA and Teamsters—did not endorse their strikes (Deto 2019, 2020a, 2020b; Forstadt 2023b; Newspaper Guild of Pittsburgh, no date; Scire 2023).

The Pittsburgh Guild's three-year contract had expired in 2017. Counting the three-year interim, the Guild's 123 members had not had a pay raise in 14 years. Between the contract's expiration and the onset of the strike, the local had filed numerous grievances and unfair labor practices against the company and protested the multiple union-avoidance meetings run by the company's law firm, King and Ballow, known for its hardball bargaining and anti-union tactics. In November 2019, the Pittsburgh Guild "took the unprecedented act" of voting no confidence in the *Post-Gazette*'s executive editor, publisher John Robinson Block; and his twin, Allan Block, the chairman of BCI, "for their escalating unconscionable treatment of employees, union members and managers alike. An indefinite byline strike … began November 20 and continues." The union also engaged in leafletting for about a year prior to the strike (Deto 2019; Newspaper Guild of Pittsburgh, no date).

Despite the 74% supermajority strike vote, the Pittsburgh Guild did not strike when the paper declared an impasse and imposed new terms and conditions in July 2020. According to the union, since 2017, "The [*Post-Gazette*'s] union-busting attorneys bargained in bad faith for three and one-half years. On July 27, 2020, the [*Post-Gazette*] unlawfully declared an impasse to negotiations, despite the Guild's bargaining noting that negotiations were not even close to an impasse" (The NewsGuild, 10/18/22).

Negotiations stalled, and the unions filed additional unfair labor practices, but on October 6, 2022, about 80 union employees in four multi-union bargaining units representing design, production, distribution, and advertising workers went on strike in response to the company's termination of their healthcare coverage. These unions had been without a contract for almost six years and had not had a raise in 16. They contended that the health insurance provider had asked for an additional $19 per week in premium costs to maintain benefits and that BCI had refused to pay it (Fu 2022f; Sainato 2022). To support their strike, the unions asked readers to cancel their subscriptions and businesses to stop advertising in the *Post-Gazette*. The Pittsburgh Guild did not participate in the work stoppage, but journalists engaged in a byline strike in solidarity. The NLRB issued multiple complaints against BCI, and in 2021, a federal appeals court upheld an arbitrator's ruling against the company for refusing to pay the increase in healthcare premiums under the expired contract that had an "evergreen" clause (Fu 2022f).

A few weeks later, on October 18, 2022, in a close vote of 38 to 36, dozens of journalists struck the *Post-Gazette*. A few dozen journalists continued to work, and some resigned from the union. Overall, more than a hundred *Post*-Gazette workers walked out. The union established a digital strike publication, the *Pittsburgh Union Progress*, and appealed to *Post-Gazette* subscribers to switch to the union publication until the strike ended. Management said that it would "continue to serve the Pittsburgh community, our readers, and advertisers, despite any work stoppage. ... We welcome our employees back at any time." This was the first major newspaper strike in the digital age and the first in Pittsburgh since 1992, when about 600 Teamsters struck the *Pittsburgh Press* after working without a contract for five months (Doyle and Zenkevich 2022; Sainato 2022; Scire 2023).

Negotiators resumed bargaining in February 2023, but the Pittsburgh Guild reported little progress at the bargaining table. In late March, the company said it would appeal the NLRB's ruling to the full board. *Post-Gazette* attorneys denied that management negotiated in bad faith and argued that the conditions it implemented in 2020 resulted from a lawful impasse. They also contended that the judge ignored the company's rationale for its bargaining proposals, as it "transitioned to a digital newspaper in order to survive." Pittsburgh Guild president Zach Tanner responded to management's claims: "It's disappointing that they'd rather pour money into attorneys and fighting us than getting us all back to work" (quoted in Forstadt 2023a).

In October 2023, about 200 workers and their supporters, including newly elected CWA president Claude Cummings, Jr.; US senator John Fetterman; and Pittsburgh city councilor Bethany Hallam, congregated outside the *Post-Gazette*'s offices to recognize the strike's one-year mark and to protest the bargaining stalemate. The company continues to appeal NLRB and court decisions that favored the unions and printed a full-page advertisement to "share the truth behind the strike," notably over disputed health benefits (Deto 2023; Forstadt 2023b; Mayo and Yorgey 2023).

The strikers remain resolute, but their ranks have declined over the past year, as some have crossed the picket line and others have found alternative employment. No settlement had been reached heading into 2024, and NLRB and court appeals await resolutions (Deto 2023; Forstadt 2023b; Mayo and Yorgey 2023).

Chainwide Protests at Gannett

In addition to strikes, Guild locals have engaged in other forms of concerted action, such as short walkouts. Gannett has been the target of these protests in response to its alleged intransigence at the bargaining table. Since 2018, the Guild has organized 18 Gannett newsrooms and currently represents over 1,000 workers across 50 bargaining units at the company, but many of the new units still do not have first contracts.

In August 2022, hundreds of Gannett journalists, representing about half of Guild-represented newsrooms, engaged in a coordinated "lunch out" in response to e-mails from top management that threatened layoffs because of Gannett's poor second-quarter performance. The NewsGuild blamed poor management and the pandemic for the company's financial situation and railed against Gannett's decision to award its CFO a $1.2 million bonus and pay CEO Mike Reed $8 million annually, or 160 times the median Gannett worker's salary. Gannett also received $16.4 million from the federal PPP, which the Guild lobbied hard to get. Instead of negotiating contracts and investing in newsrooms, the Guild contended that management authorized a $100 million stock buyback designed to increase Gannett's deflated stock price. Moreover, it noted, "Gannett continues to spend millions on union-busting law firms and violating labor and wage and hour laws, paying poverty wages, slashing newsroom staff, and failing on diversity goals" (Olson 2023; The NewsGuild, 8/11/22).

Another mass one-day protest involving over 200 Gannett employees from 14 newspapers where Guild units had been involved in protracted contract negotiations took place in November 2022, after the company announced another poor quarterly report. The union also protested a recent layoff of 400 workers. Gannett responded to the union's claims:

> Our goal is to preserve journalism and serve our communities across the country. Despite the anticipated work stoppage in some of our markets, we will not cease delivering trusted news to our loyal readers. In addition, we continue to bargain in good faith to finalize contracts that provide equitable wages and benefits for our valued employees. (Fu 2022a)

Gannett workers continued their protests over the next few months because no progress was being made at the bargaining tables. On June 1, 2023, for example, The NewsGuild announced that two dozen Gannett newsrooms and hundreds of journalists would participate in coordinated one-day strikes during the company's upcoming annual shareholder meeting "to demand that Gannett get serious about reinvesting in local news, in the largest collective action that Gannett employees have taken to date" (The NewsGuild, 6/1/23). Since the 2019 merger, the company has cut its workforce in half and closed dozens of newspapers.

Whether these or any additional mass labor actions lead to additional organizing or first contracts remains to be seen, as Gannett continues its transition to a digital publisher with an unproven business model. The ongoing and bumpy transition from print to digital led to a different type of labor problem in Cleveland.

The Slow Demise of the Cleveland NewsGuild Local 1

Conflict at the Newhouse family's Advance Publication's *Cleveland Plain Dealer* was neither overt nor typical. Rather, it stands out for the slow demise of a relatively large urban bargaining unit that was also the ANG's first local union when it formed in 1933 (Leab 1970).

The union's decline unfolded over decades and could be traced to the Newhouse family's record-setting $54.2 million ($490 million in 2023 dollars) purchase of the *Plain Dealer* in 1967, its long-standing anti-union behavior that dates to the 1930s, and, more recently, to the 1996 bargaining round that produced a rare ten-year contract that offered the Cleveland local stability in exchange for adding a no-strike clause, common in Guild contracts. Scott Stephens, former Guild executive officer but then a member of the bargaining committee and ten-year leader of the Cleveland unit, recalled that it was an unusual contract at the time: "The company was building a spacious new headquarters and a production plant. It needed predictable labor costs to manage its financial commitments, 'but it did lock us in'" (quoted in Clark 2020; Brown 2020).

When the ten-year contract expired in 2006, the parties followed up with a seven-year agreement that included lucrative buyout offers to veteran journalists. Another round of buyouts followed in 2008, which reduced the newsroom by about 60 journalists, including Stephens and his wife, a photographer. The company also laid off 50 newsroom employees, the first layoff in the *Plain Dealer*'s history. A year later, during the Great Recession, the union accepted a 12% pay cut instead of additional layoffs. During this time, Advance Publications was in the process of cutting jobs across the country, notably at its nonunion *Times-Picayune* in New Orleans, where it terminated 200 employees, including half the newsroom staff.

In 2013, Advance slashed even more jobs—about one third of the editorial staff. The union, however, signed a six-year contract (2013–2019) that increased wages by 8%. This contract followed years of pay cuts, furloughs, pension freezes, and the shrinking of the bargaining unit. Yet even after dozens of newsroom employees voluntarily accepted severance packages, management terminated another 58 Guild members (Brown 2020; Clark 2013, 2020).

The whittling down of the bargaining unit weakened Local 1, but Advance's disinvestment of the *Plain Dealer*'s newsroom and redirection of resources to a separate competing nonunion website, Cleveland.com, was unprecedented and further handicapped Local 1. The company first split reporters' beats between the two units, which led to staffers competing for stories, and then physically separated them. It also removed journalists from their relatively new downtown newsroom and demanded that they practice "backpack journalism" by working in cafés or at home. Advance also transferred designers and copy editors to its suburban production facility. In 2018, after a few more physical moves, *Plain Dealer* journalists were dispatched to the production facility, while Cleveland.com staffers were invited back to headquarters. To further divide the two staffs and weaken labor solidarity, the company discouraged the two sets of journalists from speaking with each other. According to Stephens, "Advance has very deliberately made Cleveland.com into a separate news-gathering entity, and a nonunion entity. So, while they are increasing the numbers there of nonunion news gatherers, there is continued reduction of unionized staff at the *Plain Dealer*. It's union-busting." By the end of the 2013 bargaining round, Local 1 barely had over 100 members left at the *Plain Dealer* (Brown 2020; quoted in Clark 2020).

In March 2019, in the face of continued declining revenue, the *Plain Dealer* laid off another third of the unionized newsroom and outsourced design work to its New York City–based subsidiary (Clark 2020; Ma 2018). The pandemic led to another round of 30 layoffs at the *Plain Dealer*, as well as job cuts at Cleveland.com. Only 14 journalists were left at the newspaper that had employed 340 two decades earlier. Those left were offered the option of leaving or staying to cover news only in outlying geographic areas and would be prohibited from working on Cleveland or state issues. Ten of the 14 remaining journalists accepted the company's lucrative severance package (Brown 2020; Clark 2020; Edmonds 2020). And then came the final blow to the Local 1.

On May 15, 2020, the company laid off the remaining four union journalists and offered them jobs at Cleveland.com. Local 1 posted a farewell message on Twitter: "After more than 80 years of union membership, *Plain Dealer* journalists will no longer be represented by Local One. The unit will be dissolved effective May 17. The PD newsroom will no longer exist" (Clark 2020; quoted in Jones 2020).

CONCLUSION AND FUTURE PROSPECTS

The newspaper industry has been financially stressed and volatile over the past two decades and will likely continue to be this way as it transitions from the traditional print-based product to a digital one and attempts to find a profitable business model. For example, in November 2023, Pew found that US daily newspaper circulation for print and digital formats declined by 8% and 10%, respectively, in 2021 and 2022. Total industry advertising revenue in 2022 fell 5% from 2021 to $9.8 billion for the four remaining publicly traded companies that own about 300 dailies. The total estimated circulation revenue was about the same over the same period. One positive note: the share of newspaper revenue coming from digital advertising grew from 17% in 2011 to 48% in 2022 (Pew Research Center 2023).

It is hazardous to predict the future, but a few other trends are likely to continue in the short term. These include the growing importance of investment-firm owners of newspaper chains, the further consolidation of the industry, employment losses, and the role of AI in newsrooms. In response, workers will probably continue to organize new unions and continue to fight at the bargaining table and elsewhere for a more equitable and secure workplace.

In early July 2023, Patrick Soon-Shiong sold the *San Diego Union-Tribune*, which he acquired along with the *Los Angeles Times* in 2018, to MNG, which is owned by the hedge fund Alden Global Capital. This was the fifth sale of the 154-year-old newspaper since the Copley family sold the paper to Platinum Equity in 2009 after eight decades of ownership. As soon as Alden took control, it offered buyouts to employees. Before the sale to Alden, the *Union-Tribune* employed 220 people with 108 in the newsroom, down from over 400 in 2006. But almost two weeks after the announced sale, the paper's editor and publisher and dozens of newsroom workers departed, leaving only an estimated 75 newsroom workers. Alden also sold the paper's headquarters, leaving journalists to work remotely. The *Union-Tribune* is reported to be profitable, but it retains heavy legacy pension obligations and the high costs of printing and distribution—making it a likely candidate for further cost cutting. Writing about Alden's business methods, investigative journalist Andrew Donohue notes, "You just exist in mediocrity or worse, as they drain out as many profits from the existing print product as possible and divert those profits to other investments. There is no plan for the future. There's certainly no digital transition. There's just revenue extraction" (quoted in Donahue 2023; Huntsberry and Lewis 2023; Schultz 2023; Weisberg 2023).

In early September, Alden purchased Scranton-based and family-owned Times-Shamrock Communications' four daily newspapers, a number of weeklies, and its commercial printing operations. The sale was driven by Times-Shamrock shareholders, but the Lynett family, which has owned a newspaper in Scranton since 1895, opposed the deal:

> This was a transaction that we do not support or endorse. Alden does not reflect the business principles we feel are consistent with the stewardship of any newspaper. ... We remained confident and hopeful that our current Board of Directors and management team would have been able to lead us through the industry's headwinds more effectively and humanely than a hedge fund like Alden. (*Editor & Publisher* 2023)

The NewsGuild, concerned about the duopoly of Gannett and Alden and their extraction business models, issued "comments" in September 2023 to the Department of Justice and the Federal Trade Commission on the draft merger and acquisition guidelines first issued in January 2022. In it, the Guild argues that weak anti-trust enforcement has enabled investment companies to assume control over the majority of newspapers, which is not only bad industry economics but also a threat to democracy (The NewsGuild 2023b).

The consolidation of the newspaper industry can also be seen in the outsourcing of printing and distribution operations, sometimes to other publishers hours away. Forty-five of the country's top 100 dailies now publish six or fewer days a week, and some of those and other notable newspapers have outsourced the printing of their papers as well. Outsourcing has led to poor quality, deadlines being pushed back such that the printed copy is at least a day behind the news cycle, and employment cuts (Caro 2023). For example, in February 2023, Lee Enterprises announced that the *Buffalo News* would be printed three hours away by Advance Local's *Cleveland Plain Dealer*'s printing presses. The September closure of the Buffalo plant led to the loss of about 160 jobs across eight bargaining units. In nearby Rochester, Gannett announced in January 2023 that the *Rochester Democrat & Chronicle* would be printed in New Jersey, leading to 111 layoffs (McDonnell 2023; Petro 2023).

At the *New York Times*, consolidation took still another form with the closing of its venerable sports department and its outsourcing to The Athletic, a nonunion digital-only business founded in 2016 that the Times Company purchased in January 2022 for $550 million. The Athletic employs about 400 journalists, covers over 200 sports teams, and publishes more than 150 articles daily. The *Times* sports department employed about 35 reporters and editors and was once a "pillar of American sports journalism." The move continued the integration of The Athletic into the company, which heretofore had been a separate unit. *Times* management announced that its sports journalists would be moved to other positions and that no one would be laid off (Bruell 2023b; quoted in Robertson and Koblin 2023).

The NewsGuild of New York, the local union that represents the *Times* unit, called the outsourcing move "union busting" and filed a grievance against the company. It also issued a strong statement that read in part, "We are baffled and infuriated by the Times (Co.) proposal to dissolve our storied and award-winning sports department. The announcement is a profound betrayal of our colleagues and of *Times* values" (NewsGuild of New York 2023b).

On September 18, the union held a newsroom vigil, displayed a ceremonial last edition, marched through the newsroom accompanied by a brass band, and then joined a larger outdoor rally in midtown Manhattan that featured sports reporters and union leaders. Wayne Kamidoi, an art director who designed pages for sports from 1995 through 2015, said, "Today it feels like the whole team got traded. All *Times* Guild members stand united, so we don't let another department be offloaded in a fire sale" (NewsGuild of New York 2023c).

An emergent issue, AI, has become a contentious subject of bargaining for unions, including those in airlines, hospitality, Hollywood, and in various media sectors, including newspapers (Verma and DeVynck 2023). In September 2023, the Writers Guild of America, which represents over 11,000 screenwriters, reached a deal with Hollywood studios after a 146-day strike that shuttered television and film production. The screenwriters won favorable contact language that states that AI is not a writer and gives the union control over its usage. According to Litwin (2023), the "contract establishes a precedent that an employer's use of AI can be a central subject of bargaining. It further establishes the precedent that workers can and should have a say in when and how they use artificial intelligence at work."

The actors' union, SAG-AFTRA, also struck Hollywood studios over AI and economic issues. Their strike overlapped with the screenwriter's job action. The last time these unions struck together was in 1960, when Ronald Reagan was the head of the actors' union. In early November, after 118 days, the longest strike in the union's history, the union agreed to a tentative three-year contract worth over $1 billion. SAG-AFTRA stated that it achieved "unprecedented provisions for consent and compensation that will protect members from the threat of AI." Actors were worried that AI could be used to create digital replicas of performers, replacing the need for background actors, a significant source of income for them (Barnes, Koblin and Sperling 2023; James, Lee, and Carras 2023).

The NewsGuild is equally concerned about the use and misuse of AI and the potential for job loss and has been strategizing to find ways to control it. Units in Gannett's New Jersey newsrooms, the Associated Press, *Wall Street Journal*, and *Los Angeles Times* first proposed contract language addressing AI in the summer of 2023, but so far, employers have not agreed to them (Fu 2023c).

In November 2023, The NewsGuild released the "Artificial Intelligence Member Survey Report." President Jon Schleuss's introduction stated, "A majority [of Guild members] do not trust employers to ethically implement artificial intelligence and they want to fight to make sure we do not lose jobs to automation. ... Members want strong codes of ethics and robust employee training to use AI in their jobs and identify AI-generated content in the world" (The NewsGuild, "Artificial Intelligence Member Survey Report," 2023a: 2).

Job loss is the Guild's primary concern, but it also expressed unease about glaring problems from the use and misuse of AI. Two reports released in May 2023 discovered a significant amount of misleading AI content across 125 websites, many of them "fringe news websites, content farms, and fake reviewers" with content written entirely or almost exclusively with AI tools. In addition, Gannett made a few AI-related blunders with error-laden articles on high school football games that appeared in the *Columbus Dispatch* and elsewhere. Gannett called its use of the AI tool "experimental" and suspended further articles using AI. In other news outlets, "artificial intelligence programs have screwed up simple interest calculations, botched the chronology of Star Wars movies, and produced sports stories that appeared to contain little factual information," according to *Washington Post* columnist Paul Farhi (Farhi 2023; Fu 2023c; Thompson 2023).

Not all AI use has been problematic and misleading, however, but the lack of rules and the potential for economic harm have galvanized publishers to address the unauthorized use of publisher content to train AI programs that may violate copyright laws and cause labor-related issues (Bruell 2023c; News Media Alliance 2023).

Technological change and its threat to labor have been a thread that has run through the history of newspapers since the 19th century. Newspaper publishers and The NewsGuild have both mutual and competing interests in dealing with AI and other technologies. Collective bargaining is one way in which they will attempt to address the use and effects of technological change. But labor and management will do this in an industry struggling to find stability and one that has become highly concentrated and controlled by investment firms with a history of profit extraction and a spotty record of investing in quality journalism.

ENDNOTES

1. Given the high volume of citations used from The NewsGuild's website, I will cite them as The NewsGuild or TNG with the specific dates that can be searched.
2. The top ten largest newspapers by circulation are the *Wall Street Journal, New York Times, Washington Post, New York Post, USA Today, Los Angeles Times,* (Minneapolis) *Star-Tribune,* (Long Island) *Newsday, Chicago Tribune,* and *Tampa Bay Times* (Majid 2023). Of the ten, six have unionized newsrooms.
3. The full editorial can be found at http://tinyurl.com/5srpfyub.
4. Tronc, which sometimes used the lowercase spelling, stands for "Tribune online content." The name change was ridiculed at the time, which led the company to return to its former name in 2018.
5. Unless noted otherwise, the main sources for this section are compiled into an Excel file from The NewsGuild website; The NewsGuild, "Organizing Report," 2021; and various issues of Bloomberg Law's Daily Labor Report and Labor Plus.
6. A separate University of North Carolina study of first contracts at the major chains organized between January 2017 and February 2022 found that there were 13 new units at Gannett newspapers and zero contracts, nine new units at Alden's Digital First Media and zero contracts, nine new unions at McClatchy and one new agreement, and eight new units at Lee Enterprises with six first contracts (Vassello 2022). http://tinyurl.com/2kj29hk2
7. Bloomberg Law's cross-industry analysis showed that the mean number of days to ratify a first contract had grown from 409 to 465 days, while the median time rose from 356 to 374 days. Between 2020 and 2022, however, the mean number of days increased to about 550 days. Only 47% of new units had ratified a first contract within a year (Combs 2022).

REFERENCES

Abernathy, P.M. 2020a. "Getting Readers to Pay: Questions with Iris Chyi." University of North Carolina Hussman School of Journalism and Media. December 28. http://tinyurl.com/mr3p8kmt

———. 2020b. "News Deserts and Ghost Newspapers: Will Local News Survive?" University of North Carolina Hussman School of Journalism and Media. http://tinyurl.com/22cw327n

———. 2023. "The State of Local News: The 2023 Report." Northwestern University Medill School of Journalism. November 16. http://tinyurl.com/3dnwjadc

Abernathy, P.M., and T. Franklin. 2022. "The State of Local News 2022." Northwestern University Medill School of Journalism. http://tinyurl.com/436mufuj

Alpert, L.I., and C. Lombardo. 2021. "Meet The Hedge Fund Boss Who Just Bought Tribune's Newspapers." *Wall Street Journal.* May 21. http://tinyurl.com/msc6jacy

Barnes, B., B. Koblin, and N. Sperling. 2023. "Striking Actors and Hollywood Studios Agree to a Deal." *New York Times.* November 8. http://tinyurl.com/3b78pxfy

Barthel, M. 2021. "Estimating U.S. Newspaper Circulation Is a Challenge—Especially for 2020." Pew Research Center. June 29. http://tinyurl.com/yfts55h5

Barthel, M., K.E. Matsa, and K. Worden. 2020. "Coronavirus-Driven Downturn Hits Newspapers Hard as TV News Thrives." Pew Research Center. October 29. http://tinyurl.com/y63rae9m

Benton, J. 2021. "The Vulture Is Hungry Again: Alden Global Capital Wants to Buy a Few Hundred More Newspapers." Nieman Lab. November 22. http://tinyurl.com/3p78ee8t

———. 2023. "The Scale of Local News Destruction in Gannett's Markets Is Astonishing." Nieman Lab. March 9. http://tinyurl.com/m4aku66x

Bloomberg Law. "Daily Labor Report." Various dates.

———. "Labor Plus." Various dates.

———. "Labor Plus." 2022. "Settlement Summaries—Washington Post/Communications Workers of America, Local 32035."

Bologna, M. 2018. "*Chicago Tribune* Organizing Drive Heads to Labor Board." Bloomberg Law. April 25. http://tinyurl.com/y3nhr3fz

Bologna, M., and J. Diaz. 2018. "Tronc Recognizes Chicago Tribune Guild." Bloomberg Law. May 7. http://tinyurl.com/6h6e455s

Bomey, N. August 20, 2020. "*USA TODAY* Owner Gannett Commits to Make Workforce as Diverse as America, Add New Beats on Race and Social Justice." *USA Today*. August 20. http://tinyurl.com/ymrksa2u

Bova, G. 2023. "Striking Does Work: Fort Worth Journalists Win Only Newspaper Union Contract in Texas." *Texas Observer*. January 9. http://tinyurl.com/4j98fzxz

Brenan, M. 2022. "Americans' Trust in Media Remains Near Record Low." Gallup. October 18. http://tinyurl.com/2yzyf9jy

Brown, M. 2020. "Cleveland's *Plain Dealer*: 50 Years of Union Busting." *American Prospect*. June 25. http://tinyurl.com/dbsdcdtw

Bruell, A. 2022a. "Members of *New York Times*, NBC News Digital Unions Defy Return-To-Office Plans." *Wall Street Journal*. September 12. http://tinyurl.com/yayt4sse

———. 2022b. "Google's 'News Showcase' Stalls in U.S. as Media Outlets Balk at Terms." *Wall Street Journal*. December 8. http://tinyurl.com/2mjcvn3b

———. 2023a. "Labor Strife at *New York Times* Intensifies, Dividing Staff." *Wall Street Journal*. March 19. http://tinyurl.com/yrfntfnr

———. 2023b. "*New York Times* to Close Sports Desk, Rely on the Athletic for Daily Coverage." *Wall Street Journal*. July 10. http://tinyurl.com/2puec6ax

———. 2023c. "Big News Publishers Look to Team Up to Address Impact of AI." *Wall Street Journal*. June 28. http://tinyurl.com/2p94zmcv

Caro, M. 2023. "Restart the Presses? Plant Closures and Consolidation Prompt Earlier Deadlines, Longer Drives, Higher Costs as Papers Scramble to Stay in Print." Local News Initiative, Northwestern University School of Journalism. August 10. http://tinyurl.com/53wsnjus

Channick, R. 2021a. "Hedge Fund Alden to Buy Tribune Publishing in Deal Valued at $630 Million." *Chicago Tribune*. February 16. http://tinyurl.com/bdev2e73

———. 2021b. "Tribune Publishing Offering Buyouts to Newsroom Employees, Two Days After Purchase by Hedge Fund Alden." *Chicago Tribune*. May 26. http://tinyurl.com/xa47crts

Charles, S., and L. Wilusz. 2018. "*Chicago Tribune* Newsroom Staffers Announce Intent to Unionize." *Chicago Sun Times*. April 11. http://tinyurl.com/8x9hnz8t

Chick, K. 2020. "Want Diverse Newsrooms? Unions Push for Pay Equity as a Path Forward." Nieman Reports. September 30. http://tinyurl.com/ut36z2vf

Chiglinsky, K. and G. Smith. 2019. "Warren Buffett Sees Most Newspapers as 'Toast' After Ad Decline." Bloomberg. April 23. http://tinyurl.com/2uvz7fjt

Chyi, I. 2021. "The Impact of Covid-19 on 20 U.S. Newspapers' Print and Digital Circulation." April 21. http://tinyurl.com/2cpcaf4h

Cimilluca, D., and C. Lombardo. 2019. "Gannett Closes In on Deal to Combine With GateHouse Media." *Wall Street Journal*. July 18. http://tinyurl.com/aksff2hr

Clark, A. 2013. "At the *Plain Dealer*, a Shrinking Staff Delivers Some Solid Work." *Columbia Journalism Review*. February 8. http://tinyurl.com/5b6kwa7e

———. 2020. "The Last Days of the *Cleveland Plain Dealer* Newsroom." *Columbia Journalism Review*. May 13. http://tinyurl.com/3ptckfbm

Clark, P.F., J.T. Delaney, and A.C. Frost, eds. 2002. *Collective Bargaining in the Private Sector*. Champaign, IL: Industrial Relations Research Association Series.

Combs, R. 2022. "Now It Takes 465 Days to Sign a Union's First Contract." Bloomberg Law. August 2. http://tinyurl.com/mr2prm63

Coppins, M. 2021. "A Secretive Hedge Fund Is Gutting Newsrooms." *Atlantic*. October 14. http://tinyurl.com/vkcbv66w

Dean, A. 2018. "*Denver Post* Told to Cut 30 More Newsroom Staff, Continuing Brutal Stretch of Change at Colorado's Largest News Organization." Denverite. March 14. http://tinyurl.com/ydrd2ns8

Demkovich, L. 2022. "Newspapers Were Already Hurting, and Then COVID-19 Struck. How the Pandemic Hurt the News Industry, and How Things Might Turn Around." *Spokesman-Review*. June 13. http://tinyurl.com/3tkz2hme

Denver Post Editorial Board. 2018. "Editorial: As Vultures Circle, the *Denver Post* Must Be Saved." *Denver Post*. April 6. http://tinyurl.com/5srpfyub

Deto, R. 2019. "Recent Moves by *Pittsburgh Post-Gazette* Management Have Led to a Shrinking and Increasingly Chaotic Newsroom. Can the P-G Survive?" *Pittsburgh City Paper*. December 11. http://tinyurl.com/3apskfbv

———. 2020a. "*Pittsburgh Post-Gazette* Union Journalists Will Vote to Go on Strike." *Pittsburgh City Paper*. July 29. http://tinyurl.com/mvhujsn5

———. 2020b. "Parent Union of *Post-Gazette* Union Endorses Strike, Now Awaits OK from Union Committee and President." *Pittsburgh City Paper*. September 14. http://tinyurl.com/arzvcbr6

———. 2023. "*Pittsburgh Post-Gazette* Strike Reaches 1 Year with Little Progress Made." Trib Live. October 13. http://tinyurl.com/2p822b9v

Dirks, Van Essen & April. Various years. Press Releases. https://dirksvanessen.com/press-releases

Doctor, K. 2018. "Newsonomics: Alden Global Capital Is Making So Much Money Wrecking Local Journalism It Might Not Want to Stop Anytime Soon." Nieman Lab. May 1. http://tinyurl.com/5bkt46bw

Donohue, A. 2023. "This Is the Beginning of the End for the *San Diego Union-Tribune*." Voice of San Diego. November 6. http://tinyurl.com/fw3zwk3r

Dow Jones. 2019. "IAPE & Dow Jones Agree to Three-Year Contract." Press Release. November 4. http://tinyurl.com/4mnrtv5w

———. 2022. "IAPE and Down Jones Tentatively Agree to One-Year Contract." Press Release. August 18. http://tinyurl.com/yzwxn7mk

Doyle, P., and J. Zenkevich. 2022. "*Post-Gazette* Journalists Begin Strike, as Contract Impasse Continues." WESA. October 18. http://tinyurl.com/2tufednb

Editor & Publisher. 2023. "MNG/Alden Capital Buys Times-Shamrock. Family Makes Statement to the Industry." September 1. http://tinyurl.com/mr23x86y

Edmonds, R. 2019. "The GateHouse Takeover of Gannett Has Been Finalized." Poynter. August 5. http://tinyurl.com/mubbyy7m

———. 2020. "Massive Layoffs with a Side of Union-Busting—How Advance Dismantled Its Print Staff in Cleveland." Poynter. April 30. http://tinyurl.com/3jeunad3

———. 2021. "Alden's Takeover Bid for Tribune Publishing Faces a Fresh Challenge from the NewsGuild." Poynter. January 6. http://tinyurl.com/2952vph8

———. 2022. "Lee's Slate of Directors Elected, Alden Global Capital Takeover Attempt Blocked for Now." Poynter. March 10. http://tinyurl.com/35cy96su

Eidelson, J. 2018. "*Chicago Tribune* Staff Seeks to Form Union in Challenge to Tronc." *Boston Globe*. April 11. http://tinyurl.com/mudfscmz

———. 2022. "Reuters US Reporters Are Striking for First Time in Decades." Bloomberg. August 3. http://tinyurl.com/nzvjjw9e

eMarketer. 2021. "US Triopoly Digital Ad Revenue Share, by Company, 2019–2023." Insider Intelligence. October. http://tinyurl.com/y66bjuk6

Ember, S. 2017. "*Los Angeles Times* Newsroom, Challenging Tronc, Goes Public with Union Push." *New York Times*. October 4. http://tinyurl.com/ckentrh4

Erickson, B. 2022. "The *Fort Worth Star Telegram* Strike Marks a Major Movement for Texas Newsroom Unions." *D Magazine*. November 30. http://tinyurl.com/mwa2yxmb

Ewens, M., A. Gupta, and S.T. Howell. 2022. "Local Journalism Under Private Equity Ownership." Unpublished Paper. National Bureau of Economic Research. February. https://www.nber.org/papers/w29743

Farhi, P. 2023. "AI May Be News Reporting's Future. So Far, It's Been an Embarrassment." *Washington Post*. September 22. http://tinyurl.com/259nzm3y

Fedeli, S., E. Grieco, and N. Sumida. 2018. "About a Third of Large U.S. Newspapers Have Suffered Layoffs Since 2017." Pew Research Center. July 23. http://tinyurl.com/46ju9es2

Feder, R. 2018. "Stop the Presses: *Chicago Tribune* Journalists Form Union." *Daily Herald*. April 11. http://tinyurl.com/4wtdsawh

Fischer, S. 2022. "U.S. Digital Ad Revenue Expected to Surpass Print by 2026." Axios. June 21. http://tinyurl.com/3mdy8j4e

———. 2023a. "Gannett CEO Forecasts More Daily Newspaper Sales." Axios. March 28. http://tinyurl.com/4ytf5vxm

———. 2023b. "Record Number of Media Job Cuts So Far in 2023." Axios. June 13. http://tinyurl.com/372t3zp7

Fischer, S., and K. Flynn. 2022. "Lee Quietly Slashes Jobs Following Hostile Takeover Event." Axios. March 29. http://tinyurl.com/bdsnfx82

———. 2023. "Gannett Shed Nearly Half Its Workforce Since GateHouse Merger." Axios. March 7. http://tinyurl.com/dy77w47h

Folkenflick, D. 2018a. "In Historic Move at Labor-Skeptic *Chicago Tribune*, Newsroom Pushes to Form Union." NPR. April 11. http://tinyurl.com/5n8yn6um

———. 2018b. "Under Pressure, Tronc Recognizes *Chicago Tribune* Union." NPR. May 6. http://tinyurl.com/2sb9d9hw

Forstadt, J. 2023a. "*Pittsburgh Post-Gazette* Appeals Decision Ordering Good-Faith Bargaining with Unions." WESA. March 24. http://tinyurl.com/tfydyz8c

———. 2023b. "One Year After Walking Out, Workers at the *Pittsburgh Post-Gazette* Remain on Strike." WESA. October 18. http://tinyurl.com/ye2bxuay

Fu, A. 2021a. "NewsGuild Study of 14 Unionized Gannett Newsrooms Find Gender and Racial Pay Gaps." Poynter. April 27. http://tinyurl.com/2swr6nfb

———. 2021b. "Journalists at 11 Alden Papers in Southern California Vote to Unionize." Poynter. June 11. http://tinyurl.com/7rh96jhs

———. 2021c. "'The Stakes Are Really High': Newly Unionized Newsroom Tackle the Next Challenge, Contract Negotiations." Poynter. July 20. http://tinyurl.com/mr2474tc

———. 2021d. "*New York Times* Workers Rally Outside Company Headquarters in Protest of 'Anti-Union Tactics.'" Poynter. November 17. http://tinyurl.com/yc2u9djh

———. 2021e. "2021 Was Another Successful Year for Journalism's Unionization Movement." Poynter. December 28. http://tinyurl.com/mk5pec7u

———. 2022a. "Over 200 Unionized Gannett Journalists Stage One-Day Strike." Poynter. November 4. http://tinyurl.com/ezc6hpdt

———. 2022b. "Fort Worth Journalists Launch First Open-Ended Strike at McClatchy." Poynter. November 28. http://tinyurl.com/3w45jsn4

———. 2022c. "Pay Equity Study by Tribune Unions Finds Gender and Racial Pay Gaps." Poynter. March 9. http://tinyurl.com/5n6hp6t9

———. 2022d. "Lee Enterprises Reports Growth in Digital Revenue Amid Layoffs." Poynter. May 5. http://tinyurl.com/8kj83na9

———. 2022e. "Study by Six Gannett Unions Finds Racial and Gender and Pay Inequities." Poynter. October 18. http://tinyurl.com/bdezf7fu

———. 2022f. "Unions Back to Using Walkouts as Bargaining Tactic After Two-Decade Break." Poynter. December 16. http://tinyurl.com/bdz7wp2f

———. 2023a. "The *Buffalo News* Was the Crown Jewel of Warren Buffet's News Empire. Now It's Just Another Lee Paper." Poynter. April 20. http://tinyurl.com/yma74e3u

———. 2023b. "*Los Angeles Times* Executes Largest Layoffs Under Billionaire Soon-Shiong's Ownership." Poynter. June 7. http://tinyurl.com/2rvbafpp

———. 2023c. "As AI Enters Newsrooms, Unions Push for Worker Protections." Poynter. September 18. http://tinyurl.com/aajj4bax

———. 2023d. "Hundreds of *Washington Post* Employees Stage 24-Hour Strike." Poynter. December 7. http://tinyurl.com/29ccx5zd

Funk, J. 2022. "News Publisher Lee Faces Renewed Pressure from Hedge Funds." Associated Press. April 14. http://tinyurl.com/mr37cj35

Goggin, B. 2019. "7,800 People Lost Their Media Jobs in a 2019 Landslide." *Business Insider*. December 10. http://tinyurl.com/2p8skne3

Gramlich, J. 2020. "As Newsrooms Face Coronavirus-Related Cuts, 54% of Americans Rate Media's Response to the Outbreak Positively." Pew Research Center. April 8. http://tinyurl.com/3mb-3c8b5

Greenhouse, S. 2019. "Why Newsrooms Are Unionizing Now." Nieman Reports. March 21. http://tinyurl.com/4szf2zvs

———. 2022. "Newsrooms Are Unionizing Pretty Much 'Nonstop.' Here's Why." Nieman Reports. January 19. http://tinyurl.com/2p9h4afc

Greenslade, R. 2016. "Almost 60% of US Newspaper Jobs Vanish in 26 Years." *Guardian*. June 6. http://tinyurl.com/3hm7fedd

Grieco, E. 2018a. "Newsroom Employment Dropped Nearly a Quarter in Less Than 10 Years, with Greatest Decline at Newspapers." Montana Newspaper Association. July 30. http://tinyurl.com/2tnnw6fd

———. 2018b. "Newsroom Employees Earn Less Than Other College-Educated Workers in U.S." Pew Research Center. October 4. http://tinyurl.com/mr3n8hps

———. 2019a. "U.S. Newsroom Employment Has Dropped by a Quarter Since 2008, with Greatest Decline at Newspapers." Friends of Canadian Broadcasting. July 9. http://tinyurl.com/2p9zdptc

———. 2019b. "About a Quarter of Large U.S. Newspapers Laid Off Staff in 2018." Pew Research Center. August 1. http://tinyurl.com/5n6w39cp

———. 2020. "U.S. Newspapers Have Shed Half of Their Newsroom Employees Since 2008." Pew Research Center. April 20. http://tinyurl.com/35zvk4ds

Hagey, K., L.I. Alpert, and Y. Serkez. 2019. "In News Industry, a Stark Divide Between Haves and Have-Nots." *Wall Street Journal*. May 4. http://tinyurl.com/fufvt3vj

Hagey, K., J. Trachtenberg, and L. Wise. 2020. "Without Coronavirus Aid, Local Newspapers Could Fold." *Wall Street Journal*. April 22. http://tinyurl.com/msf7fxrh

Healy, J. 2018. "*Denver Post* Editor Who Criticized Paper's Ownership Resigns." *New York Times*. May 3. http://tinyurl.com/5bxsybcm

Heaney, J. 2023. "Further Decline at the *Buffalo News*." Investigative Post. October 9. http://tinyurl.com/yc3ztzc9

Hobbs, S.R. 2013. "Newspaper Guild, *Washington Post* Agree on Tentative Contract for 820 Employees." Bloomberg Law. November 4. http://tinyurl.com/3pu6xtap

Huntsberry, W., and S. Lewis. 2023. "LA's Richest Man Sells *Union-Tribune* to Feared 'Cop Shop.'" Voice of San Diego. July 10. http://tinyurl.com/4ft96vcu

Iafolla, R. 2022. "*Pittsburgh Post-Gazette* Wrongly Laid Off Employees Promised Work." Bloomberg Law. September 21. http://tinyurl.com/2kj9y9ts

Independent Association of Publishers' Employees. No date. Website. https://www.iape1096.org

———. 2023. "Looking at the Dow Jones Pay Gap. Again." March 14. https://www.iape1096.org/2023payreport

Izadi, E., and S. Ellison. 2022. "The *Washington Post* Announces More Job Cuts Next Year." *Washington Post*. December 14. http://tinyurl.com/yc75dyu4

———. 2023. "*Washington Post* Lays Off 20 Newsroom Employees." *Washington Post*. January 24. http://tinyurl.com/mwjz4y5c

Izadi, E., and H. Scribner. 2023. "*New York Times* Staffers, Bosses Reach Agreement on New Employee Contract." *Washington Post*. May 24. http://tinyurl.com/5duuvr24

Jacob, M. 2021. "More Chain-Owned News Organizations Are Returning to Local Ownership." Poynter. July 26. http://tinyurl.com/5ayxk9ra

Jaffe, S. 2019. "The Labor Movement Comes to Virtual Reality: Unionizing Digital Media." *New Labor Forum* 28, no. 2: 36–43.

James, M. 2019. "*Los Angeles Times* Reaches Historic Agreement with Its Newsroom." *Los Angeles Times*. October 16. http://tinyurl.com/299p76ta

———. 2023. "*Los Angeles Times* to Cut 74 Newsroom Positions Amid Advertising Declines." *Los Angeles Times*. June 7. http://tinyurl.com/ycktv9pc

James, M., W. Lee, and C. Carras. 2023. "SAG-AFTRA Committee Approves Deal with Studios to End Historic Strike." *Los Angeles Times*. November 8. http://tinyurl.com/sd35a42m

Jamieson, M., A. Brenoff, D. Ferner, and M. Strachan. 2018. "How the *LA Times* Won." HuffPost. January 19. http://tinyurl.com/4nps3wc3

Jones, T. 2020. "The *Plain Dealer* Is Dissolved as Advance Local Moves Its Final Four Reporters to Non-Union Cleveland.com." Poynter. May 12. http://tinyurl.com/yc5cx685

———. 2022. "How Newsrooms Lost Their Homes." Poynter. September 29. http://tinyurl.com/3re56sy4

Kansas City News Guild. 2023. Press Release. January 6. https://kcnewsguild.org

Kanu, H.A., and J. Diaz. 2018. "*Washington Post* Reaches Tentative Agreement with Reporters' Union." Bloomberg Law. July 2. http://tinyurl.com/bp5wkun7

Kennedy, D. 2018. *The Return of the Moguls: How Jeff Bezos and John Henry Are Remaking Newspapers for the Twenty-First Century*. Lebanon, NH: University Press of New England.

Knolle, S. 2018. "Newsrooms Are Forming Unions to Create Better Pay, Better Benefits and Better Journalism." *Editor & Publisher*. May 1. http://tinyurl.com/2rvztbj3

Krupat, K.W. 2021. "Save the News: Campaigning to Preserve Jobs and Democratize Journalism: A Conversation with Jon Schleuss." *New Labor Forum* 30, no. 1 : 52–58.

Kuttner, R., and H. Zenger. 2017. "Saving the Free Press from Private Equity." *American Prospect*. December 27. http://tinyurl.com/ycxf9yyn

L.A. Times Guild. 2017. "Letter to the Newsroom: Why We're Forming a Union." October 4. http://tinyurl.com/2x6xdzbj

———. 2019. "L.A. Times Guild Reaches Agreement with Management on Historic First Contract." October 16. http://tinyurl.com/yzwd8vn6

———. 2023. "Open Letter to *L.A. Times* Management on Proposed Layoffs." June 8. http://tinyurl.com/4zcxph42

Leab, D.J. 1970. *A Union of Individuals: The Formation of the American Newspaper Guild, 1933–1936*. New York, NY: Columbia University Press.

Lenz, L. 2019. "As NewsGuild Holds Election, Members Say Union Has Been Too Passive." *Columbia Journalism Review*. May 8. http://tinyurl.com/2fym3dzk

Liedke, J. 2022. "About One in Six Journalists at News Outlets Are Part of a Union; Many More Would Join One If They Could." Pew Research Center. August 4, http://tinyurl.com/49794c4r

Litwin, A.S. 2023. "Hollywood's Deal with Screenwriters Just Rewrote the Rules Around A.I." *New York Times*. September 29. http://tinyurl.com/56rbvm3r

Lunzer, B. 2017. "Guild Reaches First-of-Its-Kind Agreement with GateHouse." The NewsGuild. December 15. http://tinyurl.com/uvmwttz3

Ma, A. 2018. "*Plain Dealer* Plans to Lay Off a Third of Unionized News Staff." WOSU. December 27. http://tinyurl.com/mrnt6t3x

Mahone, J. 2022. *Workers of the Newsroom Unite: An Analysis of Union Organizing in U.S. Local News Media, 2017 to Present*. Chapel Hill, NC: University of North Carolina Hussman School of Journalism and Media.

Majid, A. 2023. "Top 25 US Newspaper Circulations: Largest Print Titles Fall 14% in Year to March 2023." *Press Gazette*. June 26. http://tinyurl.com/yc2kcmna

Mandese, J. 2022. "Now a $15B Ad Business, Microsoft Solidifies Position in Digital's 'Big 4.'" MediaPost. January 27. http://tinyurl.com/2yzbuzp7

Mari, W. 2021. *The American Newsroom: A History, 1920–1960*. Journalism in Perspective Series. Columbia, MO: University of Missouri Press.

Matsa, K.E., and K. Worden. 2022. "Local Newspapers Fact Sheet." Pew Research Center. May 26. http://tinyurl.com/2p88exc6

Mayo, B., and T. Yorgey. 2023. "Striking *Pittsburgh Post-Gazette* Employees and Supporters Rally Outside Paper to Mark 1 Year on Strike." WTAE. October 12. http://tinyurl.com/3ekzvvxy

McAlevey, J., and A. Lawlor. 2021. "Participation & Power in Negotiations." University of California Berkeley Labor Center. May. http://tinyurl.com/55j65z75

McDonnell, S. 2023. "Plain Dealer Publishing Will Start Printing the *Buffalo News* Later This Year." Cleveland.com. February 21. http://tinyurl.com/2m62cecp

Media News Group. No date. Website. http://tinyurl.com/2vxmr7fm

Miller, G. 2021. "More Than 6,150 News Workers Were Laid Off Amid the COVID-19 Pandemic." *Columbia Journalism Review*. December 10. http://tinyurl.com/mrx5khjr

Mohajer, S.T. 2017. "The *LA Times* Flirts with Unionizing, Defying Its History." *Columbia Journalism Review*. November 21. http://tinyurl.com/msfjppv7

Mullin, B. 2023. "*Washington Post* Reaches a Contract Deal With Its Newsroom." *New York Times*. December 23.

Mullin, B., and K. Robertson. 2023. "*Washington Post* Lays Off 20 Workers." *New York Times*. January 24. http://tinyurl.com/3uev9dv2

Mutter, A.D. 2012. "Newsroom Staffing Hits 34-Year Low." Newsosaur. April 4. http://tinyurl.com/4x28drp7

NewsGuild of New York. 2017. Press release, "NewsGuild of New York Members Ratify New Four-Year Agreement at the *New York Times*." http://tinyurl.com/ehzb97bn

———. 2023a. "Breaking: NYT Guild Wins Groundbreaking Contract Agreement." May 24. http://tinyurl.com/yc7zzara

———. 2023b. "Statement: NYT Guild Responds to Disbanding of *NYT* Sports Department." July 10. http://tinyurl.com/3suz6as2

———. 2023c. "The New York Times Guild Members Bid Farewell to the Award-Winning Sports Desk." September 18. http://tinyurl.com/4fppds2p

News Media Alliance. 2023. "White Paper: How the Pervasive Copying of Expressive Works to Train and Fuel Generative Artificial Intelligence Systems Is Copyright Infringement and Not a Fair Use." News Media Alliance. https://tinyurl.com/hsbrnfv3

News Leaders Association. 2018. "2018 Diversity Survey." http://tinyurl.com/yck9ev6p

———. 2019. "2019 Diversity Survey." http://tinyurl.com/mrxtuskr

Newspaper Guild of Pittsburgh. No date. Websiter. https://pghguild.com

O'Connell, J., and E. Brown. 2019. "A Hedge Fund's 'Mercenary' Strategy: Buy Newspaper, Slash Jobs, Sell the Businesses." *Washington Post*. February 11. http://tinyurl.com/5b5u4cmc

Olson, A. 2023. "Hundreds of Journalists Strike to Demand Leadership Change at Biggest US Newspaper Chain." Associated Press. June 4. http://tinyurl.com/2bwnfae3

Peck, G. 2022. "Anti-Boycott Laws Run Afoul of the Free Press." *Editor & Publisher*. February 7. http://tinyurl.com/3fay3f5u

Petro, M. 2023. "*Buffalo News* Plans to Close Downtown Printing Facility, Move Printing to Cleveland." *Buffalo News*. February 20. https://tinyurl.com/rezbbc8t

Pew Research Center. 2016. "State of the News Media 2016." Pew Research Center. June 15. http://tinyurl.com/28re35vd

———. 2023. "Newspapers Fact Sheet." Pew Research Center. November 10. https://tinyurl.com/44unazyh

Reynolds, J. 2018a. "*Denver Post* Newsroom Slashed by 1/3 as Hedge Fund Continues Eviscerating Digital First Media Papers." Digital First Media Workers. March 14. http://tinyurl.com/3ehy5mtr

———. 2018b. "New Study: Digital First Media Leads in Profits; News Deserts Expanding." Digital First Media Workers. October 22. http://tinyurl.com/y36mtsfm

———. 2019. "Digital First Media's Profits 'Near the Top of the Industry,' Company Says in Takeover Letter." Digital First Media Workers. January 14. http://tinyurl.com/2yj9hf8r

———. 2020. "Now Alden Is Circling Lee Newspapers." The NewsGuild. January 30. http://tinyurl.com/mwtf2hfk

———. 2021a. "Tribune Board Agrees to Sell Company to Alden." Digital First Media Workers. February 17. http://tinyurl.com/bddr2smu

———. 2021b. "Tribune Papers Lose More Than 89 Positions Under Staff Buyouts." Digital First Media Workers. June 24. http://tinyurl.com/239xmbp4

Richardson, Tyrone. 2015a. "*Washington Post*, Guild Announce Tentative Two-Year Labor Agreement." Bloomberg Law. "Daily Labor Report." June 4.

———. September 14, 2015b. "Guilds Boost Efforts to Organize Digital Newsrooms." Bloomberg Law. Daily Labor Report. September 14.

———. 2015c. "Guild Goes 'Paper' Free to Reflect Changes on News-Gathering Industry." Bloomberg Law. Daily Labor Report. January 23.

———. 2016. "Digital First Media Workers Ratify Contract." Bloomberg Law. Daily Labor Report. August 15.

Robertson, K. 2021. "*New York Time*s Employees Protest over Union Fights." *New York Times*. November 16. http://tinyurl.com/37f9ecy6

———. 2023a. "The *Times* Reaches a Contract Deal with Its Newsroom Union." *New York Times*. May 25. http://tinyurl.com/2p9wvcv9

———. 2023b. "*Washington Pos*t Journalists Go on One-Day Strike." *New York Times*. December 7. http://tinyurl.com/4bbnttcj

Robertson, K., and J. Koblin. 2023. "The *New York Times* to Disband Its Sports Department." *New York Times*. July 10. http://tinyurl.com/3nd7u7v6

Robertson, K., and M. Tracy. 2020. "McClatchy, a Major U.S. Newspaper Chain, Files for Bankruptcy." *New York Times*. February 13. http://tinyurl.com/3vn7xpcz

Rosman, K., and J. Peiser. 2018. "*Denver Post* Journalists Go to New York to Protest Their Owner." *New York Times*. May 8. http://tinyurl.com/39y33sh3

Roush, C. 2022. "Dow Jones, Union Agree on One-Year Contract." Talking Biz News. August 23. http://tinyurl.com/bhxwysbd

Sainato, M. 2022. "Pittsburgh Newspaper Workers Go on Strike over Unfair Labor Practice." *Guardian*. November 11. http://tinyurl.com/4h3mesp3

Sanchez, R. 2016. "How Massive Cuts Have Remade the *Denver Post*." *5280: Denver's Mile High Magazine*. October. http://tinyurl.com/5yr3hm7v

Schleuss, J. 2019. "Candidate Statement." http://tinyurl.com/3ky55wr2

———. 2023. The NewsGuild. March 3. https://newsguild.org/members

Schneider, A. 2018. "Tronc Agrees to Let Its Virginia Newsrooms Unionize." WUVM. September 14. http://tinyurl.com/je6jmkzu

Schultz, R. 2021. "Top 10 Newspapers See Print Circ Fall by Double Digits During the Pandemic." MediaPost. April 9. http://tinyurl.com/zzdyfez4

———. 2023. "Alden's At It Again: Hedge Fund Trims Staff at *San Diego Union-Tribune*, Critic Charges." *Editor & Publisher*. November 1. http://tinyurl.com/2f34juvz

Scire, S. 2022. "Revenue for Hundreds of Local News Orgs Went Up in 2021, According to New Data." Nieman Lab. May 10. http://tinyurl.com/2c6avuyc

———. 2023. "The First Newspaper Strike of the Digital Age Stretches into a New Year." Nieman Lab. January 25. http://tinyurl.com/44z4tjmm

Shearer, E., and E. Tomasik. 2022. "After Increasing in 2020, Layoffs at Large U.S. Newspapers and Digital News Sites Declined in 2021." Pew Research Center. October 13. http://tinyurl.com/mr3pdhwy

Smith, G. 2019. "Journalism Layoffs Are at the Highest Level Since Last Recession." Bloomberg. July 1. http://tinyurl.com/3bdvj5xc

Sommer, W., and E. Izadi. 2023. "*Washington Post* Will Offer Buyouts to Cut Staff by 240." *Washington Post*. October 10. http://tinyurl.com/muusfjvx

Stanger, H.R. 2002. "Newspapers: Collective Bargaining Decline Amidst Technological Change." In *Collective Bargaining in the Private Sector*, edited by P.F. Clark, J.T. Delaney, and A.C. Frost. Champaign, IL: Labor and Employment Research Association.

———. 2013. "Hard Times and Hard Bargaining in the Newspaper Industry" In *Collective Bargaining Under Duress, Case Studies of Major North American Industries,* edited by H.R. Stanger, P.F. Clark, and A.C. Frost. Champaign, IL: Labor and Employment Relations Association.

Statista. 2022. "Number of Employees in the Newspaper Industry in the United States in 2006 and 2021, by Profession." http://tinyurl.com/mr2cn6ss

———. 2023. "Advertising Space Revenue of U.S. Newspapers from 2013 to 2021." http://tinyurl.com/32tau35j

Statt, N. 2018. "Tronc to Change Name Back to Tribune Publishing After Years of Ridicule." The Verge. June 18. http://tinyurl.com/muneset9

Sterne, P. 2015. "NewsGuild Starts $500,000 Campaign to Organize Digital Newsrooms." Politico. September 1. http://tinyurl.com/2hzb2mxy

Sullivan, M. 2018. "Is This Strip-Mining or Journalism? 'Sobs, Gasps, Expletives' over Latest *Denver Post* Layoffs." *Washington Post*. March 15. http://tinyurl.com/y6ab5cu8

Tameez, H. 2020. "Gannett Newsrooms, Whiter Than the Communities They Serve, Pledge Broad Change by 2025." Nieman Lab. August 20. https://tinyurl.com/4t32jame

Tracy, M. 2020a. "McClatchy, a Family Newspaper Business, Heads Toward Hedge-Fund Ownership." *New York Times*. July 9. http://tinyurl.com/4yr2pva4

———. 2020b. "McClatchy, Family-Run News Chain, Goes to Hedge Fund in Bankruptcy Sale." *New York Times*. August 4. http://tinyurl.com/4sm3p3bh

The NewsGuild. "News." Various dates. https://newsguild.org/category/news/

———. "History." https://newsguild.org/history/

———. "Locals." https://newsguild.org/locals/

———. "Members." https://newsguild.org/members/

———. "Organize with Us." https://newsguild.org/organize-with-us/

———. "Pay Equity." https://newsguild.org/pay-equity/

———. 2020. "Fear the Vulture: Alden Destroys News Organizations When Promising to Save Them." The NewsGuild Hedgepapers. September 10. http://tinyurl.com/3n5pp4sx

———. 2021. "Organizing Report." The NewsGuild. October.

———. 2023a. "Artificial Intelligence Member Survey Report." The NewsGuild. November.

———. 2023b. "DOJ and FTC Need to Scrutinize News Mergers." The NewsGuild. September 19. http://tinyurl.com/mr26xkzj

———. 2023c. "Reporter Top Minimum Wages," The NewsGuild. May 9. http://tinyurl.com/2s6chu6p

The Spokesman-Review. 2022. "The State of Newspapers." June 12. https://tinyurl.com/zk32sa8x

Thompson, S.A. 2023. "A.I.-Generated Content Discovered on News Sites, Content Farms and Product Reviews." *New York Times*. May 19. http0://tinyurl.com/53emjuyh

Unions of Lee Enterprises. 2023. "Statement." *Daily Montanan*. June 28. http://tinyurl.com/4pyuhaub

UnionStats. https://www.unionstats.org

US Department of Labor, Office of Labor–Management Standards. 2022. "LM-2, Schedule 13. Communications Workers of America." http://tinyurl.com/59tszv9h

US Bureau of Labor Statistics. 2016. "Employment Trends in Newspaper Publishing and Other Media, 1990–2016." Economics Daily. June 2. http://tinyurl.com/nyv2hxk6

———. 2017. "Newspaper Publishers Lose over Half Their Employment from January 2001 to September 2016." April 3. http://tinyurl.com/4ereaeu8

———. 2023. "*Occupational Outlook Handbook*: News Analysts, Reporters, and Journalists." http://tinyurl.com/35bawaap

Vassello, S. 2022. "Precarious Conditions in Local News Sparks Collective Action." University of North Carolina Hussman School of Journalism and Media. http://tinyurl.com/mwa2ztab

Verma, P., and G. De Vynck. 2023. "From Airlines to Hollywood, Workers Are Fighting to Keep AI at Bay." *Washington Post*. June 8. http://tinyurl.com/7c6jbw8m

Vranica, S. 2020. "Google, Facebook, and Amazon Gain as Coronavirus Reshapes Ad Spending." *Wall Street Journal*. December 1. http://tinyurl.com/392w2m42

Waggoner, M. 2019. "NewsGuild Plans Member Surveys." The NewsGuild. October 4. http://tinyurl.com/mue9umxt

Walker, M. 2021. "U.S. Newsroom Employment Has Fallen 26% Since 2008." Pew Research Center. July 13. http://tinyurl.com/2stm2zbw

Washington–Baltimore News Guild. 2018. "Tentative Agreement Reached." *Post Guild Bulletin*. June 30.

Washington Post Guild. "About the Guild." https://postguild.org/about-us/

Weisberg, L. 2023. "The *San Diego Union-Tribune* Sold to Alden Global Capital." *San Diego Union-Tribune*. July 10. http://tinyurl.com/36fbxbz6

Wenzel, J. 2018. "The Gutting of the *Denver Post* Is a Death Knell for Local News." *Atlantic*. May 11. http://tinyurl.com/yrmawcmz

Wikipedia. "Gannett." http://tinyurl.com/5n7yekxy

———. "New York Times Guild." http://tinyurl.com/5fdhzcrn

———. "Robert R. McCormick." http://tinyurl.com/4e4d4cs2

Zenger, H. 2018. "Hello Digital First, Goodbye Boston Herald." *American Prospect*. February 21. http://tinyurl.com/32bta3as

CHAPTER 4

Achieving Harmony: The Role of Collective Bargaining in the Symphonic Music Industry

Timothy Chandler
Louisiana State University

Rafael Gely
University of Missouri

Abstract

Collective bargaining is firmly rooted among symphony orchestras, with many major orchestras engaged in bargaining for decades. Throughout its history, symphony orchestra labor relations have been characterized by periodic, major labor–management conflicts owing in part to the unique characteristics of symphony orchestras. Like other performing arts, symphony orchestras confront low or no productivity increases while also facing escalating labor costs as well as revenues from performance sales that are insufficient to cover expenses. Consequently, persistent deficits have led to the closure of some symphony orchestras, while others have sought to remain viable by decreasing labor costs. The labor market for symphony musicians presents significant challenges in this regard. Musicians who are top performers in the field are not easily replaced, nor are they eager to forgo the high salaries their specialized skills warrant. In addition to these long-term challenges, several more recent developments, including the digitalization of music, the Great Recession of 2008, and the COVID-19 pandemic have placed significant pressure on managing boards to explore ways to reach new audiences, incorporate new technology, reduce operating expenses, and intensify fundraising efforts, further contributing to labor–management conflict. Unions have adjusted to those developments by continuing their efforts to retain work opportunities and wage gains for their members and provide them with a voice in the operations of orchestras.

INTRODUCTION

Throughout their history, symphony orchestras (SOs) have led a tenuous existence, often struggling against structural and cyclical forces that undermine their financial security and artistic fulfillment. Economic developments during the past decade have amplified these challenges, leading SOs to pursue a variety of new revenue-generating strategies and cost-cutting measures.

For its part, the American Federation of Musicians (AFM), which represents orchestra musicians, has resisted cost-cutting measures at the bargaining table, often allying with sympathetic community leaders, businesses, and other groups supportive of the arts. Despite these efforts, major concessions on economic items and employment levels were sometimes required to address persistent structural deficits, mounting debt, severe economic downturns, and, in some cases, threats of bankruptcy and closure. Major strikes involving the Detroit Symphony Orchestra (2010), the Chicago Symphony Orchestra (2019), and the San Antonio Symphony (2021), illustrate the particularly intense confrontations that sometimes characterized labor relations for SOs during the past 20 years.

In this chapter, we begin with a brief overview of the SO landscape in the United States. We then discuss the roles of musicians, managements, unions, and government in the development of industrial relations practices among SOs before examining the industry's distinctive characteristics, focusing particularly on the economics of SOs and challenges that have shaped industrial relations for SOs during the past decade. Subsequent sections focus on bargaining structure, recent contract negotiations and outcomes, and the occurrence and impact of labor–management conflict. We end with projections for the future of SO collective bargaining and SOs more generally, as well as efforts to ensure their long-term survival.

Our analyses examine 57 major orchestras that were members of the International Conference of Symphony Orchestra Musicians (ICSOM) during at least one of the four years included in our sample period (i.e., 2004–2005, N = 51; 2009–2010, N = 50; 2014–2015, N = 52; 2019–2020, N = 54). Data on finances and terms and conditions of employment for SOs in each sample year were obtained from "Wage Scales and Conditions in the Symphony Orchestra," an annual report of the AFM (American Federation of Musicians, no date). *Senza Sordino*, the quarterly newsletter of ICSOM, provided useful descriptions of various issues of import to orchestra musicians, as well as collective bargaining negotiations between local unions and SO management.

AN OVERVIEW OF THE SYMPHONY ORCHESTRA LANDSCAPE

There are some 1,600 SOs across the United States, operating in all 50 states and territories (League of American Orchestras 2020). Somewhere between 100 and 150 orchestras are considered professional orchestras. About 90% of all professional SOs have annual budgets of less than $2 million (League of American Orchestras 2020). The remaining have annual budgets ranging from $2 million to more than $20 million. While all orchestras have ties to their local communities, a relatively small number (e.g., New York Philharmonic, Chicago Symphony Orchestra) have a national and/or international reputation. This divide in budgets, missions, and reputations stratifies professional SOs into two main groups—major and regional. The major SOs, which are members of ICSOM, include about 50 orchestras with "at least 60 full-time members, a majority of whom are members of the AFM, and each of whose guaranteed minimum annual wage from playing in that orchestra is at least $25,000"

(ICSOM 2021: 3). The regional orchestras, which are members of the Regional Orchestra Players' Association (ROPA), include about 90 orchestras that have their principal office in the United States or its territories, an AFM collective bargaining agreement, ratified the ROPA bylaws, and are paying the required dues (Regional Orchestra Players Association 2018). Appendix A provides a list of the orchestras that were included in the major category for at least one year in our sample.

THE PARTIES
The Musicians
Musicians who obtain positions in major SOs are among the top performers in their field. Of the thousands of children who begin playing instruments, only a very small percentage later obtain positions in an SO (Allmendinger, Hackman, and Lehman 1996; Commons 1906; Flanagan 2012). In this sense, the labor market for SO musicians shares some features with "winners take all" markets (Frank and Cook 1995) in which relatively small differences in quality result in relatively larger differences in income and professional paths.

While both major and regional orchestra musicians are, by any reasonable measure, "gifted professional artists," they face working conditions not unlike those of workers in other industries and sometimes even more taxing. Despite their training, which most likely emphasized solo works and chamber music, symphony work is largely performed under conditions of relative anonymity (Arian 1974; Seltzer 1989). Individually, SO musicians have little control over their jobs, often struggling against employers' efforts to control costs and increase productivity and musical conductors who assert control over performance issues (e.g., the repertoire they perform). Not surprisingly, SO musicians have been primarily interested in improving and maintaining wages, both by increasing salaries and, also importantly, by increasing the number of weeks for which they are compensated. Symphony orchestra musicians have also sought to exercise some control over artistic and personnel matters to counter the authority given to conductors and orchestra managers through the bureaucratization of work.

The Symphony Orchestra Employer
In the United States, SOs are private institutions, organized as nonprofit organizations (Skolnick 2006), and led by SO associations and boards of directors that establish budgets and ensure sufficient funding to run the orchestras. A major function of symphony boards of directors is to secure donations and grants. Over time, the development/endowment offices of orchestras have grown as endowments have become a more significant portion of the operational revenues of orchestras (Kaiser 2015). This is reflected in the creation of the orchestra's executive director or president who, as managing the orchestra has become more complex, has acquired responsibilities in fundraising and development (Ruud 2000).

In addition, the employer is represented by the orchestra conductor or musical director. Through the first half of the 1900s, the "dominant maestro" model was part of SOs' efforts to attract larger audiences by the force of star power. The "prevailing theory was that while an orchestra was a collective of professional musicians, musical results were only guaranteed if a single, dominant leader (the conductor) was given the power to weld these musicians into a unified whole" (Fogel 2000:15). Under the dominant maestro model, musicians were terrorized by conductors' power, never rehearsing or performing "without fear of losing their jobs" (Ayer 2005: 34). The dominant maestro model began to recede in the latter half of the 1900s, as collective bargaining limited the absolute authority of conductors on personnel matters and provided voice to musicians in the selection and evaluation of conductors (Ayer 2005). At the same time, conductors became less attached to one particular orchestra, with some spending less than 50% of their time with their home institution while balancing time as guest conductors with other orchestras. Despite this development, conductors are still expected to manage the orchestra as they had in previous years (Fogel 2000).

The Symphony Orchestra Unions

Symphony orchestra musicians are represented by locals of the American Federation of Musicians (AFM), corresponding to the city or region where the orchestra is located. Ayer (2005) traces early organizing efforts involving symphony musicians to the formation of mutual aid societies in Baltimore, Chicago, and New York between the 1850s and 1880s, culminating in the formation of the National League of Musicians (NLM) in 1886. After the NLM rejected its invitation to membership, the American Federation of Labor created the AFM in 1896. At odds with the NLM, the AFM sought to represent "as many musicians as possible in order to control wages and working conditions" (Seltzer 1989). This tension played out over the next two decades until eventually the AFM absorbed the NLM, becoming the predominant musicians' union.

According to Commons (1906), by the early 1900s, the AFM had brought into membership "practically all instrumental musicians in the United States and Canada who play for a living." Despite early success in organizing orchestras, representation of SO musicians within the ranks of the locals was by all accounts inadequate. Seltzer (1989) notes that even as late as 1962, the participation of orchestra players in negotiations was rare, and they lacked the right to ratify their contracts. Because SO musicians generally make up a small proportion of the AFM local membership, the AFM tended to ignore the unique concerns of SO musicians (Ayer 2005). Consequently, local AFM chapters sometimes aligned more with management's interests than with the interests of SO musicians. Yet SO musicians had steady employment, unlike many other musician–members of the AFM, and contributed a disproportionate large share of the work dues in proportion to their membership count (Seltzer 1989).

As SO musicians became more involved in the collective bargaining process, they recognized the need for collaboration with other SOs. This ultimately led to the creation of ICSOM. At the time of its founding in 1962, ICSOM was seen as a potential competitor by the AFM and thus was not welcomed by the AFM leadership or SO management. In response to the perceived threat of dual unionism, the AFM sponsored several conferences to address the concerns of SO musicians, eventually absorbing ICSOM as a player association within the AFM. Symphony orchestra musicians became involved in local negotiations, leading to the establishment of the Symphony Department within the AFM and, importantly, to the AFM's commitment to grant symphony musicians the right to ratify by secret ballot their collective bargaining agreements (Ayer 2005). The local union has responsibility for negotiating the collective bargaining agreement, including overscale pay in some circumstances (e.g., minimum overscale amounts for "titled players" and "solo fees" for musicians playing a concerto in front of the orchestra). ICSOM provides training and research support.

The State

As in other industries, the state serves the role of regulator by providing the legal framework in which the collective bargaining process takes place. As private entities, SOs are covered under the National Labor Relations Act. Unionization and collective bargaining, however, were the norm among SOs decades before the National Labor Relations Board (NLRB) exerted jurisdiction over orchestras in 1974. Likely because organizing has not been a contested process among SOs, issues typically litigated during organizing drives, such as allegations of employer discrimination against employees for union activities or threats to employees during an organizing campaign, have been rare. Instead, litigation has centered on issues of bargaining structure and the status of musicians as employees. In *NLRB v. Kansas City Repertory Theatre* (2010), for example, the board rejected the employer's argument that some musicians included in a petitioned-for bargaining unit were ineligible to vote because they worked intermittently, reasoning that in many industries, such as construction, employees with little or no expectation of continued employment with a single employer engage in stable bargaining relationships, and thus the intermittent and temporary nature of their employment did not deprive those employees from the right to engage in collective bargaining. In *Lancaster Symphony Orchestra v. NLRB* (2016), a federal court of appeals enforced an NLRB decision finding that musicians were employees and not independent contractors. Noting that the "conductor exercises virtually dictatorial authority over the manner in which the musicians play," the court concluded it was clear that the employer exercised control over the means and the manner of musicians' performance, making the musicians employees under the appropriate legal standard (US Court of Appeals for the District of Columbia 2016).

In addition, federal, state, and local governments play the role of sponsors, providing either direct funding to SOs or indirect funding in the form of tax expenditures (allowing individuals and organizations to deduct contributions to SOs from their taxable income). Unlike most other countries, in the United States, direct public subsidies typically represent less than 10% of the major sources of income for SOs (Voss, Voss, Yair, and Lega 2016). Support from tax expenditures is significantly higher than from direct subsidies. Flanagan (2012) estimates that in 2005, the amount from tax expenditures for taxpayers at the 28% tax rate was close to $120 million, compared with about $4.5 million in direct support of SOs.

THE ECONOMICS OF SYMPHONY ORCHESTRAS
Structural Factors and Cyclical Impacts

Although SOs traditionally relied on ticket sales from symphony performances for operating revenues (Flanagan 2012), over time, this became increasingly unsustainable. Like other performing arts, SOs tend to experience no or low increases in productivity while also facing escalating labor costs in response to increasing salaries in other sectors of the economy. These dynamics, what economists refer to as the "cost disease" (Baumol and Bowen 1966; Flanagan 2012), are the root cause of persistent operating deficits for SOs (Arian 1974; Flanagan 2012; Kaiser 2015; Leonard 1974). Because performance revenues have accounted for a decreasing fraction of performance expenses, and broadcasting and recording income have failed to offset performance deficits, symphony management has become particularly sensitive to the public's music preferences for performances of pieces by well-known composers. This limits the breadth of music played by musicians and thus their opportunities for professional growth. In addition, SOs have sought sources of nonperformance income, including private philanthropy, investment income, and government subsidies. The lack of direct public funding and the corresponding reliance on contributed income require orchestras to cater more to big donors' business philosophies on how to manage the orchestra.

In addition to structural deficits, SOs are vulnerable to cyclical downturns. Economic recessions exacerbate normal financial problems confronting SOs through decreases in consumer spending on symphony performances, charitable giving (particularly by small-size donors), returns on endowment investments, and government subsidies. In short, business cycles impact both performance and nonperformance income. In some cases, persistent deficits, mounting debt, and other factors have led to the closure of SOs. Flanagan (2012) reports that between 1989 and 2010, a dozen major SOs ceased operations, with some eventually reopening under different names and missions. Since 2010, four additional bankruptcies have been reported in *Senza Sordino*, including the Philadelphia Orchestra, the Syracuse Symphony, the New York City Opera, and the San Antonio Symphony.

Evidence from Symphony Orchestra Budgets

A 2016 report by the League of American Orchestras, a national employer-side advocacy group, reported that 40% of the income of League members was from performances (earned income), 43% from donations and contributions (contributed income), and 17% from investment income (Voss, Voss, Yair, and Lega 2016). As for expenses, orchestras spend more than 65% of their budgets on personnel, with about two thirds of that amount related to artistic costs (Voss, Voss, Yair, and Lega 2016). From 2010 to 2014, nearly half of all League-member orchestras reported that expense growth exceeded inflation, and there was a substantial increase in other costs, including nonpersonnel costs (e.g., concert production) and rented hall expenses. Our results confirm these trends. Table 1 shows the quartiles for the projected annual budget for SOs in each year of our sample, as well as the budget surplus/deficit for each year. The median projected budget ranged from $17.9 million in 2005 to $24.7 million

Table 1
Symphony Orchestra Finances (3rd Quartile, **Median**, 1st Quartile, N)

	2004–2005	2009–2010	2014–2015	2019–2020
Projected annual budget	$32,289,168 **$17,935,662** $9,452,496.80 42	$43,345,000 **$25,000,000** $10,216,023 45	$40,799,829 **$20,880,827** $9,409,795.80 48	$50,846,627 **$24,713,922** $10,692,021 49
Previous year budget surplus/deficit	$94,910.25 **–$99,375** –1,229,822 38	$204,489.50 **–$111,475.50** –$2,060,114 46	$266,255 **$291** –$698,437 47	$480,739.25 **$20,895.50** –$129,801 50
Percentage of budget from earned income	47.75 **40** 32 42	45.05 **38.9** 32.15 46	46 **38** 31.8 47	43 **35** 29.8 49
Percentage of budget to musicians	48.25 **44** 35.75 42	45 **40** 33 45	47 **41** 34.77 47	46 **42.3** 34.75 50

"Wage Scales and Conditions in the Symphony Orchestra" (American Federation of Musicians, no date).

in 2020. Although this represents an increase of 38%, which exceeded the cumulative rate of inflation over that period (32.5%), the median projected budget declined from 2009–2010 to 2014–2015 before recovering in 2019–2020. For half the years in our sample, the median SO reported incurring deficits. Likely reflecting the onset of the Great Recession, the worst budget year was 2009–2010, when nearly 52% of SOs reported a budget deficit. The years 2014–2015 and 2019–2020 were markedly better, with approximately 60% and 68% reporting budget surpluses, respectively, although the median budget surpluses for those years were near zero.

Table 1 also shows that median earned income constituted well less than 50% of an SO's budget each year of the sample and declined over time. Moreover, for each of the four years, the median percentage budget from earned income was less than the median percentage of the budget paid to musicians, reflecting the trend toward a growing reliance on nonperformance income to cover the expenses of symphonic performances.

COLLECTIVE BARGAINING STRUCTURE AND ISSUES
Bargaining Structure
Symphony orchestras have distinct bargaining relationships with the local union and the AFM. Local unions negotiate traditional collective bargaining issues as they pertain to "live work." Since 1962 and 1975, ICSOM and ROPA, respectively, two player conferences within the AFM, have served as clearinghouses of information and support to local unions during contract negotiations with individual SOs. The AFM, on the other hand, represents SO musicians in negotiations over electronic media issues, setting terms and conditions of employment that apply when an SO does electronic media projects, such as live broadcasts and recordings (Gorman 1984).

Wages in SOs are specified as a minimum annual salary, which is a function of a minimum weekly base salary and the length of the orchestra season. The minimum salary is supplemented through various devices such as additional pay based on seniority and for musicians in leadership (principal) positions. Looking only at base pay for SO musicians, data in Table 2 show a nearly 18% increase in median minimum salary between 2005 and 2020, with nearly half (7.6%) occurring between 2005 and 2010. That was followed by a modest increase of 3.25% for 2010 to 2015 (which coincided with the aftermath of the Great Recession) and some signs of recovery from 2015 to 2020 as the average minimum salary increased 5.94%. The first and third quartile splits for each year of the data show larger increases in the lower quartile of the distribution of minimum annual salary over time and that minimum salaries were positively skewed for each year in our sample. Accounting for inflation, however, real earnings of SO musicians declined over time because of cumulative prices increasing 32.5% from 2005 to 2020 (US Inflation Calculator, no date). The erosion of real wages occurred after 2010 as SOs dealt with the financial fallout of the Great Recession. To maintain steady real earnings for SO musicians, the 2004–2005 median salary needed to increase to $60,314 in 2010, $65,558 in 2015, and $71,587 in 2020 (US Inflation Calculator, no date).

In addition to weekly wage and pay supplements, some contracts include Electronic Media Guarantee (EMG) payments to symphony musicians "in anticipation of media projects that may take place at some point during the season" (Newmark 2022). Under the typical agreement, musicians receive the EMG payment even if the SO does not do a media project during the season. The percentage of SOs reporting EMGs ranged from 40% in 2004–2005 to 80% in 2019–2020. Unlike minimum salaries, median EMG payments did not increase across most sample years. Although EMG payments were relatively stable at the top of the distribution, they fluctuated quite a lot at the median and lower quartile of the distribution. The data also show that EMG payments became more widely used as a form of compensation, with just 12 orchestras reporting in 2019–2020 that they did not rely on EMG payments.

Table 2
Compensation for Symphony Orchestra Musicians (3rd Quartile, **Median**, 1st Quartile, N)

	2004–2005	2009–2010	2014–2015	2019–2020
Minimum annual salary	$84,240.25	$88,866	$88,140	$96,585.50
	$54,020	**$58,111**	**$60,000**	**$63,562.50**
	$35,821.50	$37,739.50	$39,951.30	$42,867.25
	50		51	52
Electronic media guarantee	$3,401.25	$3,440	$4,413	$3,835
	$2,000	**$1,040**	**$2,000**	**$1,486**
	$1,000	$280	$900	$677.25
	20	27	33	40
No electronic media guarantee	29	22	14	12

"Wage Scales and Conditions in the Symphony Orchestra" (American Federation of Musicians, no date).

Length of Season

Because employee compensation is partly determined by the number of hours worked, SOs and musicians' unions have been concerned about the length of the orchestra season. Until the 1950s, orchestra seasons averaged less than 30 weeks (Leonard 1974). Over the 1960s, the season length increased to 38 weeks—but still not enough to allow SO musicians to only have one job (Lunden 1969). By the early 1970s, about a third of major orchestras had achieved 52-week contracts (Leonard 1974). Data from "Wage Scales and Conditions in the Symphony Orchestra" show 52-week contracts remain most common for SO musicians at major symphonies (American Federation of Musicians, no date), ranging from 36% of major orchestras for 2004–2005 and 2009–2010 to 31.3% in 2014–2015 (it was 34.6% in 2019–2020). Nearly two thirds of major SOs have season lengths that are shorter than 52 weeks, with all other season lengths occurring infrequently.

Staffing and Workload Restrictions

Generally, unions prefer a larger workforce and rules restricting how the workforce might be used by the employer. Employers generally prefer the opposite. Despite these preferences, symphonic music requires a specific number of instruments, and the number is relatively fixed to somewhere between 80 and 100 musicians (Symphony Nova Scotia 2022). This limits employers that want to reduce the size of the orchestra and unions that want to hire more musicians. It is thus not surprising that our data show the size distribution of orchestras remained remarkably stable. As seen in Table 3, the median orchestra size has been 80 musicians, with about a quarter of orchestras having 90 to 95 musicians and another quarter with 64 to 66 musicians. Overall, orchestras ranged from as small as 28 (for a chamber orchestra) to as large as 111.

Recognizing the limits to reducing labor costs by decreasing the number of musicians, SO management has sought to utilize orchestra musicians in ways they expect will increase efficiency. These efforts include increasing the number of days (services) musicians work in a week, adding more and different types of programs (e.g., showing popular movies with a live orchestra playing the music), increasing the number of concerts the orchestra performs during the year, "splitting" the orchestra to allow additional performances involving fewer musicians, and scheduling orchestra tours, which provide additional revenue and exposure for SOs. Because these productivity-enhancing efforts raise workload and compensation concerns for musicians, they too have become subjects of collective bargaining.

Data reported in Table 3 illustrate bargaining outcomes for some of these practices. For example, data show that the number of services (which includes rehearsals and concerts) has remained stable, with more than 50% of SOs limiting the number of services to eight per week. About 50% of SOs also reported restricting the maximum number of allowable unit splits to a median of two and the allowable minimum unit size to a median of 20 across all the years of our sample. However, some SOs reported no limits on the maximum number of allowable unit splits and no minimums on the allowable unit size. Though not presented in the table, data from "Wage Scales

Table 3
Staffing and Workload Restrictions (3rd Quartile, **Median**, 1st Quartile, N)

	2004–2005	2009–2010	2014–2015	2019–2020
Number of musicians	95.5	95	90	93
	80	**80**	**80**	**80**
	65.25	64.5	64.75	66.5
	48	49	50	53
Average number of services/ week	8	8	8	8
	8	**8**	**8**	**8**
	7	7	7	7
	49	50	50	52
Split orchestra: Maximum unit splits	3	3	3	3
	2	**2**	**2**	**2**
	2	2	2	2
	23	24	25	24
No maximum limit	9	10	12	10
Split orchestra: Minimum unit size	25	25.75	25	25
	20	**20**	**20**	**20**
	18	19.5	18	12
	24	22	24	27
No minimum limit	5	10	10	5
Maximum concerts per tour week	8	8	8	7.25
	7	**6**	**6**	**6**
	5	5	5	5
	25	30	30	30
Maximum days on tour per year	52	51.5	52	52.75
	42	**45**	**48**	**45.5**
	42	42	42	31.5
	15	12	11	14

"Wage Scales and Conditions in the Symphony Orchestra" (American Federation of Musicians, no date).

and Conditions in the Symphony Orchestra" show that, between 2003 and 2022, there were 15 reports that the maximum number of unit splits was negotiable, 21 reports that the minimum unit size was negotiable, and three reports of even splits for minimum unit size (American Federation of Musicians, no date). For orchestras reporting the maximum days allowed for touring each year, the limits remained fairly constant across our sample period; similar results were obtained for the maximum allowable concerts per tour week. Notably, provisions on touring restrictions appear in just about half of the orchestras in the sample, suggesting that either about half of the orchestras do not engage in touring, or if they do, no provisions have been negotiated restricting the practice.

Employee Benefits

Similar to other industries, SO unions have successfully negotiated a host of employee benefits for orchestra musicians. Data from "Wage Scales and Conditions in the

Symphony Orchestra" indicate that over 90% of orchestras provided health insurance, sick leave, paid vacations, and disability benefits during the period under study (American Federation of Musicians, no date). Pensions have been widely available for years, primarily through the American Federation of Musicians and Employer's Pension Fund (AFM-EPF), a defined benefit, multi-employer pension plan in which employers make all contributions (American Federation of Musicians 2020). For example, in 2004–2005, 38 of 41 SOs reported making contributions to the AFM-EPF. The corresponding figure for 2019–2020 was 44 of 54. In addition, unions in some orchestras have negotiated for orchestra-specific pension plans. These plans include both defined benefit and defined contribution plans, with the trend being toward the latter.

Unions have recently made inroads in negotiating parental leave. Since 2004, the number of orchestras offering parental leave increased by about 40% (from 27 to 40), with most of the increase occurring by 2010. This trend reflects the increased popularity and availability of family-friendly workplace policies and, in the context of SOs, the increased numbers of female SO musicians over the past 20 years (Ayer 2005; Hernandez 2022a).

Voice—Employee Selection and Dismissal

Symphony orchestra musicians possess specialized knowledge and share a sense of identity and culture with their colleagues (Couch 1989) and, like other professionals, SO musicians want input into key decisions affecting their employment, including protection against arbitrary hiring, discipline, and dismissal decisions. This desire is amplified because of the subjective nature of musical performance and the near-autocratic control conductors and music directors have traditionally held over employment decisions. Accordingly, SO musicians have demanded participation in the selection of music directors, membership and voting rights on boards of directors, and a voice in hiring and discipline decisions.

Data in Table 4 indicate that in 60% to 70% of major SOs, musicians have an advisory role in the selection of the music director, participation that appears to have increased over time. Roughly 40% of SOs grant musicians voting rights on the board. Likewise, nearly all SOs allow musician involvement on audition committees, which select musicians to fill vacant orchestra positions. Although the extent of their involvement can vary, the most common arrangement allows each committee member one vote in preliminary rounds of employee selection. This level of participation does not extend to final rounds of the selection process, when musicians are most likely to have an advisory role and, in nearly equal numbers, the musical director often has a more prominent role through the use of a weighted vote, with 2019–2020 being the exception, where one person/one vote was the most frequently reported arrangement.

Finally, Table 4 provides information regarding the use of blind auditions in the hiring of new musicians. With blind auditions, a screen masks the identities of musicians auditioning for SO positions (Sergeant and Himonides 2019). Our data show that while many orchestras (30% to 40%) report holding final auditions behind

Table 4
Voice, Employee Selection (Counts, N)

	2004–2005	2009–2010	2014–2015	2019–2020
Selection of music director	30	30	34	39
N	49	49	50	52
Orchestra board voting rights	21	20	22	23
N	27	28	29	31
Audition preliminary rounds:				
1 person, 1 vote	44	42	47	49
Mutually agree	0	0	0	0
Advise	1	2	0	0
Weighted vote	4	4	4	3
Other	0	1	0	0
N	49	48	51	52
Audition final round:				
1 person, 1 vote	10	12	13	21
Mutually agree	7	7	6	7
Advise	17	15	16	11
Weighted vote	14	14	15	13
Other	0	0	1	0
N	48	48	51	52
Audition behind screen:				
Yes	16	21	16	18
No	18	14	19	13
Discretionary	14	12	12	21
Other	0	0	4	0
N	48	49	51	52

"Wage Scales and Conditions in the Symphony Orchestra" (American Federation of Musicians, no date).

a screen, roughly equal numbers report not using the process, and for many others, the decision to use a blind-screen audition is discretionary. Blind auditions, which are consistently supported by unions, are credited for increasing the number of women musicians (Goldin and Rouse 2000), who now make up about half of all SO musicians, up from just about a third as recently as 2001 (Cuyler Consulting 2023; Tommasini 2021).

In addition to wanting input in the hiring process, SO musicians have sought to limit management's ability to terminate their employment. In SOs, a distinction is made between dismissal for artistic reasons (e.g., poor performance) and dismissal for nonartistic reasons (e.g., misconduct).

Data in Table 5 indicate that musicians have protected musicians' employment both for artistic and nonartistic reasons but in different ways. During the period under analysis, between 90% and 94% of orchestras used review committees that included musicians in cases involving dismissals for artistic reasons, with the trend moving toward committees composed exclusively by musicians. Likewise, although arbitration is the final authority for deciding dismissals for artistic reasons in at least 20% of SOs, review committees, usually a mix of musicians and management

Table 5
Union Voice, Dismissal (Counts, N)

	2004–2005	2009–2010	2014–2015	2019–2020
Process for Addressing Dismissals Based on Artistic Reasons				
Committee of musicians only	29	37	38	39
Committee of musicians plus management	16	10	10	8
Management only	0	0	0	1
No committee	0	0	1	2
N	45	47	49	50
Final Authority in Cases Involving Dismissal for Artistic Reasons				
Arbitration	18	11	11	12
Review committee	19	29	29	24
Hybrid (more than one process listed)	6	4	4	7
Management	5	5	6	6
Other	1	0	1	3
N	49	49	51	52
Process for Addressing Dismissals Based on Nonartistic Reasons				
Committee of musicians only	9	7	6	7
Committee of management only	0	0	1	3
Committee of musicians plus management	7	5	5	4
No committee	0	1	4	14
N	16	13	16	28
Final Authority in Cases Involving Dismissal for Nonartistic Reasons				
Arbitration	31	28	33	31
Review committee	3	3	2	3
Hybrid (more than one process listed)	3	5	6	5
Management	11	11	9	8
Other	1	0	1	2
N	49	47	51	49

"Wage Scales and Conditions in the Symphony Orchestra" (American Federation of Musicians, no date).

personnel, are most common. In contrast, review committees are used by only about a quarter to a third of orchestras in cases involving dismissal for nonartistic reasons. Instead, musicians have limited management's role as the final authority in nonartistic dismissal through traditional just-cause contract provisions, assigning the final decision to labor arbitrators in roughly 60% of SOs.

STRIKES/LOCKOUTS AND GENERAL STATE OF LABOR RELATIONS

Throughout the AFM's history, collective bargaining has been characterized by periodic work stoppages, which have increased over time. Before 1960, strikes involving SO musicians were very rare and concentrated among the "most prestigious" orchestras in large cities like Chicago, New York, and Philadelphia (Leonard 1974). The number of strikes increased in the 1960s and spread to orchestras in cities of varying sizes including Kansas City, Minneapolis, Rochester, and San Diego. The number and frequency of strikes remained fairly constant over the next several decades, with about ten strikes occurring per decade (Flanagan 2012). Data in Table 6, collected from *Senza Sordino,* indicate that between 2000 and 2021, there were 24 work stoppages among ICSOM orchestras, which included 14 strikes and 10 lockouts, with work stoppages lasting between five days and sixteen months.

Decisions about whether to strike might be complicated by the nature of SOs. Because money from ticket sales rarely covers the cost of a performance, a performance canceled due to a strike effectively reduces the deficit, which helps the employer by limiting the utility of the strike weapon to the union (Arian 1971). On the other

Table 6
Symphony Orchestra Work Stoppages, 2000–2020 (as reported in *Senza Sordino*)

Year	Symphony orchestra	Type of work stoppage	Duration
2021	San Antonio Symphony	Strike	Bankruptcy filed and orchestra liquidated
2019	Chicago Symphony	Strike	46 days
	Baltimore Symphony	Lockout	95 days
2018	Chicago Lyric Opera	Strike	5 days
2016	Fort Worth Symphony	Strike	3 months
	Pittsburgh Symphony	Strike	55 days
	Philadelphia Orchestra	Strike	2 days
2014	Atlanta Symphony	Lockout	9 weeks
2013	St. Paul Chamber Orchestra	Strike	191 days
	San Francisco Symphony	Strike	19 days
2012	Minnesota Orchestra	Lockout	16 months
	Atlanta Symphony	Lockout	5 weeks
	Chicago Symphony	Strike	1 day
	Indianapolis Symphony	Lockout	5 weeks
2011	Detroit Symphony	Strike	6 months
	Louisville Orchestra	Lockout	12 months
2008	Columbus Symphony	Lockout	6 months
2007	Jacksonville Symphony	Lockout	9 weeks
2005	St. Louis Symphony	Lockout	8 weeks
2004	Charlotte Symphony	Strike	8 weeks
2003	Houston Symphony	Strike	24 days
	Louisville Orchestra	Strike	5 services*
2000	NY City Ballet Orchestra	Lockout	12 days
	Florida Philharmonic**	Strike	27 days

*After not being paid for a month, musicians withheld their labor for four rehearsals and a concert.
**Though not a member now, it was a member of ICSOM in 2000.

hand, SOs are generally cherished cultural institutions in their community, a reputation that SO musicians have been able to leverage when engaging in strikes, and which makes it more costly for SO employers to endure a long work stoppage.

Three recent negotiations involving prominent SOs and their unions reveal the challenges and conflicts that often arise in collective bargaining negotiations.

The Chicago Symphony Orchestra (2019–2020)

The Chicago Symphony Orchestra (CSO), Local 10-208 of the AFM, holds a prominent place in the history of collective bargaining among SOs. The local was led by the colorful James Petrillo, who had served many years as president of the AFM. Petrillo resented SO musicians and minimized their concerns. In the 1962 negotiations, he sided with the orchestra's management and Chicago mayor Richard J. Daley against the SO musicians' demands to increase wages and the length of the orchestra season. Despite their efforts, the musicians achieved their goals at the bargaining table and gained leverage within the AFM, leading eventually to the formation of ICSOM (Ayer 2005).

Fast forward almost 60 years to negotiations in 2019, and you find evidence of continuing tension with the CSO's management. Among the issues that dominated the 2019–2020 negotiations were pensions and salaries. Management sought to switch the musicians from a defined benefit pension plan to a defined contribution plan, a move musicians viewed as an attempt to shift the risk of retirement benefits to employees (Reich 2019d). For their part, musicians wanted parity with West Coast orchestras such as those in Los Angeles and San Francisco (Reich 2019c). Prior to negotiations, the CSO Association reported that despite ticket sales increasing by over $1 million for the 2017–2018 season, the institution was still operating at a $900,000 deficit (Reich 2019a).

After about nine months of negotiations, the musicians authorized a strike, which began when the previous contract expired. The union characterized management's approach as following a "scorched earth strategy," as illustrated by management's hiring of a labor attorney who had led difficult negotiations in the airline industry in the early 2000s (Lester 2019). Musicians contended that management sought to satisfy its good-faith bargaining obligations by appearing to negotiate minor issues while refusing to compromise on critical areas (Lester 2019). Musicians accused management of distorting their demands to the public and threatening members of other unions to prevent them from assisting with closing Orchestra Hall, where the CSO performs.

The musicians in turn hired a communications firm to help with messaging to the public. They organized multiple free performances across the city, as well as several rallies in front of Orchestra Hall. A major development during the strike was support musicians received from Riccardo Muti, the CSO music director, who "shattered precedent" by joining the musicians during the first week of the strike, stating that he was "there with my musicians" and encouraging management to listen to the musicians' demands (Reich 2019b). The CSO musicians also received in-person and financial support from musicians in other SOs. Reportedly using back channels, and with substantial public pressure to resolve the conflict, Rahm Emanuel, mayor of Chicago, was convinced to intervene and mediate a resolution that resulted in the parties reaching an agreement (Lester 2019).

The negotiations produced a 13.25% wage increase over five years and allowed management to discontinue the defined benefit plan for new musicians and to transition to a defined contribution plan by freezing benefits for existing employees and giving members several years to switch to a defined contribution plan.

The Detroit Symphony Orchestra (2009–2020)

The Detroit Symphony Orchestra (DSO) is one of the oldest professional symphonic orchestras in the United States, holding its first season in 1887. In 2009, the DSO experienced the longest strike in its history and one of the longest among SOs in the country. Negotiations leading to the strike started in the middle of the 2008 financial crisis. At the time, the DSO was dealing with reduced ticket revenues, a declining donor base, and a debt burden it acquired in 2003 from expansion of the concert hall where the orchestra regularly performed (Stryker 2011b). To a large extent, the 2009–2011 negotiations were about how much wages and benefits would be cut. In early proposals, the DSO board proposed a 28% to 32% reduction in minimum wages, a change from 11 to 16 layoff weeks, and a reduction in the size of the orchestra from 96 to about 82 musicians. The musicians were willing to accept a 22% reduction in wages, up to 11 weeks of layoffs for a year, and a temporary reduction in the number of musicians to 82, followed by a gradual increase back to 88 musicians (Johnson 2010). While these proposals would likely result in difficult negotiations, the strike was attributed to management's goal of embracing a more flexible and entrepreneurial mode of operation. A particularly contentious issue for musicians was the DSO's "service conversion" proposal, which would allow management to assign musicians other duties (such as teaching, small-group performances, and library work during the year) instead of the usual rehearsals or performances by the full orchestra (McKay 2010).

After six months, which included mediation attempts by political and business leaders, the parties reached a three-year contract that included a 23% pay cut, a reduction in work weeks from 52 to 36, and a reduction in the number of musicians from 96 to 81. The parties also agreed to allocate $2 million for community outreach initiatives, allowing management to schedule musicians for such programs and giving management more flexibility to reach new audiences (Stryker 2011a).

In 2014 and 2017, on the other hand, negotiations were completed several months before the previous contracts expired and were characterized by an atmosphere of trust, with a focus on "artistic growth" (Senza Sordino 2017). Not surprisingly, the 2014 and 2017 agreements included efforts to recover wage losses from 2010. Moreover, divisive issues from earlier negotiations provided the source of innovative solutions. For instance, on the number of service weeks, the parties went from 40 weeks plus 12 guaranteed services in 2016 to 42 weeks in 2017. To help alleviate the effect of the shortened season (compared with the pre-2010 agreement), the contract provided musicians with a stipend during nonwork weeks of about $2,000. Finally, on the dispute over service conversion, musicians agreed to donate up to four services per season, to be scheduled during weeks when musicians were paid at a reduced rate, and two services that would be used for revenue-generating gala concerts (Hodges 2017). The goodwill generated in these negotiations continued in negotiations for the 2020–2023 contract, as evidenced by pay raises that increased annual salaries back above where they were nominally before the 2010 strike.

The San Antonio Symphony (2020–2022)

Founded in 1939, the San Antonio Symphony (SAS) has had, by industry standards, a difficult existence. During the past 40 years, the SAS experienced work stoppages in 1984, 1987, and 1998, and bankruptcies in 2003 and 2022. The union and the SAS Society's most recent three-year agreement was negotiated in 2019. In 2020, the parties reopened negotiations to address disruptions caused by the COVID-19 pandemic, leading to substantial reductions in pay. The parties again reopened negotiations in 2021. The reopener clause required the parties to engage in interest-based bargaining (IBB) facilitated through the Federal Mediation and Conciliation Service (Goree 2021). After failing to reach agreement through IBB, the Society proposed to cut pay 50% and convert part of the orchestra to part-time-status musicians. The union countered with a proposed pay cut of 17%, four weeks of furlough, and a joint musician–management fundraising initiative. The Society's final offer proposed to divide the orchestra into two groups—a core group of 42 musicians with an average annual base pay of $24,000 plus benefits and a group of 26 musicians with a minimum annual pay of $11,250 and no benefits, and to reduce the symphony season from 31 to 24 weeks. After the union rejected this last offer, the Society declared an impasse and imposed the terms of its offer. In response, the union filed unfair labor practice charges and declared an unfair labor practice strike (Martin 2021b). The Society likewise filed unfair labor practice charges against the union, accusing the union of failing to take the IBB process seriously (Martin 2021a).

During the strike, the union conducted frequent rallies in front of the hall where they regularly performed. The union also secured the support of ICSOM and other orchestras. In January 2022, after being on strike for nearly four months, the union offered to return to work under the terms of the existing collective bargaining agreement—but without back pay for the missing performances. The union estimated that the proposal represented a 35% to 50% concession (Katz 2022). The Society rejected the offer, canceled or postponed most performances, and terminated the health insurance of the striking players (Hernández 2021).

As other striking musicians have done, members of the SAS organized various concerts for the public. They invited Sebastian Lang-Lessing, the orchestra conductor, to participate. Lang-Lessing had expressed concerns about management's proposal, calling it "not realistic" and "immoral." After Lang-Lessing accepted the musicians' invitation to conduct two free concerts, management invoked a provision in his contract that prohibited him from making or announcing any appearances in San

Antonio within 60 days of a scheduled symphony performance and terminated his contract (Garcia 2022).

In June 2022, the Society declared bankruptcy and closed its doors. According to management, the SAS had become too costly, particularly during the COVID-19 pandemic (Hernández 2022b). Nine weeks later, a group of musicians announced the creation of the San Antonio Philharmonic, a musician-led organization. The new orchestra announced a ten-week classical season, three pops concerts, and five school performances (Nowlin 2022).

CHALLENGES FACING SYMPHONY ORCHESTRAS
Foretelling an Uncertain Future

Predictions about the future of SOs have long been largely pessimistic. In fact, shortly after the establishment of permanent orchestras in US cities, observers noted the severe financial challenges they must overcome to survive (Aldrich 1903). As these problems persisted, some predicted that at least one third, maybe even half, of major SOs could close between 1971 and 1973 (*Time* 1969). Similar dire concerns about the long-term prospects of SOs, as well as other arts organizations in the United States, have been expressed more recently (Flanagan 2012; Kaiser 2015).

The more apocalyptic of these narratives predicted that growing structural deficits, along with periodic economic downturns, would lead to more bankruptcies, leaving fewer professional SOs. Regional orchestras were expected to be especially at risk, with only the largest, most prominent orchestras standing a good chance of survival. Under the most pessimistic scenario, it was expected that there would be an "epidemic of labor problems in the orchestral world for decades to come" (Kaiser 2015: 70) as SO managements increasingly rely on hardball negotiations, threatening closure to extract concessions from unions. Despite many dire predictions of existential threats to their survival, SOs in the United States, with a few exceptions, have survived, and in many cases have thrived. Nonetheless, the nature and severity of these existential threats are once again illustrated by two recent events: the COVID-19 pandemic and the dramatic increase in inflation and accompanying threats of a looming recession.

The COVID-19 Pandemic

The COVID-19 pandemic brought the production of symphonic services to a total halt in early 2020. Once social gatherings restarted, performances were limited in the number of performers and size of the audience. Performances did not fully resume to pre-pandemic levels until 2022, leaving many orchestras hurt financially.

Collective bargaining proved its resilience and adaptability, as it has in other crises. To provide some measure of stability, multiple orchestras extended their collective bargaining agreements for one or two years (Bray 2020; Corbató 2020; Ross 2020). Recognizing the unprecedented nature of the crisis, many major orchestras continued paying musicians some, or most, of their salaries, even if performances were canceled (Carrick 2020; Hernández 2021). Moreover, orchestras relied primarily on two forms of government assistance: the Shuttered Venue Operators Grants and the Paycheck Protection Program (Noonan 2021), which nearly every orchestra received (Case 2022). Finally, recognizing management's need to generate revenue, the AFM negotiated new side letters to the IMA, allowing more flexibility in the streaming of recorded content when live performances were interrupted (Skolnick and Newmark 2020).

Inflation and Recession

As this chapter is being prepared, the United States and the rest of the world are still dealing with the economic and social disruptions caused by the pandemic. Inflation rates reached the highest level they had been in 40 years (Isidore 2022), and while they have decreased significantly, they remain higher than before the start of the pandemic (Winters 2023). Attempts by the US Federal Reserve to control inflation appear to have worked, albeit slowly, and it now appears likely that those efforts will prevent a recession. Moreover, employment growth has remained steady.

While we do not yet have a full picture of the pandemic's effects on ticket sales, there is no question that, during 2020 and 2021, ticket sales dropped. Persistent high inflation could further negatively affect ticket sales and revenues, potentially negating the improved financial positions that orchestras experienced between 2015 and 2020. At a minimum, some SOs will likely claim financial hardship from reduced revenues, though these impacts may be mitigated by pandemic relief funding from the government (Case 2022). At the same time, inflationary pressure may lead musicians to seek higher salaries to maintain purchasing power and recover concessions made at the height of the pandemic. Consequently, the next round of negotiations might be more contentious, perhaps leading to strikes, lockouts, and even bankruptcies, as illustrated by the recent experience of the SAS.

Data indicate that philanthropic giving to the arts, culture, and humanities had increased in the two years prior to the pandemic by over 13.5%, adjusted for inflation (Case 2022). The stock market also performed relatively well during the pandemic, which should have increased the wealth of foundations, corporations, and wealthy individual donors who might have been in a better position to support orchestras. Unexpectedly, owing to the elimination of production expenses from canceled performances, pandemic-related government assistance, market gains that increased endowments, and continued gifts from donors, some orchestras amassed surpluses in the 2020 to 2022 seasons.

Considering the dual effects of an unprecedented pandemic and the ever-present specter of economic uncertainty, what might be a reasonable path forward?

Fine-Tuning Symphony Orchestra Budgets for Long-Term Survival

As nonprofits, SOs are not expected to achieve large operating surpluses. However, their long-term survival depends on a proper balance between income and expenses. Given ongoing challenges with structural deficits and periodic economic downturns, financial success requires attention to three broad strategies: finding new ways to raise performance revenue, increasing nonperformance income, and slowing the growth of expenses.

Raising Performance Revenue

Because the demand for symphonic performances is highly elastic, raising ticket prices has not been a viable long-term strategy to increase revenue. Instead, SOs must continue to pursue alternative approaches. For instance, instead of relying on the sale of subscription tickets, where customers buy curated plans with predetermined performances and dates, orchestras have experimented with "customized subscriptions" in which buyers put together their own series (Waleson 2015). Customized subscriptions may raise revenues by matching more individualized consumption patterns in the digital economy, and they may also reveal customer preferences regarding specific performances, which in turn helps orchestras select repertoires that align more with the musical preferences of the public.

In addition to better serving existing patrons, SOs must expand their consumer base through more aggressive community engagement and education efforts, implementing new marketing campaigns, recording and streaming performances, and adding performances away from orchestra halls, locally, nationally, and internationally. While not explicitly redefining their mission, multiple orchestras have sought to engage with the community, reach new audiences, and demonstrate their relevance by participating in a variety of socially minded initiatives, including community health, access to food, social justice, and low-cost musical lessons.

Another innovation has come from new streams of earned income, such as renting of concert halls where SOs perform, holding music education programs for children, and contracting with third parties to produce a performance, so-called impresario activities, which have become a larger proportion of earned income, topping 34% in 2014 (Voss, Voss, Yair, and Lega 2016).

All these initiatives to increase revenue and generate new audiences for orchestras require more effort from musicians in the form of additional services for which musicians will expect appropriate compensation.

Increasing Nonperformance Income

Because of the increasing importance of nonperformance revenue to the financial well-being of SOs, there will be a greater need for SOs to become "fundraising machines" (Kaiser 2015: 86). The quest to identify and develop new donors will further shift the balance of power toward the donor base, which, as described above, might bring more confrontation to the way management conducts its affairs with employees and unions, as illustrated in the 2019 negotiations involving the Chicago Symphony Orchestra.

Slowing the Growth of Expenses
In addition to challenges on the revenue side, SOs face structural barriers to reducing operating costs. As mentioned previously, employment levels are driven primarily by the symphonic repertoire, which requires a specific number of musicians and thus are not easily reduced. SOs are also limited in their ability to decrease costs by the need to hold concerts in venues with acoustics required of a high-quality performance; the necessity for rehearsals, even though they do not produce revenue (Leonard 1974); and the costs of hiring well-known soloists and conductors, who demand premium compensation.

Because of these constraints, symphony management often emphasizes limiting wage and benefits increases or demanding reductions in the orchestra season (*Senza Sordino*, various issues). The labor market for symphony musicians presents significant challenges in this regard. Symphony musicians are among the top performers for their instruments and are not easily replaced. Nor are they eager to forgo the high salaries their specialized skills warrant. Symphony musicians also experience long employment tenure, which over time places upward pressure on wages. Thus, reducing costs by cutting salaries is not likely a viable option.

CONCLUSION

As is true in many other industries, collective bargaining proved to be an adaptable mechanism that helped orchestras and their musician employees respond to many challenges over the past century. By enabling musicians to improve wages and working conditions, collective bargaining promoted a steady and robust supply of professional musicians who can devote their careers to their symphonic jobs. By providing musicians with a voice in the operations of orchestras, collective bargaining allowed musicians to engage with donors and the broader community, securing, in that way, much-needed funding for orchestras. And finally, collective bargaining provided an avenue for unions and orchestras to creatively respond to technological changes and unexpected crises, such as the COVID-19 pandemic. Symphony orchestras and their unions have managed to survive "perilous times" before (Flanagan 2012) and, despite persistent challenges, recent successful negotiations suggest that they will do so again.

ACKNOWLEDGMENTS

The authors are listed alphabetically. We thank Julie Ayer, Kevin Case, Victor Devinatz, Felix A. Guadalupe, Rochelle Skolnick, and Gil Vernon, for their helpful comments and suggestions and Anne Tauzin for assisting with data collection. Professor Gely dedicates this chapter to his long-time music teacher, Maestro Agustín Guadalupe.

APPENDIX: MAJOR SYMPHONY ORCHESTRAS DURING SAMPLE YEARS (2004–2005, 2009–2010, 2014–2015, 2019–2020)

Symphony orchestra	Year of entry	Years in sample	Symphony orchestra	Year of entry	Years in sample
Alabama Symphony	1998	All	Louisville Orchestra	1980	All
Atlanta Symphony	1971	All	Metropolitan Opera	1962	All
Baltimore Symphony	1962	All	Milwaukee Symphony	1970	All
Boston Symphony	1962	All	Minnesota Orchestra	1962	All
Buffalo Philharmonic	1963	All	Nashville Symphony	1975	All
Charlotte Symphony	1999	All	National Symphony	1963	All
Chicago Lyric Opera	1969	All	New Jersey Symphony	1973	All
Chicago Symphony	1962	All	New York City Ballet Orchestra	1968	All
Cincinnati Symphony	1962	All	New York City Opera	1970	All
Cleveland Orchestra	1962	All	New York Philharmonic	1962	All
Colorado Symphony	1989	All	North Carolina Symphony	1972	All
Columbus Symphony	1990	All	Oregon Symphony	1971	All
Dallas Symphony	1968	All	Philadelphia Orchestra	1962	All
Detroit Symphony	1962	All	Phoenix Symphony	1974	All
Florida Orchestra	1987	All	Pittsburgh Symphony	1962	All
Fort Worth Symphony	2001	All	Puerto Rico Symphony	2003	2005, 2015, 2020
Grand Rapids Symphony	2013	2015, 2020	Rochester Philharmonic	1962	All
Grant Park Symphony	1977	All	Saint Louis Symphony	1962	All
Hawai'i Symphony	2011	2015, 2020	Saint Paul Chamber Orchestra	1984	All
Honolulu Symphony	1967	2005, 2010	San Antonio Symphony	1968	All
Houston Symphony	1965	All	San Diego Symphony	1974	All
Indianapolis Symphony	1962	All	San Francisco Ballet	1977	All
Jacksonville Symphony	1997	All	San Francisco Opera	1983	All
Kansas City Symphony	1998	All	San Francisco Symphony	1963	All
Kennedy Center Combined Orchestra	X	2020	Symphoria	2012	2015, 2020
Kennedy Center Washington National Opera	X	2020	Utah Symphony	1979	All
Kennedy Center Orchestra	X	2005, 2010, 2015	Virginia Symphony	2000	All
Los Angeles Philharmonic	1962	All			

REFERENCES

Aldrich, R. 1903. "'Permanent Orchestra' Season a Bad One." *New York Times*. May 3.

Allmendinger, J., J.R. Hackman, and E.V. Lehman. 1996. "Life and Work in Symphony Orchestras." *Musical Quarterly* 80, no. 2: 194–219.

American Federation of Musicians. 2020. "American Federation of Musicians—Employer Pension Fund, AMF-EPF Summary Plan Description." http://tinyurl.com/2ujr2kpr

———. No date. "Wage Scales and Conditions in the Symphony Orchestra." [member login required]

Arian, E. 1971. *Bach, Beethoven, and Bureaucracy: The Case of the Philadelphia Orchestra*. Tuscaloosa, AL: University of Alabama Press.

———. 1974. "Some Problems of Collective Bargaining in Symphony Orchestras." *Labor Law Journal* 25, no. 11: 666–672.

Ayer, J. 2005. *More Than Meets the Ear: How Symphony Musicians Made Labor History*. Minneapolis, MN: Syren Book Company.

Baumol, W.J., and W.G. Bowen. 1966. *The Performing Arts, the Economic Dilemma: Study of Problems Common to Theater, Opera, Music, and Dance*. New York, NY: Twentieth Century Fund.

Bray, B. 2020. "No Cuts." *Senza Sordino* 58, no. 4: 6–7.

Carrick, K. 2020. "COVID-19 Agreements: Trends and the Takeaway." *Senza Sordino* 58, no. 2: 1, 6–7.

Case, K. 2022. "Counsel's Column." *Senza Sordino* 60, no. 3: 4–5, 7.

Commons, J.R. 1906. "Types of American Labor Unions—The Musicians of St. Louis and New York." *Quarterly Journal of Economics* 20, no. 3: 419–422.

Corbató, B. 2020. "Collaboration in Grand Rapids." *Senza Sordino* 58, no. 4: 3–4.

Couch, S.R. 1989. "The Orchestra as Factory: Interrelationships of Occupational Change, Social Structure and Musical Style." In *Art and Society: Readings in the Sociology of the Arts*, edited by A.W. Foster and J.R. Blau. Albany, NY: State University of New York Press.

Cuyler Consulting. 2023. "Racial/Ethnic and Gender Diversity in the Orchestra Field in 2023: A Report by the League of American Orchestras." http://tinyurl.com/346ybdny

Flanagan, R.J. 2012. *The Perilous Life of Symphony Orchestras: Artistic Triumphs and Economic Challenges*. New Haven, CT: Yale University Press.

Fogel, H. 2000. "Are Three Legs Appropriate? Or Even Sufficient?" *Harmony*, no. 10: 11–34.

Frank, R., and P. Cook. 1995. *The Winner-Take-All Society: Why the Few at the Top Get So Much More Than the Rest of Us*. New York, NY: Free Press.

Frost, A. 2013. "Introduction: Collective Bargaining Under Duress: Case Studies of Major U.S. Industries." In *Collective Bargaining Under Duress: Cases Studies of Major U.S. Industries*, edited by H. Stanger, A. Frost, and P. Clark, 1–8. Champaign, IL: Labor and Employment Relations Association.

Garcia, G. 2022. "Dismissal of Lang–Lessing Was a Shameful Act." *San Antonio Express News*. April 20, p. A2.

Goldin, C., and C. Rouse. 2000. "Orchestrating Impartiality: The Impact of 'Blind' Auditions on Female Musicians." *American Economic Review* 90, no. 4: 715–741.

Goree, M.E. 2021. "An Intolerable Situation in San Antonio." *Senza Sordino* 59, no. 4: 1, 10.

Gorman, R. 1984. "The Recording Musician and Union Power: A Case Study of the American Federation of Musicians." *Southwestern Law Journal* 37, no. 4: 697–787.

Hernández, J.C. 2021. (Dec. 21). "The Pandemic Struck Orchestras with Underlying Conditions Hard." *New York Times*. December 21. http://tinyurl.com/jha33bec

———. 2022a. "In a 'Sea of Change,' Women of the Philharmonic Now Outnumber the Men." *New York Times*. November 22. http://tinyurl.com/wwt8rhwu
———. 2022b. "San Antonio Symphony to Dissolve Amid Labor Dispute." *New York Times*. June 17. http://tinyurl.com/yku2ajw6.
Hodges, M. 2017. "Musicians Ratify a New, Three-Year Contract with DSO." *Detroit News*. January 10. http://tinyurl.com/4vpmmt5v
International Conference of Symphony Orchestra Musicians. 2021. "Bylaws of the International Conference of Symphony Orchestra Musicians." On file with the authors.
Isidore, C. 2022. "This Is the Worst Inflation in Nearly 40 Years: But It Was Much Worse Back Then." CNN Business. January 12.
Johnson, L. 2010. "What the 2 Sides Are Proposing." *Detroit News*. August 19.
Kaiser, M. 2015. *Curtains? The Future of the Arts in America*. Waltham, MA: Brandeis University Press.
Katz, D. 2022. "Striking Musicians Propose New Offer to San Antonio Symphony." Texas Public Radio. January 12. http://tinyurl.com/4nv6db38
Lancaster Symphony Orchestra v. NLRB, 822 F.3d 563 (2016).
League of American Orchestras. 2020. "Orchestras at a Glance." http://tinyurl.com/ycx9trba
Leonard, A. 1974. "Collective Bargaining in Major Orchestras." *Industrial & Labor Relations Forum* 10: 386–417.
Lester, S. 2019. "Behind the Picket Line." *Senza Sordino* 57, no. 2: 1, 9–10.
Lunden, L. 1969. "Bargaining in Major Symphony Orchestras." *Monthly Labor Review* 92, no. 75: 17–21.
Martin, D. 2021a. "S.A. Symphony Files Complaint Against Union." *San Antonio Express News*. November 4, p. A6.
———. 2021b. "Symphony Union Accuses Board of Unfair Practices." *San Antonio Express News*. October 26, p. A3.
McKay, H. 2010. "Difficult Days in Detroit." *Senza Sordino* 48, no. 3: 6–7.
NLRB v. Kansas City Repertory Theatre, 356 NLRB No. 147 (2010).
Newmark, D. 2022. "Electronic Media Guarantees." *International Musician*. July 1. http://tinyurl.com/4839jpjp
Noonan, H. 2021. "2021 COVID-19 Legislative Relief: An Overview." *Senza Sordino* 59, no. 1: 5–7.
Nowlin, S. 2022. "The San Antonio Philharmonic Has Risen from the Symphony's Ashes. What's Next?" *San Antonio Current*. September 7. http://tinyurl.com/4p5fjuys
Regional Orchestras Players Association. 2018. "ROPA Bylaws." http://tinyurl.com/4xfj8xy2
Reich, H. 2019a. "Chicago Symphony Orchestra Strike Negotiations to Resume." *Chicago Tribune*. February 4, p. 2.
———. 2019b. "Putting the Pieces Back Together." *Chicago Tribune*. April 30, p. 1.
———. 2019c. "Striking CSO Musicians Push to Restart Negotiations." *Chicago Tribune*. April 25, p. 5.
———. 2019d. "Striking CSO Musicians, Management Make Deal." *Chicago Tribune*. April 19, p. 2.
Ross, L. 2020. "Music on Our Own." *Senza Sordino* 58, no. 4: 5–6.
Ruud, G. 2000. "The Symphony: Organizational Discourse and the Symbolic Tensions Between Artistic and Business Ideologies." *Journal of Applied Communication Research* 28, no. 2: 117–143.

Seltzer, G. 1989. *Music Matters: The Performer and the American Federation of Musicians.* Metuchen, NJ: Scarecrow Press.

Senza Sordino. 2017. "Newslets: Early Contract Settlement in Detroit." *Senza Sordino* 55, no. 1: 10.

Sergeant, D.C., and E. Himonides. 2019. "Orchestrated Sex: The Representation of Male and Female Musicians in World-Class Symphony Orchestras." *Frontiers in Psychology* 10, article 1760.

Skolnick, R. 2006. "Control, Collaboration or Coverage: The NLRA and the St. Paul Chamber Orchestra Dilemma." *Washington University Journal of Law and Policy* 20, no. 1: 403–442.

Skolnick, R., and D. Newmark. 2020. "Electronic Media for a 'COVID Season.'" *Senza Sordino* 58, no. 3: 4–7.

Stanger, H.R., A. Frost, and P. Clark, eds. 2013. *Collective Bargaining Under Duress: Cases Studies of Major U.S. Industries.* Champaign, IL: Labor and Employment Relations Association.

Stryker, Mark. 2011a. "DSO Musicians Officially OK 23% Cut." *Detroit Free Press.* April 9, p. A2.

———. 2011b. "DSO Suspends Season." *Detroit Free Press.* February 20, p. A7.

Symphony Nova Scotia. 2022. "How Is the Composition of a Symphony Orchestra Decided Upon?" http://tinyurl.com/mr89rb7d

Time. 1969. "American Orchestras: The Sound of Trouble." June 13. http://tinyurl.com/749j48wp

Tommasini, A. 2021. "To Make Orchestras More Diverse, End Blind Auditions." *New York Times*, July 16. http://tinyurl.com/29ra55h5

US Court of Appeals for the District of Columbia. 2016. *Lancaster Symphony Orchestra v. NLRB*, 822 F.3d 563.

US Inflation Calculator. No date. https://usinflationcalculator.com

Voss, Z.G., G. Voss, K. Yair, and K. Lega. 2016. "Orchestra Facts: 2006–2014: A Study of Orchestra Finances and Operations, Commissioned by the League of American Orchestras." http://tinyurl.com/5yww2ubd

Waleson, H. 2015. "Reimagining the Orchestra Subscription Model." *Symphony*, Fall: 30–35.

Winters, M. 2023. "Inflation Just Dropped to 6.5%." CNBC. January 12.

CHAPTER 5

Trucking Collective Bargaining: The Problem of Conflicting Labor Market Governance

MICHAEL H. BELZER
Wayne State University

Abstract

The commercial trucking industry plays a critical role in the US economy. Collective bargaining in this industry has changed over time in many important ways. This chapter provides an overview of unionization and collective bargaining in the US trucking industry. It also details the public policy and industry changes that have shaped bargaining in this key industry.

OVERVIEW OF THE TRUCKING INDUSTRY

Trucks account for an enormous proportion of all vehicle miles traveled in the United States. Of the 3,132.4 billion miles traveled by all highway vehicles, trucks account for 327.0 billion (10.4%) of these miles. The typical loaded tractor-trailer truck, however, weighs about 20 times as much as the typical automobile and takes up more space, putting more stress on highways. The US Department of Transportation (US DOT) Federal Motor Carrier Safety Administration (FMCSA), which regulates trucking, reports that there are 813,844 interstate motor carriers and intrastate carriers of hazardous (HAZMAT) materials. FMCSA regulations require that interstate and HAZMAT drivers have commercial driver's licenses (CDLs), and about 5.3 million drivers have CDLs ("Pocket Guide" 2023). However, many of these licenses are earned by those who train to become truck drivers and may do it for a few weeks or months, but an unknown number of such drivers walk away from trucking every year and do not use their licenses for the purposes for which the CDL was intended. Indeed, about 17% of all CDLs are used at any given time to operate heavy and tractor-trailer trucks, and at most, about one third are used by commercial truck and bus drivers at any moment.

The trucking industry has a complex structure and serves a multitude of functions. Even though some big companies occupy prominent positions in the market, the industry overall is highly decentralized and fragmented. Perhaps the most important distinction is between trucking companies that haul freight for the public—defined as shippers of goods produced or distributed by themselves but delivered by companies that do the trucking work on behalf of these shippers—and those that haul freight on their own behalf, or on their "own account"; these are called "private" or "not-for-hire" carriers. The trucking industry, *qua* industry, hauls freight within this framework. They are called "for-hire" carriers because shippers hire them to transport freight for them (Burks et al. 2010). In effect, most shippers outsource their freight hauling to for-hire motor carriers rather than try to deliver the freight themselves because it is more efficient and likely less costly.

Private carriers serve companies by delivering the products and often accompanying services that these companies produce or distribute. While some private carriers may be separately constituted as transportation divisions, they still almost entirely serve these firms. Examples might include grocery companies, which may haul their own freight from warehouse to store.[1] Walmart, which has a distribution division with highly paid tractor-trailer drivers that keeps their stores stocked properly; and industrial gas and hazardous waste companies, which value the product-handling skill and reliability of truck drivers they control as employees and consider outsourcing to trucking firms and drivers a risky proposition. These kinds of firms value this phase of their operation highly and want to make sure the shelves are ready for customers who are looking to buy the products they sell, or they service their customers in more complex and customized ways and believe that repeat customer service experience and safety are paramount.

The for-hire road transport sector is segmented according to the freight hauled as well as by the size of the shipment. The most commonly understood freight segment is general freight trucking (NAICS 4841), which accounts for 70% of all truck transportation service employment ("Truck Transportation," NAICS 484 [Table 1] 2023c), and specialized freight trucking (NAICS 4842).

Specialized freight trucking, which accounts for 30% of truck transportation employment overall, has three subsegments: used household and office goods moving (NAICS 48421; 21% of specialized freight trucking); specialized freight (except used goods) trucking, local (NAICS 48422; 46% of specialized freight trucking); and specialized freight (except used goods) trucking, long-distance (NAICS 48423; 34% of specialized freight trucking). Used goods transport—moving vans—provides interaction with consumers that is well understood but operates under a substantially different economic regulatory regime than that covering all other truckers. The last two categories of specialized freight trucking include heavy machinery, steel, and bulk solids and liquids, among others. They comprise a significant component of trucking—about 24% of truck transportation overall—and represent an important part of the trucking industry that supports industrial supply chains ("Truck Transportation" 2023c).

General freight trucking employees may be local (25%) or long distance (75%), and long-distance firms may further be subdivided into truckload (TL; 66%) and less than truckload (LTL; 34%). Local trucking can also be subdivided into TL and LTL. Local trucking may include bulk cargo (specialized) and TL general freight, as well as intermodal cargo box freight (an intermodal container is counted as a

Table 1
Number of Firms and Establishments, Employment, and Annual Payroll by State, Industry, and Enterprise Employment Size, NAICS 484 (2021)

NAICS	NAICS Description	Enterprise size (employees)	Firms	Establishments	Employment	Annual payroll ($1,000)	Average annual earnings per employee
484	**Truck Transportation**	**Total**	146,866	163,565	1,659,172	92,120,406	**$55,522**
484	Truck Transportation	< 5	113,334	113,377	137,474	6,601,517	$48,020
484	Truck Transportation	< 20	135,910	136,116	347,640	17,132,093	$49,281
484	Truck Transportation	< 500	146,187	149,319	916,512	46,677,687	$50,930
484	Truck Transportation	5,000+	180	10,158	531,654	33,339,125	$62,708
4841	**General Freight Trucking**	**Total**	97,360	110,003	1,164,852	64,664,889	**$55,513**
4841	General Freight Trucking	< 5	79,245	79,255	89,931	4,230,869	$47,046
4841	General Freight Trucking	< 20	91,071	91,148	199,440	9,840,536	$49,341
4841	General Freight Trucking	< 500	96,907	98,314	537,540	26,541,095	$49,375
4841	General Freight Trucking	5,000+	134	9,037	484,981	30,183,824	$62,237
48411	**General Freight Trucking, Local**	**Total**	40,240	41,896	294,834	13,864,147	**$47,024**
48411	General Freight Trucking, Local	< 5	31,640	31,642	37,075	1,832,752	$49,434
48411	General Freight Trucking, Local	< 20	37,277	37,298	89,295	4,398,157	$49,254
48411	General Freight Trucking, Local	< 500	40,077	40,546	228,284	10,478,654	$45,902
48411	General Freight Trucking, Local	5,000+	54	919	47,227	2,376,093	$50,312

(Table 1 continues, next three pages)

NAICS	NAICS Description	Enterprise size (employees)	Firms	Establishments	Employment	Annual payroll ($1,000)	Average annual earnings per employee
48412	**General Freight Trucking, Long-Distance**	**Total**	**57,284**	**68,107**	**870,018**	**50,800,742**	**$58,390**
48412	General Freight Trucking, Long-Distance	< 5	47,606	47,613	52,856	2,398,117	$45,371
48412	General Freight Trucking, Long-Distance	< 20	53,802	53,850	110,145	5,442,379	$49,411
48412	General Freight Trucking, Long-Distance	< 500	56,928	57,768	309,256	16,062,441	$51,939
48412	General Freight Trucking, Long-Distance	5,000+	106	8,118	437,754	27,807,731	$63,524
484121	**General Freight Trucking, Long-Distance, Truckload**	**Total**	**50,230**	**57,000**	**573,674**	**31,674,011**	**$55,213**
484121	General Freight Trucking, Long-Distance, Truckload	< 5	41,674	41,680	47,032	2,131,254	$45,315
484121	General Freight Trucking, Long-Distance, Truckload	< 20	47,174	47,221	98,028	4,846,208	$49,437
484121	General Freight Trucking, Long-Distance, Truckload	< 500	49,918	50,500	270,863	14,039,777	$51,833
484121	General Freight Trucking, Long-Distance, Truckload	5,000+	89	4,946	208,777	12,349,171	$59,150
484122	**General Freight Trucking, Long-Distance, Less Than Truckload**	**Total**	**7,100**	**11,107**	**296,344**	**19,126,731**	**$64,542**
484122	General Freight Trucking, Long-Distance, Less Than Truckload	< 5	5,932	5,933	5,824	266,863	$45,821

TRUCKING

NAICS	NAICS Description	Enterprise size (employees)	Firms	Establishments	Employment	Annual payroll ($1,000)	Average annual earnings per employee
484122	General Freight Trucking, Long-Distance, Less Than Truckload	< 20	6,628	6,629	12,117	596,171	$49,201
484122	General Freight Trucking, Long-Distance, Less Than Truckload	< 500	7,026	7,268	38,393	2,022,664	$52,683
484122	General Freight Trucking, Long-Distance, Less Than Truckload	5,000+	33	3,172	228,977	15,458,560	$67,511
4842	**Specialized Freight Trucking**	**Total**	**49,717**	**53,562**	**494,320**	**27,455,517**	**$55,542**
4842	Specialized Freight Trucking	< 5	34,092	34,122	47,543	2,370,648	$49,863
4842	Specialized Freight Trucking	< 20	44,846	44,968	148,200	7,291,557	$49,201
4842	Specialized Freight Trucking	< 500	49,400	51,005	378,972	20,136,592	$53,135
4842	Specialized Freight Trucking	5,000+	80	1,121	46,673	3,155,301	$67,604
48421	**Specialized Freight, Used Household and Office Goods Moving**	**Total**	**8,856**	**9,547**	**102,346**	**4,346,416**	**$42,468**
48421	Specialized Freight, Used Household and Office Goods Moving	< 5	5,088	5,095	7,264	311,134	$42,832
48421	Specialized Freight, Used Household and Office Goods Moving	< 20	7,539	7,591	31,274	1,189,979	$38,050
48421	Specialized Freight, Used Household and Office Goods Moving	< 500	8,832	9,392	94,668	3,908,673	$41,288

NAICS	NAICS Description	Enterprise size (employees)	Firms	Establishments	Employment	Annual payroll ($1,000)	Average annual earnings per employee
48421	Specialized Freight, Used Household and Office Goods Moving	5,000+	6	8	414	17,227	$41,611
48422	**Specialized Freight (except Used Goods) Trucking, Local**	**Total**	**30,936**	**32,217**	**225,094**	**13,071,256**	**$58,070**
48422	Specialized Freight (except Used Goods) Trucking, Local	< 5	21,886	21,897	30,293	1,589,138	$52,459
48422	Specialized Freight (except Used Goods) Trucking, Local	< 20	28,487	28,533	91,109	4,757,366	$52,216
48422	Specialized Freight (except Used Goods) Trucking, Local	< 500	30,766	31,274	193,380	10,892,416	$56,326
48422	Specialized Freight (except Used Goods) Trucking, Local	5,000+	39	489	11,774	968,439	$82,252
48423	**Specialized Freight (except Used Goods) Trucking, Long-Distance**	**Total**	**10,058**	**11,798**	**166,880**	**10,037,845**	**$60,150**
48423	Specialized Freight (except Used Goods) Trucking, Long-Distance	< 5	7,120	7,130	9,986	470,376	$47,104
48423	Specialized Freight (except Used Goods) Trucking, Long-Distance	< 20	8,828	8,844	25,817	1,344,212	$52,067
48423	Specialized Freight (except Used Goods) Trucking, Long-Distance	< 500	9,881	10,339	90,924	5,335,503	$58,681
48423	Specialized Freight (except Used Goods) Trucking, Long-Distance	5,000+	57	624	34,485	2,169,635	$62,915

US Department of the Census, Statistics of US Business; United States and states, NAICS, detailed employment. https://tinyurl.com/sx5uw533
Source: 2021 County Business Patterns. For information on confidentiality protection, sampling error, nonsampling error, and definitions, see https://tinyurl.com/2swyw37e
The Census Bureau has reviewed this data product to ensure appropriate access, use, and disclosure avoidance protection of the confidential source data (Project No. 7504501, Disclosure Review Board (DRB) approval number: CBDRB-FY24-0095).

single-unit shipment) (Levinson 2008), as well as "cartage" (local pickup and delivery of varying shipment sizes) and other LTL operations. The Census Bureau does not appear to publish information with that specificity ("Statistics of United States Business" 2023a). In addition to divisions according to radius of transport and general versus specialized freight, these category definitions revolve around shipment size, with TL freight generally involving a shipment that takes up a full trailer, and LTL freight generally incorporating a wide range of shipment sizes, where the typical shipment is likely less than 10,000 pounds and the average shipment size about 1,000 pounds. Both trailers may or may not be full, either filling the cubic volume or the weight capacity, and the work process itself is different, depending on shipment size.

While TL drivers typically pick up a single large shipment from a single shipper, LTL pickup and delivery (P and D) drivers typically deliver local freight along their route coming from a single dock and pick up freight the same day, returning it to the same dock. Dock workers at each cross-dock terminal, from which local LTL drivers take their freight every day and deliver freight every evening, consolidate freight from local P and D drivers, sort it by intercity trailer destinations, and reship freight every night to a wide network of cities that connect multiple cross-dock terminals within the company's network. The operation is quite complex and requires sales, management, and operational staff in each city in which the LTL firm operates (for a detailed explanation of how this process works, including the history of the industry, the history of regulation, and the history of industrial relations in trucking, see Belzer 2000; for additional explication of sectors and industry structure, see Burks et al. 2010).

In 1995, the US Bureau of Labor Statistics (US BLS) further complicated the understanding of trucking industrial organization as it stripped parcel delivery firms like United Parcel Service (UPS) and Federal Express (FedEx) out of trucking (trucking and courier services, except air; SIC 421) and placed them into the air transportation, scheduled, and air courier (SIC 451) segment of the air transportation industry (Belzer 2000; Chapter 5, endnote 5: 220–221). Originally, the Interstate Commerce Commission (ICC) classified UPS as a trucking company doing local delivery, and it became more clearly a trucking company over the years when it obtained common carrier service in 1922 and expanded that service within multiple cities across the United States in the 1930s and to intercity service after that. It, like FedEx, operates an extensive fleet of trucks, including intercity tractor-trailers. When the US BLS changed from SIC industry codes to the North American Industry Classification System (NAICS) in 1999 (https://www.census.gov/naics), the BLS and the Census Bureau apparently moved these two major freight carriers into courier and messenger (NAICS 492; see Table 2 in this chapter), and specifically into couriers and express delivery services (NAICS 4921). They did so, even though UPS's main business is freight, and it has only relatively recently competed in the overnight letter and ultra-small package industry associated with couriers (all trucking was local when it was founded in 1907, and UPS delivered freight; it clearly has been a trucking company for its entire history). This can be imputed from the size of the sector, as well as the large sudden shrinkage of the trucking sector, as couriers and express delivery services account for 87% of the entire courier and messenger service NAICS classification, which includes almost 1.1 million workers.

UPS, FedEx, and firms like them operate substantial LTL trucking operations on a large scale, which include local and intercity tractor-trailer freight businesses (employing tractor-trailer drivers); the supply chain industry refers to them as "integrators" because they integrate across all sectors of truck transportation. In fact, truck drivers account for 95% of all operating employees in the courier and messenger category; as truck drivers, they are regulated by the FMCSA. To the extent that truck drivers work for freight transport firms subcontracted by the courier and messenger industry, unless data collectors classify these trucking subcontractors as working in trucking, the data may be further distorted and interpretation confusing.[2]

Occupational statistics differ somewhat from industrial statistics because of the distinctions between the trucking industry and trucking occupations. Truck drivers may work in any industry that hires them because of the distinction between for-hire and private (not-for-hire) motor carriers. While truck transportation currently employs 1,659,172 workers (NAICS 484; see Table 1 in this chapter), it employs 1,386,300 "employment, production and nonsupervisory employees"; most of the remainder are supervisory and other nonproduction workers. Occupational, Employment and Wage Statistics (OEWS), reported by the US BLS, shows that there are 897,370 heavy and tractor-trailer drivers in the United States, along with an additional 62,620 truck drivers employed in "light or delivery services," a number 17.4 times smaller than the reported 1,090,906 workers in the couriers and messenger industry (NAICS 492; see Table 2 in this chapter)—most of whom drive light vehicles or work in loading and unloading capacities. All of these apparent inconsistencies make it difficult to be sure of the employment numbers.

These numbers may be distorted further because the lack of consistency in US labor market regulations allows such widespread subcontracting that there may be major gaps in the data. Surveys that have been conducted privately, such as the University of Michigan Trucking Industry Program Truck Driver Survey in 1997 (Belman, Monaco, and Brooks 2005), or publicly, such as the 2010 National Institute of Occupational Safety and Health (NIOSH) survey, suggest that substantially more than 25% of all long-haul truck drivers (LHTDs) are owner–drivers contracted to motor carriers. An estimated 65% (95% CI [confidence interval], 60%–69%) of LHTDs were company drivers, 28% (95% CI, 22%–34%) were owner–operators who leased to a motor carrier, and 7.4% (95% CI, 3.6%–11.3%) were owner–operators who operated under their own authority (Chen et al. 2015). Owner–drivers typically are not considered employees in the United States, so about one third of all long-haul drivers may fall out of the employment data, even though they should at minimum be considered self-employed, and thus still "employed." This continues to be a matter for legislation and litigation, however (Kingston 2023a, 2023b).

Table 2

Number of Firms and Establishments, Employment, and Annual Payroll by State, Industry, and Enterprise Employment Size (NAICS 492, 2021)

NAICS	NAICS description	Enterprise size (employees)	Firms	Establishments	Employment	Annual payroll ($1,000)	Average annual payroll per employee
492	**Couriers and Messengers**	**Total**	**10,355**	**16,647**	**1,090,906**	**48,077,840**	**$44,071**
492	Couriers and Messengers	< 5	5,033	5,040	5,798	492,086	$84,872
492	Couriers and Messengers	< 20	7,064	7,113	27,223	1,361,851	$50,026
492	Couriers and Messengers	< 500	10,305	10,821	237,981	7,535,093	$31,663
492	Couriers and Messengers	5,000+	11	5,314	819,507	36,646,013	$44,717
4921	**Couriers and Express Delivery Services**	**Total**	**5,592**	**11,285**	**954,109**	**40,914,977**	**$42,883**
4921	Couriers and Express Delivery Services	< 5	2,721	2,728	3,003	262,344	$87,361
4921	Couriers and Express Delivery Services	< 20	3,819	3,847	14,560	732,000	$50,275
4921	Couriers and Express Delivery Services	< 500	5,563	5,797	125,285	4,027,233	$32,145
4921	Couriers and Express Delivery Services	5,000+	7	5,179	816,103	36,444,872	$44,657
4922	**Local Messengers and Local Delivery**	**Total**	**4,786**	**5,362**	**136,797**	**7,162,863**	**$52,361**
4922	Local Messengers and Local Delivery	< 5	2,312	2,312	2,795	229,742	$82,197
4922	Local Messengers and Local Delivery	< 20	3,246	3,266	12,663	629,851	$49,739
4922	Local Messengers and Local Delivery	< 500	4,758	5,024	112,696	3,507,860	$31,127

(Table 2 continues, next page)

NAICS	NAICS description	Enterprise size (employees)	Firms	Establishments	Employment	Annual payroll ($1,000)	Average annual payroll per employee
4922	Local Messengers and Local Delivery	5,000+	6	135	3,404	201,141	$59,090
49221	**Local Messengers and Local Delivery**	**Total**	**4,786**	**5,362**	**136,797**	**7,162,863**	**$52,361**
49221	Local Messengers and Local Delivery	< 5	2,312	2,312	2,795	229,742	$82,197
49221	Local Messengers and Local Delivery	< 20	3,246	3,266	12,663	629,851	$49,739
49221	Local Messengers and Local Delivery	< 500	4,758	5,024	112,696	3,507,860	$31,127
49221	Local Messengers and Local Delivery	5,000+	6	135	3,404	201,141	$59,090

US Department of the Census, Statistics of US Business; United States and states, NAICS, detailed employment; https://tinyurl.com/4ejmrh2t; https://tinyurl.com/sx5uw533; release date 12/21/2023.

Data Source: 2021 County Business Patterns. For information on confidentiality protection, sampling error, nonsampling error, and definitions, see https://tinyurl.com/23exf59c and https://tinyurl.com/4tne6djs. The Census Bureau has reviewed this data product to ensure appropriate access, use, and disclosure avoidance protection of the confidential source data (Project No. 7504501, Disclosure Review Board (DRB) approval number: CBDRB-FY24-0095).

REGULATION AND DEREGULATION

Much has been written about the deregulation of trucking, including its motivations and consequences. However, newer analyses provide a better understanding of the relationship between compensation and safety. These analyses suggest that intense competition, which has characterized trucking since 1980, has contributed to persistent safety and health risks among commercial drivers (which will be covered in a separate section of this chapter). This section focuses on the motivation for economic regulatory liberalization.

The Motor Carrier Act of 1935 sought to correct what at the time most economists understood to be an oversupply of trucking services to the market, which probably had its roots in constrained demand, with too many underemployed workers chasing too little work, rather than an excess supply of trucking service. Having its origins in the theory of markets articulated by Jean-Baptiste Say in 1803 (Say 1834)[3] and similarly stated by John Mill in 1808 (Mill 1808),[4] Say's Law dominated the 19th century but was repudiated by John Maynard Keynes during the Great Depression of the 1930s as putting the cart before the horse—getting markets backward. Keynes paraphrased Say as stating that "supply creates its own demand" (Keynes 1936). It is reasonable to suggest that the theory underlying the Interstate Commerce Act of 1887 and the Motor Carrier Act of 1935, which brought trucking into the same regulatory regime, probably was Say's Law, and policy makers therefore may have misunderstood the underlying driving force behind markets (the pull of demand rather than the push of supply) and thus attempted to counter price deflation characterizing the Great Depression by restricting supply of the service. The movement to deregulate commerce generally, which began in the inflationary late 1970s and continued thereafter, at least through the 2008 financial crisis, manifested itself in the political drive to get rid of economic regulation as much as possible, allowing classical liberal market regulation to prevail, rather than to identify and remedy failures in otherwise competitive markets. This is the context that provides an understanding of trucking deregulation and the consequences that emerged (for the intellectual history underlying this movement, see Slobodian 2018).

Inflation during the 1970s provided the impetus for President Jimmy Carter's engagement of Alfred Kahn as a key leader in his effort to stem inflation. Many economists viewed economic deregulation as the solution to the inflation problem because regulations created during the 1930s to combat the negative growth of the Great Depression (such as the National Industrial Recovery Act of 1933 and the Motor Carrier Act of 1935), which put interstate trucking under the authority of the ICC, had become associated with an old-fashioned, anticompetitive approach to regulating industry. By the late 1970s, free market economists had come to critique this approach; this was the dawn of the neoliberal free market era in economics. It became critical to seek consumer welfare rather than general economic welfare, allowing monopoly power to re-emerge (Khan 2017).

The recessions of 1980 through 1983 initially were triggered by a combination of economic stagnation and inflation, and especially by the economic pressures associated with the second major oil crisis of the 1970s and the consequential knock-on effects associated with the Iranian Islamist revolution. In addition, the monetary crisis created by Federal Reserve Bank chair Paul Volcker, in a successful but costly effort to stamp out inflation, combined with deregulation to significantly diminish representation and reduce compensation.

The trucking industry has experienced a continuous, slow-rolling labor crisis since deregulation in 1980. Trucking companies have complained of a "driver shortage" for the past 40 years (Viscelli 2016b). Passage of the Motor Carrier Act of 1980 significantly undermined union representation, quickly driving most common carriers and signatories to the Teamsters' National Master Freight Agreement (NMFA) out of business and eventually driving a wholesale departure of experienced truck drivers out of trucking. These drivers did not return and were not sufficiently replenished to satisfy company recruitment and retention demands.

The alleged shortage really has been a long-standing recruiting and retention problem characterized by multiple factors. First, deregulation prompted an extensive churn of workers in and out of trucking (Gallup Organization 1997). Second, debt peonage expanded in the form of lease–purchase agreements designed to extract the cost of capitalizing trucking from closely managed faux contractors (Viscelli 2016a). Third, a form of indentured servitude came back into favor as a method of recruiting foreign workers to North America to drive trucks. These newly imported workers discovered that their visas were tied to their employment until they repaid labor recruiting contractors who had brought them to North America and trucking companies for company-provided training. This indentured servitude apparently is particularly prevalent in Canada (Tomlinson 2019). Finally, US trucking companies have required newly trained drivers to sign noncompete agreements that prohibit other trucking firms from hiring them if they quit before they have paid off all company training. All of the foregoing efforts to attract workers to truck driving jobs in sufficient numbers to fill out the truck driver labor market have been attempts to counter the effects of a long-term decline in truck driver compensation accompanied by an intensification of work since deregulation in 1980 (Belzer 2000). This decline, estimated at one third in 2000, is closer to 50% as of 2024, but because truck drivers are paid piecework and do not record working time accurately, hourly pay rates remain an estimate.

Institutional Roots of Failed Trucking Labor Markets

Labor markets require consistent institutional frameworks to establish a common set of "rules of the road." When the Fair Labor Standards Act (FLSA) passed in 1938, the trucking industry was a small factor in US freight transport. Most freight traveled by rail, especially over long distances, with general freight loaded in boxcars. The goal of the legislation was to create two main conditions: a minimum wage that workers could count on in order to survive, and a maximum hours provision, limiting the regular work week to 40 hours (with time-and-a-half, or a 50% pay premium, for hours greater than 40 per week), and a prohibition of child labor under age 16. The goal of the FLSA was to create more jobs for more people by disincentivizing long hours of work required of some workers, while others remained jobless. These basic features of the law have never changed ("Wages and Fair Labor Standards Act" 2011). The law applied to workers in an employment relationship, and specifically to production workers and not to "exempt" management or most professional workers, or contractors, agricultural workers (particularly farmers), or independent business operators. The FLSA also does not put any true limits on the number of hours worked but rather just on the compensation for those hours, including hours greater than the 40-hour standard that the FLSA created in law.[5]

Numerous exceptions were made, however. The motor carrier exemption is particularly important for trucking—a substantial fraction of which is now interstate under FMCSA regulations. The FLSA minimum wage provision technically applies to truck drivers, but because the "overtime" provision does not apply to truck drivers in interstate commerce, the regulations do not require trucking companies to collect the kind of data on working time that applies to other production workers. Since truck drivers commonly earn piecework compensation, hours worked is not relevant to trucking companies—the median driver earns no pay for nondriving work or labor time and spends 20 to 25 hours per week in such unpaid labor (Belman, Monaco, and Brooks 2005; Chen et al. 2015)—it is not relevant to shippers and consignees either. This makes it almost impossible to know how many hours truck drivers work and thus know their wage rate and whether it complies with the law (Levy 2023: 39–51).

Further, a federal court decision in 1960, which ruled that workers (building security workers, or night watchmen, in this case) whose total earnings divided by total work time exceed minimum wage are not entitled to pay for unpaid work time, complicates the situation.[6] Indeed, because most truck drivers are not paid for any of their nondriving labor, they have considerable incentive to log nondriving labor off duty, and thus regularly exceed FMCSA hours of service regulations at considerable health and safety risk to themselves and safety risk to the public.

The distinction for the FLSA is between truck drivers whose work has implications for safety in interstate commerce and those whose work does not. The maximum hours regulation—the 40-hour workweek, with time-and-a-half pay for overtime—does not apply to those whose work has implications for safety because FMCSA has that authority; the distinction technically is legal, not substantive. Specifically, the motor carrier exemption says that "Section 13(b)(1) of the FLSA provides an overtime exemption for employees who are within the authority of the Secretary of Transportation to establish qualifications and maximum hours of service pursuant to Section 204 of the Motor Carrier Act of 1935" ("Fact Sheet #19" 2009). Ironically, as Figure 1 shows, trucking, and true truck driver working time, hides behind FMCSA safety regulations; truck drivers typically work more than 60 hours per week, which of course is 50% more than the maximum

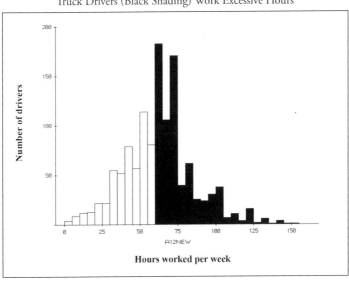

Figure 1
Truck Drivers (Black Shading) Work Excessive Hours

Hours worked per week

Median: 60 hours
Average: 61.5 hours
n = 1,254 long-haul truck drivers
Author's calculations from NIOSH Long-Haul Truck Driver Survey

workweek specified by the FLSA and the typical US workweek, and 50% greater than that which OEWS reports. While it may seem implausible to argue that the benefits associated with extremely long work hours exceed the safety and health costs, such arguments have prevailed in the US Department of Transportation regulation for decades (Belzer 2007; Saltzman and Belzer 2002, 2007).

The root of the problem lies even deeper, in the definition of "work" itself. The US Department of Labor (US DOL) defines work for all covered workers as follows:

> By statutory definition the term "employ" includes "to suffer or permit to work." The workweek ordinarily includes all time during which an employee is necessarily required to be on the employer's premises, on duty or at a prescribed workplace. ... Employees "Suffered or Permitted" to work: Work not requested but suffered or permitted to be performed is work time that must be paid for by the employer. ("Fact Sheet #22" 2008)

The work must be paid unless the employer frees the worker from work for a specific time and the employee knows in advance when work time starts and ends; and unless the worker has practical freedom to leave the place of work to go about his/her personal activity; and unless the worker is not engaged in the work for which he/she was hired, including being available for a call. In addition, all time is payable if the worker is located away from employer's place of work. In addition, wait time, and even sleep time, is part of employee's regular work unless otherwise negotiated.

The FMCSA's definition of work is much different from that of the US DOL Wage and Hour Division. Waiting time is nonwork time if "the driver is relieved of all duty and responsibility for the care and custody of the vehicle, its accessories, and any cargo or passengers it may be carrying." In addition, "during the stop, and for the duration of the stop, the driver must be at liberty to pursue activities of his/her own choosing." The FMCSA provides some examples: the off-duty driver can look at his phone, TV, or read; and the driver can sleep, eat, or take care of personal hygiene. Companies may interrupt the driver's free time and sleep time with work instructions. In addition, during a shift, off-duty time may have indeterminate start and end time, and the driver may not "practically" be able to choose his or her personal activity (personal activities of one's own choosing is "impractical" when the driver is stuck at a shipper's or consignee's distribution facility or a remote truck stop). Indeed, the decision to inform the driver that he or she is off duty may be made at the moment the company chooses or may be made on a blanket basis and defined as the time at which the driver arrives at a shipper or consignee. By definition, "if [he or she is] not doing any work (paid or unpaid) for a motor carrier and [he or she is] not doing any paid work for anyone else, [he or she] may record the time as off-duty time" ("Interstate Truck Driver's Guide" 2022).

In short, the two regulatory and institutional regimes fundamentally are at odds with each other. Since trucking draws from the same labor market as other industries draw, and since the truck driving occupation can be found across multiple industries, including construction, the labor market is governed by contradictory frameworks. What workers expect from a job in construction, for example, they probably will not find in trucking except at the local level. Even then, truck drivers will be expected to work very long days because FMCSA's regulations allow a 14-hour workday that is far longer, and over the weeks far less sustainable, than nontrucking jobs. This makes it doubly difficult to recruit and retain drivers. A truck driver's employment is more like a seven-day-per-week lifestyle involving many weeks or months on the road and away from home; truck driving has become less than a job and more like the lifestyle of a seafarer.

The problems created by this anomaly in the law came to the attention of the White House in 2021, during the COVID-19 supply chain crisis. President Joe Biden commissioned a supply chain study to identify causes and solutions to this problem (Belzer 2021a, 2021b). Policy Goal 40 in the study report recommended that Congress amend the FLSA to eliminate the trucking exemption (Executive Office of the President 2022 [Table 9]: 85). In response, Congressman Andy Levin placed the Guaranteeing Overtime for Truckers Act before Congress. Although Congressman Levin was districted out in 2022, the proposed law remains pending in the US House of Representatives as H.R. 6359 and in the US Senate as S. 4823 in the 118th Congress. The law has this simple text: "Section 13(b)(1) of the Fair Labor Standards Act of 1938 (29 U.S.C. 213(b)(1)) is repealed."[7]

The Teamsters Union

The International Brotherhood of Teamsters (IBT, or Teamsters Union) has historically represented commercial truck drivers in the United States and Canada. The term "teamsters" hearkens back to the pre-industrial era when wagons hitched to a team of horses and driven by workers called teamsters were important means of moving goods and people, generally over short distances. With the invention of the internal combustion engine, trucks replaced wagons as a major mode of commercial transportation. The union that organized and represented truck drivers in the 20th century retained the name, Teamsters, with horses' heads in the logo.

The challenges in trucking collective bargaining stem from multiple factors. Industrial structure and organizing, as well as labor and regulatory law, were important to the establishment of an industry-wide union. The Teamsters Union successfully organized a very fragmented and localized industry for several reasons.

First, the establishment of economic regulation in 1935 put boundaries around the industry and limited competition. This set of boundaries allowed the industry to grow steadily from within, based on infrastructure, technological progress, and economic growth within a confined market that restricted entry from the outside, and among both trucking company owners and union leaders who understood each other. In a development that foreshadowed the post-1980 decline in union density, the union's threat-effect worked on behalf of truck drivers in the regulatory-exempt sector (agricultural and other raw materials) from which the TL sector later arose after deregulation in 1980.

Second, the Teamsters Union originally was a craft union, and an early member of the American Federation of Labor. Daniel Tobin, the Teamsters general president for almost five decades in the first half of the 20th century, wanted the union just to represent "skilled" local drivers hauling ice, beer, coal, fuel oil, and other local commodities; he did not want freight drivers—especially long-haul drivers—in the union because he considered them unskilled. This attitude prevailed until the mid-1930s, when he eventually acceded to drivers' demands for representation. He even sent a young Jimmy Hoffa to Minneapolis to bust heads and get control of Trotskyist organizers who had led an aggressive unionizing drive, especially throughout the Midwest, but Hoffa returned a convert (not to socialism but to organizing). By the end of that decade, this organizing had caught on, and Secretary–Treasurer Sandy O'Brien of Local 710 in Chicago (and a member of the Teamsters International Executive Board) had become a convert as well, leading negotiations for the "eleven-state over-the-road contract"—the first multistate IBT contract—with support from General President Tobin. Michigan was represented on the negotiating committee by future Teamsters General President Jimmy Hoffa (Dobbs 1973: 177–187).

This organizing could not have occurred without certain features of the new National Labor Relations Act (NLRA) of 1935 (also known as the Wagner Act), which covered the trucking industry. Rather than being covered by the Railway Labor Act (RLA), trucking was covered by the NLRA because, at the time, it was a very local industry, and long-distance trucking was new, difficult, and relatively slow (it took five days to get from Chicago to New York, for example, due to the lack of horsepower in trucks, as well as the rudimentary US highway system). Airlines were covered under the RLA, in contrast, because it seemed clear that this industry was likely to become national and would need the universal wall-to-wall coverage provided by the RLA, as well as the very restricted right to direct economic action.

The Teamsters Union—especially under the influence of militant socialists like Dobbs—took advantage of the political and legal environment that allowed the use of the secondary boycott. Secondary strikes allowed Teamsters Union organizers to "leapfrog" from city to city, threatening to shut down operations that Teamsters served, creating a force multiplier for organizers. The secondary boycott was a key target of the National Labor Management Relations Act (NLMRA) of 1947 (also known as the Taft–Hartley Act). The passage of Taft–Hartley seriously undermined the Teamsters Union by banning the secondary boycott (strike), but by the time it went into effect, the Teamsters Union had already developed a significant organizing and contract machine that the regulated carriers found difficult and disadvantageous to challenge.

After Taft–Hartley, the Teamsters Union introduced "hot cargo" clauses into their contracts, which allowed Teamsters Union members to refuse to haul struck goods. The Labor Management Reporting and Disclosure Act of 1959 (also known as the Landrum–Griffin Act) banned hot cargo clauses in collective bargaining contracts, further reducing Teamster bargaining leverage. Again, while this blunted union expansion, the framework of the NMFA was already present, and Jimmy Hoffa negotiated what became the central common carrier freight contract in 1964. In 1967, he negotiated a second successful National Master Freight Contract Agreement (Levinson 1980). That same year, Hoffa was convicted of attempted bribery, jury tampering, conspiracy, and mail and wire fraud and was sentenced to 13 years in federal prison (Levinson 1980).

In the decade following Hoffa's imprisonment, legal, economic, and political pressures continued to weigh on the Teamsters Union, and on the trucking industry, keeping them both off balance. The union faced many challenges during this period, including instances of corruption within its leadership ranks, growing employer resistance to unions, and broad political support for deregulation—a product of the intellectual neoliberal "thought collective" (Slobodian 2018). As a result, the Teamsters' influence began to wane. By the time deregulation of industry became US government policy under the nation's first neoliberal president, Jimmy Carter, the Teamsters had no ready response.

Over time, commercial truck drivers have made up a declining share of the Teamsters' membership. Today, the union represents a wide range of occupations, including warehouse workers, airline pilots, healthcare workers, railroad workers, government employees, and Hollywood film crews. No longer a union made up primarily of truckers, the union is now a general union with a transport focus.

The decline in the percentage of Teamsters working in trucking is reflected in the decline in union density in that industry since the economic deregulation of the interstate trucking industry by the Motor Carrier Act of 1980 and the intrastate deregulation mandated by the Federal Aviation Administration Authorization Act of 1994.[8] Before deregulation, about 60% of all truck drivers were represented by unions (Hirsch 1993), but union density dropped precipitously after 1980 (Table 3). In 2022, 7.2% of all eligible (production) employees in the truck transportation industry were unionized, and 15.8% of the courier and messenger industry were union members; they were almost always represented by the Teamsters (Table 4). Table 5 shows employment and unionization for the entire road freight transport sector (Hirsch, Macpherson, and Even 2024). The high level of representation in the courier and messenger industry most likely reflects the influence of the IBT, which represents UPS workers as well, but the trend in this part of the surface freight truck transportation industry also has declined by more than half.

Truck owner–operators and owner–drivers (mostly of tractor-trailers) play an important role in industrial union density because owner–drivers generally are not considered employees and have not been eligible to join unions since 1970.[9] As subcontracting has increased since 1980, and as multiple schemes and lax regulation have allowed practices resembling debt peonage and indentured servitude to proliferate, an increasing fraction of truck drivers have become "faux" independent (nonemployee) workers, subject to market pressure and control by motor carriers with operating authority and the freight business (Viscelli 2016a: 105–189).

While the IBT was founded jointly in 1901 by employee teamsters as well as individual teamsters who owned their own teams of horses and wagons, the union

Table 3
Membership, Coverage, Density, and Employment, Trucking Industry, 1983–2022

Year	CIC	Industry name	Obs	Employment	Members	Covered	Mem	Cov
1983	410	Trucking service	2,203	1,117,169	421,385	442,013	37.7%	39.6%
1984	410	Trucking service	2,484	1,302,408	404,791	433,664	31.1%	33.3%
1985	410	Trucking service	2,635	1,386,493	420,006	442,622	30.3%	31.9%
1986	410	Trucking service	2,537	1,385,572	374,293	404,021	27.0%	29.2%
1987	410	Trucking service	2649	1,466,315	368,062	391,384	25.1%	26.7%
1988	410	Trucking service	2,645	1,543,802	379,544	403,468	24.6%	26.1%
1989	410	Trucking service	2,667	1,576,313	378,013	402,566	24.0%	25.5%
1990	410	Trucking service	2,820	1,627,262	394,043	423,223	24.2%	26.0%
1991	410	Trucking service	2,783	1,624,478	399,238	428,696	24.6%	26.4%
1992	410	Trucking service	2,736	1,632,276	368,634	388,449	22.6%	23.8%
1993	410	Trucking service	2,819	1,725,577	384,671	408,530	22.3%	23.7%
1994	410	Trucking service	2,797	1,848,681	397,879	423,353	21.5%	22.9%
1995	410	Trucking service	2,696	1,830,895	390,111	418,257	21.3%	22.8%
1996	410	Trucking service	2,506	1,906,915	444,619	471,452	23.3%	24.7%
1997	410	Trucking service	2,631	2,024,239	436,068	465,281	21.5%	23.0%
1998	410	Trucking service	2,615	2,041,186	423,754	440,014	20.8%	21.6%
1999	410	Trucking service	2,704	2,084,122	434,235	457,238	20.8%	21.9%
2000	410	Trucking service	2,859	2,196,065	411,533	434,687	18.7%	19.8%
2001	410	Trucking service	2,918	2,113,172	407,265	430,473	19.3%	20.4%

*CIC for truck transportation created in 2003. Workers totaling 578,635 transferred from trucking service to couriers and messengers, shrinking the trucking sector correspondingly. As subsequent trucking growth occurred mainly in this subsector; couriers and messengers grew from 28% to 43% of all road freight transport.

Data sources: The Current Population Survey (CPS) Outgoing Rotation Group (ORG) earnings files. Employed wage and salary workers, ages 16 and older. Variable definitions are: CIC = Census industry code used in CPS; Obs = CPS sample size; Employment = wage and salary employment; Members = employed workers who are union members; Covered = workers covered by a collective bargaining agreement; Mem = percentage of employed workers who are union members; Cov = percentage of employed workers who are covered by a collective bargaining agreement.

Year	CIC	Industry name	Obs	Employment	Members	Covered	Mem	Cov
2002	410	Trucking service	3,201	2,154,986	396,288	420,748	18.4%	19.5%
2003	6170	Truck transportation	2,129	1,495,202*	181,914	196,031	12.2%	13.1%
2004	6170	Truck transportation	2,116	1,525,478	167,493	178,193	11.0%	11.7%
2005	6170	Truck transportation	2,259	1,673,273	182,020	191,324	10.9%	11.4%
2006	6170	Truck transportation	2,186	1,622,556	194,128	205,173	12.0%	12.6%
2007	6170	Truck transportation	2,117	1,615,125	171,458	183,236	10.6%	11.3%
2008	6170	Truck transportation	2,090	1,632,270	166,219	178,060	10.2%	10.9%
2009	6170	Truck transportation	1,810	1,362,909	130,923	143,109	9.6%	10.5%
2010	6170	Truck transportation	1,802	1,380,245	127,313	139,216	9.2%	10.1%
2011	6170	Truck transportation	1,875	1,464,659	140,887	146,773	9.6%	10.0%
2012	6170	Truck transportation	1,872	1,486,891	132,149	142,469	8.9%	9.6%
2013	6170	Truck transportation	1,866	1,480,981	134,997	151,732	9.1%	10.2%
2014	6170	Truck transportation	1,965	1,570,923	141,025	156,253	9.0%	9.9%
2015	6170	Truck transportation	1,888	1,587,272	149,455	162,161	9.4%	10.2%
2016	6170	Truck transportation	1,991	1,672,707	152,400	174,144	9.1%	10.4%
2017	6170	Truck transportation	1,908	1,634,801	153,312	169,709	9.4%	10.4%
2018	6170	Truck transportation	1,832	1,590,562	131,032	139,271	8.2%	8.8%
2019	6170	Truck transportation	1,764	1,631,809	119,674	144,163	7.3%	8.8%
2020	6170	Truck transportation	1,591	1,608,391	147,095	161,688	9.1%	10.1%
2021	6170	Truck transportation	1,653	1,709,068	119,673	133,761	7.0%	7.8%
2022	6170	Truck transportation	1,573	1,772,275	126,971	144,218	7.2%	8.1%

1983 through 1991 uses 1980 Census Industry codes. 1992 through 2002 uses 1990 Census Industry codes. 2003 through 2008 uses 2002 Census Industry codes. 2009 through 2013 uses 2007 Census Industry codes. 2014 through 2019 uses 2012 Census Industry codes. 2020 forward uses 2017 Census Industry codes. HIrsch, Macpherson, and Even (2024).

Table 4
Union Membership, Coverage, Density, and Employment, Couriers and Messengers, 2003–2022

Year	Industry name (CIC 6380)	Obs	Employed	Members	Covered	Mem	Cov
2003	Couriers and Messengers	781	578,635	194,777	200,233	33.7%	34.6%
2004	Couriers and Messengers	756	573,965	186,900	199,312	32.6%	34.7%
2005	Couriers and Messengers	804	600,258	189,735	197,344	31.6%	32.9%
2006	Couriers and Messengers	785	621,282	171,216	183,428	27.6%	29.5%
2007	Couriers and Messengers	812	676,940	196,782	210,900	29.1%	31.2%
2008	Couriers and Messengers	809	669,777	190,993	204,579	28.5%	30.5%
2009	Couriers and Messengers	757	620,633	180,187	193,467	29.0%	31.2%
2010	Couriers and Messengers	749	593,147	163,611	172,620	27.6%	29.1%
2011	Couriers and Messengers	795	650,925	177,046	186,520	27.2%	28.7%
2012	Couriers and Messengers	756	641,425	183,820	196,503	28.7%	30.6%
2013	Couriers and Messengers	770	658,469	176,456	185,962	26.8%	28.2%
2014	Couriers and Messengers	799	696,804	195,133	204,698	28.0%	29.4%
2015	Couriers and Messengers	797	697,838	177,478	186,794	25.4%	26.8%
2016	Couriers and Messengers	857	766,303	230,594	241,358	30.1%	31.5%
2017	Couriers and Messengers	781	715,589	179,600	189,650	25.1%	26.5%
2018	Couriers and Messengers	794	743,550	160,447	167,247	21.6%	22.5%
2019	Couriers and Messengers	880	889,298	183,037	201,079	20.6%	22.6%
2020	Couriers and Messengers	942	1,033,708	209,250	224,943	20.2%	21.8%
2021	Couriers and Messengers	1,177	1,345,537	214,123	235,951	15.9%	17.5%
2022	Couriers and Messengers	1,083	1,324,903	209,913	223,088	15.8%	16.8%

Hirsch, Macpherson, and Even (2024).

Table 5
Union Membership, Coverage, Density, and Employment by Road Freight Transport Industry, 2003–2022

Year	Industry (CIC 6130)	Fraction of unionized road freight transport, by road freight transport subsector	Industry (CIC 6380)	Fraction of unionized road freight transport, by road freight transport subsector	Total road freight transport employees	Total road freight transport union members	Total road transport union density
2003	Truck Transportation	72.1%	Couriers and Messengers	27.9%	2,073,837	376,691	18.2%
2004	Truck Transportation	72.7%	Couriers and Messengers	27.3%	2,099,443	354,393	16.9%
2005	Truck Transportation	73.6%	Couriers and Messengers	26.4%	2,273,531	371,755	16.4%
2006	Truck Transportation	72.3%	Couriers and Messengers	27.7%	2,243,838	365,344	16.3%
2007	Truck Transportation	70.5%	Couriers and Messengers	29.5%	2,292,066	368,240	16.1%
2008	Truck Transportation	70.9%	Couriers and Messengers	29.1%	2,302,047	357,212	15.5%
2009	Truck Transportation	68.7%	Couriers and Messengers	31.3%	1,983,542	311,110	15.7%
2010	Truck Transportation	69.9%	Couriers and Messengers	30.1%	1,973,392	290,924	14.7%
2011	Truck Transportation	69.2%	Couriers and Messengers	30.8%	2,115,584	317,933	15.0%
2012	Truck Transportation	69.9%	Couriers and Messengers	30.1%	2,128,316	315,969	14.8%
2013	Truck Transportation	69.2%	Couriers and Messengers	30.8%	2,139,450	311,453	14.6%
2014	Truck Transportation	69.3%	Couriers and Messengers	30.7%	2,267,727	336,158	14.8%
2015	Truck Transportation	69.5%	Couriers and Messengers	30.5%	2,285,110	326,933	14.3%
2016	Truck Transportation	68.6%	Couriers and Messengers	31.4%	2,439,011	382,994	15.7%

(Table 5 continues, next page)

Year	Industry (CIC 6130)	Fraction of unionized road freight transport, by road freight transport subsector	Industry (CIC 6380)	Fraction of unionized road freight transport, by road freight transport subsector	Total road freight transport employees	Total road freight transport union members	Total road transport union density
2003	Truck Transportation	72.1%	Couriers and Messengers	27.9%	2,073,837	376,691	18.2%
2004	Truck Transportation	72.7%	Couriers and Messengers	27.3%	2,099,443	354,393	16.9%
2005	Truck Transportation	73.6%	Couriers and Messengers	26.4%	2,273,531	371,755	16.4%
2006	Truck Transportation	72.3%	Couriers and Messengers	27.7%	2,243,838	365,344	16.3%
2007	Truck Transportation	70.5%	Couriers and Messengers	29.5%	2,292,066	368,240	16.1%
2008	Truck Transportation	70.9%	Couriers and Messengers	29.1%	2,302,047	357,212	15.5%
2009	Truck Transportation	68.7%	Couriers and Messengers	31.3%	1,983,542	311,110	15.7%
2010	Truck Transportation	69.9%	Couriers and Messengers	30.1%	1,973,392	290,924	14.7%
2011	Truck Transportation	69.2%	Couriers and Messengers	30.8%	2,115,584	317,933	15.0%
2012	Truck Transportation	69.9%	Couriers and Messengers	30.1%	2,128,316	315,969	14.8%
2013	Truck Transportation	69.2%	Couriers and Messengers	30.8%	2,139,450	311,453	14.6%
2014	Truck Transportation	69.3%	Couriers and Messengers	30.7%	2,267,727	336,158	14.8%
2015	Truck Transportation	69.5%	Couriers and Messengers	30.5%	2,285,110	326,933	14.3%
2016	Truck Transportation	68.6%	Couriers and Messengers	31.4%	2,439,011	382,994	15.7%
2017	Truck Transportation	69.6%	Couriers and Messengers	30.4%	2,350,391	332,912	14.2%
2018	Truck Transportation	68.1%	Couriers and Messengers	31.9%	2,334,112	291,479	12.5%
2019	Truck Transportation	64.7%	Couriers and Messengers	35.3%	2,521,108	302,711	12.0%

Year	Industry (CIC 6130)	Fraction of unionized road freight transport, by road freight transport subsector	Industry (CIC 6380)	Fraction of unionized road freight transport, by road freight transport subsector	Total road freight transport employees	Total road freight transport union members	Total road transport union density
2020	Truck Transportation	60.9%	Couriers and Messengers	39.1%	2,642,099	356,345	13.5%
2021	Truck Transportation	56.0%	Couriers and Messengers	44.0%	3,054,605	333,797	10.9%
2022	Truck Transportation	57.2%	Couriers and Messengers	42.8%	3,097,178	336,884	10.9%

Hlrsch, Macpherson, and Even (2024).

represented both owner–operators and owner–drivers for about seven decades (including the decades during which the NLRA and NLMRA were passed). However, in the late 1960s and 1970s, judges repudiated the law in support of specialized carriers that wanted to reduce Teamster bargaining power (Belzer 2000). Although the data are spotty, it appears that the use of owner–drivers as contractors has increased substantially since deregulation. While the IBT remains the sole representative of unionized truck drivers and dock workers, the fact that for the past 50 years the courts have held that what now constitute about 35% of all long-haul truck drivers are not eligible for collective bargaining means that union density among truck drivers has declined and will remain low. This has significantly reduced union bargaining leverage.

Preventing more than a third of all long-haul truck drivers from exercising the right to the representation to which they are entitled in our employer–employee industrial relations model by excluding them from coverage of the NLRA while also stripping them of rights to workers compensation, unemployment compensation, and Social Security coverage remains powerful motivation to subcontract the work rather than hire employees. Unionization is much lower than it would be in almost any other industry simply because a large portion of the workforce has been deprived of the right of representation.

This is an important incentive for companies such as Amazon, Federal Express, and others to continue to exploit the subcontracting business strategy intensively. While IBT General President Sean O'Brien has declared the union's intent to organize Amazon and other major nonunion freight transport companies (Soroff 2022), the barrier created by pervasive subcontracting in trucking has made this challenge especially difficult. While technically it is illegal for companies to retaliate against workers exercising their collective bargaining rights, if workers organize any contractor firm, the company controlling the business (such as Amazon, Federal Express, or any other freight delivery company that uses owner–drivers to power its core freight transport business) can simply terminate the business contract between it and the newly organized contractor, effectively overthrowing the NLRA by eliminating the workers' practical right to organize and bargain collectively. Reformers have attempted to resolve this contradiction through legislation and litigation for more than five decades.

The contradiction appears to have been resolved by a decision of the United States District Court in the Southern District of California, although plaintiffs have appealed the judge's ruling to the 9th Circuit Court of Appeals. On April 30, 2018, the California Supreme Court ruled in *Dynamex Operations West, Inc. v. Superior Court* that the rule distinguishing employment from legitimate subcontracting (the Borello test) was unworkably vague and implemented an "ABC test," which drew a brighter line defining employment. In effect, the California Supreme Court considered the then-current definition of employment to have created a pervasive problem of worker misclassification. Under the ABC test, most owner–drivers employed by trucking companies should be considered employees and not independent businesses.[10] The California legislature codified the Supreme Court *Dynamex* decision into law by passing Assembly Bill 5 (AB5) shortly thereafter. The California Trucking Association and others sued to block AB5. The district court initially granted a preliminary injunction blocking AB5, but the Ninth Circuit reversed that decision. After losing in the Ninth Circuit, the plaintiffs appealed to the Supreme Court, which denied *certiorari* in 2022, returning the case to the district court for resolution. The March 15 district court decision upheld California's right to regulate the employment relationship to promote labor welfare in the state based on its police powers.[11]

An expert declaration for the AB5 case articulated a practical resolution for this conflict. In California, if trucking companies still wish to hire owner–drivers and manage them directly like they do employees, they can hire the owner–drivers as employees, and the owner–drivers can lease their trucks to the motor carriers that employ them. In other words, truck drivers can own their trucks and lease them to the trucking companies for which they work. They would earn a profit from their capital investment while earning a living wage, and the carriers can pay separate checks for each activity. This "two-check" system, which carriers used for 75 years to hire owner–drivers who operated under the motor carrier's authority, allows companies to hire drivers with their own trucks, allows truckers to drive their own trucks (operating a truck-leasing business), and requires that motor carriers pay those drivers separately for their labor and for the value of the trucks they lease to the carriers.[12]

COLLECTIVE BARGAINING AFTER 1980: WINNOWING THE PARTIES

The first NMFA was created in 1964, after a quarter of a century of steady organizing and both local and regional bargaining. The process started with the famous Minneapolis 1934 trucking strike (Dobbs 1972) and continued during the first multistate over-the-road contract negotiated and signed in 1938 (Dobbs 1973). The NMFA, at its height, represented between 800 and 1,000 motor carriers and between 300,000 and 500,000 truck drivers, which included most truck drivers and dock workers (including owner–drivers) working for common carriers of general freight as well as for private carriers

(James and James 1965; Leiter 1957; Levinson 1971, 1980). At the time of deregulation, which changed the structure of the trucking industry permanently, the Teamsters Union represented about 60% of all truck drivers (Hirsch 1993).

The NMFA declined after deregulation because most of the represented general freight motor carriers that existed at that time went out of business. Most failed within the first three years, as the industry restructured into separate LTL and TL sectors. The TL sector became almost completely nonunion quickly, as TL trucking companies and drivers from the regulatory-exempt sector (haulers of specialized freight and agricultural goods) flowed into general freight and drove prices down based on significantly lower compensation for truck drivers, while shifting away from the Teamsters' "miles and hours" contracts to pay only by the book mile (not even the practical mile), with little or no pay for nondriving work, or pay only a percentage of the freight revenue. At the same time, the LTL sector, created out of the reconstructed general freight common carrier sector after the disappearance of the common carrier concept, consolidated into a very few very large regional and national LTL carriers (Belzer 2000).

The Teamsters Union has been haunted by links between Teamsters leaders and organized crime. In 1988, the Justice Department sued the Teamsters under the Racketeer Influenced and Corrupt Organizations Act of 1970 (RICO), alleging that the union was dominated by organized crime. In 1989, immediately before going to trial, the Teamsters agreed to a consent decree giving the Justice Department control over the union. One feature of this control was an agreement to impose one-member-one-vote elections for national leadership. In 1991, Ron Carey was elected Teamsters general president on a platform to reform the union and end long-standing corruption. In 1994, he led the first strike of the NMFA in decades. The union won the strike, as well as a 1997 strike against UPS (Belzer 2002). In many ways, these successful strikes represented a new high-water mark for the Teamsters Union (Belzer 2000), but they did not reverse the slide in representation.

As multiple Teamster-represented LTL companies failed or sold out to other trucking companies during the subsequent decade, the number of carriers represented was winnowed down to just a few much larger companies. Yellow Freight System purchased Roadway in a leveraged buyout; Yellow purchased US Freightways (which included multiple well-run and profitable unionized companies such as New Penn and Holland), after which Yellow Freight was renamed YRC Worldwide (until 2021, when the name reverted to Yellow Corporation); and Yellow Corporation declared bankruptcy in 2023 following two decades of poor management.[13] By 2023, only ABF Freight System (formerly known as Arkansas-Best Freight System) remained of the NMFA carriers,[14] and references to a "master" agreement simply covered the remaining company across the entire United States. Arguably the Yellow bankruptcy, which occurred after decades of Teamster-granted concessions, had left the company paying less than market compensation (even against nonunion companies) and its ongoing failure forced the Teamsters to choose between managing standards on behalf of its sole remaining profitable unionized major freight company—ABF—and letting Yellow go. It let Yellow go.

UPS also survived and prospered during the last quarter century. Extremely profitable and very well run, UPS has beaten the competition and provided top wages and benefits to workers despite competition from nonunion firms, many of which rely on deep cost-cutting and escape from liability via subcontracting (Bandler et al. 2019; Callahan 2019a, 2019b). In 2023, newly elected IBT general president Sean O'Brien and his allies in the long-standing reform organization Teamsters for a Democratic Union waged a high-pressure bargaining campaign against UPS. The campaign included threats of a national strike that were backed with a program of strike preparation events and activities. The union eventually won a strong contract without a strike that reversed decades of givebacks conceded by national Teamsters leaders beginning four decades earlier.

The 2023 UPS–Teamsters contract included the following:

- $2.75 more per hour in 2023 and $7.50 more in total for the 340,000 full- and part-time employees by the contract's end in 2028
- Wage increases for full-timers that will keep UPS Teamsters the highest-paid delivery drivers in the nation, improving their average top rate to $49 per hour
- General wage increases for part-time workers that will double the amount obtained in the previous UPS–Teamsters contract, and existing part-time workers will receive a 48% average total wage increase over the next five years
- Starting wages of $21 an hour for new part-time workers
- Elimination of the two-tiered pay system in which newer employees doing the same jobs were paid less
- Measures to address safety and health concerns, including the addition of air conditioning, fans, heat exhaust shields, and air induction vents in delivery trucks
- The addition of 7,500 new full-time Teamster jobs and the filling of 22,500 positions to establish more opportunities for part-timers to transition to full-time work (International Brotherhood of Teamsters 2023).

With the victory against UPS, O'Brien clearly was sending a message to Amazon workers that the Teamsters Union was strong and militant.

Organizing Amazon, and other carriers that rely on subcontracting as their primary means of conducting business, will require a major initiative in organizing strategy, such as the community-based type of organizing suggested by President O'Brien (Soroff 2022). Organizing and bargaining contracts also will require a significant effort to restore the employment relationship, which courts have gone so far to undermine. This will require committed political leadership that has not materialized in the United States over the past five decades.

"SAFE RATES" AND THE GLOBAL PROMOTION OF COLLECTIVE BARGAINING

Growing concerns about road transport safety in the United States and elsewhere began during the 1980s, as the traditional trucking industry structure transformed after economic deregulation, leading to the rapid decline of the common carrier sector of trucking and the failure of traditional common carrier firms. They were replaced by truckers from the specialized trucking industry sector and the regulatory-exempt sector, who quickly scrambled in at low rates to cream freight from the common carriers. These truck drivers were not union members and, coming out of agricultural hauling, often had little understanding of the safety, workplace, and compensation culture in the industry sector they replaced. As the tables in this chapter have shown, the change in industrial structure fueled a decline in union membership, compensation, and applicant "character," leading to a new phenomenon in trucking employment: the inability to hire the kind of responsible drivers needed to drive tractor trailers, especially in intercity and interstate commerce (Belzer 1995).

Research began on this issue in the 1980s in Australia—a country like the United States, but which had experienced deregulation much earlier. The early research showed a strong connection between pay and safety (Hensher, Batellino, Gee, and Daniels 1991). At the same time, the General Accounting Office found similar results in the United States. The GAO found that trucking companies' economic health (measured by seven specific financial ratios), as well as driver compensation, associated with lower crash risk (General Accounting Office 1991). In 2000, the Motor Accidents Authority of New South Wales commissioned a major inquiry, which demonstrated a strong link between compensation and safety (Quinlan 2001). Multiple papers and official Australian government reports emerged following this inquiry. During the same period, the US DOT Office of Motor Carriers (later replaced by FMCSA) commissioned a study on this relationship. That study, in three parts, found a strong relationship between compensation and safety using multiple data sets from multiple sources (Belzer, Rodriguez, and Sedo 2002).

The dislocation left by global economic deregulation of trucking, including the diminution of the institutions for worker-interest representation in the United States and globally, has left a chronically dysfunctional labor market that exhibits very high turnover, chronically high crash rates, and poor worker health, in addition to an inability to recruit and retain truck drivers. Members of the International Transport Workers' Federation, the "democratic, affiliate-led federation recognized as the world's leading transport authority" (https://www.itfglobal.org/en) have been engaged for decades in a global effort to establish a regulatory framework that seeks to transform the commercial motor vehicle drivers' occupation (both truck and bus) into "decent work" by linking compensation to road safety. This culminated in a series of reports and meetings sponsored by the International Labour Organization (ILO) ("The Road to Social Dialogue" 2019b).

Tripartite negotiations in 2015 at the ILO led to two resolutions that were approved by consensus. The relevant resolution called on

> the Governing Body to request the International Labour Office … to conduct further research in consultation with tripartite experts in the sector on best practices including on the Safe Rates model; … and convene, when appropriate, a tripartite meeting

of experts to elaborate and adopt a code of practice or guidelines on best practices in road transport safety with the objective of protecting the community and road transport workers from all health and safety hazards, preventing accidents and promoting safe and fair remuneration. ("Conclusions on Safety" 2016; "Resolution Concerning" 2016).

The International Labor Office developed a response for participants to review, based on research and consultation. In 2019, the ILO convened a "Meeting of Experts," which considered the accumulated evidence and adopted a final report in support of the "safe rates" strategy. That report included the following ILO consensus: "The Safe Rates model represented a best practice to address the growing supply chain pressures by recognizing the link between the value of transport services and road safety outcomes, and by ensuring supply chain accountability"("Final Report" 2019a). This broad consensus understanding led to a report that recommended significant guidelines for safe road transport operation ("Guidelines on the Promotion" 2020).

The problems associated with the relationship between compensation and safety are not unique to the United States and are prevalent elsewhere. Trucking unionization in Europe is similarly fraught with challenges, for example, because the transnational European Union structure contributes to the fracturing of collective bargaining and transnational labor protections within the European Union (Belzer and Thörnquist 2021), again, especially in fragmented industries like trucking. Trucking in developing countries is similarly characterized by fragmented markets and intense market pressure tending to drive small carriers and truck drivers to the low road.

Australia, which has had an expert system of industrial tribunals for more than 100 years (Anderson and Quinlan 2008: 121 ff.; Gardner 1995), has recently begun implementation of a model that will bring the whole trucking industry under a common "award" regime, in the interest of balancing the nationwide labor market for these workers with the comparable labor markets for similarly situated workers in other industries. In the "Closing the Loopholes Bills" [Fair Work Legislation Amendment (Closing Loopholes) Act 2023], introduced the Albanese Labour Government in September 2023 and passed in two separate components as the third tranche of labor law reforms on December 7, 2023, and February 8, 2024 (Feltham et al. 2023; Karp 2024), key features associated with creating labor market governance institutions bring long-haul truckers closer to the level paid to intrastate drivers and make collective bargaining for interstate drivers more plausible in Australia. This comprehensive institutional framework has important implications for collective bargaining in the United States and elsewhere, as institutions provide a necessary counterbalance to the "creative destruction" wrought by unfettered markets.

CONCLUSION

Collective bargaining in US trucking has special features due to persistent contradictions in the country's trucking labor market regulation and institutions. The problem exists because our political system hampers lawmakers from changing the law to reflect a changing economic order and empower the interests of workers. Decades of efforts to reform labor and employment law in a way that would enforce the principles of the NLRA, and even the FLSA, have been stymied by lobbying from business interests that prefer to retain the power advantage in the relationship, giving workers and their representatives very little hope that reform can happen. The problem of regulatory capture looms in the background as well, in critiques from historians on the left (Kolko 1963, historian) and the right (Stigler 1971, economist), as industry efforts to cultivate a regulatory system that supports their perceived interests seem to swamp the public interest. In the case of trucking, the very odd 85-year-old exclusion of interstate trucking from the FLSA, as well as the conflicting messages sent by US DOL and US DOT regulations defining "work," is just one case out of many reflecting our institutional paralysis.

During and after the COVID-19 pandemic, the United States experienced labor market disruptions with multiple origins, and those became particularly acute in trucking in significant part because of the contradictory legal framework discussed in this chapter. The trucking industry, with an average firm size of approximately five trucks, is particularly fragmented and prone to the kind of bargaining asymmetry that has plagued many fragmented industries, but trucking is an "industry on roller skates." The workplace is mobile, and relationships are fragile and easily disrupted by competitive forces. Collective bargaining developed in trucking only because of a particular confluence of factors, such as a restrictive economic regulatory regime that constrained free competition and a nascent labor law regime that established the right to organize during the Great Depression—a right that slowly dissipated in response to hostile political forces. Those forces continue to control the legislative environment as well as the court system, making organizing and bargaining fraught.

While the detailed workplace standards involving collective forms of worker representation in the United States might seem impossible, basic labor standards in the country would enable unions and other worker-interest representatives to create order within the supply chain that would resolve the alleged labor shortage and bring US truck drivers a modicum of security and prosperity. Such standards seem out of reach in the United States, however, as even a simple one-sentence FLSA amendment that eliminates the overtime exclusion afforded to almost all other US production workers continues to appear out of reach. This suggests that if the Teamsters have any hope of organizing the trucking industry again, it will require an all-hands effort engaging the support of the public and political supporters of independent worker-interest representation and collective bargaining.

ENDNOTES

1. Some such grocery and distribution companies subcontract their distribution operations to firms specializing in this kind of distribution to save money, or perhaps to avoid or break union representation.

2. While these distinctions may seem hair splitting, they have major implications for classification and analysis of labor markets. Census data on unionization show that for this purpose, the trucking service industry again was split into truck transportation, and courier and messenger, in 2003, creating significant confusion in industry measurements (see Tables 3–5).

3. "A product is no sooner created, than it, from that instant, affords a market for other products to the full extent of its own value" (138). Originally published 1803 in French. https://tinyurl.com/4zapvk47

4. "Commerce Defended (1808)." https://tinyurl.com/3e94xswr

5. "Wages and the Fair Labor Standards Act." https://tinyurl.com/58cva8d3

6. 1960. *United States v. Klinghoffer Bros. Realty Corp.*, United States Court of Appeals for the Second Circuit, 285 F.2d 487, 490 (2d Cir. 1960).

7. "H.R. 6359: Guaranteeing Overtime for Truckers Act." https://tinyurl.com/mv6r26ea; "S. 4823: Guaranteeing Overtime for Truckers Act." https://tinyurl.com/3sky9vfk

8. 49 U.S. Code §14501. https://tinyurl.com/3z39x8dp

9. Complete legal research is beyond the scope of this chapter, but key cases include the following: *National Labor Relations Board, Petitioner v. Deaton Truck Line, Inc., Respondent*. Federal Appeals Court Decisions, Second Series. United States Court of Appeals for the Fifth Circuit, 163 (1968).

United States Steel Corp., Plaintiff, and Bethlehem Steel Corp., Jones and Laughlin Steel Corp., Wheeling-Pittsburgh Steel Corp., National Steel Corp., Republic Steel Corp., and Youngstown Sheet and Tube Co., Intervening Plaintiffs v. Fraternal Association of Steelhaulers, a/k/a Fraternal Association of Special Haulers, William J. Hill, National Chairman, Fraternal Association of Steelhaulers of Western Pennsylvania, William J. Hill, Chairman, Milton E. Schaudt, Executive Vice President, David Haugh, Secretary, R.H. Wilson, Robert W. Schwirian, Clyde Mostoller, Harry Ludwig, E.E. Stoner and Paul Burns, individually and as members of a class representing owners of steel hauling rigs, Defendants. United States District Court for the Western District of Pennsylvania (1970).

United States Steel Corp., Plaintiff, and National Steel Corp., Republic Steel Corp., Wheeling-Pittsburgh Steel Corp., Bethlehem Steel Corp., Jones and Laughlin Steel Corp. and Youngstown Sheet and Tube Co., Intervening Plaintiffs v. Fraternal Association of Steelhaulers a/k/a Fraternal Association of Special Haulers, William J. Hill, National Chairman, Fraternal Association of Steelhaulers of Western Pennsylvania, William J. Hill, Chairman, Milton E. Schaudt, Executive Vice-President, David Haugh, Secretary, R.H. Wilson, Robert W. Schwirian, Clyde Mostoller, Harry Ludwig and E.E. Stoner, Individually and as members of a class representing owners of steel hauling rigs, Appellants. Federal Appeals Court Decisions, Second Series. United States Court of Appeals for the Third Circuit, 1046 (1970). *Conley Motor Express, Inc., a corporation, Appellee, v. Harry M. Russell, Walter J. Dennis, William B. Bain, William Senge, Roger Keadle, John Molenda, Earl Burgoon, Henry Cooper, John A. Jones, and William Schwartz, Appellants*. Federal Appeals Court Decisions, Second Series. United States Court of Appeals for the Third Circuit, 124 (1974).

10. *Dynamex Operations West, Inc. v. Superior Court*. ABC test defined on p. 7. https://tinyurl.com/tx5bj6ye

11. Bluebook: *California Trucking Ass'n et al. v. Bonta et al.*, No. 3:18-cv-02458 (S.D. Cal. Mar. 15, 2024). ABC test restated on p. 4. https://tinyurl.com/58whcs5d; Westlaw: *California Trucking Ass'n v. Bonta*, __ F.Supp.3d __, 2024 WL 1249554 (S.D. Cal. Mar. 15, 2024).

12. Declaration of Dr. Michael H. Belzer, Dkt. 173-1, *California Trucking Association v. Bonta*, No. 18-2458 (S.D. Cal.), filed June 20, 2023. https://www.michaelbelzer-saferates.com
13. "Yellow Corporation." https://en.wikipedia.org/wiki/Yellow_Corporation
14. "ABF Freight System." https://en.wikipedia.org/wiki/ABF_Freight_System

REFERENCES

Anderson, G., and M. Quinlan. 2008. "The Changing Role of the State: Regulating Work in Australia and New Zealand 1788–2007." *Labour History* 95: 111–132. https://doi.org/10.2307/2751631

Bandler, J., P. Callahan, D. Burke, K. Bensinger, and C. O'Donovan. 2019. "Inside Documents Show How Amazon Chose Speed over Safety in Building Its Delivery Network." ProPublica and BuzzFeed News. https://tinyurl.com/4mnd5nxw

Belman, D.L., K.A. Monaco, and T.J. Brooks. 2005. *Sailors of the Concrete Sea: A Portrait of Truck Drivers Work and Lives*. East Lansing, MI: Michigan State University Press.

Belzer, M.H. 1995. "Collective Bargaining After Deregulation: Do the Teamsters Still Count?" *Industrial and Labor Relations Review* 48, no. 44: 636–655.

———. 2000. *Sweatshops on Wheels: Winners and Losers in Trucking Deregulation*. Oxford, UK, and New York, NY: Oxford University Press.

———. 2002. "Trucking: Collective Bargaining Takes a Rocky Road." In *Collective Bargaining in the Private Sector*, edited by P.F. Clark, J.T. Delaney, and A.C. Frost, 311–342. Champaign, IL: Labor Relations and Research Association.

———. 2007. "Truck Driver Hours of Service, Interim Final Rule; 72 FR 71247." December 17 [comments]. Regulations.gov. https://doi.org/10.13140/RG.2.2.22750.66882

———. 2021a. "Building Back Better in Commercial Road Transport: Markets Require 'Safe Rates' Regulation." Roundtable of Truck Driver Retention and Supply Chain. US Department of Transportation and US Department of Labor. July 8. https://tinyurl.com/yc63rxrh

———. 2021b. "Building Back Better in Commercial Road Transport: Markets Require Fair Labor Standards." Motor Carrier Safety Advisory Council. US Department of Transportation, Federal Motor Carrier Safety Administration. July 19. https://tinyurl.com/ywnkht8d

Belzer, M.H., D.A. Rodriguez, and S.A. Sedo. 2002. "Paying for Safety: An Economic Analysis of the Effect of Compensation on Truck Driver Safety." Washington, DC: United States Department of Transportation, Federal Motor Carrier Safety Administration. September 10. https://tinyurl.com/bdhpnhw6

Belzer, M.H., and A. Thörnquist. 2021. "Economic Liberalisation of Road Freight Transport in the EU and the USA." In *The Regulation and Management of Workplace Health and Safety: Historical and Emerging Trends*, edited by P. Sheldon, S. Gregson, R. Lansbury, and K. Sanders, 52–79. New York, NY: Routledge.

Burks, S.V., M.H. Belzer, Q. Kwan, S.G. Pratt, and S. Shackelford. 2010. "Trucking 101: An Industry Primer." TRB Transportation Research Circular. Washington, DC: Transportation Research Board.

Callahan, P. 2019a. "How Amazon Hooked America on Fast Delivery While Avoiding Responsibility for Crashes." ProPublica. September 5. https://tinyurl.com/2bxkd2zs

———. 2019b. "The Human Cost of Amazon's Fast, Free Shipping." *New York Times*. September 5. https://tinyurl.com/yc2zszvx

Chen, G.X., W.K. Sieber, J.E. Lincoln, J. Birdsey, E.M. Hitchcock, A. Nakata, C.F. Robinson, J.W. Collins, and M.H. Sweeney. 2015. "NIOSH National Survey of Long-Haul Truck Drivers:

Injury and Safety." *Accident Analysis and Prevention* 85: 66–72. https://doi.org/10.1016/j.aap.2015.09.001

Dobbs, F. 1972. *Teamster Rebellion.* New York, NY: Monad Press.

———. 1973. *Teamster Power.* New York, NY: Monad Press.

Executive Office of the President. 2022. "Supply Chain Assessment of the Transportation Industrial Base: Freight and Logistics." February. https://tinyurl.com/2v8n7ddv

Feltham, B., A. Gray, M. Kellock, A. Rooding, R. Rosedale, A. Weber, and P. Willox. 2023. "Closing Loopholes Bill—Our Summary of the Proposed New Laws." https://tinyurl.com/znnmafep

Gallup Organization. 1997. "Empty Seats and Musical Chairs: Critical Success Factors in Truck Driver Retention." ATA Foundation. October. https://tinyurl.com/47vbbmun

Gardner, M. 1995. "Labor Movements and Industrial Restructuring: Australia, New Zealand, and the U.S." In *The Comparative Political Economy of Industrial Relations*, edited by K.S. Wever and L. Turner, 33–69. Madison, WI: Industrial Relations Research Association.

General Accounting Office. 1991. "Promising Approach for Predicting Carriers' Safety Risks." GAO/PEMD-91-13. April 4. Washington, DC: United States Congress, General Accounting Office.

Hensher, D.A., H.C. Battellino, J.L. Gee, and R.F. Daniels. 1991. "Long Distance Truck Drivers On-Road Performance and Economic Reward." December. Sydney, Australia: Institute of Transport Studies, Graduate School of Management and Public Policy. https://tinyurl.com/4ryv3fj6

Hirsch, B.T. 1993. "Trucking Deregulation and Labor Earnings: Is the Union Premium a Compensating Differential?" *Journal of Labor Economics* 11, no. 2: 279–301.

Hirsch, B.T., D.A. Macpherson, and W.E. Even. 2024. "Union Membership and Coverage Database." https://www.unionstats.com

International Brotherhood of Teamsters. 2023. "Teamsters Ratify Historic UPS Contract." Press Release. August 22. https://tinyurl.com/bdzev8j4

James, R., and E.D. James. 1965. *Hoffa and the Teamsters: A Study of Union Power.* Princeton, NJ: D. Van Nostrand.

Karp, P. 2024. "Closing Loopholes Bill: The Right to Disconnect and Five Other Changes Coming to Australian Workplaces." *Guardian.* February 8. https://tinyurl.com/2ernznhy

Keynes, J.M. 1936. *The General Theory of Employment, Interest, and Money.* Cambridge, UK: Macmillan Cambridge University Press, for the Royal Economic Society.

Khan, L.M. 2017. "Amazon's Antitrust Paradox." *Yale Law Journal* 126, no. 3: 710–805.

Kingston, J. 2023a. "15 States Jump into California's Ongoing AB5 Legal Battle; Attorneys General from Mostly Democratic States Seek 'to Correct the Mistaken and Harmful Panel Decision' on Independent Contractor Law." FreightWaves. May 11. https://tinyurl.com/52h9ck82

Kingston, J. 2023b. "Lawyers Will Square Off on California Trucking's Latest AB5 Exemption Request; Monday Hearing Will Be Before Judge Who Granted Initial AB5 Request in 2019." FreightWaves. November 10. https://tinyurl.com/425yd96v

Kolko, G. 1963. *The Triumph of Conservatism: A Reinterpretation of American History, 1900–1916.* New York, NY: The Free Press.

Leiter, R.D. 1957. *The Teamsters Union: A Study of Its Economic Impact.* New York, NY: Bookman Associates.

Levinson, H.M. 1971. "Collective Bargaining and Technological Change in the Trucking Industry." In *Collective Bargaining and Technological Change in American Transportation*, edited by H.M. Levinson, C.M. Rehmus, J.P. Goldberg, and M.C. Kahn, 1–84. Evanston, IL: Northwestern University Transportation Center.

———. 1980. "Trucking." In *Collective Bargaining: Contemporary American Experience*, edited by G.G. Somers, 99–149. Champaign, IL: Industrial Relations Research Association.

Levinson, M. 2008. *The Box: How the Shipping Container Made the World Smaller and the World Economy Bigger*. Princeton, NJ: Princeton University Press.

Levy, K. 2023. *Data Driven: Truckers, Technology, and the New Workplace Surveillance*. Princeton, NJ: Princeton University Press.

Mill, J. 1808. *Commerce Defended*. London, UK: C. and R. Baldwin.

Quinlan, M. 2001. "Report of Inquiry into Safety in the Long Haul Trucking Industry." Sydney, Australia: Motor Accidents Authority of New South Wales. November. https://tinyurl.com/5bthb56u

Saltzman, G.M., and M.H. Belzer. 2002. "The Case for Strengthened Motor Carrier Hours of Service Regulations." *Transportation Journal* 41, no. 4: 51–71.

———. 2007. "Truck Driver Occupational Safety and Health: 2003 Conference Report and Selective Literature Review." April 24–25, 2003. Washington, DC: US Department of Health and Human Services, Public Health Service, Centers for Disease Control and Prevention, National Institute for Occupational Safety and Health (NIOSH). http://www.cdc.gov/niosh/docs/2007-120

Say, J.-B. 1834 (1803). *A Treatise on Political Economy, or, The Production, Distribution, and Consumption of Wealth*. Philadelphia, PA: Grigg and Elliot.

Slobodian, Q. 2018. *Globalists: The End of Empire and the Birth of Neoliberalism*. Cambridge, MA: Harvard University Press.

Soroff J. 2022. "The Interview: Teamsters General President Sean O'Brien. How Do You Defeat Amazon? We Ask That and Other Burning Questions of Boston's Own Sean O'Brien, the Most Powerful Labor Leader in All the Land." City Life. February 8. https://tinyurl.com/yxm9fkhv

Stigler, G.J. 1971. "The Theory of Economic Regulation." *Bell Journal of Economics and Management Science* 2, no. 1: 3–21. https://doi.org/10.2307/3003160

Tomlinson, K. 2019. "How an Immigration Scheme Steers Newcomers into Canadian Trucking Jobs—and Puts Lives at Risk." *Globe and Mail*. October 5. https://tinyurl.com/y5zmn84t

Viscelli, S. 2016a. *The Big Rig: Trucking and the Decline of the American Dream*. Oakland, CA: University of California Press.

———. 2016b. "Truck Stop: How One of America's Steadiest Jobs Turned into One of Its Most Grueling." *Atlantic*. May 10. https://tinyurl.com/47w2zpfm

Additional Reports, Documents, and Legislation Cited

"2021 Statistics of United States Business (SUSB) Annual Data Tables by Establishment Industry." 2023. https://tinyurl.com/sx5uw533

"2023 Pocket Guide to Large Truck and Bus Statistics." December 2023. US Department of Transportation, Federal Motor Carrier Safety Administration. https://tinyurl.com/32uwbd2m

"Conclusions on Safety and Health in the Road Transport Sector." 2016. Tripartite Sectoral Meeting on Safety and Health in the Road Transport Sector, October 12–16, 2015, Geneva, Switzerland. https://tinyurl.com/48kdrtkw

"Fact Sheet #19:" The Motor Carrier Exemption under the Fair Labor Standards Act (FLSA). 2009. https://tinyurl.com/4nwehs4s

"Fact Sheet #22: Hours Worked Under the Fair Labor Standards Act (FLSA)." 2008. US Department of Labor, Wage and Hour Division.

"Final Report." Meeting of Experts to Adopt Guidelines on the Promotion of Decent Work and Road Safety in the Transport Sector. Geneva, Switzerland: International Labour Office.

"Guidelines on the Promotion of Decent Work and Road Safety in the Transport Sector." Meeting of Experts to Adopt Guidelines on the Promotion of Decent Work and Road Safety in the Transport Sector. September 2019. Geneva, Switzerland: International Labour Office.

"Interstate Truck Driver's Guide to Hours of Service." 2022. US Department of Transportation, Federal Motor Carrier Safety Administration.

"Resolution Concerning Best Practices in Road Transport Safety." 2016. Tripartite Sectoral Meeting on Safety and Health in the Road Transport Sector, October 12–16, 2015, Geneva, Switzerland. https://tinyurl.com/48kdrtkw

"The Fair Labor Standards Act of 1938, as Amended." 2011. 29 CFR Chapter V. US Department of Labor, Wage and Hour Division.

"The Road to Social Dialogue: A Compendium of the ILO's Work in the Road Transport Sector (1938–2015)." Meeting of Experts to Adopt Guidelines on the Promotion of Decent Work and Road Safety in the Transport Sector. September 2019. Geneva, Switzerland: International Labour Office. https://tinyurl.com/2p98bfp3

"Truck Transportation: NAICS 484." 2023. https://www.bls.gov/iag/tgs/iag484.htm

CHAPTER 6

Labor Relations in the Healthcare Industry: A Portrait of Contradictions

ARIEL AVGAR
Cornell University

ADRIENNE E. EATON
REBECCA K. GIVAN
Rutgers University

ADAM SETH LITWIN
Cornell University

Abstract

This chapter provides a review of labor relations in the healthcare industry in the United States. The authors offer a broad overview of a range of contextual factors that influence the way in which labor relations plays out in this setting. They highlight a number of patterns and trends related to healthcare expenditures, labor markets, financialization, and unionization within the healthcare context. In addition, the chapter offers an overview of key labor and management actors with an assessment of power dynamics and strategic approaches. Building on this overview, the authors detail the implications associated with labor relations processes, distinguishing between conflict and cooperation. Finally, the chapter reviews existing evidence on the outcomes associated with unionization and labor relations in the healthcare context. Taken together, this review points to a number of significant contradictions that help explain some of the inextricable challenges policy makers and practitioners face in this crucial industry. The chapter builds on a long-held employment relations–based argument that workplace factors, including labor relations, are critical to the delivery of high-quality care and that these have been mostly absent from policy discussions about how best to fix a broken healthcare system. The authors conclude that a more careful attention to a set of labor relations contradictions might offer a path forward.

INTRODUCTION: THE HEALTHCARE INDUSTRY CONTEXT

For most people in the United States, healthcare is the very first and the very last system they interact with. Even the healthiest among us turn to hospitals and medical offices for immunizations, annual physical exams, and other routine services. We all have a stake in this system as potential patients. As employment relations scholars, we contend that labor relations factors—the manner in which employers and unions engage with one another through collective bargaining, strikes, and partnership (Ahmed et al. 2022)—strongly shape the state of our healthcare system. Understanding these employment and labor relations factors is critical to having a complete understanding of healthcare systems and healthcare outcomes for patients, workers, and organizations. In this chapter, we provide a review of the state of labor relations in healthcare. We begin with an overview of the healthcare system in the United States, including trends in employment and unionization. We then outline the key labor relations actors, focusing on employers, unions, and the public sector. Next, we focus on core labor–management processes, with an emphasis on conflict and cooperation. Finally, we examine the array of outcomes associated with labor relations in this essential sector.

In painting a portrait of labor relations in the US healthcare system, a number of contradictions emerge. Ours is a system characterized by fragmentation alongside consolidation; by massive economic investments alongside mixed, uneven patient care outcomes; and by supposed worker centrality or essentiality alongside the deterioration of working conditions. In what follows, we highlight these and other contradictions that characterize the healthcare system and that stand at the heart of where labor and management might focus their joint efforts.

Healthcare Expenditures

A description of the state of healthcare in the United States should start with the macro economy in general and the labor market in particular, which present a host of additional reasons for broad interest and concern regarding this sector. On the macro side, healthcare accounts for nearly one fifth of all economic activity in the United States, hovering at 18.3%. As Figure 1 shows, that cost has grown larger and larger since 1960, cresting at 20% during the COVID pandemic. Not surprisingly, these costs have long troubled policy makers, generating demands that they "bend the cost curve," effectively halting its near linear growth. More concretely, taxpayers cough up over half of that $4.3 trillion directly by funding Medicare and Medicaid, our insurance programs for the elderly, disabled, and indigent. That might not be very alarming, except that at $12,555 per year, the United States spends far more per capita than any other developed country. Switzerland comes the closest, at $8,049 (Organisation for Economic Co-operation and Development 2023). However, given those investments, Switzerland also far outscores the United States on the sector's most fundamental performance indicators, such as life expectancy (84 years versus 77.3) (Organisation for Economic Co-operation and Development 2023), infant mortality (3.51 death per 1,000 live births versus 5.12) (US Central Intelligence Agency 2023), and maternal mortality (1.2 deaths per 100,000 live births versus 23.8) (Organisation for Economic Co-operation and Development 2023). Suffice it to say, our nation's investments in its healthcare system do not appear to translate into commensurate improvements in patient care quality.

Figure 1
Healthcare Expenditures as a Share of Gross
Domestic Product in the United States, 1983–2021

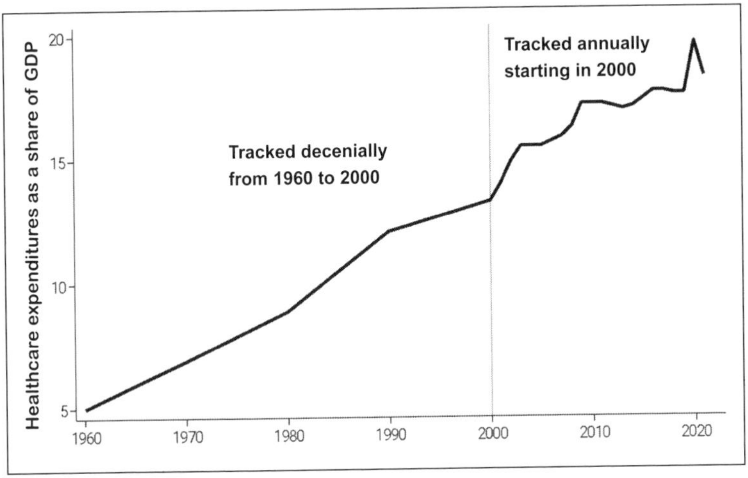

[Chart: Healthcare expenditures as a share of GDP, 1960–2020. Tracked decenially from 1960 to 2000. Tracked annually starting in 2000.]

US Centers for Medicare and Medicaid Services (2023).

Healthcare Labor Market

Not surprisingly, the healthcare sector, which plays such an outsized role in the macro economy, is also a dominant actor in the labor market. With a labor force exceeding 17 million people, the sector accounts for 12.3% of all employment in the United States, eclipsing manufacturing's 10.4% share. In fact, since the US Bureau of Labor Statistics began collecting sector-disaggregated employment data in 1983, healthcare employment growth has far exceeded that of the economy at large (Figure 2).

More critically, over the next decade, the government projects that healthcare and social assistance will exhibit the most pronounced growth of all sectors, contributing significantly to the overall job gains projected for the period spanning from 2022 through 2032. In fact, the sector will account for approximately 45% of all employment growth during that period. Demand for nurse practitioners (NPs) in particular will grow faster than that of any other job in the economy, save wind turbine service technicians, at a rate of 45% (US Bureau of Labor Statistics 2023b). At the lower end of the sector's wage distribution, the number of home health and personal care aide jobs is expected to grow by 22% (US Bureau of Labor Statistics 2023a).

Even as concerns and uncertainty proliferate around the extent to which robots and artificial intelligence (AI) could displace millions of workers, there are no projections of dramatic decreases in the demand for front-line healthcare workers. While AI could assist skilled workers in performing their jobs, allowing them to shift their attention to more complex cases and more complicated tasks, robotics has yet to advance in its efforts to undertake myriad, nonroutine, self-directed physical tasks

Figure 2
Relative Employment Growth in the United States, 1983–2022

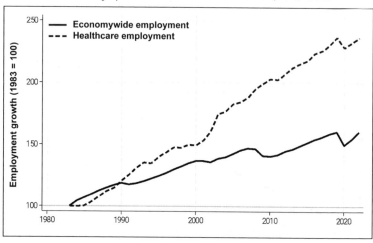

US Bureau of Labor Statistics Current Population Survey via https://www.unionstats.com. See Hirsch and Macpherson (2003) for complete methodology.

in unfamiliar, ever-changing environments. Therefore, while one should not ignore the possibilities for technological solutions to sectoral labor market shortages, it would be wrong to think that technology in and of itself could solve healthcare's "wicked" problems or somehow render healthcare workers redundant en masse. More simply, technology per se will neither address the sector's woes nor economically injure its workforce (Litwin 2020).

Healthcare Workforce Demographics

Driving this workforce demand is demographics. Significant demographic changes will have profound implications for the quantity and composition of healthcare services in the coming decades. One of the main reasons for this change is the aging of the population, as baby boomers reach retirement age and life expectancies increase. According to the US Census Bureau, the number of residents aged 65 and older is projected to nearly double from 52 million in 2018 to 95 million by 2060, increasing their share of the total population from 16% to 23% (Vespa, Armstrong, and Medina 2018). This trend will result in a higher prevalence of chronic diseases, disability, and multi-morbidity among older adults, as well as a greater need for long-term and end-of-life care (Ortman, Velkoff, and Hogan 2014).

Another important demographic factor that will affect the healthcare system is the increasing diversity of the population in terms of race, ethnicity, and immigration status. The United States is becoming more racially and ethnically diverse: the share of non-Hispanic Whites is projected to decline from 60% in 2018 to 44% by 2060, while the share of Hispanics will increase from 18% to 28%, and the share of Asians will increase from 6% to 9% (Vespa, Armstrong, and Medina 2018). Moreover, the United States is home to more than 44 million immigrants who account for about 14% of the total population and represent a wide range of countries, cultures, languages, and health needs (Radford and Noe-Bustamante 2019). These demographic shifts pose challenges and opportunities for the healthcare system because they require more culturally competent and linguistically appropriate care, as well as more attention being paid to health disparities and social determinants of health among different groups.

A third demographic factor that will influence the demand for healthcare services is the changing composition of households and families. The United States has witnessed a decline in marriage rates and an increase in divorce rates, resulting in more single-person households and more blended families. Additionally, the United States has experienced a decline in fertility rates and an increase in childlessness, leading to smaller family sizes and fewer potential caregivers for older adults (Ortman, Velkoff, and Hogan 2014).

Financialization of Healthcare

While demographics are driving change on the demand side, the usual forces of profit-maximization—bolstered by the imperatives of financialization—are catalyzing developments on the supply side. What began as a wave of consolidation—single hospitals into larger groups and then those groups into larger, integrated community health systems—has transformed into a system adept at capturing every bit of value in the system. Consolidation refers to the process of merging or acquiring healthcare entities, such as hospitals, physician groups, insurers, or pharmaceutical companies. Financialization refers to the increasing influence of financial actors and markets on the healthcare sector, such as private equity firms, hedge funds, or venture capitalists. Both consolidation and financialization have accelerated in recent years, especially during the COVID-19 pandemic, as healthcare organizations faced financial pressures and sought economies of scale or new sources of capital (Welch et al. 2022).

The upshot has been an increase in the market power of healthcare entities, which enables them to exert greater control over prices, quality, and access to healthcare services. Studies have shown that hospital consolidation leads to higher prices for patients, employers, and insurers, without improving quality or efficiency (Baker, Bundorf, and Kessler 2016). Similarly, physician consolidation results in higher prices and lower quality for consumers (Baker, Bundorf, and Kessler 2014). Moreover, insurer consolidation reduces competition and choice for consumers and providers, while increasing premiums and deductibles (Dafny, Ho, and Lee 2019). Furthermore, financialization introduces new actors and interests into the healthcare sector, which may prioritize profit over patient care or public health. For example, private equity firms have been involved in acquiring hospitals, nursing homes, physician practices, and other healthcare entities, often cutting costs, reducing staff, increasing prices, or engaging in aggressive billing practices (Harrington and Edelman 2023).

Another effect of consolidation and financialization is the change in the structure and governance of healthcare entities, which may affect their mission, culture, and accountability. Consolidation often leads to the formation of large and complex health systems or networks, which may span different regions, markets, or sectors. These systems may have advantages in terms of coordination, integration, or innovation, but they may also face challenges in terms of management, regulation, or oversight. For instance, some health systems may become too big to fail or too powerful to regulate, posing systemic risks or anti-trust concerns (Cutler and Morton 2013). Financialization also alters the ownership and governance of healthcare entities, which may affect their incentives, performance, or transparency. For example, some healthcare entities may become more responsive to shareholders or investors than to patients or communities, or they may adopt short-term or risky strategies that undermine long-term sustainability or social responsibility (Appelbaum and Batt 2020).

Unionization in Healthcare

Having described shifts in employer power, we turn to the state of unionization in this sector. Consolidation and financialization in the wake of the strong and abiding demand for healthcare services engendered by demographic shifts has understandably made the sector relatively ripe for organizing and raises clear questions about countervailing sources of power that might offset the considerable expansion of employer leverage. While private sector union density has eroded precipitously since the early 1980s, as shown in Figure 3, healthcare unions have managed to maintain their strength in the sector. Healthcare union density now trumps that of manufacturing, 13.2% versus 7.9%, respectively. That places healthcare far ahead of the private sector writ large, where just 6% of workers now claim union membership. Healthcare's headline union density measure—8.2%—buries some important variation within the sector. Figure 4 drills down by partitioning healthcare into the four subsectors—medical offices, hospitals, homecare, and nursing homes.[1] This makes clear that hospitals are the real force driving the sector's high density—not surprising, given their size and work structures.

Figure 5 adds more dimensionality to our understanding of intra-industry variation. Panel A breaks down overall employment in the sector for 2022, the most recent year for which we have data. It reveals that nearly 60% of all healthcare employment occurs in hospitals and homecare, the two subsectors that outperform relative to the overall private sector in terms of union density. Of course, this raises the possibility that medical offices and nursing homes are difficult to organize. To the extent that sectoral growth will take place in nursing homes or that more medical services once delivered in hospitals could soon be delivered in medical offices, unions will need to think harder about strategies for succeeding in settings less amenable to organizing. Panel B, which breaks down union membership by subsector, drives this point home. Fully two thirds of all union members in the sector work in hospitals. But only 7.7% work in nursing homes, suggesting that nursing homes may be the next place for healthcare unions to focus as they aim to grow their ranks.

Figure 3
Union Membership as a Share of Workers Employed
in the United States, 1983–2022

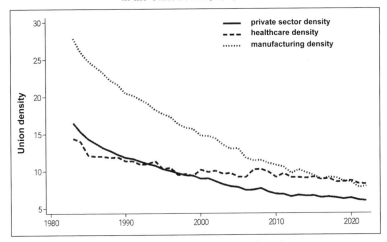

US Bureau of Labor Statistics Current Population Survey via https://www.unionstats.com.
See Hirsch and Macpherson (2003) for complete methodology.

Figure 4
Breakdown of Healthcare Employment and Union Membership
in the United States in 2022, by Subsector

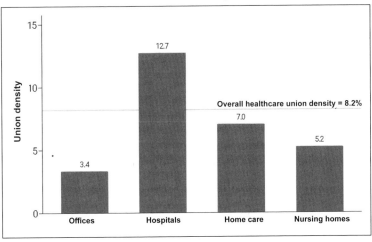

US Bureau of Labor Statistics Current Population Survey via https://www.unionstats.com.
See Hirsch and Macpherson (2003) for complete methodology.

Figure 5
Breakdown of Healthcare Employment and Union Membership in the United States in 2022, by Subsector

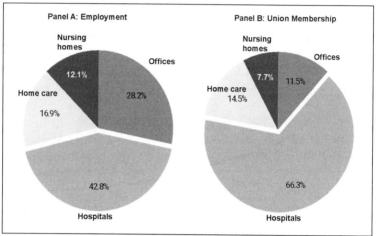

Note: Total employment in healthcare in the United States in 2022 was 17,367,780 people, of which 1,428,299, or 8.2%, were union members.

US Bureau of Labor Statistics Current Population Survey via https://www.unionstats.com. See Hirsch and Macpherson (2003) for complete methodology.

KEY ACTORS: EMPLOYERS, HEALTHCARE SYSTEMS, AND UNIONS

Employers and Healthcare Systems

The above overview of the state of healthcare in the United States sets the stage for a review of the key actors who play a role within the labor relations system. One of the most important structural features of the US healthcare system is its multi-payer and multi-provider character. Compared with most other national healthcare systems in developed countries, the United States is incredibly decentralized and fragmented across a mostly privatized landscape. The United States has over 6,000 acute care hospitals and more than 28,000 nursing homes organized under hundreds of local and regional healthcare systems (American Hospital Association 2024). This fragmentation has clear implications for the interactions between labor and management and poses a significant challenge for unions seeking to organize across thousands of independent healthcare organizations. At a very basic level, it means that unions seeking to organize front-line workers must engage across an array of separate systems adopting a range of labor relations strategies.

As noted, healthcare remains the largest and fastest growing sector in the US economy (Rhyan, Turner, and Miller 2020). While approximately two thirds of healthcare in the country is purchased by government entities (including public healthcare programs and employment-based health insurance for public employees), the vast majority of healthcare, whether primary, acute, hospital, or nursing care, is provided by private entities (Himmelstein and Woolhandler 2016). This patchwork of providers includes nonprofit and for-profit healthcare systems, many of which, as noted above, have gone through significant consolidation in recent years (Fulton et al. 2022). This creates unique challenges for collective bargaining because systems may include multiple ongoing bargaining units or unionized and nonunionized workers performing the same work across different sites. Exacerbating the challenge of a fragmented landscape, unions in healthcare must contend with organizing and bargaining in varied contexts that span different occupational groups and a range of employer strategies and in the absence of industry-wide leverage.

Given the consolidated, privatized, and fragmented nature of the US healthcare system, there are many areas in which single, local, or regional healthcare systems have become dominant. The massive University of Pittsburgh Medical Center system in Pennsylvania, for example, employs 95,000 people and operates dozens of hospitals and hundreds of clinics and doctors' offices (UPMC 2023). HCA, one of the largest healthcare systems in the United States, owns 186 hospitals and operates thousands of facilities (HCA Healthcare 2020). These healthcare systems can become near-monopolistic providers, as well as serve as the major employer and economic engine in many small and deindustrialized communities (Winant 2021). Major public healthcare systems are also significant employers. The Veterans Health Administration, for example, employs over 400,000 people (Department of Veterans Affairs 2022). The New York City public healthcare system, NYC Health + Hospitals, employs 45,000 people (NYC Health + Hospitals 2023). What might, at first blush, appear to be a paradox, the US healthcare system comprises separate and fragmented systems and healthcare organizations that, themselves, have increased their regional and, in some cases, multiregional consolidated power. As such, unions find themselves dealing with a system that lacks integration but affords employers with considerable bargaining power.

Complicating the employer landscape further, some managed care organizations (known as health maintenance organizations, or HMOs) function as both health insurers and healthcare providers, generally providing care within a closed system in which the HMO owns the facilities and directly employs or contracts with the staff providing the care. Kaiser Permanente, the largest of these organizations, covers over 12 million patients (or "members") and employs over 200,000 people, the majority of whom are unionized (Kaiser Permanente 2023).

Workers and Unions

As noted above, close to one in ten US workers is employed in the healthcare sector (Smith and Blank 2023). The largest occupational group is RNs, who represent 3.4 million of the total 14.7 million employees (Smith and Blank, 2023). Overall, 13.2% of healthcare workers are unionized (Ahmed et al. 2022), a number slightly higher than the unionization rate for workers as a whole. However, this average hides massive differences across states. For example, 21.5% of healthcare workers were unionized in the Northeast, compared with only 11.4% and 5.2% in the Midwest and South, respectively (Ahmed et al. 2022).

Healthcare workers are represented by over two dozen different unions, some operating at the state and local levels, such as the California Nurses Association, and others national in scope. Some, such as National Nurses United (NNU), represent only a single occupational group, in this case RNs, while others, like the Service Employees International Union (SEIU), represent healthcare workers across the occupational spectrum. As shown in Table 1, SEIU represents over one million healthcare workers, and the NNU represents over 200,000 workers. Together, SEIU, NNU, the American Federation of Teachers, and the United Food and Commercial Workers represent millions of healthcare workers across multiple occupational groups.

Nationally, RNs are represented by over 20 unions. In addition to the unions mentioned above, these include the Steelworkers, Teamsters, and Operating Engineers. Emerging organizing efforts over the past few years have led to many new bargaining units composed of single occupational groups, such as RNs, or interns and residents. In other cases, different occupational groups are working together to form unions in their workplace, as doctors, RNs, and physician assistants are doing at PeaceHealth in Oregon. In the face of growing employer power through consolidations and other patterns and trends discussed in this chapter, multi-occupational models offer a strategic advantage to enhance labor's capacity to bargain effectively. One of the challenges in doing so more robustly is addressing the dramatically different issues and concerns that animate organizing for different occupational groups, from physicians to homecare workers. In addition, regulatory constraints, described later, give occupational unionization efforts a clear advantage. Cross-occupational coalitions, like those among Kaiser Permanente unions, offer another option.

Despite these challenges, union organizing in the healthcare industry has seen growing worker interest and collective action over the past few years. This trend began prior to the pandemic and has accelerated as a result of the crisis. While overall

Table 1
Major Unions Representing Healthcare Workers in the United States

Union	Total membership	Healthcare membership
National Nurses United	225,000	225,000
Service Employees International Union	2,000,000	1,100,000
American Federation of Teachers	1,720,000	70,000
American Federation of State, County and Municipal Employees	1,300,000	350,000
American Federation of Government Employees	750,000	Total unknown; includes over 300,000 within the Veterans Administration

AFSCME Research and Collective Bargaining Services Department, "About AFT Healthcare," https://tinyurl.com/28zy4jh; National Nurses United, https://tinyurl.com/298tfypd.

union density in the healthcare industry has remained relatively stable over the past decade, petitions filed with the National Labor Relations Board (NLRB) suggest a growing interest on the part of front-line healthcare workers in organizing collectively (Ahmed et al. 2022).

One interesting area that has seen recent changes impacting labor relations and collective bargaining is the employment status and working conditions of physicians. For decades, the majority of physicians were self-employed, working as independent contractors or separate business entities, receiving payment based on services provided, and billing patients or insurers directly (Kane 2021). As of 2022, 50% of physicians were employees, a dramatic increase from the 41.8% of physicians who were employees as recently as 2012. In 2022, just 44% of physicians were practice owners, down from 61% just two decades earlier (Kane 2023). In recent years, however, this has changed rapidly. The majority of physicians today are now directly employed by healthcare organizations and are entitled to the workplace protections (including the right to organize collectively) afforded all employees. The massive investment of private equity into healthcare has accelerated this trend, with large private equity–owned corporations buying out small physician-owned practices and restructuring with these physicians as direct employees (Scheffler, Alexander, and Godwin 2021). Staffing firms (also significantly owned by private equity), directly employ physicians at hospitals as well, creating another example of the fissuring of work, where multiple entities function as the de facto employer but the staffing firm is the de jure employer (Geyman 2023).

These employment changes have contributed to a notable organizing push on the part of physician interns, residents, and fellows since the onset of the pandemic. The groups have primarily, but not exclusively, chosen to affiliate with the Committee of Interns and Residents (CIR, part of SEIU). CIR has grown by over 50% since 2020 (Mateus 2023), and house staff at some of the country's most prestigious and well-resourced hospitals and health systems, such as Mass General, Penn Health, and Stanford University, have chosen to organize, generally winning their NLRB elections in landslides in spite of full-throated and aggressive employer opposition.

At the Allina healthcare system in Minnesota and Wisconsin, some 400 physicians at primary care clinics joined with their nurse practitioner and physician assistant colleagues in voting to unionize in the fall of 2023. They joined a group of 100 physicians at Allina's Mercy Hospital who had voted to unionize earlier the same year (Nesterak 2023). Physicians voted to unionize by large margins, expressing concerns about numerous issues, including staffing levels, workloads and productivity requirements, and insufficient support staff.

In addition to unions, many professional healthcare workers have strong and influential professional associations. These organizations often wield significant lobbying power and influence credentialing and entry into the professions. The American Medical Association represents about 20% of practicing physicians but exerts a great deal of legislative pressure and is very well funded, thanks to sources of income beyond membership dues (Givan 2016). Specialty medical associations play a significant role in the professional arena for doctors. Other healthcare professionals from physical therapists to nurses also participate in professional associations, some of which provide individualized insurance or legal support, but they are generally completely separate from healthcare unions.

In addition to physicians, healthcare unions have seen gains in organizing other occupational groups, including low-wage workers such as homecare workers and certified nursing assistants. The healthcare system in the United States has increasingly turned to models of care that move away from acute hospital care and toward care that is provided at home. This shift has required a significant expansion of workers who assist patients outside of healthcare institutions such as hospitals and nursing homes (Bestsennyy, Chmielewski, Koffel, and Shah 2022). Despite their centrality to the healthcare system's approach to patient care and the growing demand, homecare workers are, for the most part, invisible and employed in very poor and precarious working conditions. These employment trends and working conditions have clear implications for union organizing strategies that are increasingly focusing on this low-wage occupational group. Thus, for example, 1199SEIU has been increasingly focused on unionization efforts of homecare workers.

The need to address a broad range of worker needs, from front-line low-wage workers to physicians, helps to explain some of the reluctance on the part of unions to expand a cross-occupational organizing approach.

THE ROLE OF PROCESS: CONFLICT AND COLLABORATION IN HEALTHCARE LABOR RELATIONS

How do employers and unions engage with one another through collective bargaining and labor–management relations? There are two key ways in which the collective bargaining process in healthcare differs significantly when compared to other industries, owing to the legal regulation of bargaining in the industry. First, as a result of an NLRB rule enacted in 1989, there is a preference for occupation-based bargaining units in hospitals (i.e., units of RNs, physicians, other professionals, technicians, skill maintenance, business office/clerical, or guards and other nonprofessional employees). Units can certainly be combined for purposes of bargaining if both parties agree, as they are for national, programwide bargaining at Kaiser Permanente, for instance, or more informally coordinated when unions are able to align contract expiration dates.[2] This fragmentation of bargaining also helps explain the wide array of unions that represent healthcare workers.

Second, because of the potential risks of strikes disrupting patient care, there are special legal provisions for work stoppages at hospitals and other healthcare facilities. The National Labor Relations Act offers most private sector employees a broad right to strike, while simultaneously allowing them to be permanently replaced, but Section 8(g) of the act requires unions to give healthcare employers and the Federal Mediation and Conciliation Service (FMCS) a ten-day notice prior to a strike. This is ostensibly so employers can make arrangements to protect the continuity of patient care. Unions are also required to give the FMCS earlier notice for hospital bargaining renewals and reopeners. Neither party is supposed to use economic weapons during the notice period. As such, one of the primary tools through which unions can secure leverage vis-à-vis employers is constrained in healthcare compared to other settings. This constraint is compounded both by public opinion regarding strikes in healthcare and the role that healthcare workers' professional identity plays in using strikes as a tactic of last resort (Essex, Milligan, Williams, and Weldon 2022). Despite these constraints, healthcare unions appear to be making increased use of strike activity in recent years as a way of forcing improved working conditions for their members.

Healthcare unions and their members have leveraged collective bargaining to address a range of issues that include traditional items like pay and benefits, as well nontraditional issues. In fact, healthcare unions have long argued that patient care can be improved by addressing working condition issues such as understaffing and mandatory overtime. Accordingly, many healthcare unions emphasize the need to operate on both fronts—improving the terms and conditions of healthcare workers while also advocating for measures that will address patient care shortcomings (Clark 2016). Nurses continue to fight for safe staffing and limits on the number of patients assigned to each nurse.

The impact of the pandemic on healthcare workers has undoubtedly been significant. Concerns about burnout and short-staffing, especially among nurses, have intensified (Rotenstein, Brown, Sinsky, and Linzer 2023). The shortage has led to a reliance on temporary and travel nurses, an arrangement where hospitals contract with outside agencies who recruit and employ nurses on a short-term basis to fill staffing needs. In general, these nurses receive higher pay than staff nurses (sometimes several multiples of the hourly pay of staff nurses). The reliance on these short-term nurses can exacerbate problems for staff nurses, amplifying the appeal of becoming a travel nurse and reaping higher wages while making no commitment to remain with an employer for a significant period (Yang and Mason 2022). As a result, one of the central collective bargaining issues for healthcare unions has been the use of traveling, temporary nurses and other forms of outsourcing and subcontracting of work. In fact, this issue played a central role in the recent Kaiser Permanente strike. One of the central ways in which unions are attempting to advance both worker needs and patient care is by bargaining provisions that guarantee adequate staffing levels and limit outsourcing and subcontracting.

As is the case in most industries, labor and management in healthcare have numerous tools available to address the conflicting, and sometimes mutual, challenges they face. These tools range from the conflictual to the collaborative. The healthcare setting in the United States offers examples of both extremes. On the one hand, strikes, walkouts, and other expressions of substantial labor–management strife are increasingly common in healthcare and have intensified in the years since the pandemic. On the other hand, some of the most notable examples of labor–management partnership in the United States have emerged and have been institutionalized in this industry (Eaton, Givan, and Lazes 2016).

Labor–Management Conflict in Healthcare

One of the ways in which healthcare unions have won gains for their members, both in terms of working conditions and the quality of patient care, is through strikes and strike threats. Such actions have yielded strong contract language requiring a range of protections, including enforceable nurse-to-patient ratios. Thus, for example, at Mount Sinai and Montefiore hospitals in New York City, striking nurses won strong contracts and have begun to use their newly acquired enforcement mechanisms, including expedited arbitration, with the possibility of fines levied on the hospitals when they are out of compliance.

Strikes in healthcare labor relations appear to have increased during and after the COVID-19 pandemic. The years following the pandemic have been noted by many as a period of labor strife (Eaton 2024). Many observers called the surge of strike activity in fall 2020 "Striketober," and more recently, journalists have described the summer of 2023 as the "strike summer" or "hot labor summer," referring to the many instances of overt labor–management conflict, including screenwriters and actors, as well as a threatened strike of 340,000 UPS workers and an early fall strike by the United Auto Workers (UAW) (about 150,000 workers).

Several aspects of healthcare strikes are worth noting. First, despite the increased attention to strikes and the assessments of a sea change in US labor relations in general and in healthcare in particular, the proportion of negotiations that have ended in a strike remains a small fraction of the total contracts negotiated. Nevertheless, there have been a number of large, well-publicized strikes that have had an outsized influence beyond the boundaries of any particular organization or labor–management relationship. Table 2 shows the numbers of strikes each year from 2019 through 2023, along with two years of comparison from a decade ago and from two decades ago, using Bloomberg data (Bloomberg Law 2024). Table 3 uses data from the Cornell ILR Labor Action Tracker to provide a breakdown for the level of strike activity across different states in the United States between 2020 and 2023.

Although it is difficult to discern a clear trend, the number of strikes in healthcare increased in 2022 from the year before, and with the Kaiser Permanente and other strikes, 2023 also saw significant strike activity. Of note is the fact that many of the largest strikes in recent years took place in California. This probably reflects the fact that the state has numerous large, unionized healthcare systems, including the University of California system, Kaiser Permanente, and Sutter. It is interesting that, according to one healthcare publication, twice as many healthcare workers threatened to strike in 2022 than actually went on strike (Mensik 2023).

Many of the post-pandemic strikes have centered on staffing-related concerns because the US healthcare system as a whole struggled to retain front-line workers as a result of the pandemic. Nevertheless, this is not a new issue for hospitals, nursing homes, and other healthcare organizations, particularly when it involves RNs. According to the Cornell Labor Action tracker, which reports 122 healthcare strikes in 2021 through 2023, the most frequently mentioned issue was pay (90), followed by staffing (77), health and safety (32), and, ironically, employee healthcare (32)

Table 2
Healthcare Strikes in the United States

Year	Number of strikes/lockouts (started in the listed year)	Total workers involved	Size range	Average size (rounded)
2023 (through 9/15)	27	21,211	11–3,500	786
2022	38	44,345	40–15,000	1,167
2021	29	53,077	24–40,000	1,830
2020	23	25,875	40–8,000	1,125
2019	28	107,480*	10–38,000**	3,839
2012	37	59,071	24–21,000	1,597
2011	33	64,167	25–29,000	2,005
2002	37	13,012	5–1,500	352
2001	40	30,454	40–4,500	761

*The big number in 2019 comes from the University of California healthcare system. This was one of several one-day strikes in that system in 2019.

**Includes three zeros, which distorts the average size.

(Kallas 2022). Cornell's data also indicate that healthcare strikes constitute more than 10% of the overall number of strikes during that period. More research is clearly needed to tease out how best to interpret these trends.

A more detailed assessment of major recent strikes raises some interesting issues regarding the state of labor relations in healthcare. In 2019, the American Federation of State, County and Municipal Employees carried out a series of one-day strikes against the University of California healthcare system (which consists of five hospitals). While the union asserted the strikes concerned outsourcing and other practices related to contractors, the actions also took place in the midst of ongoing negotiations; management representatives repeatedly argued that the strikes were really a demonstration of union power in that context. The union had also filed unfair labor practice charges against the system for failure to bargain with the union prior to engaging with the contractors. These strikes involved tens of thousands of workers in a wide variety of occupations from relatively low-skilled clerical and janitorial jobs to higher-skilled technicians, case managers, audiologists, and other direct care providers.

A similarly large (40,000 employees) and brief COVID-era strike also took place at Kaiser Permanente in November 2021. The strike was conducted by three locals of the Office and Professional Employees International Union that represent mainly clerical employees. Interestingly, this action was described by a Bloomberg publication as a sympathy strike in support of Operating Engineers who, by that time, had been on strike for two months.

Table 3
Breakdown of States with Largest
Strike Activity (2020–2023)

State	Strike activity (%, largest to smallest)
California	23.2
New York	11.6
Pennsylvania	6.3
Washington	5.6
Connecticut	5.3
Minnesota	5.3
Massachusetts	5
Michigan	3.8
New Jersey	3.4
Illinois	3.1
Oregon	3.1
Missouri	2.2
Nevada	2.2
Rhode Island	1.9
Hawai'i	1.9
Ohio	1.6
Colorado	1.3
Maryland	0.9

Another notable COVID-era strike took place in September 2022 among RNs in major Minnesota cities represented by the Minnesota Nurses Association (MNA). This was a multi-employer strike across seven systems and 16 hospitals. It lasted three days, and the issues included wages, benefits, staffing, paid family leave, and scheduling. A second strike among these workers was averted when MNA won major gains, particularly in pay and a role in staffing decisions, in December of that year.

The largest healthcare strike in US history took place in October 2023 at Kaiser Permanente, with 85,000 members of the Coalition of Unions walking off the job for three days. The pressure of this strike, and the threat of another one in November 2023, resulted in an agreement announced in mid-October. The gains achieved by the unions were substantial, including a 21% wage increase over four years, which was designed to improve retention and address the dramatic staffing shortage that has impacted front-line workers and their ability to care for patients. This strike occurred within the context of the most well-established labor–management partnership in healthcare, a reminder that conflict and cooperation are both features of that relationship.

The shorter strikes described above do appear to be typical for healthcare strikes. Of the 52 strikes Bloomberg lists for 2023, only six lasted more than a week. The longest was over four months long and involved a local of the United Steelworkers representing nurses at Robert Wood Johnson/Barnabas Hospital in New Brunswick, New Jersey. Consistent with recent trends, the main issues were staffing, wages, and benefit costs; the union claimed wins on all three issues. Of the 38 strikes listed for 2022, only seven lasted longer than a week. In this case, the longest was a strike of six months that took place at Kaiser Permanente in Hawai'i.

Interestingly, Kallas argues that the "fixed duration" strike has become a strategic tool for nurses' unions and one that "protect[s] the economic interests of nurses and advance[s] their role as patient care advocates, while still imposing financial and reputational costs on employers" (2023: 69). The logic of protecting patient care probably extends to other healthcare strikes as well. In 2022, Essex, Milligan, Williams, and Weldon reviewed 15 studies examining the impact of healthcare strikes across several countries on patient morbidity. These studies ranged over several decades, involved a variety of different occupations, and examined different patient outcomes. The studies concluded that there is little evidence for any impact, either positive or negative.

Labor–Management Cooperation in Healthcare

On the opposite spectrum from strikes is the collaborative approach represented by labor–management partnerships (LMPs)—an arrangement in which both sides seek to advance collaborative and problem-solving approaches with the goal of enhancing mutual gains. There is no database in the United States of partnerships in healthcare or other industries. Eaton, Givan, and Lazes argued that healthcare was "one of the few sectors where [partnership] had continued to grow and develop" (2016: 143). They describe in some depth six "critical cases" of healthcare partnerships:

- University of Massachusetts Memorial Hospital/SHARE
- University of Vermont Medical Center/Vermont Federation of Nurses and Health Professionals
- Los Angeles Department of Health Services/SEIU
- Maimonides Medical Center/CIR
- New York State Nurses Association and 1199/SEIU, multiple employers in NYC/CIR
- Kaiser Permanente/Coalition of KP Unions

They also list three other "important" cases, including a multi-employer, multi-union partnership in the Twin Cities of Minnesota (now defunct), the multi-facility relationship between the League of Voluntary Hospitals and Nursing Homes/1199SEIU in New York City, and the Allegheny Health Network/SEIU in western Pennsylvania. The key cases all involve both union leaders and workers in various kinds of joint committees. All focus on improvement to patient care, among other objectives.

The challenges faced by these partnerships, documented by the authors of this chapter, include the 24/7 nature of healthcare work that makes worker involvement difficult, the issues faced by less-skilled employees exercising voice when working in concert with highly educated professionals, and the fragmentation of union representation and differing union strategies within the same employer. All six cases have produced a number of positive outcomes for workers and patients. Others have described partnership as particularly "precarious" and therefore difficult to sustain (Kochan et al. 2008); thus, it is interesting to note that at least five of the six key cases continue to exist, if not always thrive.

It is important to note that the Kaiser Permanente labor–management partnership has been particularly challenged by a split of the original union coalition into two groups and the apparent shifts in both management and union bargaining strategy. Kaiser Permanente has experienced strikes from some of the partnership unions over the past few years, including the major strike in October 2023 discussed above.[3] CIR has also changed strategy recently, though we think it is likely they will continue to pursue joint strategies for increasing the quality of care.

It is also important to note another employment/employment relations innovation in healthcare that is also not common and, in fact, nonexistent in hospitals. This innovation is worker-owned healthcare cooperatives. Eaton and Scharf argue that worker cooperatives are "an emergent organizational form that offers a fundamentally different, more equitable, and worker-centered approach to organizing health work and providing patient or client care" (2023: 8). Two of the cases they review are unionized cooperatives in which unions have played a role.

Interestingly, Kaiser Permanente has partnered with the cooperative holding company Obran (which has a healthcare division) and Project Equity to help its suppliers convert to worker-owned businesses. This development has the multidimensional goals of preserving and building wealth in the communities they operate in, preserving their supplier network in the face of generation transitions, and improving health and other outcomes for the workers involved. Examples include Cooperative Homecare Associates, the largest worker cooperative in the United States; others that provide homecare, physical therapy, psychotherapy, and acupuncture practices; and three suppliers to larger systems: a laundry, a staffing cooperative, and Obran (Eaton and Scharf 2023).

Healthcare is a powerful illustration of the range of labor–management models available to the parties. While this industry is recognized as fertile ground for labor–management experimentation, especially around efforts to establish partnership and cooperatives, the dominant model remains a traditional one and includes arm's-length and adversarial modes of interaction. In fact, as illustrated by the strike activity in 2021 and 2023, even collaborative models, such as the Kaiser Permanente partnership, have episodes of traditional conflict embedded into the relationship. This is a reminder that labor relations in healthcare are fluid, varied, and complex.

WHAT DO UNIONS DO IN HEALTHCARE?

Labor relations scholars have long been interested in the effects that unions have on a host of outcomes, both for workers and employers. In the healthcare context, this central question has an added level of complexity, given the importance of patient outcomes as a measure of labor relations effectiveness. As noted above, most healthcare unions seek to advance two outcome categories—patient quality of care and working conditions. One of the dominant arguments made by employment relations scholars and unions is that these two outcomes are inextricably linked.

Addressing working conditions for front-line healthcare workers advances patient care outcomes and improving quality of patient care spills over into worker-related improvements. This relationship is driven by the central role that workers play in delivering patient care. Workers delivering care while employed in poor working conditions and/or contending with stress and burnout are more likely to make errors and less likely to meet patients' needs fully. Research on labor relations in healthcare has produced a significant body of evidence supporting the benefits that unions have for both outcomes—working conditions and patient care.

What do healthcare unions do for workers and their working conditions? As has been clearly established in a well-documented body of literature, unions have a significant effect on a range of worker outcomes, from pay to job security (Ahmed et al. 2022; McNicholas, Shierholz, and Poydock 2021). Research on the effects of healthcare unions is consistent with these general findings. Although far less robust, existing studies on the effects of unions on worker pay in healthcare have shown that unionized workers have higher weekly earnings and hourly wages and are more likely to have health insurance coverage.

In a recent study, Ahmed and colleagues (2022) examined unionization rates in healthcare and associated outcomes between 2009 and 2021. They found a significant effect on earnings and noncash benefits for unionized healthcare workers. Dill and Tanem (2022) conducted a similar analysis for direct healthcare workers between 2010 and 2020 and found that unionized workers earned about 7.8% higher wages than their nonunion counterparts did. Interestingly and unusually, the authors of that study found a lower wage premium for Black unionized direct care workers than for White workers.

The union wage effect is also supported by research Sojourner and colleagues (2015) conducted regarding nursing homes. Likewise, Bender, Mridha, and Peoples (2006) examined wage effects for unionized hospital janitors and found a significant wage differential when compared with nonunion janitors in the industry. Those authors maintain that this difference is driven, for the most part, by the risk compensation negotiated for unionized janitors. Unions, they argue, affect wages by, among other things, bargaining over occupational risks that are not compensated for in nonunion healthcare settings.

In addition to wages and benefits, unions have been shown to affect decisions regarding staffing levels through collective bargaining (Krachler, Auffenberg, and Wolf 2021). Comparing union strategies in Germany and the United States, Krachler and colleagues found that many of the effects of unions on staffing-level decisions occur at the organizational level and are not significantly affected by national-level institutions. Accordingly, unions have the capacity to address one of the most persistent challenges in healthcare that affects both workers and patient care.

Unions also appear to increase organizational adherence to health and safety regulations. Dean, McCallum, Venkataramani, and Michaels (2023) examined nursing home compliance with Occupational Safety and Health Administration requirements to report worker injuries and illness, comparing unionized and nonunion facilities between 2016 and 2021. They found that two years after unionization, nursing homes saw an increase of over 30% in compliance with this reporting requirement. Given that reporting and awareness of worker injuries are critical in addressing organizational safety issues, these findings suggest an important link between unions and safer working conditions for healthcare workers.

Alongside the effects of unions on worker pay and other working conditions, there is a body of evidence linking unions to better quality of care. One of the seminal studies in this area of inquiry, by Ash and Seago (2004), found a significant relationship between hospitals with unionized registered nurses in California and lower mortality following heart attacks. Using data from all acute care hospitals in California, the authors found that mortality rates in unionized hospitals are 5.5% lower than nonunion hospitals, after controlling for a variety of factors. Although Ash and Seago did not provide direct evidence regarding possible mechanisms for this effect, their finding lends support for the argument that unions address a range of workplace concerns that likely affect the conditions in which front-line workers deliver care.

Dube, Kaplan, and Thompson (2016) provided additional support for this argument also using data from California hospitals between 1996 and 2005. The authors examined patient outcomes following a union election compared with those in which a union failed to win recognition. They found that a host of patient care outcomes, seen as sensitive to nursing care, improved in hospitals that unionized compared with that did not. Interestingly, the authors also found that unionization attempts were more likely in hospitals that experienced deteriorating patient care quality. Once this factor is considered, patient care quality outcomes were better in unionized hospitals than in nonunion hospitals that did not experience a unionization attempt. This study adds to the portrait of how unions might affect patient care outcomes. In particular, it appears as though unionization efforts increase as patient care quality erodes and that unions are capable of improving quality.

Another window into the role that unions play in affecting patient care emerged during the pandemic, with a particular focus on COVID-related mortality rates. Dean, McCallum, Venkataramani, and Michaels(2023) used proprietary data from unionized and nonunion nursing homes in 48 states and found a significant relationship between unionization and resident mortality and worker infection rates. They noted that mortality rates in unionized nursing homes during COVID were 10% lower than those in nonunion ones. Furthermore, worker infection rates were close to 7% lower for union workers than their nonunion counterparts. What this study suggests is that unionized nursing homes implemented measures that protected both patients and workers during the pandemic. It pointed to a likely preparedness of unionized healthcare organization that is more effective during a time of crisis.

What is lacking in the existing body of research is a stronger and clearer link between unionization and the mechanisms that affect patient care outcomes. As noted, the existing literature points to a very strong association between unionization and improved care and is suggestive regarding the link to the emphasis unions place on working conditions, safety, and staffing levels. One mechanism sometimes highlighted by union advocates and others is the protection of worker voice, including voice about patient care failures (Kochan and Kimball 2019). Nevertheless, additional research is needed to shed light more explicitly on the varied mechanisms by which union status affects patient care quality.

DISCUSSION AND CONCLUSION: AN INDUSTRY RIFE WITH LABOR RELATIONS CONTRADICTIONS

This review of labor relations in the healthcare industry points to a number of glaring contradictions that, taken together, help explain some of the inextricable challenges policy makers and practitioners face. The many challenges of delivering high-quality patient care despite massive economic investments are well documented. What has been elusive are ways to overcome systemic shortcomings. The chapter builds on a long-held employment relations–based argument that workplace factors, including labor relations, are critical to the delivery of high-quality care and that, more often than not, these are absent from policy discussions about how best to fix a broken healthcare system (Avgar, Eaton, Givan, and Litwin 2016, 2020). More careful attention to a set of labor relations contradictions might offer a path forward.

First, the chapter highlights the two seemingly contradictory trends in healthcare of fragmentation across myriad private and independent healthcare organizations and systems, as well as the pattern of regional consolidation within systems. In some ways, this pattern of fragmented, privatized, and consolidated healthcare systems creates an especially unruly healthcare system. On the one hand, the existence of separate and independent healthcare systems competing with one another, whether as for-profits or nonprofits, creates a well-documented challenge of healthcare integration. It makes it virtually impossible to ensure coordination across different parts of our healthcare system. On the other hand, consolidation within the larger healthcare systems, with some managing over 200 hospitals, provides private and, sometimes, public actors with a great deal of bargaining power that is not always leveraged to enhance patient care outcomes. In the context of the chapter's focus, this bargaining power also creates challenges for unionization, which, as outlined above and summarized below, has the potential to increase patient care quality.

Second, labor relations in the healthcare industry offers a tale of two models. The vast majority of labor–management relations in this sector can be characterized as traditional or conflictual, with an indication of a growing reliance on strikes and collective action as a means of reconciling competing interests. However, the healthcare industry in the United States has seen some of the most long-standing examples of labor–management partnership and collaboration. The mutual concern for patient outcomes and the link between worker interests and quality of care have created a strong foundation on which to establish thriving partnerships where both sides are able to set aside their reflexive adversarial default settings. And, despite the volumes of labor relations research pointing to the concrete advantages associated with labor–management partnership, this model is still very much the exception. Labor relations researchers would do well to continue to explore the barriers that limit the diffusion and institutionalization of a partnership model that has the potential to advance gains for workers, employers, and patients.

Finally, the most glaring contradiction to emerge from our review is the gap between the role that unions can—and have been shown to—play in advancing both patient and worker gains and the relatively modest density across the industry. While unionization in the healthcare industry outpaces the overall density and while there appears to be an increased interest in organizing across different healthcare occupational groups, especially since the pandemic, the vast majority of this sector remains nonunion. Evidence regarding the link between unionization and patient care prompts the question why this is not pursued as a proven tool to address the long-standing failings of our healthcare system, especially when compared with those in other developed countries.

These contradictions present an opportunity to promote scholarship that continues to document the ways in which unions and labor–management approaches in the healthcare industry can serve to address persisting challenges. And they suggest the need for a robust and meaningful engagement with policy makers and practitioners around these inherent contradictions and ways in which they might be reconciled to the benefit of patients, workers, and healthcare organizations.

ENDNOTES

1. "Offices" includes the following census industry codes: 7970 "offices of physicians," 7980 "offices of dentists," 7990 "offices of chiropractors," 8070 "offices of optometrists," 8080 "offices of other health care practitioners," and 8090 "outpatient care centers." "Hospitals" are 8191 "general medical and surgical hospitals" and 8192 "psychiatric and substance abuse hospitals." "Home care" includes 8170 "home health care services" and 8180 "other health care services." And "nursing homes" includes 8270 and "skilled nursing facilities" and 8290 "residential care facilities."

2. The New York State Nurses Association provides an example of such an alignment with its contracts at different private hospitals in New York City.

3. Kaiser Permanente has experienced numerous strikes in recent years by the California Nurses Association/NNU, who are not part of the coalition and have never been part of the labor–management partnership.

REFERENCES

Ahmed, A., K. Kadakia, A. Ahmed, B. Shultz, and X. Li. 2022. "Trends in Labor Unionization Among US Health Care Workers, 2009–2021." *JAMA* 328, no. 124: 2404–2411.
American Hospital Association. 2024. "Fast Facts on U.S. Hospitals, 2024." https://tinyurl.com/2ddbe3pw
Appelbaum, E., and R. Batt. 2020. "Private Equity Buyouts in Healthcare: Who Wins, Who Loses?" Institute for New Economic Thinking Working Paper Series 118. https://tinyurl.com/y4wtzm39
Ash, M., and J.A. Seago. 2004. "The Effect of Registered Nurses' Unions on Heart-Attack Mortality." *ILR Review* 57, no. 13: 422–442.
Avgar, A.C., A.E. Eaton, R.K. Givan, and A.S. Litwin. 2016. "Editorial Essay: Introduction to a Special Issue on Work and Employment Relations in Health Care." *ILR Review* 69, no. 14: 787–802.
———. 2020. "Paying the Price for a Broken Healthcare System: Rethinking Employment, Labor, and Work in a Post-Pandemic World." *Work and Occupations* 47, no. 13: 267–279.
Baker, L.C., M.K. Bundorf, and D.P. Kessler. 2014. "Vertical Integration: Hospital Ownership of Physician Practices Is Associated with Higher Prices and Spending." *Health Affairs* 33, no. 15: 756–763.

———. 2016. "The Effect of Hospital/Physician Integration on Hospital Choice." *Journal of Health Economics* 50: 1–8.

Bender, K.A., H.A. Mridha, and J. Peoples. 2006. "Risk Compensation for Hospital Workers: Evidence from Relative Wages of Janitors." *ILR Review* 59, no. 12: 226–242.

Bestsennyy, O., M. Chmielewski, A. Koffel, and A. Shah. 2022. "From Facility to Home: How Healthcare Could Shift by 2025." February 1. McKinsey & Company. https://tinyurl.com/4kpn8en6

Bloomberg Law. 2024. "Work Stoppages in Health Services [unpublished raw data]." https://tinyurl.com/2thmby3j

Clark, P. 2016. "Nurse Union Strategies for Improving the Quality of Patient Care." In *The Evolving Healthcare Landscape: How Employees, Organizations, and Institutions are Adapting and Innovating*, edited by A.C. Avgar and T.J. Vogus. Champaign, IL: Labor and Employment Relations Association.

Cutler, D.M., and F.S. Morton. 2013. "Hospitals, Market Share, and Consolidation." *JAMA* 310, no. 118: 1964–1970.

Dafny, L., K. Ho, and R.S. Lee. 2019. "The Price Effects of Cross-Market Mergers: Theory and Evidence from the Hospital Industry." *RAND Journal of Economics* 50, no. 12: 286–325.

Dean, A., J. McCallum, A.S. Venkataramani, and D. Michaels. 2023. "The Effect of Labor Unions on Nursing Home Compliance with OSHA's Workplace Injury and Illness Reporting Requirement." *Health Affairs (Millwood)* 42, no. 19: 1260–1265. https://doi.org/10.1377/hlthaff.2023.00255

Department of Veterans Affairs. 2022. "Annual Report on the Steps Taken to Achieve Full Staffing Capacity." https://tinyurl.com/2r3e7fyr

Dill, J., and J. Tanem. 2022. "Gender, Race/Ethnicity, and Unionization in Direct Care Occupations." *American Journal of Public Health* 112, no. 111: 1676–1684.

Dube, A., E. Kaplan, and O. Thompson. 2016. "Nurse Unions and Patient Outcomes." *ILR Review* 69, no. 14: 803–833.

Eaton, A.E. 2024. "Work in the Pandemic and Beyond." In *Reflections on the Pandemic: COVID and Social Crises in the Year Everything Changed*, edited by T. Politano, 237–246. New Brunswick, NJ: Rutgers University Press.

Eaton, A.E., and A. Scharf. 2023. "Introduction." In *Just Health: Case Studies of Worker Cooperatives in Health and Care Sectors*. E-Book. https://tinyurl.com/2fcna4ey

Eaton, A.E., R.K. Givan, and P. Lazes. 2016. "Labor–Management Partnerships in Health Care: Responding to the Evolving Landscape." In *The Evolving Healthcare Landscape: How Employees, Organizations, and Institutions are Adapting and Innovating*, edited by A.C. Avgar and T.J. Vogus. Champaign, IL: Labor and Employment Relations Association.

Essex, R., W. Milligan, G. Williams, and S.M. Weldon. 2022. "The Impact of Strike Action on Patient Morbidity: A Systematic Literature Review." *International Journal of Health Planning and Management* 37, no. 13: 1311–1326. https://doi.org/10.1002/hpm.3418

Fulton, B.D., D.R. Arnold, J.S. King, A.D. Montague, T.L. Greaney, and R.M. Scheffler. 2022. "The Rise of Cross-Market Hospital Systems and Their Market Power in the US: Study Examines the Increase in Cross-Market Hospital Systems and Their Market Power in the US." *Health Affairs* 41, no. 111: 1652–1660.

Geyman, J. 2023. "Private Equity Looting of US Health Care: An Under-Recognized and Uncontrolled Scourge." *International Journal of Social Determinants of Health and Health Services* 53, no. 12: 233–238.

Givan, R.K. 2016. "Who Regulates? Physicians and the Regulation of Health Care." In *The Evolving Healthcare Landscape: How Employees, Organizations, and Institutions are Adapting and Innovating*, edited by A.C. Avgar and T.J. Vogus. Champaign, IL: Labor and Employment Relations Association.

Harrington, C., and T.S. Edelman. 2023. "Private Equity and Nursing Home Care: What Policies Can Be Adopted to Address the Growing Problems?" *Public Policy and Aging Report* 33, no. 12: 44–48.

HCA Healthcare. 2020. "HCA Healthcare Fact Sheet." https://tinyurl.com/3v7843kj

Himmelstein, D.U., and S. Woolhandler. 2016. "The Current and Projected Taxpayer Shares of US Health Costs." *American Journal of Public Health* 106, no. 13: 449–452. https://doi.org/10.2105/ajph.2015.302997

Hirsch, B.T., and D.A. Macpherson. 2003. "Union Membership and Coverage Database from the Current Population Survey: Note." *ILR Review* 56, no. 12: 349–354.

Kaiser Permanente. 2023. "Fast Facts." https://tinyurl.com/2yvphmxm

Kallas, J. 2022. "Labor Action Tracker 2022." The ILR School, Cornell University. https://tinyurl.com/msdxzszr

———. 2023. "Retooling Militancy: Labour Revitalization and Fixed-Duration Strikes." *British Journal of Industrial Relations* 61, no. 11: 68–88.

Kane, C. 2021. "Policy Research Perspectives." American Medical Association. https://tinyurl.com/jkyne2sy

———. 2023. "Recent Changes in Physician Practice Arrangements: Shifts Away from Private Practice and Towards Larger Practice Size Continue Through 2022." American Medical Association. https://tinyurl.com/4c2vpzf3

Kochan, T.A., P. Adler, R. McKersie, A. Eaton, P. Segal, and P. Gerhart. 2008. "The Potential and Precariousness of Partnership: The Case of the Kaiser Permanente Labor Management Partnership." *Industrial Relations: A Journal of Economy and Society* 47, no. 1, 36–65.

Kochan, T.A., and W.T. Kimball. 2019. "Unions, Worker Voice, and Management Practices: Implications for a High-Productivity, High-Wage Economy." *RSF: The Russell Sage Foundation Journal of the Social Sciences* 5, no. 15: 88–108.

Krachler, N., J. Auffenberg, and L. Wolf. 2021. "The Role of Organizational Factors in Mobilizing Professionals: Evidence from Nurse Unions in the United States and Germany." *British Journal of Industrial Relations* 59, no. 13: 643–668.

Litwin, A.S. 2020. "Technological Change in Health Care Delivery: Its Drivers and Consequences for Work and Workers." Berkeley, CA: UC Berkeley Labor Center.

Mateus, B. 2023. "Behind the Sharp Rise in US Resident Physicians Organizing into Unions." World Socialist. https://tinyurl.com/jp922k7n

McNicholas, C., H. Shierholz, and M. Poydock. 2021. "Union Workers Had More Job Security During the Pandemic, but Unionization Remains Historically Low." Economic Policy Institute. https://tinyurl.com/225ra5vj

Mensik, H. 2023. "The Largest Healthcare Worker Strikes Waged—and Avoided—in 2022." Healthcare Dive. https://tinyurl.com/3rcec5xu

Nesterak, M. 2023. "Allina Health Clinicians Vote by Overwhelming Margin to Unionize in Historic Election." *Minnesota Reformer*. October 13. https://tinyurl.com/56t5s3v3

NYC Health + Hospitals. 2023. "About NYC Health + Hospitals." https://tinyurl.com/3rvxtw3c

Organisation for Economic Co-operation and Development. 2023. https://stats.oecd.org

Ortman, J.M., V.A. Velkoff, and H. Hogan 2014. "An Aging Nation: The Older Population in the United States." US Department of Commerce, Economics and Statistics Administration, US Census Bureau.

Radford, J., and L. Noe-Bustamante. 2019. "Facts on U.S. Immigrants, 2017." Pew Research Center's Hispanic Trends Project.

Rhyan, C., A. Turner, and G. Miller. 2020. "Tracking the US Health Sector: The Impact of the COVID-19 Pandemic." *Business Economics* 55, 267–278.

Rotenstein, L.S., R. Brown, C. Sinsky, and M. Linzer. 2023. "The Association of Work Overload with Burnout and Intent to Leave the Job Across the Healthcare Workforce During COVID-19." *Journal of General Internal Medicine* 38, no. 8: 1–8. https://doi.org/10.1007%2Fs11606-023-08153-z

Scheffler, R.M., L.M. Alexander, and J.R. Godwin. 2021. "Soaring Private Equity Investment in the Healthcare Sector: Consolidation Accelerated, Competition Undermined, and Patients at Risk." SSRN. https://tinyurl.com/5xfhtd2j

Smith, S., and A. Blank. 2023. "Healthcare Occupations: Characteristics of the Employed." US Bureau of Labor Statistics. https://tinyurl.com/4yzjt32c

Sojourner, A.J., B.R. Frandsen, R.J. Town, D.C. Grabowski, and M.M. Chen. 2015. "Impacts of Unionization on Quality and Productivity: Regression Discontinuity Evidence from Nursing Homes." *ILR Review* 68, no. 14: 771–806.

University of Pittsburgh Medical Center. 2023. "UPMC Facts and Stats." https://tinyurl.com/bdfxjf4p

US Bureau of Labor Statistics. 2023a. "Home Health and Personal Care Aides." *Occupational Outlook Handbook.* https://tinyurl.com/z8w75tsu

———. 2023b. "Employment Projections—2022–2023." https://tinyurl.com/k4yw65tn

US Centers for Medicare and Medicaid Services. 2023. "National Health Expenditure Data." https://tinyurl.com/4hnd774e

US Central Intelligence Agency. 2023. *The World Factbook.* https://tinyurl.com/4hfwx26a

Vespa, J., D.M. Armstrong, and L. Medina. 2018. "Demographic Turning Points for the United States: Population Projections for 2020 to 2060." Washington, DC: US Department of Commerce, Economics and Statistics Administration, US Census Bureau.

Welch, W.P., J. Ruhter, A. Bosworth, N. De Lew, and B.D. Sommers. 2022. "Changes of Ownership of Hospital and Skilled Nursing Facilities: An Analysis of Newly-Released CMS Data." U.S. Department of Health and Human Services.

Winant, G. 2021. *The Next Shift: The Fall of Industry and the Rise of Health Care in Rust Belt America.* Cambridge, MA: Harvard University Press.

Yang, Y.T., and D.J. Mason. 2022. "COVID-19's Impact on Nursing Shortages, the Rise of Travel Nurses, and Price Gouging." Health Affairs Forefront. https://tinyurl.com/y2vvuw58

CHAPTER 7

Teachers and Unions: Collective Bargaining in the Schools and the Politics of Public Education

CLIFFORD B. DONN
BRENDA J. KIRBY
Le Moyne College

Abstract

State-level legal frameworks shape teacher unionization and bargaining, varying from encouraging to prohibiting these activities. Public school teacher unionization levels differ across states because of these legal differences. Historically, two national unions, the American Federation of Teachers and the National Education Association, have competed for teacher allegiance, with some state branches merging. Bargaining issues such as pay and health insurance are common, while others, such as duties beyond the classroom and job security, are unique to public education. In the 21st century, the "education reform" movement has politicized issues around unions and collective bargaining. Some states have faced legal challenges to teacher union activities, while others have seen grassroots protests over pay and working conditions. Attempts to control teacher speech and the challenges of the COVID-19 pandemic add further complexities to the landscape of public education.

INTRODUCTION

The public education industry touches millions of families across every area of the United States. Millions of children attend public schools and depend on those schools to prepare them for life. Millions of adults serve as teachers and administrators, as well as in a variety of other roles in public schools.

Our economy, our democracy, and our culture all depend on an educated and informed citizenry. Public schools provide the means of accomplishing that for a large majority of the population.

The success of this industry, like the success of any other, depends heavily on the employees who work in it. Teachers are the key employees in this industry because it is teachers who directly deliver the educational services that the industry is designed to provide. While teachers and the public schools in which they work have come under attack in recent decades, there is actually a long history of such criticism of teachers and public schools. However, in the most recent periods, teachers and public schools have also faced some unique challenges (Cuevas 2022; Gelberg 1997; Goldstein 2015; Levin 2022; López et al. 2023; Miller, Liu, and Ball 2023).

The purpose of this chapter is to discuss and analyze collective bargaining in public education in the United States, paying close attention to the historical development, challenges faced by teachers and their unions, and current issues in bargaining teacher contracts.

OVERVIEW OF THE INDUSTRY

Since the early 1800s, there has been recognition of the need for public schools. Starting with the creation of a Massachusetts State Board of Education to oversee local schools and require the enrollment of all children, a national movement was born (Goldstein 2015: 23–24). According to Gelberg, "by the 1890s it was clear that business supported the idea of having schools shape youngsters into future employees" (1997: 39), an idea that has continued into our contemporary view of the purpose of public education and has led to private enterprises attempting to define the problems with education as not providing a sufficiently compliant workforce and to provide solutions (Gelberg 1997: 132). The goals of this system at its origins were similar to those of today—to prepare students to live in a democratic society and for the world of work. These goals often seemed to contradict each other, and sometimes they still do.

In addition, there are sharp political disagreements among those who would like to see schools prepare students for our democratic society. Some believe that schools should focus on celebrating the United States and its history and on the positive aspects of that history. Those who hold such beliefs sometimes object strongly to those who feel that students should be taught to analyze our history and institutions critically and to point out where we have fallen short of our ideals. As will be discussed in this chapter, this has given rise to political challenges against teachers and public schools in recent years, as well as in the more distant past.

Public education is a huge industry with one of the most decentralized structures imaginable. There are approximately 19,254 public school districts in the United States (US Department of Education 2021). According to the National Center for Educational Statistics, as of 2020–21, there were 98,557 public schools in operation, serving 49.5 million students (US Department of Education 2022).

According to Riser-Kotsitsky (2019), about 6.8% of public school students attended charter schools, and 5.5 million students were in private schools as of 2019. In 2019, 3.23% of students were home schooled, but by 2021 it was 5.4%—reflecting the COVID-19 pandemic. By 2015–16, minority students for the first time exceeded White students as a majority of public school students, and by 2021, White students made up just over 45% of total public school enrollment. The graduation rate when first tracked in 2010–11 was approximately 79%, but it has risen to 87% in 2019–20.

A charter school is technically a public school that is not subject to many state and school district policies. It is run much more independently than most public schools. Charter schools were originally proposed in the United States in 1988 by American Federation of Teachers president Albert Shanker. He suggested them as publicly funded schools that would allow more voice for teachers to experiment and innovate in their teaching. He hoped that successful innovations would then be widely adopted by conventional public schools. While in their early form, charter schools were often promoted by unions and union supporters, in the more recent period they have become an instrument of union opponents and corporate interests, emphasizing managerial control, and reducing teacher voice (Kahlenberg and Potter 2014–2015). How did this change come about?

PUBLIC SCHOOL TEACHERS UNIONS

Public education employs millions of workers, and the key group of employees—teachers—numbered around three million as of fall 2021 (US Department of Education 2021), approximately 77% of them women and approximately 80% White (Riser-Kotsitsky 2019). The majority of public school teachers (69% to 70%) belong to a union or employee association (US Department of Education 2016). However, this is much lower than the estimated 90% membership in the 1970s, when teachers were the most unionized profession in the United States. This decline is related to the overall decline in unionization rates in the United States and other factors related to public employment generally (changes in state legislation to limit and discourage public employee unionization) and public education specifically (attacks on teacher collective bargaining, as discussed later in this chapter). It also reflects growth in charter schools and home schooling.

Two national unions have traditionally dominated teacher representation and competed for the allegiance of teachers—the American Federation of Teachers (AFT) and the National Education Association (NEA). A large majority of unionized teachers are in states and districts with collective bargaining rights with locals of one of those two unions (Goldstein 2015: 134).

The precursor to the AFT, the Chicago Teachers Federation, was founded in 1897 and was the first "teachers-only" union in the country (Goldstein 2015: 67, 69). In 1915, the Chicago Board of Education adopted a rule prohibiting teachers from joining "organizations affiliated with a trade union" (Goldstein 2015: 83–84). This led the Chicago Federation of Teachers to found the AFT in 1916, which grew rapidly (Goldstein 2015: 84). The AFT was especially important in major cities, and its power base ultimately became its New York City local, the United Federation of Teachers (UFT) (Weiner 2012: 60–61, 192).

The NEA dates from 1857; it was founded in Philadelphia as the National Teachers Association. It originally included school administrators, college professors, and presidents along with teachers (Goldstein 2015: 69). It was largely focused on promoting "professionalism" in education. It became the NEA in 1870, when it merged with several other groups, including one representing school superintendents (Provenzo and Provenzo 2008: 534).

In 1921, the NEA partnered with the American Legion to counter the AFT, which both organizations thought was too radical (Goldstein 2015: 95). In 1939, responding to a push by the American Legion, the House of Representatives Un-American

Activities Committee investigated Communist influence in the AFT. Waves of these investigations occurred from 1917 to 1960, targeting thousands of teachers (Goldstein 2015: 96). In the 1950s, the NEA reoriented itself to focus more on representing teachers than administrators. This seemed to reflect a growing acceptance of the differences in interests between these two groups.

In 1949, the New York State legislature adopted a law that permitted school districts to dismiss teachers who belonged to "subversive organizations." Teachers could be and were dismissed with no evidence of any inappropriate behavior in the classroom but solely because of their personal political beliefs (Goldstein 2015: 104–106). Issues related to such political firings occupied the concerns of both of the major unions and led to a push for job protection from arbitrary terminations unrelated to classroom performance (Taylor 2011).

The UFT adopted more militant tactics than its left-wing predecessor, The Teachers Union, which considered strikes inappropriate for professionals, but the UFT was more moderate politically (Goldstein 2015: 107).

While NEA is larger, much of the leadership of the teachers union movement has come from the smaller AFT (Weiner 2012: 96). The NEA adopts more reliably liberal positions than the AFT does (Weiner 2012: 165). The competition for teacher membership in the two unions was a legacy of older debates about the appropriateness of unionization for professional employees such as teachers. However, those debates have largely subsided, and in some states, the two national unions have even merged (e.g., Florida and New York).

The overwhelming majority of teachers who are unionized belong to affiliates of those two unions. Most of the bargaining is done by the local affiliates. One of the issues that has led to the politicization of teacher unionization and collective bargaining is that the teachers unions have become a major constituency in the Democratic Party. Sometimes, up to 10% of delegates to Democratic Party conventions are teachers, and their unions have become major financial contributors to the party (Goldstein 2015: 161).

In some states, public school teachers are among the most highly unionized employees in the state, but in others, they are overwhelmingly unrepresented or may belong to a union but have no right to engage in collective bargaining. For example, several states have over 90% of their teachers organized (e.g., Vermont and Washington), while some, such as Arkansas and South Carolina, have less than 30% organized (US Department of Education 2017–2018). This largely reflects the different legal frameworks governing public education unions and bargaining. The legal frameworks governing teacher unionization and bargaining are primarily determined at the state level and range from frameworks that encourage unionization and bargaining to frameworks that prohibit bargaining entirely. Some states that permit or encourage collective bargaining also permit strikes by teachers, while others prohibit strikes by teachers and often by other public employees as well (e.g., New York). Examples of states that prohibit strikes and collective bargaining by teachers include North Carolina, Texas, and Virginia. A few of the states that permit teacher strikes include

Alaska, California, Illinois, and Pennsylvania. Some states, such as Arizona and Utah, have no statutes that explicitly address either the issue of strikes or collective bargaining (Sanes and Schmitt 2014).

States have a variety of laws governing public employee collective bargaining. In a number of states, such as Tennessee, teachers unions are legally limited to an advisory role (Bascia and Osmond 2012: 2). Other states, such as Virginia, allow public employees to unionize and negotiate with public employers, but the employers are not permitted to sign legally enforceable contracts. States may have laws that govern multiple occupations or separate laws for separate occupations (e.g., New York). Some have no law at all or have laws prohibiting collective bargaining for most public employees (e.g., Mississippi). These laws have changed frequently since 2011 (Hebdon, Slater, and Masters 2013: 256–257).

States that prohibit public employees from unionizing and/or bargaining with their employers have been of concern to some international agencies that consider such laws to contravene international human rights principles. Of particular concern is the case of North Carolina, where the law prohibits public agencies from reaching any contract or agreement with a union (Novitz 2009: 145–146).

According to Robert Hebdon, "after 2008, the issue of public sector compensation became the pretext for an assault on public sector compensation, jobs, unions, and the institution of collective bargaining. Sadly, the rigorous research on the topic was largely ignored as the rhetoric of the political debate escalated out of control." (Hebdon, Slater, and Masters 2013: 260–261). Much of this research shows that teachers are significantly underpaid compared with similarly educated professionals (one estimate for 2018 was that the differential was over 20%) and that unions impose far fewer limits on school districts than many critics presume (Allegretto and Mishel 2019; Donn, Donn, Goldberg, and Kirby 2014). In a number of states with Republican governors and state legislatures, these issues became major public controversies (Donn 2012).

BARGAINING STRUCTURE

One difficulty in successful bargaining within the public education industry is its size and its highly decentralized structure. It employs hundreds of thousands of workers, and the key group of employees (teachers) can number anywhere from a dozen to thousands. The typical bargaining structure is based on the individual school district, but teachers unions typically attempt to negotiate a single collective bargaining agreement that covers all teachers in a single school district, regardless of how many schools there are in the district. The exception is charter schools, which are public schools legally permitted to operate largely independently. Most charter schools do not have collective bargaining agreements with teachers unions (Weiner 2012: 75). However, charter schools have grown, and a growing minority of those have become unionized as teachers in those schools have sought greater voice in wages, hours, and working conditions (Goldstein 2015: 223).

Educational reformers often believe charter schools are especially promising because they usually operate without unions and outside the restrictions established by school district bureaucracies. In addition, they are often exempt from many of the state policies that regulate public schools (Rubinstein and McCarthy 2021: 250–251). Most studies, however, have demonstrated that charter schools do not, on average, produce better results for students than ordinary public schools. School vouchers (another policy that is popular with critics of public education) tend to produce even poorer results for students (Carnoy 2017; Dobbie and Fryer 2016; Rubinstein and McCarthy 2021: 253).

The educational reform movement (which involves *inter alia* opposition to teacher collective bargaining and supports merit pay for teachers and measuring teacher performance in terms of student test outcomes) has not produced positive results for students, and harsh criticisms of teachers have led to teachers leaving the profession faster than ever and have made it harder to recruit new teachers (Rubinstein and McCarthy 2021: 254). Evidence from a RAND Corporation study shows that evaluating teachers based on student test scores, a goal of "reformers," has no measurable impact on teacher quality or student achievement (Rubinstein and McCarthy 2021: 253).

MAIN BARGAINING ISSUES

Teacher collective bargaining originated as a response to arbitrary and sexist behavior by school managers (Bascia and Osmond 2012: 1). In later periods, teacher discontent that began to manifest with the New York City teachers strike of 1962 was overall about "the ability of centralized, bureaucratic administration to wield power with impunity" (Gelberg 1997: 79)—that is, teacher collective bargaining often focuses on pay and benefits, but behind those more mundane issues are often questions of authority, independence, and job security. Some widely discussed teacher strikes had strong racial overtones, sometimes with minority communities seeking greater input into the running of local schools and teachers concerned about their job security (Goldstein 2015: 137–163).

Much teacher collective bargaining parallels the bargaining issues that exist in many other industries. Thus, pay and benefits are important issues in most negotiations. Health insurance and its rising costs has been a particularly contentious issue for decades. Issues of autonomy, professional control, and modes of evaluation, however, are also important bargaining topics. This includes, for example, issues of how much control teachers have over how they teach in the classroom. It also includes questions about who conducts teacher evaluations and what is included (e.g., student test results).

Because of the highly decentralized bargaining structures in public education, pay levels vary considerably within individual states. Such differences often reflect the affluence of various communities because local schools are often largely funded with local property taxes. Thus, in New York State, there is a very large difference in pay levels between suburban school districts, on the one hand, and rural and urban school districts, on the other. In starting salaries for those with master's degrees, suburban teachers earn 39% more—and that difference grows over time (Colvin, Klingel, Boehme, and Donovan 2013).

One issue that has risen in importance several times over the years, only to fade again, is "merit pay." At various times, such pay systems have been widely discussed and implemented in a number of districts. Traditionally, in most school districts, teacher pay is largely determined by two factors—seniority and education. Usually, there is a salary grid based on years of service and degrees and graduate college credits possessed by the teacher.

Critics argue that such systems provide little incentive for teachers to work hard or to develop more effective skills. They believe that merit pay systems would result in better education outcomes for children. However, merit pay systems are difficult to design for teachers because teacher performance is difficult to measure. Determining merit based on student outcomes is difficult because student outcomes are affected by a variety of factors unrelated to teacher performance, such as poverty, unemployment, and lack of housing (Ravitch 2013). Many school districts in the 1980s experimented with a variety of types of merit pay and career ladders, but over the following decade, most of those systems disappeared, having had little to no positive impact on student outcomes and being very hard to administer without negative impacts on teacher morale and retention.

Albert Shanker, the long-term and iconic president of the AFT, endorsed a version of merit pay for teachers, though it was not universally applauded by his constituents. In fact, he was basically forced to recant, claiming he had been misunderstood (Weiner 2012: 123). Most of the merit pay plans and related career ladders that were adopted had died out by the end of the 1980s (Goldstein 2015: 178). One more recent attempt that involved evaluation pegged in part to student achievement and pay based on evaluation was instituted in Dallas in 2015. Early evaluation seems to indicate some positive and lasting effects on student achievement. (Hanushek et al. 2023)

Related to issues of authority and independence is the question of professionalism. "From the time of the pro-efficiency reforms until the 1960s, school boards and managers called teachers 'professionals' in order to keep them cooperative, servile, and antiunion" (Gelberg 1997: 82). School managers used the word "professional" to criticize anything teachers did that the managers did not like, accusing the teachers of being "unprofessional." Administrators often called disobedience "unprofessional," essentially reversing the meaning of the word (Gelberg 1997: 83). The concept of professionalism was used early on as a weapon against unionization and collective bargaining—that is, teachers were told that unionism and collective bargaining were inappropriate for professionals such as teachers. In the 1920s, many school administrators tried to model their management practices on Frederick Taylor's scientific management approach, the very antithesis of treating teachers as professionals (Goldstein 2015: 86–87).

The key to understanding issues related to teacher job security is the much-maligned and much-misunderstood concept of "tenure." The first teachers to win tenure rights were in New Jersey in 1909. This was seen by advocates as a "good government" reform after years in which teachers were appointed as part of the political patronage system (Goldstein 2015: 85). Previously, female teachers could be fired for offenses such as getting married, getting pregnant, or wearing pants (Stephey 2008). In some places, issues of teacher tenure are negotiated in collective bargaining, while in others (New York, for example), the issue is addressed extensively in state law. In simple terms, the public perception that tenure means a "job for life" is simply incorrect. The basic meaning of tenure is that a teacher cannot be discharged without reasonable cause and that they have due process rights in defending themselves if an employer attempts to discipline or terminate them.

In some areas, there has been increased bargaining about class sizes, mandated evaluation procedures, and a role for teachers in schoolwide curriculum decisions. Also, issues of teacher preparation time and professional development activities have grown in importance at the bargaining table (Bascia and Osmond 2012: 1–2).

Still, teacher working conditions have often eroded since the 1970s because of unpredictable funding and frequent policy changes as newly elected political leaders attempt to change directions (Bascia and Osmond 2012: 2). The strike wave beginning in 2018 reflected the erosion of salaries and working conditions and the fact that a growing number of issues that had been decided at the local level are now being determined at the state or even at the federal level (Bascia and Osmond 2012: 5).

Seniority layoffs were extensively criticized during the Great Recession (2007–2009). With considerable financial distress, school districts often felt the necessity for layoffs, but there were numerous objections to seniority rules that required newer teachers (who many critics of the layoffs claimed were often the best teachers) to be laid off first. There were attempts to either eliminate seniority-based layoffs or, at the least, to require that measures of competency be considered along with seniority (Alter 2010; Hernandez 2011).

In 2010, Wisconsin governor Scott Walker tried to crush the teachers unions in his state and supported legislation severely limiting the right of public employees to engage in collective bargaining, arguing that highly paid teachers and other public employees were robbing low-income workers whose taxes supported the salaries and pensions of public employees. Other states took similar actions, including Florida, Indiana, Kansas, Ohio, Michigan, and New Jersey (Donn 2012; Taylor 2020: 83). Some of this also happened in Democrat-controlled states (Taylor 2020: 84).

The belief of the education reform movement that teacher collective bargaining agreements handcuff administrators and hamper the efficient allocation of teacher resources has been examined in a number of studies in recent years. Some of these have looked at collective bargaining agreements in particular states. Most have found a more nuanced picture than that presented by the education reform movement. This is true even if one assumes, as most of the education reformers seem to do, that while teachers unions have interests beyond the education of students, educational administrators do not (for just a few examples, see Cohen-Vogel and Osborne-Lampkin 2007; Donn 2019; Donn, Karper, and Kirby 2011; Goldhaber et al. 2013; Koski and Horng 2007; Strunk 2011; and Strunk and Grissom 2010). There is also evidence that school districts without teacher collective bargaining agreements often use many of the same "restrictive" policies that are used by districts with such agreements (Donn, Donn, Goldberg, and Kirby 2014).

Developments in Teacher Pay

A Nation at Risk, the 1983 report of the National Commission on Excellence in Education, attacked the supposed mediocrity of the education that most public schools provided and the teachers who provided it (Goldstein 2015: 165). Albert Shanker and NEA president Mary Futtrell both played roles in writing this report, although Futtrell signed it reluctantly and did not endorse a proposal for national certification of teachers that Shanker supported. (Weiner 2012: 124–125).

A Nation at Risk helped create a movement for national standards in education and helped lead to the growth of the federal role in public education (Goldstein 2015: 165). One of the principal recommendations of the report was to implement merit pay for teachers (Goldstein 2015: 170). In the early 2000s, some school districts began again to experiment with variations of merit pay, often with union support. In Minneapolis, the teachers union cooperated with the Republican governor to develop a plan in which some teachers worked with mentors and teachers could get bonuses for raising student achievement. One reason behind these experiments is that the US Department of Education was making considerable extra funding available to some districts implementing such plans. The NEA continued to oppose these plans, while the AFT was willing to consider them, but not if the administrators alone decided which teachers received extra pay (Dillon 2007).

There is clear evidence that higher teacher pay is associated with better student outcomes (Baker 2012; Goldstein 2015: 263). It is not clear to what extent this reflects stronger teacher motivation (as the education reformers usually argue), the ability of higher-paying districts to recruit better teachers, or some other mechanism. However, it should be noted that the United States is unusual in that teachers are paid much less than other professionals (Allegretto and Mishel 2016, 2019; Goldstein 2015: 264). For example, research conducted by the Economic Policy Institute concluded that teachers are underpaid compared with comparably educated workers. The gap between teachers and comparably educated professionals is between 3.4% and 35.9%, depending on the state. The highest gaps are in Colorado and Oklahoma and the smallest are in Rhode Island and Wyoming (Economic Policy Institute 2022). Interestingly, a national poll in 2018 found that over three quarters of the US population also believed teachers were underpaid (Karp and Sanchez 2020: 193).

STRIKES/LOCKOUTS AND GENERAL STATE OF LABOR RELATIONS

Between 1960 and 1980, there were over 1,000 teacher strikes in the United States (Goldstein 2015: 135). One New York City teacher strike in 1962 involved more than half of its 40,000 teachers and was called after a large majority of UFT membership voted to support it. The UFT became the teachers' bargaining agent after winning a vote by a two-thirds' majority in December 1961. The strike was illegal under the

Condon–Wadlin Act; however, strikers were not dismissed, but they could have been. The strike had been in effect only one day when New York City secured a restraining order against it (*Time* 1962).

A series of teacher strikes in 1968 in New York City involved over 60,000 teachers—many of these strikes pitting teachers and their desire for job security against minority groups seeking community control of schools. Those were the largest teacher strikes to date (Goldstein 2015: 151).

In 1970, Newark, New Jersey, was the site of perhaps the longest and most violent teacher strikes in US history. The strikes were initially spurred by the injury of a student crossing the road after school. Previously, teachers would have helped the students across the street, but the recently negotiated collective bargaining agreement had largely freed teachers from such "nonprofessional" duties. The community was outraged, and the result was a series of strikes (Goldstein 2015: 160).

Some widely discussed teacher strikes had strong racial overtones, sometimes with minority communities seeking greater input into the running of local schools and teachers concerned about their job security. The Oceanhill–Brownsville strike in 1968 in Brooklyn, New York, and those in 1970 and 1971 in Newark, New Jersey, are outstanding examples (Goldstein 2015: 151, 159; Weiner 2012: 134).

In 2004, US Secretary of Education Rod Paige called the NEA a "terrorist organization" for its criticism of "No Child Left Behind," the education policy of the George W. Bush administration. Paige later said his language was inappropriate, but he went on to attack the union for using "obstructionist scare tactics" (Toppo 2004).

A more recent strike wave began in 2018 and involved both legal and illegal strikes. Some illegal ones were largely victorious when community support prevented school districts and authorities from bringing down the full weight of the law against the strikers and their unions (Kolins Givan 2020: 253). May 2018 saw a continuing series of teacher strikes in Colorado and North Carolina, following statewide strikes in Arizona, Kentucky, Oklahoma, and West Virginia. "They were rebellions against the austerity and privatization that has been driving federal and state economic policy for decades. … [M]any of the walkouts were more akin to mass political protests, seeking broad changes in public policy, than to labor strikes against a single employer such as a school district." This strike wave reflected the fact that, while much of the funding for schools is raised locally, states have the ultimate responsibility (Karp and Sanchez 2020: 191). Many of these strikes, especially in states where they are prohibited by law, were framed by the strikers as aimed at forcing state legislatures to allocate more money for public education as strikers argued that they often spent their own money for supplies for their students and that their salaries had lagged far behind those of other professionals. In a number of these strikes, teachers gained raises (Richards 2022). It is interesting to note that many of these strikes were spontaneous, conducted by nonunionized teachers in states that don't provide for teacher collective bargaining. More recently, a legal strike involving both teachers and education support personnel took place in Minneapolis in early 2022 and lasted for three weeks (Shockman and Krueger 2022).

COLLECTIVE BARGAINING INNOVATIONS

Both the AFT and NEA have nationally attempted to engage in a variety of innovative changes designed to enhance teaching. Most innovation has taken place at the local level (Kerchner 2003: 237; Rubinstein and McCarthy 2021: 255). There is research supporting a strong inverse relationship between educational collaboration and teacher turnover, especially in schools in impoverished areas. There is also evidence that such collaboration improves student achievement (Rubinstein and McCarthy 2021: 258, 261).

Some unions have adopted a "new unionism" approach that attempts a more collaborative bargaining approach while increasing the scope of bargaining to cover professional issues and reform agendas (Bascia and Osmond 2012: 9). However, this kind of collaboration can be difficult because state laws that govern teacher collective bargaining often restrict the involvement of unions in a variety of noncompensation aspects of the work environment (Kerchner 2003: 239). "There is no legally required role for teacher unions in standard setting, induction, professional development, or quality assurance" (Kerchner 2003: 242).

The AFT has supported standards based on student achievement, and most local teachers unions have been involved in teacher development activities. New York City and Minneapolis have been good examples of building long-term relationships that are increasingly based on student standards and achievement (Kerchner 2003: 243–245). "The Minneapolis Public Schools and the Minneapolis Federation of Teachers have also created a residency: a one-year program that provides for a reduced teaching load and increased professional development for newly licensed teachers." Teaching interns are matched with experienced teachers (Kerchner 2003: 246). Both AFT and NEA locals have adopted forms of peer review of senior teachers (Kerchner 2003: 247).

A union-related group has tried to promote some aspects of the educational reform movement agenda. The Teacher Union Reform Network (TURN) was founded in 1995 and includes both AFT and NEA locals (Kerchner 2003: 255). It is led by Adam Urbanski, who was president of the Rochester, New York, teachers union when that local had negotiated an extremely unusual collective bargaining agreement focusing on ways to improve student outcomes by supporting teachers. However, TURN has not spread far—having only about 200 member locals nationwide (Teacher Union Reform Network 2023).

Merit pay and career ladders, previously discussed, have been adopted in the collective bargaining agreements of some school districts. However, most of these have died out. Another approach that has been adopted in the collective bargaining agreements of some districts is peer evaluation (Goldstein 2015: 241). Teachers unions that support reform often focus on mentoring programs pairing new teachers and those in need of remediation with effective senior teachers and creating incentives for other types of activities by senior teachers to improve the quality of overall teaching (Bascia and Osmond 2012: 11).

However, policy makers sometimes become enamored of an approach that has found success in one or two particular districts and then try to mandate that approach statewide or even nationwide. "When American policy makers require every public school to use the same strategies—typically without confirming if their favored approaches are actually effective for kids—they reduce the discretion of the most motivated teachers" (Goldstein 2015: 261).

POLITICS AND PUBLIC EDUCATION

In the 1980s and 1990s, critics of teachers unions became more politically sophisticated in exploiting the clash between unions' visions of themselves as fighters for underdog workers and the view that some of the public takes of unions as defenders of peculiar privileges, like tenure (Goldstein 2015: 163). Because of criticism of unions as raising costs, reducing student achievement, and being obstacles to reform initiatives, unions and teachers came under greater public criticism and greater scrutiny by politicians (Bascia and Osmond 2012: 6).

Indeed, potential 2024 Republican presidential candidate Mike Pompeo recently called AFT president Randi Weingarten "the most dangerous person in the world" (Levin 2022). It serves an important political purpose to blame teachers unions for undesirable educational outcomes rather than to focus on several underlying causes such as poverty, hunger, homelessness, racism, and inequality in school funding. Rather than addressing the fundamental problems children face in their education, reformers provide "horror tales" about tenure and collective bargaining agreements (Weiner 2012: 19). A principal goal of reformers has been to improve teaching by eliminating teacher tenure and consideration of seniority (Fensterwald 2016; Kerchner 2003; Stephey 2008; Weiner 2012: 191). Silicon Valley technology entrepreneurs continue to invest in new technology and innovation and support so-called reforms "that promote privatization, high stakes testing, characterization, and the substitution of software for teachers" (Kolins Givan 2020: 254).

In the 21st century, a new series of issues has arisen. Some of them relate to the education reform movement mentioned earlier, which asserts that public schools are failing our children and that unions and collective bargaining are among the principal reasons for these failures (see Moe 2006 for an example of this argument). In fact, the so-called crisis in public education or failure of the schools is largely a creation of the critics. There is very little convincing evidence for the existence of this crisis, and it can be documented that, in many ways, educational outcomes are better than they have been for decades, or even ever (Best 2011; Kerchner 2003: 235; Ravitch 2013: 44–81). These issues have become politicized, and in some states, teachers unions have found the legal basis for their activities under attack. On the other hand, some states that have largely forbidden teacher unionization and collective bargaining have found their teachers engaging in grassroots, spontaneous protests and even strikes motivated by what teachers see as inadequate pay, overwork, and generally persistent underfunding of public education (such as the 2018 strikes described previously).

Other issues unique to public education involve attempts by state governments and others to control what teachers say to their students. In the 2020s, a new controversy emerged over the teaching of racial issues in US history. Elementary and secondary schools were both accused of teaching so-called critical race theory (CRT). Critics have argued that such teaching was designed to make White children feel guilty or bad about being White. This critique was often pushed by organized partisan groups who made the term "critical race theory" (which, in fact, is a concept that emerged in law schools and was never used in primary or secondary school curricula) a shorthand for anti-White racism and "wokeness" (Williams 2022). The critics derided any version of racial history that has the potential to make majority students uncomfortable (or that contradicts the more sanitized versions that they had learned in school), and some states, such as Florida, have taken action to outlaw its presentation in public schools. In one particularly egregious example, Florida education regulations now require that students be taught that enslaved African Americans learned skills from slavery that they were able to use for their own benefit. While teachers unions in Florida have objected strenuously, the requirements were part of Florida governor Ron DeSantis's "war on woke" in his presidential campaign. Given the complete control that DeSantis and his allies have over the Florida state legislature, protests from the unions have been utterly ineffective (Peoples, Farrington, and Stafford 2023).

Almost 900 school districts nationwide were targeted by anti-CRT campaigns. This issue already played a role in elections, with a Republican candidate for governor of Virginia making CRT a major issue in his campaign and winning an unexpected victory (Williams 2022: 55).

These controversies had, by early 2023, already generated 64 new state laws limiting or controlling what children could be taught. A RAND Corporation study found that a fourth of a nationally representative sample of English, mathematics, and science teachers reported revising their teaching materials to "limit or eliminate" discussions of race and gender. There is also evidence that teachers are becoming warier about addressing issues of policing (Natanson 2023).

There have also been political efforts to control whether and how students are taught about issues related to human sexualities and gender identities, along with various issues raised by having transgender students in schools. Politicians have taken it upon themselves to determine related curricular issues, such as when and how such issues can be addressed. Indeed, the Florida law dealing with this issue was popularly called "Don't Say Gay" (Chmielewski and Coster 2023). In the words of Weiner, "a key aim of the neoliberal project … is to destroy teachers' autonomy and the space this creates in schools for critical thought and for ideas of freedom and social justice" (2012: 21).

The issues of teacher unionization and collective bargaining themselves have become highly political in the 2000s. Teachers unions have become one of the principal sources of support (financial and logistic) for the Democratic Party, and as such they have been attacked in a number of states controlled by Republicans. Some of those states (e.g., Wisconsin and Ohio) took actions designed to weaken teachers unions and collective bargaining (Donn 2012).

Democratic administrations have often adopted as much of the corporate education reform agenda as Republican administrations have. Thus, the Obama administration's "Race to the Top" provided extra money for school districts that evaluated teachers in terms of demonstrated growth in measurable student achievement (Goldstein 2015: 213; Rubinstein and McCarthy 2021: 247, 249).

During the 1990s and into the 2000s, schools came under pressure from conservative politicians and from private interest groups who wanted to reduce spending through the privatization of public schools (Bascia and Osmond 2012: 6). The Trump administration's Secretary of Education Betsy DeVos strongly promoted privatization (Rubinstein and McCarthy 2021: 252). DeVos was the rare Secretary of Education with no background in public education.

According to Rubinstein and McCarthy, "despite their popularity with policy makers, these neoliberal approaches to school reform have not only had a negative impact on school climate by undervaluing teachers—dismissing their professional input and attacking their unions—they have also failed to produce the promised results" (2021: 253).

Corporate executives and politicians essentially seemed to believe that education's purpose is preparation for employment (Weiner 2012: 67). The culture wars of the 2000s have spread this belief more widely, at least among conservative activists. The Bush administration's program, "No Child Left Behind," was an example of this belief, stating that the "purported aim of increasing educational opportunity masks its real purpose: to create a privatized system of public education that has a narrow, vocationalized curriculum enforced through the use of standardized tests" (Weiner 2012: 148). However, it should be noted that the "No Child Left Behind" legislation passed both houses of Congress in 2001 with overwhelming bipartisan support (Rubinstein and McCarthy 2021: 251).

Therefore, one of the principal challenges for teachers and their unions is that both major political parties seem to support the bulk of the corporatist educational agenda. They both support the notion that students in US public schools are falling behind and that teachers are the principal reason.

CHALLENGES FROM THE PANDEMIC

Beginning in early 2020, the COVID-19 pandemic created immense and unprecedented challenges for teachers and the school districts where they work. Many states moved to virtual instruction during the pandemic, and such decisions were often controversial. Many teachers had little or no experience with systems of online instruction, and in some cases, teaching from home was complicated by a lack of appropriate technology (for students and teachers alike), childcare, and other competing needs. Unions struggled to develop policies and positions to keep their members (and students) safe, assist teachers in developing the skills they needed, and help them acquire the technologies they needed for their new roles.

In many places, this issue became intertwined with political issues as school shutdowns became controversial, and states tried to find a balance between the need to educate students and the need to protect their health. Teachers also faced this dilemma, but, in some cases, seemed to feel that the health of teachers was not a consideration for some state and local governments.

CONCLUSIONS

It is clear that many of the controversies about teacher unionization and collective bargaining, as well as about public education in general, echo long-standing disputes about the role of education in US society and politics. That controversy, at its base, is between those who believe the primary purpose of public education is to provide an enlightened and critical citizenry to participate in our democracy and those who believe the purpose of public education is primarily to create a well-prepared workforce. The issue of preparing students to participate in democracy is also disputed between those who believe that schools should promote critical thinking and those who believe schools should promote a patriotic view of the United States that minimizes discussion of inequities in US history and in the country's political and social systems. The issue of preparing students to participate in the economy is also subject to dispute between those who seem to want schools to prepare a creative workforce and those who seem to want schools to prepare an obedient or even docile workforce.

However, there are other challenges to teacher collective bargaining and to public schools that are unique to the contemporary period. Clearly, the COVID-19 pandemic provided a whole series of those. The controversies over critical race theory, however, as well as how and when to address sexualities and gender identities are, if not new, clearly in new forms and may have become more politically salient now than they have been for decades. These issues make the future of teacher unionism and collective bargaining more uncertain than it has been for decades.

REFERENCES

Allegretto, S., and L. Mishel. 2016. "The Teacher Pay Gap Is Wider Than Ever." Economic Policy Institute. August 9. https://tinyurl.com/6zt6syz4

———. 2019. "The Teacher Weekly Wage Penalty Hit 21.4 Percent in 2018, a Record High." Economic Policy Institute. April 24. https://tinyurl.com/2695sacj

Alter, J. 2010. "Will Obama Take the Next Step on Teachers?" *Newsweek*. May 3.

Baker, B. 2012. "Revisiting the Age-Old Question: Does Money Matter in Education?" Report. Albert Shanker Institute. https://eric.ed.gov/?id=ED528632

Bascia, N., and P. Osmond. 2012. "Teacher Unions and Educational Reform: A Research Review." Center for Great Public Schools, National Education Association. https://tinyurl.com/bd9mthk8

Best, J. 2011. *The Stupidity Epidemic: Worrying About Students, Schools, and America's Future*. New York, NY: Routledge.

Carnoy, M. 2017. "School Vouchers Are Not a Proven Strategy for Improving Student Achievement." Economic Policy Institute. February 28. https://tinyurl.com/4bjwb5rm

Chmielewski, D., and H. Coster. 2023. "Florida Governor DeSantis Ends 'Corporate Kingdom' of Walt Disney World." Reuters. February 27.

Cohen-Vogel, L., and L. Osborne-Lampkin. 2007. "Allocating Quality: Collective Bargaining Agreements and Administrative Discretion over Teacher Assignment." *Educational Administration Quarterly* 43, no. 4: 433–461.

Colvin, A., S. Klingel, S. Boehme, and S. Donovan. 2013. "New York State Teacher Salary Report." ILR School, Cornell University. December. https://tinyurl.com/tmwnr3ca

Cuevas, J. 2022. "The Authoritarian Threat to Public Education: Attacks on Diversity, Equity and Inclusion Undermine Teaching and Learning." *Journal of Language and Literacy Education* 13, no. 2: 1–6.

Dillon, S. 2007. "Long Reviled, Merit Pay Gains Among Teachers." *New York Times.* June 18. https://tinyurl.com/5n8aucvm

Dobbie, W., and R.G. Fryer. 2016. "Charter Schools and Labor Market Outcomes." Working Paper No. 600. July. Princeton University, Industrial Relations Section.

Donn, C.B. 2012. "The Attack on Public Sector Bargaining Rights and Unions in the United States: The Case of Public School Teachers." *Management Re-Imagined: Proceedings of the 11th World Congress.* Brussels, Belgium: International Federation of Scholarly Associations of Management.

———. 2019. "Management of Educational Personnel Under the Taylor Law: Evidence from Teacher Collective Bargaining Agreements in Public School Districts in New York State." In *The Taylor Law at 50: Public Sector Labor Relations in a Shifting Landscape,* edited by J.F. Wirenius. Albany, NY: New York State Bar Association.

Donn, C.B., R. Donn, L. Goldberg, and B.J. Kirby. 2014. "Teacher Working Conditions With and Without Collective Bargaining." *Nevada Law Journal* 14, no. 2, article 1. https://scholars.law.unlv.edu/nlj/vol14/iss2/11

Donn, C.B., M. Karper, and B.J. Kirby. 2011. "Teacher Collective Bargaining and the Flexible Deployment of Teaching Resources: Evidence from Cities in New York State." *Proceedings of the Annual Meeting, Labor and Employment Relations Association.* Champaign, IL: Labor and Employment Relations Association.

Economic Policy Institute. 2022. "The Five Top Charts of 2022," Chart 2—How Underpaid Are Teachers in Your State?" Economic Policy Institute. December 16. https://tinyurl.com/ybwy83f4

Fensterwald, J. 2016. "California High Court Lets Rulings Stand on Teacher Tenure, School Funding Lawsuits," EdSource. August 26. https://tinyurl.com/7xyy6c4w

Gelberg, D. 1997. *The "Business" of Reforming American Schools.* Albany, NY: State University of New York Press.

Goldhaber, D., L. Lavery, R. Theobald, D. D'Entremont, and Y. Fang. 2013. "Teacher Collective Bargaining: Assessing Internal Validity of Partial Independence Item Response Measures of Contract Restrictiveness." *SAGE Open* 3, no. 2. https://doi.org/10.1177/215824401348

Goldstein, D. 2015. *The Teacher Wars: A History of America's Most Embattled Profession.* New York, NY: Anchor Books.

Hanushek, E.A., J. Luo, A.J. Morgan, M. Nguyen, B. Ost, S.G. Rivkin, and A. Shakeel. 2023. "The Effects of Comprehensive Educator Evaluation and Pay Reform on Achievement." Working Paper 31073. National Bureau of Economic Research. March. http://www.nber.org/papers/w31073

Hebdon, R., J.E. Slater, and M.F. Masters. 2013. "Public Sector Collective Bargaining: Tumultuous Times." In *Collective Bargaining Under Duress: Case Studies in Major North American Industries,* edited by H.R. Stanger, P.F. Clark, and A.C. Frost. Champaign, IL: Labor and Employment Relations Association.

Hernandez, J.C. 2011. "Critics Say Cuomo's Plan for Teacher Evaluations Falls Short." *Syracuse Post-Standard.* March 6.

Kahlenberg, R.D., and H. Potter. 2014–2015. "Restoring Shanker's Vision for Charter Schools." *American Educator.* Winter. American Federation of Teachers. https://tinyurl.com/yvhmpmrp

Karp, S., and A. Sanchez. 2020. "The 2018 Wave of Teacher Strikes: A Turning Point for Our Schools?" In *Strike for the Common Good: Fighting for the Future of Public Education*, edited by R. Kolins Givan and A. Schrager Lang, 191–197. Ann Arbor, MI: University of Michigan Press.

Kerchner, C. 2003. "The Modern Guild: The Prospects for Organizing Around Quality in Public Education." In *Going Public: The Role of Labor-Management Relations in Delivering Quality Government Services*, edited by J. Brock and D.B. Lipsky, 235–265. Champaign, IL: Labor and Employment Relations Association.

Kolins Givan, R. 2020. "Afterward: The Strikes Continue …" In *Strike for the Common Good: Fighting for the Future of Public Education*, edited by R. Kolins Givan and A. Schrager Lang, 253–255. Ann Arbor, MI: University of Michigan Press.

Koski, W.S., and E.L. Horng. 2007. "Curbing or Facilitating Inequality? Law, Collective Bargaining and Teacher Assignment Among Schools in California." Getting Down to Facts: A Research Project to Inform Solutions to California's Education Problems. https://tinyurl.com/399zxnc2

Levin, B. 2022. "Mike Pompeo Boldly and Insanely Claims Teachers' Union Leader Is 'the Most Dangerous Person in the World'—Ahead of Kim Jong Un." *Vanity Fair*. November 22. https://tinyurl.com/22yzeskr

López, F., A. Molnar, R. Johnson, A. Patterson, L. Ward, and K. Kumashiro. 2021. "Understanding the Attacks on Critical Race Theory." National Education Policy Center. http://nepc.colorado.edu/publication/crt

Miller, R., K. Liu, and A.F. Ball, 2023. "Misunderstanding the Campaign Against CRT: Absurdity and White Supremacy in Attacks on Teaching and Teacher Education." *Thresholds* 46, no.1: 139–156. https://tinyurl.com/wewk3m9d

Moe, T.M. 2006. "Union Power and the Education of Children." In *Collective Bargaining in Education: Negotiating Change in Today's Schools*, edited by J. Hannaway and A.J. Rotherham, 229–258. Cambridge, MA: Harvard Education Press.

Natanson, H. 2023. "Slavery Was Wrong and 5 Other Things Some Educators Won't Teach Anymore." *Washington Post*. March 6. https://tinyurl.com/5n6v9f2b

National Commission on Excellence in Education. 1983. "A Nation at Risk: The Imperative for Educational Reform. A Report to the Nation and the Secretary of Education." National Commission on Excellence in Education. https://tinyurl.com/ynfcjzxb

Novitz, T. 2009. "Workers' Freedom of Association." In *Human Rights in Labor and Employment Relations: International and Domestic Perspectives*, edited by J.A. Gross and L. Compa, 123–154. Champaign, IL: Labor and Employment Relations Association.

Peoples, S., B. Farrington, and K. Stafford. 2023. "DeSantis Is Defending New Slavery Teachings. Civil Rights Leaders See a Pattern of 'Policy Violence.'" Associated Press. July 27. https://tinyurl.com/2r65pj7t

Provenzo, E.F., and A.B. Provenzo, eds. 2008. *Encyclopedia of the Social and Cultural Foundations of Education*. Thousand Oaks, CA: Sage. https://doi.org/10.4135/9781412963992

Ravitch, D. 2013. *Reign of Error: The Hoax of the Privatization Movement and the Danger to America's Public Schools*. New York, NY: Alfred A. Knopf.

Richards, E. 2022. "Schools Primed for 'Militant Teacher Strikes' over Post-COVID Pay, Benefits and Respect," *USA Today*. March 20.

Riser-Kotsitsky, M. 2019. "Education Statistics: Facts About American Schools." *Education Week*. January 3 (corrected November 22, 2021; updated January 9, 2024). https://tinyurl.com/2rmy3fwa

Rubinstein, S.A., and John E. McCarthy. 2021. "The Future of US Public School Reform: Elevating Teacher Voice." In *Revaluing Work(ers): Toward a Democratic and Sustainable Future*, edited by T. Schulze-Cleven and T.E. Vachon, 247–270. Champaign, IL: Labor and Employment Relations Association.

Sanes, M., and J. Schmitt. March 2014. "Regulation of Public Sector Collective Bargaining in the States." Center for Economic and Policy Research. March. https://tinyurl.com/y76kn9ud

Shockman, E., and A. Krueger. 2022. "Deal Reached to End Minneapolis Teachers Strike: Classes Expected to Start Tuesday." Minnesota Public Radio News. March 25. https://tinyurl.com/bde7df4j

Stephey, M.J. 2008. "Tenure." *Time*. November 17. https://tinyurl.com/2363n7pv

Strunk, K.O. 2011. "Are Teachers' Unions Really to Blame? Collective Bargaining Agreements and Their Relationships with District Resource Allocation and Student Performance in California." *Education Finance and Policy* 6, no. 3: 354–398. https://doi.org/10.1162/EDFP_a_00039

Strunk, K.O., and J.A. Grissom. 2010. "Do Strong Unions Shape District Policies? Collective Bargaining, Teacher Contract Restrictiveness, and the Political Power of Teachers' Unions." *Educational Evaluation and Policy Analysis* 32, no. 3: 389–406. https://doi.org/10.3102/016237371037666

Taylor, C. 2011. *Reds at the Blackboard: Communism, Civil Rights and the New York Teachers Union*. New York, NY: Columbia University Press.

———. 2020. "The Long History of Attacking Teachers' Unions and Public Education." In *Strike for the Common Good: Fighting for the Future of Public Education*, edited by R. Kolins Givan and A. Schrager Lang, 76–87. Ann Arbor, MI: University of Michigan Press.

Teacher Union Reform Network. 2023. Website. https://www.turnweb.org

Time. "Education: Biggest Teacher Strike." 1962. April 20. https://tinyurl.com/mhfm4ymc

Toppo, G. 2004. "Education Chief Calls Teachers Union 'Terrorist Organization.'" *USA Today*. February 23.

US Department of Education, National Center for Education Statistics. 2016. National Teacher and Principal Survey, "Public School Data File, 2015–16."

———. 2017–2018. National Teacher and Principal Survey, "Public School Teacher Data File, 2017–18."

———. 2021. Common Core of Data. "Public Elementary/Secondary School Universe Survey, 2020–21: Local Education Agency Universe Survey, 2020–21, Provisional Version 1a," and "State Nonfiscal Survey of Public Elementary/Secondary Education: 2020–21, Provisional Version 1a."

———. 2022. Common Core of Data. "Public Elementary/Secondary School Universe Survey, 2009–10 through 2019–20," "Private School Universe Survey, 2010–11 Through 2020–21," and "Integrated Postsecondary Education Data System, Fall 2010 Through Fall 2020, Institutional Characteristics Component."

Weiner, L. 2012. *The Future of Our Schools: Teachers Unions and Social Justice*, Chicago, IL: Haymarket Books.

Williams, P. 2022. "Annals of Education: Class Warfare—School Boards Are Being Attacked by Partisan Saboteurs" *New Yorker*. November 7: 52–63.

CHAPTER 8

Police Collective Bargaining: An Integral Part of US Law Enforcement

Paul F. Clark
Pennsylvania State University

Abstract

Law enforcement is an essential service provided by government. It is also a labor-intensive undertaking. In 2022, there were 787,565 officers employed by state, county, and local police forces in the United States. The police workforce is not only large and present in every community, but it is also one of the most heavily unionized workforces in the nation. More than half of all US police officers, 55.5 percent, belong to a union. This means that the terms and conditions of employment for a majority of officers, including pay, benefits, and working conditions, are determined through collective bargaining. This chapter provides an overview of police collective bargaining. It looks at the legal framework underlying the process, as well the main parties engaged in bargaining in this sector—police unions and police management. It examines the bargaining process itself and the various mechanisms for resolving bargaining impasses. And it examines the outcomes of bargaining and how those outcomes impact the nature and practice of policing across the country.

INTRODUCTION

Law enforcement is an essential service provided by government. Police officers are given the power and authority to enforce the law and prevent and investigate criminal activities. They are expected to use this power to protect citizens and their property and hold individuals who break the law accountable for their actions. The fair and effective use of this delegated power helps maintain order and peace in society.

The modern system of law enforcement is a labor-intensive undertaking. While technology plays an increasing role in this system, policing still is largely dependent on the presence and the decision making of police officers.[1] Police departments or agencies of local, counties, states, and the federal government have more than 900,000 officers (Brooks 2023; Gardner and Scott 2022).

The police workforce is not only large and present in every community, but it is also one of the most heavily unionized workforces in the nation. More than half of all US police officers, 55.5%, belong to a union (Hirsch, Macpherson, and Even

2024). This means that the terms and conditions of employment for a majority of officers, including pay, benefits, and working conditions, are determined through collective bargaining. At a time when US society is dealing with a range of concerns about police and policing, including a significant shortage of officers, the effectiveness of police tactics and strategies, and high-profile cases of police misconduct, an understanding of police collective bargaining is necessary to understand the US law enforcement system and its impact on US society.

This chapter provides an overview of police collective bargaining. It focuses specifically on bargaining by sworn police officers (as opposed to other law enforcement personnel, such as civilian police employees, prison guards, and parking officers) at the local and state government levels. The chapter looks at the legal framework underlying the process, as well the main parties engaged in collective bargaining in this sector—police unions and police management. It examines the bargaining process itself and the various mechanisms for resolving bargaining impasses. And it examines the outcomes of bargaining and how those outcomes impact the nature and practice of policing across the country.

OVERVIEW OF US LAW ENFORCEMENT
Federal Government

Law enforcement in the United States is considered one of the most important services that local and state governments provide to their citizens. The Tenth Amendment to the US Constitution states that "[t]he powers not delegated to the United States by the Constitution, nor prohibited by it to the states, are reserved to the states" (US Senate, no date). This, in effect, cedes the authority for policing at the state and local levels to state governments. State governments then provide police services at the state level and delegate that authority to local governments to provide policing in their communities.

The federal government does have some limited police powers under Articles 1 and 8 of the Constitution. These powers are restricted to the enforcement of federal laws that cover the entire country. Congress has created several federal law enforcement agencies, including the Federal Bureau of Investigation (FBI); Bureau of Alcohol, Tobacco, and Firearms (BATF); Secret Service; and US Capitol Police to enforce federal law (The Policy Circle, no date). Many federal government employees, including the US Capitol Police, are granted limited collective bargaining rights under the Federal Service Labor–Management Relations Statute (Office of Congressional Workplace Rights 2022). However, employees of the FBI, BATF, and Secret Service are not covered by the statute and do not have collective bargaining rights (US Federal Labor Relations Authority, no date).

State and Local Government

The designation of most police powers to state governments by the US Constitution is an example of "dual sovereignty," a central tenet of federalism in which power is shared by national and state governments. This serves to balance the power between the two levels. Because it is generally thought that decisions about policing services in a community are best made by that community, local governments administer police services in their locality with assistance from state government (this is the case in 49 of the 50 states; Hawai'i is the only state without a state police agency). Where criminal activity extends across state borders, the federal government has the power to assist the states.

As a result of the legal framework for policing created by the Constitution, the United States has one of the most decentralized law enforcement systems in the world. The most recent statistics indicate that there are 787,565 police officers working in 17,541 state and local police forces (Gardner and Scott 2022) in the United States to serve 336 million people (Table 1) (Congressional Budget Office 2023). That is one police force for every 19,155 people.

Because state and local governments have police powers, most municipalities in the United States (cities, counties, towns, villages, boroughs, and townships) have their own police department. Urban police forces tend to be very large; forces in rural areas tend to be very small. New York City has 35,047 officers, Chicago has 14,058, and Los Angeles has 9,522 (Lange 2022). Overall, in 2018, there were 80 police forces in the United States with 1,000 or more police officers. The most common size (the mode) of police forces in the United States is 10 to 24 officers (5,104 forces fell in this category). However, there were 2,391 forces with two to four officers, and 795 police forces consisted of just one officer (Gardner and Scott 2022).

Table 1
State and Local Law Enforcement Full-Time
Sworn Officers by Size of Department

Size of agency	No. of agencies	No. of full-time sworn officers
All sizes	17,541	787,565
1,000 or more	80	227,884
500–999	107	72,178
250–499	243	83,514
100–249	838	122,939
50–99	1,395	93,196
25–49	2,719	90,132
10–24	5,104	71,969
5–9	3,869	20,383
2–4	2,391	5,002
1	795	768

Gardner and Scott (2022).

INITIAL EFFORTS OF POLICE TO ORGANIZE AND BARGAIN

The first organization formed to support and advocate for police officers was the Patrolmen's Benevolent Association (PBA). The PBA was founded in New York City in 1892 as a fraternal organization. In its early years, it formed additional chapters in nearby cities such as Paterson, New Jersey; and Schenectady, New York. The PBA raised money for police widows, provided funeral insurance, and advocated politically for better treatment for officers. For example, in 1901, it helped win the eight-hour day for New York City police (DiSalvo 2020).

The next significant police organization to form was the Fraternal Order of Police (FOP). The first FOP "lodge" was organized in 1915 in Pittsburgh to improve the working lives of police officers. Lodges quickly formed in other cities, and in 1917, existing local lodges formed the national FOP. Like the PBA, the FOP's initial focus was on advocating for police through the political process (Walsh 2001).

The earliest effort to organize police officers for the purpose of collective bargaining took place in the years just after World War I, when the American Federation of Labor (AFL) chartered police unions in more than 30 cities. The campaign was in response to widespread dissatisfaction among police officers who worked long hours for low pay. Boston was among the cities in which the organizing efforts were met with great enthusiasm by officers (Levine 1988).

When the Boston police commissioner learned of the organizing effort, he suspended a dozen officers because of their union activity. This resulted in nearly 75% of the Boston police department walking out on strike. The Boston Police Strike of 1919 was condemned by both the governor of Massachusetts (Calvin Coolidge) and the president of the United States (Woodrow Wilson) as gravely endangering the public. Coolidge quickly broke the strike and the union when he permanently fired the strikers (Levine 1988).

The political and public fallout from the unsuccessful Boston strike caused the AFL to withdraw the charters of the police unions it had established. While union activity among police ceased for a time, the two main benevolent and fraternal police organizations that had been formed earlier, the PBA and the FOP, carried on. These organizations did not yet push for collective bargaining rights, but they did advocate politically for better pay and working conditions for officers (DiSalvo 2020).

During the 1940s and 1950s, affiliate unions of the AFL and the Congress of Industrial Organizations (CIO) renewed their efforts to organize local police unions in major US cities. These efforts were strongly opposed by police chiefs because of the locals' affiliation with the broader labor movement. It would not be until the 1960s that the first police officers would gain the right to bargain collectively. And because police departments viewed recognition of the independent fraternal and benevolent organizations as a way to block AFL-CIO affiliates from gaining a foothold among police, it would be local chapters of the PBA and the FOP that would be the first to win these rights (Levine 1988).

In 1964, the first organization representing police gained collective bargaining rights when the mayor of New York City recognized and subsequently signed a contract with the PBA. In return, the New York City PBA agreed not to affiliate with a union and not to strike. PBAs in Boston and Detroit quickly gained recognition and signed collective bargaining agreements. By the early 1970s, 11 cities had granted the right to collective bargaining to police officers represented by either the PBA or the FOP (Levine 1988).

LEGAL FRAMEWORK FOR POLICE COLLECTIVE BARGAINING

In 1935, Congress passed the National Labor Relations Act, granting the rights to organize unions, bargain collectively, and strike to most private sector workers. However, the act did not extend those rights to the public sector, or government, employees. It was not until the late 1960s and 1970s that public employees across the country, including police, began to clamor for the same rights that private sector workers had won in 1935 and that police in New York City had been granted in 1964. In 1968, Pennsylvania passed the first state law granting police the right to bargain collectively. The law, Act 111, however, banned strikes by police and provided compulsory interest arbitration as an alternative way of resolving impasses between municipalities and police unions and associations (Decker 1968).

Including Pennsylvania, police officers have gained collective bargaining rights in 42 states and the District of Columbia (Table 2) (National Conference of State Legislatures, no date; DiSalvo 2021). Some states have public sector bargaining statutes that grant police the right to bargain or to "meet and confer" (the two terms are largely interchangeable). In other states, this right was granted by case law based on court decisions. And four states—Georgia, North Carolina, South Carolina, Tennessee—have laws that specifically prohibit police collective bargaining. If a state does not have a statute that either grants or prohibits collective bargaining by law enforcement officers, the decision to grant this right is sometimes delegated to local jurisdictions (counties or municipalities). In many of these states, local governments have chosen to engage in bargaining with police unions (National Conference of State Legislatures, no date).

While most states grant collective bargaining rights to police officers, no state grants them the right to strike. The "essentiality and sovereignty doctrines" are commonly cited as the fundamental rationales for the ban on the right to strike for police. The essentiality argument makes the case that police services protect the lives, liberty, and property of individual citizens as well as the community at large. The protections provided are so crucial that any withdrawal of those services, as in the case of a police strike, would threaten the fundamental welfare of society (Denholm 2016; Wellington and Winter 1969). This is the same argument that Massachusetts governor Calvin Coolidge voiced in his opposition to the Boston Police Strike of 1919 when he stated, "There is no right to strike against the public's safety, by anyone, anywhere, at any time" (Ross 1969: 15).

Table 2
Legality of Police Collective Bargaining by State

States with law making police collective bargaining legal	States with law making police collective bargaining illegal	States with no law regarding police collective bargaining
Alaska	Georgia*	Alabama
Arizona	North Carolina	Colorado
Arkansas	South Carolina	Mississippi
California	Tennessee*	Wyoming
Connecticut		
Delaware		
District of Columbia		
Florida		
Hawai'i		
Idaho		
Illinois		
Indiana		
Iowa		
Kansas		
Kentucky		
Louisiana		
Maine		
Maryland		
Massachusetts		
Michigan		
Minnesota		
Missouri		
Montana		
Nebraska		
Nevada		
New Hampshire		
New Jersey		
New Mexico		
New York		
North Dakota		
Ohio		
Oklahoma		
Oregon		
Pennsylvania		
Rhode Island		
South Dakota		
Texas		
Utah		
Vermont		
Virginia		
Washington		
West Virginia		
Wisconsin		

*Despite having laws that prohibit police collective bargaining, police departments in Atlanta, Georgia; Macon County, Georgia; Memphis, Tennessee; and Nashville, Tennessee have negotiated contracts with police unions.

National Conference of State Legislatures, no date; DiSalvo 2021.

The sovereignty doctrine states that governments are granted exclusive authority in specific areas by the Constitution that creates them (i.e., the federal government by the US Constitution and state governments by state constitutions). The doctrine further argues that those governments cannot delegate or share those decision-making powers with others. This principle has been used to argue that granting the right to strike would give police officers the power to force local governments to make decisions that they would otherwise not make. This would violate the authority of the government to make such decisions exclusively (Ross 1969).

The denial of the right to strike by state governments, however, is problematic in a fundamental way. Collective bargaining rights have been granted over the years because the right to bargain over wages, benefits, and working conditions is seen as providing a number of benefits to workers. This right gives workers a voice in their work lives, keeps wages and benefits competitive, and reduces turnover. Bargaining between employers and employees is a process of give and take. Neither side gets everything they want as the parties compromise in order to obtain some of their objectives for bargaining. However, a strong argument can be made that authentic bargaining only occurs when the bargaining power of each party is relatively balanced; otherwise, the party with significantly more power has very little incentive to make concessions.

In most employee–employer relationships, the only power workers have comes from disrupting (or threatening to disrupt) the employer's ability to produce and sell a product or provide a service by withdrawing their labor. During negotiations, the possibility that employees might engage in a strike forces an employer to weigh the cost of being unable to operate versus the cost of meeting some of the employees' demands for higher wages or better benefits. The simple threat of a strike helps balance the power between the two parties. However, if the possibility of a strike is not present in bargaining, employers have no incentive to make any concessions to employees. Collective bargaining in the absence of the right to strike is sometimes referred to as "collective begging" on the part of employees.

Because police and their unions do not have the right to strike, states often grant them alternative dispute resolution mechanisms.

THE PARTIES

Three parties are directly involved in every collective bargaining relationship. The two main parties are the employer and the labor organization that represents employees in that employer's workplace. Because collective bargaining is an adversarial process that is conducted according to a series of rules and regulations, it is necessary to have a neutral third party that enforces and interprets those rules and regulations. In police collective bargaining, the third party is usually a state government agency created for that purpose.

Police Labor Organizations

As noted previously, the first type of labor organization to represent police officers was fraternal organizations such as the PBA and the FOP, which formed in the late 1800s and early 1900s. AFL unions began to organize police following the end of

World War I. However, it would not be until the early 1960s that the first organizations representing police gained the right to collective bargaining. And in the decades that followed, police unionism grew significantly in all parts of the country. Today, law enforcement is one of the most heavily unionized sectors of the US economy. Its 55.5% union density rate is significantly above the national rate of 10%. Most city and state police forces in the United States are represented by a union. Police in many small municipalities are also union members. The only occupation that has a higher rate of union density is firefighters, at 63.9% (Hirsch, Macpherson, and Even 2024).

Many of the organizations representing police officers are small, local, independent unions unaffiliated with any national organization. There are, however, a handful of national and state police unions that have significant memberships (Table 3). The largest such organization is the FOP, which has 354,000 members in 2,100 lodges (local unions) in every state as well as in Puerto Rico and Washington, DC (Fraternal Order of Police, "A History," no date). Because the police departments that employ its members are either at the municipal or state level, bargaining takes place at those levels (there is no national police bargaining). The FOP is a decentralized organization; its structure reflects the decentralized nature of bargaining in law enforcement. In most respects, the FOP's local lodges operate independently of the national FOP. The national organization provides services in a range of areas to the lodges, including training, benefits, and political action. It also serves as the national voice of its members, lobbying Congress and government agencies on their behalf (Fraternal Order of Police, "About," no date).

The second-largest national organization of police officers is the National Association of Police Organizations (NAPO). NAPO is not a true national union. Rather, it is a coalition of more than 1,000 independent police unions and associations from across the United States. It has a membership of 241,000. Much like the FOP, NAPO affiliates bargain their own contracts with local and state police departments. The national organization assists local unions by engaging in legislative advocacy, political action, and education (National Association of Police Organizations, no date).

A third national police organization is the International Union of Police Associations (IUPA). The IUPA has a membership of approximately 100,000 and is distinct from the other national police organizations in one very significant way—it is the only labor organization made up exclusively of police officers that is an affiliate of the AFL-CIO. Founded in 1954, the IUPA consists of local unions nationwide. The local unions represent, and bargain for, police officers employed by local, county, and state police forces. Much like the national FOP and NAPO, the national IUPA speaks for its members on national police issues, provides services to local unions, and engages in political action and lobbying (International Union of Police Associations 2023). Because of its affiliation with the AFL-CIO, it represents the interests of the law enforcement profession within the US labor movement.

Table 3
Police Labor Unions

National unions	Membership*
Fraternal Order of Police (FOP)	355,000
National Association of Police Organizations (NAPO)	241,000
International Union of Police Associations (IUPA) (AFL-CIO)	100,000
National Sheriffs' Association (NSA)	20,000
International Brotherhood of Teamsters (IBT)	20,000
Service Employees International Union (SEIU) Local 5000, International Brotherhood of Police Officers	10,000
American Federation of State, County and Municipal Employees (AFSCME) (AFL-CIO)	Not available
Communications Workers of America (CWA) (AFL-CIO)	Not available
United Food and Commercial Workers (UFCW) (AFL-CIO)	Not available
American Federation of Government Employees (AFGE) (AFL-CIO)	Not available
United Steelworkers of America (USWA) (AFL-CIO)	Not available
United Auto Workers (UAW) (AFL-CIO)	Not available
International Union of Painters and Allied Trades (IUPAT) (AFL-CIO)	Not available
United Mine Workers of America (UMWA) (AFL-CIO)	Not available
International Association of Machinists (IAM) (AFL-CIO)	Not available
State unions	
Pennsylvania FOP	40,000
Illinois FOP	3,000
Combined Law Enforcement Associations of Texas	27,000
California Peace Officers' Association	3,000
Local unions	
Police Benevolent Association New York City (PBA NYC)	24,000
Philadelphia FOP Lodge #7	14,000
New York City Sergeants Benevolent Association (SBA)	11,000
Los Angeles Police Protective League	9,900
Chicago FOP Lodge #7	8,000
Houston Police Officers Union, FOP Lodge 110	5,000
Washington, D.C., Police Union	3,600
Phoenix Law Enforcement Association	2,700

*Membership statistics are self-reported figures largely found on union websites.
Brannick and Holman (2022).

The National Sheriffs' Association (NSA) is a fourth national organization. It represents 20,000 deputy sheriffs across the country and operates similarly to other national police organizations (National Sheriffs' Association, no date).

Eleven primarily nonpolice national unions, such as Service Employees International Union (SEIU), the American Federation of State, County and Municipal Employees (AFSCME), and the United Auto Workers (UAW), also represent police officers in collective bargaining. Nine of these unions are affiliated with the AFL-CIO, while two are not affiliated. In all cases, the police represent a very small portion of these unions' overall membership and a very small portion of total police union membership.

In addition to national police unions, a number of statewide police unions have substantial memberships. Two of the largest are state affiliates of the FOP in Pennsylvania and Illinois. Two others are unaffiliated state organizations that bring together independent local unions in Texas and California. These state organizations perform roles similar to national unions by providing services to their affiliates, such as legal representation, lobbying and political action expertise, assistance in collective bargaining, and education and training programs.

As mentioned earlier, many police officers belong to independent local unions unaffiliated with national organizations. Even where local unions of police are affiliated with the FOP or the IUPA, the locals largely operate independently from their national organization, as their bargaining always takes place with their local police department. While most of these unions are small, with 5 to 50 members, police union locals in major cities can be substantially larger. For example, the PBA in New York City represents police officers and has 24,000 members. The police sergeants in New York City have their own union, the Sergeants Benevolent Association (SBA), which bargains for roughly 11,000 sergeants. The Philadelphia FOP Lodge #7 is also very substantial, with 14,000 members.

Last, when talking about police unions, it is important to understand that they are generally different in significant ways from nonpolice unions. One longtime police union leader stressed this difference when he called police unions "the duck-billed platypus of the labor movement" (Delord and York 2017). Because the differences are substantial, nonpolice unions generally do not consider police unions to be part of the larger US labor movement. The reasons for this include the fact that, in the 1800s and 1900s, police officers regularly used violence to disperse union gatherings, marches, and picket lines at the behest of employers. For that reason, historically, they were shunned by other unions (Clark 2020).

It is also true that today, the vast majority of police unions and their members do not see themselves as having much in common with nonpolice unions. Police unions are insular in that they are generally only concerned with protecting the interests of their members without consideration for other workers. The fact that police unions and police union members are significantly more politically conservative than members of other unions also sets them apart from other labor organizations (Clark 2020).

For instance, a poll in the fall of 2016 found that 84% of police officers planned to vote for Donald Trump and that all police unions endorsed Trump for that election

(Griffith 2016). This contrasts sharply with the fact that only 39% of all union voters voted for Trump (Leary and Maher 2019) and every other union that made an endorsement supported Hillary Clinton (Vote Smart, no date).

Police Managers and Government Employers

Police departments, or departments of public safety (DPS), as they are sometimes called, and the government responsible for them, are the second primary party involved in the collective bargaining relationship. As mentioned earlier, the US system of law enforcement is the most decentralized policing system in the world.[2] There are 17,541 state, county, and local police departments in the United States. Given the police workforce's high rate of union density, that means that more than 9,700 individual police departments engage in collective bargaining.

Police departments are sometimes referred to as paramilitary organizations. This implies that such departments are structured and operate, in some respects, like military forces. In fact, the two do have much in common, including the fact that most members of these groups wear uniforms when on duty, they both organize their workforce by ranks, and the hierarchy created by ranks bestows power on higher-ranked members to compel lower-ranked members to obey "orders." They are also empowered to use compulsion or violence to carry out their responsibilities. And after 9/11, the US "war on terror" policies led many police departments to accept donations of heavy arms and vehicles from the military (Shults, no date).

At the top of this hierarchy are police chiefs (or directors of DPS) and sheriffs and their seconds in command, deputy police chiefs (or deputy DPS directors) and chief deputy sheriffs. At the bottom are police officers. In the middle of the hierarchy are sergeants, detectives, lieutenants, and captains. Which ranks are considered management is an important issue for the purposes of collective bargaining. In the private sector, managers do not have the right to bargain, and they are not union members. Depending on the state law that regulates the bargaining process, managers at the rank of sergeant, lieutenant, detective, and captain may have bargaining rights. In some cases, they are represented by their own union (e.g., the New York City Lieutenants' Benevolent Association [LBA], and in other cases, they are represented by the same union that represents officers. In those cases, the union will negotiate for both officers and managers.

Like the bargaining teams of police unions, the composition of employer bargaining teams can vary greatly depending on the size of the force, the government unit involved, and its geographic location. One key point in this regard is that police unions actually negotiate with the government entity that the police department serves. This might be the state, city, county, town, village, or borough government.

The employer bargaining team might be led by a senior administrator, such as the director of labor and employment relations, or human resources; a deputy mayor; or an appointed city manager. It is also common for government employers to hire a professional negotiator to lead bargaining. These negotiators are often attorneys or consultants with significant bargaining experience. A bargaining team might also include members with special knowledge about the issues being discussed, such as a representative of the police department (deputy chief or chief deputy sheriff) and professional staff, such as the finance or budget director. And while it is not common, at least at the state or large-city level, for an elected official to lead negotiations, elected leaders—mayors, county commissioners, or elected executives, and at the state level, governors—usually are the ultimate decision makers in bargaining. Elected legislative bodies—like a town or city council—might also have to have to give final approval to a negotiated agreement.

State Government Boards and Agencies

As suggested earlier, collective bargaining is an adversarial process created either by legislation or case law that involves two main parties—employers and unions. Such processes usually involve a neutral third party that serves to interpret and enforce the law that governs the process, much as sporting events use a referee or umpire to ensure that the teams play by the rules. More than half of the states have created state agencies to play this role.

Because these agencies serve a function for public sector unions and employers at the state level that the National Labor Relations Board serves for private sector unions and employers at the national level, many of them are referred to as state labor relations boards. For example, in Pennsylvania, the agency that oversees police collective bargaining is the Pennsylvania Labor Relations Board; the board serving this function in Illinois is the Illinois Labor Relations Board. In some states, they are also sometimes called state public employment relations boards (e.g., the New York Public Employment Relations Board or the California Public Employment Relations Board).

These agencies have the responsibility of interpreting and enforcing state public sector labor law. Among their duties are conducting union representation elections, certifying bargaining units, and protecting the rights of public employees, including police, to organize and bargain. They also may play a key role when the parties reach a bargaining impasse. In many states, the state board (or another state agency) will select and assign mediators and fact finders to help the parties resolve their deadlock. If a state provides the option of interest arbitration when impasses occur, it is very often the responsibility of the state labor board to assign an arbitrator and oversee that process.

THE COLLECTIVE BARGAINING PROCESS
Bargaining Units

One of the issues on which the state laws that grant police the right to bargain vary is which ranks of officers have bargaining rights. And because this varies from state to state, so does the issue of which ranks are eligible for membership in the various police unions. In New York City, in addition to the officers' (PBA) and the sergeants' (SBA) unions, New York City police lieutenants have their own union (LBA), as do the detectives and captains who are represented, respectively by the Detectives'

Endowment Association (DEA) and the Captains' Endowment Association (CEA). The PBA and the SBA negotiate separate contracts; the LBA and the CEA bargain as a coalition. But many police unions include ranks above that of police officer. For example, the DC Police Union represents officers, detectives, and sergeants in Washington, D.C. And the New York Finger Lakes Region Police Officers Local 195 includes officers, sergeants, detectives, lieutenants, and captains as members. When Local 195 bargains a contract, it does so on behalf of all the different ranks represented by the union (City of Auburn, New York 2023). Since police sergeants, lieutenants, and captains are all considered middle management, potential conflicts of interest must be considered when these managers are in the same unit as the people they manage.

Police local unions generally represent only the members employed by one police department; thus, most police labor negotiations involve the local union bargaining with the police department that employs its members. The composition of the union's bargaining team can vary greatly depending on the size of the police force and whether the union is negotiating with a large city or county, a midsize town, or a small borough or village. The president of the local will usually play a leading role in bargaining. If a local is affiliated with a larger labor organization like the FOP, IUPA, or a national union, the local president might be assisted by professional union staff with bargaining experience. Because many police union locals are unaffiliated, they often hire professional negotiators to advise them. These advisors might be attorneys or former police union leaders with significant bargaining experience. A local union bargaining team may also include other local officers or members (Clark 2023).

Table 4
States That Require Police Collective Bargaining Sessions to Be Open to the Public

| Florida |
| Mississippi |
| Montana |
| Nebraska |
| Nevada |
| North Dakota |
| Tennessee |
| Texas |
| Kansas |
| Minnesota |

Brannick and Holman (2022).

Sunshine Laws

In the private sector, collective bargaining takes place behind closed doors, and the proceedings are confidential. Because funding for public employee compensation and benefits comes from tax revenues, ten states have "sunshine laws" that require police negotiations to be open to the public (Table 4). These laws are designed to create a more transparent process. In those states, however, representatives of management and the union are each allowed to hold private executive sessions to discuss bargaining strategy (Brannick and Holman 2022).

Scope of Bargaining

One of the concerns that local governments have about bargaining with public sector unions is that it requires them to share their power to make decisions regarding the provision of public services. Beyond increasing the cost of police services by negotiating better salaries and benefits, police unions are interested in negotiating other employment-related issues of concern to their members. These might include policies related to staffing, discipline, scheduling, uniform policies, and other issues. Bargaining thus becomes an effort to balance the public's interest in the provision of police services with the efforts of police unions to improve conditions for their officer-members (Sackman 1977).

Some states, however, have taken steps to limit the "scope of bargaining," which restricts the issues over which the parties are permitted to bargain. For example, Hawai'i and the District of Columbia have passed measures prohibiting police unions and police departments from negotiating over discipline. Nebraska "prohibits collective bargaining provisions that limit the discretion of the [State Police] to use records of prior misconduct for the past ten years in determining appropriate disciplinary action" (US Conference of Mayors, no date). In recent years, there have been efforts in numerous states to make discipline and discipline-related issues management prerogatives that are outside the scope of bargaining. Those efforts have largely failed, and discipline remains a common subject of police bargaining (Kurtz and Glock 2020).

Bargaining Power Dynamics

As suggested earlier, unions draw their bargaining power from the threat of a strike. The possibility of a strike brings balance to the bargaining relationship and forces employers to consider concessions to the union. Police unions, however, do not have the right to strike. So, how do they get an employer to take their demands seriously? Two factors give police unions power at the bargaining table.

State laws that provide police unions with the opportunity to take impasses to interest arbitration are a source of bargaining leverage for police unions. This is because most government employers are reluctant to have the salary, benefits, and terms of employment they must provide decided by a third-party arbitrator. The possibility of interest arbitration serves as an incentive for employers to make concessions to the union and retain final authority to determine the terms of a contract.

Even when interest arbitration is not available to police unions, the union's political influence is a second factor that forces governments to take police union demands at the bargaining table seriously. Since the earliest days of police collective bargaining, police unions have recognized the potential they have for influencing the political process in their communities. Police negotiations take place between a police union and a local or state government entity. In every case, the people ultimately making the final decisions for those entities are elected officials. Being able to influence those elected officials is critical to police unions' efforts to improve the salaries, benefits, and working conditions of their members. As Juris and Feuille put it, "collective bargaining with a political overlay gives the police union an inordinate amount of power" (1973: 177) relative to the government entity with which it is bargaining.

Police officers represent something that carries great weight in US politics—the principle of law and order. Most candidates for public office, whether Democrat or Republican, do not want to be labeled as soft on crime or unsupportive of police. The endorsement of the local police union is highly sought after by most politicians. They understand that angering the union by taking a stand against its demands at the bargaining table risks jeopardizing the support of the union in the next election. And if an elected official does receive the endorsement of the local police union and goes on to win their race, it would be naïve to think that this would not impact the positions that the official, or the representatives he sends to the bargaining table, takes in negotiations.

In addition to candidate endorsements, police unions use dues money collected from their members to lobby politicians to support pro-police legislation. They also use such funds for "get out the vote" efforts to make sure that their members vote on election day and to publicize the candidates who have received their endorsements.

Police unions cannot, however, donate dues money directly to candidates. For that purpose, most police unions of any size have formed political action committees that solicit voluntary contributions from members that can then be given directly to candidates. The amount of these contributions has been rising. A 2020 news story reported that police unions in the country's three largest cities—New York, Los Angeles, and Chicago—spent $87 million dollars in combined lobbying costs and campaign contributions in the previous 20 years (Perkins 2020). Being able to help elect the politician you will be bargaining with gives police unions significant leverage. Some observers have questioned the ethics of this situation, but it remains a key dynamic of police collective bargaining.

Bargaining Issues
Economic Issues

Police unions bargain over a wide range of issues that fall into two general categories—economic and noneconomic issues. Economic issues are those that have a direct monetary cost, and noneconomic issues focus more on policies as well as process and procedure issues.

Pay is considered a very high-priority economic issue in police negotiations. In recent years, collectively bargained police compensation has increased rapidly. Headlines such as "Detroit Police Tentative Contract Comes with Big Raises" (Sahouri 2022), "St. Louis Police in Line for Largest Raises in Recent Memory" (Huguelet 2023), and "West Palm Police Employees Getting Huge Raises" (Washington 2021) have become commonplace.

Traditionally, police union demands for pay increases have been backed up by comparability studies showing that their members are underpaid compared to officers in nearby communities (Figure 1). Union negotiators might also argue that police pay in their community is falling behind the cost of living. They would further argue that these shortcomings need to be addressed to prevent their police force from losing officers to nearby communities that value their officers more.

Figure 1

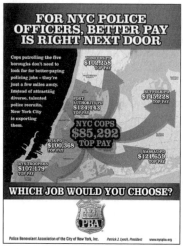

Police Benevolent Association of the City of New York (no date).

In response, the negotiators for the local government might argue that the tax base of the community is limited and that little or no additional tax revenue can be raised to fund significant increases in officers' salaries; only a minimal raise might be possible at best. If the union and the employer do not come to an agreement, a bargaining impasse might be declared. In that case, the dispute would go to some form of mediation and/or fact finding. If the state law regulating police bargaining includes a provision for interest arbitration, the final terms of the contract might be determined through that process.

The deaths of George Floyd and Breonna Taylor at the hands of police in 2020, and other high-profile examples of police misconduct, have brought heightened scrutiny to US law enforcement and generated calls for police reform. This movement initially put police unions on the defensive. It also resulted in a wave of resignations and retirements by officers across the country, resulting in a growing national shortage of police officers that quickly reached the crisis stage. And it was accompanied by a spike in violent crime across the country (Saric 2022).

Almost all police departments that have come to the bargaining table in recent years have done so with a seriously understaffed police force. Any employer who cannot fill job openings quickly realizes that to attract applicants, it needs to increase compensation. This kind of tight labor market (one in which unemployment is low and employers cannot fill job openings) gives unions an advantage in collective bargaining. As a result, bargaining does not focus on whether the employer will offer a significant pay increase—but rather on how significant that raise will be. This explains the headlines about police receiving big pay increases mentioned earlier.

In the present environment, unions will push hard to maximize member pay. This includes increasing the starting salaries for new police officers. In 2022, the Detroit police union negotiated an increase in starting salaries for officers from $43,000 to $53,000. Raising the issue of comparability with surrounding communities, the mayor of Detroit said that the increase would "make us competitive with other area police departments" (Ramirez and Hunter 2022).

Police unions will also focus their efforts on significantly increasing the base pay of current officers. In addition, union negotiators will propose raising supplements to base pay rates for performing specialty duties such as K-9, special weapons and tactics, and undercover work. Officers can often also earn additional supplements by completing training programs or academic degrees.

Given the importance of retaining current officers, longevity pay increases will also be a high priority for police unions in negotiations. Longevity pay takes the form of additional pay supplements for each year of service completed. Police unions argue that to retain and recruit officers in today's environment, police departments need to provide opportunities for their officers to increase their earnings with extra pay. This often takes the form of premium pay—overtime for working beyond the usual work hours, a shift differential for working undesirable hours (evening or overnight shifts or weekends),[3] or pay for working on a holiday. Premium pay can greatly increase the yearly income of officers.

Pay for time not worked, including sick leave, vacations, personal days, and paid holidays, is an additional type of economic issue typically included in police labor agreements.

Benefits are another category of economic bargaining issues important to labor negotiations. Police unions are using their increased leverage to negotiate better benefits packages. A high priority in this regard is maintaining the high-quality healthcare plans police officers enjoy, while resisting management efforts to shift a greater portion of the cost to them through increased premiums, co-payments, and deductibles. Contracts also usually include dental and vision benefits.

Pensions are also a part of any police labor agreement. Most police contracts provide the possibility of retirement after 25 years of service, with most officers typically retiring around age 50. Early retirement was originally instituted to make up for the low pay police received at one time; today, it is seen as an important recruitment and retention benefit. For that reason, police unions often negotiate healthcare and pension benefits that help "bridge" the period between retirement and when officers become eligible for Medicare. In recent years, these bridges have taken the form of 401(k) deferred compensation programs that pay into a voluntary employee beneficiary association (Clark 2023).

Other benefits commonly found in police collective bargaining agreements are reimbursements for uniforms, educational and training costs, and cell phone stipends, as well as life insurance, survivors' benefits, and short- and long-term disability insurance. Some police departments also provide officers with a take-home car.

Noneconomic Issues

Noneconomic bargaining issues are issues included in a labor agreement that do not have a direct monetary cost. Examples of noneconomic issues that would typically be subject to negotiations between a police union and a police department are seniority rights, promotion processes, scheduling, union dues deduction, workplace safety and health, military leave, unpaid leave, time off to conduct union business, and body cameras.

Some of these issues could be considered the purview of management, so employers may be reluctant to bargain over them. But police unions have had a lot of success in negotiating such issues. Why have police departments been willing to give up unilateral authority to decide how these issues will be handled? Pretty clearly, the leverage police unions have at the bargaining table is sometimes so significant that they are not willing to settle for just big increases in pay and other economic issues. When union negotiators are convinced that management cannot afford the cost of additional pay increases or economic benefits, they will turn their attention to noneconomic issues such as discipline or scheduling that will not increase police department budgets, at least in the short run (Fegley 2020).

One issue that is generally considered to be a management function is staffing levels. As police departments have seen the number of officer vacancies grow steadily in recent years, they have had to reduce staffing levels and require officers to work overtime to provide the minimal police coverage necessary to maintain law and order. Being forced to work 16- to 18-hour shifts in an effort to provide minimal coverage represents a safety and health issue for officers. They are placed in greater danger, as their physical and mental reactions dull from exhaustion. This leads to increased stress and eventual burnout. Negotiating about the safety and health problems that their members face is a high priority for police unions, so it is increasingly common to see them making proposals for minimum staffing levels and restrictions on mandatory overtime to protect their members.

Another noneconomic issue that has garnered a great deal of attention in recent years is police officer discipline. Over the past decade, many police unions have negotiated restrictions to discipline processes. These restrictions are valued by police unions and their members because, in their view, they make the discipline process fairer. Coincidentally, they may also make it more difficult to punish officers for misconduct, which means increased job security. Police departments are willing to make such concessions because they are budget neutral (meaning they do not cost the departments anything to implement, at least initially). Rushin (2017) found that 156 of 178 police contracts he analyzed included at least one restriction that made it harder to discipline officers charged with misconduct.

Table 5 presents data from a 2020 study by Fegley about the most common restrictions on discipline found in police contracts in 81 large cities. Among the findings are that 61.73% of those contracts included provisions that instituted delays as to when officers accused of misconduct can be interviewed by their departments,

Table 5
Police Officer Protections in 81 Large Cities with Union Contracts
and 16 Large Cities without Collective Bargaining Agreements

	Protections	
	Union contracts (n = 81)	No collective bargaining agreement (n = 16)
Restrictions/delays on interrogations	61.73%	18.75%
Gives officers very broad access to information	50.62%	18.75%
Limits oversight and discipline	81.48%	6.25%
Erases misconduct records	53.09%	6.25%

Fegley (2020).

81.48% had language that limits oversight and discipline, and 53.09% of the contracts contained provisions that required erasing instances of previous discipline from an officer's personnel file after a given period (often as little as one to two years).

Since 2006, the nation's largest police departments have fired at least 1,881 officers for misconduct that betrayed the public's trust, from cheating on overtime to unjustified shootings. *The Washington Post*, however, found that departments have been forced to reinstate more than 450 of these officers because their discipline was overturned in arbitration, the final step of the discipline process (Kelly, Lowery, and Rich 2017). In some cases, the officers who returned to duty have continued to engage in misconduct. Many observers have blamed the disciplinary restrictions negotiated by police unions for these officers being returned to duty (Melendez 2021). Such restrictions include disqualifying misconduct complaints that are submitted too many days after an incident occurs or when an investigation takes too long to complete, preventing the consideration of past disciplinary action involving an officer, and limiting disciplinary consequences for officers (Rushin 2017).

In the wake of the Floyd and Taylor deaths caused by police, questions have been raised about whether the restrictions on discipline negotiated by police unions have made it more difficult to hold police officers accountable for serious acts of misconduct. This has led to calls that such language be removed from collective bargaining agreements and that discipline be designated as a prohibited item of bargaining (Kurtz and Glock 2020).

DISPUTE RESOLUTION

In the process of negotiations, sometimes the parties reach a point where neither side is willing to compromise further. Such a deadlock is legally termed an "impasse." When nonpolice employees have the right to strike, they can withdraw their labor to break an impasse. Because police do not have this option, most state laws governing police collective bargaining provide several impasse resolution mechanisms to help break such deadlocks. Mediation is the first mechanism introduced when impasses occur. In this process, an experienced, neutral mediator meets with the parties to help them resolve their differences. Mediators try to facilitate communications between the parties, provide realistic assessments of the positions the parties have taken, and suggest alternative solutions to the problems the parties cannot solve themselves (Williams 1979).

Mediators, however, have no power to compel the parties to change their positions. Thus, mediation is not always successful in resolving impasses. If mediation does not resolve the dispute, numerous states require police unions and local governments to submit their dispute to a fact-finding process. Fact finding again uses a neutral third party, or sometimes a panel of individuals, with experience in collective bargaining. The fact finder either conducts a hearing or asks the parties to submit their final offers or negotiating positions in writing, along with supporting data. The fact finder reviews the positions of the parties and makes a recommendation that the fact finder believes constitutes a fair and reasonable settlement. Fact finders' reports are usually not binding on the parties, but they are often made public in an effort to put pressure on the parties to accept the fact finders' recommendations. In some states, this is the end of the collective bargaining process. In several states, the dispute moves to the final impasse resolution step—interest arbitration (Ricketson 2013).

Unlike mediation and fact finding, interest arbitration is binding on the parties. In this process, the parties follow a clearly defined procedure for appointing a neutral third party, or sometimes a panel of three, to hear the case. In interest arbitration, the arbitrator or arbitration panel holds a hearing at which the police union and the police department/municipality each present their positions on what the contract should contain in terms of wages, benefits, and other issues in contention.

There are at least three variations of interest arbitration used by states. "Final offer by item" arbitration enables the arbitrator to pick either the employer's or the union's final position on each item in dispute. In this version, the arbitrator could, for example, pick the employer's final offer on compensation and the union's final offer on healthcare insurance, overtime pay, and paid holidays. In the second version, "final offer by package," the arbitrator must pick either the employer's or the union's entire final offer. They cannot pick and choose between issues. And in the third version of interest arbitration, the arbitrator can choose any position on any issue. In other words, the arbitrator could choose some of the employer's positions on some issues and some of the union's positions or all of either side's final positions, or he could choose positions that are halfway between each or some other variation (Ricketson 2013).

Interest arbitration is a mechanism designed to encourage both sides to genuinely bargain and attempt to resolve their differences themselves. However, research suggests that sometimes it can actually impede bargaining in two ways. First, it can cause the parties to refrain from compromising on issues in order to position themselves for arbitration. This "chilling effect" occurs when the parties believe interest arbitration will result in a better outcome than actual bargaining. Second, if parties have previously used interest arbitration in negotiations, they can come to rely on the process to resolve their bargaining differences and, as a result, make little effort to settle their differences through negotiations. Because the parties come to be dependent on or "addicted" to arbitration, this is called the "narcotic effect." In both cases, interest arbitration actually impedes genuine bargaining, rather than encouraging it (Kochan and Baderschneider 1978; Ricketson 2013).

SIGNIFICANT RECENT POLICE NEGOTIATIONS

The police contract that covers the greatest number of officers in the country is the one negotiated between the New York City PBA and the City of New York. Between 2017 and 2023, the two parties were unable to agree on a new contract, and the officers continued to work under the previous agreement. In 2023, they agreed on a revised agreement that would provide officers with a 28.25% total increase for the period 2017 through mid-2025 (some of that increase would be paid retroactively for the prior years, when they had not received a raise). Police at the highest pay grade with numerous years of experience would see their salary increase to $131,500 per year (Sommerfeldt and Gartland 2023).

The new contract also includes a six-month pilot program that will offer a new shift structure that offers 10-hour and 12-hour shifts to a limited number of officers. New York City's mayor was quoted as saying that "the contract allows the New York Police Department to complete with the private sector and other agencies to recruit the best to join the finest" (Sommerfeldt and Gartland 2023).

Another 2023 contract settlement that provides insight into bargaining in the midst of a critical shortage of officers is the labor agreement between the King County (Seattle, Washington) Sheriff's Department and the King County Police Officers Guild. This contract was negotiated in the second half of 2022, when the Sheriff's Department had 100 vacant positions and deputies were being forced to work 16-hour shifts multiple days a week (Swaby 2022). The new agreement covers 2023 and 2024 (Pauley 2022).

The contract attempted to address the department's shortage by emphasizing both the recruitment of new deputies and the retention of current deputies. Starting salaries for new hires increased from $73,402 to $85,249. Starting deputies without experience also receive a $7,500 signing bonus; new hires with experience receive a $15,000 bonus (Pauley 2022).

Current deputies in the department received a total increase of 20% over three years, including a retroactive salary increase of 6%, an increase of 10% for 2023, and an additional 4% increase for 2024. Depending on years of service, base pay ranged from the starting salary of $85,249 to a top base pay rate of $119,372 (Pauley 2022).

In addition, deputies received boosts in pay beyond their base pay for performing specialty duties and for gaining additional education and training. For example, deputies performing K-9, bomb disposal, diving, marine, or flight duties received an additional 10% in pay. Detectives received a 6% or 8% increase, depending on their rank. Motorcycle deputies earned an additional 3%, plain clothes officers 4%, and hostage negotiators 5%. Also, deputies earning an associate's degree received a 2% supplement, those earning a bachelor's garnered a 4% increase, and a master's degree was worth 6% in additional pay (King County 2023).

Longevity pay was also included in the contract. In each of their fifth through fifteenth years of service, deputies received either an additional 1% or 2% pay increase each year.

And as is the case in most police contract negotiations, premium pay and pay for time not worked was improved (King County, Washington 2023).

A third example of police bargaining differs significantly from the situation in New York City and Seattle. A Texas state law prohibits its public employees from engaging in collective bargaining. However, a 1973 change to the law allows political subdivisions in the state to choose to engage in collective bargaining with their employees. The City of Austin agreed to negotiate with a union representing its police in 1995. Since then, they have negotiated several agreements with the union (Delord and Sanders 2006).

The most recent contract expired on March 31, 2023. Prior to the expiration of that contract, city and police negotiators agreed on a four-year contract. However, city leaders postponed signing the contract because of an upcoming May voter referendum on civilian oversight of police. The referendum passed overwhelmingly, but a subsequent politically inspired lawsuit delayed its implementation. And the City of Austin believes it cannot sign a contract until it knows for sure the lawsuit's outcome (Seipp 2024).

So, almost a year after the police contract expired, no agreement was negotiated to take its place. The result is low morale among Austin's police force, which has resulted in increased resignations from the department at a time when the city already faces a police shortage. The Austin situation demonstrates the manner in which police bargaining can be influenced in negative ways by local politics (Seipp 2024).

THE FUTURE OF POLICE COLLECTIVE BARGAINING

The first police collective bargaining agreement in the United States was signed by the New York City PBA and New York City in 1964. And the first statewide law authorizing police collective bargaining was passed in Pennsylvania in 1968. Since then, police departments and police unions in almost all major cities and in 44 states have negotiated labor agreements that set mutually agreed-to compensation, benefits, and working conditions.

Because of the considerable support the police enjoy from the public, police unions have accumulated significant political power at the local, state, and national levels in the collective bargaining process despite the fact that they are legally prohibited from striking.

In just the past three to five years, the resignations and retirements of police officers have left police forces across the country severely understaffed. The need for police departments to make the recruitment of new officers and the retention of current officers a top priority has increased the leverage of police unions at the bargaining table. As a result, we are seeing police contracts that contain well-above-average pay and benefits. We also see police unions using their bargaining power to negotiate improved terms and conditions of employment. And in a number of areas, we see them using their clout to change policies and practices that have traditionally been considered solely the discretion of management. One area in particular that has raised significant concerns is officer discipline. Some states already prohibit police unions from bargaining about discipline, and there have been a number of proposals to make that prohibition the rule and not the exception. However, it is not yet clear whether such efforts will be successful and what their impact would be (Kurtz and Glock 2020).

Collective bargaining has become such an integral part of the US system of law enforcement that it is not possible to fully understand that system without understanding how police unions and police departments come together to establish basic standards of employment for the officers who serve and protect. This chapter provided insight into the history, the parties, the legal framework, the power dynamics, the process, and the outcomes of police bargaining. Because the system of law enforcement touches everyone's lives, these basic insights are of value to all.

ENDNOTES

1. In this chapter, the term "police officer" or "officer" is used to designate police personnel in the lowest-ranking sworn position in a municipal police department. Officers make up the majority of sworn officers in police forces. The term "deputy sheriff" is generally used to designate the lowest-ranking sworn position in a county police force. A trooper is the lowest-ranking, fully qualified officer in state police forces.

2. The UK system of law enforcement, by comparison, is much more centralized. There are only 45 police forces in the United Kingdom. Forty-three of these are "territorial forces" covering geographic regions in England and Wales. They serve on average 1,319,000 people each (Statista). Scotland and Northern Ireland have one police force to cover both regions (Police.uk, no date).

3. Increasingly, officers are working four 10-hour or three 12-hour shifts a week. A shift differential would compensate those who work during the least attractive times of day.

REFERENCES

Brannick, P., and A. Holman 2022. *The Battle for Worker Freedom in the States: Grading State Public Sector Labor Laws,* 3rd ed. Harrisburg, PA: Commonwealth Foundation. http://tinyurl.com/vsnubftw

Brooks, C. 2023. "Federal Law Enforcement Officers, 2020—Statistical Tables." US Department of Justice, Bureau of Justice Statistics. September. http://tinyurl.com/adtu7zey

City of Auburn, New York, and New York Finger Lakes Region Police Officers Local 195. 2023. "Collective Negotiations Agreement, 2022–2026." http://tinyurl.com/28k7dars

Clark, P. 2020. "Why Police Unions Are Not Part of the American Labor Movement." The Conversation. August 25. http://tinyurl.com/mpetw2zk

———. 2023. "Interview with Police Union Negotiator Rockne Lucia." Conducted by Paul Clark. July 7.

Congressional Budget Office. 2023. "The Demographic Outlook: 2023 to 2053—Congressional Budget Office." April. https://www.cbo.gov

Decker, K. 1968. "The Right to Strike for Pennsylvania's Public Employees—Its Scope, Limits and Ramifications for the Public Employer." *Duquesne Law Review* 17, no. 3: 755–775. http://tinyurl.com/bdzd93s9

Delord, R., and J. Sanders. 2006. "Police Labor-Management Relations (Vol. I): Perspectives and Practical Solutions for Implementing Change, Making Reforms, and Handling Crises for Managers and Union Leaders." Report. August. US Department of Justice, Office of Community Oriented Policing Services. http://tinyurl.com/4mubjzue

Delord, R., and R. York. 2017. *Law Enforcement, Police Unions, and the Future: Educating Police Management and Unions About the Challenges Ahead.* Springfield, IL: Charles C. Thomas.

Denholm, D. 2016. "The Case Against Public Sector Unionism and Collective Bargaining." *Government Union Review* 18. http://tinyurl.com/3sjejut5

DiSalvo, D. 2020. "The Trouble with Police Unions." *National Affairs.* Fall. http://tinyurl.com/ycydyv2d

———. 2021. "Interest Groups, Local Politics, and Police Unions." *Interest Groups and Advocacy* 11: 263–277. https://doi.org/10.1057/s41309-021-00146-9

Fegley, T. 2020. "Police Unions and Officer Privileges." *Independent Review* 25, no. 2: 165–186. http://tinyurl.com/7uebrbfd

Fraternal Order of Police. No date. "About the Fraternal Order of Police." http://tinyurl.com/22auwa7j

———. No date. "A History of the Fraternal Order of Police." http://tinyurl.com/5n7p2dt3

Gardner, A.M., and K.M. Scott. 2022. "Census of State and Local Law Enforcement Agencies, 2018—Statistical Tables." US Department of Justice, Bureau of Justice Statistics. October. http://tinyurl.com/3pjtax2n

Griffith, D. 2016. "The 2016 POLICE Presidential Poll." Police Law Enforcement Solutions. September 2. http://tinyurl.com/fhewabbu

Hirsch, B., D. Macpherson, and W. Even. 2024. "Union Membership, Coverage, and Earnings from the CPS." https://unionstats.com

Huguelet, A. 2023. "St. Louis Police in Line for Largest Raises in Recent Memory." *St. Louis Post-Dispatch.* March 3. http://tinyurl.com/39a8s3pa

International Union of Police Associations. 2023. Website. https://iupa.org

Juris, H., and P. Feuille. 1973. *Police Unionism: Power and Impact in Public Sector Collective Bargaining.* Lexington, MA: D.C. Heath.

Kelly, K., W. Lowery, and S. Rich. 2017. "Fired/Rehired: Police Chiefs Are Often Forced to Put Officers Fired for Misconduct Back on the Streets." *Washington Post.* August 3. http://tinyurl.com/bdh6dt75

King County, Washington. 2023. "Agreement Between King County, Washington and King County Sheriff's Office Marshals' Guild." http://tinyurl.com/bddrbhsj

Kochan, T., and J. Baderschneider. 1978. "Dependence on Impasse Procedures: Police and Firefighters in New York State." *Industrial and Labor Relations Review* 31, no. 4: 431–449. https://doi.org/10.2307/2522233

Kurtz, D., and J. Glock. 2020. "Reforming America's Police Unions to Ensure Justice." Cicero Institute. September 9. http://tinyurl.com/mr2ffd4e

Lange, C. 2022. "The Largest Police Forces in the US." *Wall Street Journal.* December 23. http://tinyurl.com/msk2udzk

Leary, A., and C. Maher. 2019. "Democrats Labor to Stem Flow of Union Voters to Trump." *Wall Street Journal*. September 2. http://tinyurl.com/2krjf758

Levine, M.J. 1988. "Historical Overview of Police Unionization in the United States." *Police Journal* 61, no. 4: 334–343.

Melendez, P. 2021. "'Florida's Worst Cop' Was Just Fired for Misconduct—for the Seventh Time." Daily Beast. May 28. http://tinyurl.com/5yttj63u

National Association of Police Organizations. No date. Website. http://tinyurl.com/ywvueymz

National Conference of State Legislatures. No date. "Collective Bargaining: Statutory Summary." http://tinyurl.com/y55rysua

National Sheriffs' Association. No date. Website. https://www.sheriffs.org

Office of Congressional Workplace Rights. 2022. *Fraternal Order of Police, District of Columbia Lodge No. 1 US Capitol Police Labor Committee v. United States Capitol Police*, Case No. 20-LMR-01 (CA). Office of Congressional Workplace Rights. April 4. http://tinyurl.com/yv34h7vp

Pauly, S. 2022. "New Agreement Gives King County Sheriff's Office Raises and Body Cams." Center Square Washington. November 9. http://tinyurl.com/yczaemyv

Perkins, T. 2020. "Revealed: Police Unions Spend Millions to Influence Policy in Biggest US Cities." *Guardian*. June 23. http://tinyurl.com/4ujtzdrs

Police Benevolent Association of the City of New York. No date. "Fighting for a Fair Contract." http://tinyurl.com/yajf2r34

Police.uk. No date. "UK Police Forces." http://tinyurl.com/mf3dfdf9

Ramirez, C., and G. Hunter. 2022. "Detroit City Officials, Police Reach New Contract Deal with Pay Raises." *Detroit News*. September 30. http://tinyurl.com/bdd3rtry

Ricketson, D. 2013. "Interest Arbitration Impasse Rates." Paper 28, Seminar Research Paper Series. DigitalCommons@URI. http://tinyurl.com/7pty8bsm

Ross, A.M. 1969. "Public Employee Unions and the Right to Strike." *Monthly Labor Review* 92, no. 3: 14–18. http://tinyurl.com/4mfks4me

Rushin, S. 2017. "Police Union Contracts." *Duke Law Journal* 66, no. 6: 1191–266. http://tinyurl.com/59mvw7fu

Sackman, M. 1977. "Redefining the Scope of Bargaining in Public Employment." *Boston College Law Review* 19, no. 1: 135–205.

Sahouri, A. 2022. "Detroit Police Officers Would Get $10K Raises Under New Tentative Contract Agreement." *Detroit Free Press*. September 30. http://tinyurl.com/ykmm9e42

Saric, I. 2022. "Police Departments Struggle with Staffing Shortages." Axios. August 8. http://tinyurl.com/3v23czj7

Seipp, S. 2024. "Will the Austin Police Union and City Reach a Long-Term Contract This Year? What We Know." *Austin American-Statesman*. January 8. http://tinyurl.com/bdh7rk49

Shults, J. No date. "Is Paramilitary Structure Bad?" http://tinyurl.com/4mnmrbxr

Sommerfeldt, C., and M. Gartland. 2023. "NYC, NYPD Union Reach New Contract After Seven Years of Disagreement." Police1. April 5. http://tinyurl.com/22mfky69

Statista. No date. "Number of Police Officers in the United Kingdom in 2022, by Police Force." Statista. http://tinyurl.com/3upfnd8s

Swaby, N. 2022. "Coalition of Law Enforcement Guilds Emphasizes King County 'Public Safety Crisis.'" K5 News. September 7. http://tinyurl.com/4fx8d5hp

The Policy Circle. No date. "Understanding Law Enforcement." http://tinyurl.com/4uw243f4

US Conference of Mayors. No date. "Transparency and Accountability to Reinforce Constitutional Policing." http://tinyurl.com/jhcr5umy

US Federal Labor Relations Authority. No date. "Federal Service Labor-Management Relations Statute." http://tinyurl.com/mr3ux8h4
US Senate. No date. "Constitution of the United States." http://tinyurl.com/54nnna7y
Vote Smart. No date. "Hillary Clinton's Ratings and Endorsements." http://tinyurl.com/2x3serum
Walsh, J. 2001. *The Fraternal Order of Police*. Nashville, TN: Turner.
Washington, W. 2021. "West Palm Police Employees Getting Huge Raises—Up to 29 Percent—in New Contract." *Palm Beach Post*. June 16. http://tinyurl.com/4fp6pujp
Wellington, H., and R.K. Winter Jr. 1969. "The Limits of Collective Bargaining in Public Employment." *The Yale Law Journal* 78, no. 7: 1107–1127. http://tinyurl.com/4j3bpc6f
Williams, A.S. 1979. "Alternatives to the Right to Strike for Public Employees: Do They Adequately Implement Florida's Constitutional Right to Collectively Bargain?" *Florida State University Law Review* 7, no. 3: 475–504. http://tinyurl.com/werxvu2v

CHAPTER 9

Collective Bargaining in the Grocery Industry and the Growth of the Nonunion Sector

MICHAEL SCHUSTER
Syracuse University

Abstract

The retail grocery industry is composed of three elements: the stores that sell directly to consumers, the companies or distribution centers that supply the stores, and company-owned manufacturing facilities that make branded products to be sold in stores. Forty-three percent of the market is occupied by strong regional players. Thirteen percent of employees are represented by unions. The others are, for the most part, or entirely, nonunion. The industry is experiencing significant disruptions from the growth of online grocery shopping. This trend was greatly enhanced by the recent pandemic. The largest union, the United Food and Commercial Workers Union, has locals in most regions of the United States and Canada. These regions can have hundreds of individual stores, with employment ranging from 100 to 400 employees. At the distribution level, bargaining tends to be individual site or multi-employer through the Teamsters union. At the manufacturing level, bargaining is generally conducted at the plant level, although there are multisite master agreements at Kellogg, General Mills, and Kraft Heinz. In several areas of the United States, there is regional coordinated bargaining among several employers. Collective bargaining is primarily over wages, retirement and healthcare benefits, and flexibility. Represented employers tend to have lower starting wages than nonunion competitors, with more generous healthcare and retirement benefits. Employers have been seeking to lower the cost of benefits to put more resources into entry level and early seniority pay. The industry has seen only infrequent strikes.

INTRODUCTION

The retail food (grocery and specialty) and beverage industry is an $850 billion industry (Ozbun 2023) employing 3.2 million workers (US Department of Labor 2022), with more than 115,000 locations (US Department of Agriculture 2022). The industry is composed of four segments: the stores that sell directly to consumers, where most grocery purchases are made; the company or third-party-owned distribution centers that supply the stores; company-owned manufacturing facilities that produce private-label branded products sold in the stores; and finally, the growth of fulfillment centers and delivery personnel to complete online customer purchases.

The three most common positions in grocery stores are cashiers, first-line supervisors, and stock clerks and order fillers. Training requirements for entry-level positions are minimal. Customer-facing positions, such as cashiers and deli and bakery workers, require more training and skill because most stores are focused on enhancing the customer service experience. Supervisory positions (department heads, assistant managers) require more education and experience because issues of inventory control, staffing, scheduling, supervision, and merchandising are paramount. The industry is almost evenly split by gender (49% female, 51% male). The average work week for employees is 42.3 hours for full-time and 22.6 hours for part-time (Deloitte and Datawheel 2023).

It is important to note that there are other food manufacturers and suppliers in the grocery value chain, including third-party private-label manufacturers and well-known, highly advertised branded producers such as Kellogg, Kraft Heinz, General Mills, Conagra Foods, Coca-Cola, and PepsiCo. Tyson, Perdue, and Hormel serve the meatpacking industry. The branded companies provide considerable revenue to the grocery chains through trade funding and promotions. This takes the form of payments for shelf space, displays, and coupons. While all of these segments are important to the industry, the focus of this chapter is confined to the retail employers and the unions that represent their employees.

The industry is highly competitive, with a large number of diverse competitors serving a variety of grocery distribution channels and consumer purchase options. There are the traditional, longtime industry grocery leaders—Kroger, Albertsons, Ahold, Publix, and Meijer—and an additional group of more recent entrants—Walmart, Whole Foods, Costco, Aldi, Target, and Trader Joe's. Stores such as Wegmans and H-E-B have developed a strong regional presence.

Walmart (including Sam's Club) is the industry leader, with an estimated market share of 25.6%, followed by Kroger (9.9%), Costco (7%), and Albertsons (5.7%) (Repko 2022). Forty-three percent of the market is occupied by strong regional players such as Wegmans. Kroger, Albertsons, Ahold, Meijer, Stater Bros, Cub, and Giant are union represented. Costco has a large contingent (10%) of represented employees. The others are, for the most part, entirely nonunion. Publix (nonunion) is the largest employee-owned company in the United States (80% of the stock is owned by current and former employees). Also included in the composition of the industry are specialty food and convenience stores such as 7-Eleven, Speedway, and Circle K. Today, most large drugstore chains (Walgreens, CVS) have large retail food and beverage departments. The grocery stores compete with drug stores for prescription and over-the-counter medications. Table 1 provides a detailed summary of the 30 largest employers in the industry, their sales, and number of stores.

The retail grocery business is low margin (Biery 2018). Employers have tended to offset these low margins by expanding hard goods sales (such as clothing and kitchen equipment) and other services, including prepared foods, floral departments,

Table 1
Top 30 Retailers (Grocery, Mass, Convenience, Drug, and Dollar Stores) by Annual Sales, in US Dollars (billions)

Rank	Company	2019–20	2020–21	Change (%)	Store banners	Store count
1	Walmart	399.8	433.9	8.53	Walmart, Sam's Club	5,342
2	Amazon	164.74	236.28	43.42	Whole Foods Market, Amazon Fresh, Amazon Go	539
3	Kroger	122.29	132.5	8.4	Kroger, Ralphs, Dillons, Smith's, Roundy's, King Soopers, Fry's, QFC, City Market, Owen's, Jay C, Pay Less, Baker's, Gerbes, Harris Teeter, Pick 'n Save, Copps, Metro Market, Mariano's, Fred Meyer, Food 4 Less, Foods Co.	2,742
4	Costco	111.75	122.14	9.3	Costco	559
5	Walgreens Boots Alliance	104.53	107.7	3	Walgreens, Duane Reade	9,021
6	Target	77.13	92.4	19.8	Target	1,897
7	CVS	86.61	91.2	5.3	CVS	9,960
8	Albertsons	62.45	69.69	11.6	Albertsons, Safeway, Vons, Jewel–Osco, Shaw's, Acme, Tom Thumb, Randalls, United Supermarkets, Pavilions, Star Market, Carrs and Haggen	2,277
9	Ahold Delhaize USA	44.84	51.84	15.6	Stop & Shop, Food Lion, Giant/Martin's, Hannaford, Giant Food, Peapod	1,970
10	Publix Super Markets	38.12	44.86	17.7	Publix Super Markets, GreenWise Market	1,269
11	Couche-Tard	37.84	43.36	13.59	Circle K, Corner Store, Couche-Tard, Mac's, Kangaroo Express, CST, On the Run, Holiday Stationstores	9,414
12	Dollar General	27.75	33.75	19.49	Dollar General	17,266
13	C&S Wholesale Grocers	31.49	33.64	6.5	—	—
14	Loblaw	33.76	37.6	11.4	Loblaws	2,439
15	H-E-B	27.93	31.75	13.7	H-E-B	351
16	Seven & i Holdings	18.52	27.29	47.35	7-Eleven, Stripes, Aplus, Speedway	13,839
17	Sobeys	25.14	26.59	5.77	Sobeys, Farm Boy, Foodland, FreshCo, Price Chopper, Lawtons Drugs	1,933

(Table 1 continues, next page)

Rank	Company	2019–20	2020–21	Change (%)	Store banners	Store count
18	United Natural Foods	22.31	26.51	18.85	Cub Foods, Shoppers	71
19	Dollar Tree	23.61	25.51	8.03	Dollar Tree, Family Dollar, Dollar Tree Canada	15,68
20	Meijer	19.06	20.95	9.87	Meijer, Bridge Street Market, Woodward Corner Market	253
21	Aldi	16.86	18.44	9.36	Aldi	2,070
22	Wakefern Food Corporation	16.62	18.37	10.5	Price Rite Marketplace, ShopRite, The Fresh Grocer, Gourmet Garage, Dearborn Market	363
23	Trader Joe's*	15.27	16.5	8.05	Trader Joe's	530
24	Rite Aid	15.62	16.36	4.8	Rite Aid	2,510
25	B.J.'s Wholesale Club Holdings	12.89	15.1	17.13	BJ's Wholesale Club	221
26	Metro	13.28	14.26	7.4	Metro (Plus), Super C, Food Basics, Adonis, Première Moisson, Les 5 Saisons, Marché Richelieu, Brunet Pharmacies, Metro Pharmacy, Drug Basics, PJC Jean Coutu, PJC Santé, PJC Santé Beauté	1,601
27	Hy-Vee	10.91	12.15	11.4	Hy-Vee	265
28	Wegmans	9.73	10.68	9.8	Wegmans	105
29	Associated Wholesale Grocers	9.38	10.63	13.4	Homeland, United Supermarkets, Cash Saver and Price Chopper	6
30	Giant Eagle	9.48	10.35	9.2	Giant Eagle (+Express), Market District (+Express), GetGo, Ricker's, Giant Eagle	474

Data compiled by *Supermarket News* (2021) and by IGD, a UK-based analysis and insight organization for the food and consumer goods industry.

pharmacies, and gas stations. Walmart, Target, Kroger, and Costco stores are an example of this new business model. The warehouse channel (Costco, BJ's, and Sam's Club) utilizes a membership business model—charging lower prices, with a substantial portion of their profits generated by membership fees. Others tend to replicate this to a lesser, but growing, extent. The convenience segment of the grocery business has a lower volume, higher margin business model and relies heavily on fuel sales. The traditional grocery stores, along with the membership clubs, offer fuel at discount prices to attract and retain customers.

The fourth segment, online shopping, has grown significantly in recent years and currently represents 14.4% ($128 billion) of sales in 2022 (Arcieri 2022). This part of the business comprises personal shoppers, fulfillment centers, and delivery drivers. Some online sales also provide for customer store pickup. Amazon's purchase of Whole Foods in 2017 and Walmart's online business created a greater urgency among their competitors to grow their online shopping presence. The COVID-19 pandemic acted as an accelerant of the trend toward greater online shopping. This has forced Albertsons, Kroger, and others to enter the online space. The online market is expected to reach $188 billion in sales by 2024 (Ozbun 2022).

A BRIEF HISTORY OF THE GROCERY STORE

Today's grocery store is the result of shifting consumer preferences, technological changes, industry consolidation, and new entrants, as well as an expanded grocery store business model. The modern self-service grocery store replaced the labor of the small store clerk with that of the customer. The first grocery store (Piggly Wiggly) opened in 1916 in Memphis, Tennessee (Trinidad 2020). Prior to this time, customers provided a list of desired items, which were retrieved by store employees. In contrast, the new business model encouraged customers to roam the store with each item priced to inform customers of the cost of their purchases.

By the 1920s, small chains of groceries, including Kroger, Loblaws, and A&P, had developed a regional presence with uniform branding and customer loyalty. These chains primarily sold dry goods. Meats and produce were sold in separate venues. The industry began to be disrupted with the first supermarket (King Kullen in Queens, New York, 1930) (Farrell 2020). In addition to the traditional dry goods, the store sold meats, produce, baked goods, and dairy. This was facilitated by the growing presence of automobiles for travel to and from the market and refrigeration for store and home storage. The invention of the shopping cart in 1937 (replacing the handheld basket) encouraged additional customer purchases (Farrell 2020). By the 1950s, an international aisle was added, with items such as spaghetti, pasta sauce, and La Choy chow mein (Trinidad 2020). The bar code (better known as the uniform product code, or UPC) was developed and patented in 1952, but the scanning technology needed for its effectiveness did not occur until 1974 (Weightman 2015). This was a major technological invention that allowed for greater employee productivity and more accurate inventory control.

During the 1960s, supermarkets began providing customers with trading stamps (a loyalty program) that could be used toward future promotional purchases. Loyalty cards later replaced these in the 1990s. By the early 1970s, grocery stores began operating for more extended hours, including 24/7. In 1976, membership-based superstores were introduced (Price Club, now Costco) and charged customers for the privilege of shopping in their stores. Walmart founded Sam's Club in 1983 and opened its first supercenters in 1988, combining both grocery and hard goods, along with additional businesses discussed below.

The supermarket's evolution into the supercenter added pharmacies, banking, photo development, floral departments, prepared foods, gas stations, and car maintenance. More recently, fast food franchises, vision care, and hard goods have been added to the mix. The industry evolved further with online shopping (Peapod Digital Labs, no date), although it took many more years for its acceptance to catch on.

As more consumers became conscious of, and concerned with, industrial farming processes and techniques, the preference for organically produced products grew. Although there were earlier providers, Whole Foods (1980) set a course for the industry. In 2002, the US government issued regulations defining organic products. This led to a significant expansion in organic sales from $8.6 billion in 2002 to $49 billion in 2017, when Amazon acquired Whole Foods, the organic grocery market leader (Farrell 2020). Today most traditional stores have added significant shelf space for organic products. The Amazon acquisition followed the 2015 Albertsons–Safeway merger, the most significant consolidation to date. The combined Albertsons had 250,000 employees, 2,230 stores, 19 manufacturing facilities, and 27 distribution facilities in 34 states and the District of Columbia (Safeway 2015).

UNION REPRESENTATION

The industry is governed by the National Labor Relations Act and other federal and state employment legislation. The Affordable Care Act has impacted the bargaining over healthcare benefits eligibility as a result of the large number of part-time employees. State minimum wage laws and federal and state requirements for overtime pay eligibility impact employee work hours and earnings. This had an effect on lower levels of management (department heads and assistant managers). In addition, the food safety regulation of stores, distribution, and production facilities through the Food and Drug Administration is significant (US Food and Drug Administration 2022). There is also a presence of state food regulation to varying degrees.

The major union is the United Food and Commercial Workers Union (UFCW), with 1.2 million members, 835,000 (in the United States and Canada) of whom work in grocery. The balance of the UFCW is composed of meatpacking, healthcare, chemicals, distillery, and retail. Two other unions, the Bakery, Tobacco, Confectionery, and Grain Millers (BCTGM), with 63,000 members (Center for Union Facts 2023), and the International Brotherhood of Teamsters (IBT), with 1.3 million members, comprise most of the rest of the industry. The UFCW combined three formerly independent unions—the Retail Clerks International Association (RCIA) and the Amalgamated Meat Cutters (AMC), both affiliated with the American Federation of Labor (AFL), and the Retail, Wholesale, and Department Store Union (RWDSU), a CIO affiliate formed in 1937. All three joined the AFL-CIO in 1955. In 1979, the RCIA and the AMC merged to form the UFCW. Thereafter, the RWDSU became a semi-autonomous affiliate of the UFCW in 1993. The BCTGM represents a small number of employees in the manufacturing locations of grocery retailers. The UFCW and IBT grocery industry membership is highly concentrated in a handful of longtime represented employers. The IBT has a much more diversified membership beyond the grocery industry.

As with many other industries, union representation has steadily declined as a percentage of the workforce. Milkman (2022) persuasively demonstrates that there has been a long-term decline in union representation, from 40% in the 1960s to 28% in 1986. More recently, it has been 17.7% in 2021 and 13.0% in 2021. Most of the decline is attributable to the growth of the nonunion sector of the grocery industry and the lack of success in organizing new entrants. However, hiring during the pandemic reversed this trend temporarily, but the downward trend continued as the pandemic abated (Figure 1).

STATE OF ORGANIZING IN THE INDUSTRY

Recent National Labor Relations Board (NLRB) statistics show slight increases in union election success for the UFCW and the IBT. It should be noted that these data are union specific and not necessarily industry specific. Table 2 shows the number of elections, number of union wins and losses, workers eligible, and workers organized for the period 2018 through 2022. In 2022, The IBT won 66.2% of 219 elections, adding 4,947 new employees to their roles. The UFCW won 70.3 % of 158 elections, adding 2,552 new employees.

The IBT (Table 3) also contested 35 decertification elections, winning 31.4% and losing 899 members (net gain over losses: 4,048). The UFCW contested 13 decertification elections, losing 785 members (net gain over losses: 1,767) (Bloomberg Law 2023).

Recently, employees at four Trader Joe's stores (Hadley, Massachusetts; Minneapolis, Minnesota; Louisville, Kentucky; and Oakland, California) voted to unionize under the auspices of Trader Joe's United, an independent union formed at the Hadley location (Crowe 2023). The union reports that the locations are negotiating their contracts separately but on parallel tracks. As of this writing, agreements have yet to be reached. However, there are news reports that employees at the Hadley location

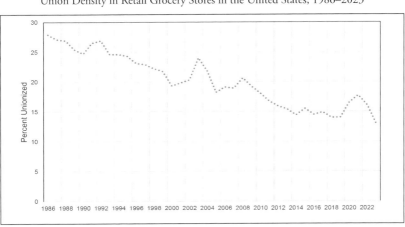

Figure 1
Union Density in Retail Grocery Stores in the United States, 1986–2023

Hirsch, Macpherson, and Even 2024.

Table 2
NLRB Representation Elections, UFCW and Teamsters, 2018–2022

Year	No. elections held	No. union wins	No. union losses	Union wins (%)	No. workers eligible	No. workers organized
United Food and Commercial Workers						
2018	82	44	38	53.7%	7,264	2,730
2019	72	41	31	56.9%	5,233	3,169
2020	71	41	30	57.7%	4,454	2,410
2021	74	51	23	68.9%	2,700	1,544
2022	158	111	47	70.3%	4,281	2,552
Total	457	288	169	63.0%	23,932	12,405
International Brotherhood of Teamsters						
2018	253	163	90	64.4%	9,248	5,362
2019	254	169	85	66.5%	9,653	6,326
2020	199	121	78	60.8%	7,889	3,496
2021	211	135	76	64.0%	8,797	5,280
2022	219	145	74	66.2%	8,565	4,947
Total	1,136	733	403	64.5%	44,152	25,411

Bloomberg Law (2023).

Table 3
NLRB Declassification Elections, UFCW and Teamsters, 2018–2022

Year	No. elections held	No. union wins	No. union losses	Union wins (%)	No. workers eligible	No. workers organized
United Food and Commercial Workers						
2018	13	5	8	38.5%	888	497
2019	9	3	6	33.3%	2,077	515
2020	9	4	5	44.4%	396	271
2021	10	5	5	50.0%	844	141
2022	13	5	8	38.5%	1,073	288
Total	54	22	32	40.7%	5,278	1,712
International Brotherhood of Teamsters						
2018	40	8	32	20.0%	1,874	639
2019	41	9	32	22.0%	1,453	377
2020	30	15	15	50.0%	1,545	1,228
2021	35	12	23	34.3%	1,676	1,043
2022	35	11	24	31.4%	1,512	613
Total	181	55	126	30.4%	8,060	3,900

Bloomberg Law (2023).

were attempting to decertify the union (Wilson 2024a), and a Chicago location had filed an election petition (Inklebarger 2024). More grassroots organizing is evidenced by workers at several New Seasons Markets on the West Coast forming another independent union—the New Seasons Labor Union. The UFCW attempted to organize workers at the New Seasons Market in Portland, Oregon, but was unsuccessful in its first attempt and has filed NLRB unfair labor practice charges against the company (Hamstra 2023b).

The IBT has had two recent successful organizing drives on the West Coast, where 300 warehouse employees at the Smart & Final distribution center (375 stores, 24,000 employees) and 220 employees at United Natural Foods were organized (Mitchell 2023).

Costco is the result of a merger of Price Club and Costco in 1993. At the time of the merger, Price Club employees were represented by the IBT. Approximately 18,000 (10%) Costco employees recently negotiated a national agreement (Reuters 2022), and recently, Costco distribution centers in Norfolk, Virginia (200 employees) and Sumner, Washington (150 employees) were successfully organized by the IBT.

Although there has been recent success in organizing one Amazon distribution center on Staten Island by the independent Amazon Labor Union, Amazon and Whole Foods are nonunion, with only sporadic union activity elsewhere, which has largely been unsuccessful. The RWDSU (a UFCW affiliate) has lost two elections in Bessemer, Alabama. Organizing activities at Walmart, Target, and other retailers have been infrequent and unsuccessful. There tend to be more aggressive organizing efforts at warehouse distribution centers, but the retail stores and online segments are primarily untouched.

Union opposition by the major nonunion employers has been fierce and, at times, the subject of unfair labor practice charges. Walmart (4,717 US stores; 1.6 million US employees) has remained nonunion through a combination of advanced human resources management techniques, strong management commitment to maintaining union-free status, and, sometimes, aggressive tactics. An example would be the post-2000 UFCW election victory involving ten butchers at a Walmart Supercenter in Jacksonville, Texas. Walmart terminated store meat-cutting throughout the company, offering customers prepackaged "case-ready meat," which had become a widespread industry trend (Wartzman 2022). Once that occurred, there was no longer a basis for a separate bargaining unit. The change retained the company's nonunion status and sent a message to employees interested in unionizing. The enormous size of Walmart and its financial and managerial resources make it a difficult target for organizing.

Other unions have taken up the fight with Walmart. The Service Employees International Union led a political campaign ("Walmart Watch") against Walmart. This was not an effort to organize Walmart employees as much as it was a public relations effort to embarrass the company to pay higher wages and improve benefits and working conditions.

Whole Foods (Amazon) reportedly has an aggressive approach to maintaining union-free status with its 95,000 employees, referred to as team members. Whole Foods claims to provide an industry-competitive starting wage of $15 per hour, competitive benefits, and career advancement opportunities. According to published articles, the company utilizes more than 24 metrics to create a heat map to rank its 510 stores on the degree of risk they pose for unionization. The heat map classifies three areas of risk: external, store, and team member sentiment. Examples of external risks include local union membership size, "labor incident tracking," which monitors local organizing and union activity; the store's ZIP code poverty rate; and the unemployment rate. Store risks are reported to include average store compensation, average sales, and worker compensation claims. Team member sentiment is collected from internal surveys that measure the quality and safety of the work environment, as well as respect and support from management (Peters 2020). As part of a highly sophisticated approach to union avoidance, corporate resources are directed to those locations with the objective of "mitigating risk."

CHALLENGES FACING THE INDUSTRY IN RECENT YEARS

The industry is experiencing significant disruption owing to the growth of online grocery shopping, including home delivery. In 2022, online grocery accounted for 14.5% of grocery shopping, up from 6.8% pre-pandemic, and is expected to grow to 20% by 2026 (Hamstra 2023a). This portion of the industry is almost exclusively nonunion because deliveries are served by nonunion automated warehouses and nonunion drivers for home delivery. Amazon is the industry leader, followed by Walmart in online market share. Most of the major grocery retailers now offer some form of online shopping. The shift to online shopping makes brick-and-mortar stores less relevant, which is where union penetration is the most far reaching.

The industry is having considerable difficulty hiring and retaining employees. The retail side of the industry uses large numbers of part-time employees to adapt to shoppers' schedule preferences. Retail shopping patterns are heavily skewed to weekends. Store shelf stocking often occurs during overnight hours. The average workweek for production and nonsupervisory employees is 28 hours (US Department of Labor 2023a). Industry data show a 2021 turnover rate of food retail employees of 48%, down from 58% in 2020. Part-time turnover was reported to be 67% (Nelson 2022). Entry-level wages of nonunion employers have tended to be higher, while benefits for union-represented employees have tended to be more generous. High turnover is also a problem for the unions attempting to organize workers because there are fewer full-time workers to organize their colleagues. In distribution, the work is very physical (lifting requirements), the hours of work are less appealing (nights and weekends), and in some areas, employees experience harsh work environments (refrigerators and freezers).

Represented employers and unions are challenged to balance wage rates and benefits. Because the industry relies on significant numbers of part-time employees for whom the supermarket is often a first job or one that offers sufficient flexible hours for part-time work or a second job, the hiring wage and early progression are key features in the acquisition and maintenance of the workforce. There is less interest among workers in healthcare and retirement benefits. However, the stores rely on their full-time employees for stability and management. Department heads, for example, are typically part of the bargaining unit. The full-time employees made an industry/employer career choice and most often seek to ensure that the collective bargaining agreements provide sufficient funds for vacation, healthcare, and retirement benefits. Full-time, long-service employees tend to have more significant sway in local union bargaining decision making. Thus, the nonunion employer may provide a higher starting rate of pay, with smaller costs for benefits, while the represented employer tends to provide a significantly better and more expensive benefits packages.

Worker safety is another area of growing concern. Accident rates are higher in the grocery industry when compared with retail in general. In 2020, the grocery industry reported 4.0 total recordable accidents per 100 employees, compared with 3.1 for retail overall. Cases away from work were 2.8 per 100 employees compared with 1.1 for retail employers overall (US Department of Labor 2022, 2023b).

Recent mass shootings at grocery stores in Colorado, Texas, and upstate New York have highlighted safety concerns and caused companies to increase the presence and visibility of security personnel. The pandemic also brought employee health and safety issues to the forefront.

Customer theft, known as "shrinkage," has become a severe industry problem that also endangers employees. Most major retailers have human resource policies that discourage or prohibit employees from confronting shoplifters out of concern for employee safety. The dangers posed by customer theft stem from two sources: individuals stealing for personal use and, more recently, organized crime stealing for resale. Because the retail grocery industry is a low-margin business, with customer theft increasing and limited company capacity to contain it, companies have closed stores in high-crime (primarily urban) areas. This has resulted in "food deserts," where the ability to purchase groceries is severely limited.

For example, Whole Foods announced the temporary closing and eventual relocation of its flagship San Francisco store out of concerns about employee safety and the high cost of theft. Target and Walgreens report similar concerns, and Walgreens has recently developed a new store anti-theft model with most of the merchandise behind counters and customers ordering at a kiosk. Employees then provide the merchandise ordered. Interestingly, this approach is a return to the original store clerk model described in the introduction.

INDUSTRY CONSOLIDATION AND BARGAINING STRUCTURE

In part, to generate efficiencies and overcome the low-margin nature of the industry, the 1990s brought industry consolidation, with larger national chains acquiring small regional chains (US Department of Agriculture 2000). From 1996 through 1999, there were 385 grocery store mergers (Trinidad 2020; Woody 2013) and, by 2009, the four top chains—Walmart, Kroger, Costco, and SuperValu—accounted for more than 50% of all sales. Ownership has also become more international, with Trader

Joe's and Aldi being German owned, and Stop & Shop, Giant, and Food Lion being part of the Dutch conglomerate Ahold Delhaize (Trinidad 2020).

Where organized, the retail grocery bargaining structure is regional. The UFCW has local unions in most regions of the United States and Canada. These regions can have multiple employers, hundreds of individual stores, and employment ranging from 50 to 400 employees, depending on the site and market of the store. In several areas of the United States, there is regional coordinated bargaining among several employers. This primarily occurs on the West Coast.

At the distribution level, bargaining tends to be at individual sites, but there are some multiple-site master agreements through the IBT. Local negotiations supplement those master agreements. As previously noted, Costco has a national agreement, but its coverage is limited to about 10% of its workforce. At the manufacturing level, bargaining is generally conducted at the plant level, although there are multi-site master agreements at Kellogg, General Mills, and Kraft Heinz with the BCTGM.

Consolidation has shifted bargaining power. Before consolidation, there was greater financial pressure on the employer. During negotiations between a smaller, regional employer, and the union, a strike, or the threat of a strike, would force the closure of most or all of the employer's operations. With consolidation, other divisions of the company can continue to provide revenue and workforce during a strike (Milkman 2022). However, strikes do cause a loss of sales, as many customers are reluctant to cross picket lines. Additionally, customers who begin to shop elsewhere might not return to the struck employer once the labor dispute ends. In distribution, the stores served by a striking warehouse can be served by other distribution centers, although with higher transportation costs.

MAIN BARGAINING ISSUES

Bargaining in the industry typically centers on wages, retirement, healthcare benefits, compensation for time not worked, and flexibility. The primary focus, however, is on wages and benefits. Average hourly earnings for nonsupervisory employees were $17.01 per hour (US Department of Labor 2023a). Represented employers tend to have lower starting wages than nonunion competitors, including more generous healthcare and retirement benefits and pay for time not worked. Represented employers have been seeking to limit increases in the cost of benefits to put more resources into entry-level and early seniority pay. Much of the industry has Taft–Hartley health and welfare plans, many of which cover small numbers of employees and are inadequately funded. Employers have been seeking to consolidate plans to achieve economies of scale, a larger risk pool, and utilization of better technology as a means to lower their costs.

Contracts provide extensive language as to the definition of the bargaining unit—those employees covered by the agreement and those excluded. Contract language reflects the business model of the employer. The UFCW and Albertsons–Vons 2019–2022 contract states:

> It is recognized by the Employer and the Union that the bargaining unit … is composed of several segments consisting of food markets, discount stores, drug stores and shoe stores. With reference to such segments, it is agreed that negotiations shall be conducted in each segment, separate and apart from any other segment and that any economic action undertaken by the Union or Employer shall not extend to or include or in any way involve any other segment. … Other exclusions may include the employees of suppliers who handle specific categories of merchandise (for example, bread, soft drinks, potato chips and related snacks). (UFCW/Albertson–Vons 2019)

Employers have sought to offset the costs of economic improvements through productivity and flexibility changes described in the following section. Other bargaining outcomes include jurisdiction over work, union security, discharge and discipline, seniority and overtime, paid time off, new locations, successors and assigns (if all, or part, of the bargaining unit is sold to another employer), flexibility (ability to assign work under contract rules), and operational changes (degree of management rights to make changes without negotiations/discussions with the union).

PRODUCTIVITY AND TECHNOLOGICAL CHANGE

In a highly competitive, low-margin industry, labor productivity is an essential element that drives profitability. The retail grocery industry has already expanded self-checkout to most stores and replaced in-store butcher shops with pre-cut selections and packaging at meat-processing facilities. Self-checkout requires fewer front-of-store personnel, thus reducing staffing costs. They also free up store space, allowing for more merchandising. However, the downside has been increased customer theft. Survey data suggest that as many as 20% of customers have stolen at the self-checkout line. Another study suggests that items in the self-checkout lane not being scanned totals about 4% of item value. One large retail grocer is reported to have removed self-checkout, and others have cut back. The industry is reportedly working with theft control vendors to address this issue (Gitnux 2023; IT Retail 2022). Labor shortages related to COVID-19 allowed for elimination of full-service ordering at deli counters and replacement with in-store pre-cut selections. Some stores have yet to return to full-service deli counters, while others have increased pre-cut selections. Stores (particularly strong regional participants) in more-affluent markets continue to use in-store meat-cutting and full-service delis as a competitive advantage. Other productivity gains have resulted from contracting out store functions, including floral department staffing, prepared foods, and store maintenance.

At distribution centers, automated picking and the use of in-house autonomous vehicles have enabled productivity gains. For online distribution, automated fulfillment centers are an essential element of the business model. H-E-B is reported to have tested augmented-reality eyeglasses that provide employees with more real-time information and visual cues to increase efficiency (Turcsik 2018). Further productivity gains may be expected when, and if, autonomous vehicles are used on highways to deliver goods from warehouses to the stores. Whether home delivery of online purchases can be automated remains to be seen.

Walmart has announced major capital investment plans to automate distribution and fulfillment centers. Walmart also reports that it has plans to automate 65% of its stores (Wilson 2023b). Such adjustments may fit well with changing patterns in consumer sentiment regarding the store experience they wish to have.

STRIKES/LOCKOUTS

The industry has seen infrequent strikes. There was a ten-day strike in 2022 at King Soopers (a Kroger division) involving 8,000 workers. In 2019, there was an 11-day strike at Stop & Shop (Ahold Delhaize) involving 31,000 employees. In 2003, a five-month strike and lockout in Southern California involving 70,000 supermarket workers ended in concessions by the union, with employers implementing reductions in benefits. Subsequent negotiations restored many of the benefits.

Strikes are infrequent because collective bargaining power tends to favor employers. First, the vast majority of the industry is nonunion, so a strike against a union employer serves to benefit the nonunion competitor who receives the sales of the struck union employer. Because of the regional nature of the bargaining, employers with a national presence have resources and revenue from other regions (known as banners). Management personnel as well as contract strike breakers can keep the more profitable stores operating during strikes.

The union is at a disadvantage if its members are spread over numerous workplaces separated by many miles. This makes strike communication and coordination more difficult. Because retail grocery is a lower-wage industry, most workers are unlikely to have personal savings to sustain themselves financially during a strike. Most of the part-time workforce has only a marginal commitment to the industry and can obtain alternate employment with similar wages elsewhere. In communities where there is strong support for labor and workers, customers frequently support the strikers by refusing to cross picket lines.

COLLECTIVE BARGAINING INNOVATIONS

During the pandemic, the UFCW was able to negotiate substantial pay raises ($2 per hour) at Albertsons and Kroger-owned stores. This was partly due to recognition of the essential nature of these employees. Some other retailers followed. In addition, the UFCW achieved significant health and safety improvements, along with other health, welfare, and financial assistance benefits (United Food and Commercial Workers International Union 2020). Beyond this, most collective bargaining is very traditional. Some contracts make provisions for labor–management committees to address issues during the contract, but there is no evidence as to their effectiveness.

THE UNIQUE CASE OF PUBLIX

Publix, founded in 1930, is the largest employee-owned company in the United States. The company operates more than 1,300 stores in the southeast United States; the majority (800) are in Florida, generating an estimated $47 billion in sales in 2021. Publix employment is estimated to be 227,000 and none of its workers are unionized. Approximately 205,000 (90%) employees are shareholders. Stock is granted annually to staff, who are also permitted to purchase additional shares in the company. Employees own 80% of the stock of the company. The balance is held by the founding family (Jenkins) and board members. The company establishes the share price quarterly, and employees who wish to cash out must sell their shares back to the company. Employees receive quarterly dividends (most recently 0.37 per share). It has been estimated that the average employee holds $150,000 in stock. Longer-term employees may have substantially more (Bary 2022).

There is little or no academic research on Publix because the company maintains a very low profile. The academic literature that exists suggests that employee ownership leads to a more engaged and committed culture. Clearly, Publix's financial performance, which shows much higher net margins than its competitors, would support that. Publix is also reported to own considerable real estate as well as its manufacturing and distribution facilities. The company benefits from stable, long-tenure management, which is also no doubt a function of the company's ownership structure. It is interesting that other companies have not imitated this successful organizational structure.

KROGER–ALBERTSONS MERGER

On October 18, 2022, Kroger announced it would acquire Albertsons for $24.6 billion. Kroger is number two in market share, and Albertsons is number four, behind Walmart and Costco, respectively (Table 1). The combined company would have approximately 5,000 stores, 66 distribution centers, 52 manufacturing plants, and 1,000 fuel centers. It would be the fifth-largest pharmacy, with 4,000 locations, and would operate in 48 states and the District of Columbia (Repko 2022). Kroger–Albertsons would employ more than 700,000 employees and would be the largest private sector unionized employer in the United States. Both companies operate under multiple banners. The new company would hold a 15% market share—number two behind Walmart. A goal of the consolidation is to increase efficiencies and manage costs across its footprint.

At the time of this writing, the proposed merger was under review by the Federal Trade Commission (FTC) and had generated congressional and some state oversight. The merger has been criticized by consumer groups, suppliers, and political groups. Consumer groups fear that the merger would lead to higher grocery prices, while suppliers fear an increasing imbalance in bargaining power between suppliers and the two chains. Kroger argues that it plans on spending $500 million to lower prices and $1 billion in wage and benefit improvements (Wilson 2023b).

On February 26, 2024, the FTC issued an administrative complaint and authorized a lawsuit in federal court to oppose Kroger's acquisition of Albertsons. The FTC charged that the merger would eliminate the "fierce competition" between the two companies, resulting in higher grocery prices, lower-quality products and services, and a narrowing of locations for consumers to shop for groceries.

The FTC also noted that Kroger and Albertsons are the two largest employers of union-represented grocery labor and that they compete against each other for labor, and where they overlap, "poach" workers from each other. Thus, a merger would suppress wages and benefits. The FTC further noted that a combined Kroger–Albertsons would gain increased bargaining leverage over their unions, increasing the company's ability to impose subpar terms and conditions of employment. (Federal Trade Commission 2024).

The Kroger and Albertsons in separate responses to the FTC complaint were threefold: (1) the FTC ignored previous Kroger acquisitions that lowered prices for consumers; (2) the FTC was "willfully blind to the realities of current competition," ignoring other grocery operators listed earlier in this chapter (e.g., Walmart, Costco, Whole Foods/Amazon), thus distorting the competitive market; and (3) ignoring the divestiture of 413 stores plus other assets to C&S Wholesale Grocers to ensure competition (increased to 579 stores).

Kroger further asserted that there is no union grocery labor market and that it competes for labor, particularly entry-level employees across a variety of employers. Kroger further asserted that the merger would likely increase union bargaining leverage.

It appears that this case will be decided based on how the grocery industry is defined. If defined by traditional grocery stores, the merger is likely to be defeated. However, the industry now includes Walmart and others previously referenced, which would make the merger more likely. The UFCW and IBT have taken public positions in opposition to the merger (United Food and Commercial Workers International Union 2023), citing job security concerns.

Further industry consolidation is underscored by the August 2023 Aldi announcement that it would purchase 400 Winn-Dixie and Harveys Supermarket stores in five southeastern states. Aldi is a low-cost, discount retailer. With planned expansion, Aldi was expected to have 2,400 stores by the end of 2023. Aldi is a nonunion employer (Silverstein 2023; Wilson 2023a).

FUTURE PROJECTIONS FOR COLLECTIVE BARGAINING IN THE INDUSTRY

The economics of the grocery industry will remain low margin and highly competitive (even if the Kroger–Albertsons merger is approved), with economies of scale being an important driver of profitability and, thus, the ability to increase wages and benefits. Those companies that can differentiate themselves in terms of price, quality, and/or merchandising are likely to have an advantage. Unless something drastically changes, the industry will likely continue to be dominated by nonunion employers. Critical will be union efforts to organize Walmart, Whole Foods, and the others. Represented employers will be challenged to maintain wages and benefits and remain competitive, unless there is a breakthrough in organizing the 80% to 85% of the industry that is nonunion. Because of the competitive landscape, employers are likely to continue to aggressively resist union organizing efforts through effective human resource management techniques and strong corporate commitment to union-free status.

The shape of the industry will also present challenges because growth of online purchasing will continue to threaten traditional stores, and thus employment growth will be adversely affected. Total grocery sales are forecasted to grow by 7.4% annually over the next five years. Online is expected to grow 11.7% over the same period, and its share of the total grocery market will increase to 13.6% from 11.2% by 2027 (Brick Meets Click 2023). This is both a union challenge and opportunity. The online channel requires large fulfillment centers that might be attractive organizing opportunities for unions. However, as Amazon experience has shown, organizing those centers may prove difficult, in part because of intensive technology use reducing employment. Delivery drivers may also prove to be a second source of unionization, but organizing here has been sparse to date.

As it has historically, the retail grocery industry will continue to struggle with hiring and turnover of employees. There will be continued wage competition between grocery stores and other employers such as fast food that hire entry-level employees. This may lead to new approaches to attract workers, such as programs providing college tuition. And unions will need to manage the challenge posed by the different preferences for wages and benefits of junior employees(wages) and senior employees (benefits). Finally, continued technological implementation will create a need for employees with different skill sets, which could also affect potential interest in unions as well as customers' experience in stores.

REFERENCES

Arcieri, K. 2022. "Online Groceries Accelerate Market Share Gains as Pandemic Upends US Shopping." S&P Global. January 25. https://bit.ly/3vvDsQ2

Bary, A. 2022. "Employee-Owned Publix Offers a Lesson for Other Supermarket Chains." *Barrons*. January 23. https://bit.ly/3HncZHf

Biery, M.E. 2018. "These Industries Generate the Lowest Profit Margins." *Forbes*. April 16. https://bit.ly/3U1Xc8e

Bloomberg Law. 2023. "Labor Data Series NLRB Election Statistics Year-End 2022." Report. Arlington, VA: Bloomberg Industry Group.

Brick Meets Click. 2023. "Tracking Online Grocery's Growth." Brick Meets Click. June 13. https://bit.ly/3O5bdOy

Center for Union Facts. 2023. "Facts and Stats About the Labor Movement." Union Facts. June 15. https://www.unionfacts.com

Crowe, E. 2023. "Trader Joe's Employees Mark Unionization Win in California." *Progressive Grocer*. April 25. https://tinyurl.com/yc4zxey9

Deloitte and Datawheel. 2023. "Grocery Stores." Data USA. July 20. https://bit.ly/3O2qOP3

Farrell, K. 2020. "How We Wound Up with Supermarkets: A History of the Grocery Store." 10Best. April 21. https://bit.ly/48yW802

Federal Trade Commission. 2024. "FTC Challenges Kroger's Acquisition of Albertsons." February 26. https://tinyurl.com/mrascnmb

Gitnux. 2023. "The Most Surprising Self-Checkout Theft Statistics and Trends in 2023." Gitnux. July 12. https://bit.ly/3U0Ve7V

Hamstra, M. 2023a. "Digital Grocery Sales Hit $128B." *Supermarket News.* March 13. https://bit.ly/426qBjK

———. 2023b. "Workers at Third Trader Joe's Vote to Unionize." *Supermarket News.* January 30. https://bit.ly/48KSHTI

Hirsch, B.T., D.A. Macpherson, and W. Even. 2024. "Union Membership and Coverage Database." Unionstats. http://unionstats.com

Inklebarger, T. 2024. "Trader Joe's in Chicago Files to Unionize." *Supermarket News.* April 9. https://tinyurl.com/p5hxxhur

IT Retail. 2022. "Self-Checkout Criminals on the Rise in 2021." *IT Retail.* November 29. https://bit.ly/4aUGM7E

Milkman, R. 2022. "Grocery Unions Under the Gun in New York City and the Nation." *New Labor Forum* 31, no. 2: 17–26. https://doi.org/10.1177/10957960221091482

Mitchell, R. 2023. "Smart & Final Warehouse Workers Vote to Unionize." *Supermarket News.* February 14. https://bit.ly/426L3AT

Nelson, A. 2022. "Retailers, Suppliers Continue to Struggle to Get and Keep High-Quality Workers." *Supermarket Perimeter.* November 30. https://bit.ly/423d0K2

Ozbun, T. 2022. "Online Grocery Shopping Sales in the United States from 2019 to 2024." Statista. January 27. https://bit.ly/3O2ZkZw

———. 2023. "Grocery Store Sales in the United States from 1992 to 2022." Statista. March 17. https://bit.ly/3Sn1jL2

Peapod Digital Labs. No date. "Who We Are." https://tinyurl.com/5fpms5s6

Peters, J. 2020. "Whole Foods Is Reportedly Using a Heat Map to Track Stores at Risk of Unionization." The Verge. April 20. https://bit.ly/422gKvm

Repko, M. 2022. "Kroger Agrees to Buy Rival Grocery Company Albertsons for $24.6 Billion." CNBC. October 14. https://bit.ly/3Sk4K55

Reuters. 2022. "Teamsters Union Reaches National Contract with Costco." Reuters. October 25. https://bit.ly/421vQkp

Safeway. 2015. "Albertsons and Safeway Complete Merger Transaction." PR Newswire. January 30. https://prn.to/3tSmPhc

Silverstein, S. 2023. "Aldi's Purchase of Winn-Dixie Sets Up a Powerful Force in Grocery, Report Says." Grocery Dive. August 30. https://bit.ly/3S2zvKi

Supermarket News. 2021. "Top 50 Food and Grocery Retailers by Sales." *Supermarket News.* July 7. https://bit.ly/3TYu3e4

Trinidad, K. 2020. "History of the Supermarket Industry in America." Stacker. March 13. https://bit.ly/3vBQJqo

Turcsik, R. 2018. "H-E-B Tests Smart Glasses." *Supermarket News.* February 1. https://bit.ly/48wFvlv

UFCW/Albertsons-Vons. 2019. "Retail Food, Meat, Bakery, Candy and General Merchandise Agreement Between UFCW Union Locals 135, 324, 770, 1167, 1428, 1442 & 8-Gs and Albertsons, LLC. Vons Companies, Inc." Contract. https://bit.ly/3HkYaF6

United Food and Commercial Workers International Union. 2020. "Kroger, UFCW Announce Increased Pay, Benefits for Grocery Workers on Front Lines of Coronavirus Outbreak." August 24. https://bit.ly/3HkCBnX

———. 2023. "America's Largest Union of Essential Grocery Workers Announces Opposition to Kroger and Albertsons Merger." May 5. https://bit.ly/4aZfixw

US Department of Agriculture. 2000. "Consolidation in Food Retailing: Prospects for Consumers & Grocery Suppliers." Economic Research Service/USDA Agricultural Outlook. August, 18–22. https://bit.ly/48tYgWO

———. 2022. "Retail Trends." USDA ERS Retail Trends. November 1. https://bit.ly/3RRwuwo

US Department of Labor. 2022. "The Employment Situation, March 2022." US Bureau of Labor Statistics. April 1. https://bit.ly/3O4yGPQ

———. 2023a. "Current Employment Statistics, CES (National)." US Bureau of Labor Statistics. February. https://www.bls.gov/ces

———. 2023b. "Industries at a Glance: Food and Beverage Stores: NAICS 445." US Bureau of Labor Statistics. May. https://bit.ly/3HgnBaV

US Food and Drug Administration. 2022. "A Cooperative Program." Retail Food Protection. December 28. https://bit.ly/3tVXAus

Wartzman, R.N. 2022. "A Brief History of the Attempts to Unionize Walmart." Literary Hub. November 13. https://bit.ly/3SivSkR

Weightman, G. 2015. "The History of the Bar Code." *Smithsonian Magazine.* September 23. https://bit.ly/3tVulI6

Wilson, B. 2023a. "Aldi Acquires Winn-Dixie, Harveys Supermarket Stores." *Supermarket News.* August 16. https://bit.ly/3O3KG4c

———. 2023b. "Kroger Gives Updates on Merger, Fresh Program." *Supermarket News.* June 23. https://bit.ly/3O51wj9

———. 2024a. "Some Employees at 1st Unionized Trader Joe's Now Want to Reverse Course." *Supermarket News.* March 8. https://tinyurl.com/4yxeb8fm

———. 2024b. "Costco Workers Make Historic Move to Join Union." *Supermarket News.* April 22. https://tinyurl.com/3jxenttt

Woody, S. 2013. "Revisiting the US Food Retail Consolidation Wave: Regulation, Market Power and Spatial Outcomes." *Journal of Economic Geography* 13, no. 2: 299–326. https://www.jstor.org/stable/26158702

CHAPTER 10

Emerging Labor Relations in High-Tech Industries

DAVID LEWIN
University of California, Los Angeles

TINGTING ZHANG
University of Illinois Urbana-Champaign

Abstract

High-tech industries employ a large share of science, technology, engineering, and mathematics workers. However, with the growing implementation of information technology in the workplace, tech workers are widely employed elsewhere, such as in service industries. High-tech companies are privately owned and, as such, are subject to the National Labor Relations Act. Yet high-tech workers are traditionally viewed as hard to organize. One reason is the legal framework governing private sector unionization. That framework applies to employees but not to independent contractors. Another reason is the traditional lack of interest in unionization among high-tech employees. Such employees often receive wage premiums and expansive fringe benefits, and they have considerable labor market mobility. Nonetheless, tech workers are increasingly using collective action to support prosocial activism. Unlike employees in other sectors, the main bargaining issues for tech workers are issues other than job security, compensation, and work control. For example, Google employees recently demanded that employment arbitration be made optional, and Google acceded to that demand. In light of these developments, we believe that the high-tech sector is a potential high-growth sector for union organizing and collective bargaining in the years ahead. Managerial control of employees in this sector has gradually weakened, and tech workers are increasingly comfortable using collective action to demand a greater voice in the workplace. Whether unionism will be the main voice mechanism in this regard remains to be seen, but this chapter closely examines the prospects for unionism and other forms of employee voice in this sector.

OVERVIEW OF THE INDUSTRY

There is no universal definition of what constitutes a high-tech industry. The US Bureau of Labor Statistics (BLS) defines a high-tech industry based on the following attributes: (1) employing a large share of STEM (science, technology, engineering, and mathematics) workers, (2) investing a significant share of physical and human capital in research and development, (3) using high-tech production methods, and (4) producing high-tech goods and services (Wolf and Terrell 2016). However, this definition is broad and rather arbitrary.

To more fully grasp the difficulty involved in defining a high-tech industry, consider the opposite—that is, a low-tech industry. What exactly is a low-tech industry? The BLS does not provide a definition in this regard, nor does any other source that we identified or reviewed. Stated differently, if something is claimed to be "high," then ideally it must be distinguishable from something that is "low"— and, indeed, from something that is "medium." Otherwise, almost any industry can be claimed to be high-tech. Note that this conundrum is similar to that involving so-called best practices. Much literature exists proclaiming and purporting to identify best practices in numerous functional areas of organizations, such as strategy, information technology, sales and marketing, finance, accounting, research and development, and of course human resources, labor relations, and employment relations. But this literature also fails to distinguish best practices from average practices and worst practices.

Nonetheless, in the United States, high-tech typically evokes such giant companies as Apple, Google, Meta, Microsoft, Amazon, Nvidia, and Tesla. Table 1 lists the 20 top US high-tech companies measured by their market capitalization as of February 2024. These global companies are clearly leaders, but they represent only a subset of companies in this "industry." In fact, high-tech includes a wide variety of industries based on the North American Industry Classification System (NAICS), ranging from electronics and semiconductor and related device manufacturing to software publishers, Web search portals and other information services, media streaming distribution services, social networks, other media networks and content providers, and even miscellaneous retailers and taxi and ridesharing services (Table 1, Column 4). With a couple of outliers, the large majority of market-recognized high-tech companies are producers of computer-related devices, software development, and services related to the Internet of Things. High-tech companies have also experienced much faster contraction and expansion than those in other industries. For instance, OpenAI, a San Francisco-based startup, reached $2 billion in annualized revenue in 2023 and is expected to double this figure by 2025, following the launch of ChatGPT in November 2022 (Murgia and Hammond 2024). The semiconductor industry has also seen a boost from AI adoption, with four of the top 20 US high-tech companies in early 2024, measured by market capitalization, belonging to this sector and delivering above-average growth compared to other leading tech companies.

A focus on companies' market capitalization, products, and services, however, fails to capture the dynamics of high-tech, and we therefore propose to expand the definition of "high-tech industry" by adding occupations within the companies in this industry (Heckler 2005; Roberts and Wolf 2018). In this regard, the Information Technology Association of America, the leading professional association of the high-tech workforce, recognizes eight clusters of workers using emerging technologies

Table 1
Top 20 U.S. High Tech Companies by Market Cap (as of February 27, 2024)

Rank	Company	Market Cap	Industry Code (NAICS)
1	Microsoft	$3.027 T	513210 Software Publishers
			41511 Custom Computer Programming Services
2	Apple	$2.820 T	334220 Radio and Television Broadcasting and Wireless Communications Equipment Manufacturing
			334111 Electronic Computer Manufacturing
3	Nvidia	$1.967 T	334413 Semiconductor and Related Device Manufacturing
4	Amazon	$1.802 T	459999 All Other Miscellaneous Retailers
			445110 Supermarkets and Other Grocery Retailers (except Convenience Retailers)
5	Alphabet (Google)	$1.733 T	541511 Custom Computer Programming Services
6	Meta Platforms (Facebook)	$1.241 T	519290 Web Search Portals and All Other Information Services
7	Tesla	$636.09 B	336110 Automobile and Light Duty Motor Vehicle Manufacturing
			336390 Other Motor Vehicle Parts Manufacturing
8	Broadcom	$606.81 B	334413 Semiconductor and Related Device Manufacturing
9	Oracle	$306.17 B	513210 Software Publishers
10	Salesforce	$289.91 B	513210 Software Publishers
			519290 Web search Portals and All Other Information Services
11	AMD	$287.61 B	334413 Semiconductor and Related Device Manufacturing
12	Netflix	$260.37 B	516210 Media Streaming Distribution Services, Social Networks, and Other Media Networks and Content Providers

(Table 1 continues, next page)

Rank	Company	Market Cap	Industry Code (NAICS)
13	Adobe	$249.72 B	513210 Software Publishers
14	Cisco	$195.61 B	334118 Computer Terminal and Other Computer Peripheral Equipment Manufacturing
			541512 Computer Systems Design Services
15	Intuit	$187.40 B	513210 Software Publishers
16	Intel	$180.66 B	334413 Semiconductor and Related Device Manufacturing
			334118 Computer Terminal and Other Computer Peripheral Equipment Manufacturing
17	Qualcomm	$176.66 B	533110 Lessors of Nonfinancial Intangible Assets (except Copyrighted Works)
18	IBM	$169.47 B	334118 Computer Terminal and Other Computer Peripheral Equipment Manufacturing
			334111 Electronic Computer Manufacturing
19	Applied Materials	$168.78 B	333242 Semiconductor Machinery Manufacturing
			334413 Semiconductor and Related Device Manufacturing
20	Uber	$163.52 B	485310 Taxi and Ridesharing Services

Companies Market Cap (no date); North American Industry Classification System (no date).

(Moncarz 2002). Those clusters are programming and software engineering, technical support, enterprise systems, database development and administration, Web development and administration, network design and administration, digital media, and technical writing. Relatedly, a recent Deloitte report indicates that the high-tech workforce comprises six key occupations—namely, computer and information system managers, computer and mathematical scientists, computer hardware engineers, electrical engineers, electronics engineers (except computer), and electronics and electronic engineering technicians (Barua 2021). Because it is difficult to find relevant data on some of these occupations, we narrowed our focus to companies in which the predominant employee group comprises skilled professionals who use advanced technology to produce information technology (IT) products and services. In the NAICS, the majority of these companies are classified as being in the IT sector and, specifically, part of professional, scientific, and technical services (NAICS 54 group).[1]

In the United States, the IT sector is rapidly growing and has become a significant economic driver (Henry-Nickie, Frimpong, and Sun 2019; Muro et al. 2015). Although this industry accounts for only about 6 percent of the total US economy, it is widely recognized as "a growth powerhouse" (Henry-Nickie, Frimpong, and Sun 2019). Many of these companies' products are so well integrated into our daily life that they have become verbs, as in the cases of Google and Zoom. The high-tech industry has also been a leader in the development of new industries and a major source of innovation (e.g., ChatGPT), driving job growth and improving the quality of life. The industry includes a wide range of companies, from large multinational corporations to small startups, all working to develop new information-related technologies and services. The NAICS classifies approximately 246,500 US entities as operating in computer system design and related services (NAICS 5415).[2] These companies are responsible for a small but critical portion of the country's economic output, employing millions of workers, and producing many of the products and services we use every day. The latest US Census found that approximately 4.6 million people worked in IT occupations in 2016, a tenfold increase over 1970 (Beckhusen 2016).

With the growing implementation of IT in the workplace, high-tech workers are widely employed outside the high-tech companies themselves (Roberts and Wolf 2018). In fact, 92% of all IT workers are employed in non-IT companies, including in retail and service industries (Moncarz 2002). Recognizing this fact, consider that some elements of high-tech are embedded in the operations of many companies that are not thought of as being in the high-tech industry (Muro et al. 2015). This includes automobile manufacturing companies such as Ford and Toyota; construction equipment companies such as Caterpillar and John Deere; cable, satellite, and streaming service companies such as Direct TV and Netflix; accounting firms such as KPMG and PricewaterhouseCoopers; and professional services firms more broadly. It also includes retailing companies such as Walmart and Kroger, and insurance companies such as Allstate, State Farm, and GEICO. Each of these firms relies heavily on IT but is not typically thought of as being in the high-tech industry. In other words, the boundaries of this industry are fluid and malleable.

CHALLENGES FACING THE INDUSTRY IN RECENT YEARS

The US high-tech sector has grown rapidly over recent decades. The stock market value of the top five high-tech firms (Apple, Microsoft, Google, Amazon, and Meta) increased from $1.13 trillion in 2012 to $7.51 trillion in 2020 (*Wall Street Journal* 2021) (Figure 1). In 2021, the total market value of these five companies ($9.3 trillion) was smaller than only the GDPs of the United States and China (*Wall Street Journal* 2021). The BLS projects that computer and peripheral equipment manufacturing and computer system design and related services will grow by 19% and 5%, respectively, between 2019 and

Figure 1
The Growth in Leading Tech Companies, 2013–2021

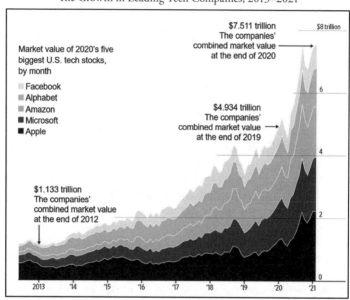

Wall Street Journal (2021).

2029 (Torpey 2021). Over the same period, transportation, travel accommodation, food services, and nonresidential construction are projected to shrink.

Not surprisingly given these figures, the high-tech workforce has grown significantly over the past two decades. More than three million US workers were employed in IT between 2001 and 2007 (Wright 2009). According to the BLS Occupational Employment and Wage Statistics survey, the average annual growth for computer and mathematical science employment was close to 3% between 2000 and 2020, much higher than the 1% annual growth in other sectors (Barua 2021). High-tech jobs are also clustered geographically, as high-tech companies are concentrated in major cities, such as New York, San Francisco, and Seattle (Fallah, Partridge, and Rickman 2014). Similarly, changes in high-tech employment vary substantially across states (Adkisson 2015; Muro et al. 2015; Muro and You 2022).

The COVID-19 pandemic was detrimental to many businesses in the United States and globally. However, multinational corporations in the high-tech sector recorded massive growth in business during 2020, while the US economy as a whole contracted (Cassagnol 2021; Torry 2020; Weed 2021). Part of this business success was attributed to increased product and service demands owing to the rising use of remote work arrangements (Stadler 2022). In one example, Apple's profit during the second quarter of 2021 ($21.7 billion) was nearly twice the total pre-pandemic annual revenues of the five largest US airline companies (Ovide 2021). In another example, Amazon reported a $109 billion growth in e-commerce revenue. To put this into context, the same increase would take Walmart nine years to achieve (Ovide 2021). The rapid profit growth led high-tech companies to expand their businesses significantly and aggressively hire more top talent. Tech-sector workers were also deemed essential workers during the pandemic because their jobs were considered a part of the critical infrastructure workforce (Torpey 2020). Thus, their work hours were not constricted, unlike the hours of many other workers. They were also mainly doing remote work because the nature of their work is not bound by the physical location of their workplaces (Dalton and Groen 2022).

However, the growing demand for talent and, consequently, the need to pay higher wages, also led to significantly higher business operating costs. Coupled with plateaued product and service demand, major high-tech companies reported a heavy loss of revenue and announced mass layoffs beginning in the fourth quarter of 2022 (Goswami 2022). Figure 2 documents the number of mass layoffs and the number of employees affected in the high-tech sector between January 2022 and February 2024. More than 400,000 high-tech employees in more than 2,000 companies were reported to have been laid off during this period (Layoffs Tracker 2024). Many were concerned that these layoffs indicated the end of the rapid growth of the high-tech sector. Others argued that this massive human capital composition shift reflected some top high-tech companies' strong business commitment to new, advanced, disruptive technologies, such as artificial intelligence (Chowdhury 2023). Yet the large number of active job vacancy postings in the United States during this time implied an overall substantial labor shortage in these occupations (Anderson 2022), and many workers who were laid off were able to find new jobs in the tech sector relatively quickly.

THE PARTIES

As mentioned earlier, the broadly defined high-tech sector comprises both large multinational corporations and small, midsize enterprises (those with fewer than 500 employees). The overwhelming majority of high-tech firms are privately owned, though the largest of them are publicly traded on one or another stock exchange.

Figure 2
Mass Layoffs in the Tech Sector, January 2022–February 2024

Layoffs Tracker (2024).

The core employee groups in most of these firms are highly skilled professional workers doing innovative, creative work. However, increasing numbers of larger high-tech companies are hiring contractors and employees of professional service firms. High-tech workers increasingly work in nonstandard employment settings, such as contract work, temporary employment, and employment with professional service firms (Sheng 2018; Van Jaarsveld 2004). For example, since 2018 Google has employed more contract workers than direct employees (Sheng 2018; Tech Equality Collaborative 2022). Large high-tech corporations also hire various types of employees other than high-tech workers, including professionals who specialize in other business functions and other service and support workers. Again, for example, there are 273 Apple retail stores across the country[3] that employ thousands of retail sales representatives. These are not high-tech workers, per se.

Several unions have attempted to organize high-tech workers. The Communications Workers of America (CWA) is one of the more successful unions in this regard. In 2020, the CWA launched a national technology and gaming union organizing campaign known as the Campaign to Organize Digital Employees (CODE-CWA) (Dean 2020). The CODE-CWA campaign organized several successful strikes and union drives in the high-tech sector, particularly in the gaming industry. Other large unions, such as the Teamsters, the Service Employees International Union, and the Office and Professional Employees International Union, have also attempted to organize specific segments of workers in large high-tech companies or small regional high-tech companies. Other independent unions, such as the Amazon Labor Union (ALU) or minority, noncertified unions, such as the Alphabet Workers Union, have also attempted to organize and build solidarity among various types of high-tech workers.

It is difficult to ascertain the effects of unionization on high-tech. Figure 3 shows union membership coverage of the tech sector derived from individual self-reported status using the Current Population Survey. Union coverage based on industry or occupation grouping suggests that the IT industry has below average unionization rates and that union coverage has been declining during the past decades. The BLS (2024) reports that 4.7% of private sector workers in computer and mathematical occupations were represented by labor unions in 2023, down slightly from 4.8% in 2021. However, we are unable to identify any contract coverage of tech workers exclusively in the collective bargaining agreement repository managed by the BLS Office of Labor–Management Standards (OLMS). The most recently certified unions in the high-tech companies we identified on a case-by-case basis tend to have very small memberships (see subsequent discussion). Hence, we suspect that the majority of unionized high-tech workers are covered by collective bargaining agreements in other types of industries, not necessarily in the high-tech industry. The apparent discrepancy between individual and business-level union density in the high-tech sector should be further investigated.

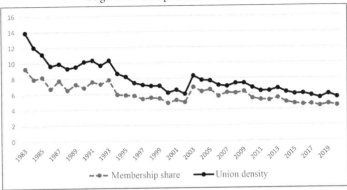

Figure 3
Union Membership and Coverage Rates,
High-Tech Occupations, 1983–2021*

*Data derived based on Union Membership and Coverage Database from the Current Population Survey, by occupations (Hirsch, Macpherson, and Even 2024).

THE LEGAL FRAMEWORK

Most high-tech companies are privately owned and, as such, are subject to the National Labor Relations Act (NLRA). More broadly, high-tech companies (as well as other companies) outsource various functions, such as IT and customer relationship management, and the related work is not performed by the companies' employees. Because the NLRA applies to employees but not to independent contractors, the National Labor Relations Board (NLRB) has limited jurisdiction over union organizing and labor disputes in many high-tech firms.

Platform companies, such as rideshare and food delivery service companies, add further complexity to the legal framework regulating labor–management relations in high-tech firms. In 2018, the California Supreme Court rendered a decision in the Dynamex case that established a three-factor test, known as the ABC test, to determine whether workers providing labor services to these companies were independent contractors or employees.[4] These three factors are as follows:

- The worker is free from the control and direction of the hiring entity in connection with the performance of the work, both under the contract for the performance of the work and in fact.
- The worker performs work that is outside the usual course of the hiring entity's business.
- The worker is customarily engaged in an independently established trade, occupation, or business of the same nature as that involved in the work performed.

The second factor has drawn the most attention because rideshare and food delivery company drivers clearly perform work that is part of the usual course of the hiring entity's business. Hence, under a strict interpretation of this factor, such drivers would be classified as employees.

In 2019, the California State Legislature enacted into law Assembly Bill AB 5 (AB5), which was specifically aimed at ridesharing and food delivery companies such as Uber, Lyft, DoorDash, Instacart, and Postmates. The law basically adopted the Supreme Court's three-factor test for determining whether workers—drivers—for these types of companies are independent contractors or employees.[5]

However, in 2020, Proposition 22 was placed on the California ballot. It asked voters to indicate whether they supported the continuation of the independent contractor status of drivers for rideshare and food delivery companies. Unsurprisingly, the proposition was heavily supported by the rideshare and food delivery companies. In November 2020, California voters voted in favor of the proposition by a margin of 58% to 42% (Ballotpedia, no date). Nonetheless, in August 2021, a California court ruled that Proposition 22 was unconstitutional. Had this ruling stood, it would have negated voter approval of the proposition. However, in March 2023, the California First District Court of Appeal issued a ruling upholding Proposition 22 (Gedye 2023). Hence, as of the date of this writing, drivers for rideshare and food delivery companies based in California continue to be treated as independent contractors.

Well before the enactment of AB5 in California, specifically in 1989, the California Supreme Court issued a decision in *Borello v. the California Department of Industrial Relations* in which it ruled that a worker "is classified based on whether the hiring entity has 'all necessary control over the manner and means' of obtaining desired results, even if this control is 'not direct or actually exercised'" (Out of the Box Solutions, no date). In explaining its decision, the court identified 11 factors that constituted a test of such control. Nonetheless, the criterion of control remains the main determinant of whether an individual who performs labor services for a company (or nonprofit organization or public entity) is an independent contractor or employee. A determination in this regard, in turn, depends on the extent to which independent contractors exercise autonomy and discretion in performing their work.

STATE OF ORGANIZING IN THE INDUSTRY

High-tech firms are claimed to be "one of the most union-resistant segments of the American economy" (Hossfeld 1995; Robinson and McIlwee 1989: 116; Van Jaarsveld 2004), and there are many possible reasons for this. To illustrate, high-tech companies engaged in aggressive union-busting strategies as early as the 1990s (Hossfeld 1995). In addition, high-tech firms are increasing their use of nonstandard employment arrangements (Van Jaarsveld 2004), and multiple worksites are common for midsize and large companies (Van Jaarsveld 2004); both pose a challenge to organizing. The flexible and frequently changing organizational structures of high-tech companies also present challenges to union organizing (Carré, duRivage, and Tilly 1995; Van Jaarsveld 2004).

More problematically, high-tech workers are traditionally viewed as lacking the desire to unionize (Isler 2007; Milton 2003; Van Jaarsveld 2004). Their professional identity, which emphasizes merit, individuality, flexibility, and self-actualization, has traditionally made them less interested than other workers in collective actions

(Dorschel 2022; Marks, Chillas, Galloway, and Maclean 2020; Milton 2003; Van Jaarsveld 2004). High-tech workers have specific technical skills and substantial human capital; these are in high demand and rewarded in the labor market. Most high-tech sector occupations require a bachelor's degree for entry. Because of their technical skills, high-tech employees often hold strong individual economic power in salary negotiations with employers and receive relatively high salaries and substantial fringe benefits (Muro et al. 2015; Van Jaarsveld 2004). High-tech workers also have considerable labor market mobility because their technical skills and human capital are readily transferable across companies and industries (Milton 2003; Van Jaarsveld 2004). The BLS reports that workers in the same occupation (e.g., computer systems analyst) could be employed in as many as 180 different industry groups (Torpey and Watson 2014).

Another factor influencing—limiting—high-tech worker support for unionization is the stock option arrangements covering many such workers. The typical—indeed, widespread—arrangement in high-tech companies is the issuance of a four-year stock option vesting plan that is provided to new employees and renewed for continuing employees. In the parlance of the gambling game craps, stock options are a form of "betting on the come." This means that high-tech workers bet that the value of their stock options will rise, perhaps substantially, during their employment. If this occurs or is expected to occur, it in turn implies that high-tech workers, such as artificial intelligence programmers, are not particularly concerned about whether they are paid relatively low wages and thus are not especially likely to seek unionization and collective bargaining to raise wages. The recent acquisition of Activision Blizzard by Microsoft provides a case in point: the value of vested and unvested stock options of employees of both of these companies rose considerably as a result of this transaction (Browning and McCabe 2023).

High-tech workers use their technical skills to solve problems and develop new products and services. Thus, they have relatively more control over their work and the tasks they perform (Milton 2003; Van Jaarsveld 2004) and also have a strong sense of ownership of their designs. Although this stems from their ability to control their work, it also makes them more susceptible to some undesirable workplace practices, such as long working hours, high-pressure work environments, and extremely tight deadlines, because these work practices are viewed as commitments to their craft. Management often portrays these workers as "part of the company" because of their ability to create core innovative products and services. Both the industry and workers in it view the high-tech sector as a "fun and creative" work environment (Milton 2003).

The millennial generation of high-tech workers, however, has certain characteristics and preferences that may change these traditional work norms. Millennials highly value work–life balance, which makes them more resistant to the intensive work demands embraced by previous generations (Dorschel 2022). They also have more left-leaning political views and are self-identified as "purveyors of the social good" (Sheehan and Williams 2023: 455). Therefore, they are relatively more concerned about income inequality, lack of diversity and inclusion, and diminishing or lack of ethical standards in the high-tech sector and at the societal level (Dorschel 2022; Rothstein 2021). They increasingly self-categorize themselves as "workers" and are more sympathetic to vulnerable groups, such as workers performing nonstandard work, gig workers, and other support workers (e.g., service staff) in their companies (Dorschel 2022). These characteristics may make it easier to build solidarity among such workers.

At the present time, however, organizing efforts in the high-tech sector seem less of a priority for either unions or high-tech workers themselves (Hossfeld 1995). Any such efforts seem more like an extension of organizing drives in other industries with a strong union presence or organizing potential. Telecommunications was the first high-tech industry sector to be exposed to unionization, and it occurred between the 1970s and the early 2010s. The major organizing effort targeted the semiconductor manufacturing industry and IBM (Early and Wilson 1986; Wright 2020). In addition, between 2014 and 2020, several unions, including the Teamsters and the Retail, Wholesale and Department Store Union, attempted to organize Amazon warehouse workers because of their resemblance to a mass production workforce (Greenhouse 2021). In 2019, 80 Google high-tech contractors organized to form a union. They were motivated by their lack of benefits, even though they worked alongside full-time employees (Lecher 2019). Although Google commented that "whether HCL's [the contractor] employees unionize or not is between them and their employer," this certification marked a significant win in organizing high-tech contractors hired by a vendor company but working for a high-tech giant.

Since the beginning of 2020, there have been several successful organizing drives targeting the high-tech workers who are the main workforce in these companies. Video Workers Unite formed the first video game union, including both full-time and contract workers in the United States and Canada, through voluntary recognition by their employer in December 2021 (Carpenter 2021). Quality assurance workers from two studios at Activision Blizzard in separate locations won their NLRB union elections after being denied voluntary recognition in 2022, amid acquisition talks between Activision and Microsoft (Liao 2022). On January 3, 2023, Microsoft voluntarily recognized its ZeniMax Studio's quality assurance workers when they signed union authorization cards and voted with a large majority to form a union (Communication Workers of America 2023c). ZeniMax Workers United/CWA became the first Microsoft studio to form a union and is the largest quality assurance workers' union in the United States gaming industry. These workers believed that their union would "put an end to sudden periods of crunch, unfair pay, and lack of growth opportunities within the company" (Communication Workers of America 2023c). Workers at TCGPlayer, which was acquired by eBay in November 2022, formed the first certified union at eBay through certification voting in March 2023 (Communication Workers of America 2023d). Several nonprofit high-tech firms providing services for labor movements, community organizing, and social movements were also certified during 2021. MissionWired, "one of the largest and most prominent digital direct marketing firms in progressive politics," voluntarily recognized their workers' union in August 2023 after a majority of workers signed representation cards (Communication Workers of America 2023b). The Alphabet Workers Union (AWU), established in January 2021, now has more than 800 members.[6] Deemed a minority union, the AWU is not registered with the NLRB and cannot collectively bargain. However, the campaign resulted in the unionization of several small high-tech companies. By the end of 2021, more than half a dozen high-tech companies had been unionized through employer voluntary recognition. However, a higher percentage of voluntary recognition does not imply that employers will not resist unionization. For instance, when the largest tech worker union, the New York Times Tech Guild, was overwhelmingly ratified in March 2022, the employer denied the union's initial request for recognition (Kochan et al. 2022).

High-tech workers in the public sector have tried to form unions as well. The majority of workers at Nava PBC, a company dealing with digital issues in the public sector, asked their employer to acknowledge their union affiliation with the Office and Professional Employees International Union Tech Workers Union Local 1010. The 171 employees at Nava unionized "to improve transparency in the company, ensure equal pay, boost employee well-being and retention, and attract new talent in a competitive industry" (Quinnell and Gallant 2022).

As previously discussed, high-tech companies operate in various industries. Hence, their employees include not only the high-skilled tech workers but also workers in sectors such as retail and services. By the end of 2022, there were 17 legally recognized unions in the broader high-tech sector, including the Google (Compass Group) Cafeteria Workers Union, Facebook Shuttle Drivers Union, and Kickstarter United, among others.

Collective labor actions mushroomed during the pandemic. The ALU, an independent labor union formed in April 2021, is probably the most surprising one. Less than one year later, ALU successfully organized an Amazon warehouse with more than 5,000 employees in Staten Island, New York, and became the first Amazon union in the United States, which was described as "one of the biggest victories for organized labor in a generation" (Weise and Scheiber 2022). The NLRB subsequently certified the ALU as the exclusive representative for "all hourly full-time and regular part-time fulfillment center associates employed at the Employer's JFK8 building" (National Labor Relations Board 2022). In August 2021, Apple Together, a grassroots worker group, organized an online protest, and hundreds of current and formal employees, mostly on the retail side, shared their experience of workplace incivility, sexual harassment, pay discrimination, and other problems at work. Dozens of Apple retail store workers in three states staged a walkout on Christmas Eve in 2021, demanding pandemic hazard pay and more paid sick leave, among other requests (Ruiz-Grossman 2021). In early 2020, a dozen Instacart part-time in-store shopper employees voted for the first gig workers union. Less than a year later, Instacart laid off 2,000 grocery store workers, including all of its union members (Schiffer 2021a).

Non-high-tech companies have seen labor activity organized by tech workers as well. One of the closest adjacent industries is news media, which has undergone significant technology changes. At the start of 2020, the CWA, the largest communications and media labor union in the United States, launched the Campaign to Organize Digital Employees (CODE-CWA). In early 2022, The New York Times Tech Guild workers certified their union through a NLRB election and became the union representing the largest number of high-tech workers, with more than 1,100 members (Coster 2022).

BARGAINING STRUCTURE

The overwhelming majority of high-tech companies are in the private sector. As previously mentioned, the sector has widely varied sizes of firms. The high-tech giants typically have workplaces dispersed all over the globe. These companies also open branches across all tech hubs in the United States (Hossfeld 1995; Van Jaarsveld 2004), which opens the possibility of having a decentralized bargaining structure. Spotify currently has collective agreements with two unions based on companies acquired by Spotify (Carman 2021). Another collective agreement was established between a single employer, Glitch, and a group of workers performing homogeneous tasks in a single workplace (Communication Workers of America 2021). In small high-tech firms with a single workplace, it is more common to have a collective agreement between a single employer and workers performing various types of jobs.

MAIN BARGAINING ISSUES

For most high-tech workers, wages and benefits seem less of a concern because of the high average earnings in this sector (Torpey and Watson 2014; US Bureau of Labor Statistics 2022). In the United States, the average annual earnings of most high-tech workers are over $100,000, except for several support occupations (US Bureau of Labor Statistics 2022). Over the past two decades, high-tech workers have earned, on average, 40% more than workers in other professions (US Bureau of Labor Statistics 2022; Zavodny 2021). Because of the unique characteristics of their jobs and their professional approach to their work, some IT workers are even willing to work for lower pay in order to use emerging, interesting IT systems (Tambe, Ye, and Cappelli 2020). Indeed, the recent Financial Independence, Retire Early movement has apparently caught on among many younger workers employed in high-paying tech jobs, who seek to rapidly accumulate wealth and then retire relatively early. This preference most likely reduces such employees' interest in unionization and collective bargaining.

However, not all high-tech employees are making above-average salaries. Some high-tech workers who provide cutting-edge technological services are paid close to minimum wage, mainly because they are hired by professional service companies or firms picking up outsourcing contracts from the major high-tech firms. To illustrate, thousands of contract employees at an AI training vendor of Google received their first-ever pay raise from $10 an hour to $14 to $14.50 an hour on January 1, 2023 (Nieva 2023). A recent report shows that a leading AI company received a $10 billion investment from Microsoft and then outsourced its content-labeling work to companies that hired workers in Kenya, Uganda, and India, where those workers were paid between $1.32 and $2 per hour (Perrigo 2023). Therefore, some high-tech workers are motivated to unionize in order to promote pay equity and transparency in internal company policies (Shuler 2020).

High-tech workers, especially those working for top multinational corporations, are known to enjoy substantial perks on top of standard healthcare insurance and other benefits. These corporations provide flexible work schedules, free intern housing, shuttle transportation, unlimited vacation time, paid time off for volunteering, and childcare support. Their campus-style headquarters provide free food, gyms, cooking classes, barbers and hairdressers, massages, and laundry services. These companies try to create a family environment so as to motivate and retain their employees. Since 2020, many high-tech companies have allowed workers whose jobs can be performed remotely to convert their jobs to be permanently remote (Barrero, Bloom, and Davis 2021). Many smaller high-tech companies, including startups, also provide good benefits. Thus, union organizing strategies centered around the grievances of insufficient benefits or poor working conditions have been less effective for high-tech workers. However, tech workers are interested in collective action to ensure that existing benefits are not stripped away in future. For example, one goal of Vodeo's collective agreement is to lock in the four-day workweek policy (Carpenter 2021).

For most high-paid employees in the high-tech sector, the main bargaining items are framed around issues other than compensation and benefits. Instead, tech workers are organizing because they want to have a say on how their work should be done (Carpenter 2021). For example, they may "demand changes both in who their firms do business with, and how" (Kugler 2021: 19; Rothstein 2021). As mentioned previously, high-tech workers enjoy relatively high work control, leading some to argue that they have "adopted management's discourse and transformed it into resources for collective action" (Rothstein 2021: 16). To illustrate, Google employees recently demanded that employment arbitration be optional, and Google agreed. Other collective actions by high-tech workers have challenged managerial controls and focused on broader social issues, such as sales to migrant detention camps, secret contracts with the US Department of Defense, gun sales, business decisions negatively impacting climate change, transphobia, and hate speech (Oswalt 2020). Although such demands have not yet been collectively bargained, ensuring that workers have a voice in the workplace about these and related issues is a central employment relations issue for many high-tech workers.

The global COVID-19 pandemic generated some interesting twists on employment relations between high-tech companies and their high-tech workers. During the pandemic, most firms allowed employees to work remotely, and many of those firms intended to continue this practice after the pandemic, thereby weakening managerial control of such employees. However, many high-tech employees report longer hours, lower job satisfaction, and even burnout while working remotely (Gibbs, Mengel, and Siemroth 2023). Relatedly, large numbers of employees began to resign from their jobs in late 2020, leading to increased bargaining power of the remaining employees.

Although larger corporations performed quite well financially during the pandemic (Cassagnol 2021) and awarded substantial bonuses to their employees, many small and midsize tech firms laid off workers because of limited business opportunities and increased labor costs. The lack of job security in the high-tech sector thus became more salient. At the same time, however, labor shortages enabled laid-off workers to secure other jobs quite quickly.

Overall, employment relations in high-tech industries have worsened, with high-tech employees recognizing the increasing inequality within the sector and the power imbalance between management and labor. The mass layoffs across high-tech companies that began in the second half of 2022 may exacerbate the situation. High-tech giants, such as Google and Twitter, exercised at-will employment clauses, terminating thousands of employees via email messages often sent in the middle of the night and locking workers out of the companies' systems immediately. Hence, job protection and job security are likely to become main bargaining issues for high-tech workers in the near future.

STRIKES/LOCKOUTS AND GENERAL STATE OF LABOR RELATIONS

Since collective representation in the high-tech sector is in its infancy, minimal collective labor conflicts, in the form of strikes or lockouts, have fallen under the jurisdiction of the NLRA/NLRB. Although no strikes or lockouts have been recorded in unionized workplaces in the high-tech industry, several collective actions led by high-tech workers could be considered lawful unfair labor practice strikes. On November 1, 2018, 20,000 Google employees, including full-time employees, temporary workers, independent contractors, and vendors (Kugler 2021) from 50 office sites worldwide, walked out of their offices to publicly protest Google's inappropriate handling of sexual harassment claims (Wakabayashi, Griffith, Tsang, and Conger 2018). The company responded more or less positively to the one-hour strike. Google then changed some of its company policies, but the strike organizers claimed they faced retaliation for organizing collective action. In another example, the CWA filed an unfair labor practice lawsuit alleging that Activision Blizzard engaged in union-busting activities, and the NLRB sided with the union (Communication Workers of America 2023a; Holt 2022). In a pre-acquisition conversation with Microsoft, Activision Blizzard, a leading game-developing company, reported multiple employee physical and virtual walkouts between 2021 and 2022 to protest workplace incivility and mistreatment by management. The workers raised strike funds through a GoFundMe account to cover wage losses during the strike.

High-tech workers are increasingly using collective actions to support prosocial activism (Changfong-Hagen 2020; Nahmias 2021) and have organized several high-profile work interruptions and stoppages (Nahmias 2021). Because these stoppages occurred in nonunionized high-tech firms and the protest issues were not directly involved in workplace grievances, these collective actions were not protected under the NLRA. In the Activision Blizzard case, workers demanded management's responses to social issues and organizational policy changes, including protesting layoffs and the vaccine mandate, seeking abortion and LGBTQ support, and demanding that the CEO step down for mishandling sexual misconduct claims. Similar employee walkouts occurred in other high-profile tech firms, such as Netflix. Netflix's one-day walkout was organized by the company's Trans* Employee Resource Group to protest an offensive Netflix show. Employees demanded the company take down offensive content, support racial justice, and invest more in trans talent and content (Rae 2022).

Because those labor actions were brief, the companies didn't have much time to respond to workers' actions, including use of replacement workers. Nonetheless, most companies involved in those labor actions made organizational policy changes in response to workers' collective demands.

KEY BARGAINING OUTCOMES

The OLMS does not have any record of collective bargaining agreements in the high-tech sector, but several voluntarily recognized unions have reported reaching collective agreements with their companies. In this regard, we identified key bargaining outcomes through union and company releases and news articles.

In March 2021, employees at Glitch, a small US tech company, signed the high-tech sector's first collective bargaining agreement. Workers at Glitch were represented by the CWA (Schiffer 2021b). Although a full copy of this agreement is not yet available on the US Department of Labor website, it is widely reported that it ensures basic union protections for workers and a continuous voice in the workplace. Unlike traditional collective agreements in other sectors, the agreement does not focus on higher wages (Schiffer 2021b). Instead, Glitch workers wanted "to have a lasting voice at this company and lasting protections" (Communication Workers of America 2021). Therefore, the CWA bargained for significant job security protections; Glitch workers are now entitled to "just cause" protections, grievance procedures, severance pay, and call-back rights (Communication Workers of America 2021). The collective agreement also locks in existing benefits.

In July 2021, HCL Technologies employees, vendor contractors at Google, ratified their first three-year collective agreement after winning a union election in 2019. The main focus of their contract is on traditional labor issues, such as wages, job security, and working conditions (United Steelworkers 2021). Two unions, the Ringer Union and the Gimlet Union, representing white-collar workers for contractors, reached a three-year collective agreement with Spotify in 2021. The agreements include clauses related to minimum salary, annual salary increases, just-cause terminations, severance pay, diversity hiring, limitations on the use of contractors, and formation of a labor–management committee (Carman 2021). However, those unions did not secure any intellectual property protections, which is a major issue for union members (Carman 2021).

Unlike other high-tech companies that are actively engaging in anti-union activities, Microsoft is now committing to respect employees' legal rights to form or join a union and will take "creative and collaborative approaches with unions when employees wish to exercise their rights" (Smith 2022). Microsoft and the CWA signed a union neutrality agreement in 2022 (Carpenter 2022; Scheiber 2024). In late 2023, Microsoft went further and formed a partnership with the AFL-CIO on issues related to AI and the future of the workforce (Microsoft 2023; Scheiber 2024).

FUTURE PROJECTIONS FOR COLLECTIVE BARGAINING IN THE HIGH-TECH INDUSTRY

In light of these developments, the high-tech sector apparently is a potentially high-growth sector for union organizing and collective bargaining in the years ahead. Tech jobs are considered to set the standard for a "good job" (Sheehan and Williams 2023). Consequently, incorporating tech workers into the labor movement will enhance the bargaining power of other unionized workforces. Managerial control of employees in this sector has gradually weakened, and high-tech workers are increasingly comfortable using collective action to demand a greater voice in the workplace, as illustrated by the numerous examples provided in this chapter. But whether unionism will be the main voice mechanism in this regard remains to be seen.

Tech workers' "bread-and-butter" workplace issues may differ from those of other workers who are the primary focus of the traditional labor movement. Where high-tech employees are covered by stock option plans, the potential of large payoffs from such plans acts to discourage employee support for unionism and collective bargaining. Similarly, labor markets featuring high demands for high-tech employees provide such employees with exit opportunities and inter-employer mobility, thereby again discouraging employee support for union organizing and collective bargaining.

Technological change is yet another factor that calls into question high-tech employees' support of unionism and collective bargaining. Although technological change has and will continue to eliminate certain jobs and functions and change the content and contours of other jobs, it also generates new, largely unanticipated forms of work, such as that performed by "influencers" who gain followers—sometimes large numbers of followers—on social media. Influencers are neither employers nor employees in the traditional sense of these terms, yet they produce services of a certain type. However, it is difficult to imagine a union of influencers coming into being.

But as industrial relations scholars know well, it has historically been difficult to predict the eruption and growth of unionism and collective bargaining. This was true of the emergence and growth during the 1930s of the Congress of Industrial Organizations (CIO), which challenged the dominance of the American Federation of Labor (AFL) for workers' unionization and collective bargaining coverage. It was also true of the emergence and very substantial growth of public employee unions and collective bargaining (especially among public school teachers) during the 1960s and 1970s. Although unionism and collective bargaining have recently emerged among high-tech industry employees, the growth of unionism and collective bargaining in this industry in the years ahead will depend on how well such institutions can meet the needs of the relatively young high-tech employee workforce; changes in extant, dated labor laws; and the depth and breadth of future technological changes. "Betting on the come" in this regard is thus a risky bet but an intriguing one as well.

ENDNOTES

1. We excluded engineering occupations because they are more common and more difficult to measure.
2. https://www.naics.com/six-digit-naics/?v=2022&code=54
3. https://www.apple.com/retail/storelist
4. *Dynamex Operations West, Inc. v. Superior Court of Los Angeles*, April 30, 2018.
5. Notably, AB5 excluded from coverage occupations and specialty areas practiced by doctors, lawyers, architects, engineers, accountants, insurance agents, real estate agents, hair stylists, freelance journalists, financial specialists (such as brokers), commercial fisherman, tow truckers, dog groomers, and school tutors. This clearly indicates that the focus of AB5 is on rideshare and food delivery companies and their drivers (California Legislative Information 2019). Other exclusions, or carve outs, were considered during the discussion of AB5 before it was enacted into law. These included owner–operators who work for multiple companies delivering supplies to construction sites and port truck drivers who work for Southern California transportation companies (Roosevelt, Dillon, and Bhuiyan 2019). For a related analysis, see Bearson, Kenney, and Zysman (2021).
6. Alphabet is the parent company of Google.

REFERENCES

Adkisson, R.V. 2015. "State-by-State Variations in High-Tech Employment Through the Great Recession." *Social Science Journal* 52, no. 3: 348–357.

Anderson, S. 2022. "Tech Job Openings Remain High, but Congress Is Not Taking Action." *Forbes*. September 27. https://bit.ly/48vT70D

Ballotpedia. No date. "California Proposition 22, App-Based Drivers as Contractors and Labor Policy Initiatives (2020)." https://bit.ly/3Sk1RRv

Barrero, J.M., N. Bloom, and S.J. Davis. 2021. "Why Working from Home Will Stick." Working Paper No. 28731. National Bureau of Economic Research.

Barua, A. 2021. "The Tech Workforce Is Expanding—and Changing—as Different Sectors Battle for Talent." Deloitte Insight. December 16. https://bit.ly/48ApxH7

Bearson, D., M. Kenney, and J. Zysman. 2021. "Measuring the Impacts of Labor in the Platform Economy: New Work Created, Old Work Reorganized, and Value Creation Reconfigured." *Industrial and Corporate Change* 30, no. 3: 536–563.

Beckhusen, J. 2016. "Occupations in Information Technology." Report No. ACS-35. US Census Bureau. August 16. https://bit.ly/47Ax2fY

Browning, K., and D. McCabe. 2023. "Microsoft Closes $69B Activision Deal, Overcoming Regulators' Objections." *New York Times*. October 13. https://bit.ly/3RZ9D22

California Legislative Information. 2019. "AB-5 Worker Status: Employees and Independent Contractors." https://bit.ly/3vDnWlo

Carman, A. 2021. "Gimlet and Ringer Unions Detail Their First Historic Contracts with Spotify." Verge. April 7. https://bit.ly/3HiyB7y

Carpenter, N. 2021. "North America Has Its First Video Game Union at Vodeo Games." Polygon. December 15. https://bit.ly/47CR4X2

———. 2022. "Tech Is Notoriously Anti-Union. Microsoft Is Taking a Different Approach—Neutrality." Polygon. June 13. https://bit.ly/4aPBhHg

Carré, F.J., V.L. duRivage, and C. Tilly. 1995. "Piecing Together the Fragmented Workplace: Unions and Public Policy on Flexible Employment." In *Union and Public Policy: The New Economy, Law, and Democratic Politics*, edited by Lawrence G. Flood, 13–34. Westport, CT: Greenwood Press.

Cassagnol, D. 2021. "U.S. Tech Industry Revenue to Jump 4.3% in 2021 After Record Year in 2020, Says CTA." Consumer Technology Association. January 11. https://bit.ly/3U3lj6E

Changfong-Hagen, K. 2020. "'Don't Be Evil': Collective Action and Employee Prosocial Activism." HRLR Online. *Columbia Human Rights Law Review* 188–224.

Chowdhury, H. 2023. "We're About to Find Out Whether AI Might Replace Those 200,000 Laid-Off Tech Workers as Silicon Valley Prioritizes Efficiency." *Business Insider*. March 16. https://bit.ly/47HvOiR

Communication Workers of America. 2021. "CWA Members at Glitch Secure First-Ever Contract for Tech Workers." March 4. https://bit.ly/4aPGTBk

———. 2023a. "National Labor Relations Board Finds Merit Charges Against Blizzard for Illegal Union-Busting." March 31. https://bit.ly/48YsLnP

———. 2023b. "Organizing Update." September 14. https://bit.ly/4aRM3Nr

———. 2023c. "Quality Assurance Workers at Microsoft's ZeniMax Studios Establish Company's First Union with Communications Workers of America, Become Largest Certified Video Game Studio in U.S." January 3. https://bit.ly/3O3ngMw

———. 2023d. "Workers at TCGPlayer Celebrate Groundbreaking Win, TCGUnion/CWA Becomes First Certified Union at eBay." March 10. https://bit.ly/41Yg75M

Companies Market Cap. No date. "Largest Tech Companies by Market Cap." https://bit.ly/3HkQoej

Coster, H. 2022. "*NY Times* Union Members Walk Out After Contract Talks Miss Deadline." Reuters. December 8. https://bit.ly/4aV5gOa

Dalton, M., and J.A. Groen. 2022. "Telework During the COVID-19 Pandemic: Estimates Using the 2021 Business Response Survey." *Monthly Labor Review*. US Bureau of Labor Statistics. March. https://doi.org/10.21916/mlr.2022.8

Dean, S. 2020. "Major Union Launches Campaign to Organize Video Game and Tech Workers." *Los Angeles Times*. January 7. https://bit.ly/48UUlSJ

Dorschel, R. 2022. "A New Middle-Class Fraction with a Distinct Subjectivity: Tech Workers and the Transformation of the Entrepreneurial Self." *Sociological Review* 70, no. 6: 1302–1320.

Early, S., and R. Wilson. 1986. "Organizing High Tech: Unions and Their Future." *Labor Research Review* 1, no. 8: 47–65. https://hdl.handle.net/1813/102472

Fallah, B., M.D. Partridge, and D.S. Rickman. 2014. "Geography and High-Tech Employment Growth in US Counties." *Journal of Economic Geography* 14, no. 4: 683–720.

Gedye, G. 2023. "Court Upholds Prop. 22 in Big Win for Gig Firms Like Lyft and Uber." Cal Matters. March 13. https://bit.ly/3O7a49f

Gibbs, M., F. Mengel, and C. Siemroth. 2023. "Work from Home and Productivity: Evidence from Personnel and Analytics Data on Information Technology Professionals." *Journal of Political Economy Microeconomics* 1, no. 1: 7–41.

Goswami, R. 2022. "Tech's Reality Check: How the Industry Lost $7.4 Trillion in One Year." CNBC. November 25. https://bit.ly/47wrgMo

Greenhouse, S. 2021. "Amazon Crushed the Alabama Union Drive—Can the Teamsters Do Better?" *Guardian*. https://bit.ly/3PszEWS

Heckler, D.E. 2005. "High-Technology Employment: A NAICS-Based Update." *Monthly Labor Review* 128: 57–72.

Henry-Nickie, M., K. Frimpong, and H. Sun. 2019. "Trends in the Information Technology Sector." Brookings Institution. https://bit.ly/3PszEWS

Hirsch, B., D. Macpherson, and W. Even. 2024. "Union Membership, Coverage, and Earnings from the CPS." https://unionstats.com

Holt, K. 2022. "Activision Blizzard Found to Have Withheld Raises from Unionizing Raven Software Workers." Engadget. October 4. https://bit.ly/3tKYudb

Hossfeld, K. J. 1995. "Why Aren't High-Tech Workers Organized?" In *Working People of California*, edited by Daniel Cornford, 405–432. Berkeley, CA: University of California Press.

Isler, J.M. 2007. "A Tale of Two 'Unorganizables.'" *Qualitative Sociology* 30, no. 4: 443–458.

Kochan, T., J. Fine, K. Bronfenbrenner, S. Naidu, J. Barnes, Y. Dias-Linhart, J. Kallas, J. Kim, A. Minster, D. Tong, P. Townsend, and D. Twiss. 2022. "U.S. Workers' Organizing Efforts and Collective Actions: A Review of the Current Landscape." Worker Empowerment Research Network. June. https://bit.ly/3U1jBmc

Kugler, L. 2021. "The Unionization of Technology Companies." *Communications of the ACM* 64, no. 8: 18–20. https://doi.org/10.1145/3469285

Layoffs Tracker. 2024. https://layoffs.fyi

Lecher, C. 2019. "Google Tech Contractors in Pittsburgh Just Voted to Unionize." Verge. September 24. https://bit.ly/3U2YPm6

Liao, S. 2022. "Raven Software Employees Win Union Election." *Washington Post*. May 23. https://bit.ly/3U4xz6G

Marks, A., S. Chillas, L. Galloway, and G. Maclean. 2020. "Confusion and Collectivism in the ICT Sector: Is FLOSS the Answer?" *Economic and Industrial Democracy* 41, no. 1: 167–188.

Microsoft. 2023. "AFL-CIO and Microsoft Announce New Tech-Labor Partnership on AI and the Future of the Workforce." https://bit.ly/3v6MOSN

Milton, L.P. 2003. "An Identity Perspective on the Propensity of High-Tech Talent to Unionize." *Journal of Labor Research* 24, no. 1: 31–53. https://doi.org/10.1007/s12122-003-1028-8

Moncarz, R. 2002. "Training for Techies: Career Preparation in Information Technology." *Occupational Outlook Quarterly*. US Bureau of Labor Statistics. Fall. https://bit.ly/3U1kICo

Murgia, M., and G. Hammond. 2024. "OpenAI on Track to Hit $2bn Revenue Milestone as Growth Rockets." *Financial Times*. February 8. https://bit.ly/3xa1W20

Muro, M., J. Rothwell, S. Andes, K. Fikri, and S. Kulkarni. 2015. *America's Advanced Industries: What They Are, Where They Are, and Why They Matter*. Washington, DC: Brookings Institution.

Muro, M., and Y. You. 2022. "Superstars, Rising Stars, and the Rest: Pandemic Trends and Shifts in the Geography of Tech." Brookings Institution. March 8. https://bit.ly/3U5SW7F

Nahmias, G. 2021. "Innovations in Collective Action in the Labor Movement: Organizing Workers Beyond the NLRA and the Business Union." MIT Work of the Future Working Paper 13-2021. Cambridge, MA: Massachusetts Institute of Technology.

National Labor Relations Board. 2022. "Case Search Results." https://bit.ly/3IJj4hI

Nieva, R. 2023. "After Months of Protest, Google Search Quality Raters Finally Get a Raise." *Forbes*. January 11. https://bit.ly/3HFAwDz

North American Industry Classification System (NAICS). No date. https://www.naics.com/search

Oswalt, M.M. 2020. "Short Strikes." *Chicago Kent Law Review* 95: 67–102.

Out of the Box Solutions. No date. "Explaining How the Borello Test Relates to Worker Classification." https://bit.ly/3U2G421

Ovide, S. 2021. "Big Tech Has Outgrown This Planet." *New York Times*. July 29. https://bit.ly/48UrlKL

Perrigo, B. 2023. "Exclusive: OpenAI Used Kenyan Workers on Less Than $2 per Hour to Make ChatGPT Less Toxic." *Time.* January 18. https://bit.ly/47HEqWS

Quinnell, K., and A. Gallant. 2022. "Workers at Nava PBC Form Largest Union in Civic Tech." AFL-CIO. March 29. https://bit.ly/3Hm4Ani

Rae, M. 2022. "Netflix Employees Walk Out over Company Culture." SAGE Business Cases Originals. January 3. https://doi.org/10.4135/9781529600322

Roberts, B., and M. Wolf. 2018. "High-Tech Industries: An Analysis of Employment, Wages, and Output." *Beyond the Numbers: Employment & Unemployment* 7, no. 7. https://bit.ly/3TDPrVt

Robinson, J.G., and J.S. McIlwee. 1989. "Obstacles to Unionization in High-Tech Industries." *Work and Occupations* 16, no. 2: 115–136.

Roosevelt, M., L. Dillon, and J. Bhuiyan. 2019. "A Bill Giving Workplace Protection to a Million Californians Moves One Step Closer to Law." *Los Angeles Times.* August 30. https://bit.ly/3SkxmuU

Rothstein, S.A. 2021. "How Workers Mobilize in Financializing Firms: A Theory of Discursive Opportunism." *British Journal of Industrial Relations* 60, no. 1: 57–77. https://doi.org/10.1111/bjir.12608

Ruiz-Grossman, S. 2021. "Apple Workers Walk Out on Christmas Eve, Demanding Better Working Conditions." Huff Post. December 24. https://bit.ly/3S3xGgp

Scheiber, N. 2024. "Why Microsoft Has Accepted Unions, Unlike Its Rivals." *Wall Street Journal.* February 2024. https://nyti.ms/4co9Dlm

Schiffer, Z. 2021a. "Instacart Is Firing Every Employee Who Voted to Unionize." Verge. January 21. https://bit.ly/3tXR9ab

———. 2021b. "Glitch Workers Sign Tech's First Collective Bargaining Agreement." Verge. March 2. https://bit.ly/4b0kst8

Sheehan, P., and C.L. Williams. 2023. "Unionizing High Tech: Opportunities and Obstacles." *Work and Occupations* 50, no. 3: 452–460.

Sheng, E. 2018. "Silicon Valley's Dirty Secret: Using a Shadow Workforce of Contract Employees to Drive Profits." CNBC. October 22. https://bit.ly/3vMji4k

Shuler, L. 2020. "Activision Blizzard Game Workers Take Collective Action to Reduce Pay Inequities." AFL-CIO. August 5. https://bit.ly/3O5Dch0

Smith, B. 2022. "Microsoft Adopts Principles for Employee Organizing and Engagement with Labor Organizations." Microsoft on the Issues. June 2. https://bit.ly/3tTrM9w

Stadler, C. 2022. "Pandemic Winners: The 10 Best Performing U.S. Companies." *Forbes.* January 18. https://bit.ly/48xnN1p

Tambe, P., X. Ye, and P. Cappelli. 2020. "Paying to Program? Engineering Brand and High-Tech Wages." *Management Science* 66, no. 7: 3010–3028. https://doi.org/10.1287/mnsc.2019.3343

Tech Equality Collaborative. 2022. "Shining a Light on Tech's Shadow Workforce." Report. Contract Worker Disparity Project. January. https://bit.ly/3vMkt3K

Torpey, E. 2020. "Essential Work: Employment and Outlook in Occupations That Protect and Provide." *Career Outlook.* US Bureau of Labor Statistics. September. https://bit.ly/3U2LnyO

———. 2021. "Effects of the Pandemic on Projected Employment in Selected Industries, 2019–29." *Career Outlook.* US Bureau of Labor Statistics. February. https://bit.ly/3TYVHrh

Torpey, E., and A. Watson. 2014. "Careers with Options: Occupations with Jobs in Many Industries." *Career Outlook.* US Bureau of Labor Statistics. Spring. https://bit.ly/3O7gghz

Torry, H. 2020. "U.S. Economy Contracted at Record Rate Last Quarter; Jobless Claims Rise to 1.43 Million." *Wall Street Journal.* July 30. https://bit.ly/3vk9y1B

United Steelworkers. 2021. "USW Tech Workers Ratify Historic First Contract at HCL." July 29. https://bit.ly/4b0mF7U

US Bureau of Labor Statistics. 2021. "A Look at Union Membership Rates Across Industries in 2020." February 25. https://bit.ly/48wZxMM

———. 2022. "May 2022 National Industry-Specific Occupational Employment and Wage Estimates, NAICS 541500—Computer Systems Design and Related Services." *Occupational Employment and Wage Statistics.* https://bit.ly/420ph1A

———. 2024. "Union Members—2023." News Release. January 23. https://bit.ly/3SuxckV

Van Jaarsveld, D.D. 2004. "Collective Representation Among High-Tech Workers at Microsoft and Beyond: Lessons from WashTech/CWA." *Industrial Relations: A Journal of Economy and Society* 43, no. 2: 364–385. https://doi.org/10.1111/j.0019-8676.2004.00334.x

Wakabayashi, D., E. Griffith, A. Tsang, and K. Conger. 2018. "Google Walkout: Employees Stage Protest over Handling of Sexual Harassment." *New York Times.* November 1. https://bit.ly/4afCGpy

Wall Street Journal. 2021. "How Big Tech Got Even Bigger." February 6. https://bit.ly/3SkXXb9

Weed, J. 2021. "As Big Tech Grows in the Pandemic, Seattle Grows with It." *New York Times.* October 12. https://bit.ly/3O1hdYP

Weise, K., and N. Scheiber. 2022. "Amazon Workers on Staten Island Vote to Unionize in Landmark Win for Labor." *New York Times.* April 1. https://bit.ly/3S1ZIbN

Wolf, M., and D. Terrell. 2016. "The High-Tech Industry, What Is It and Why It Matters to Our Economic Future." *Beyond the Numbers: Employment & Unemployment* 5, no. 8. US Bureau of Labor Statistics. https://bit.ly/47FmqfP

Wright, A. 2020. "Don't Call It a Trend: A Brief History of Organizing in Tech." OneZero. February 17. http://tinyurl.com/2c32e9hx

Wright, B. 2009. "Employment, Trends, and Training in Information Technology." *Career Outlook.* US Bureau of Labor Statistics. https://bit.ly/47x8tk9

Zavodny, M. 2021. "The Earnings of IT Professionals Compared with Other Professionals." Policy Brief. National Foundation for American Policy. June. https://bit.ly/3tYqs59

CHAPTER 11

Labor Relations and Collective Bargaining in the Museum Industry

Daniel J. Julius
Case Western Reserve University, Rutgers University, and Yale University

Jai Abrams
University of Connecticut

James N. Baron
Yale University

Abstract

This chapter presents information on union organizing and collective bargaining in the US museum sector. With a few exceptions, this is a recent phenomenon, with many cases occurring in the past five years. The chapter summarizes research data gathered through structured interviews with over 45 museum CEOs, board members, and union leaders, and it provides a comprehensive picture of current issues and concerns to those organizing and those leading these institutions. The authors focus on the status of collective bargaining as well as the underlying causes and consequences of unionization in this cultural sector. Advice for individuals leading these organizations and for those studying them is presented. Three major issues stand out. First, collective bargaining in museums resembles what has occurred in other mission-driven cultural organizations—for example, zoos, aquariums, botanical gardens, symphony orchestras, dance companies, libraries, colleges, and universities. Second, as museums have enlarged the focus of their mission, they have experienced changes in the types of people recruited to work in them, many of whom may not share traditional notions of the role of museums and who are sympathetic to social unionism ideologies (even though bargaining issues are primarily bread-and-butter concerns). Third, museum leaders find themselves in an increasingly constrained and challenged position: caught between employees who may not share a sense of the mission of the museum and seek more decision-making authority, while still relying on individual board members for significant portions of revenues.

INTRODUCTION

This chapter examines unionization over the past four years in US art museums. The main data presented here are informed through discussions with 45 museum leaders, as well as representatives of arts organizations, board members, and union representatives. We supplement these data with a variety of sources.

Although underlying tensions causing recent labor–management conflict in museums have existed for the past 50 years, they have been exacerbated by post-pandemic–related factors and are particularly evident in museums undergoing unionization. Although very few museums were unionized prior to the past four years, and while initial labor relationships between the parties could be characterized as rocky, our experience suggests that over time, unions work effectively with museum leadership with minimal conflict. We anticipate that, in the coming years, collective bargaining with museum workers will be institutionalized and function with little disruption.

In the current environment, themes associated with social justice have assumed a new urgency for museum workers. Union organizing reflecting social justice concepts appeals to workers whose views align with "social unionism," even though issues generating labor conflict in this sector are those traditionally conceptualized as "bread-and-butter" issues.

OVERVIEW OF THE MUSEUM INDUSTRY

A major challenge in presenting an overview of the museum industry is the limitations of available data and information, including incomplete and outdated sources and conflicting definitions, which make it difficult to take an accounting of the number of museums and how they are categorized. Museums are ubiquitous; there are more museums in the United States than McDonald's fast-food establishments and Starbucks combined (Ingraham 2014). The Institute of Museums and Library Services (IMLS) data, as of 2018, reveal 30,171 museums in the United States (Institute of Museum and Library Services 2018). IMLS files from 2014 list 35,144 active museums (Institute of Museum and Library Services 2014). That number includes museums of all disciplines, such as arboretums, botanical gardens, and nature centers; historical societies, historic preservation organizations, and history museums; science and technology centers; planetariums; children's museums; art museums; general encyclopedic museums; natural history and natural science museums; and zoos, aquariums, and wildlife conservation centers. The largest categories are historical societies/museums and unclassified/general museums at 48% and 33% of the total, respectively (Figure 1). The US Bureau of Labor Statistics estimates there are 37,700 curators, archivists, and museum workers (US Bureau of Labor Statistics, no date) and 172,300 museum/historical site personnel. The median salary for museum workers is $47,360. Of all museum workers, 12.6% are represented by unions for purposes of collective bargaining. Figure 1 also shows the number and type of museums documented by the IMLS Museum Universe Data File (Institute of Museum and Library Services 2018).

The largest number of museums are situated in states with greater populations and in wealthier urban centers, where patrons support cultural institutions in ways not normally possible in less populated and rural environments. For a variety of economic and political reasons, these are often regions and states with higher degrees of union density and less resistance to unionization. These locations are populated with people

Figure 1
American Museums by Discipline

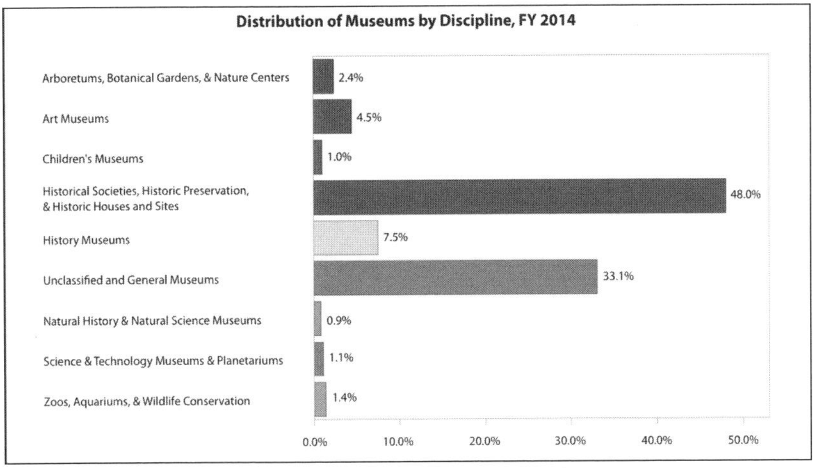

Distribution of Museums by Discipline, FY 2014

Discipline	Percentage
Arboretums, Botanical Gardens, & Nature Centers	2.4%
Art Museums	4.5%
Children's Museums	1.0%
Historical Societies, Historic Preservation, & Historic Houses and Sites	48.0%
History Museums	7.5%
Unclassified and General Museums	33.1%
Natural History & Natural Science Museums	0.9%
Science & Technology Museums & Planetariums	1.1%
Zoos, Aquariums, & Wildlife Conservation	1.4%

Museum Universe Data File, FY 2014 Q3, Institute of Museum and Library Services.

with the interests, skills, and education required for museum work (and universities with programs preparing graduates for such). Museum employees in universities are often represented by unions as well. Examples include the City University of New York, George Washington University, Harvard University, Wayne State University, the University of Illinois Chicago, and Yale University. All of these institutions are located in cities with high numbers of museums. Figure 2 reports the number of US museums by state.

CHALLENGES FACING THE INDUSTRY

Museums are undergoing a re-examination of their missions, impacting the relationship they have with patrons and the community, as well as the labor–management environment. This re-examination includes how museums present themselves to the public, how to create empathetic visitor environments, and how to implement protocols concerning shared decision making. The dynamic referred to here is fueled by a variety of factors, including changing attitudes toward the purpose and value of museums, political polarization in the United States, and the accompanying "culture wars" resulting in a hypercritical focus on the role of educational and cultural organizations. The reassessment also reflects new sensitivities to structural inequities in society, particularly around race and gender, and the role played by museums in continuing or reaffirming structural inequality. This latter topic manifests itself in tensions over how collections were (and are) acquired, exhibited, and, in some cases, deaccessioned. For example, in response to federal legislation, the Museum of Natural History in New York City closed a large exhibit of Indigenous artifacts until and unless permission to view these objects is obtained from tribal leaders. Similar actions are being taken in other states as well, having to do with the return of human remains and native artifacts (American Alliance of Museums 2023; CBS News 2024; *Time* 2024).

Figure 2
Museums by State

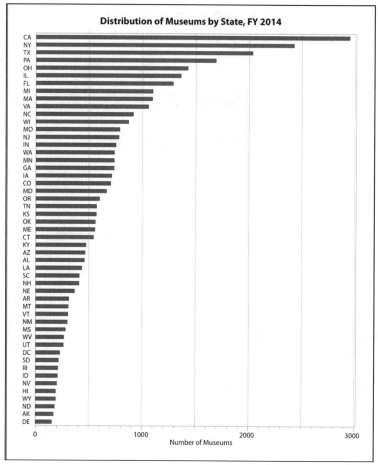

Museum Universe Data File, FY 2014 Q3, Institute of Museum and Library Services.

Questions about which constituencies should be involved in decision making are brought into sharp relief. Conflict around shared governance is further exacerbated by what many museum leaders and labor representatives perceive as changing attitudes toward work (and working on site) by employees recruited into museum workforces. Senior museum leaders are finding themselves in positions where they are being asked to rethink relationships with their workforce and their communities in order to create visitor-friendly *and* employee-friendly environments. Also being reviewed is the role of boards and how to manage board expectations because boards may now be obligated to cast a more discerning eye on sources of donor funding. Museums also are faced with developing ways to engage and react to employee and union demands over compensation, wage equity, working hours, flex time, career ladders, and the like—many issues previously placed on back burners because of more pressing concerns (Dionne 2022; Grau 2020; Raicovich 2021; Szántó 2020). In such a fluid and disruptive time, the position of museum executive has become exceedingly challenging.

In summary, museum leaders find they need more effective management structures and decision-making protocols enabling teams to develop and implement organizational policies. These include the institutionalization of new modes of access to collections as viewing and education moves online; the need to enhance diversity, equity, and inclusion in museum workforces; identification of alternative revenue sources in response to lost revenues initially driven by the pandemic; confronting challenges inherent in the post-pandemic workplace (desires for remote work, less workplace commitment, "quiet quitting," and the like); and, simultaneously, addressing unionization efforts. Industry leaders, we believe, find themselves with limited authority and resources to effectively resolve these pressing matters (Connelly 2022; Faine 1986; Schonfeld and Sweeney 2019).

During the pandemic, unemployment across the country climbed to its highest rate (10.8%) since the government has been keeping records, and many employees exited the labor force to care for family members and protect themselves from the coronavirus. Some have speculated that worker disengagement and discontent, particularly in museums, were at an all-time high. Lately, scholars and the media have discussed the issue where employees do the bare minimum required, drawing firm boundaries around work rather than striving to overachieve. Younger workers, in particular, are thought to be influenced by perceptions of wealth inequality, a lack of socioeconomic mobility (the loss of confidence in a college degree), and heightened perceptions of disparities and inadequacies in compensation among museum workers (Emba 2022; Marcus 2021; Swaim 2022).

Competition for labor helped push up wages by nearly 5% in the private sector in 2021, a continuing trend that, in the case of this industry, has reinforced the need to implement initiatives to attract and retain employees, including assistance with repaying student debt, more focused career development ladders, and financial support for employees traveling for medical care. Employers across a wide spectrum of organizations, including museums, are experimenting with three- or four-day workweeks without cutting salaries. Fueled by pandemic-related factors, museum employees engaging in remote or hybrid work tripled between 2019 and 2021, and predictions abound regarding how many jobs will become fully remote in the next decade (Gallup 2022; Miller 2021).

The pandemic labor exodus struck the nonprofit mission–driven sector particularly hard and labor shortages worsened. The American Alliance of Museums anticipated labor and skills shortages would be a major disruptor in the coming years. In 2022, 69% of nonprofits cited staffing challenges, leaving social service nonprofits unable to meet acute needs created or exacerbated by the pandemic (Congressional Research Services 2021; American Alliance of Museums 2022a; *NonProfit Times* 2022).

Labor–management relationships are presently shaped by decisions made during an earlier period when leaders were obligated to take actions in crisis mode without the benefit of engaging in more inclusive and shared governance. In museums that were experiencing union organizing drives, or where employees were already represented, the implementation and impact of innovative approaches to health benefits and working hours, furloughs, which workers were deemed "essential," and policies on vaccinations, masks, and the like had to be negotiated and often generated labor strife. Workplace pressures are still cascading and leading many to think about how to create more supportive and equitable workforce environments such as committing to paid internships for a broad range of positions (thereby reducing economic barriers to entering the field). Larger museums in urban centers are taking steps to significantly raise salaries, provide flexible work hours, and navigate the technical, legal, and financial complexities of supporting a widely distributed remote workforce.

Traditional sources for recruiting museum employees have also changed. No longer exclusively from more privileged backgrounds, newer employees may bring distinct perspectives to work. Contemporary employees are younger and more diverse in race, gender, and economic background than their counterparts in prior generations. These employees compare their salaries and working conditions to peers in other industries, such as high tech or financial services. Many no longer view the museum as a familial or elite organization engaged in fostering connoisseurship and preserving cultural perspectives and history. Some may find fault with museum collections accumulated, in their view, through colonial violence or capitalist exploitation that legitimizes oppression of marginalized populations and obfuscates history. This latter group harbors views susceptible to union organizers bargaining in the name of the "common good"—that is, unions focused on historical inequalities and social justice issues not only for bargaining unit members, but for nonmembers in other industries as well (Bargaining for the Common Good 2018, 2022). In fact, these themes have been emphasized by organizers in a variety of settings, such as at Minneapolis's historic Walker Art Museum, the San Francisco Museum of Modern Art, and the Tacoma Art Museum, to name a few.

THE PARTIES AND ORGANIZING ISSUES

Unions involved in organizing museums represent a cross-section of employee organizations that represent workers in both the public and private sectors in the cities where museums are located. These unions include, among others, the American Federation of State, County and Municipal Employees (AFSCME), Office and Professional Employees International Union (OPEIU), Service Employees International Union (SEIU), and United Auto Workers (UAW). The underlying causes of employee discontent have remained remarkably similar over the years, leading in many cases to a receptive environment for unionization. Among the more salient issues are employee perceptions of inadequate compensation, unfair compensation systems, the lack of known career mobility ladders, leadership turnover, arbitrary leadership styles, and resistance of leaders and donors who question the legitimacy of unionization.

Such perceptions are most acute, for example, when facilities are expanded or expensive collections purchased, while employee compensation levels remain low.

The behaviors and attitudes referenced here are perceived by employees as an unwillingness of management to look closely at what they believe are inadequate monetary and human resources concerns and bespeak a general lack of empathy for workers while publicly focusing on "empathetic" visitor environments. Other factors having an impact on organizing efforts include the increased prevalence of women in museum workforces that, according to some accounts, has strengthened these sentiments in addition to less than inclusive and meaningful shared decision-making processes, the desire for greater consultation or involvement in major financial or facility-related initiatives, and what are thought to be inconsistent management behaviors resulting in favoritism toward individuals who make special deals to secure better working relationships.

To be sure, these employee concerns have existed for a long time. Had they been addressed in a timelier manner, museums might not have remained inhospitable to organizing efforts. No doubt the impact of COVID and concomitant loss of revenues brought several underlying issues to the forefront. It comes as no surprise, therefore, that key issues framing the core of negotiations are wages and benefits, paid leaves, flexible work schedules, and decision-making protocols. Organizers have been effective in bringing these issues to the forefront as well as calling for a greater focus on gender equality, racial and climate justice, equitable wages for workers in other sectors, promotional and advancement opportunities for marginalized populations, and structural inequality in society (Alloway 1975; Guarino 2021; Small 2022).

Fissures, cracks, competition, and tension in the labor movement are hardly new. In the past 25 years, the breakup of traditional alliances and jurisdictional territories protected under the AFL-CIO umbrella resulted in decentralization and more autonomy of various unions. The breakaway of these groups led to a new federation, Change to Win, in 2005, comprised of unions organizing in different sectors and now unencumbered by prior restrictions regarding which employee groups could be legitimately targeted. Many of the unions have engaged in newer organizing efforts designed to leverage workers in a specific labor market, and they have younger, more idealistic leaders who are more effective in the use of online media technology. A number of unions active in museums have witnessed a decline in their traditional membership bases (the UAW, for example) and seek to organize workers in education or the mission-driven sector, searching for new workers—and dues-paying union members (Bargaining for the Common Good 2018; McCartin, Corrigan, and Luff 2014).

In the museum cases we observed, employees are receptive to organizers promoting change on key societal issues for members and nonmembers alike (for example, an increased minimum wage for employees not represented by a particular union). Social justice in the museum environment often revolves around correcting historical injustices to various social groups and addressing institutionalized racism, salary inequities, and questioning the legitimacy of capitalism itself. After all, major museum donors have frequently accumulated their fortunes and collected and donated their art under rules and circumstances now being reappraised. In fact, in many of the organizing campaigns in various cities—from Chicago to New York to Portland—the presence of wealthy and elite donors and patrons and how they accumulated their fortunes is contrasted with the behavior and resources of those working at museums. Such concerns and issues have become an underlying rally cry for organizers. We note, however, that if by social justice the parties mean the protection of employees from arbitrary management decision making, unfair terminations or unfair and inequitable grievance and arbitration provisions, such matters are often central to labor–management relationships. If, however, social justice is used at the bargaining table to negotiate more expansive antidiscrimination protections, fair trade policies, antipoverty initiatives, antiglobalization campaigns, race, gender, and human rights issues, defunding the police, and the like, such concerns are not easily accommodated in bargaining. The further away social justice is from the heart of the labor–management relationship, the more likely union demands will be found not mandatorily negotiable and challenged by employer representatives. They will normally be set aside by union negotiators (who know select issues are not mandatory subjects of bargaining), particularly if compensation packages are improved. This has been the case in New York City at the Brooklyn Museum, the Solomon R. Guggenheim Museum, The New Museum, and the Whitney Museum, but also elsewhere, at the Carnegie Museum in Pittsburgh, the Los Angeles Museum of Contemporary Art, the Milwaukee Art Museum, the Portland Museum of Art in Maine, and the Walker Art Center in Minneapolis.

LEGAL FRAMEWORK AND STATUS OF UNIONS IN MUSEUMS

Unions are most often found in larger independent "encyclopedic" museums that invariably operate under the National Labor Relations Act, but there are also museums that are public entities, which are covered by various state labor laws. These include, for example, those at public universities. Unions and unionization were uncommon in museums until the 1970s. The earliest organizing efforts took place at the Minneapolis Institute of Art, the Museum of Modern Art (MOMA) in New York City, and the San Francisco Museum of Art. Events and outcomes at the MOMA were thought to influence a variety of other organizing efforts throughout the fine arts museum sector.

We hypothesize that labor organizing came to these locales in the 1970s just as employees in other mission-driven organizations were also unionizing, particularly in higher education and the public sector. These dynamics occurred in cities located in states with enabling labor legislation and elected officials more sympathetic to labor's needs. The presence of other unions and organized industries in these locales aided organizers working in museums. The institutions mentioned are larger, with significant workforces and are thus attractive to organizers. The 1970s also witnessed a rise in crime in large urban centers and financial cycles that made it more difficult to address pressing employee issues, particularly in industries reliant on visitor revenues and donors. Leaders were obligated to make decisions without adequate consultation, to balance budgets—and one reaction was unionization on the part of employees to safeguard rights won during earlier times, as well as to preserve benefits and push back on what was no doubt perceived by employees as arbitrary decision making on the part of those leading museums (Faine 1986; Pynes 1997; Connelly 2022).

Museums that have been organized in recent years are still situated in union-friendly states or cities, such as Baltimore, Los Angeles, Minneapolis, New York City, Philadelphia, Pittsburgh, and SanFrancisco (Ginsburgh and Throsby 2006; Seaman and Young 2018). These places share institutional and demographic similarities that support unionization, such as employees in nonprofit organizations and in professional, service, and municipal industries. These cities boast high concentrations of unions in the public sector, where favorable state labor legislation, administrative agencies, and indebted political leaders are reluctant to thwart unionization.

Although there is considerable scholarship on the economics and funding of arts and cultural institutions, much less scholarly attention has been directed toward labor relations and collective bargaining. Those who have written on labor topics in arts organizations or public contexts have distinguished labor relations from what occurs in the private sector. These authors observe differences in market factors and supply chain issues. Museums normally incur lower operating deficits when closed rather than open. Labor–management conflict does not affect the financial position of major funding agencies, donors, or visitors in the same way that it does in the private or services sector. Professional workers (i.e., curators, educators, and archivists) are difficult to replace in the event of a strike, which, in the labor–management arena, gives workforces more influence in the bargaining environment (Baumol and Bowen 1966).

A January 2024 status report regarding museums engaged in union organizing activities and negotiations is provided (Table 1). As of 2021, approximately 13% of museums nationwide were unionized, an increase from 11% in 2018 (Hirsch, Macpherson, and Even, no date). Labor–management processes and outcomes in museums resemble what has occurred in select public and private organizations such as colleges and universities, symphony orchestras, and related industries, where professional and craft-type employees are organized. In independent larger comprehensive museums, the most common arrangement is a single employer/single workplace bargaining structure. There are instances of single employer/multiple-site structures, but they are not common.

To those viewing the institutional landscape from afar, it would appear labor conflict in museums occurs between "management" and a "union" representing employees. Although true in a legal sense, these two groups often share the same concerns and may hold similar positions on important negotiation matters. Disruption may result from conflicts of interest between museum leadership and employees on one side, and funding agencies, donors, corporations, and foundations on the other. This is not a traditional labor–management dichotomy, and the museum CEO is invariably caught in the middle. Inadequate funding models for nonprofit organizations—who depend on volunteers, wealthy individuals, or foundations—remain a salient matter, as has been the case for decades.

Table 1
Status of Unions in Art Museums as of January 2024: Unionized Art Museums

Museum name	City/State	Museum website	Year unionized	Negotiation stage	Union
Art Institute of Chicago	Chicago, IL	artic.edu	2022	CBA	AICWU
Asian Art Museum of San Francisco	San Francisco, CA	asianart.org	Pre-pandemic	CBA	SEIU 1021
Baltimore Museum of Art	Baltimore, MD	artbma.org	2022	In negotiations	AFSCME District Council 67
Bronx Museum of the Arts	New York, NY	bronxmuseum.org	2005	CBA	UAW Local 2110
Brooklyn Museum	New York, NY	brooklynmuseum.org	2021	CBA	UAW Local 2110
Carnegie Museum of Art	Pittsburgh, PA	cmoa.org	2020	CBA	UMW
Columbus Museum of Art	Columbus, OH	columbusmuseum.org	2022	In negotiations	AFSCME Council 8
Dia Art Foundation	New York/Beacon, NY	diaart.org	2022	In negotiations	UAW Local 2110
Fine Arts Museums of San Francisco	San Francisco, CA	famsf.org	Pre-pandemic	CBA	SEIU 1021
Frye Art Museum	Seattle, WA	fryemuseum.org	2019	In negotiations	AWU
Guggenheim Museum	New York, NY	guggenheim.org	2019	CBA	IUOE Local 30
Hispanic Society Museum	New York, NY	hispanicsociety.org	2021	CBA	UAW Local 2110
Jewish Museum	New York, NY	thejewishmuseum.org	2022	CBA	UAW Local 2110
Massachusetts Museum of Contemporary Art	North Adams, MA	massmoca.org	2021	CBA	UAW Local 2110
Milwaukee Museum of Art	Milwaukee, WI	mam.org	2020	CBA	IAMAW Lodge 66
Minneapolis Institute of Art	Minneapolis, MN	artsmia.org	1971	CBA	SEIU 26

MUSEUMS

Museum	Location	Website	Year	Status	Union
Museum of Contemporary Art, Los Angeles	Los Angeles, CA	moca.org	2019	CBA	AFSCME District Council 36
Museum of Fine Arts, Boston	Boston, MA	mfa.org	2020	CBA	UAW Local 2110
Museum of Modern Art	New York, NY	moma.org	1971	CBA	UAW Local 2110
New Museum of Contemporary Art	New York, NY	newmuseum.org	2019	CBA	UAW Local 2110
Philadelphia Museum of Art	Philadelphia, PA	philamuseum.org	2020	CBA	AFSCME District Council 47
Portland Museum of Art	Portland, ME	portlandmuseum.org	2021	CBA	UAW Local 2110
San Francisco Museum of Modern Art	San Francisco, CA	sfmoma.org	1972	CBA	OPEIU Local 29
Tacoma Art Museum	Tacoma, WA	tacomaartmuseum.org	2023	In negotiations	AFSCME Council 28
The Andy Warhol Museum	Pittsburgh, PA	www.warhol.org	2020	CBA	UMW
The Metropolitan Museum of Art	New York, NY	metmuseum.org	Pre-pandemic	CBA	AFSCME District Council 37
Walker Art Center	Minneapolis, MN	walkerart.org	2020	CBA	AFSCME Council 5
Walters Art Museum	Baltimore, MD	thewalters.org	2023	In negotiations	AFSCME Maryland Council 3
Whitney Museum of American Art	New York, NY	whitney.org	2021	CBA	UAW Local 2110

Union Name Key
AFSCME: American Federation of State, County and Municipal Employees
AICWU: Art Institute of Chicago Workers United
AWU: Art Workers Union
IAMAW: International Association of Machinists and Aerospace Workers
IUOE: International Union of Operating Engineers
OPEIU: Office and Professional Employees International Union
SEIU: Service Employees International Union
UAW: United Auto Workers
UMW: United Museum Workers

LABOR CONFLICT AND CONTRACT SETTLEMENTS

Have museum managements fought unionization, and is opposition in the museum sector different than in other industries? The answer depends on who is asked and what sources are consulted. Union organizers, or those writing with labor sympathies, suggest widespread opposition. Here again, however, there are gaps in the data that make it more difficult to assess the level of opposition in museums per se. According to US Bureau of Labor Statistics data (no date), unfair labor practice charges across all sectors are up 16% in 2023. No doubt this reflects tenuous relationships in the museum sector as well. However, if National Labor Relations Board (NLRB) data between 1993 and 2022 are examined, we find that strikes in the sector where museums are found (arts, entertainment, and recreation) are among the lowest (barely a handful) compared with other sectors during the same time period. In our discussions with museum executives, we did not find strong desires to oppose unions, although several leaders perceived unionization drives as a personal affront and believe labor–management processes are not beneficial for museums. There have also been some very difficult strikes lasting long periods; the Fine Arts Museum in Boston and the Philadelphia Museum of Art two examples.

Sentiments concerning labor opposition versus accommodation are similar to those voiced by executives and leaders in other mission-driven and educational organization—particularly in the earlier phases of unionization—and therefore not surprising. The normal bargaining process involved in reaching a first-time contract can take considerable time (between one and two years) and generate tense relationships during negotiations (Julius and DiGiovanni 2016). Most strikes in the museum sector, when they have occurred, were settled in a matter of months, and we believe that the average time to reach a first-time contract coincides with that in other industries. Rather than characterize the stance of museum managements as oppositional, we argue what has transpired during negotiations, particularly for first-time contracts, more closely resembles the normal bargaining process in comparable organizations. A recent Bloomberg Law study found that the average time to negotiate a first time contract took between 409 and 465 days (Combs 2022). We tend to believe that the data are, on average, appropriate for museums as well.

We examined museums that settled contracts in the past three years. Bargaining agents include the UAW, AFSCME, and independent unions, and bargaining units most often comprised professional, technical, curatorial, and administrative staff. Settlements examined are from the Academy Museum in California; the Art Institute in Chicago; the Brooklyn Museum, the Jewish Museum, the Hispanic Society Museum & Library, MOMA, and The New Museum in New York City; the Museum of Fine Arts in Boston; the Philadelphia Museum of Art; and the Tacoma Art Museum. We found a group of issues that were most often at the front and center of negotiations. The main ones are "bread and butter" economics, including retroactive and across-the-board wage increases, addressing wage disparities, one-time bonuses, tuition reimbursement, longevity pay, raising the floor for minimum hourly pay, and holding healthcare premium costs down. Other salient topics include the right of employees to engage in hybrid work on flexible schedules; leaves of absence, most notably parental leave; access to career ladders; and childcare-related benefits. The average wage increases in the contracts studied ranged between 14% and 24% over a multi-year period, normally two to three years. The minimum hourly base pay increased between $17 and $20 per hour. We did not examine whether compensation increases were related to bargaining agent status (Boucher 2021; Cascone 2023a, 2023b; Connelly 2022; Giordano 2022).

In all cases, strikes were settled without long-term detriment to communities where museums reside. We found three cases where admission fees for visitors were raised and attributed to labor contract settlements—at the Guggenheim and Whitney Museums in New York and at the Philadelphia Museum of Art. One museum, the Marciano Art Foundation, attributed its closure to labor strife. We also heard anecdotes of the departure of senior executives and board members following prolonged labor conflict.

Ever-present issues involving confidentiality and transparency are brought into sharp relief during bargaining. Not surprisingly, we found that when the parties found ways to communicate more effectively, build trust, and reward collaborative and ethical behavior, collective bargaining was used to advance innovation and initiative-taking responses to address serious internal and external matters, as has been the case in other organized sectors.

COLLECTIVE BARGAINING INNOVATION

There is an adage among labor relations practitioners that one's point of view is determined by what side of the table one sits at. Another quip about bargaining tables and mission-driven cultural organizations is applicable here: the need for a table with enough sides to accommodate all constituencies with a rightful claim to the museum would necessitate a round table. With these two "table" caveats in mind, we suggest collective bargaining remains an inherently complex phenomenon for museums as well as other industries. Outcomes are influenced profoundly by personalities, context, and a history of relationships; the use of power, influence, and communication focused on changing people's opinions; the configuration of bargaining units; the legislation serving as the legal umbrella for negotiations; and the experiences, skills, and autonomy of the chief negotiators.

Museum leaders find themselves in a difficult position if a particularly hard-nosed employer negotiator from an employer-side law firm takes a wrong step or says the wrong thing. In such cases, the museum itself can be shamed and leaders' reputations trashed. Union organizers use such scenarios in media campaigns as negotiations devolve into a public relations war. One example comes from the nonmuseum field. We recently observed how labor–management relations at the healthcare provider Kaiser Permanente in Northern California deteriorated with mental health clinicians and nurses, resulting in a bitter strike lasting several months that involved negative public relations for Kaiser. Statewide politicians got involved, and regulators commenced investigations. Kaiser patients began telling horror stories to the press about treatment received. Kaiser's messaging to the public was poor, and they were not able to communicate their position to stakeholders in a coherent way, which reinforced the view they were not in a hurry to resolve the conflict. Labor relations had previously been harmonious, with Kaiser frequently being cited as an example of union–management collaboration. It may be years before the hospital system recovers the trust of members, and it is likely that a turnover in senior leadership has occurred (Greenhouse 2021; King 2021; McClurg and Silvers 2022).

PROJECTIONS FOR COLLECTIVE BARGAINING IN MUSEUMS

In general, predictions should be made with caution. Collective bargaining in any sector relies on a multiplicity of factors—internal, external, environmental, political, and, of course, economic. Should a Republican return to the White House in 2024, the composition of the NLRB will change in the near term, which will have a pronounced (dampening) impact on union organizing efforts in private independent institutions. The current Biden administration has been supportive of labor, and unions have made headway in industries previously resistant to organizing efforts. In the public sector, changes to state labor laws have become a flashpoint in polarized states. The fact that Wisconsin, a birthplace of unionization, is at present a right-to-work state amply illustrates this point. With these caveats in mind, barring catastrophic upheaval in society or war, we expect that union organizing in this sector will continue to be successful. We offer three reasons for this prediction.

First, the kinds of employees taking positions in mission-driven cultural organizations, particularly younger, well-educated individuals, are more sympathetic to unions and, at least in the near future, still feeling the economic pinch of inflation, high housing costs, and heavy student loan debt. Museum employees who were educated in the elite university sector, traditionally the wellspring for large numbers of museum workers, come from campuses where unionization is increasingly common among graduate students and undergraduates. Chances are high that students graduating from elite schools possess the skills and willingness to organize, use social media effectively, and have already been in a union or are sympathetic to social justice and related arguments used by organizers. Overall, the next generation of museum workers will be willing to mobilize for higher wages and social concerns.

Second, unions active in the museum sector face declines in their traditional sources of membership. These unions will seek new dues-paying members, and larger independent museums are fertile ground for organizing efforts. This is not to suggest that social justice concerns or traditional union organizing are simply a ruse for union dues; there are many idealists, pragmatists, and believers in what the labor movement has done and represents, and unions have been shown to increase wages, enhance the quality of working life for members, promote more democratic involvement, improve health and safety, and offer other major advantages to society.

Third, for a variety of reasons, this is not an industry likely to aggressively oppose unionization, although it would appear during negotiations that relationships can be rancorous. Executives who manage these types of mission-driven organizations are often themselves sympathetic to higher compensation and other job-related benefits for museum employees. In most of the cases that we studied, unions were able to negotiate a first-time contract after organizing. We did not examine the amount of time it took to negotiate the first contracts but suspect the time needed is consistent with comparable industries, such as higher education. Museums face widespread difficulty in retaining skilled and professional employees. Taking a strong anti-union stance might alienate these groups. Yet those leading these organizations also confront the harsh economic realities of museum finances, which rely primarily on visitors and board members. Social mission organizations like museums cannot be as readily assessed in terms of the efficiency of their operations as private sector enterprises can be. Accordingly, more weight tends to be placed on how the organization is structured and how it treats core stakeholders in gauging the legitimacy and effectiveness of museum leaders. Those in leadership positions are not, in our estimation, inclined to support concerted anti-union activities, believing instead that labor strife rips the fabric of the organization in ways detrimental to those who work there, as well as visitors and the community.

With the above three points in mind, we would predict a robust future for union organizers in this sector.

ACKNOWLEDGMENTS

We thank the leaders of AAM, as well as the Yale School of Management, for support of our research. We wish to thank Susan J. Schurman, Distinguished Professor, School of Management and Labor Relations (SMLR) at Rutgers University; and Tobias Schulze-Cleven and Mingwei Liu, also at SMLR, for their comments. An earlier working paper on this topic was distributed through the Center for Global Work and Employment at SMLR.

REFERENCES

Alloway, L. 1975. "Museums and Unionization." Artforum International. February. https://tinyurl.com/29fm2w4v

American Alliance of Museums. 2022a. "National Snapshot of Covid-19 Impact on United States Museums." February 8. https://tinyurl.com/yhhwjcez

———. 2022b. "The Unionization of Museums: What Management and Staff Need to Know." May 6. https://tinyurl.com/b4s5e3aw

———. 2023, June 27. "2023 Annual National Snapshot of United States Museums." June 27. American Alliance of Museums. https://tinyurl.com/4j83rt8w

Bargaining for the Common Good. 2018. "Concrete Examples of Bargaining for the Common Good." December 1. https://tinyurl.com/25899ayu

Bargaining for the Common Good, Executive Committee on Behalf of the Advisory Committee. 2022. "Introducing Bargaining for the Common Good—Non Profit News." *Nonprofit Quarterly.* September 7. https://tinyurl.com/5f4mjhs5

Baumol, W.J., and W.G. Bowen. 1966. "Performing Arts, the Economic Dilemma: A Study of Problems Common to Theater, Opera, Music, and Dance." Twentieth Century Fund.

Boucher, B. 2021. "After a Bitter Battle, the Guggenheim and Its New Union Have Struck a Deal for Improved Pay and Benefits." Artnet. February 17. https://tinyurl.com/3h73m8j3

Cascone, S. 2023a. "Hispanic Society Museum Workers Approved a New Union Contract, Ending a Grueling Two-Month Strike." Artnet. May 22. https://tinyurl.com/ynvwuz3h

Cascone, S. 2023b. "Unionized Workers at New York's Jewish Museum Ratified Their First Contract, Improving Pay and Time Off." Artnet. October 12. https://tinyurl.com/28axs7t5

CBS News. 2024. "Museum of Natural History Closing Two Native American Exhibition Halls." January 26. https://tinyurl.com/3aaf6368

Combs, R. 2022. "Analysis: Now It Takes 465 Days to Sign a Union's First Contract." Bloomberg Law. August 2. https://tinyurl.com/3sp8bryx

Congressional Research Services. 2021. "Unemployment Rates During the Covid-19 Pandemic." https://tinyurl.com/yc9fwc8h

Connelly, J.F. 2022. "Strike at the Museum: A Report on Museum Labor Unions." Master's Thesis, State University of New York College at Buffalo. https://tinyurl.com/3zhdetcj

Dionne, E.J., Jr. 2022. "Opinion: Unions Are on a Roll. And They Unite a Divided Nation." *Washington Post*. September 4. https://tinyurl.com/3ftwrrvn

Emba, C. 2022. Opinion: Lost in the College-Major-Regret Story: It's Not About the Majors." *Washington Post*. September 25. https://tinyurl.com/56kv2cft

Faine, H.R. 1986. "Cooperative Bargaining in Nonprofit Arts Organizations." *Journal of Arts, Management and Law* 16, no. 1: 47.

Gallup. 2022. "State of the Global Workplace: 2022 Report." https://tinyurl.com/2z5z66wa

Ginsburgh, V.A., and D. Throsby. 2006. *Handbook of the Economics of Art and Culture*. Amsterdam, Netherlands: North Holland.

Giordano, R. 2022. "New Philadelphia Museum of Art Director Addresses the 17-Day Strike and Unveils Matisse Exhibit." *Philadelphia Inquirer*. October 12. https://tinyurl.com/mk3tcaxh

Grau, D. 2020. *Living Museums: Conversations with Leading Museum Directors*. Berlin, Germany: Hatje Cantz.

Greenhouse, S. 2021. "'A Slap in the Face': Nurses' Strike Signals Kaiser's End as Union Haven." *Guardian*. November 13. https://tinyurl.com/5n87f95j

Guarino, M. 2021. "'We Are in Crisis Mode': Museum Workers Are Turning to Unions over Conditions They Say Are Untenable." *Washington Post*. November 4. https://tinyurl.com/63azyvnn

Hirsch, B., D. Macpherson, and W. Even. No date. "Union Membership, Coverage, and Earnings from the CPS." https://www.unionstats.com

Ingraham, D. 2014. "There Are More Museums in the U.S. Than There Are Starbucks and McDonalds—Combined." *Washington Post*. June 13. https://tinyurl.com/3n4cyww6

Institute of Museum and Library Services. 2014. "Government Doubles Official Estimate: There Are 35,000 Active Museums in the U.S." May 19. https://tinyurl.com/bdpeav6h

———. 2018. "Museum Data Files." https://tinyurl.com/389hvd6x

Julius, D.J., and N. DiGiovanni. 2016. "What Factors Affect the Time It Takes to Negotiate Collective Bargaining Agreements?" *Journal of Collective Bargaining in the Academy* 8, article 6.

King, R. 2021. "Kaiser Permanente Strike of Nearly 32,000 Workers Halted After Last-Second Deal Reached." Fierce Healthcare. November 15. https://tinyurl.com/bduyep8w

Marcus, J. 2021. "Will That College Degree Pay Off? A Look at Some of the Numbers." *Washington Post*. November 1. https://tinyurl.com/mrxzx9nn

McCartin, J.A., K. Corrigan, and J. Luff. 2014. "Bargaining for the Future: Rethinking Labor's Recent Past and Planning Strategically for Its Future." Kalmanovich Institute for Labor and the Working Poor, Georgetown University. https://tinyurl.com/48ran5cm

McClurg, L., and E. Silvers. 2022. "Kaiser Mental Health Workers Strike for Third Day in Fight for Increased Staffing and Wages." KQED. August 17. https://tinyurl.com/3nx6smw3

Miller, S. 2021. "U.S. Labor Costs Up 1.3% in Third Quarter." Society for Human Resource Management. October 29. https://tinyurl.com/ye24cvfj

NonProfit Times. 2022. "Changes Become Permanent in Brave New NPO World." March 28. https://tinyurl.com/5xk86nr4

Pynes, J.E. 1997. "The Anticipated Growth of Nonprofit Unionism." *Non-Profit Management & Leadership* 7, no. 4: 355–371.

Raicovich, L. 2021. *Culture Strike: Art and Museums in an Age of Protest.* Brooklyn, NY: Verso.

Schonfeld, R.C., and L. Sweeney. 2019. "Organizing the Work of the Art Museum." Research Report. Ithaka S+R. https://doi.org/10.18665/sr.311731

Seaman, B.A., and D.R. Young. 2018. *Handbook of Research on Nonprofit Economics and Management*, 2nd ed. Cheltenham, UK: Edward Elgar.

Small, Z. 2022. "U.S. Museums See Rise in Unions Even as Labor Movement Slumps." *New York Times.* February 21. https://tinyurl.com/224amheu

Swaim, B. 2022. "The War on Work." *Commentary.* November. https://tinyurl.com/56tw6dtj

Szántó, A. 2020. *The Future of the Museum: 28 Dialogues.* Berlin, Germany: Hatje Cantz.

Time. 2024. "NYC Natural History Museums Closes Native American Displays Amid New Federal Regulations." January 27. https://tinyurl.com/ymtrt8u8

US Bureau of Labor Statistics. No date. *Occupational Outlook Handbook.* September 26. https://tinyurl.com/39ypfcr7 (see also, US Bureau of Labor Statistics, no date, "Trends In Work Stoppages." https://tinyurl.com/3npvsy52

CHAPTER 12

The Status of Unionization Among Undergraduate Students

Daniel J. Julius
Case Western Reserve University, Rutgers University, and Yale University

Nicholas DiGiovanni
Morgan, Brown & Joy

Jai Abrams
University of Connecticut

Abstract

This chapter focuses on the status, causes, and consequences of unionization of undergraduate student employees in colleges and universities. Collective bargaining for undergraduate employees is, with a few exceptions, new in higher education and may presage potentially wide-ranging implications for undergraduate education as well as the way colleges and universities are managed. A multiplicity of factors is explored for reasons undergraduates (including student athletes) are embracing labor unions. Five issues are most salient. First, unraveling student educational issues from their concerns as employees is not straightforward and, while the parties are working to diligently to keep these realms separate, overlapping jurisdictions exist. Second, except for several institutions, primarily public, students are organizing at the most prestigious private schools—institutions thought immune from unionization owing to their autonomy, prestige, and resources. Third, with a few public exceptions, full-time faculty at institutions where undergraduates are organizing tend not to be unionized, and potential conflicts of interest could arise between faculty and students attributable to collective bargaining. Fourth, access to binding arbitration and other traditional labor mechanisms will result in student employees gaining more power and influence than they have had in the past. Student employees may eventually achieve parity with other represented campus employees. Last, should Republicans win the White House occur in 2024, the current NLRB board and legal precedents, now favorable to employee definitions covering students in the private sector, may change, with implications for private schools.

INTRODUCTION

The union movement and organized labor have flourished in the past few years. For example, the success of recent labor strikes involving screenwriters and actors, the United Auto Workers' successful strike activity, hospitality workers in Las Vegas, and the rapid organizing efforts at Starbucks, Amazon, and other corporations that, until recently, were considered hostile territory for organizing efforts, have been noteworthy. While overall numbers of the US workforce represented by unions are still considerably below percentages of unionized workers in the 1950s era—10% now versus about 25% then—recent successes in a variety of sectors are reversing years of decline. These trends, however, do not accurately reflect what has occurred in higher education.

Although there has been evidence of unionization in colleges and universities as early as 100 years ago (Cain 2020), and staff unions were found in private institutions commencing in the late 1930s (Julius and DiGiovanni 2019), unionization of college teaching faculty began very fleetingly in the late 1940s (Herbert, Apkarian, and van der Naald 2020). These trends did not begin in earnest until the passage of enabling state labor legislation beginning in the 1960s and extending into the 1970s and 1980s (Garbarino and Aussicker 1975). Collective bargaining among professors and graduate students was, until much more recently, largely a public sector phenomenon beginning at community colleges and public comprehensive state systems, although major exceptions soon became evident. For example, by the late 1960s and early 1970s, faculty organized in land-grant universities in New England and at Rutgers University, Temple University, the University of Delaware, Wayne State University, the University of Cincinnati, in public systems such as the City University of New York and State University of New York, a number of Jesuit and other private schools, and flagship universities in Florida, Oregon, University of California Santa Cruz, and several others. Institutions where faculty and other academically related employees joined unions are primarily in states with enabling state labor legislation, where other groups of state and private sector employees are unionized, where there is less resistance to unionization in general, where elected officials are beholden to union voters, and where systemwide units invariably include flagship institutions (where faculty are less inclined to support collective bargaining) into larger bargaining unit configurations (Julius and DiGiovanni 2019).

Graduate student unionization at first occurred in larger land-grant institutions in states with enabling legislation and where faculty at comprehensive state institutions in those locales joined unions as well—for example, the University of Oregon, the University of Wisconsin, and Rutgers University. In addition to such activity in the public sector, a new wave of unionization is under way among graduate and undergraduate student workers at elite private schools, a consequence of the 2016 *Columbia* decision by the National Labor Relations Board in which it was determined that such workers have the right to unionize (Columbia University 2016). The former may not be surprising as far as graduate students are concerned because these institutions are major centers for graduate education. However, undergraduate unionization is taking place not only in larger comprehensive state systems, such as California State University, but at smaller elite schools in the private sector, such as Dartmouth, Kenyon, and Reed (Herbert and Apkarian 2021; National Center for the Study of Collective Bargaining in Higher Education and the Professions, various dates).

Currently, it is estimated that 35% to 40% of the teaching professoriate is now organized for purposes of collective bargaining, and organizing among adjunct, part-time, and academically related employees shows no signs of abatement (Herbert and Apkarian 2021). Unions are also making headway at institutions such as Michigan State University, the University of Pittsburgh, and Miami of Ohio, schools where faculty were thought to exhibit greater degrees of autonomy, lighter teaching loads, higher compensation, and meaningful shared governance (i.e., the type of schools where faculty historically resisted formal union representation) (Ladd and Lipset 1974).

In this chapter, we are particularly interested in two questions: First, where have undergraduate students organized for purposes of collective bargaining and where are they presently covered by labor agreements? Regarding the first question, there are two major formats: unions comprising only undergraduates, and institutions where undergraduates are hired into employee classifications already represented by existing bargaining agents (Figure 1). The latter is more common than many might expect. Second, what impact, if any, does membership or involvement in unionization have on the undergraduate student experience—for example, graduation and attrition rates, alumni involvement, attitudes toward faculty or the institution, compensation, tuition, class time, shared governance, decision-making protocols, and the like?

Figure 1
Distribution of Bargaining Agents

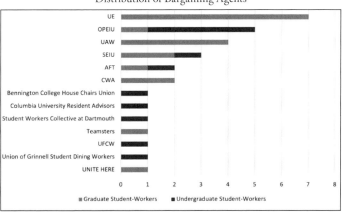

National Center for the Study of Collective Bargaining in Higher Education, Hunter College, CUNY, Newsletter 2024.

THE LEGAL FRAMEWORK

Collective bargaining is governed in the public sector under the jurisdiction of state labor legislation in states where such legislation has been enacted. In the private sector, matters are governed under the National Labor Relations Act (NLRA). The unionization of graduate students and postdocs at private elite schools, such as Harvard, Yale, Columbia, Brown, Dartmouth, Tufts, Georgetown, the University of Chicago, MIT, and Stanford, among others, has occurred in the past few years: 23 bargaining units of graduate student assistants have been formed in the past two years[1] (National Center for the Study of Collective Bargaining in Higher Education and the Professions, various dates). Most of this activity is the result of the 2016 National Labor Relations Board (NLRB) decision in the Columbia University case (Columbia University 2016), where the NLRB reversed earlier precedents and held that students who carry out work functions on campus can be considered employees under the NLRA and allowed to unionize. The fact that they are primarily students and, indeed, must maintain student status to be a teaching or research assistant, does not mean they could also not be considered employees with the right to join a union. While that decision involved graduate students working as research and teaching assistants, the NLRB's rationale applied with equal force to undergraduate students who may hold campus jobs—the group we focus on here.

UNDERGRADUATE ORGANIZING IN HIGHER EDUCATION

While large-scale formalized and legal union activity among undergraduates is relatively recent, labor issues and unions on campus are not new. In 1914, for example, undergraduate student workers at the University of Wisconsin Commons called for a work action after being discharged by management for belonging to a union (University of Wisconsin Student Workers Union 1914). In the 19th century and well into the 20th, students were routinely hired as employees at many of the colleges where they attended school. The *Daily Illini*, the University of Illinois Urbana-Champaign's student newspaper, recounts a union action by custodians in 1917, who asked for an increase of six cents an hour in wages (Cain 2017, 2020). Whether undergraduates were active in that action remains unknown, but the possibility that some student workers were involved is highly likely. Organized staff unions were organized at Ivy League schools in the late 1930s, soon after the passage of the NLRA (NLRA 1935). Although there is strong suspicion of student involvement there, we lack conclusive data that undergraduates were involved.

In the mid- to late 1960s and early 1970s, a time when major labor legislation was passed in numerous states enabling public employee unionization, including legislation covering faculty in the private sector (Cornell University 1970), much was written about the potential impact of faculty collective bargaining on undergraduates and graduate students (Shark 1972; Ladd and Lipset 1974). At that time, the focus was on the potential impact on students where faculty were unionized, not on labor union organizing efforts among undergraduates as employees.

This is not to suggest that students were not demonstrating or organizing—it was the 1960s after all—but they were not forming traditional unions composed of student employees. Those writing on students and collective bargaining suggested that gains in compensation for full-time faculty and staff would result in higher tuition and other financial costs for students and that strikes would impede educational progress and curtail classroom time. One of the most important impacts was thought to be in areas of shared governance, where leading voices at that time believed students could now be excluded from governance decisions concerning teaching, evaluation of faculty, and program development (Garbarino and Aussieker 1975; Ladd and Lipset 1974).

During that era, students were actively involved with state legislatures and governing boards in several states, to safeguard student rights as enabling legislation covering public employee unionization was developed. In some locales, students sought "observer status" (statutorily permitted to attend negotiation sessions). These efforts were successful in several jurisdictions—for example, in Oregon. Students lobbied for other constraints on the parties in order not to be excluded from governance and campus matters as trustees, senior administrators, and legislators responded to collective bargaining.

In the early years of unionization, it was common for both labor and management to invite undergraduate students to the bargaining table to rally them to one side or the other. Two respected scholars of that era and authors of Carnegie Commission studies on unionization in higher education, Garbarino and Aussieker (1975), argued that students were at risk or threatened by faculty bargaining because they feared a bilateral bargaining relationship would erode hard-won gains made in governance during the turbulent 1960s (Ladd and Lipset 1974).

Graduate students were active at various land-grant institutions, including a major strike at the University of Wisconsin in 1971. The first formal graduate student contract was signed at Wisconsin in 1970, and it was estimated that a quarter of the members in faculty units at Rutgers and the City University of New York (CUNY) were graduate students. The relationship between student activism of the 1960s and the origins of graduate student or faculty unionization has still not been adequately explored. Still, many predictions about the impact of academic collective bargaining on undergraduate students have not come to pass (Julius and DiGiovanni 2019; Julius and Gumport 2002).

The earliest known confirmed example of students hired as employees in classifications represented by labor unions is found in the mid-1960s at CUNY, where students were hired on occasion as clerical and other part-time workers represented by the American Federation of State, County and Municipal Employees (AFSCME) District Council 37. In the 1990s, there was evidence that students worked in classifications (dining halls, dormitories) represented by unions in the University of California system. The first contract covering undergraduates (part-time students only) occurred at the University of Oregon in 1972. The first contract covering full-time undergraduates was negotiated at the University of Massachusetts in the early 2000s (resident assistants and peer mentors).

The success of recent campaigns may be attributed to several factors, including growing public support for organized labor, with high percentages of young adults approving of unions (Hunt 2024; McCarty 2023); the centrality of social justice issues in student-worker organizing; the impact of the COVID-19 pandemic on campus working conditions and its broader effect on public awareness of labor issues; and essential support from unions such as the United Automobile Workers, the United Electrical Workers, and the Service Employees International Union (Herbert and Apkarian 2017; Herbert, Apkarian, and van der Naald 2020; Herbert and van der Naald 2021).

Unionization has been shown to increase compensation, which is certainly important to those facing high student debt. We believe also that, in select public jurisdictions, the availability of electronic voting favors a yes vote, as does the requirement in legislation or trustee policy that public sector universities remain neutral during organizing campaigns. This is the case in California and Michigan. In some cases, such as at Wesleyan University, an elite liberal arts institution in Connecticut, the university voluntarily recognized a union of undergraduates working in dining halls. Senior leaders in smaller private institutions like Wesleyan may not oppose student unionization in part because they do not want to engender disruptions in relationships with undergraduates, who may later become contributing alumni.

Unions organizing undergraduates (independent, unaffiliated, or established unions) have been effective using social justice and other rallying points that appeal to younger workers, many of whom are from privileged backgrounds and are inexperienced in labor matters but who are amenable to arguments emphasizing social unionism. Issues attributed to working conditions, student debt, low compensation, and COVID-19 have also pushed students to see the labor movement in a positive light (Perkins 2022). Herbert and colleagues found in a comparison of 2022–2023 with the nine-year period prior to 2022 a recent surge in undergraduate and graduate student organizing. The new student bargaining units established since January 2022 represent a nearly 50% increase over the total number of graduate and undergraduate student-worker units organized over the entire 2013–2021 period (Herbert and van der Naald 2021).

Finally, we note that unions traditionally associated with representing college and university faculty, such as the American Association of University Professors, National Education Association, and American Federation of Teachers, have shied away from organizing undergraduate students. Although it has not been stated publicly, we believe the potential exists for student demands for more control over educational decisions, for greater compensation, for the right to be treated with dignity and respect, and for job protection using just-cause criteria for dismissal, may ultimately conflict with the role and responsibilities of faculty. Unions representing teaching and other academically related employees may not desire to embrace another employee group where potential conflicts of interest may exist with other units represented by these bargaining agents.

COLLEGE ATHLETES: STUDENTS? EMPLOYEES? OR BOTH?

Although the NLRA was enacted in 1935, the NLRB did not assert jurisdiction over private colleges and universities until 1970 in the *Cornell* decision (Cornell University 1970). Even though the Wagner Act authorizing private sector collective bargaining was passed in 1935, the NLRB did not actually decide to assert jurisdiction over private colleges and universities until 1970.

While it first found that graduate teaching assistants could be considered employees under the NLRA in its 2000 *New York University* decision, the NLRB reversed course in 2004 in the *Brown* decision, where it found that because student workers were primarily students, they should not have the right to unionize.

This was the state of the law until 2016 when the Obama NLRB ruled in the *Columbia* decision that, even though student workers were primarily students, they still could be considered employees with a right to unionize under the NLRA. That decision remains good law today and, as noted, led to a proliferation of new graduate-assistant bargaining units as well as undergraduate student-worker bargaining units.

One consequence of *Columbia* was the possibility that student athletes could be deemed employees if they were viewed as providing services to the institution in exchange for compensation, such as athletic scholarships. The NLRB first dealt with that issue in the 2015 *Northwestern* case, where it refused to directly reach the question of employee status for student athletes, but it nevertheless declined to assert jurisdiction in the case because doing so would create labor instability and not effectuate the purpose of the NLRA to permit a single team bargaining unit and to do so when that team is but one of many in a league that included some public sector institutions. Additionally, assertion of NLRB jurisdiction and a finding that a single college team bargaining unit is appropriate raised substantial public policy concerns, including preventing international students from participating in college athletics in the United States based on visa work-hour restrictions (Northwestern 2015).

The only other case thus far that has dealt with the issue of employee status for student athletes was a recent decision from Region 1 of the NLRB involving the Dartmouth College men's basketball players, who sought the right to unionize. That decision (*Trustees of Dartmouth College* 2024) held that the players were indeed employees under the NLRA and had the right to unionize. The regional director's decision was based on the following factors:

- The basketball players at issue perform work that benefits Dartmouth. Even if the basketball program is not particularly profitable (unlike some larger university athletic programs elsewhere), the profitability of any given business does not affect the employee status of the individuals who perform work for that business. The basketball program clearly generates alumni engagement—and financial donations—as well as publicity, which leads to student interest and applications.
- Dartmouth exercises significant control over the basketball players' work. The players are required to provide their basketball services to Dartmouth only. The

student-athlete handbook details the tasks athletes must complete and the regulations they may not break. While it is true that Dartmouth itself must follow restrictions placed on it by the NCAA and the Ivy League, Dartmouth has significant ability to make decisions within the framework of those restrictions.
- The Dartmouth men's basketball team performs work in exchange for compensation. It is true that they do not receive the athletic scholarships enjoyed by the football players at Northwestern University. However, they receive the benefits of "early read" for admission prior to graduating from high school. They also receive equipment and apparel—including basketball shoes valued in excess of $1,000 per player per year—as well as tickets to games, lodging, meals, and the benefits of Dartmouth's Peak Performance program.
- Compensation can include various fringe benefit payments. The Dartmouth players receive numerous fringe benefits, including academic support, career development, sports and counseling support, sports nutrition, leadership and mental performance training, strength and conditioning training, sports medicine, and integrative health and wellness. Players are eligible to receive up to four free tickets for each regular season home game and two free tickets for each away game. Because the NLRB does not consider the size of the compensation when making the determination of whether compensation is "received," it is immaterial that these payments and benefits may be less than the value of full scholarship.

Dartmouth filed a request for review with the full NLRB, asking it to reverse the regional director's decision on multiple grounds, including the lack of real compensation and the substantial restrictions on the college's "control" of the players' activities. As of this writing, the NLRB has not decided whether to take the case.

Should undergraduate athletes eventually be unionized, a host of other questions and issues could arise at the bargaining table and may concern revenues associated with particular sports, relationships with coaches, academic eligibility for players, and long-term benefits in the event of injury. The implications for students and how athletics are managed in colleges and universities could be far reaching.

THE CURRENT STATUS OF STUDENT UNIONS IN HIGHER EDUCATION

While a national clearinghouse for the compilation of data regarding the extent of union representation in higher education among undergraduates does not yet exist, data gathered through the National Center for the Study of Collective Bargaining in Higher Education and the Professions is ongoing and represents an important and, we believe, most current source of information. We have augmented National Center data through our own research (Table 1), which is the most current at the time these charts were assembled in May 2024.

Here we offer several observations on the data presented in Table 1. Most obvious is the fact that undergraduate students are being organized by unions not often found representing

Table 1
Undergraduate Student Unionization (status as of May 2024)

Institution	Type	Category of student worker in unit	Agent	Status	State
Barnard College	A	Resident hall advisors	OPEIU	3	New York
Bennington College	A	Students serving as house chairs	IND	1	Vermont
Boston University	B	Resident assistants	SEIU	2	Massachusetts
Bucknell University	A	Resident assistants	OPEIU	2	Pennsylvania
California State University*	D	Student assistants	SEIU	2	California
City University of New York	D	Clerical, part-time employees	DC 37	1	New York
Columbia University	B	Teaching assistants/research assistants Student resident advisors	UAW IND	1 2	New York
Dartmouth College**	B	Dining hall workers Basketball players Student employees, Office of Residential Life	IND SEIU IND	1 2 4	New Hampshire
Drexel University	B	Resident assistants	OPEIU	2	Philadelphia
Emerson College	A	Resident advisors	OPEIU	2	Massachusetts
Fordham University	A	Resident advisors	OPEIU	1	New York
Georgetown University	B	Resident assistants	OPEIU	2	Washington, DC
Grinnell College	A	All student workers	IND	4	Iowa
Hamilton College	A	Admissions workers	UFCW	2	New York
Harvard University	B	Students working in libraries, cafés, and select administrative offices	UAW	3	Massachusetts
Kenyon College	A	Student employees	IND	4	Ohio
Mount Holyoke College	A	Resident hall advisors	UFCW	2	Massachusetts
New York University	B	Resident assistants	IND	4	New York
Occidental College	A	Select undergraduate student workers	SEIU	4	California
Pomona College	A	Student employee dining workers	UH	4	California
Reed College	A	Housing advisors	OPEIU	4	Oregon
Rensselaer Polytechnic Institute	B	Resident assistants	OPEIU	2	New York
Skidmore College	A	Resident assistants	SEIU	2	New York
Smith College	A	Resident assistants House advisors/coordinators and apartment managers	OPEIU UFCW	2 2	Massachusetts
St. John's College	A	All undergraduate and graduate student workers	CWA	2	Maryland
Swarthmore College	A	Resident assistants	OPEIU	2	Pennsylvania
Temple University	C	Regular student employees	IND	2	Pennsylvania
The New School	B	Regular and part-time student employees	UAW	1	New York
Tufts University	B	Resident hall advisors	OPEIU	3	Massachusetts
University of California	D	Readers and tutors	UAW	1	California
University of California, San Diego	C	Dining hall workers	UAW	1	California

(Table 1 continues, next page)

Institution	Type	Category of student worker in unit	Agent	Status	State
University of California, Santa Barbara***	C	Readers and tutors Dining hall workers	UAW UAW	1 4	California
University of Southern California	B	Football and basketball players	IND	4	California
University of Massachusetts, Amherst	C	Resident assistants and peer mentors	UAW	3	Massachusetts
University of Oregon	C	Part-time student workers	IND	3	Oregon
University of Pennsylvania	B	Resident advisors	OPEIU	2	Pennsylvania
Wesleyan University	A	Resident hall workers and other student workers	IND	3	Connecticut
Worcester Polytechnic Institute	B	Resident and housing advisors	UAW	2	Massachusetts

Institutional Type
A: Private Liberal Arts Colleges/Universities
B: Private Comprehensive Colleges/Universities
C: Public Colleges/Universities
D: Public System

Unit Status
1: In unit with graduate students or other employees
2: Unit Certified, ongoing negotiations
3: Contract covers undergraduates only
4: Union activity among undergraduates

Acronyms
AFSCME: American Federation of State, County and Municipal Employees
CWA: Communications Workers of America
DC 37: District Council (affiliated with AFSCME)

Acronyms (cont.)
IND: Independent Union
IAM: International Association of Machinists and Aerospace Workers
OPEIU: Office and Professional Employees International Union
SEIU: Service Employees International Union
UAW: United Auto Workers
UFCW: United Food and Commercial Workers
UH: Unite Here

Notes
*Unit of 20,000 composed of undergraduates, represented by SEIU.
**Basketball players seeking representation; NLRB hearing officer determined they are eligible to unionize.
***Undergraduates working in select system-wide units. Union activity among undergraduate dining hall workers.

faculty—for example, the American Association of University Professors, National Educational Association, or American Federation of Teachers. We believe that the potential for a conflict of interest between those units is real. Several of these unions, do, however, represent graduate students, adjunct faculty, or part-time employees. Unions organizing undergraduate populations are at the forefront of social justice and social unionism, and they are seeking new dues-paying members as their traditional employee bases decline.

With only a handful of exceptions (mostly in the public sector), full-time faculty at public and private schools where undergraduates are unionizing are not members of labor unions, although graduate students, postdocs, and various categories of teachers at those institutions may be represented by unions. Undergraduates are seeking to unionize at institutions, certainly in the private sector, where full-time faculty have relatively high compensation, lighter teaching loads, decision-making autonomy, meaningful shared governance, and high prestige. Student workers at such institutions are feeling the pinch of higher inflation, post-pandemic insecurity, and student debt, and are receptive to union efforts to demand fairer and more equitable compensation. They believe they have nothing to lose by joining a labor union; no one else may be adequately addressing the concerns they believe are important. University leaders at the institutions are vulnerable to the charge that not enough resources are being spent on students, even though many students receive financial aid of some kind. It may also be the case that unionization in the high-prestige liberal arts sector elucidates a chasm between wealthier privileged students and poorer counterparts as institutions seek to diversify student bodies. In this, as in other matters, administrators cannot seem to agree on effective responses and appear to be constrained by many factors.

As undergraduate unions gain a foothold in the most prestigious schools, it is interesting to reflect that those writing on collective bargaining in the early years incorrectly posited that high prestige negated the need for unionization (Ladd and Lipset 1974). The resources and autonomy associated with high prestige for full-time, tenure-track faculty may not extend to students or staff studying or working at these institutions. The latter may see the university as just another employer.

Finally, undergraduates are being organized largely in locales where there is significant union activity and in states which, by and large, are union friendly. It comes as no surprise that organizing drives are occurring at schools in California, Connecticut, Massachusetts, New York, Oregon, and Pennsylvania, for example, where unionization is robust in many sectors and bargaining agents have people and other resources at hand.

MAIN BARGAINING ISSUES AND COMPENSATION INCREASES

In a qualitative fashion, we examined a current representative sample of contracts covering undergraduates and, in one case, an agreement covering undergraduate and graduate students. The contracts we studied were negotiated at the University of Massachusetts—undergraduate students working as resident assistants and peer mentors (bargaining agent, United Automobile, Aerospace and Agricultural Implement Workers, Local 2322), Tufts University (undergraduate and graduate students working as resident advisors in student housing represented by OPEIU, Local 153), Dartmouth College (full-time and regular part-time student employees working in dining halls, represented by an independent union, the Dartmouth College Collective), and Mount Holyoke College (undergraduates employed as resident advisors or resident fellows represented by the United Food and Commercial Workers, Local 1459).

Our analysis leads us to conclude that collective bargaining potentially offers undergraduate student employees more power and influence than they may have possessed prior to collective bargaining. While that assertion will come as no surprise to those familiar with collective bargaining, it may surprise those unfamiliar with bargaining protocols and contracts.

For example, in all cases, student workers are now given access to robust grievance procedures, sometimes with generous grievance definitions, which allow a union to bring such cases to binding arbitration. In two cases, binding arbitration applies to an "interpretation" of the contract with which the union disagrees and may be applied to outcomes of unfavorable investigations involving discrimination and harassment. In other contracts, student employees were able to file grievances over whether the college is treating them with dignity and respect, whether gender-neutral bathrooms and showers were available or whether the institution is providing a healthy and safe workplace. While such clauses may sound harmless to those unfamiliar with the language of collective bargaining, they are potentially wide-open doors for arbitration and could result in removing educational and financial decisions from college leaders and faculty to external arbitrators, courts, and third-party agencies. However, as of this time, no cases appeared to have risen to the level of arbitration. One reason, we believe, is that bargaining relationships are very new.

One contract contains a clause on gender inclusivity, dignity, and respect—language normally thought to be beyond what is construed as normal "boilerplate" matters concerning wages, hours, and working conditions. Some of these issues go beyond mandatory subjects of bargaining, and the contracts we studied were, with one exception, first-time agreements. In successor contracts, it is probable that negotiators will discuss issues such as dismissal for academic reasons, classroom protocols, and perhaps an expansion of matters that may be taken to arbitration. These and other clauses could result in grievances where undergraduate student employees may potentially be on a collision course with faculty who have a great deal to say over such matters.

The contracts we reviewed also cover traditional employee concerns, including leaves of absence, job descriptions, meal plans, working schedules, and a variety of other employee benefits. One matter considered a traditional boilerplate issue concerns union security and the requirement for student workers to join a union or pay fees to a union as a condition of continued employment [a provision seen in private sector contracts since the Supreme Court banned such provisions in the public sector in its 2018 *Janus* decision (*Janus v. AFSCME* 2018)]. Students working as represented employees may eventually gain parity in select areas with other organized institutional workers.

Wage increases were between 1% and 5 %, although it was not possible to ascertain the increase in hourly wages and stipends in all cases, and we suspect they are in fact much higher than 1% to 5%, especially in the first year of an initial contract. We did not find cost of living or escalator clauses, but we did see provisions related to housing waivers, longevity payments, free parking, and paid leaves.

KEY BARGAINING OUTCOMES AND INNOVATIONS

Few recent academic studies have focused exclusively on the impact of unionization on undergraduate students. Given that undergraduate labor unions are, with a few exceptions, a recent phenomenon, this is hardly surprising. In discussions with those responsible for managing these contracts, they were hard pressed to identify specific impacts of labor union activity on the undergraduate student experience. Therefore, predictions about long-term impacts are exploratory at best and should be made with caution. The experience of graduate student unionization may be instructive. In those cases, the impact of collective bargaining on institutional governance, productivity, the teaching learning environment, prestige rankings, or the teacher mentor relationship has been minimal overall, although isolated cases demonstrate the potential for such to occur. In all, it remains difficult to isolate the impact of collective bargaining from other internal and external forces affecting the academy (Julius 2021; Julius and Gumport 2002).

In the short term, we believe unionization may result in greater empowerment and protection of students as employees, and certainly contracts will provide greater parity with other institutional employees, including higher compensation for those working in unionized positions. Students may also find that they have a greater voice over working conditions, scheduling, and other job requirements. Being in a union may also result in greater job protections and access to formal grievance procedures, including binding arbitration to resolve employment-related disputes.

On the other hand, students may lose benefits or flexibility. For example, one contract covering undergraduates clearly states that no individual employment arrangements with student employees may be made without a union agreement. Education-related benefits will have to be untangled from employee-related benefits. Students are now likely to pay union dues or fees, at least in many private sector institutions, prohibiting such provisions in the public sector. Moreover, income will be taxable, whereas in past years, trade-offs on housing allowances may not have been framed as taxable income. While wages for on-campus union jobs may rise, students may no longer have the autonomy to develop individualized employment relationships. Still, in the near future, students will continue to focus on the positive benefits of unionization. Their experiences over time will tell whether such sentiments continue.

Regarding internal university governance and decision-making processes, unions of undergraduate student employees may lead to increased bureaucracy and formalization of decision making. Authority for student affairs (on matters covered in labor contracts) will migrate from offices of student life to legal and labor relations professionals. Student affairs professionals will need training and professional development to manage effectively in unionized settings, much the same as academic administrators needed when full-time faculty unionized. Institutional leaders may lose authority to third parties over select aspects of student affairs, particularly in systems where bargaining is managed in system offices, including bargaining agent representatives, courts, arbitrators, mediators, and the like who are central to bargaining relationships.

Students working as employees in bargaining units will have a different relationship than nonunionized students with the institution. They will be obligated to adhere to the terms and conditions set forth in the labor contract and may have different avenues than their nonunion peers to address conflicts related to employment. Unionization among undergraduates, particularly in the private sector, is common in the most prestigious colleges and universities in the United States. There will inevitably be long-term implications for voting behavior and, we suspect, increasingly pro-union sentiments as younger adults at elite schools continue to embrace more liberal and left-leaning views supported by the labor movement today.

We do not yet know whether collective bargaining will impact the student–mentor relationship between faculty and students. We highly doubt this will be the case because, unlike graduate student unionization, undergraduate student bargaining units do not implicate the educational process (DiGiovanni in Julius 2022). Nor do we know the impact, if any, on undergraduate student governance processes and systems, classroom protocols, grading policies, attrition rates, alumni support, or other aspects and outcomes of the undergraduate experience. Of course, there is potential for an impact on these matters, but it will depend on what the parties negotiate in the contract (a process that, most know, can be complicated and potentially lengthy) and, of course, how bargaining relationships are managed.

Finally, undergraduate unionization will further constrain the decision-making prerogatives of school leaders and impact organizational cultures in ways yet unanticipated. Despite best efforts by faculty and administrative leaders, it is possible that the growing student-worker movement may expand into larger discussions at the bargaining table—not just about pay and working conditions but about the entire student experience. Already, graduate student unions are pushing the boundaries of bargaining subjects that they want to discuss at the table and place them into labor contracts. Issues such as racism on campus, the use of campus police, general financial aid and funding, academic performance standards, and other nontraditional—and, in most cases, nonmandatory—topics of bargaining are inching their way into negotiations. Expanding collective bargaining into a forum to discuss all student-related topics could be unsettling to many, particularly faculty members who normally have authority over some of these areas.

Managed effectively, however, collective bargaining can facilitate long-range planning, resource allocation, the management of employees, and conflict resolution. How the parties manage and adapt labor relations processes will determine outcomes.

ACKNOWLEDGMENTS

An earlier and shorter version of this paper was published in the *Journal of Collective Bargaining in the Academy,* Volume 15, March 2024.

ENDNOTES

1. These include new graduate student assistant units at Boston University, Cal Tech, Clark University, Cornell University, Dartmouth University, Duke University, Fordham University, Johns Hopkins University, MIT, New Mexico State University, Northeastern University, Stanford University, Syracuse University, Yale University, University of Alaska, University of Chicago, University of Maine, University of Minnesota, University of New Mexico, University of Southern California, Washington State University, Western Washington University, and Worcester Polytechnic Institute. These are in addition to major graduate student assistant units formed at Brandeis University, Brown University, Columbia University, Georgetown University, Harvard University, New York University, The New School, and the University of Connecticut in the preceding five years.

REFERENCES

Cain, T.R. 2017. "Campus Unions: Organized Faculty and Graduate Students in U.S. Higher Education." *ASHE Higher Education Report* 43, no. 3: 1–163. https://doi.org/10.1002/aehe.20119

———. 2020. "Collective Bargaining and Committee A: Five Decades of Unionism and Academic Freedom." *Review of Higher Education* 44, no. 1: 57–85. https://doi.org/10.1353/rhe.2020.0035

Garbarino, J.W., and B. Aussieker. 1975. "Faculty Bargaining: Change and Conflict." Carnegie Commission on Higher Education, Ford Foundation. New York, NY: McGraw-Hill.

Herbert, W.A., and J. Apkarian. 2017. "Everything Passes, Everything Changes: Unionization and Collective Bargaining in Higher Education." *Perspectives on Work* 21: 30–35. https://tinyurl.com/36xuj2pp

Herbert, W.A., J. Apkarian, and J. van der Naald. 2020. "Supplementary Directory of New Bargaining Agents and Contracts in Institutions of Higher Education, 2013-2019." https://tinyurl.com/mrxw9w6n

Herbert, W.A., and J. van der Naald. 2021. "Graduate Student Employee Unionization in the Second Gilded Age." In *Revaluing Work(ers): Toward a Democratic and Sustainable Future*, edited by T. Schulze-Cleven and T. Vachon. Champaign, IL: Labor and Employment Relations Association.

Hunt, F. "Colleges Contend with Tidal Wave of New Undergraduate Unions." 2024. *Chronicle of Higher Education*. March 7.

Julius, D.J. 2021. "Collective Bargaining and Social Justice in the Post-Covid Era." UC Berkeley Research and Occasional Papers Series. https://tinyurl.com/5xhu3jxy

———, ed. 2022. *Collective Bargaining in Higher Education: Best Practices for Promoting Collaboration, Equity and Measurable Outcomes*. New York, NY: Routledge Press.

Julius, D.J., and H. DiGiovanni Jr. 2019. "Academic Collective Bargaining: Status, Process, and Prospects." *Academic Labor: Research and Artistry* 3. Article 11. https://tinyurl.com/3kpy7he7

Julius, D.J., and P.J. Gumport. 2002. "Graduate Student Unionization: Causes and Consequences." *Review of Higher Education* 26, no. 2: 187–216.

Ladd Jr., E.C., and S.M. Lipset. 1974. *Professors, Unions, and American Higher Education*. New York, NY: McGraw-Hill.

National Center for the Study of Collective Bargaining in Higher Education and the Professions. Various dates. Newsletters, 2022–2024. Hunter College, City University of New York.

National Labor Relations Act. 29 U.S.C. §§151–169 (1935). Title 29, Chapter 7, Subchapter II, United States Code.

Perkins, K. 2022. "Unionization Is Catching On Among Undergraduate Student Workers." All Things Considered, NPR. June 7. https://tinyurl.com/bder2vxs

Shark, A. 1972. "A Student's Collective Thought on Bargaining." *Journal of Higher Education* 43, no. 7: 552–558.

University of Wisconsin Student Workers Union, 1914. "Not a Strike, but a Lockout." Lockout Flier.

Court Cases and National Labor Relations Board Rulings

Cornell University and Association of Cornell Employees—Libraries, Cornell University and Staff Association of the Metropolitan District Office, School of Industrial Relations, Cornell University and Civil Service Employees Association, Syracuse University and Service Employees International Union, Cases 3-RC-4768, 3-RM-440, 3-RM-441, 3-RM-442, AND 3-RM 433. 183 NLRB 329 (June 12, 1970).

Janus v. AFSCME. 2018. 585 U.S. —, 138 S. Ct. 2448.

New York University and International Union, United Automobile, Aerospace and Agricultural Implement Workers of America, AFL-CIO, Case No. 2-RC-22082. 332 NLRB 1205 (October 31, 2000).

Northwestern University and College Athletes Players Association (CAPA), Petitioner, Case 13-RC-121359. 362 NLRB 1350 (August 17, 2015).

The Trustees of Columbia University in the City of New York and Graduate Workers of Columbia–GWC, UAW, Case 02-RC-143012. 364 NLRB No. 90 (August 23, 2016).

Trustees of Dartmouth College and Service Employees International Union, Local 560, Case No. 01-RC-325663, 337 NLRB 34 (March 5, 2024).

COMMENTARIES

COMMENTARY: AUTOMOBILES, CONSTRUCTION, AND TRUCKING: CORE INDUSTRIES IN IRRA/LERA RESEARCH VOLUMES ON COLLECTIVE BARGAINING

Howard R. Stanger
Canisius University

The automobile, construction, and trucking industries have been mainstays in IRRA/LERA research volumes on collective bargaining. This commentary compares and contrasts developments in labor relations and collective bargaining across these three important sectors.

The automobile industry has a significant economic impact on the American economy, but its influence extends globally, owing to long supply chains and extensive competition from domestic—American and transplant—and foreign manufacturers. The industry generated directly and indirectly 9.6 million jobs that paid $650 billion in payroll compensation in 2022. Since the mid-20th century, the industry has also been trendsetter in labor–management relations. But since the 1970s, the Big 3 American car companies—General Motors, Ford, and Chrysler (now Stellantis)—have lost market share to foreign manufacturers operating outside and inside the United States, and very recently to electric vehicle (EV) manufacturers such as Tesla.

Changes in the competitive landscape and economic recessions have hurt the main union, the United Auto Workers (UAW), over the past 40+ years. From a peak of close to 1.6 million members in the late 1970s, the UAW's membership current stands at about 383,000. Overall union density in the industry fell from 58.5% in 1983 to 15.8% in 2022. Hourly employment in the Big 3 declined from 400,000 in 2001 to 150,000 by 2022. Moreover, internal union leadership scandals in 2017 harmed the reputation and efficacy of the UAW. But the federal government's move to reform the union has led to the direct election of UAW leaders, including the reform candidate Shawn Fain, who has taken a more militant approach to organizing and collective bargaining.

After undertaking strategic strikes and public relations campaigns against the Big 3 in the fall of 2023, the UAW signed lucrative contracts for its members that helped to erase some of the concessions the union had made over the past four decades. The UAW is using the gains it made at the bargaining table with the profitable Big 3 to organize the growing nonunion sector, mainly in the American South, which could continue the long history of "pattern bargaining" in this industry with company-wide labor agreements.

Masters, Goeddeke, and Gibney note in their chapter that the future of the UAW and the Big 3 depends on making a successful transition to electric vehicles (EVs), the state of the global automobile industry, and whether the UAW can increase union density in both the traditional combustible engine and growing EV sectors.

In contrast to the unionized automobile industry, bargaining in the construction industry is conducted on a more decentralized basis, with unions negotiating with multiple employer associations that represent the (mostly) small employers in various subsectors of the industry. But similar to automobiles, construction unions face the threat of a large and growing nonunion sector and weakened labor market institutions. Despite these challenges, Belman and Erlich show in their chapter that construction unions have held their ground and maintained higher wages relative to unorganized construction workers and manufacturing workers in general.

As with the automobile industry, the construction industry is important to the US economy, representing between 4% and 5% of GDP, but it is highly fragmented, with numerous small employers and a handful of large ones. Residential construction is virtually nonunion, while the various specialty branches have strong union presences. There are 15 building trades unions that represent over 4 million workers, and each one negotiates its own labor agreement. Until the 1970s, union market share exceeded 80%, but since then the industry has bifurcated: outside major metropolitan areas in the Northeast, Midwest, and West Coast, union density is very low. For example, density in the broad construction industry declined from 38.1% in 1973 to 12.6% in 2023.

In addition, the employer structure is multilayered, with subcontractors employing the bulk of the construction labor force. These employers are most concerned with labor relations and labor costs. One older but increasingly rare feature in American labor relations is the presence of employer associations in the construction industry owing to small employer size and larger craft unions. Collective agreements are negotiated separately for each trade and mainly at the local level, although pattern bargaining extends across the crafts and regions.

The benefits of pattern bargaining to construction unions (as well as employers) have been compromised by the growing and widespread use of independent contractors, multitiered subcontracting, and immigrant labor to lower labor costs. Here, public policies related to IRS tax codes and immigration have created incentives for employers to misclassify workers as independent contractors to avoid tax and workers compensation insurance obligations and to pay foreign-born (mostly Hispanic immigrant) labor "off the books," especially in the South, where the Hispanic construction labor force dominates. Belman and Erlich note that between 12.4% and 20.5% of the construction labor force were either misclassified as independent contractors or paid off the books in 2017, saving employers between $6.6 to 17.3 million in 2017. One of the clear lessons that emerge from this chapter is that the erosion of labor market institutions and the regulatory framework are critical to the health and well-being of workers and the strength of unions and is responsible for a number of negative outcomes, including wage theft. The breakdown of labor market institutions also has been a problem for workers in the trucking industry, as discussed below.

In the face of these threats, construction unions have been able to maintain standards by having a productivity advantage over nonunion shops, recruiting members of underrepresented groups, and altering government policies to shape perceptions of employers about union labor. Unions also have engaged in more cooperative relations with employers and reduced the amount of labor disputes through long-standing dispute resolution systems similar to those in the printing and garment trades from the early 20th century. The construction industry experience shows both the resiliency of unions and the effective use of labor–management cooperation practices.

Much the same as the automobile and construction industries, the commercial trucking industry is a vital part of the US economy that has been greatly and negatively impacted by public policies. In trucking, deregulation and overtime pay eligibility issues owing to contradictions in laws have hurt drivers. According to Belzer, "Decades of efforts to reform labor and employment law in a way that would enforce the principles of the National Labor Relations Act, and even the Fair Labor Standards Act, have been stymied by lobbying from business interests that prefer to retain the power advantage in the relationship, giving workers and their representatives very little hope that reform can happen. The problem of regulatory capture looms in the background as well."

Similar to construction, the trucking industry is highly decentralized, with many small operators and only a few large ones and an extensive multilayered network of subcontractors. Unlike construction, however, there is one main union, the International Brotherhood of Teamsters. The Motor Carrier Act of 1980 deregulated this once highly regulated industry and created intense competition that has contributed to worsening economic and safety outcomes, the demise of many trucking companies, the departure of skilled drivers, and the loss of many Teamster-represented jobs. Where collective bargaining currently is present, it has become decentralized. The centralized National Master Freight Agreement (NMFA) that formed in 1964 and involved numerous companies and the Teamsters Union has been reduced to a single firm, ABF Freight Systems, after the Yellow Corporation went out of business in 2023. At its height, the NMFA represented between 800 and 1,000 companies and between 300,000 and 500,000 workers.

Before deregulation, about 60% of truckers were unionized. In 2022, only 7.2% of production employees in truck transportation were unionized. The Teamsters Union is no longer primarily composed of truck drivers and dock workers. It does, however, have high representation in the courier and messenger sector because of its representation of workers at United Parcel Service (UPS), where the parties negotiate a national master labor agreement.

Recent internal union politics and labor relations at UPS parallel those of the automobile industry. The same way that reform candidate Shawn Fain won the presidency of the UAW and subsequently took a tougher stance against the Big 3, Sean O'Brien, a candidate from the decades-old reform group Teamsters for a Democratic Union, won the presidency of the Teamsters and quickly engaged in a high-pressure bargaining campaign against UPS that produced a rich contract for union members that reversed years of concessions. Like the UAW's new approach to the Big 3, the Teamsters' campaign included threats of a national strike against UPS that were backed with a program of strike preparation events and activities. The same way that Fain sent a strong message to nonunion auto companies after signing strong contracts with the Big 3, O'Brien delivered a similar message to Amazon after signing a new contract with UPS. But, as Belzer makes clear, "organizing Amazon, and other carriers that rely on subcontracting as their primary means of conducting business, will require a major initiative in organizing strategy, such as the community-based type of organizing" and changes in the legal and regulatory framework that have weakened the union and labor market institutions in the trucking industry. Moreover, although Belzer does not discuss the elimination of drivers by technology, by the end of 2024, it is expected that fully autonomous (driverless) trucks will be operating in Texas. Whether they prove safe enough for Texas and the rest of country to replace truck drivers remains to be seen. If they pass their road test, driverless trucks will pose a threat to drivers and the Teamsters greater than deregulation.

These three chapters reveal that growing union density and strengthening collective bargaining will require more than stronger union leadership, extensive organizing, and new and militant bargaining strategies. It also will necessitate reforms of the legal and regulatory framework and the rebuilding of labor market institutions. The cases of automobiles, construction, and trucking reveal that the road to the revitalization of unions and collective bargaining will be rocky and may have to navigate around a few dead ends along the way.

COMMENTARY: REGENERATING THE NEWSGUILD

Nicholas Bedell
The NewsGuild

Howard Stanger's chapter provides a detailed description of workplace trends in the newspaper industry over many years. The situation appears grim, as journalists and ethical journalism have been sacrificed for short-term profit to feed corporate greed. Additionally, the industry, in the face of declining ad revenue, is hell-bent on abandoning the print product and converting to a largely digital one.

Over the course of the past eight years, The Newspaper Guild (TNG) has experienced a "phone ringing off the hook" moment in terms of organizing interest. Journalists have reached out to TNG at an unprecedented rate from all corners of the news ecosphere. In follow-up correspondence and conversations, journalists universally describe conditions at the outlet they work for as low paid and deeply unfair, and they routinely point to the fact that the outlet is unsuccessful in fulfilling its stated mission. They seek to organize a union because they see it as the best vehicle for having their collective voice heard and, most importantly, considered, as they seek to reimagine what a well-functioning newsroom looks like in this dynamic moment.

The object of TNG is defined in its constitution, and the organizing and bargaining of the past eight years have been in service of this vision:

> The purpose of the Guild shall be to advance the economic interests and to improve the working conditions of its members; to guarantee, as far as it is able, equal employment and advancement opportunity in the industry and constant honesty in news, editorials, advertising, and business practices; to raise the standards of journalism and ethics of the industry; to foster friendly cooperation with all other workers; and to promote industrial unionism in the jurisdiction of the Guild.

Once TNG takes on a campaign, workers build an organizing committee and collectively compose a mission statement that a super-majority signs onto. It is in these documents that the aspirations of journalists reside and the source material for a rising movement finds its voice.

The *Morning Call* mission statement illustrates the issues and concerns expressed:

> As *Morning Call* journalists and support staff, we are proud of the work we do to serve our readers as the Lehigh Valley's leading newspaper. We shine a light on injustices, share stories that lift the spirit and cover breaking news that affects our communities. Our ability to cover the Lehigh Valley, however, has been continuously compromised by the drive to maximize profit at the expense of

what we do. We have lost dozens of veteran journalists, depriving us of decades' worth of expertise. Those who remain cope with stagnant wages, exponentially increased work responsibilities and declining benefits. We face constant insecurity about our futures.

The strongest defense against these threats is a unified workforce.

From the *Florida Times-Union* mission statement:

> The workers of The *Florida Times Union* intend to unionize with the NewsGuild Communication Workers of America. We are doing so to protect the mission of the newspaper—to expose injustices, to explore the nuances of modern life and keep a watchful eye over those in power. We cannot fulfill that mission without demanding the same transparency at our own workplace and from our own corporate owners.
>
> It is the men and women of the newsroom who make this newspaper so special, yet our current and past owners have actively harmed the newsroom. Our objective is to preserve a level of dignity for those who work to produce a newspaper that has value. We don't just work in Jacksonville; we live here. This is our community, too, and we believe that it deserves a vibrant ambitious newspaper.

From the *Los Angeles Times* mission statement:

> The *Los Angeles Times* is an essential institution. As employees, we take enormous pride in the journalism we produce, fighting each day to serve our readers and make our product better. We give our community a voice, and we deserve a voice as well. That's why we are forming a union with the NewsGuild, the organization that represents our peers at *The New York Times*, the *Washington Post*, the *Wall Street Journal*, Reuters, the Associated Press and many others.
>
> A union is the best way for us to protect ourselves and ensure that we have a say in the critical decisions that shape our journalism.

TNG's collective bargaining program—how workers organize and coordinate their fights at individual outlets or chains and what those demands are—finds its roots in these quotes. TNG has realized that the need for change in the industry is urgent and that journalists' demands cannot be advanced only in the silos of individual bargaining. What journalists want is to do work for the public good. They are not interested in maximizing profit and extractive income for a nameless predatory hedge fund. It is with this in mind that TNG is advancing a "bargaining for the common good" model for negotiations.

With the mission statements in mind, The TNG Common Good Demands that have been put forward at multiple tables, including Gannett, are the following:

- **Staff That Is Adequate in Number—Hiring:** In the past decade, thousands of papers have shut their doors, and half of all journalist jobs have disappeared. Existing newsroom staff have been cut to the bone, and current workers are doing too much with too little—at Gannett outlets, media workers are producing top-tier journalism in lowest-tier conditions. Gannett must immediately increase hiring into newsrooms across the country and make real a commitment to local journalism and local journalists.
- **Diverse in Perspective—Diversity, Equity, and Inclusion:** In-depth, committed local news coverage requires newsrooms that have a diversity of views, cultures, and perspectives. As Gannett hires across the chain, it must seek to create newsrooms diverse in perspective and skilled in navigating the communities being covered.
- **Developing Expertise in Craft—Sustainable Jobs:** Gannett must commit to sufficient compensation to enable media workers to live and thrive in the communities they cover. The sustained deep and vital connections required to produce in-depth local news, along with the experience and training that feeds that growth, can exist only if media workers have secure jobs and fair compensation. Additionally, media workers must be afforded the benefits and paid time off that support a healthy work–life balance.

To support and deepen the reach of bargaining for the common good, TNG has launched a national campaign funded by the Communication Workers of America (CWA) to address news deserts. News deserts are the predictable result of the destruction caused by the shrinkage of local news coverage that results from layoffs and the systematic defunding of newsrooms. This campaign looks to build partnerships with the public, subscribers and readers, allied organizations, unions, and membership across all of CWA to advance issue awareness broadly, political action internally, and advocate for state and federal legislative fixes alongside bargaining demands.

Journalists have recognized that the journalism they trained to do—that they have gone into debt to master, that they have pursued as a passion without thought to achieving financial fortune—is heading toward extinction. They also understand that they have to do something if it is going to be rebuilt, reimagined, and reconstructed.

The desire you hear ringing in your ears as you read these excerpts is one that seeks to completely remake the institutions of news gathering, given the horrors inflicted on it by the current ownership models. The detailed recounting of organizing and bargaining in this chapter illustrates TNG's evolving strategy to raise the issue of the destruction of news-gathering institutions and the carnage of US democracy that inevitably follows. TNG has come to realize that while short-term, modest gains can be made in terms of working conditions and wages—and that this is the primary work of the union—the current ownership model is no longer compatible with meeting the requirements of our constitution, which guarantees the citizens of the United States a free press. TNG members are the most equipped stakeholders to lead us as we restructure the news industry so that it will be ambitious, diverse, transparent, and a steady voice in, and of, our nation's communities.

COMMENTARY: LABOR RELATIONS IN THE HEALTHCARE INDUSTRY

Marge DiCuccio
Allegheny General Hospital/Allegheny Health Network

There is no doubt that the cost of healthcare has escalated to an unsustainable level, and serious changes are necessary if the United States is to provide healthcare to all members of society. As noted in the chapter, there are many contributors to the situation, one of which is the costs generated when a hospital has a unionized workforce. There are several obvious and hidden costs, including legal costs, dues paid to the union by employees, and opportunity costs.

Legal costs encompass the need for additional internal and external legal staff to manage contract negotiations and subsequent legal actions related to contract disputes. In my experience, the hospital's primary focus during labor negotiations is to ensure covered employees leave negotiations with a compensation package that will not only be competitive in the market at the time the contract is negotiated but also one that will remain competitive for the duration of the contract. A secondary focus is to avoid any type of work stoppage that would negatively impact patient care. In addition, throughout the course of the contract, there tend to be disagreements related to interpretation of the contract. These disagreements are solved through several steps of due process, including grievances, arbitration, and mediation, which require legal resources to proceed through the process.

In each of the three organized hospitals where I have provided leadership, there is no doubt that my union colleagues, both those employed by the union and staff members who assume leadership roles representing their fellow team members, have a passion for the labor mission and for quality patient care. It is important to recognize that labor unions are also extensive organizations that require funding to spread their mission to new organizations and to influence political processes in ways that support the mission and constituents. One of the primary sources of funding is dues paid by the members to the union, although money from dues may not be used for electoral purposes. A large hospital's employees can provide millions of dollars of funding for a union not only to represent the local members but also to organize other hospitals and to influence lawmakers in ways that benefit the members. When a hospital is recruiting top talent, the cost of dues needs to be factored into total compensation if it is to remain competitive in the market. In my experience, the staff being recruited are generally not as invested in union representation because they were not employed when the conditions that led the staff members to organize existed. Their relationship with the hospital is based on the current working conditions, not those from many years before.

Opportunity costs are experienced when an organization needs to respond quickly to market pressures in times of high demand for specific employee types, such as a nursing shortage driven by an unforeseen pandemic. When employees are represented by a union, the hospital must negotiate any changes in compensation or working conditions with representatives of the union. These negotiations are time consuming and normally place an organization in a challenging position to respond quickly to market pressures. The time lapse can lead to insufficient staff members to accommodate the patients requiring care, resulting in a loss of income for the organization. It is important to be clear that the unions I have worked with want the organization to be successful and are not purposefully delaying the organization's response to unforeseen pressure. The fact is that adding a third party into decision making is likely to add additional time, even if unintended. These three examples bring to light that labor unions are complex organizations that add both obvious and hidden costs to the nation's healthcare system.

The chapter prominently discusses the two types of labor relationships that can exist: a traditional relationship and a labor–management partnership. Based on my experience, there is a continuum involving partnerships that is not dichotomous or stationary in time. My union and leadership colleagues alike would agree that we have invested extraordinary time and financial resources in creating a culture where problems can be solved outside of the formal negotiation and/or arbitration process.

My latest partnership journey began ten years ago in the common space of improving quality and patient outcomes by using Lean methodology and nursing unit–based teams. This is no different from similar types of groups and initiatives I have co-led in nonunion organizations, except for the need to ensure that the union is an equal participant in the planning and implementation of the initiative. I believe that these groups were critical in the organization's successful Magnet© journey by driving improved patient outcomes and staff ownership of their nursing practice. (Magnet© is a designation given by the American Nurses Credentialling Center to hospitals that meet the standards of high nursing outcomes and autonomy in nursing practice. In other words, the hospital is a magnet that attracts nurses.) The day-to-day interactions and activities occurring between labor and management within the hospital are very cordial and professional. The cost of this model has been absorbed by the hospital for the most part, and at the beginning of the experiment, the offset to the cost was expected to be seen in streamlined, interest-based labor negotiations and less need for the grievance process. The original benefits expected by the organization were not realized because of several factors, including changes in both union and elected nurse leadership, the desires of the active union membership, and the composition of the union negotiating teams.

Partnerships often falter when there are changes in the founding members. In our case, both the union leadership and the elected nurse leaders turned over within two years of the start of the partnership. The elected nurse leadership (president, vice presidents, etc.) were seen to be "too close to hospital leadership" by many of the nurses and therefore were not re-elected following the first contract negotiation after the formation of the partnership. The newly elected leaders struggled to find value in this type of partnership and were less committed to it. This didn't impact the organization's quality work, though it did limit the parties' ability to move past quality.

This brings us to the second issue, the desires of active union members. It is common that most nurses are not active in their union's activities, despite their appreciation for the union's representation during contract negotiations. In our case, most of the active members were nurses who were on staff when the union was voted into the organization or had a strong belief in unionization. This type of employee highly values the traditional relationship that exists between management and the union and is suspect when the traditional relationship becomes blurred by a partnership. These staff members are likeliest to vote for officers of the union and lean toward officers that represent traditional union values. The lack of interest in these elections by staff members who value partnership leads to more traditional leaders. That, in turn, makes it difficult to sustain partnerships.

Finally, in my experience, the composition of the negotiating team very much drives the processes used during negotiations. Staff members who are willing to commit significant time and face emotional challenges within our organization tend to gravitate to traditional negotiations and are less interested in interest-based bargaining. This means that all the tools available to the union, including the threat of a strike, are likely to be utilized. Most organizations that invest the resources to develop a labor–management partnership up front are expecting to avoid the cost of work-stoppage plans and contentious contract negotiations. In the case of most of these partnerships, this goal is not realized, which can cause the partnership to unravel from the hospital's perspective. I do believe there is a benefit to the partnership on a day-to-day basis; however, delivering streamlined negotiations and fewer grievances and arbitrations is more complex than simply forming a partnership.

The current healthcare environment is significantly more complex than ever before, and increasing union penetration will add to the cost and complexity of the environment. And while I agree with the chapter authors that it is worthwhile to partner with unions when the opportunity presents, it is important to have realistic expectations regarding the potential outcomes that are likely to be achieved. Partnerships are not a panacea.

COMMENTARY: TEACHERS AND UNIONS

Gregory C. Hutchings, Jr.
Howard University

Teacher unions have been around since 1857, when the largest and oldest teachers' union in the United States, the National Education Association (NEA), was founded. However, it wasn't until a century later that Black/African American teachers were permitted to join teacher unions, when the second oldest and second largest teachers' union, the American Federation of Teachers (AFT), became the first to offer full membership to people of color. Today, nearly 70% of US public school teachers are members of a teachers' union.

The authors of the chapter provide a solid overview of the bargaining structures and activities taking place in the United States. Their insights are useful and relevant to everyone interested in education. The structuring, however, overlooks some critical issues that have become interwoven into education today. As a result, my commentary focuses on those critical issues to explain, in part, some of the challenges facing educators, unions, and schools today.

As a nation, we are currently experiencing sensational politics in education that are similar to the Civil Rights Movement era. Books are being banned from schools, educators are being terminated or threatened to be terminated for using words such as diversity, equity, inclusion, and antiracism. Literally, we are witnessing a "déjà vu" situation in which the United States of America is still battling racism and fighting for the rights of Black people, Indigenous people, and people of color.

The anti–critical race theory (CRT) movement is being influenced by political influencers such as Virginia governor Glenn Youngkin, who won his gubernatorial election on false information about CRT and continues to influence anti-CRT and anti-Black actions that negatively impact education in Virginia. Just as in the Commonwealth of Virginia, the racial narrative in the United States continues to promote White supremacy and oppress other races with the most significant impact on Black and Brown people.

Educators join the profession to help young people of all races be their best and strive to change the world, one child at a time. Yet the national phenomenon of educational inequities continues to have a profound impact on our educational systems across the country. Black people, Indigenous people, and students of color in the US educational system continue to experience academic disparities, lack of opportunity, and gaps in academic performance, as well as higher rates of suspensions, expulsions, and special education placements than their White counterparts. Teacher unions across America should be focused on ensuring that these educational disparities are not preventing students, especially those who are Black, Indigenous, and students of color, from having an equitable educational experience relative to their White counterparts in US schools.

It seems that teacher unions are so preoccupied with fighting for their own rights that the well-being of our young students is being overshadowed. Teacher compensation, benefits, and rights are important to ensure that educators are treated fairly and well compensated, as are best practices to recruit the top educators for our schools. However, the federal government should be involved in ensuring that federal dollars are being used to provide additional compensation for educators so that they have competitive salaries for all teachers across the United States and incentives to join the education profession. The findings of one study suggest otherwise:

- Our current educational system for funding public schools shortchanges students, especially those from low-income backgrounds.
- Funding inadequacies and inequities are magnified during and after a recession in the United States.
- Increased federal spending on education in the United States after recessions has been able to mitigate funding shortfalls and inequities.
- Increased federal spending from Congress on education could help boost economic recovery.
- Public education can stabilize our economy and overhaul the school finance system by ensuring a larger role for the federal government in education funding.

Teacher unions should be advocating and unapologetically fighting for the federal government to take a larger role in their involvement in education spending in the United States. We are in a national crisis with teacher shortages, significant academic disparities, gun violence in schools, and most importantly, the continued oppression of Black people, Indigenous people, and people of color through systemic racism in education. It behooves our teacher unions to come together as one entity and leave no opportunity for "divide and conquer" in public education through our multiple teacher unions.

According to the National Center for Education Statistics, there have been significant changes in enrollment trends for the overall composition of US public school students. Specifically, from the fall of 2010 through the fall of 2021, the student population in our public schools have become less White (from 52% to 45%), less Black (from 16% to 15%), less Native American (from 1.1% to 0.9%), more Hispanic (from 23% to 28%), more Asian (from 4.6% to 5.4%), and there are more students of two or more races (from 2% to 5%). By contrast, the data also show that, of the public school teachers in the United States during the 2020–21 school year, 80% were White, 9% Hispanic, 6% Black, 2% Asian, and 2% of two or more races (fewer than 1% of teachers were Native American or Pacific Islanders).

These data are significant because they demonstrate that US public schools are now a majority of non-White students being taught primarily by White women. Representation matters in education, and therefore the importance of diversity in education matters, which means we must understand the implications of teacher unions on public education for Black students, Indigenous students, and students of color in the US educational system as well as teacher union members who are Black people, Indigenous people, and people of color.

Being that the majority of our teachers in America are White women and nearly 70% of teachers are a part of a union, how do we ensure that the voices of Black people, Indigenous people, and people of color are being represented within the advocacy of teacher unions? It's more than just putting social justice as one of the unions' priorities or advocating not to ban certain books in schools. Teacher diversity has been a secondary focus of teacher policy. Like racial and ethnic achievement gaps, lack of teacher diversity is a problem in nearly all schools and districts. This requires intentional efforts to have Black teachers, Indigenous teachers, and teachers of color be a part of the decision making and strategy building as well as insights from students who are Black, Indigenous, and people of color.

How do teacher unions ensure that there are intentional efforts to include the perspectives, experiences, and needs of Black people, Indigenous people, and people of color? There is limited research on this topic, and it is time to bring diverse perspectives to the forefront of teacher unions across the United States. Furthermore, an intentional effort to increase the diversity of teachers in public schools across the country should be a pressing priority. Teacher unions should be working directly with historically Black colleges and universities (HBCUs) to develop teacher pipelines to diversify the teaching profession. There should be teacher training programs in every urban school system across the country sponsored by the two major teacher unions, the NEA and AFT, where teacher preparation programs for Black people, Indigenous people, and people of color who represent teens, young adults, and second-career professionals thrive and are constantly recruiting the next generation of teachers. The NEA has already started diversity educator programs, such as the Educator Diversity Collective; however, there needs to be a more streamlined process that is associated with HBCUs in America.

Teacher unions across the country have a place in public education and should be commended for their efforts over the years with regard to catapulting the education sector as a respected profession. In addition, teacher unions have advocated for civil rights and equal pay for women, as well as ensuring working conditions are adequate for students and teachers. For more than 150 years, teacher unions have been at the forefront of education. It is important that these unions use their prestige and power to change the narrative of divisiveness in public education and ensure that our democracy is preserved for future generations, especially for Black people, Indigenous people, and people of color in public schools across the United States. A focus on diversifying the teaching profession and advocating for an equitable education for all students should be the hallmark of teacher unions. This will require vision, integrity, and passion; however, it is my belief that, together, we can make a difference and ensure that an equitable education is a reality for all students, regardless of their life circumstances, ZIP codes, learning abilities, or socioeconomic status.

COMMENTARY: POLICE COLLECTIVE BARGAINING

John T. Delaney
Saint Vincent College

Forty years ago, my postdoctoral project was a US Department of Justice–funded study on the effects of collective bargaining and interest arbitration on policing. It involved a massive effort to collect bargaining outcome data, union contracts, and arbitration awards covering police in US cities with more than 25,000 residents. The results of our analyses indicated that a large percentage of police were unionized and that they benefited from bargaining and arbitration. Bargaining increased police compensation, fringe benefits, and nonwage outcomes. An examination of union contracts showed language favorable to police on issues ranging from grievance procedures to discipline. In addition, evidence showed that the use of arbitration is associated with better outcomes for unionized police. My colleagues and I concluded that collective bargaining was a powerful tool for police and their unions. Paul Clark's chapter indicates that it is still a powerful tool and that police unions continue to use collective bargaining to secure good outcomes for officers.

Having such a tool may be necessary, however, given the situations that police officers face. Law enforcement is a difficult job that is not always an attractive career. Historically, requirements for serving as a police officer have varied across jurisdictions and departments, and college degrees have not always been required for applicants. Today, for the reasons mentioned by Clark, police departments face a shortage of job candidates. At a time when substantial training for police has been advocated, the shortage has precluded an increase in standards; in some cases, agencies have reduced requirements for hiring or admission to a police academy to secure a sufficient number of police officer candidates. The shortage has also caused some agencies to use mandatory overtime as a way of ensuring that an adequate number of officers is available at all times. This places pressure on officers because they have less time off to decompress from jobs that can vary from boringly routine to incredibly dangerous.

Consistent with the results of our Department of Justice report four decades ago, collective bargaining is helpful to officers in that it can ensure a specific set of rules or processes are used when problems occur that may lead to discipline, public scrutiny, or decisions on outcomes. The safeguards built into bargaining inevitably create questions for people skeptical of a particular police action or concerned about police misconduct more generally. When police managers and officials support officers who were involved in questionable situations, skeptical people often assume that there is a conspiracy to hide the truth. Social media posts provide whatever assertions people wish to make—in support of or opposition to the officer involved or the action in question. This environment makes the protections provided by union contracts more important to police officers.

It is important to recognize that police are different from other public employees in critical ways. They are expected to respond to a variety of situations ranging from minor nuisances to dangerous encounters with armed individuals. They have the power to restrain and use force on people. And they are expected to exercise good judgment in all cases. In 1967, the Supreme Court provided police with qualified immunity to address the difficult situations they face in which the constitutional rights of others may be abused. Although this aspect of constitutional law has been criticized regularly, it has not been changed by Congress. Moreover, recent polling suggests that most interactions with police are a positive experience (68%, 70%, and 82% for Black, Hispanic, and White adults, respectively).

At the same time, those experiencing negative interactions have a different view of policing. And in recent years, substantial criticism has occurred in the face of police misconduct. The deaths of George Floyd and Breonna Taylor, mentioned by Clark in the chapter, are two of the highest-profile events that caused a public outcry. Unfortunately, they are only a few of many problematic encounters that have occurred, especially in situations involving interactions between officers and non-White individuals. The encounters have created an atmosphere that makes collective bargaining more important to officers and the public less trusting of the contractual agreements that are made.

One aspect of policing today that was not covered in our Department of Justice report is the pervasive use of social media and real-time technology, such as body cameras and dashcams, that provides video and audio recordings of interactions between officers and people. Today's shot-spotter systems create a powerful tool for locating where gunshots have been fired, allowing a rapid police response. When officers respond, they are often filming and being filmed. However, the clarity of a video can be overshadowed by the context, as some interactions involve substantial nuance that requires careful judgment by a police officer. And one misstep can lead to tragedy. Those tragedies have often caused debate that bargaining has created barriers to holding police accountable for their actions.

Despite concerns about bargaining and dispute resolution procedures being used to protect bad police, it is possible to use bargaining more directly to help repair relationships between police unions and the public. We could do so in three ways. First, states and local governments can adjust their bargaining regulations specifically to handle issues of discipline, arbitrator decision authority in misconduct situations, and the use of technology (e.g., turning on the body camera). Such regulations will influence contract language and interpretation, which will affect outcomes. Specific adjustments here can protect officers' rights while ensuring public accountability within the boundaries set by state legislators.

Second, decisions must be made regarding the interaction and cooperation of police agencies, officers, and unions with elected and appointed police review boards that have been created in some localities. In some instances, there is no cooperation between these entities, which reduces public trust and generates ongoing friction between the police and the public. This does not serve hard-working, effective police officers or individuals in the community concerned about disparities in law enforcement tactics, approaches, or biases. Unless elected officials address this issue, ongoing friction ensures an undercurrent of disrespect for police in many places.

Third, decisions must be made regarding the education police need as well as the training required—both in an academy and on a regular follow-up basis. If determinations are made to create nonpolice response units for certain emergency calls, it is important to cross-train experts in those areas with police. All responders must coordinate effectively to provide the services expected by the public. Recent situations involving mass shootings have provided unfortunate guidance in that officers now need to be prepared to confront an armed individual by themselves before backup arrives. The training for such encounters is often inadequate, and department or agency policies differ across jurisdictions, creating additional danger to officers and the individuals they are seeking to protect. Many of these matters would typically be management prerogatives. They must blend seamlessly with collective agreements, however, to ensure that the outcome is in the best interest of all.

It will also be important for police agencies to make concerted efforts to recruit officers who are as diverse as the communities they serve. Officers also need to possess a variety of skills instead of a singular warrior mentality because police are often first on the scene in situations involving people in distress. In this regard, even something as basic as the nature of uniforms has been suggested to be important: some preferred by police agencies are more militaristic, which may invoke fear on the part of segments of the public.

The chapter on police provides a good overview of police unions, bargaining, and outcomes. It reaffirms the value of bargaining to police officers. At the same time, with the new technologies, challenges, and demands facing officers, more attention could be paid to how bargaining could help improve policing, which would better serve officers and the public.

COMMENTARY: THE RETAIL GROCERY INDUSTRY

Ruth Milkman
City University of New York

It is no secret that private sector union density in the United States has been in free fall for decades. Although this is often seen as the result of new technology and/or the export of jobs to the Global South, there are many relatively "low-tech" place-bound industries in which union density has also declined precipitously. One of them is the retail grocery industry, the focus of Michael Schuster's excellent chapter. He provides a useful overview of the dynamics of this industry and the current state of collective bargaining within it, along with a brief discussion of recent union organizing efforts. His account of the impact of the COVID-19 pandemic on the retail grocery sector is especially fascinating—although the extent to which the changes that took place during the lockdowns will endure into the post-pandemic era remains unclear. The chapter also highlights the case of Publix supermarkets, a vast, employee-owned grocery chain based in the Southeast, which is largely absent from the research literature on the industry.

Between 1986 and 2019, as Schuster's Figure 1 shows, the unionization rate in the retail grocery industry fell steadily (with some interruptions, most notably in 2003), although it remains the most highly organized segment of the retail sector. Over the period shown in Figure 1, union density in the retail grocery industry was cut in half, dropping from 27.9% to 14.0%—mirroring the nation's private sector as a whole, in which density was also halved over this period, falling from 13.8% in 1986 to 7.0% in 2019.

However, the retail grocery unionization rate reversed course during the pandemic lockdowns, rising to 17.7% in 2021 (the last data point shown in Figure 1). Schuster attributes this uptick to "hiring during the pandemic." By all accounts, retail grocery firms did hire more workers during the lockdown period, but that occurred in both unionized and nonunion stores. The density uptick in 2020 and 2021 shown in Figure 1 suggests that hiring in unionized groceries outpaced that in nonunion stores during those two years. But in 2022, the long-term downward trend resumed, as retail grocery density fell to 16.1%—still above the pre-pandemic level but not by much.

The true level of unionization in the retail grocery sector, however, is substantially lower than Figure 1 suggests—although it's hard to say exactly how much lower. This is no fault of Schuster's. We all rely on the same source of data on unionization rates: the US Current Population Survey's Outgoing Rotation Group (CPS-ORG). Thanks to Barry Hirsch, David McPherson, and William Even, disaggregated CPS-ORG data are easily accessible on the website www.unionstats.com. Drawing on that source, Schuster's Figure 1 shows the data for Census Industrial Category (CIC) 4970, "Grocery Stores." So far, so good.

But CIC 4970 does *not* include the largest single firm selling retail groceries—namely, the intransigently anti-union Walmart corporation, which entered the grocery business in 1988 and then proceeded to gain rapidly in market share. As Schuster notes, by the early 2020s, Walmart (along with its subsidiary, Sam's Club) accounted for about one-quarter of the US retail grocery market, more than any other company. In the CPS-ORG data (and thus on unionstats.com), Walmart is classified under CIC 5391, "General Merchandise Stores, Including Warehouse Clubs and Supercenters," which had a unionization rate of only 2.8% in 2022. The CIC 5391 rate would be even lower if not for its inclusion of the partly unionized Costco, which, as Schuster notes, is another major player, accounting for 7% of the nation's retail grocery market. Other firms in CIC 5391, like Target and K-Mart, also sell groceries to consumers and are just as resistant to unionism as Walmart, even if they have attracted far less public attention on that score. In recent years, large drugstore chains such as CVS and Walgreens have also begun selling groceries. They are classified in CIC 5070, "Pharmacies and Drug Stores," with a 2022 unionization rate of 4.6%.

But Walmart is unrivaled as the primary competitive threat to the nation's legacy unionized supermarkets, most of whose workers are represented by the United Food and Commercial Workers (UFCW). In recent years, criticism of Walmart has been relatively muted, as public attention has increasingly shifted to another notoriously anti-union company, Amazon, which has begun to make significant inroads in the retail grocery sector. Amazon acquired Whole Foods in 2017 and sells groceries via "Amazon Fresh" and through its general fulfillment centers as well. Amazon's share of the retail grocery market is still modest, but it is on a rapid growth path, as Schuster's Table 1 shows. Whole Foods (and the much smaller Amazon Go) *is* part of CIC 4970, and thus included in Figure 1, but the rest of Amazon's retail grocery business instead falls under CIC 5593, "Electronic Shopping and Mail-Order Houses," which had a 0.9% unionization rate in 2022.

In short, the data in Figure 1 are woefully incomplete, including only a portion of Amazon's retail grocery operations—and entirely omitting the single largest player in the industry, Walmart, as well as other nonunion companies selling groceries to consumers. The fragmented CIC classification system makes it extremely difficult to specify the true rate of union density in the overall retail grocery sector, but it is certainly well below what is shown in Figure 1. Even the data in that figure present a stark contrast to the 1960s, when about 40% of all US retail grocery workers were unionized.

Not only has union density declined dramatically in the industry over the past half-century, but the pay and benefits that unionized workers enjoy have also been substantially eroded, even where the UFCW retains a foothold. Competitive pressure from Walmart and other nonunion firms has generated steadily increasing pressure—at least prior to the pandemic—on the UFCW to make concessions in collective bargaining with the legacy union supermarkets, whose traditional business model has become less and less viable. As a UFCW staffer told me in a 2020 interview, "The union operators have higher costs because they're actually investing in their workforce. They're providing better wages and benefits than the nonunion employer."

That statement demands one qualification: as Schuster points out, starting pay is often *higher* at stores like Whole Foods or Trader Joe's than in unionized supermarkets, which appeals to many of the young workers such stores recruit, who do not envision long-term careers in the industry. But workers who accumulate seniority in unionized stores eventually attain much higher wage rates, along with far superior fringe benefits, than in the nonunion stores. Indeed, by the turn of the 21st century, unionized supermarket worker pay and benefit costs (including health insurance and pensions) were about 30% higher than Walmart's.

Ironically, and presumably unintentionally, the 2010 Affordable Care Act (ACA) added to the difficulties facing unionized grocery store workers. Historically, UFCW contracts provided defined benefit pension plans and excellent health insurance benefits for full-time workers, and only slightly less comprehensive benefits for part-timers. But once the ACA required employers to offer health insurance only to workers averaging 30 hours or more a week, the unionized supermarket firms were incentivized to dramatically increase the part-time share of their workforce, and they proceeded to do precisely that. Part-time union jobs not only have inferior fringe benefits but, as in the nonunion sector, are typically subject to unpredictable and fluctuating schedules.

In short, as unionization declined, and unrelenting competitive pressures hollowed out pay and benefit standards for the dwindling ranks of remaining union members, retail grocery store jobs across the nation were transformed from relatively well-paid jobs with excellent benefits into far less desirable, more precarious ones. Today, only a minority of workers in the industry are unionized, and the vast nonunion majority have generally inferior compensation (apart from higher starting hourly wages in many cases) and neither employment security nor the ability to voice their on-the-job concerns freely to management.

Schuster points out that the COVID-19 pandemic not only brought an uptick in unionization in the industry, as noted above, but also higher wage rates in the form of "hazard pay," reflecting increased public attention to the challenges facing grocery store workers who were among those branded "essential." Even after the lockdowns ended, persistent labor shortages enabled the UFCW to negotiate significant contract improvements, most notably in Southern California and New England in 2022, and to launch several successful strikes.

The pandemic also helped fuel rising public support for unions generally and galvanized a burst of new labor organizing efforts among workers at retail companies such as Starbucks, Apple, and Amazon, attracting widespread media and public attention. These recent union drives have been disproportionately led by young workers, many of them college educated—precisely the demographic that nonunion grocers such as Trader Joe's and Whole Foods have long recruited to staff their stores. As Schuster notes, among these recent organizing campaigns are several targeting just such employers.

The most successful of these campaigns have been led by independent unions. For example, in mid-2022, workers at a Trader Joe's in Hadley, Massachusetts, formed "Trader Joe's United," which went on to launch organizing campaigns around the country and won National Labor Relations Board (NLRB) elections at Trader Joe's stores in Hadley, Minneapolis, Louisville, and Oakland (while losing elections at a few other locations). But collective bargaining efforts at Trader Joe's have stalled amid reports of managerial foot-dragging. Another independent union, also led by young workers, recently won elections at several New Seasons markets in the Portland, Oregon, area; it too is facing vigorous resistance at the bargaining table. The first and largest such organizing campaign (although only partly focused on retail groceries) was that of the independent Amazon Labor Union, which won an NLRB election on Staten Island in April 2021; like the others, it has faced strong management opposition at every turn.

To date, none of these efforts has yielded a first contract, and their scale has been far too modest to move the needle on union density in the grocery industry. It is too early to know whether such organizing efforts will continue in the face of the unrelenting managerial pushback they routinely engender. Despite the lack of any concrete results at the bargaining table, these efforts have brought renewed public attention to the dysfunctional state of US labor law. Nevertheless, at this writing, there is no basis to dispute Schuster's concluding prediction that "the industry will likely continue to be dominated by nonunion employers."

COMMENTARY: ACHIEVING HARMONY

Rochelle G. Skolnick
American Federation of Musicians

On December 8, 2022, the Fort Wayne Philharmonic musicians elected orchestra committee walked out of yet another fruitless bargaining session after announcing to the employer's bargaining team that the musicians were beginning a strike. The musicians of the orchestra had voted overwhelmingly the previous month to authorize that strike. The strike lasted three months and was the first ever in the nearly 80-year history of the Fort Wayne Philharmonic. When it ended on March 7, 2023, the musicians had accomplished everything they set out to accomplish in the strike. The resulting deal included historic gains in compensation, but more important, musicians had defeated a push by their employer to greatly expand management rights and to diminish musicians' ability to resolve issues and disputes that arise during the term of the contract.[1]

This comment narrows the focus from the wider context Chandler and Gely develop in their excellent analysis of collective bargaining in the symphonic industry to draw insights from the recent labor history of the Fort Wayne Philharmonic, including the musicians' three-month strike. This case study moves us from the comparatively rarified air of the International Conference of Symphony and Opera Musicians (ICSOM) of major orchestras to one of the 86 Regional Orchestra Players Association (ROPA) orchestras referenced in passing by Chandler and Gely. The ROPA orchestras and their musicians share much in common with their larger, better-paid counterparts in ICSOM. This comment also takes the reader "behind the curtain" to provide insight into typical American Federation of Musicians (AFM) bargaining practices and highlights the way the bargaining in Fort Wayne—and especially the musicians' organizing work in support of that bargaining—relates to the labor movement in 2023, as expressed in the symphonic industry.

The Fort Wayne Philharmonic has been in existence since 1944, with predecessor organizations in existence since 1924.[2] It is consistently within the top ten ROPA orchestras in terms of annual budget, with a budget typically around $5.5 million. It has an unusually large endowment of approximately $30 million for an orchestra of its size. In the 2019–2020 season, the orchestra employed 44 full-time musicians, who were paid a minimum annual salary of just over $26,000, and 19 "per service" musicians who were guaranteed employment for 81 services (and minimum annual compensation of just under $10,000) during the orchestra's 33-week season. Musicians receive pension contributions to the AFM and employers pension fund, and full-time musicians are eligible to participate in the employer's health insurance plan at subsidized rates.

The musicians of the Fort Wayne Philharmonic are represented by Local 58 of the American Federation of Musicians and have been since 1958, when they obtained their first collective bargaining agreement (CBA). As is now almost universally the practice in the industry and codified in the AFM bylaws,[3] Local 58 recognizes a committee of orchestra musicians elected by their peers not only to serve as "liaison between the orchestra players and the Local" but also to sit at the bargaining table side by side with local officers in contract negotiations and to assist the local in contract administration and enforcement. As is common in the symphonic industry, the orchestra committee in Fort Wayne functions more or less as union steward and as the conduit for the voices of all bargaining unit musicians, vis-à-vis both the local union and the employer.[4] The orchestra committee is threaded throughout the CBA, fulfilling various roles in contract administration. It is also written into the contractual grievance process.[5]

In preparation for bargaining, orchestra committees survey their colleagues and formulate proposals based on the resulting data and other factors, including any disputes that have arisen during the term of the existing contract and prevailing economic forces. Taken together with the ratification required by AFM bylaws for all symphonic CBAs, this representative committee structure gives orchestra musicians a high degree of democratic input and direct control over their own contract negotiations and enforcement of the resulting contracts.

Orchestra committees and AFM locals with symphonic CBAs receive support for collective bargaining from the AFM International Union's Symphonic Services Division (SSD), which collects and makes available to AFM members an archive of CBAs and other labor-education resources. The division also maintains the "Wage Scales and Conditions in the Symphony Orchestra," which compiles certain key terms and conditions from each of the CBAs of the three symphonic player conference orchestras and makes them available in chart format and through an interactive database that allows musicians to cross-reference and compare these terms and conditions across and among orchestras. SSD also offers the services of a staff of three professional (nonlawyer) negotiators who assist orchestra committees and locals in all stages of bargaining, along with legal support for their work. Each year, SSD negotiators assist in bargaining 30 to 40 contracts with regional orchestras in the United States.[6] The AFM also maintains a Symphony–Opera Orchestra Strike Fund, which provides musicians in participating orchestras a weekly benefit for up to 15 weeks of a strike or lockout.

As Chandler and Gely highlight in their paper, symphonic labor disputes in the present moment often have ties to the parties' labor history. The Fort Wayne Philharmonic strike of 2022–2023 was the product of an often troubled labor history between the parties that became truly fractious during the first year of the COVID-19 pandemic. When the pandemic erupted in the spring of 2020, the musicians of the Fort Wayne Philharmonic were engaged in bargaining a successor CBA with one that had expired August 31, 2019. The committee and Local 58 representatives were assisted in bargaining by SSD negotiator Chris Durham, who had worked with the musicians in Fort Wayne for decades. The parties began bargaining in late June 2019 and engaged the services of a mediator from the Federal Mediation and Conciliation

Services (FMCS) in December 2019. They were moving closer to a deal by February 2020 when the employer presented a comprehensive proposal that closed the gap between its prior positions and the musicians' position on economics and other key issues. From the musicians' perspective, all that remained was to iron out a few last details and do some wordsmithing, and bargaining would be complete.

Unfortunately, COVID intervened. Before the musicians could respond to the employer's February 2020 proposal, COVID closed concert halls and brought a halt to all live performance activities. The musicians pivoted immediately to consideration of the terms for virtual performances, special allowances for distribution of electronic media content, and safety protocols to allow some smaller-scale work to continue. Rather than meeting with musicians to engage in these talks, the employer in April rescinded its February proposal, citing the uncertainty generated by the pandemic. Even after this rescission, management stonewalled, refusing to meet with musicians but paying their wages for the remainder of the spring of 2020, aided by money from a CARES Act Paycheck Protection Program loan.

When the parties finally met on July 15, it was only to allow the employer to inform the musicians that concerts had been cancelled and they would be furloughed without compensation until at least the start of 2021. During this same period, the majority of symphony orchestra musicians elsewhere had bargained modifications to their CBAs to allow work to proceed virtually and/or on a smaller scale, with safety protocols in place and special electronic media provisions bargained by the AMF, as touched on by Chandler and Gely.[7] Those musicians continued to be compensated, most of them at rates somewhat reduced by agreement from those provided in existing CBAs.

Almost immediately after announcing the furloughs, the employer began to hear from donors concerned about musicians going without wages for the fall season. In response, the employer reached out to musicians to begin talks about "how to engage musicians during the furlough." The parties came close to reaching agreement on terms similar to those that had been hammered out by other orchestras, but as the substantive terms for the fall of 2020 were agreed on, the form of the agreement became an issue. The musicians proposed to extend the expired CBA and include the terms for the fall of 2020 in a side letter that would expire one day before the CBA extension it modified. This would ensure that, at expiration of the short-term deal, the terms of the expired CBA would once again be the status quo that would govern the parties' relationship postexpiration, pursuant to *NLRB v. Katz*, 369 US 736 (1962). The employer, on the other hand, refused to extend the CBA at all and wanted the terms of the short-term deal to serve as the post-expiration status quo. The employer's approach would have jettisoned the entirety of the parties' mature 36-page CBA in favor of a three-page document outlining basic terms for a three-month period. The union viewed this as destructive and unworkable. The parties were unable to resolve this dispute prior to the employer's self-imposed August 31 deadline. Rather than declare impasse and implement its own proposal, which would at least have provided the musicians with nine weeks of work and compensation during the 18-week fall season, the employer followed through on its plan to completely furlough the musicians.[8] The musicians remained furloughed without any compensation until June 2021.

While the musicians were furloughed, the parties restarted bargaining a successor CBA. On September 28, 2020, the employer presented a comprehensive proposal for a new agreement. That proposal sought to reduce the number of musicians on contract from 63 to 15 and eliminate employer-provided health insurance and pension contributions. It also included noneconomic proposals to erode the musicians' working conditions, including the removal of industry-standard provisions concerning musician input into certain artistic decisions and protections against arbitrary terminations of musicians for artistic reasons. The employer's September 28, 2020, proposal represented a radical departure from the one it had made in February of that same year, with terms far less favorable to musicians.

This proposal, which the union viewed as unlawfully regressive,[9] coupled with the fact that the musicians had been furloughed without pay during a global pandemic, provided the musicians with strong issues around which to organize themselves and appeal to the community. The musicians formed several committees to manage various tasks. A self-care committee helped the musicians organize their resources to support one another with activities such as babysitting, car repairs, and home maintenance. Outreach and media committees took charge of producing the musicians' Players' Voice newsletter (available by email to anyone who signed up to receive it), created a "power map" identifying allies and other sources of support for the musicians, and oversaw their website and Facebook page. A concerts committee led the work of presenting musician-produced concerts to the public, filling the void left by the employer's concert cancelations. And an action committee organized demonstrations at various sites around Fort Wayne, including Philharmonic board members' businesses. The musicians' activities and their outreach to members of the press garnered significant and largely favorable press coverage through the winter of 2020 and spring of 2021. Providing additional support, Local 58 reinforced its connections to state and local labor federations.

The musicians' public actions culminated in a May 1, 2021, rally in front of the Allen County Courthouse attended by community members, representatives of other labor unions, musicians from throughout the Midwest, and local politicians. Meanwhile, prompted by Region 25 of the National Labor Relations Board's February 24, 2021, issuance of a complaint against the employer concerning the employer's September 28 regressive proposal, the parties reopened talks aimed at reaching agreement on a deal that would put musicians back to work in the summer of 2021 through the end of the 2021–2022 season. On May 21, 2021, with the assistance of an FMCS mediator, the parties reached an agreement on terms for a deal nominally effective from September 1, 2019, through August 31, 2022. The musicians went back to work a month later. The deal, which actually covered only an 11-month period of work from June 2021 through May 2022, paid the musicians more for that period than they had ever earned.[10] It incorporated most of the changes the parties had agreed on in bargaining prior to the pandemic shutdowns but cut the season length from 33 to 28 weeks for the 2021–2022 season. The musicians mostly viewed it as a success under the circumstances, with one major exception: the employer refused to build into the agreement a restoration of the 33-week season length, signaling that it remained attached to a vision of a shorter, less costly season going forward. Because of this, the musicians predicted that the next round of bargaining (which would begin just over a year later) would be difficult, as they sought to recover weeks of work and compensation.

Armed with this foresight, the musicians never deactivated the internal organizing infrastructure they had built to weather the pandemic shutdowns and related labor disputes. Bargaining for a new contract began in August 2022. Despite the fact that the parties were bargaining in a period of record inflation and beginning with a five-week-shorter season length than in 2019, the employer came to the table seeking a freeze in wages and weeks of work. The employer also sought to convert to part-time status three of the orchestra's 44 full-time positions and to create a more restrictive attendance policy, limiting musicians' ability to supplement their income through other employment. Of equal concern was an employer proposal to greatly expand the CBA's management rights provision and to eliminate part of the grievance process that required the parties to negotiate "a reasonable and mutually agreeable settlement in good faith" when "a question arises the disposition of which is not otherwise provided for" in the CBA.[11] Musicians, for their part, sought recovery from the cuts they had agreed to during the pandemic bargaining, including increases in weekly salary and per-service wage rates, and restoration of lost weeks of work.

By the time the committee exercised the authority they had been given by the bargaining unit to call a strike on December 8, 2022, the parties had held nine bargaining sessions over more than three months and were still far apart. The strike led the Philharmonic to cancel the weekend's holiday pops concerts[12] but, thanks to their robust organizational structure, the musicians quickly planned and presented their own holiday concert at a local church to a capacity audience on December 10, with a second concert on December 18. The musicians also launched pickets, which were well attended by both the musicians themselves and numerous supporters from the community and other labor organizations. The musician-produced concerts and pickets drew attention from the press and the public. The musicians also began collecting benefits from the AFM Strike Fund.[13]

With the strike in progress, the parties continued to bargain, finally closing the gap between their positions, at least with regard to wages. By January 7, 2023, the parties had agreed on wage increases amounting to 3.75% in each year of a four-year agreement. Notwithstanding this accord, the employer's other proposals kept the parties apart for another two months. Of particular interest was the employer's insistence on its changes to management rights and grievance provisions—and the musicians' messaging around these issues. Far from the kind of "bread-and-butter" issues such as wages and benefits that usually drive work stoppages, these remaining issues were largely theoretical and very much "inside baseball" for labor professionals.

Conventional wisdom would have suggested that solidarity among the bargaining unit and engagement by the public and press would falter once an agreement was reached on wages. Defying the odds, the musicians managed to message successfully around these issues both internally and externally, decrying the employer's proposal to replace "industry standard workplace bargaining rights with dictatorial power in the hands of management"[14] and similar rhetoric, while also emphasizing the employer's robust financial position, including an endowment approaching $30 million. Press coverage increased, with local news outlets publishing both news stories and op-ed pieces about the strike and the future of the institution.

Finally, on March 7, the parties reached an agreement. The employer withdrew its proposals to cut full-time musicians, to modify the attendance policy, and to change the management rights and grievance provisions. The final agreement included the wage increases previously agreed to and afforded the employer additional flexibility in scheduling. Although the number of work weeks remained below the pre-pandemic level, the parties agreed to increase that number from 28 to 30. The new agreement was ratified overwhelmingly by the musicians, who gave their first post-strike performances on March 14.

The musicians in Fort Wayne are hardly alone among orchestra musicians in their willingness to engage in concerted activities in support of their bargaining aims. In 2023, musicians from orchestras of all sizes took public action in support of their bargaining positions. For example, the musicians of the Minnesota Opera orchestra engaged in a robust leafletting and social media campaign during a period of difficult bargaining, drawing attention by entering the opera pit en masse to audience cheers prior to a performance of Donizetti's "The Daughter of the Regiment." The musicians went so far as to take a strike authorization vote and make picket signs, but ultimately, a strike was narrowly averted. The musicians of the Philadelphia Orchestra leafletted to patrons and demonstrated their solidarity by wearing bright blue t-shirts emblazoned with Local 77 insignia to a rehearsal at which orchestra board members were in attendance, also demonstrating their solidarity. Philadelphia Orchestra Music Director Yannick Nezet-Seguin showed his solidarity with musicians by wearing the same t-shirt, echoing Riccardo Muti's support for Chicago Symphony musicians during their strike.[15] The parties finally reached agreement without resorting to a strike, although there, too, the musicians had authorized their bargaining team to call one if necessary. Collective action is flourishing on the organizing front as well, with the musicians of both the Colorado Music Festival and the Eastern Music Festival voting overwhelmingly in 2023 to be represented by locals of the AFM.[16]

A groundswell of collective action among orchestra musicians is not really surprising at a time when a Gallup poll shows that public support for labor unions is at a 57-year high, and the president of the United States walked the picket line with striking members of the United Auto Workers. Chandler and Gely point out that numerous factors are creating uncertainty about the future of symphony orchestras, but one thing appears certain: the musicians of AFM-represented orchestras are well equipped to meet the challenges of the future with collective action.

ENDNOTES

1. Bloomberg Law placed the Fort Wayne settlement ninth on a list of the largest pay increases in union contracts between September 2022 and August 2023. (Combs, R. 2023. "Analysis: Is a 36% Raise Too High? It Wasn't for These 23 CBAs." Bloomberg Law. September 26. https://tinyurl.com/44n8924t
2. "About the Phil." https://fwphil.org/about-the-phil
3. AFM bylaws, Article 5, Section 37.
4. Article 1.02 of the CBA recognizes the existence of the orchestra committee and provides that it "shall serve as the liaison between the Philharmonic, the Musicians and the Local concerning Contractual matters, including negotiation of the Master Agreement, and shall perform such other duties as are assigned to it by the provisions of this Agreement." Although the CBA provides for a number of types of committees on which musicians participate, in Article 5.06 the employer "acknowledges that only the Orchestra Committee may represent the official views of the collective Musicians."
5. Article 18 of the CBA.
6. Two additional SSD staff members provide similar assistance to Canadian orchestra musicians.
7. These special provisions were included in side letters to the Integrated Media Agreement between the AFM and the Employers' Electronic Media Association, to which the Fort Wayne Philharmonic is signatory.
8. On October 5, 2020, Local 58 filed an unfair labor practice charge against the employer with Region 25 of the NLRB alleging that the furloughs constituted unlawful unilateral changes. On January 22, 2021, Region 25 dismissed the charge, finding that emergent circumstances regarding the pandemic had privileged the employer to implement the furloughs.
9. In fact, On November 10, 2020, the union filed an unfair labor practice charge alleging that the employer's September 28, 2020, proposal constituted regressive bargaining, in part because many of the noneconomic proposals bore no relation to any possible COVID-related economic hardship for the employer that might have justified less favorable terms for musicians. Region 25 agreed with the union, finding merit in the charge and issuing a formal complaint against the employer on February 24, 2021. The case was set for hearing on June 2, but on the eve of trial, the union agreed to withdraw the charge in connection with the parties' agreement on terms for the 2019–2022 CBA.
10. This compensation included "furlough offset pay" of $4,000 for each full-time musician and $2,000 for each per-service musician.
11. Article 18.02.
12. Employers in the symphony orchestra industry have never succeeded in engaging replacement workers to take the place of striking musicians. The AFM maintains an "international unfair list" on which employers are placed at the request of a local that has a primary labor dispute with that employer. AFM members are instructed not to work for an employer on the unfair list. Because of the high degree of union density in the symphonic sector, placement on the unfair list makes it virtually impossible for an orchestra to hire replacement musicians. Further, given that ticket sales constitute only about a third of a typical symphony orchestra budget, performing concerts almost always costs the institution more than it nets. These factors lead orchestra employers to simply cease operations during a musicians' strike.
13. The musicians had increased the level of their participation in that fund in anticipation of a potential work stoppage. Those benefits, along with numerous donations from members of the community and other AFM musicians around the country, helped sustain the musicians during the three-month strike.

14. "Philharmonic Management Thwarts Resolution in Latest Talks with Musicians." 2023. Press Release. February 5. https://tinyurl.com/5d3885pj

15. Such public shows of support from music directors are quite rare. Music directors usually place themselves above the fray of a labor dispute.

16. Organizing drives are especially notable given the already-high union density in the symphonic sector.

COMMENTARY: LABOR RELATIONS IN MUSEUMS AND AMONG STUDENTS

John T. Delaney
Saint Vincent College

In the 1950s, at the peak of union density in the United States, the labor movement primarily served workers who had not attended college. Those workers may have been skilled tradespeople in construction, truck drivers, or assembly line workers in a factory, among others. They banded together and leveraged support from a union and collective bargaining to protect their interests in a working relationship with a powerful employer. Whether the worker was young or old, the union contract provided collective rights and protections. And it seemed that such protections were not needed by college-educated workers because they constituted the management levels that ran the organizations populated by unionized workers.

By the early 2000s, technology improvements, employer opposition, lessening government and legal support for unionization, and other factors shaped a different and smaller labor movement. Many of the ideal-type workers ripe for unionization in the 1950s no longer belonged to unions, precipitating a dramatic decline in union density. The situation created a crisis for organized labor and led to much speculation among labor relations observers on what type of representation workers wanted and what the future held for the union movement.

At the same time, the college-educated segment of society grew over the years, and social justice causes supported by unions aligned with the sentiments of many young, college-educated workers. Students supported various union efforts, including product boycotts and justice marches. In addition, union growth occurred in some sectors requiring higher levels of education, such as nursing, and unions invested more in efforts aimed at younger, highly educated workers outside of the for-profit sector. As the chapters on museums and college students illustrate, labor has gotten some traction in those sectors. Stimulated initially by concerns about social justice and the effects of the pandemic, workers in those sectors showed interest in having a say in the terms and conditions of their employment.

The chapter by Julius, Abrams, and Baron illustrates the situation in museums over the past few years. It explains how changes in the management and operation of museums, lagging compensation, and employees' sense of growing inequality increased interest in unionization among museum employees. Those employees—younger, more diverse than prior museum workers, well educated, and less frequently from privileged backgrounds—had an interest in using collective action to improve working conditions at their museum. And most museums avoided the aggressive anti-union approaches used by private sector employers, precipitating an increase in unionization.

The chapter by Julius, DiGiovanni, and Abrams on unionization among undergraduate students provides an overview of a sector where interest in unions has increased rapidly. Recognition of graduate-student bargaining units, initially in public universities in states with favorable labor laws, has spread over the years to other universities, including some elite institutions. While undergraduate bargaining units typically did not exist, some undergraduates became union members by taking a job in an organized unit of a university. In recent years, however, policy changes by the National Labor Relations Board (NLRB) have facilitated organizing by undergraduate workers and opened a new avenue for union growth. The situation is ever more interesting given the desire by some student athletes to unionize.

These two chapters provide much context for speculation about the labor movement's future. Across the chapters, a common theme emerges. In each of these sectors, shared governance is a fundamental part of the industry. In museums, the employees and the managers all support the mission of the museum, whether historical or focused on art or another specialty. In colleges, students are exposed to a liberal view of the purpose of education—one emphasizing academic freedom, examination of all perspectives, and open discussion. The view is often supported by their faculty, who hold similar views, as well as university policies. The context of shared governance supports by extension the notion that employees, including student workers, should be treated equitably and potentially have a say in their employment terms.

Higher levels of education among workers in these sectors likely supports views on the importance of shared governance. The age of workers may also be relevant because younger workers dominate in lower job levels and express strong views on why elements of unfairness, including student debt and inequality in society, should be reduced or eliminated. Such workers are sympathetic toward unions. The general views of these workers about equity and fair outcomes combine with their willingness to take action and employers' unwillingness to use anti-union tactics to generate union organizing victories.

Although student workers have been represented by unions in various universities and roles for many years, the interesting new development is an expansion toward undergraduates and the unknown factor of whether college athletes are eligible to unionize. Julius, DiGiovanni, and Abrams note the potential for conflicts between unions organizing students and those organizing faculty as faculty control over academics, including evaluation of research assistants, could be questioned by unions supporting undergraduate students. In my view, this issue will be overshadowed by two others in the coming years.

First, it is likely that NLRB policy on undergraduate unionization will continue to change and evolve. It will change based on the views of NLRB members appointed by presidents with liberal or with conservative views. This unsettled situation will create a laboratory for research and an opportunity to understand the effects of unionization on undergraduate students and the way it develops. If students view college jobs as temporary, their interest in work outcomes may wane even as their interest in liberal causes remains. At the same time, with strong sentiment against student debt, undergraduate unions could push for approaches that constrain the ability of universities to provide the quality of education that is expected. Collective bargaining with undergraduates could be a vehicle that shifts college debt costs from the government to universities. This in turn could hasten the demise of many colleges and reduce the quality of others. Even the elite schools that may be open to unionization of undergraduates will face risks from their negotiated contracts.

Second, the crisis over college athletics ensures that any instances of bargaining by sports teams or athletes more generally will be covered substantially in the media. With issues associated with name-image-likeness (NIL) money and the transfer portal already disrupting college athletics, the potential for bargaining to set parameters for all athletes, including those with little NIL power, could bring about a dramatic change in college sports. In combination with the huge increase in legalized sports betting, the path for college athletics is already narrow, and unionization of undergraduate athletes could fundamentally challenge universities.

Unionization among undergraduates could also disintegrate if bargaining unit members seek outcomes that are broader than the context that bargaining can support. If students want more than wages, benefits, and other terms and conditions of employment, they may disagree on what to seek, which could reduce support for the union. They could also cause faculty to push back against pressure regarding a say in grades or other classroom conditions.

Although unionization among museum employees is a sectoral matter that will evolve in ways that may help the labor movement, the long-term effect of unionization among undergraduates could be monumental. In the 1960s and 1970s, students supported liberal causes, including unions. Organized labor supported social causes that were viewed as just and garnered support from students in return. Over the years, however, those students did not become aggressively pro-union. As Boomers aged, they became more conservative. The unknown here is whether extensive unionization of undergraduates in the 2020s would produce strong pro-union views among a large part of the population in the 2040s and beyond. If so, the investment by unions in undergraduates could alter labor's future. In such a case, over a period of 150 years, the labor movement will have gone from a supporter of craft and factory workers to one engaging educated workers in the professions, offices, and virtual spaces. What a transformation.

Workers in museums and student workers might have been curiosities in labor volumes in the past. They are central in this one, reflecting a change in the labor movement and orientation of young and highly educated people. Continuing developments in these sectors will provide predictions on union growth and suggest whether temporary unionization gains today will generate a stronger labor movement in the future.

COMMENTARY: EMERGING LABOR RELATIONS IN HIGH-TECH INDUSTRIES

Adrienne E. Eaton and Hanna Xue
Rutgers University

We commend the authors for their insights into the high-tech industry. Compared with many industries, describing labor relations in this sector is difficult, and the authors provided many compelling and useful examples of organizing and bargaining cases. We learned much from the chapter and offer this commentary as a supplement instead of a major critique.

We will focus our comments on four points. The first addresses the definition of the industry and its associated occupations. The second involves the intertwining issues of identity-based organizing and collective action and forms of organization. The identity piece takes its inspiration from a call for more focus in industrial relations scholarship on issues of identity and intersectionality. Closely related to this point, we also seek to expand the field's thinking about new forms of labor organization and collective bargaining. The third issue involves the traditional unionization of IT occupations that are organized as part of other units, including in the public sector. We think there may be something to be learned from this phenomenon, drawing on our own workplace as an example. Finally, we end with a paragraph on a new agreement between Microsoft and the AFL-CIO.

What Is the High-Tech Sector?

The authors of the chapter define this sector as including companies producing "computer-related devices, software development and services related to the Internet of Things" plus eight occupational "clusters of workers using emerging technologies," ranging from programmers and software engineers to technical support, Web development, network design, and beyond. We think the focus on high-tech workers and occupations may make more sense than focusing on entire companies. Part of the problem with the company focus is that many companies with a significant high-tech component, such as Uber, Lyft, DoorDash, Handy, Taskrabbit, and Amazon—despite their protests otherwise—fundamentally provide a service (transportation, food delivery, cleaning, household tasks, retail) enabled by their digital platform. We recognize that the programmers and coders who maintain the platform or digital infrastructure should be viewed as part of the high-tech sector, but it's less clear that drivers, cleaners, deliverers, and warehouse workers should be. In traditional industrial relations theoretical terms, a central purpose of unions is to take wages out of competition. Amazon's competition, in their central business, for instance, is the rest of the retail sector, and Uber and Lyft (out)compete the taxi industry. We also note that it is very tempting to focus on the low-wage workers involved in these platforms, given that there is a lot of attention to, and much written on, organizing at Amazon and among driving and delivery platforms like Uber—and less activity among high-tech workers themselves.

Identity
Gender

Perhaps the most salient identity issue in high-tech firms, those we think of as constituting Silicon Valley and employing large numbers of coders, is gender. Sexual harassment is mentioned in the chapter but is likely a symptom of a much broader problem with organizational culture. Infamously, in 2017, Google software engineer James Damore circulated a memo criticizing the company's diversity policies by arguing that biological differences, not discrimination, accounted for the lack of representation of women in tech positions. While the publication of this memo elicited serious backlash leading Google to terminate Damore's employment, the memo reflects the reality that women attempting to break into the high-tech industry must face—a culture of hostility and resistance to gender diversity initiatives. Historically, women not only accounted for 40% of computer science degrees awarded in the 1980s, but they also made essential early contributions to the field, such as writing the very first computer program. Today, however, women account for only 22% of computer science degrees and remain staggeringly underrepresented in tech for a variety of complex structural and systemic reasons.

The organizational culture in high-tech exposes women to constant and widespread sexual harassment and discrimination. Lawsuits against Activision Blizzard, one of the country's largest video game companies, resulting from the company's treatment of women, as well as gender-based harassment and discrimination claims, exemplify these issues. In 2021, an initial lawsuit filed against Activision by the State of California uncovered a "pervasive 'frat boy' workplace culture" at the company that created a "breeding ground for harassment and discrimination." The Equal Employment Opportunity Commission (EEOC) filed an additional lawsuit around the same time, after a two-year investigation discovered countless incidents of sexual harassment, such as comments and groping, and that the Human Resources Department treated these complaints in a "perfunctory and dismissive manner." Human Resources also failed to keep complaints confidential, resulting in multiple incidents of retaliation through layoffs, deprivation of projects, and forced transfers to different units for victims of harassment or discrimination. Both lawsuits also revealed that management constantly assigned women to lower-paid positions with fewer opportunities for advancement. Amid these lawsuits, a media report that the CEO knew about rampant sexual misconduct but refused to notify the board of directors led over 100 Activision employees to walk out, demanding his resignation. While Activision eventually settled its lawsuit with the EEOC in 2022, the Communications Workers of America (CWA) called the $18 million settlement "woefully inadequate," with many other company critics agreeing. Importantly, gender equity and sexual harassment represented salient issues in union organizing at Activision later that year.

In addition to workplace retaliation, there has also been intense public backlash against women in high-tech speaking out about the harassment and discrimination they face. For example, the Gamergate campaign (2014–2015) involved online death threats, sexual harassment, and stalking, especially toward women openly criticizing the industry's mistreatment of them.

Calls to end mandatory arbitration policies represent an important way through which collective action in the high-tech industry has tried to target a major barrier to discouraging widespread sexual harassment and discrimination. In an industry afflicted by sexual misconduct, activists argue that mandatory arbitration allows offenders to escape accountability and consequences by forcing victims to settle privately instead of taking their cases to public courts. On November 1, 2018, over 20,000 Google employees walked out of their jobs in protest against the "lenient treatment of executives accused of misconduct," demanding an end to mandatory arbitration in harassment and discrimination cases in addition to ending pay and opportunity inequity and increasing transparency. The walkout represented an important point of inflection: later that month, Google announced they would end mandatory arbitration, and Facebook followed suit quickly thereafter. In 2022, continued demands to end mandatory arbitration and increase accountability for companies led Congress to pass a bill banning companies from using the practice to handle cases of sexual misconduct.

Race/Ethnicity

A central problem in the high-tech sector as it concerns race is the very small percentage of the workforce that is Black. The Silicon Valley Index showed that Black workers are the least represented minority group in the Silicon Valley high-tech workforce, constituting only 2% of the workforce at many of the top firms.[1] Other research provides similar statistics and reflects on their meaning for Black workers in the sector. In 2018, Black employees made up only 2.8% of Google's technical roles and 4.8% of their entire workforce.

Given the low number of Black employees in the sector, much of the labor activism (broadly defined) focuses on hiring. For instance, Jesse Jackson and Rainbow Push began a campaign in 2014 to push high-tech companies to diversify hiring at all levels. Judging by the lack of change in the numbers, the campaign has not been particularly successful.

Within tech companies, activism has come from Black employee resource groups (ERGs). During the height of the Black Lives Matter protests following the murder of George Floyd in 2020, many US corporations, including those in the high-tech sector, began to confront their records on racial issues and respond to internal and external activist pressure. Interestingly, ERGs, long thought to be focused on mentoring and peer-to-peer support, became the vehicle for collective action and corporate response. *The Washington Post* ran a story in June 2020 for which they interviewed several current and former leaders of ERGs, reporting that they were being asked to bear the burden of diversity work, often effectively taking on a second job. As one former ERG leader put it, "We joined the ERG because we needed help, but we became the help." The article describes companies relying on ERGs to "host panels on race, vet company statements, allocate donations to racial justice nonprofits, and shepherd new diversity initiatives." At the same time, ERGs pushed companies to commit to hiring more executives from "underrepresented groups," offering Juneteenth as a paid holiday and sharing demographic data.

Caste

Another salient issue around identity has arisen within the large Indian community that works in the high-tech sector, especially in California and in the Silicon Valley. According to the Migration Policy Institute, nearly 89,000 Indians live in the Silicon Valley, and a vast majority work in the tech industry. Researchers have emphasized the prominence of caste issues, reporting that Indian workers with bachelor's degrees made up 27% of tech workers in Santa Clara and San Mateo counties in 2021. This issue has resulted in some collective action, though not, as far as we know, within the traditional union and collective bargaining framework.

The issue of Hindu caste discrimination in the Silicon Valley received widespread media and public attention in 2020, when the State of California filed a discrimination lawsuit against Cisco Systems and two of its engineers for caste discrimination. The complainant was a Dalit, known in India as "untouchables"; he alleged pay discrimination, reduced opportunities, and retaliation for raising these issues within the company.[2] The nongovernmental organization Equality Labs has organized to fight caste discrimination, including through legislative proposals in a number of states, the best known of which is the recently governor-vetoed bill in California. Shortly after the Cisco lawsuit was filed, "more than 250 Dalits from Google, Facebook, Microsoft, Apple, Netflix, and dozens of others in Silicon Valley [came] forward to report discrimination, bullying, ostracization, and even sexual harassment by colleagues who are higher-caste Indians. The data included multiple complaints from Dalit employees at other large companies such as Twitter, Dell, Uber, and Lyft, as well as smaller tech-sector companies."

A Dalit interviewed for a *Vice* story claimed that "Brahmin Indians ... have established powerful cliques within many of Silicon Valley's biggest companies" and exclude Dalits from career opportunities and social interactions at work. "I think that every single tech company is vulnerable," Thenmozhi Soundarajan, director of Equality Labs, told *Vice*. Later that same year, in another collective action, 30 women Dalit engineers working in Silicon Valley, issued a statement published by the *Washington Post* alleging "that they routinely face caste discrimination" and urging American companies to adopt caste as a protected category to eradicate caste-based discrimination in the US tech industry.

An Example of High-Tech (IT) Workers in Non-High-Tech Organizations

The authors of the chapter note that they "suspect that the majority of unionized high-tech workers are covered by collective bargaining agreements in other types of industries, not necessarily in the high-tech industry." We share this suspicion. Several IT job titles at our own university are union represented, strangely enough, by the Health Professional and Allied Employees (HPAE) union, an affiliate of the American Federation of Teachers. To make a long, complex story reasonably short, in the early 1990s, HPAE organized a non-nurses professional unit at the independent New Jersey state medical school, including several IT titles. (Nurses had been organized some years earlier.) Interestingly, the union created a space within the organization for the IT group, including a "chair" for IT workers, a position still in existence today.

In 2013, the medical school officially merged into Rutgers. Although Rutgers is heavily unionized, the IT staff had not been successfully organized. The 2018 New Jersey Workplace Democracy Enhancement Act expanded coverage, effectively providing the opportunity for public sector unions to accrete previously excluded groups of workers into their relevant units.[3] Through various grievances, unfair labor practice charges, and negotiations, 125 new Rutgers IT workers were brought into the medical school unit. Following negotiations, a memorandum of agreement incorporated them into the collective bargaining agreement. (There are still dozens of contested titles in the process of being legally sorted out.)

In an interview, a representative from HPAE made several observations about the IT unit members. First, they tend to be "fiercely independent" and not terribly interested or active in the union and are less likely to join than some of the other professionals, especially nurses. The primary "special" issues that have arisen in representing this group come from the constantly changing skill demands. Relatedly, the employer sent many hospital-based IT workers for expensive training to Epic (the major electronic medical records platform) headquarters. Several of these workers then jumped ship to other hospitals, pushing the employer to negotiate with the union a provision that workers who left sooner than six months from the completion of the training would have to refund half the cost of the training. More generally, there is a sense that both parties need to pay more attention to skill development for this group, and the rapidly changing systems and related skill requirements make layoff rules based on seniority and bumping rights difficult to manage. These observations suggest difficulties in representing (and organizing) these workers that likely exist in other contexts as well.

CONCLUSION

Finally, we note that if the labor movement, no matter how it is defined, is to grow, it must take on the high-tech sector. Since the chapter was finalized, there has been an interesting development in the relationship between the traditional labor movement and one important high-tech firm. In December 2023, Microsoft, the AFL-CIO, the American Federation of Teachers, and CWA announced a new partnership around AI and the future of the workforce. According to the parties' news release, this agreement builds on the neutrality agreement between CWA and Activision and Zenimax discussed in the chapter; among other things, it "provides a neutrality framework for future worker organizing by AFL-CIO affiliate unions." Importantly though, it goes beyond workers and organizing at Microsoft and includes three broad goals: AI education for workers and students, a mechanism for feedback from labor leaders and workers to AI developers at Microsoft, and joint policy and skills development.

ENDNOTES

1. The Silicon Valley Index "Indicators" website, drawing on Census Bureau data, actually shows only 1% of the "Tech Talent in the Core Working Age Group (25–44)" in 2021 were Black; 3% were Hispanic or Latino. https://tinyurl.com/mkcen9w9

2. The case against the Cisco engineers was eventually dropped, but the case against Cisco still active in 2023.

3. Sections 5(a) and (b) of the WDEA expanded coverage under a collective bargaining agreement to include "all regular full-time and part-time employees of the public employer who perform negotiations unit work ... without regard to job title, job classification or number of hours worked."

About the Contributors

EDITORS

Paul F. Clark is a professor and former director at the School of Labor and Employment Relations, Penn State University. In 2022, he received a grant from the National Academy of Arbitrators to study police discipline and misconduct processes. In addition to research on collective bargaining in policing, he has also conducted studies of employment relations in the coal, steel, and healthcare industries. He is a past president of the Labor and Employment Relations Association.

John T. Delaney is vice president for academic affairs at Saint Vincent College. He has served in a variety of university administrative positions since 1996. Delaney is an expert in business education, with a background in labor–management relations, especially public sector labor relations and dispute resolution. He has written extensively on collective bargaining, negotiations, dispute resolution, and union political action. as well as issues related to ethics in business. Delaney has given expert testimony to the National Labor Relations Board and the Subcommittee on Labor of the US Senate Committee on Labor and Human Resources.

Howard R. Stanger is a professor of management in the Wehle School of Business, Canisius University. His research has focused on historical and contemporary labor relations in printing, newspapers, and digital media. Stanger also has published articles and book chapters on Buffalo's Larkin Company, employers' associations, and other business and labor history topics. This is his third contribution (2002, 2013, and 2024) to IRRA's/LERA's annual research volume on industry-focused collective bargaining.

CONTRIBUTORS

Jai Abrams, formerly a research assistant at the School of Management at Yale University and engineering undergraduate at Wesleyan University, is now completing his degree at the University of Connecticut.

Ariel Avgar is a professor at the ILR School at Cornell University and senior associate dean for outreach and sponsored research. His research focuses on two primary areas within employment relations. First, he explores the role that employment relations factors play in the healthcare industry. He examines the effects of a variety of workplace innovations, including new technology, delivery-of-care models, and innovative work practices, on patients, front-line employees, and organizational performance. Second, he studies conflict and its management in organizations, with a focus on the strategic choices made by firms. In addition, his research investigates the adoption and implementation of organization-level conflict management practices and systems. His research has been published in a number of journals, including *Industrial and Labor Relations Review*, *Industrial Relations*, *British Journal of Industrial Relations*, *Ohio State Journal on Dispute Resolution*, *International Journal of Conflict Management*, and the *International Journal of Human Resource Management*. He served as law clerk for the president of the Israeli National Labor Court before being admitted to the Israeli Bar. Prior to joining ILR, he was an associate professor and assistant professor at the School of Labor and Employment Relations at the University of Illinois Urbana-Champaign.

James N. Baron is the William S. Beinecke Professor of Management (and professor of sociology, by courtesy) at Yale University. His research interests include human resources; organizational design and behavior; social stratification and inequality; work, labor markets, and careers; economic sociology; and entrepreneurial companies. Before coming to Yale in 2006, he taught at Stanford's Graduate School of Business. He was co-director of the Stanford Project on Emerging Companies, a large-scale longitudinal study of the organizational design, human resource management practices, and financial and nonfinancial performance measures of entrepreneurial firms in Silicon Valley. Papers based on the project appeared in leading disciplinary journals, and an overview of the project in *California Management Review* won the 2003 Accenture Award for making "the most important contribution to improving the practice of management." Baron is the author, with Stanford economist David M. Kreps, of a textbook, *Strategic Human Resources: Frameworks for General Managers*.

Nicholas Bedell joined The NewsGuild as administrative director in March 2021. Before that, he was the director of campaigns for the Transport Workers Union. His union career started in 1990 as a labor educator in the Needle Trades Unions, and he has worked in a variety of capacities over the years for multiple unions—as new organizing lead, staff representative, and director of union education.

Dale Belman is a professor in the School of Human Resources and Labor Relations at Michigan State University. He conducts research on unions and labor market regulation. *What Does the Minimum Wage Do?*, forthcoming from the Upjohn Institute for Employment Research, reviews the past decade of research on the effect of the minimum wage on employment, hours, earnings, and other outcomes. Belman has also written about the construction industry, truckers and trucking, public sector employment, and minimum- and low-wage work. Belman is president of the Institute for Construction Economics Research.

Michael H. Belzer is a professor of economics at Wayne State University. He created and then chaired the Transportation Research Board (TRB) Committee on Trucking Industry Research for more than 12 years. He has served on the National Institute for Occupational Safety and Health National Occupational Research Agenda Sector Council for Transportation, Warehousing and Utilities since 2006. Belzer is author of *Sweatshops on Wheels: Winners and Losers in Trucking Deregulation*, co-author of *Truck Driver Occupational Safety and Health: 2003 Conference Report and Selective Literature Review*, and numerous peer-reviewed articles on trucking industry economics, labor, occupational safety and health, infrastructure, and operational issues. He testified to the Australian Parliament in 2011 and again in 2021 in support of legislation that created a new regulatory regime for Australia intended to take compensation out of competition in an otherwise competitive, deregulated trucking industry. He also testified before the US House of Representatives Committee on Small Business in 2012, calling on the Departments of Labor and Transportation to harmonize the definition of work.

Timothy Chandler is department chair and professor in the Rucks Department of Management, Louisiana State University. His teaching interests include labor relations, negotiations, alternative dispute resolution, and regulation of employment practices. His research focuses on private and public sector labor relations and the regulation of employment practices.

Marge DiCuccio serves as the chief nursing officer of Allegheny General Hospital. An experienced nurse leader, she has previously held several senior-level positions. She is a current member and former board member, including past chair, of the Southwest Pennsylvania Organization of Nurse Leaders. She is a current member and former board member of the Pennsylvania Organization of Nurse Leaders. DiCuccio is a member of the American Organization for Nursing Leadership and the Association of Critical Care Nurses. She serves as a trustee of Robert Morris University.

Nicholas DiGiovanni has handled cases and issues in virtually all aspects of labor and employment law. Over the course of his career, he developed a particular niche in labor and employment matters affecting colleges and universities, focusing especially on collective bargaining with faculty, staff, and graduate student unions; proceedings before state and federal labor board agencies; arbitration cases; advice on union organizing; and management training. DiGiovanni successfully litigated at the National Labor Relations Board the managerial status of full-time faculty members at Tufts University Medical School and Elmira College under the standards of the Supreme Court's *Yeshiva University* case. He has also negotiated dozens of initial and successor faculty, staff, and graduate student collective bargaining agreements at both public and private institutions, including community colleges, private four-year institutions, and R1 doctoral research universities.

Clifford B. Donn is a professor in the Department of Anthropology, Criminology and Sociology at Le Moyne College. He has been at Le Moyne since 1982, where he was a member of and chaired the Department of Industrial Relations and Human Resource Management, was director of the international studies program, and served as director of the study abroad program. He has taught both graduate and undergraduate courses in the economics and education departments in the MBA program and the integral honors program. Donn's principal research interests are dispute resolution, comparative trade unionism, labor and employment issues in the oceangoing maritime industry, collective bargaining among public school teachers, and unionization and collective bargaining among part-time college faculty members. He has written and edited books on these subjects as well as published articles in *Industrial and Labor Relations Review*, *Industrial Relations*, and *Journal of Industrial Relations*, among others. He has presented papers at conferences in Australia, Canada, China, England, Ireland, Japan, and the United States.

Adrienne E. Eaton is the dean of the School of Management and Labor Relations at Rutgers University. She is a past president of the Labor and Employment Relations Association. She is a member of the editorial board for the *Labor Studies Journal* and past editor-in-chief of the Labor and Employment Relations Association. She has also served as a member of the New Jersey Public Employment Relations Commission and is a past president of the Rutgers AAUP-AFT. The Labor and Employment Relations Association named her a LERA Fellow in 2017 in recognition of her research on union and worker participation in management decision making, neutrality and card-check agreements in union organizing, and other key labor issues. Eaton remains active in a number of areas of research, including labor–management partnerships in healthcare. She has published numerous journal articles and book chapters on this topic and co-authored the book *Healing Together: The Kaiser Permanente Labor–Management Partnership*. Her groundbreaking research concerning the negotiation, effectiveness, and outcomes of neutrality and card-check agreements has been published in *Industrial and Labor*

Relations Review, Perspectives on Work, in a book chapter, and in technical reports and cited in congressional floor debates.

Mark Erlich is a fellow at the Harvard Law School's Center for Labor and a Just Economy. He retired as executive secretary-treasurer of the New England Regional Council of Carpenters, a 20,000-member organization, in 2017. A member of Carpenters Local 40 since 1975, he worked at his craft as an apprentice, journeyman, foreman, and superintendent. He won election as the business manager of his local in 1992 and head of the Regional Council in 2005. While leading the union, Erlich also chaired the New England Carpenters Benefits Funds and the New England Carpenters Training Fund. He was a vice president of the Massachusetts AFL-CIO and the Massachusetts Building Trades, and he continues to serve as a board member of MassINC. In addition to his career in the trades and the labor movement, Erlich has written and lectured extensively on labor issues. He is the author of three books, *The Way We Build: Restoring Dignity to Construction Work*, *With Our Hands: The Story of Carpenters in Massachusetts*, and *Labor at the Ballot Box*. He has also written dozens of essays, articles, and op-eds on labor history, contemporary union issues, and politics in academic publications, as well as popular journals and newspapers.

Rafael Gely is the James E. Campbell Missouri Endowed Professor of Law at the University of Missouri School of Law, where he has taught since 2008. Before joining the faculty at the University of Missouri, Gely taught at the University of Cincinnati College of Law, the Chicago-Kent College of Law, and the Department of Management at the Mays College of Business at Texas A&M University.

Ray Gibney joined Penn State Harrisburg in 2007, where he is currently an associate professor of management in the School of Business Administration. His primary teaching responsibilities focus on human resource management. Prior to joining Penn State Harrisburg, Gibney worked as a consultant with firms such as PeopleSoft and Coopers & Lybrand. He has consulted on various HR-related issues across diverse industries. His particular research interests include employee–employer relationships and labor unions. He holds memberships in the Academy of Management, Southern Management Association, and Labor and Employment Relations Association.

Rebecca K. Givan is an associate professor of labor studies and employment relations in the School of Management and Labor Relations at Rutgers University. Her research expertise is in US and comparative labor relations and healthcare work and the public sector. She has published widely on employment relations in healthcare, comparative welfare states, and labor studies in journals such as *Social Forces*, *ILR Review*, and *British Journal of Industrial Relations*. Her recent book, *The Challenge to Change: Reforming Health Care on the Front Line in the United States and the United Kingdom*, was published in 2016.

Frank Goeddeke, Jr., an assistant professor at Wayne State University, has taught at nearly a dozen postsecondary institutions over more than two decades. He has been published in several journals, including the *Journal of Organizational Behavior* and *Organizational Research Methods*. He has held a number of professional positions in his career, including associate dean, skilled tradesperson, flight instructor, union president, industry researcher, union organizer, university administrator, and accreditation manager. Additionally, he served as a US Peace Corps volunteer in Mongolia. Goeddeke is a Quality Matters online course peer reviewer and holds the Quality Matters Online teaching certification. His research and teaching interests are in organizational behavior, labor relations, and research methods.

Gregory C. Hutchings, Jr. is a nationally recognized educational leader, anti-racism activist, and published author who advocates for Black, Indigenous, and People of Color and racial equity in education. He is the founder and chief executive officer of Revolutionary ED and currently serves as an assistant professor and program coordinator in the School of Education's Educational Leadership and Policy Studies program. Hutchings has over 24 years of combined educational experience as a college admissions counselor, teacher, school principal, central office administrator, superintendent, and college professor. He specializes in anti-racism in education, educational leadership, strategic planning, strategic thinking, professional learning, school board and superintendent relations, and executive coaching.

Daniel J. Julius is a visiting professor at the Weatherhead School of Management at Case Western Reserve University; Senior Fellow, Center for Global Work and Employment at Rutgers University; and Visiting Fellow in the School of Management at Yale University. He is an expert in the areas of labor management relations, collective negotiations, human resource management and conflict resolution. He is experienced in establishing and maintaining partnerships in international higher education, implementing shared governance, crisis management, long-range planning, and managing institutional accreditation. He has served as provost and academic/senior vice president at three public and private universities/systems and has been the senior systemwide administrator responsible for labor and human resources for two public higher education systems. Earlier in his career he was director of the Center for Higher Education at Teachers College, Columbia University. More recently he has engaged in research and worked extensively with senior leaders in mission-driven cultural organizations. He is developing executive education and related professional development programs at Rutgers University in these areas and serving as a consultant on research projects and organizational design for numerous institutions.

Brenda J. Kirby teaches social psychology, psychology and the law, research methods, and a senior seminar on the psychology of stereotypes, prejudice, and discrimination at Le Moyne College. She is also an active mentor for students doing independent research, including departmental honors research. Kirby's research students regularly present at professional meetings and go on to do graduate work in psychology. Her research is in two areas: looking at issues of prejudice and discrimination, especially related to sexual orientation, social class, and race, and looking at issues of justice system practices and jury decision making.

David Lewin is the Neil H. Jacoby Professor Emeritus of Management, Human Resources and Organizational Behavior at the UCLA Anderson School of Management. Prior to joining UCLA, he was professor and faculty director of the PhD program and faculty director of the Human Resource Research Center at the Columbia University Business School. Lewin has published many books and journal articles on human resource management, employee relations, labor markets, and compensation. His books include *Human Resource Management: An Economic Approach*, *The Oxford Handbook of Participation in Organizations*, *Contemporary Issues in Employment Relations*, *The Modern Grievance Procedure in the United States*, *The Human Resource Management Handbook*, *Advances in Industrial and Labor Relations* Volume 27, and the *Handbook of Qualitative Research Methods on Human Resource Management: Innovative Techniques*. Lewin is a former president of the Labor and Employment Relations Association and is a Fellow of the National Academy of Human Resources. He also presently serves as a managing director and head of the Labor & Employment and Human Capital Practices of the Berkeley Research Group, and he frequently serves as an expert witness in litigation matters involving issues of no-poaching and noncompete agreements, executive compensation, wrongful termination and retaliation, independent contractor versus employee status, and age, gender, race, disability, and religious discrimination.

Adam Seth Litwin is an associate professor of industrial and labor relations at Cornell's ILR School and serves as an associate editor at its flagship journal, the *ILR Review*. Litwin's research, anchored in industrial relations, examines the determinants and impacts of labor relations structures and technological change. As a technologist, he also writes on issues involving technological change, work, and workers in the healthcare sector, having been honored by the Aspen Institute, the Alfred P. Sloan Foundation, the Labor and Employment Relations Association, and the International Labor and Employment Relations Association, among others. He has published a mix of empirical and conceptual studies intersecting the areas of labor relations and technological change, in industrial relations and medical journals. At Cornell, he teaches undergraduate and graduate core courses in labor relations, as well as electives focused on the evolution and impact of technological change on workers, organizations, and society at large. Litwin joined Cornell's ILR faculty in the fall of 2014 after serving as a standing faculty member at Johns Hopkins University.

Marick F. Masters is a professor of business in the Department of Management and Information Systems at the Mike Ilitch School of Business at Wayne State University. Masters's research and teaching interests lie in negotiations and conflict resolution, unions, business and labor political action, federal sector labor–management relations, human resource management and employee relations, workplace privacy, and workplace violence. He has published four books (*Unions at the Crossroads*, *The Complete Guide to Conflict Resolution in the Workplace*, *The UAW: An Iconic Union Falls in Scandal*, and *Trade Union Finance: How Labor Organizations Raise and Spend Money*) and more than 100 articles, proceedings, and columns. Masters has directed several executive education programs, served on the boards of several professional associations, co-hosted a radio program, and been a guest columnist for several publications. He is a senior partner in Albright, Irr, and Masters, a consulting firm based in New London, Connecticut. His research and teaching interests are in negotiations, business, and labor political activities, and union finances.

Ruth Milkman is a sociologist of labor and labor movements who has written on a variety of topics involving work and organized labor in the United States, past and present. Her most recent books are *Immigrant Labor and the New Precariat* and *On Gender, Labor and Inequality*. She has written extensively about low-wage immigrant workers, analyzing their employment conditions as well as the dynamics of immigrant labor organizing. After 21 years as a sociology professor at UCLA, where she directed the Institute for Research on Labor and Employment from 2001 to 2008, Milkman returned to New York City in 2010. She is currently Distinguished Professor of Sociology at the CUNY Graduate Center and at the CUNY School of Labor and Urban Studies, where she chairs the Labor Studies Department.

Michael Schuster, managing partner of CHRS, LLC, is professor emeritus of management and human resources at the Martin J. Whitman School of Management at Syracuse University. He is a former Fulbright Scholar from the London School of Economics and Political Science. He also served as professor of strategic management and head of the Management Department at the US Coast Guard Academy. Schuster is one of the recognized authorities in compensation and human resource management strategy, incentive compensation, gain sharing, variable pay, and other performance-driven compensation systems. He has completed the most intensive longevity-oriented research on performance-based pay program effectiveness in the United States and is often cited in books and articles on the subject. He has a long history of successfully working with companies seeking to change compensation systems, including individual and large-group bonus plans, sales incentives, modifying gainsharing plans, conversions of individual incentives to nonincentives, and reducing the overall costs of compensation.

Rochelle G. Skolnick is an attorney at the union-side labor and employment law firm of Schuchat, Cook & Werner in St. Louis. She works in all areas of the firm's practice, handling labor arbitrations, administrative proceedings, and state and federal lawsuits. Since 2009, she has served as counsel to the Symphonic Services Division of the American Federation of Musicians. She regularly presents seminars on labor and employment law topics, including the duty of fair representation, grievance and arbitration, disability rights, sexual harassment, and healthcare reform.

Hanna Xue is a graduate student in the Rutgers University School of Management and Labor Relations, working on her PhD in labor, work, and society.

Tingting Zhang is an assistant professor in the School of Labor and Employment Relations at the University of Illinois Urbana-Champaign. Her research within industrial relations focuses on the role of information communication technology, such as social media, in labor movements and union renewal. In employment relations, she studies various training and development mechanisms both within and outside organizations, examining how occupational regulation and the emergence of nondegree credentials influence the career outcomes of marginalized groups, including women and immigrants. Her work has been published in several scholarly journals, including *British Journal of Industrial Relations*, *Industrial Relations Journal*, *International Migration Review*, and *International Journal of Training and Development*, among others.

LERA Executive Board Members 2024–25

President
Jim Pruitt, Kaiser Permanente

President-Elect
John Budd, University of Minnesota

Past President
Dennis Dabney, Dabney Law LLC

Secretary-Treasurer
Andrew Weaver, University of Illinois Urbana-Champaign

Editor-in-Chief
J. Ryan Lamare, University of Illinois Urbana-Champaign

National Chapter Advisory Council Chair
William Canak, Middle Tennessee State University (retired)

Legal Counsel
Steven B. Rynecki

Executive Board Members
Sharon Block, Harvard Law
Andrea Cáceres, SHARE/AFSCME
Robert Chiaravalli, Strategic Labor and HR, LLC
Julie Farb, AFL-CIO
Maria Figueroa, SUNY Empire State College
Eliza Forsythe, University of Illinois Urbana-Champaign
Ruben Garcia, University of Nevada, Las Vegas
Janet Gillman, Oregon Employment Relations Board
Beverly Harrison, Arbitrator/Mediator
John Johnson, Southeastern Pennsylvania Transportation Authority
Glenard Middleton, AFSCME MD Council 67
Deborah Moore-Carter, City of Baltimore
Monique Morrissey, Economic Policy Institute
Dionne Pohler, University of Saskatchewan
Sean Rogers, University of Rhode Island
Hal Ruddick, Alliance of Health Care Unions
Lionel Sims, Jr., Kaiser Permanente
Maite Tapia, Michigan State University
Christy Yoshitomi, Federal Mediation and Conciliation Service

A Better Way to Work →→→→→→→

Kaiser Permanente and the Alliance of Health Care Unions thank all our managers, physicians and employees — including more than 50,000 union-represented workers — for 27 years of partnership.

Affordable, quality care. It started in California's shipyards and steel mills in World War II; today we continue that tradition across the country. Kaiser Permanente is America's largest non-profit health care delivery organization. Kaiser Permanente and the Alliance of Health Care Unions are proud to work together to ensure Kaiser Permanente is the best place to work and the best place to receive care.

In 2021, we affirmed our Labor Management Partnership in a new four-year agreement, which includes important new provisions committing to joint work on staffing, racial justice, and promoting the affordability of health care. The new national agreement covers more than 57,000 members of AFSCME, AFT, IBT, ILWU, IUOE, KPNAA, UFCW, UNITE HERE, and USW, in every market where Kaiser Permanente operates.

The International Union, United Automobile, Aerospace and Agricultural Implement Workers of America (UAW) is one of the largest and most diverse unions in North America, with members in virtually every sector of the economy. UAW-represented workplaces range from multinational corporations, small manufacturers and state and local governments to colleges and universities, hospitals, and private non-profit organizations. The UAW has almost 400,000 active members and more than 580,000 retired members in the United States, Canada, and Puerto Rico.

President: Shawn Fain | **Secretary-Treasurer:** Margaret Mock
Vice Presidents: Chuck Browning | Mike Booth | Rich Boyer

UAW-Ford Labor Management Committee Trust

Powered By Our People
mycareer.ford.com

A FOCUS ON RESEARCH
ilr.cornell.edu/research

Cornell University's ILR School is the preeminent educational institution in the world focused on work, labor and employment. ILR-generated research – conducted by the largest number of full-time faculty members focused on work-related topics of any institution in the U.S. – influences public policy, informs organizational strategy and improves professional practice.

ILR faculty and students have produced research on a diverse range of topics, including sexual harassment, remote work, fostering creativity in the workplace, migrant worker rights, the pitfalls of AI and the dangers facing workers in the global apparel and fishing industries.

We are also home to the Catherwood Library, The Kheel Center for Labor-Management Documentation & Archives, and over 15 centers and institutes focused on bridging the gap between research and practice.

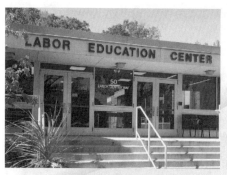

Leading the Way with LERA

Rutgers School of Management and Labor Relations (SMLR) is proud to partner with LERA through an established tradition of leadership and service to the association across executive, editorial and committee roles. Through our academic programs, research initiatives, and outreach programs, Rutgers SMLR is a leading source of expertise on the world of work, building effective and sustainable organizations, and the changing employment relationship.

Rutgers SMLR is pleased to continue our collaboration with LERA to offer a unique lens to explore the evolution of work and the Future of Work(ers).

smlr.rutgers.edu

Proud supporter of LERA

Forging new research frontiers since 1922

From the Hoover administration to the Biden administration, Princeton's Industrial Relations Section has been a hub for policymakers, companies, researchers, and activists seeking best-in-class data and research on the labor market and the relationship between industry and workers.

https://irs.princeton.edu
https://irs100.princeton.edu